The Crosscultural, Language, and Academic Development Handbook

A Complete K–12 Reference Guide

FOURTH EDITION

Lynne T. Díaz-Rico
California State University, San Bernardino

Kathryn Z. Weed
Late of California State University, San Bernardino

Allyn & Bacon

Boston • New York • San Francisco
Mexico City • Montreal • Toronto • London • Madrid • Munich • Paris
Hong Kong • Singapore • Tokyo • Cape Town • Sydney

Executive Editor: *Aurora Martínez Ramos*
Editorial Assistant: *Jacqueline Gillen*
Executive Marketing Manager: *Krista Clark*
Editorial Production Service: *Omegatype Typography, Inc.*
Composition Buyer: *Linda Cox*
Manufacturing Manager: *Megan Cochran*
Electronic Composition: *Omegatype Typography, Inc.*
Interior Design: *Omegatype Typography, Inc.*
Photo Researcher: *Annie Pickert*
Cover Designer: *Linda Knowles*

For related titles and support materials, visit our online catalog at www.pearsonhighered.com.

Between the time Website information is gathered and then published, it is not unusual for some sites to have closed. Also, the transcription of URLs can result in typographical errors. The publisher would appreciate notification where these errors occur.

Library of Congress Cataloging-in-Publication Data

Díaz-Rico, Lynne T.
   The crosscultural, language, and academic development handbook : a complete K–12 reference guide / Lynne T. Díaz-Rico, Kathryn Z. Weed.—4th ed.
      p. cm.
   Includes bibliographical references and index.
   ISBN-13: 978-0-13-715409-8 (pbk.)
   ISBN-10: 0-13-715409-7 (pbk.)
   1. English language—Study and teaching (Higher)—Foreign speakers—Handbooks, manuals, etc.   2. Multicultural education—United States—Handbooks, manuals, etc.
3. Language and education—United States—Handbooks, manuals, etc.   4. Education, Bilingual—United States—Handbooks, manuals, etc.   I. Weed, Kathryn Z.   II. Title.
   PE1128.A2D45   2010
   428.0071'73—dc22   2008046055

Printed in the United States of America

10 9 8 7 6 5 4 3 2   HAM   13 12 11 10

Credits appear on p. 390, which constitutes an extension of the copyright page.

Allyn & Bacon
is an imprint of

www.pearsonhighered.com   ISBN-10: 0-13-715409-7
                                       ISBN-13: 978-0-13-715409-8

Dedication

I dedicate this edition to Kathryn Weed.
Her devotion to excellence,
her generosity of spirit,
and her daily cordiality
set a standard for what it means to
be a true colleague.

—LTD-R

About the Author

Lynne T. Díaz-Rico is a professor of education at California State University, San Bernardino (CSUSB). Dr. Díaz-Rico obtained her doctoral degree in English as a second language at InterAmerican University in Puerto Rico and has taught students at all levels from kindergarten to high school. At CSUSB, Dr. Díaz-Rico is coordinator of the Masters in Education, Teaching English to Speakers of Other Languages Option program. She is actively involved in teacher education and gives presentations at numerous professional conferences on such subjects as intercultural education, critical language analysis, and organization of schools and classrooms for educational equity. Her current research interest is the use of language in complex, particularly crosscultural, contexts.

Contents

Part One
Learning: Learning about the Learner, Language Structure, and Second-Language Acquisition   1

CHAPTER 1   Learning about the Language Learner   2

CHAPTER 2   Learning about Language Structure   29

CHAPTER 3   Learning about Second-Language Acquisition   49

Part Two

Instruction: Oracy and Literacy for English-Language Development, Content-Area Instruction, and Bilingual Education

67

Part Three
Assessment   177

CHAPTER 7   Language and Content-Area Assessment   178

Part Four
Culture: Cultural Diversity in the United States, the Intercultural Educator, and Culturally Responsive Schooling   211

CHAPTER 8   Cultural Diversity   212

CHAPTER 9   The Intercultural Educator   234

CHAPTER 10 Culturally Responsive Schooling   264

Part Five
Policy: Language Policy and Special Populations of English Learners   301

CHAPTER 11 The Role of Educators in Language Policy   302

CHAPTER 12   **Culturally and Linguistically Diverse Learners and Special Education**   321

Introduction

The presence of many linguistic and ethnic minority students in the United States has challenged educators to rethink basic assumptions about schooling. School models and methods based on the notions that students share the same cultural background and speak the same language are no longer sufficient to meet the needs of today's students. The urgent need to provide a high-quality education for students in the United States whose native language is not English calls for increased expertise on the part of classroom teachers, administrators, and community leaders.

In the past, schools were designed for native speakers of English. Today's students come from diverse cultural and linguistic backgrounds. But the cultural patterns of schools and classrooms may not ensure that all students have equal opportunity to succeed. Culture is a part of the educational process that has been invisible but that can no longer remain so. By understanding the influence of culture, educators can avoid inadvertently advantaging those students who share the dominant culture while neglecting those students whose cultures differ from the mainstream. Culture includes more than the habits and beliefs of students and teachers; the school itself is a culture in which the physical environment, daily routines, and interactions advantage some and alienate others. Educators now need a foundation of cultural awareness and second-language acquisition theory in order to adapt schools to the needs of multicultural and multilingual students.

Crosscultural, Language, and Academic Development: A Model for Teacher Preparation

Much has been written, both general and specific information, about the effect of culture on schooling, second-language acquisition, and ways to help English learners achieve access to the core curriculum. To synthesize this wealth of information, a means of organizing this knowledge is needed. The figure on page xv represents the central elements of this book and their relationship to one another.

In the figure, *learning* occupies the central area (Part One). Understanding the learner, the language to be learned, and the process of learning a second language helps teachers to meet the needs of individual learners.

Instruction is the second major area that organizes knowledge about teaching English learners (Part Two). Instruction for English learners falls into three categories: oracy and literacy for English-language development, content-area instruction (also known as "sheltered" instruction or specially designed academic instruction in English—SDAIE), and theories and methods for bilingual education.

Assessment practices are influenced by instruction and policymaking, and, in turn, assessment affects learning. Assessment of students is the way to determine if curricular content is appropriate and teaching methods are successful. Through assessment, one can ascertain what learning has taken place. The placement of students as a

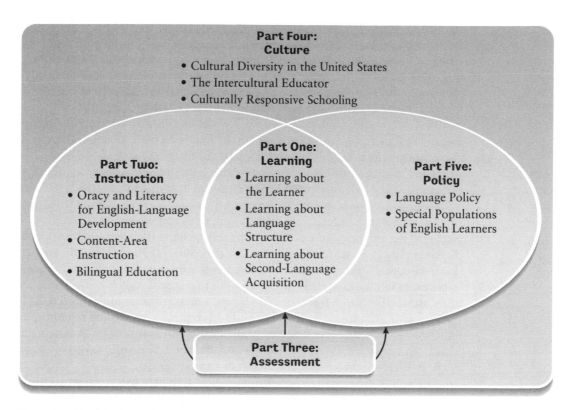

Theoretical Model for Crosscultural, Language, and Academic Development

function of assessment affects the organization and management of schooling; thus assessment involves not only issues of pedagogy and learning but also policy. Assessment is covered in Part Three.

Culture permeates the activities of learning, instruction, and policymaking. Fundamental insights into cultural diversity in the United States, the role of the intercultural educator, and the means for creating culturally appropriate pedagogy are provided in Part Four.

The fifth area, *policy,* denotes the organization and management of schooling, elements that affect the operation of schools. Because the policies affecting schooling can be better understood with a background on the influence and importance of culture, policy for English learners is discussed in Part Five.

Chapter 12 discusses policies and practices in the relationship between English-language development (ELD) and special education. This chapter addresses effective curriculum, teaching methods, assessment, organization, and management of instruction.

Teachers can be resources within their schools and districts on matters pertaining to English-language and academic development for their multicultural and multilinguistic students. A framework that organizes crosscultural, language, and academic development in terms of learning, pedagogy, and policy contributes to teachers' abilities to describe, communicate, and teach others about this field.

In addition to changes in the model (see figure on page xv) and expanded and updated information, this fourth edition adds new classroom-related vignettes (Example of Concept) and instructional modifications (Adapted Instruction) to help the classroom teacher work successfully with culturally and linguistically diverse students. The concepts and information provided in this text not only encompass those necessary for examinations such as California's CLAD, but also for newer exams such as California Teacher of English Learners (CTEL).

Care has been taken to use acceptable terminology to denote school students whose primary language is not English, as well as terms to denote various racial and ethnic groups. The terms *Hispanic* and *Hispanic American* denote those whose ancestors originated in Spain or Spanish America, and who now represent twenty-six separate nationalities and a variety of racial groups (Bruder, Anderson, Schultz, & Caldera, 1991). Research has shown that the ethnic labels for Hispanics are complex. In open-ended interviews, Latino adolescents were asked for their ethnic label preferences. In many cases, they did not commit to a specific label, instead indicating that they ascribed to more fluid, flexible labels. On average, students selected "Latino," "Mexican American," "Hispanic," and "Mexican," when asked to choose only one label. When selecting "American," "Chicano," "Salvadoran," or "Guatemalan," students always added a second term (Zarate, Bhimji, & Reese, 2005). *European American* is used in preference to *White* or *Anglo* to denote those whose ancestral background is European. *African American* is similarly used to refer to those whose ancestors came from Africa. Other ethnic group labels follow a similar logic. In some cases, data are cited that classify groups according to other labels; in these cases, the labels used in the citation are preserved.

Like the changes in terminology for racial and ethnic groups, terminology for students learning English as an additional language has undergone change. Over the years, these students have been called *language minority, limited-English proficient (LEP), non-English proficient (NEP), English-as-a-second-language (ESL) learner, English-language learner (ELL),* and *learners of English as a new language.* In this book, both the terms *English learner* and *culturally and linguistically diverse (CLD) student* are used. The term *English-language development (ELD)* is used to denote classrooms and programs that promote English learners' language and academic learning.

Burgeoning information in the areas of culture and linguistic/academic development has made *The Crosscultural, Language, and Academic Development Handbook* a difficult yet useful synthesis. The result, I believe, is a readable text that brings into focus the challenges and possibilities in educating new Americans. Principles and practices that promote crosscultural understanding are relevant for all.

New With This Edition!

Help your students get better grades and become better teachers.

MyEducationLab (www.myeducationlab.com) is a research-based learning tool that brings teaching to life. Through authentic in-class video footage, interactive simulations, rich case studies, examples of authentic teacher and student work, and more, MyEducationLab prepares students for teaching careers by showing what quality instruction looks like.

MyEducationLab is easy to use! At the end of every chapter in the textbook, you will find the MyEducationLab logo adjacent to activities and exercises that correlate material you've just read in the chapter to your viewing of multimedia assets on the MyEducationLab site. These assets include:

- **Video.** The authentic classroom videos in MyEducationLab show how real teachers handle actual classroom situations.
- **Case Studies.** A diverse set of robust cases illustrates the realities of teaching and offers valuable perspectives on common issues and challenges in education.
- **Simulations.** Created by the IRIS Center at Vanderbilt University, these interactive simulations give you hands-on practice at adapting instruction for a full spectrum of learners.
- **Lesson Plans.** Specially selected, topically relevant excerpts from texts expand and enrich your perspectives on key issues and topics.
- **Classroom Artifacts.** Authentic PreK–12 student and teacher classroom artifacts are tied to course topics and offer you practice in working with the actual types of materials you will encounter daily as teachers.
- **Lesson and Portfolio Builders.** With this effective and easy-to-use tool, you can create, update, and share standards-based lesson plans and portfolios.

Acknowledgments

A book like this could not have been written without the help and support of numerous individuals. The teachers and students with whom I have worked have given me insights and examples. My colleagues have shared their experiences and expertise. In addition to those who gave so much support to previous editions, I would also like to thank those who have made this fourth edition a reality. It goes without saying I owe homage to the California Commission on Teacher Credentialing for their work in designing California's CLAD credential and its revision, the CTEL authorization.

I want to thank the teacher education and TESOL master's students at CSUSB as well as my colleagues in TESOL and in the Department of Language, Literacy, and Culture at CSUSB who have enriched my understanding of the teaching–learning process as it relates to second-language learners, and who have participated with me in research and curriculum development.

I am grateful also to those who provided helpful reviews of the manuscript for this edition: Emilio Garza, California State University, Bakersfield; Walton King, Clearwater Christian College; and Sam Perkins, Barry University.

To all those who have provided linguistic and cultural support not only to English learners but also to those who have struggled to adapt to a new culture, I salute you. To the researchers and authors who provided valuable insights into this process, my deepest thanks for your pioneering efforts. Finally, I thank series editor Aurora Martínez Ramos and the rest of the Allyn & Bacon staff for their efforts in producing this book.

part one

Learning

Learning about the Learner, Language Structure, and Second-Language Acquisition

Part One represents learning the foundations of instruction: knowledge about the learner, about the structure of language, and about the process of acquiring a second language. Chapter 1 introduces the learner, with a focus on the psychological factors in language learning that make individual language learners unique, as well as the sociocultural factors that situate the learner in the context of cultural patterns that may influence groups of learners to react in similar ways to classroom instruction. Chapter 2 introduces language structure and functions. Chapter 3 offers insights from classic and contemporary research in language acquisition and development, particularly in the context of the classroom. The figure below highlights Part One of the theoretical model presented in the introduction.

Theoretical Model for CLAD Learning: Learning about the Learner, Language Structure, and Second-Language Acquisition

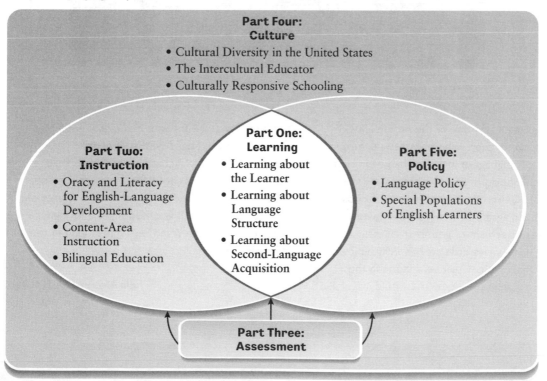

Part Four:
Culture
- Cultural Diversity in the United States
- The Intercultural Educator
- Culturally Responsive Schooling

Part Two:
Instruction
- Oracy and Literacy for English-Language Development
- Content-Area Instruction
- Bilingual Education

Part One:
Learning
- Learning about the Learner
- Learning about Language Structure
- Learning about Second-Language Acquisition

Part Five:
Policy
- Language Policy
- Special Populations of English Learners

Part Three:
Assessment

1

Learning about the Language Learner

English learners comprise a growing proportion of school children in the United States.

In sixth grade, I had one of the first in a lucky line of English teachers who began to nurture in me a love of language, a love that had been there since my childhood of listening closely to words. Sister Maria Generosa did not make our class interminably diagram sentences from a workbook or learn [a] catechism of grammar rules. Instead she asked us to write little stories imagining we were snowflakes, birds, pianos, a stone in the pavement, a star in the sky. What would it feel like to be a flower with roots in the ground? Sister Maria filled the board with snowy print . . . until English . . . became a charged, fluid mass that carried me in its great fluent waves, rolling and moving onward, to deposit me on the shores of my new homeland, I was no longer a foreigner with no ground to stand on. I had landed in the English language.

Julia Alvarez (2007, p. 34)

Because of her English-language development teachers, Julia Alvarez is a writer. She can communicate her memories, her joys, her terrors—those ideas and feelings that make her human. Learning a second language connects people across cultures, making it possible for immigrants to achieve their dreams and aspirations. This cross-cultural process enriches everyone.

Teachers in the United States are increasingly expected to educate students whose native languages are not English and whose cultural backgrounds vary considerably from that of the American mainstream culture. Although the teaching profession includes educators from minority cultures in the United States as well as from other countries, the core of the profession remains the white, middle-class, usually monolingual teacher who can benefit from teacher education that includes specialized methods and strategies for the effective education of culturally and linguistically diverse (CLD) students.

Moreover, research has documented the effectiveness of long-term primary-language education. However, numerous classrooms contain students speaking various home languages. Thus English-language development (ELD) classrooms that require modified instruction in English become increasingly important. Teachers with a strong interest in language acquisition and a sense of compassion for the difficulties faced by CLD students are often the most successful in promoting their academic success.

Schools, as institutions within a society, perform an important role in socializing students and helping them gain the knowledge, skills, roles, and identities they need for success. Students who enter school must develop a high level of English proficiency, and teachers are challenged to develop students' English skills during the K–12 period of schooling. The first part of this chapter presents current demographic trends. The chapter then introduces the English learner and offers ways for teachers to inform themselves about these learners' needs.

English Learners: Demographic Trends

The profession of teaching has changed dramatically in the early twenty-first century; many more classrooms contain English learners, students whose home language is not English and who are not classified as "fluent English proficient" based on test scores and other criteria. By 2025, one in every four students will initially be classified as an English learner. A quick overview of the demographics of English learners in the United States can help teachers to visualize the numbers of these learners and their distribution in the schools.

Throughout the United States, 47 million people (18 percent of the population) speak a language other than English at home (U.S. Census Bureau, 2003c). Although the largest percentage of non–English speakers (37 percent) lives in the West, English learners and their families are increasingly living in places such as the Midwest (9 percent) and the South (15 percent) that have not previously needed to hire ELD teachers. The previous concentration of English learners in the West and Southwest has shifted; during 1997–2007, sixteen states had a 200 percent increase in English learners (Rahilly & Weinmann, 2007).

California had the largest population percentage of non-English-language speakers; 43 percent speak a language other than English at home. Following

California are New Mexico, Texas, New York, Hawaii, Arizona, and New Jersey (see Table 1.1). Other states—Florida (3.5 million), Illinois (2.2 million), and Massachusetts (1.1 million)—also have large populations of non-English-language speakers. The majority of English learners in the United States are Spanish speaking (28.1 million); Asian and Pacific Islanders constitute the second-largest demographic group of English learners.

The National Clearinghouse for English Language Acquisition and Language Instruction Educational Programs (NCELA) put the number of children of school age with a home language other than English at 9,779,766—one of every six children of school age—and 31 percent of all American-Indian/Alaska Native, Asian/Pacific Islander, and Hispanic students enrolled in public schools (National Center for Education Statistics, 2005). Of these language-minority students, in 2005–2006, 5,074,572 do not yet have sufficient proficiency in English to be able to succeed academically in traditional all-English-medium classrooms (NCELA, 2007). Los Angeles Unified School District leads all other school districts in the nation both in the number (326,040) of English learners (in 2006–2007), number of languages (56), and percent of total enrollment (40 percent), followed by New York City; Dade County, Florida; Chicago; Houston; Dallas; San Diego; and Long Beach. In 2008, California, with a school enrollment of approximately 1.6 million English learners, led the states in need for English-learner services at the K–12 level. In California, 85 percent of English learners are Spanish-speaking, and 83 percent of these Spanish-speaking learners are from Mexico. The majority of them live in Southern California, the San Francisco Bay area, and the Central Valley. Los Angeles Unified School District has 32 percent of all English learners (EdSource, 2008).

The national distribution of English learners by grade levels is as follows: Grades PreK–3, 44 percent; grades 4–8, 35 percent; grades 9–12, 19 percent; and alternative schools, 2 percent (Rahilly & Weinmann, 2007). Of children who speak a language other than English at home, 81 percent are U.S.-born or naturalized U.S. citizens (Lapkoff & Li, 2007).

Table 1.1

States with the Highest Percent of Population Speaking a Language Other Than English

State	Population of Non-English-Language Speakers (in millions)	Percent of the State's Population
California	12.4	39.5
New Mexico	0.5	36.5
Texas	6.0	31.2
New York	5.0	28.0
Hawaii	0.3	26.6
Arizona	1.2	25.9
New Jersey	2.0	25.5

Source: www.census.gov/population/www/cen2000/phc-t20.html/tab04.pdf

These population demographics indicate that all states need to provide services for English learners, with the need greatest in California, New Mexico, New York, and Texas, serving Hispanics or Asian/Pacific Islanders. The linguistic and cultural variety of English learners suggests that more and more teachers serve as intercultural and interlinguistic educators—those who can reach out to learners from a variety of backgrounds and offer effective learning experiences.

Psychological Factors That Influence Instruction

Learners do not learn language in a vacuum. They learn it by interacting with others. Psychological and sociocultural factors play important roles in a learner's acquiring and using a second language. Teachers who are aware of these individual (psychological) and group (sociocultural) factors are able to adapt instruction to meet the individual needs of the learners so that each student can achieve academic success. Figure 1.1 offers an outline that can help teachers organize the factors they know about a given learner.

Psychological factors are traits specific to individuals that enable them to acquire a second language (L2). Learners use the assets of their personalities to absorb the ambiance of the culture, to process the language they hear, and to create meaningful responses. Psychological factors can be divided into three categories: *background* factors, *social–emotional* factors, and *cognitive* factors. Teachers can help students be aware of those psychological factors that further their language learning and can work with students to ensure that these factors promote rather than impede their learning.

The Learner's Background

Naming Practices and Forms of Address. A learner's name represents the learner's individuality as well as a family connection. People feel validated if their names are treated with respect. Teachers who make the effort to pronounce students' names accurately communicate a sense of caring. Students may be asked to speak their names into a tape recorder so the teacher can practice privately. Expecting students to say their names again and again so the teacher can rehearse may be embarrassing for both parties.

Naming practices differ across cultures. The custom in the United States is to have a first (or given), middle, and last (or family) name. On lists, the first and last names are often reversed in order to alphabetize the names. In other parts of the world, naming practices differ. In Vietnam, for example, names also consist of three parts, in the following order: family name, middle name, and given name. The names are always given in this order and cannot be reversed because doing so would denote a different person—Nguyên Van Hai is different from Hai Van Nguyên. In Taiwan the family name also goes first, followed by given names. Puerto Ricans, as well as other Hispanics, generally use three names: a given name, followed by the father's surname and then the mother's surname. If one last name must be used, it is generally the father's surname. Thus, Esther Reyes Mimosa can be listed as Esther Reyes. If the first name is composed of two given names (Hector Luis), both are used. This person may

Figure 1.1 English-Learner Profile

Psychological Factors

The Learner's Background

Learner's name _____Age _____ Gender (M / F)

Grade _____ L1 proficiency _____

Type of bilingualism _____

Previous L2 experience _____

Assessed L2 level: Reading _____ Writing _____ Listening _____ Speaking _____

Prior academic success _____

Likes/dislikes _____

Social–Emotional Factors

Self-esteem _____

Motivation _____

Anxiety level _____

Attitudes toward L1/L2 _____

Attitudes toward the teacher and the class _____

Cognitive Factors

Stage of L2 acquisition _____

Cognitive style/Learning style _____

Learning strategies _____

Sociocultural Factors

Family acculturation and use of L1 and L2_____

Family values _____

Institutional support for L1 _____

Sociocultural support for L1 in the classroom environment _____

have a brother who is Hector José; for either to be called simply Hector would represent a loss of identity.

In many cultures, adults are referred to by their function rather than their name. In Hmong, *xib fwb* means "teacher," and Hmong children may use the English term *teacher* in the classroom rather than a title plus surname, as in "Mrs. Jasko." Middle-class European-American teachers may consider this to be rude rather than realizing this is a cultural difference.

Osgood (2002) suggests ways to enlist native-English-speaking students to make friends with newcomers: Challenge them to teach a new student their names and to learn the new student's first and last names, using recess, lunchtime, or free time to accomplish this task.

Adapted Instruction: Students' Names

- Understand the use and order of names and pronounce them correctly.
- Don't change a student's name, apply a nickname, or use an "English" version of a student's name (even at the student's request) without first checking with a member of the student's family.

Age. Second-language acquisition (SLA) is a complex process that occurs over a long period of time. Although many people believe that children acquire a second language more rapidly than adults, recent research counters this notion. While it is true that the kind of instruction varies greatly according to the age of the learner, there is little evidence to indicate that biology closes the door to learning a second language at certain ages (see Singleton & Ryan [2004] and Han [2004] for further discussion of age-related issues in SLA, as well as the Point/Counterpoint box on page 8).

First-Language Proficiency. Research has shown that proficiency in the first language (L1) helps students to achieve in school. In order to learn a student's strengths in the first language, a teacher, primary-language-speaking aide, or parent who is fluent in the language of the student may observe a student working or playing in the primary language and take notes on the child's language behavior, or schools may rely on formal testing. Knowledge about the student's linguistic and academic abilities may assist the teacher in second-language academic content instruction.

Acceptance of the first language and use of the first language to support instruction promotes a low-anxiety environment for students. A lower anxiety level in turn promotes increased learning.

Adapted Instruction: First-Language Proficiency

- Monitor students' fluency in their primary languages and share concerns with parents if students appear to be dysfluent in their home languages.
- In cooperative groups, allow use of the first language so that students can discuss concepts.

Types of Bilingualism. Cummins (1979) analyzed the language characteristics of the children he studied and suggested that the level of bilingualism attained is an important factor in educational development. *Limited bilingualism,* or subtractive bilingualism, can occur when children's first language is gradually replaced by a more dominant and prestigious language. In this case, children may develop relatively low

Point/Counterpoint:

What Is the Best Age for Second-Language Acquisition?

For adults, learning a second language can be a frustrating and difficult experience. In contrast, it seems so easy for children. Is there a best age for learning a second language?

POINT: Children Learn Second Languages Easily.
Those who argue that a child can learn a second language more rapidly than an adult generally ascribe this ability to the *critical period hypothesis*—that the brain has a language-acquisition processor that functions best before puberty (Lenneberg, 1967)—despite the fact that the critical period hypothesis has not been proved.

Evidence from child second-language studies indicates that the language children speak is relatively simple compared to that of adults; it has shorter constructions with fewer vocabulary words and thus appears more fluent. Moreover, adults are often unaware that a child's silence indicates lack of understanding or shyness, and they underestimate the limitations of a child's second-language acquisition skills. One area that seems to be a clear advantage for children is phonology: The earlier a person begins to learn a second language, the closer the accent will become to that of a native speaker (Oyama, 1976).

COUNTERPOINT: Adults Learn Languages More Skillfully Than Children. Research comparing adults to children has consistently demonstrated that ado-
lescents and adults outperform children in controlled language-learning studies (e.g., Snow & Hoefnagel-Hoehle, 1978). Adults have access to more memory strategies; are, as a rule, more socially comfortable; and have greater experience with language in general. The self-discipline, strategy use, prior knowledge, and metalinguistic ability of the older learner create a distinct advantage for the adult over the child in language acquisition.

Marinova-Todd, Marshall, and Snow (2000) analyzed misconceptions about age and second-language learning and reached the following conclusions: "[O]lder learners have the potential to learn second languages to a very high level and introducing foreign languages to very young learners cannot be justified on grounds of biological readiness to learn languages" (p. 10). "Age does influence language learning, but primarily because it is associated with social, psychological, educational, and other factors that can affect L2 proficiency, not because of any critical period that limits the possibility of language learning by adults" (p. 28).

Implications for Teaching
Teachers need to be aware that learning a second language is difficult for children as well as for adults. Helping children to feel socially comfortable reduces their anxiety and assists acquisition.

levels of academic proficiency in both languages. The most positive cognitive effects are experienced in *proficient bilingualism*, when students attain high levels of proficiency in both languages. This is also called *additive bilingualism*.

Adapted Instruction: Promoting Additive Bilingualism

- Seek out or prepare handouts that encourage families to preserve the home language.
- Make sure classroom or community libraries feature books in the home language and encourage students to check out books in both languages.
- Welcome classroom visitors and volunteers who speak the home language, and ask them to speak to the class about the importance of proficiency in two languages.

Previous L2 Experience. English learners in the same grade may have had vastly different prior exposure to English, ranging from previous all-primary-language instruction to submersion in English—including students with no prior schooling at all. Moreover, no two students have been exposed to exactly the same input of English outside of class. Therefore, students' prior exposure to English and attainment of proficiency are often highly varied.

Students who have been overcorrected when first learning English may have "shut down" and be unwilling to speak. It may take time for a more positive approach to L2 instruction to produce results, combined with a positive attitude toward L1 maintenance.

Assessed L2 Level. An important part of the knowledge about the learner that a teacher amasses as a foundation for instruction is the student's assessed level of proficiency in listening, speaking, reading, and writing in English. This can be obtained during the process of assessment for placement. In California, the California English Language Development Test (CELDT) (online at www.cde.ca.gov/ta/tg/el) is the designated placement instrument; other states have other ways to assess proficiency. (See each state's Department of Education Website.) No matter the source of information, the student's L2 level is the beginning point of instruction in English.

Adapted Instruction: Assessing L2 Proficiency Levels

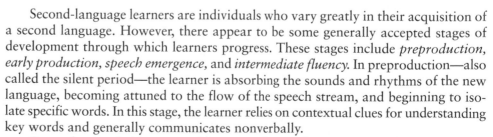

- Be aware that a student's listening/speaking proficiency may surpass that of reading and writing, or vice versa.
- Assess each language skill independently.
- Use a measure such as the Student Oral Language Observation Matrix (SOLOM) to assess students' oral proficiency.
- Use *The English–Español Reading Inventory for the Classroom* (Flynt & Cooter, 1999) to provide a quick assessment of reading levels in two languages.

Second-language learners are individuals who vary greatly in their acquisition of a second language. However, there appear to be some generally accepted stages of development through which learners progress. These stages include *preproduction, early production, speech emergence,* and *intermediate fluency.* In preproduction—also called the silent period—the learner is absorbing the sounds and rhythms of the new language, becoming attuned to the flow of the speech stream, and beginning to isolate specific words. In this stage, the learner relies on contextual clues for understanding key words and generally communicates nonverbally.

Once a learner feels more confident, words and phrases are attempted—the early production stage. Responses can consist of single words ("yes," "no," "OK," "you," "come") or two- or three-word combinations ("where book," "no go," "don't go," "teacher help"). Students can sometimes recite simple poems and sing songs at this point. In the third stage, speech emergence, learners respond more freely. Utterances become longer and more complex, but as utterances begin to resemble sentences, syntax errors are more noticeable than in the earlier stage ("Where you going?" "The boy running."). Once in intermediate fluency, students begin to initiate and sustain conversations and are often able to recognize and correct their own errors.

Regardless of the way one labels the stages of second-language acquisition, it is now recognized that, in natural situations, learners progress through predictable stages, and learners advance through them at their own pace. Undue pressure to move through the stages rapidly only frustrates and retards language learning.

Adapted Instruction: Matching Instruction to Students' L2 Levels

Ideally, classroom activities match the students' second-language acquisition levels.

Beginning Level (preproduction stage)
- Provide concrete activities featuring input that is augmented by pictures, real objects, carefully modified teacher speech, and frequent repetition of new vocabulary.

Early Intermediate and Intermediate Levels (early production and speech emergence)
- Ask questions that evoke responses of single words and brief phrases.
- Provide opportunities for students to use their primary language as they acquire the second language.

Early Advanced Level
- Engage students in opportunities to speak with greater complexity, read several pages of text even though they may have limited comprehension, and write paragraphs.
- Offer a curriculum that supports and explicitly teaches learning strategies (see Chapter 5).

Prior Academic Success. A valid predictor of school success is prior academic success. By reading a student's cumulative academic record, a teacher may get a sense of the student's strengths and weaknesses. This can be augmented by observations of the student during academic activities and interviews of family members and former teachers. It is important for the current teacher to assemble as complete a record of students' prior schooling as possible to best inform instructional decisions.

Likes/Dislikes. Inquiring about students' favorite academic subjects, television shows, and extracurricular activities is one way of bridging adult–child, teacher–student, or intercultural gaps. Getting-to-know-you activities can be based on the following questions: Who/what is your favorite [native-language/culture] singer? Actor? Video game? Outdoor game? Storybook? Grocery store? Holiday? What do you like about it? Students can write about favorite subjects, and teachers can then use these culturally familiar ideas in math story problems and other content.

Psychological Factors: Social–Emotional

The affective domain, the emotional side of human behavior, is the means through which individuals become aware of their environment, respond to it with feeling, and act as though their feelings make a difference. This emotional dimension helps determine how language acquisition and communication take place. The affective factors discussed here are self-esteem, motivation, anxiety, and learner attitudes.

Self-Esteem. A large part of one's feelings revolve around how one feels about oneself, one's self-esteem. High self-esteem may *cause* language success or *result from* language success. Many teachers, however, intuitively recognize that self-esteem issues play important roles in their classrooms, and they encourage students to feel proud of their successes and abilities. Self-esteem enhancement, such as efforts to empower students with positive images of self, family, and culture, may facilitate language learning. Teachers also strive to ensure that learners feel good about specific aspects of their language learning (e.g., speaking, writing) or about their success with a particular task.

Self-esteem is particularly at risk when learning a second language, because so much identity and pride are associated with language competence. Schools that honor the primary languages and cultures of students and help students to develop additive bilingualism foster strong identities; schools in which students face disrespect and discrimination hinder students' social and emotional development (Cummins, 2001).

Children who do poorly in school face daily degradation to their sense of self-esteem as they often receive low grades, and experience disapproval from their teachers and even social ostracism from peers (McKay, 2000). A healthy sense of success is necessary not only to master academics, but also to feel valuable to society.

Example of Concept: Building Self-Esteem

Anita Alvarez was a Spanish-speaking first-grade student at the beginning stages of English-language acquisition. She was shy and retiring, and Mrs. Figueroa noticed that she seldom took advantage of opportunities to chat with her peers. Anita seemed to have good sensorimotor abilities and to be particularly adept at building three-dimensional models following printed diagrams. When Mrs. Figueroa observed that Mary, another student in the class, had a lot of difficulty in constructing objects, she teamed Anita with Mary; and, with Anita's help, Mary completed her project successfully. Noting this success, Mrs. Figueroa publicly praised her to the class and referred students to her for help. Mrs. Figueroa was pleased to see that, subsequently, Anita talked more with other students and seemed to acquire English at a faster rate.

Many classroom activities can be used to enhance students' self-esteem. In the Name Game, students introduce themselves by first name, adding a word that describes how they are feeling that day—using a word that begins with the same letter as their first name (the teacher may provide English learners with an alphabetized list of adjectives). Each subsequent person repeats what the others have said in sequence. Another activity, Name Interviews, lets students work in pairs to use a teacher-provided questionnaire. This includes questions such as, "What do you like about your name? Who named you? Were you named for someone? Are there members of your family who have the same name?" and more (Siccone, 1995).

Adapted Instruction: Fostering Self-Esteem in Classroom Groups

Weber (2005) suggests ways that classroom teachers can "create a tone that encourages thought" (p. 16). These ideas can also foster students' self-esteem. Students will

- feel free to express their minds, in respect, and without any attack in response
- contribute freely to ideas and feel valued in small teams and in class
- show positive attitudes to others' different ideas, even when they disagree

The ability to take risks, to "gamble," may facilitate second-language acquisition. Educators believe that those who are willing to guess at meaning when it is not clear and to be relatively unconcerned about making errors will progress in language skills more rapidly than their more inhibited peers. As Brown (2000) pointed out, however, students who make random guesses and blurt out meaningless phrases have not been as successful. It appears that moderate risk takers stand the best chance at language development.

Motivation. "The impulse, emotion, or desire that causes one to act in a certain way" is one way to define motivation. Gardner and Lambert (1972) postulated two types of motivation in learning a second language: *instrumental,* the need to acquire a language for a specific purpose such as reading technical material or getting a job, and *integrative,* the desire to become a member of the culture of the second-language group. Most situations involve a mixture of both types.

Generally, in classrooms, teachers may believe that motivation is a trait or a state. As a *trait,* motivation is seen as being relatively consistent and persistent and is attributed to various groups: parents, communities, or cultures. Students are motivated to learn English by such incentives as the desire to please—or not to shame—their families or by the drive to bring honor to their communities. As a *state,* motivation is viewed as a more temporary condition that can be influenced by the use of highly interesting materials or activities, or by contingencies of reward or punishment (Tharp, 1989b).

Adapted Instruction: Motivating Students

- Give pep talks to remind students that anything worth doing may seem difficult at first.
- Provide students with a list of encouraging phrases to repeat to themselves as self-talk.

Anxiety Level. Anxiety when learning a second language can be seen as similar to general feelings of tension that students experience in the classroom. Almost everyone feels some anxiety when learning a new language—that is, they have feelings of self-consciousness, a desire to be perfect when speaking, and a fear of making mistakes. Using a foreign language can threaten a person's sense of self if speakers fear they cannot represent themselves fully in a new language or understand others readily. Anxiety can be debilitating. As one student recalled,

> During these several months after my arrival in the U.S.A., every day I came back exhausted so I had to take a rest for a while, stretching myself on the bed. For all the time, I strained every nerve in order to understand what the people were saying and make myself understood in my broken English. I sometimes have to pretend to understand by smiling, even though I feel alienated, uneasy, and tense. (Barna, 2007, p. 71)

Because anxiety can cause learners to feel defensive and can block effective learning, language educators strive to make the classroom a place of warmth and friendliness, where risk-taking is rewarded and encouraged and where peer work, small-group work, games, and simulations are featured. Highly anxious learners must divide their attentional resources into both learning and worrying about learning. This reduces the ability to concentrate and be successful at learning tasks. Accepting English learners' use of both languages during instruction may help reduce their anxiety about speaking English (Pappamihiel, 2002).

Example of Concept: Reducing Anxiety

In a series of lessons, Mr. Green has students write a letter to an imaginary "Dear Abby," relating a particular difficulty they have in language learning and asking for advice. Working in groups, the students read and discuss the letters, offer advice, and return the letters to their originators for follow-up discussion.

Adapted Instruction: Ways to Deal with Excessive Student Anxiety

- Monitor activities to ensure that students are receiving no undue pressure.
- Avoid having anxious students perform in front of large groups.
- When using a novel format or starting a new type of task, provide students with examples or models of how the task is done.
- Occasionally make available take-home tests to lower unnecessary time pressures for performance.
- Teach test-taking skills explicitly and provide study guides to help students who may need extra academic preparation.
- To increase energy levels in class, give students a brief chance to be physically active by introducing stimuli that whet their curiosity or surprise them.

Source: Adapted from Woolfolk (2007).

Attitudes of the Learner. Attitudes play a critical role in learning English. Attitudes toward self, toward language (one's own and English), toward English-speaking people (particularly peers), and toward the teacher and the classroom environment affect students (Richard-Amato, 2003). One's attitude toward the self involves cognition about one's ability in general, ability to learn language, and self-esteem and its related emotions. These cognitions and feelings are seldom explicit and may be slow to change.

Attitudes toward language and those who speak it are largely a result of experience and the influence of people in the immediate environment, such as peers and parents. Negative reactions are often the result of negative stereotypes or the experience of discrimination or racism. Peñalosa (1980) pointed out that if English learners are made to feel inferior because of accent or language status, they may have a defensive reaction against English and English speakers. Students may also experience ambivalent feelings about their primary language. In some families, parents use English at the expense of the primary language in the hope of influencing children to learn English more rapidly. This can cause problems within the family and create a backlash against English or English speakers.

Students' attitudes toward the primary language vary; some students may have a defensive reaction or ambivalent feelings toward their own primary language as a result of internalized shame if they have been made to feel inferior. Peers may incite attitudes against the L1 or may try to tease or bully those who speak the same primary language with a different dialect.

Attitudes toward the teacher and the classroom environment play an important role in school success in general and English acquisition in particular. One way to create a sense of belonging is to assign a new student to a home group that remains unchanged for a long time. If such groups are an ongoing aspect of classroom social organization, with rules of caring, respect, and concern already in place, then the home group provides an ideal social group to receive newcomers and help them develop interdependence, support, and identity (Peregoy & Boyle, 2008).

Teachers can do much to model positive attitudes toward the students' primary language (see Chapter 8). A teacher–family conference may be advisable if a student continues to show poor attitudes toward the first or second language or the school. (Chapter 10 offers a range of strategies for involving the family in schooling.)

Psychological Factors: Cognitive

The cognitive perspective helps educators understand language learners as people who are active processors of information. Language is used in school in expanded ways: to create meaning from print, to encode ideas into print, to analyze and compare information, and to respond to classroom discussion. All of these activities involve cognitive factors. Students learn in many different ways using a variety of strategies and styles. This section addresses students' cognitive styles, learning styles, and learning strategies.

Cognitive Style. A cognitive style refers to "consistent and rather enduring tendencies or preferences *within* an individual" (Brown, 1987, p. 79). Tharp (1989b) suggested two cognitive styles that have relevance for classrooms: visual/verbal and holistic/analytic. Schools expect and reward verbal more than visual, and analytic more than holistic styles. For students who learn by observing and doing rather than through verbal instructions, schools may be mystifying until they catch on to a different cognitive style. Similarly, students with more holistic thought processes learn by seeing the "big picture."

Learning Styles. Many researchers have documented differences in the manner in which learners approach the learning task. These preferences serve as models for instructors in their efforts to anticipate the different needs and perspectives of students. Once learning styles have been identified, instructors can use the information to plan and to modify certain aspects of courses and assignments. Hruska-Riechmann and Grasha (1982) offer six learning styles: competitive versus cooperative, dependent versus independent, and participant versus avoidant. For Sonbuchner (1991), learning styles refer to information-processing styles and work environment preferences. Table 1.2 lists learning style variables that have been divided into four categories—cognitive, affective, incentive, and physiological—according to Keefe (1987).

Table 1.3 provides a list of learning style Websites that feature learning style information, diagnostic checklists, and ideas for adapted instruction. The teacher who builds variety into instruction and helps learners to understand their own styles can enhance students' achievement.

Adapted Instruction: Teaching to Diverse Learning Styles

Although in the typical classroom it is not possible to tailor instruction precisely to meet individuals' needs, some modifications can be made that take learning styles into account.

■ Students who are dependent may benefit from encouragement to become more independent learners; the teacher may offer a choice between two learning activities, for example, or reduce the number of times a student has to ask the teacher for help.

■ Students who are highly competitive may be provided activities and assignments that encourage collaboration and interdependent learning.
■ Students who show little tolerance for frustration can be given a range of tasks on the same skill or concept that slowly increases in complexity, with the student gradually gaining skill and confidence.

Learning Strategies. Aside from general language-acquisition processes that all learners use, there are individual strategies that learners adopt to help them in the acquisition process. Second-language-acquisition research divides individual learner strategies into two types: communication and learning. Learning strategies include the techniques a person uses to think and to act in order to complete a task. Extensive work in identifying learning strategies has been done by O'Malley and Chamot (O'Malley, Chamot, Stewner-Manzanares, Kupper, & Russo, 1985a, 1985b), who have incorporated specific instruction in learning strategies in their Cognitive Academic Language Learning Approach (CALLA; see Chapter 5). Communication strategies

Table 1.2

Variables That Constitute Learning Style Differences

Cognitive	Affective	Incentive	Physiological
• Field independent/field dependent • Scanning (broad attention) v. focusing (narrow) • Conceptual/analytical v. perceptual/concrete • Task constricted (easily distracted) v. task flexible (capable of controlled concentration) • Reflective v. impulsive • Leveling (tendency to lump new experiences with previous ones) v. sharpening (ability to distinguish small differences) • High cognitive complexity (multidimensional discrimination, accepting of diversity and conflict) v. low cognitive complexity (tendency to reduce conflicting information to a minimum)	• Need for structure • Curiosity • Persistence • Level of anxiety • Frustration tolerance	• Locus of control (internal: seeing oneself as responsible for own behavior; or external: attributing circumstances to luck, chance, or other people) • Risk taking v. caution • Competition v. cooperation • Level of achievement motivation (high or low) • Reaction to external reinforcement (does or does not need rewards and punishment) • Social motivation arising from family, school, and ethnic background (high or low) • Personal interests (hobbies, academic preferences)	• Gender-related differences (typically, males are more visual–spatial and aggressive, females more verbal and tuned to fine-motor control) • Personal nutrition (healthy v. poor eating habits) • Health • Time-of-day preferences (morning, afternoon, evening, night) • Sleeping and waking habits • Need for mobility • Need for and response to varying levels of light, sound, and temperature

Source: Based on Keefe (1987).

Table 1.3

Websites That Feature Learning Style Information, Diagnostic Inventories, and Ideas for Adapted Instruction

Website	Source	Content
www.chaminade.org/inspire/learnstl.htm	Adapted from Colin Rose's 1987 book *Accelerated Learning*	Users can take an inventory to determine if they are a visual, auditory, or kinesthetic and tactile learner.
www.engr.ncsu.edu/learningstyles/ilsweb.html	North Carolina State University	Users can take a learning styles questionnaire with 44 items to self-assess.
http://volcano.und.nodak.edu/vwdocs/msh/llc/is/4mat.html	Living Laboratory Curriculum	Explains how to use McCarthy's 4-MAT system.
www.usd.edu/trio/tut/ts/style.html	University of San Diego	Learn about learning styles (auditory, visual, and kinesthetic); identify your own learning style.

are employed for transmitting an idea when the learner cannot produce precise linguistic forms, whereas learning strategies relate to the individual's processing, storage, and retrieval of language concepts (Brown, 2000).

Communication strategies include avoiding sounds, structures, or topics that are beyond current proficiency; memorizing stock phrases to rely on when all else fails; asking a conversant for help or pausing to consult a dictionary; and falling back on the primary language for help in communication. The last strategy, often called *code switching*, has been studied extensively because it permeates a learner's progression in a second language. Code switching—the alternating use of two languages on the word, phrase, clause, or sentence level—has been found to serve a variety of purposes, not just as a strategy to help when expressions in the second language are lacking.

Baker (2001) lists ten purposes for code switching: (1) to emphasize a point, (2) because a word is unknown in one of the languages, (3) for ease and efficiency of expression, (4) as a repetition to clarify, (5) to express group identity and status and/or to be accepted by a group, (6) to quote someone, (7) to interject in a conversation, (8) to exclude someone, (9) to cross social or ethnic boundaries, and (10) to ease tension in a conversation. Code switching thus serves a variety of intentions beyond the mere linguistic. It has important power and social ramifications.

According to Buell (2004), "Code-switching is a key marker of social identities, relations, and context. When a speaker uses or changes a code, she is signaling who she is, how she relates to listeners or readers, how she understands the context and what communication tools are available to her" (pp. 99, 100). Code switching can be seen not only in spoken conversations but also in mass media, literature, in science textbooks, and so on. Students' writing and other discourse practices are apt to be complex, multilayered, and sometimes contradictory. Understanding students in the full splendor of their code-switching and use of dialect, peer-influenced, or idiosyncratic language is part of the joy of teaching.

Example of Concept: Code Switching

Jennifer Seitz, a third-grade teacher, uses Alicia's primary language, Spanish, as a way to help Alicia learn English. A recent Spanish-speaking immigrant to the United States, Alicia has acquired whole phrases or words in English from a fellow student and intersperses these when speaking Spanish to gain access to her peer group. On the playground, she has been heard to repeat in Spanish something just said in English, perhaps to clarify what was said or to identify with two groups. She often uses English when learning concepts in the classroom, but uses Spanish when she is discussing the concept with another student or when the conversation involves a personal matter. The content of the instruction and the interpersonal link between speakers seem to be the main factors in her language choice.

Although language purists look down on language mixing, a more fruitful approach is letting children learn in whatever manner they feel most comfortable, so that anxiety about language will not interfere with concept acquisition. In fact, a teacher who learns words and expressions in the students' home language is able to use the students' language to express solidarity and share personal feelings when appropriate.

Adapted Instruction: Accommodating Students' Psychological Needs

To adjust for individual psychological factors, teachers can provide verbal reassurances to timid students, alternative learning activities to address multiple intelligences, explicit opportunities to help students express their strong abilities, and additional mediation for students who need to achieve despite a possible weak ability in a specific area.

Sociocultural Factors That Influence Instruction

Language learning occurs within social and cultural contexts. A part of the sense of mastery and enjoyment in a language is acting appropriately and understanding cultural norms. Learners adapt patterns of behavior in a new language and culture based on experiences from their own culture. Home culture patterns of behavior can be both helpful and limiting in learning the second-language community's patterns of interaction. Thus, sociocultural factors—how people interact with one another and how they carry out their daily business—play a large role in second-language acquisition.

If, as many believe, prolonged exposure to English is sufficient for mastery, then why do so many students fail to achieve the proficiency in English necessary for academic success? Some clues to this perplexity can be found beyond the language itself, in the sociocultural context. Do the students feel that their language and culture are accepted and validated by the school? A well-meaning teacher, with the most up-to-date pedagogy, may still fail to foster achievement if students are socially and culturally uncomfortable with, resistant to, or alienated from schooling.

As students learn a second language, their success is dependent on sociocultural factors. These factors are explored here with a view toward helping teachers facilitate student learning by bridging the culture and language gaps.

Family Acculturation and the Use of First and Second Languages

Acculturation is the process of adapting to a new culture. English learners in the United States, by the mere fact of living in this country and participating in schools, learn a second culture as well as a second language. How the acculturation proceeds depends on factors beyond language itself and beyond the individual learner's motivation, capabilities, and style—it usually is a familywide phenomenon.

In studying students' differential school performance, Ogbu (1978) draws a distinction between various types of immigrant groups. *Castelike minorities* are those minority groups that were originally incorporated into society against their will and have been systematically exploited and depreciated over generations through slavery or colonization. Castelike minorities traditionally work at the lowest paying and most undesirable jobs, and they suffer from a job ceiling they cannot rise above regardless of talent, motivation, or achievement. Thus, academic success is not always seen as helpful or even desirable for members of these groups.

On the other hand, *immigrant minorities* who are relatively free of a history of depreciation, such as immigrants to the United States from El Salvador, Guatemala, and Nicaragua, believe that the United States is a land of opportunity. These immigrants do not view education as irrelevant or exploitative but rather as an important investment. Therefore, the internalized attitudes about the value of school success for family members may influence the individual student.

Schumann (1978) developed the acculturation model that asserted, "the degree to which a learner acculturates to the target language group will control the degree to which he acquires the second language" (p. 34). He listed the following social variables that he concludes are important factors in acculturation:

- The primary-language and English-language groups view each other as socially equal, of equal status.
- The primary-language and the English-language groups both desire that the L1 group assimilate.
- Both the primary-language and English-language groups expect the primary-language group to share social facilities with the English-language group.
- The primary-language group is small and not very cohesive.
- The primary-language group's culture is congruent with that of the English-language group.
- Both groups have positive attitudes toward each other.
- The primary-language group expects to stay in the area for an extended period.

Schumann's model demonstrates that the factors influencing a student's L1 and L2 use are complicated by sociocultural variables stemming from society at large. For example, one can infer from the model that a family living in a predominantly primary-language community will exert fewer pressures on the children to speak English.

Adapted Instruction: Learning about the Family

- If possible, visit the student's home to observe the family's degree of acculturation.
- Note the family's media consumption:

    What television shows does the family watch, in which language?
    Do family members read books, magazines, or newspapers, and in which languages?

A family's use of L1 and L2 is also influenced by the relative status of the primary language in the eyes of the dominant culture. In modern U.S. culture, the social value and prestige of speaking a second language varies with socioeconomic position; it also varies as to the second language that is spoken.

Many middle-class parents believe that learning a second language benefits their children personally and socially and will later benefit them professionally. In fact, it is characteristic of the elite group in the United States who are involved in scholarly work, diplomacy, foreign trade, or travel to desire to be fully competent in two languages (Porter, 1990). However, the languages that parents wish their children to study are often not those spoken by recently arrived immigrants (Dicker, 1992). This suggests that a certain bias exists in being bilingual—that being competent in a "foreign language" is valuable, whereas knowing an immigrant language is a burden to be overcome.

There are many ways in which a second-class status is communicated to speakers of other languages, and because language attitudes usually operate at an inconspicuous level, school personnel and teachers are not always aware of the attitudes they hold. For example, the interlanguage of English learners—the language they use as they learn English—may be considered a dialect of English. Students learning English express themselves in many different dialects, depending on the language they hear in their homes and communities. These forms of English vary in the pronunciation of words, the selection of vocabulary that is used, and the way that words are arranged in sentences.

Some teachers only accept Standard English, the English found in textbooks. They may view nonstandard forms as less logical, less precise, or less elegant; sometimes they may even stigmatized these forms as corrupt or debased. Worse, they may view those who speak nonstandard English as less intelligent or less gifted linguistically. Research has shown that incorporating nonstandard language use in the classroom is often a helpful bridge to the learning of Standard English. When students feel that they are accepted and are confident of their language skills, they are more likely to want to acquire a second language (Siegel, 1999).

If teachers devalue the accent, syntax, or other speech characteristics of students as they learn English, English learners receive the message that their dialect is not accepted.

If teachers use dialect to evaluate students' potential or use proficiency in Standard English to predict school achievement, it is possible that the teacher's own attitude toward the students' dialects—either positive or negative—has more to do with students' cognitive and academic achievement than does the dialect.

Adapted Instruction: Recognizing Biases

- Recognize areas in which there may be differences in language use and in which those differences might create friction because the minority group's use may be deemed "inferior" by the majority.
- Be honest about your own biases, recognizing that you communicate these biases whether or not you are aware of them.
- Model correct usage without overt correction, and the student in time will self-correct—*if* the student chooses Standard English as the appropriate sociolinguistic choice for that context.

Family Values and School Values

As student populations in U.S. schools become increasingly diversified both linguistically and culturally, teachers and students have come to recognize the important role that attitudes and values play in school success. At times, the values of the school may differ from those of the home. Not only the individual's attitudes as described above, but also the family's values and attitudes toward schooling, influence a child's school success.

Example of Concept: Family Values

Amol is a third-grade student whose parents were born in India. As the only son in a male-dominant culture, he has internalized a strong sense of commitment to becoming a heart surgeon. His approach to classwork is painstaking. Often he is the last to finish an assignment during class. The teacher's main frustration with Amol is that he cannot quickly complete his work. However, when talking with Amol's family, the teacher notes that his parents seem pleased with his perfectionism and not at all concerned with his speed at tasks. In this respect, home and school values differ.

In this example, the teacher epitomizes a mainstream U.S. value: speed and efficiency in learning. Teachers may describe students of other cultures as being lackadaisical and uncaring about learning, when in fact they may be operating within a different time frame and value system.

Other values held by teachers and embodied in classroom procedures have to do with task orientation. The typical U.S. classroom is a place of work in which students are expected to conform to a schedule, keep busy, maintain order, avoid wasting time, conform to authority, and achieve academically in order to attain personal worth. Working alone is also valued in school, and children may spend a great deal of time in activities that do not allow them to interact verbally with other people or to move physically around the room.

Children need to find within the structure and content of their schooling those behaviors and perspectives that permit them to switch between home and school cultural behaviors and values without inner conflict or crises of identity (Pérez & Torres-Guzmán, 2002). Teachers need to feel comfortable with the values and behaviors of their students' cultures in order to develop a flexible cultural repertoire within the context of teaching.

The danger of excluding the students' culture(s) from the classroom is that cultural identity, if not included, may become oppositional. Ogbu and Matute-Bianchi (1986) described how oppositional identity in a distinctly Mexican-American frame of reference influenced the performance of Mexican-American children. They attributed achievement difficulties on the part of some Mexican-American children to a distrust of academic effort. When schools were segregated and offered inferior education to this community, a general mistrust of schools caused a difficulty in accepting, internalizing, and following school rules of behavior for achievement. This element of resistance or opposition is not always overt but often takes the form of mental withdrawal, high absenteeism, or reluctance to do classwork.

Schools with high concentrations of English learners often deprive children of the use of their cultural knowledge and experience, even when staff are well meaning. It is easy to give lip service to the validation of the students' cultures and values. However, teachers should not use examples drawn from one culture and not another, use literature that displays pictures and photographs of one culture only, and set up classroom procedures that make some students feel less comfortable than others. This is unfair and damaging. The implementation of a rich and flexible cultural repertoire is the strategy that can allow cultures to mix constructively and promote achievement.

Adapted Instruction: Accommodating Students' Cultures

> Dalle and Young (2003) suggest that teachers check with families to see if family cultures have any "taboos" that would make students uncomfortable performing certain activities; discuss with family members the support available for homework, and arrange for after-class supervision if needed; and explain key concepts using ideas that are familiar from the students' perspective.

Institutional Support for the Primary Language and Those Who Speak It

Educators may view a student's ability to speak a home language other than English as an advantage or as a liability toward school success. Those who blame bilingual students for failing in school often operate from the mistaken beliefs that students and/or their parents are uninterested in education; that students who are raised as native speakers of another language are handicapped in learning because they have not acquired sufficient English; or that cultural differences between the ways children learn at home or among their peers and the ways they are expected to learn at school interfere with school learning.

In fact, schools often operate in ways that advantage certain children and disadvantage others, causing distinct outcomes that align with social and political forces in the larger cultural context. Institutional support for the primary language and students who speak it is a prime factor in school success for these students.

Some social theorists see the culture of the school as maintaining the poor in a permanent underclass and as legitimizing inequality (Giroux, 1983). In other words, schooling is used to reaffirm class boundaries. This creates an educational class system in which minority students—or any students who are not successful in the classroom—emerge from their schooling to occupy the same social status as their parents.

Example of Concept: The Way Schools Use Language to Perpetuate Social Class Inequality

Consider this account from Erickson of a fourth-grade class that was electing student council representatives.

Mrs. Lark called for nominations. Mary, a monolingual English-speaking European-American student, nominated herself. Mrs. Lark accepted Mary's self-nomination and wrote her name on the board. Rogelio, a Spanish-speaking Mexican-American child with limited English proficiency, nominated Pedro. Mrs. Lark reminded the class that the representative must be "outspoken." Rogelio again said "Pedro." Mrs. Lark announced to the class again that the representative must be "a good outspoken citizen." Pedro turned red and stared at the floor. Mrs. Lark embarrassed Rogelio into withdrawing the nomination. No other Mexican-American child was nominated, and Mary won the election. Pedro and Rogelio were unusually quiet for the rest of the school day.

Source: Adapted from Erickson (1977, p. 59).

Incidents like the one in Mrs. Lark's classroom are generally unintentional on the teacher's part. A beginning step in helping all students feel fully integrated into the class and the learning environment is for teachers to become sensitive to their own cultural and linguistic predispositions.

Nieto and Bode (2008) identified numerous structures within schools that affect English learners: tracking, testing, the curriculum, pedagogy, the school's physical structure and disciplinary policies, the limited roles of both students and teachers, and limited parent and community involvement.

Tracking. The practice of placing students in groups of matched abilities, despite its superficial advantages, in reality often labels and groups children for years and allows them little or no opportunity to change groups. Secondary school personnel who place English learners in low tracks or in nonacademic ELD classes preclude those students from any opportunity for higher-track, precollege work. In contrast, a supportive school environment offers equal education opportunity to all students, regardless of their language background.

Testing. Students who respond poorly on standardized tests are often given "basic skills" in a remedial curriculum that is essentially the same as the one in which they were not experiencing success. A supportive school is one that offers testing adaptations for English learners as permitted by law; for example, academic testing in the primary language, extended time for test taking, and fully trained testing administrators.

Curriculum Design. Only a small fraction of knowledge is codified into textbooks and teachers' guides, and this is rarely the knowledge that English learners bring from their communities (see Loewen, 1995). In addition, the curriculum may be systematically watered down for the "benefit" of children in language-minority communities through the mistaken idea that such students cannot absorb the core curriculum. A supportive environment is one that maintains high standards while offering a curriculum that is challenging and meaningful.

Pedagogy. The way students are taught is often tedious and uninteresting, particularly for students who have been given a basic skills curriculum in a lower-track classroom. The pressure to "cover" a curriculum may exclude learning in depth and frustrate teachers and students alike. Pedagogy that is supportive fully involves students—teachers make every effort to present understandable instruction that engages students at high levels of cognitive stimulation.

Example of Concept: A School Culture That Disconnects, Bores, and Controls—for Teachers and Students Alike

Order predominated at the traditional high school that Wells (1996) studied. Control trumped creativity. Teachers were not encouraged to voice their educational philosophies or innovate. Instruction was driven by textbooks, with few opportunities for students to write. Reading became an exercise in searching for answers to chapter questions or worksheet blanks. Little inquiry, exploration, or reflection was asked of students. Pope (2002) came to a similar conclusion. Students, for the most part, experienced little genuine engagement. They did schoolwork because they had to—there was little evidence of curiosity or interest. If this is the case for the average middle-class high school, conditions can only be worse in inner-city schools, where the majority of immigrant students are educated.

The Physical Structure of the School. Architecture also affects the educational environment. Many inner-city schools are built like fortresses to forestall vandalism and theft. Rich suburban school districts, by contrast, may provide more space, more supplies, and campuslike schools for their educationally advantaged students. Supportive schooling is observable—facilities are humane, well cared for, and materially advantaged.

Disciplinary Policies. Certain students may be punished more often than others, particularly those who wear high-profile clothing, have high physical activity levels, or tend to hold an attitude of resistance toward schooling. Rather than defining students' predilections as deviant or disruptive, teachers can channel these interactions into cooperative groups that allow children to express themselves and learn at the same time, thus supporting rich cultural and linguistic expression.

The School Culture. The most powerful regularities about school are not found in the formalities such as course offerings and schedules. They are found in the school culture—such unspoken elements as the respect shown by students for academic endeavor, the openness that the teachers show when the principal drops in to observe instruction, and the welcome parents feel when they take an active role in the school. In its 1996 report *What Matters Most: Teaching and America's Future*, the National Commission on Teaching and America's Future argued that without a formal overhaul of school culture in America, students cannot learn well. This is a warning that applies especially to the aspects of school culture that promote success for English learners.

The Limited Role of Students. Students may be excluded from taking an active part in their own schooling, and alienation and passive frustration may result. However, in addition to language barriers, cultural differences may preclude some students from participating in ways that the mainstream culture rewards. The accompanying Example of Concept illustrates the ways in which the limited role of students is disempowering.

Example of Concept: The Limited Role of Students

Natisha has not said a word to any of her teachers since the beginning of school. It's not that she was a "bad" student; she turned in assignments and made Bs. She certainly didn't cause her teachers trouble. Therefore Mr. Williams, her high school counselor, was somewhat surprised to hear she was dropping out of school.

Natisha described her school experiences as coming to school, listening to teachers, and going home. School was boring and not connected to her real life. Nothing she was learning in school could help her get a job. She knew from more than ten years of listening to teachers and reading textbooks that her chances of becoming a news anchorwoman or even a teacher were about the same as winning the lottery.

School had helped silence Natisha. Classes provided no meaningful experience for her. The content may have been important to the teachers, but she could find no relationship to her own world.

Source: Adapted from Gollnick & Chinn (2006, p. 355).

The Limited Role of Teachers. Teachers of CLD students may be excluded from decision making just as students are disenfranchised. This may lead teachers to have negative feelings toward their students. A supportive environment for CLD students is supportive of their teachers as well.

Limited Family and Community Involvement. Inner-city schools with large populations of English learners may exclude families from participation. Parents may find it difficult to attend meetings, may be only symbolically involved in the governance of the school, or may feel a sense of mismatch with the culture of the school just as their children do. In circumstances like these, school personnel, in consultation with community and parent representatives, can begin to ameliorate such perceptions by talking with one another and developing means of communication and interaction appropriate for both parent and school communities.

Example of Concept: Building Home–School Partnerships

When students began skipping classes in high school, several teachers and staff became concerned. The district's ELD and bilingual staff and several school principals met individually with students and parents to search for the reasons the school system wasn't working. Community meetings were held with parents, teachers, school principals, central office administrators, and the school superintendent to strengthen the home–school partnership, and included informal potluck suppers and teacher- and parent-facilitated roundtable discussions. Numerous suggestions and positive actions came from these meetings—including the powerful links that were made between the district and the families (Zacarian, 2004a, pp. 11–13).

A supportive classroom environment for CLD students is less effective if the environment or practices of the school are discriminatory. Chapter 11 offers ways in which teachers can exercise influence within the school and society at large to support the right of CLD students to receive an effective education.

Sociocultural Support for L1 in the Classroom Environment

Various sociocultural factors influence the support that is offered for the primary language and its speakers in the classroom. Teaching and learning in mainstream classrooms are often organized with social structures that deny the ways in which students are most likely to learn. Tharp (1989b) describes the typical North-American classroom. Students are seated in ranks and files, and a teacher-leader instructs the whole group. Many students are not productive and on-task in this environment. They may benefit more from the opportunity to interact with peers as they learn, speaking their primary language if necessary to exchange information.

Cooperative learning has positive results in the education of CLD students (Kagan, 1986). Positive race relations among students and socialization toward pro-social values and behaviors are potential outcomes of a cooperative-learning environment. Cooperative learning may restore a sense of comfort in the school setting to children of a variety of cultures. Students may gain psychological support from one another as they acquire English, and this support can help the students work as a group with the teacher to achieve a workable sociocultural compromise between the use of L1 and L2 in the classroom.

Adapted Instruction: Supporting the Primary Language

- Feature the primary language(s) of students on bulletin boards throughout the school and within the classroom.
- Showcase primary-language skills in written and oral reports.
- Involve primary-language speakers as guests, volunteers, and instructional assistants.

This chapter introduced the English learner and highlighted a variety of factors that a teacher must consider to design and deliver effective instruction. Some of these factors lie within the student, and others are factors in society at large that affect the individual, the family, and the school. The teacher as an intercultural, interlinguistic educator learns everything possible about the background of the students and marshals every available kind of support to advance the education of English learners. The United States is expected to need at least two million teachers by 2011 (Chan, 2004). These teachers can greatly benefit from specific techniques in crosscultural, language, and academic development for English learners. ■

LEARNING MORE

Further Reading

Carolyn Nelson (2004), in the article "Reclaiming Teacher Preparation for Success in High-Needs Schools," describes her first year of teaching in an inner-city school in Rochester, New York. This article offers a memorable glimpse at her daily challenges in a school comprised largely of Puerto Rican and African-American students. She details the strengths of the elementary teacher education curriculum at San José State in the context of preparing teachers as problem-solving intellectuals, a point of view that imparts a balance to the "prescriptive, curriculum-in-a-box" approaches to teaching.

Web Search

The U.S. Census Bureau's Website "Minority Links" (online at www.census.gov/pubinfo/www/hotlinks.html) features demographic information on special populations (Hispanic/Latino, Asian, Native Hawaiian and other Pacific Islander, and American Indian/Alaska Native) that includes demographics by regional, state, and local areas.

Exploration

Find out about the number of English learners in your local school district by visiting a local school district office, or look it up in the demographics section of the State Department of Education Website in your state. Visit a school in a neighborhood that serves CLD students, or visit your neighborhood school and ask if there are English learners being served. If there are local teachers who specialize in the education of English learners, ask them about professional development opportunities in that field.

Experiment

Give a fifteen-word list in a foreign language to three different individuals: a primary school student (age 6–11), a middle school student (age 12–14), and an adult (age 18 or older). Let them study the words for five minutes and then ask them to recall the list. Compare the success of these learners. Ask them what strategy they used to complete the memory task. Which learner had more success? Which learner had more strategies?

PEARSON
myeducationlab
The Power of Classroom Practice
www.myeducationlab.com

Culture and Self-Esteem

This video discusses that it is important for English-language learners to retain their self-esteem. Often they are made to feel inferior to students from different cultures. Teaching culture should go both ways.

> To access the video, go to MyEducationLab (www.myeducationlab.com), choose the Díaz-Rico and Weed text, and log in to MyEducationLab for English Language Learners. Select the topic Diversity, and watch the video entitled "Culture and Self-Esteem."

Answer the following questions:
1. How would you define "self-efficacy"? What role does the teacher play in fostering this?
2. What are the possible consequences of teaching without concern for an individual's native culture?
3. What specific teaching strategies should a teacher include to ensure that all students are made to feel valued?

2 | Learning about Language Structure

Language is dynamic—and young people are usually on the cutting edge of language change.

When I'm Fifteen

When I'm fifteen . . .
I want to be a moon fixer—
The pieces that fall off
To glue them back on.
And I'll be a tree pushermover
'Cause they lean over too far.
I want to kill bugs
And put flies on them,
And catch cats and
Put them back in their houses.

Sebastian G-E, age 4
Trilingual: Hungarian, English, French

Language—what it can do for us! It allows us to express hopes and dreams, as this young boy has done in his chat with a friend. It takes us beyond the here and now. It connects one individual to another. It communicates the heights of joy and the depths of despair. Language belongs to everyone, from the preschooler to the professor. Almost all aspects of a person's life are touched by language: Everyone speaks and everyone listens. People argue about language, sometimes quite passionately and eloquently. Language is universal, and yet each language has evolved to meet the experiences, needs, and desires of that language's community.

Understanding language structure and use builds teachers' confidence and provides them with essential tools to help their students learn (see figure on page 1). One of the fascinating facts about language is that speakers learn their first language without understanding how language "works." Thus, native speakers can converse fluently but may not be able to explain a sound pattern, a grammatical point, or the use of a certain expression to get their needs met. To them, that is "just the way it is."

This chapter explores these various aspects of language and provides examples and suggestions to help English-language-development (ELD) teachers pinpoint student needs and provide appropriate instruction. Such knowledge also helps teachers recognize the richness and variety of students' emerging language.

Language Universals

At last count, 6,809 languages are spoken in today's world (SIL International, 2000). Although not all of these have been intensely studied, linguists have carried out enough investigations over the centuries to posit some universal facts about language (Fromkin, Rodman, & Hyams, 2003, p. 18).

Language Is Dynamic

Languages change over time. Vocabulary changes are the most obvious: Words disappear, such as *tang* and *swik*. Words expand their meanings, such as *chip* and *mouse*. New words appear, such as *visitability* and *cyberbalkanization*. But languages change in many ways, not just in semantic meaning. Pronunciation (phonology) changes. We recognize that pronunciation in English has altered over time because the spelling of some words is archaic: We no longer pronounce the *k* in *know* or the *w* in *write;* at one time, the vowel sounds in *tie, sky,* and *high* did not rhyme. Even common words such as *tomato* and *park* are pronounced differently depending on which part of the country the speaker is from, indicating that part of the dynamics of language comes from dialectical differences.

Morphological (word form) changes have occurred in English, such as the gradual elimination of declension endings in nouns and verbs. Only the change in form of the third person ("he goes") remains in the declension of present-tense verbs, and only the plural shift remains in the inflection of nouns. Syntactically, as the inflections dropped off nouns, word order became fixed. Pragmatically, the fusing of the

English second person into the single form *you* avoided many of the status distinctions still preserved in European languages.

Teachers who respect the dynamic nature of language can take delight in learners' approximations of English rather than be annoyed by constructions that can be considered mistakes. When a student writes, "When school was out he fell in love with a young girl, July" (meaning "Julie"), rather than correcting the misspelling, a teacher can consider that "July" may be a better way to spell the name of a summer love!

Language Is Complex

Without question, using language is one of the most complex of human activities. The wide range of concepts, both concrete and abstract, that language can convey—and the fact that this ability is the norm for human beings rather than the exception—combines with its dynamic quality to provide the human race with a psychological tool unmatched in power and flexibility.

No languages are "primitive." All languages are equally complex, capable of expressing a wide range of ideas, and expandable to include new words for new concepts.

Language is arbitrary. The relationships between the sounds and the meanings of spoken languages and between gestures and meanings of sign languages are, for the most part, not caused by any natural or necessary reason (such as reflecting a sound, like "buzz" for the sound that bees make when they fly). There is no inherent reason to call an object "table" or "mesa" or "danh t." Those just happen to be the sounds that English, Spanish, and Vietnamese speakers use.

Language comes easily to human beings. Every normal child, born anywhere in the world, of any racial, geographical, social, or economic heritage, is capable of learning any language to which he or she is exposed.

Language is open-ended. Speakers of a language are capable of producing and comprehending an infinite set of sentences. As we will see later, these facts help teachers recognize that their learners are proficient language users who can and will produce novel and complex sentences and thoughts in their own and their developing languages.

All Languages Have Structure

All human languages use a finite set of sounds (or gestures) that are combined to form meaningful elements or words, which themselves form an infinite set of possible sentences. Every spoken language also uses discrete sound segments, such as /p/, /n/, or /a/, and has a class of vowels and a class of consonants.

All grammars contain rules for the formation of words and sentences of a similar kind, and similar grammatical categories (for example, noun, verb) are found in all languages. Every language has a way of referring to past time; the ability to negate; and the ability to form questions, issue commands, and so on.

Teachers who are familiar with the structure of language can use this knowledge to design learning activities that build the language of English learners in a systematic way. Linguistic knowledge—not only about English but also about the possibilities inherent in languages that differ from English—helps teachers to view the language world of the English learner with insight and empathy.

Phonology: The Sound Patterns of Language

Phonology is the study of the system or pattern of speech sounds. Native speakers know intuitively the patterns of their mother tongue and when given a list of nonsense words can recognize which are possible pronunciations in their language.

Example of Concept: Could It Be English?

Which of the following are *possible* English words and which would be *impossible* because they do not fit the English sound system?

dschang   borogrove   jëfandikoo
nde   takkies

Phonemes

Phonemes are the sounds that make up a language. They are the distinctive units that "make a difference" when sounds form words. For example, in English the initial consonant sounds /t/ and /d/ are the only difference between the words *tip* and *dip* and are thus phonemes. The number of phonemes in a language ranges between twenty and fifty; English has a high average count, from thirty-four to forty-five, depending on the dialect.

Each language has permissible ways in which phonemes can be combined. These are called *phonemic sequences*. In English, /spr/ as in *spring,* /nd/ as in *handle,* and /kt/ as in *talked* are phonemic sequences. Languages also have permissible places for these sequences: initial (at the beginning of a word), medial (between initial and final position), and final (at the end of a word), or in a combination of these positions. English, for example, uses /sp/ in all three positions—*speak, respect, grasp*—but uses /sk/ in only two—*school, describe.* Spanish, on the other hand, uses the sequence /sp/ medially—*español*—but never initially. This would explain why, in speaking English, native-Spanish speakers may say "espeak." Not all of the permissible sequences are used in every pattern. For example, English has /cr/ and /br/ as initial consonant clusters. *Craft* is a word but—at present—*braft* is not, although it would be phonologically permissible. *Nkaft,* on the other hand, is not permissible because /nk/ is not an initial cluster in English.

Phonemes can be described in terms of their characteristic point of articulation (tip, front, or back of the tongue), the manner of articulation (the way the airstream is obstructed), and whether the vocal cords vibrate or not (voiced and voiceless sounds). Table 2.1 shows the English stops (sounds that are produced by completely blocking the breath stream and then releasing it abruptly). The point placements given in the chart relate to the positions in the mouth from which the sound is produced. Other languages may have different points. The point for /t/ and /d/ in Spanish, for example, is labiodental, with the tongue just behind the upper teeth. Not all languages

Table 2.1

Point of Articulation for Voiced and Voiceless English Stops

| | Labial | | Dental | | | |
Point	Bilabial	Labiodental	Interdental	Alveolar	Palatal	Velar
Voiceless	p			t		k
Voiced	b			d		g

distinguish between voiced and voiceless sounds. Arabic speakers may say "barking lot" instead of "parking lot" because to them /p/ and /b/ are not distinguishable.

Although learners may be able to articulate all the phonemes in their native language, they do not necessarily have phonemic awareness—such knowledge as what is a sound unit, how many phonemes there are in a given word, and how one phoneme may change the sound of an adjacent one.

Example of Concept: Teaching Phonemic Awareness

Heilman (2002) suggests the Bring *t* to the Party activity to teach students how to think, subvocalize, and manipulate the sound /t/:

The teacher pronounces a word. Students add the /t/ sound in front of the word to form a different word:

able ➜ table
all   ➜ tall
rain ➜ train

Source: Heilman (2002, p. 45)

Pitch

Besides the actual formation of sounds, other sound qualities are important in speech. Pitch, the vibration of the vocal chords, is important in distinguishing meaning within a sentence: "Eva is going," as a statement, is said with a falling pitch, but when it is used as a question, the pitch rises at the end. This use of pitch to modify the sentence meaning is called *intonation*. Languages that use the pitch of individual syllables to contrast meanings are called *tone languages*. Pitch, whether at the word level or at the sentence level, is one of the phonological components of a language that plays an important role in determining meaning.

Stress

Stress, the increase in vocal activity, also modifies the meaning of words. Speakers of English as a second language must learn to properly stress syllables in a word or words in a sentence, because in American English, syllables and words are not said with equal stress: particular syllables and words are emphasized with a higher pitch, a louder volume, and/or a longer vowel.

There are some rules to follow when learning what to stress. For example, in compound words, the first syllable is stressed: *checkbook, take-out, cell phone*. When saying proper nouns, the rule is opposite: the last word in a phrase is stressed: Statue of Liberty, Golden Gate Bridge, President Clinton. A similar rule is followed for abbreviations: the last initial is emphasized: Ph.D., IBM, HBO. With homonyms, the first syllable is accented for nouns, the second for verbs: *Project/project, record/record* (Wilner & Feinstein-Whitaker, 2008).

One aspect of English pronunciation that is often difficult for English learners is the fact that English speakers not only reduce the vowels in unaccented syllables to the schwa sound, but also de-emphasize unimportant words in a sentence, creating a strong contrast that highlights the focus of meaning. Contractions—shortened forms of pronoun–auxiliary verb combinations—are one form of de-emphasis, and reductions are another ("n" for *and*; "'e" for *he*; "'er" for *her*). These elements may require focused listening training, especially because pronouns carry important contextual information, without which a listener may become confused (Gilbert, 2006).

Correct pronunciation is one of the most difficult features of learning a second language. Teachers who overemphasize correct pronunciation when learners are in the early stages of learning English may hinder the innovative spirit of risk taking that is preferable when a learner is trying to achieve fluency. Instead, teaching intonation through fun activities such as chants and songs brings enjoyment to language learning.

Native speakers are seldom if ever explicitly taught the phonological rules of their language, yet they know them. Phonological knowledge is acquired as a learner listens to and begins to produce speech. The same is true in a second language. A learner routinely exposed to a specific dialect or accent in English views it as the target language.

The Sound System as Written Language

Spelling in English has long been difficult, but some anomalies persist for a reason. Related words with similar spellings may have contrasting phonemes, such as *medical* and *medicine* (the c is pronounced as k in one and as s in the other). Silent letters are not always better eliminated; for example, g in *sign* is silent, but it remains as a holdover from its relative, the g that is pronounced in *signify*. People may complain that homonyms should be spelled the same, but the visual distinction serves a purpose to clarify meanings when written. Moreover, even if they were spelled the same, some homonyms would still diverge in some dialects (the words *are* and *our* are homonyms only in certain dialects). Therefore the current spelling system, while inconsistent, is not always illogical (Freeman & Freeman, 2004).

No language has a writing system in which letters exactly represent the corresponding sounds. One letter may have two sounds, and a sound may be written more than one way. Linguists use phonemic transcription to represent sounds in a consistent

Did You Know?

Linguists use the International Phonetics Alphabet (http://en.wikipedia.org/wiki/International_Phonetic_Alphabet) to describe phonemes precisely. Student dictionaries also have phonetic conventions that are specific to that book.

way, using slash marks to indicate phonemes (for example, /m/ for the first phoneme in *make*). For even more precise rendering, linguists use a phonetic transcription, employing brackets. For example, some people pronounce *which* and *witch* alike, using the phoneme /w/. Others distinguish these words using a [w^h] sound for *which*.

Morphology: The Words of Language

Morphology is the study of the meaning units in a language. Many people believe that individual words constitute these basic meaning units. However, many words can be broken down into smaller segments—morphemes—that still retain meaning.

Morphemes

Morphemes are the basic building blocks of meaning. *Abolitionists* is an English word composed of four morphemes: *aboli* + *tion* + *ist* + *s* (root + noun-forming suffix + noun-forming suffix + plural marker). Morphemes can be represented by a single sound, such as /a/ (as a morpheme, this means "without" as in *amoral* or *asexual*); a syllable, such as the noun-forming suffix -*ment* in *amendment;* or two or more syllables, such as in *tiger* or *artichoke*. Two different morphemes may have the same sound, such as the /er/ as in *dancer* ("one who dances") and the /er/ in *fancier* (the comparative form of *fancy*). A morpheme may also have alternate phonetic forms: The regular plural -*s* can be pronounced either /z/ (*bags*), /s/ (*cats*), or /iz/ (*bushes*).

Morphemes are of different types and serve different purposes. *Free morpheme*s can stand alone (*envelop, the, through*), whereas *bound morphemes* occur only in conjunction with others (-*ing, dis-, -ceive*). Most bound morphemes occur as *affixes*. (The others are bound roots.) Affixes at the beginning of words are *prefixes* (*un-* in the word *unafraid*); those added at the end are *suffixes* (-*able* in the word *believable*); and *infixes* are morphemes that are inserted into other morphemes (-*zu-* in the German word *anzufangen,* "to begin").

Part of the power and flexibility of English is the ease with which families of words can be understood by knowing the rules for forming nouns from verbs and so forth—for example, knowing that the suffix -*ism* means "a doctrine, system, or philosophy" and -*ist* means "one who follows a doctrine, system, or philosophy." This predictability can make it easier for students to learn to infer words from context rather than to rely on rote memorization.

Example of Concept: Working with Morphemes

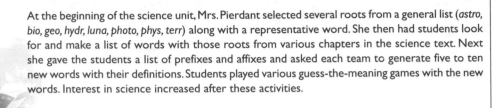

At the beginning of the science unit, Mrs. Pierdant selected several roots from a general list (*astro, bio, geo, hydr, luna, photo, phys, terr*) along with a representative word. She then had students look for and make a list of words with those roots from various chapters in the science text. Next she gave the students a list of prefixes and affixes and asked each team to generate five to ten new words with their definitions. Students played various guess-the-meaning games with the new words. Interest in science increased after these activities.

Word-Formation Processes

English has historically been a language that has welcomed new words—either borrowing them from other languages or coining new ones from existing words. Studying processes of word formation heightens students' interest in vocabulary building.

Example of Concepts: Creating New Words

Product names often use existing morphemes combined in ways to create a new word that fits within the English sound system and evokes a positive image for the product. For example, "Aleve" connotes "alleviate," as in making a headache better.

Clipping. Clipping is a process of shortening words, such as *prof* for *professor* or the slangy *teach* for *teacher*. Learning two words for one gives students a sense that they are mastering both colloquial and academic speech.

Acronyms. In English, *acronyms* are plentiful, and many are already familiar to students—UN, CIA, and NASA, for example. A growing list of acronyms helps students increase their vocabulary of both the words forming the acronyms and the acronyms themselves. Who can resist knowing that *scuba* is a *self-contained underwater breathing apparatus?*

Computer Shorthand. Acronyms are also used to text or type using a computer or cell phone. Examples include BRB (be right back), CYL (catch you later), CYT (see you tomorrow), IMHO (in my humble opinion), LMK (let me know), NM (never mind), ROFL (rolling on the floor laughing), and WTH (what the heck). For a glossary of chat room abbreviations, go to www.petrospec-technologies.com/Herkommer/chatword.htm.

Blends. Words formed from parts of two words are called blends—for example, *smog* from *smoke* + *fog*, *brunch* from *breakfast* + *lunch*, and *blog* from *web* + *log*. The prefixes *e-* and *i-* have combined to form many new words and concepts over recent decades (e.g., *e-commerce* and *iTunes*). Students can become word detectives and discover new blends through shopping (Wal-Mart?) or advertisements, or add to their enjoyment of learning English by finding new words and creating their own. The study of morphology adds fun to learning English as well as word power.

Syntax: The Sentence Patterns of Language

Syntax refers to the structure of sentences and the rules that govern the formation of a sentence. Sentences are composed of words that follow patterns, but sentence meaning is more than the sum of the meaning of the words. Sentence A, "The teacher asked the students to sit down," has the same words as sentence B, "The students asked the teacher to sit down," but not the same meaning.

All native speakers of a language can distinguish syntactically correct from syntactically incorrect combinations of words. This syntactic knowledge in the native language is not taught in school but is constructed as native speakers acquire their language as children. This internal knowledge allows speakers to recognize the sentence "'Twas brillig and the slithy toves did gyre and gimble in the wabes" in Lewis Carroll's poem "Jabberwocky" as syntactically correct English, even though the words are nonsense.

Fortunately, speakers of a language who have this knowledge of correct and incorrect sentences can, in fact, understand sentences that are not perfectly formed. Sentences that contain minor syntactic errors, such as the preschool student's poem cited at the beginning of this chapter, are still comprehensible.

Adapted Instruction: English Syntax and Chinese Speakers

English learners with Chinese as a mother tongue may need additional teacher assistance with the following aspects of English:

- Verb tense: *I see him yesterday.* (In Chinese, the adverb signals the tense, not the verb, and the verb form is not changed to mark tense; so in English changing the verb form may prove to be difficult for the learner.)
- Subject–verb agreement: *He see me.* (In Chinese, verbs do not change form to create subject–verb agreement.)
- Word order: *I at home ate.* (In Chinese, prepositional phrases come before the verb—the rules governing the flexibility in adverb-phrase placement in English are difficult for many learners.)
- Plurals: *They give me 3 dollar.* (In Chinese, like English, the marker indicates number, but in English the noun form changes as well.)

Whereas syntax refers to the internally constructed rules that make sentences, *grammar* looks at whether a sentence conforms to a standard. An important distinction, therefore, is the one between standard and colloquial usage. Many colloquial usages are acceptable sentence patterns in English, even though their usage is not standard—for example, "I ain't got no pencil" is acceptable English syntax. It is not, however, standard usage. Through example and in lessons, teachers who are promoting the standard dialect need to be aware that students' developing competence will not always conform to that standard and that students will also learn colloquial expressions they will not always use in the appropriate context (see the Appropriate Language section later in this chapter).

Adapted Instruction: Teaching Grammar

Grammar need not be a difficult or boring subject. Grammar rules for forming verb tenses in English, for example, are easy to learn; only about fifty commonly used verbs are irregular, and the rules for irregular verbs have their own consistency (see Jesness, 2004). Parts of speech are used in a regular way. Teachers who take the time to become proficient in discussing the rules of grammar are much more effective teachers of English to speakers of other languages. There are many amusing ways to teach grammar, like asking absurd questions ("Do you sleep in the doghouse?") to help students use negative sentences ("No, I don't.").

Example of Concept: Colloquial versus Standard Usage

As Mrs. Ralfe hears students using new colloquial phrases, she has them write them on the left half of a poster hanging in the room. At the end of the day, she and the students discuss the phrases and how to say them in a more standard fashion. The students then write the standard phrase on the right side of the poster.

Semantics: The Meanings of Language

Semantics is the study of meanings of individual words and of larger units such as phrases and sentences. Speakers of a language have learned the "agreed-upon" meanings of words and phrases in their language and are not free to change meanings of words at will, which would result in no communication at all (Fromkin et al., 2003).

Some words carry a high degree of stability and conformity in the ways they are used (*kick* as a verb, for example, must involve the foot—"He kicked me with his hand" is not semantically correct). Other words carry multiple meanings (e.g., *break*), ambiguous meanings (*bank,* as in "They're at the bank"), or debatable meanings (*marriage,* for example, for many people can refer only to heterosexual alliances, and to use it for nonheterosexual contexts is not only unacceptable but inflammatory to them). For second-language acquisition, the process of translating already-recognized meaning from one language to the next is only part of the challenge.

Another challenge is that the English language is extraordinarily rich in synonyms. One estimate of English vocabulary places the number at over three million words. Fortunately, only about 200,000 words are in common use, and an educated person uses about 2,000 in a week (Wilton, 2003). The challenge when learning this vast vocabulary is to distinguish denotations, connotations, and other shades of meaning.

Adapted Instruction: Denotations and Connotations

- With students, generate a list of eight to ten thematically linked words, such as colors.
- Have students define each word using objects, drawings, or basic definitions (denotation).
- Elicit or provide connotative (the implied, emotional) meanings of the words, for example: *red* = irritated or angry.
- During their independent reading, have students be alert to the connotative use of the words. Add representative sentences to the chart.

About two-thirds of English words did not originate in English, but are borrowed from around the world. English has borrowed words for beasts (*aardvark,* from Afrikaans, *zebra* from Bantu), for food and drink (*coffee* from Arabic, *pretzel* from German, *paprika* from Hungarian), or clothes (*khaki* from Hindi), for dances (*tango* from Ibibio, *hula* from Hawai'ian), spiritual ideas (*messiah* from Hebrew), vices (*cigar* from Maya), politics (*caucus* from Iroquois, *fascist* from Italian), and for miscellaneous ideas (*berserk* from Norse, *sleazy* from Latvian, *kowtow* from Mandarin). Visit www.krysstal.com/borrow.html to find other examples. Our world would be impoverished without these loanwords to discuss spice, samba, and the martial arts!

Adapted Instruction: Borrowed Words

Making charts of English words that English learners use in their first language and words English has borrowed from the students' native languages increases everyone's vocabulary and often generates interesting discussions about food, clothing, cultural artifacts, and the ever-expanding world of technology.

Speakers of a language must also make semantic shifts when writing. It may be understandable when a speaker uses the colloquial "And then she goes . . ." to mean "she says," but in written English, one must make a semantic shift toward formality, using synonyms such as "she declared," "she remarked," and "she admitted." A teacher who encourages this type of semantic expansion helps students acquire semantic flexibility.

Example of Concept: Learning Synonyms

Each week, Mrs. Arias selects five to eight groups of synonyms from a list (Kress, 1993). During time spent at a language center, pairs of students choose two groups to study. They look up the words and write definitions, write a story incorporating the words (five) in each group, or develop games and quizzes for their classmates to play. At the end of the week, students report on their learning.

Semantics also includes word meanings that have become overused and trite. A list of clichés to avoid in the near future: proactive, utilized, closure, über, basically, whatever, touch base, absolutely, and no problem (*Los Angeles Times,* 2008, p. M2).

So what does it mean to "know" a word? The meaning of words comes partially from the stored meaning and partially from the meaning derived from context. In addition, knowing a word includes the ability to pronounce the word correctly, to use the word grammatically in a sentence, and to know which morphemes are appropriately connected with the word. This knowledge is acquired as the brain absorbs and interacts with the meaning in context. For English learners, acquiring new vocabulary in semantically related groups helps them make connections and retain important concepts.

Adapted Instruction: Vocabulary Teaching and Concept Development

The following graphic organizers help students not only with vocabulary but also with how concepts relate to one another:

- *Concept maps.* The concept is in the center, and definitions, examples, and details are linked around it.
- *Key word or topic notes.* The key word is in the left column with notes in the right.
- *Thinking tree.* The topic is at the top of the "tree" and the main ideas are branches coming down. From the main ideas twigs are added as details.

Did You Know?

Sometimes it is helpful when teaching English for teachers to know about the similarities between English and the students' home language. For example, Spinelli (1994) pointed out that like English, Spanish has constructions in which words in phrases make idioms whose meanings cannot be predicted from

knowing the individual words; for example, in Spanish, *hacer* ("to make") and *cola* ("tail") can be use together to make the idiom *hacer cola,* "to form a line." This is similar to phrasal verbs in English; for example, "put up with" means "to tolerate."

Pragmatics: The Influence of Context

Pragmatics is the study of communication in context. It includes three major communication skills. The first is the ability to use language for different functions—greeting, informing, demanding, promising, requesting, and so on. The second is the ability to appropriately adapt or change language according to the listener or situation—talking differently to a friend than to a principal, or talking differently in a classroom than on a playground. The third ability is to follow rules for conversations and narrative—knowing how to tell a story, give a book report, or recount events of the day. Because these pragmatic ways of using speech vary depending on language and culture (Maciejewski, 2003), teachers who understand these differences can help learners to adjust their pragmatics to those that "work" when speaking English.

Language Functions

Halliday (1978) distinguished seven different functions for language: *instrumental* (getting needs met); *regulatory* (controlling others' behavior); *informative* (communicating information); *interactional* (establishing social relationships); *personal* (expressing individuality); *heuristic* (investigating and acquiring knowledge); and *imaginative* (expressing fantasy). Providing English learners with opportunities to engage in the various functions is critical for them to develop a full pragmatic range in English.

Adapted Instruction: Promoting Language Functions

- *Instrumental:* Analyze advertising and propaganda so that students learn how people use language to get what they want.
- *Regulatory:* Allow students to be in charge of small and large groups.
- *Informative:* Have students keep records of events over periods of time, review their records, and draw conclusions; for example, keeping records of classroom pets, weather patterns, or building constructions.
- *Interactional:* Have students work together to plan field trips, social events, and classroom and school projects.
- *Personal:* Encourage students to share thoughts and opinions.

- *Heuristic:* In projects, ask questions that no one, including the teacher, knows the answer to.
- *Imaginative:* Encourage "play" with language—the sounds of words and the images they convey.

Source: Adapted from Pinnell (1985).

Appropriate Language

To speak appropriately, the speaker must take into account the gender, status, age, and cultural background of the listener. The term *speech register* is often used to denote the varieties of language that take these factors into consideration. For example, in the classroom in which the teacher's assistant is an older woman who shares the language and culture of the children, students may converse with her in a manner similar to the interactions with their own mothers, whereas their discourse with the teacher could reflect usage reserved for more formal situations. A reverse of these registers would be inappropriate.

Example of Concept: Learning to Be Appropriate

In preparation for a drama unit, Mrs. Morley has her students develop short conversations that might occur with different people in different situations, such as selling ice cream to a child, a teenager, a working adult, and a retiree. Pairs of students perform their conversations and the class critiques the appropriateness of the language. Students develop a feel for appropriate expressions, tones, and stances before working on plays and skits.

Conversational Rules

Numerous aspects of conversation carry unexamined rules. Conversations generally follow a script. There are procedures for turn taking, for introducing and maintaining topics, and for clarifying misunderstandings.

Scripts. Every situation carries with it the expectations of the speakers involved and a script that carries out those expectations. (Note: When linguists use the term *script,* they mean a predictable sequence of events, not a written dialogue that actors follow.) In a restaurant, for example, the customers pause at the front counter to see if someone will escort them to their seat. They anticipate being asked, "How many (people in the party)?" To continue the script, when they are seated, they expect to be approached by a waitperson, given a menu, and asked if they would like a drink before ordering. This interchange follows a predictable sequence, and pragmatic knowledge is needed to carry out the parts of the dialogue. Other contexts, such as fast-food restaurants, have different scripts.

Classroom procedures have patterns, and one of the important tasks of kindergarten and first-grade teachers is to teach children how to initiate and respond appropriately in the school setting. Confusion and possibly a sense of alienation can arise for English learners who are used to the school patterns in their own countries and find a different one in U.S. schools. It may take time—and explicit coaching—for students to learn the set of behaviors appropriate for a U.S. school context.

Turn Taking. Speakers of a language have internalized the rules of when to speak, when to remain silent, how long to speak, how long to remain silent, how to give up "the floor," how to enter into a conversation, and so on. Linguistic devices such as intonation, pausing, and phrasing are used to signal an exchange of turns. Some groups of people wait for a clear pause before beginning their turn to speak, whereas others start while the speaker is winding down (Tannen, n.d.). It is often this difference in when to take the floor that causes feelings of unease and sometimes hostility. A speaker may constantly feel that he is being interrupted or pushed in a conversation or, conversely, that he has to keep talking because his partner does not join in when appropriate.

Topic Focus and Relevance. These elements involve the ability of conversationalists to explore and maintain one another's interest in topics that are introduced, the context of the conversation, the genre of the interchange (storytelling, excuse making), and the relationship between the speakers.

Conversational Repair. This involves techniques for clearing up misunderstandings and maintaining conversation. For example, a listener confused by the speaker's use of the pronoun *she* might ask, "Do you mean Sally's aunt or her cousin?" With English learners, the alert teacher will notice quizzical looks rather than specific conversational interactions that signal lack of understanding.

Classroom Discourse. Although classroom discourse patterns vary greatly across cultures, they also show some remarkable similarities. For example, research on classrooms shows that teachers talk about 70 percent of the time, and when they talk, about 60 percent of the time they ask questions that students are expected to answer. Often these questions are *display questions* that ask students to answer quickly with information that has been memorized. Typically, students are given less than one second to respond (Andrews, 2001).

Many students have difficulty learning the classroom discourse patterns of another culture:

> I had difficulty with the opinion in the class where peoples in groups discuss about subject. I was surrounded by Americans with whom I couldn't follow their tempo of discussion half of the time. I have difficulty to listen and speak, but also with the way they handle the group. I felt uncomfortable because sometimes they believe their opinion strongly. I had been very serious about the whole subject but I was afraid I would say something wrong. I had the idea but not the words. (Barna, 2007, p. 68)

Nonverbal Communication

A complex nonverbal system accompanies, complements, or takes the place of the verbal. "An elaborate and secret code that is written nowhere, known by none, and understood by all" is Edward Sapir's definition of nonverbal behavior (quoted in

Miller, 1985). This nonverbal system involves sending and receiving messages through gesture, facial expression, eye contact, posture, and tone of voice. Because this nonverbal system accounts for a large part of the emotional message given and received, awareness of its various aspects helps teachers to recognize students' nonverbal messages.

Body Language

Body language, the way one holds and positions oneself, is one way teachers communicate their authority in the classroom. Standing in front of the room, they become the focus of attention. In turn, students' body language communicates that they are paying attention (eyes up front and hands folded is the standard way teachers expect attentive students to act). Students who look industrious are often seen as more effective academically.

In a parent conference, for example, cultural differences in body language may impede communication. Parents may need to be formally ushered into the classroom and not merely waved in with a flick of the hand. Parents from a culture that offers elaborate respect for the teacher may become uncomfortable if the teacher slouches, moves his or her chair too intimately toward the parent, or otherwise compromises the formal nature of the interchange.

Gestures

Gestures—expressive motions or actions made with hands, arms, head, or even the whole body—are culturally based signs that are often misunderstood. Gestures are commonly used to convey "come here," "good-bye," "yes," "no," and "I don't know." In European-American culture, for example, "come here" is signaled by holding the hand vertically, palm facing the body, and moving the index finger rapidly back and forth. In other cultures, it is signaled by holding the hand in a more horizontal position, palm facing down, and moving the fingers rapidly back and forth. "Yes" is generally signaled by a nod of the head, but in some places a shake of the head means "yes." This can be particularly unnerving for teachers if they constantly interpret the students' head shakes as rejection rather than affirmation.

Example of Concept: Teaching Gestures

Preteach and demonstrate the twelve gestures that accompany the phrases below. Form groups in circles of four or five. Give each a set of twenty-four cards (two each of the twelve gestures). A student from each group picks a card and acts out the gesture on the card. The other group members must try to guess the expression that goes with the card. When someone has guessed correctly, the turn passes to the next person in the circle. The first group to get through all the cards wins the game.

1. Come with me.
2. There he/she/it is.
3. I'm waiting . . .

---

4. Nice to meet you.
5. I love you.
6. OK.
7. Good job.
8. That's enough.
9. Calm down.
10. Hurry up.
11. Shhhh.
12. I don't care.

Source: Adapted from Saslow & Ascher (2006).

Facial Expressions

Through the use of eyebrows, eyes, cheeks, nose, lips, tongue, and chin, people nonverbally signal any number of emotions, opinions, and moods. Smiles and winks, tongue thrusts, and chin jutting can have different meanings depending on the context within a culture as well as across cultures. Americans, for example, are often perceived by others as being emotionally superficial because of the amount of smiling they do, even to strangers. In some cultures, smiles are reserved for close friends and family.

Adapted Instruction: Learning about Facial Expressions

- Have students make lists of expressions that are neutral, pleasing, or offensive.
- Discover and discuss how the findings of English learners may differ from those of their native-English speaking peers.

Eye Contact

Eye contact is another communication device that is highly variable and frequently misunderstood. Both insufficient and excessive eye contact create feelings of unease, yet it is so subject to individual variation that there are no hard-and-fast rules to describe it. Generally, children in European-American culture are taught not to stare but are expected to look people in the eye when addressing them. In some cultures, however, children learn that the correct way to listen is to avoid direct eye contact with the speaker. In the following dialogue, the teacher incorrectly interprets Sylvia's downcast eyes as an admission of guilt because, in the teacher's culture, eye avoidance signals culpability.

Teacher: Sylvia and Amanda, I want to hear what happened on the playground.
Amanda: (looks at teacher) Sylvia hit me with the jump rope.

Teacher: (turning to Sylvia) Sylvia, did you hit her?
Sylvia: (looking at her feet) No.
Teacher: Look at me, Sylvia. Am I going to have to take the jump rope away?
Sylvia: (continuing to look down) No.

By being aware that eye contact norms vary, teachers can begin to move beyond feelings of mistrust and open up lines of communication. If a student's culture mandates that a young person not look an adult in the eye when directly addressed, the teacher may need to explain to the student that in English the rules of address call for different behavior.

Communicative Distance

People maintain distance between themselves and others, an invisible wall or "bubble" that defines a person's personal space. Violating a person's space norm can be interpreted as aggressive behavior. In the United States, an accidental bumping of another person requires an "excuse me" or "pardon me." In Arab countries, such inadvertent contact does not violate the individual's space and requires no verbal apology.

Adapted Instruction: Learning about
Communicative Distance

- *Interviews*. Students interview others and ask questions such as "What distance is too close for a friend? For a family member?" "At what distance do you stand to an adult, a teacher, or a clerk?"
- *Observations*. Students observe people, videos, pictures, and television and compare these people's distance behavior in relation to the situation, culture, sex of participants, and so forth.

Source: Adapted from Arias (1996).

Conceptions of Time

In the mainstream culture of the United States, individuals' understanding of time may be at odds with that of students of other cultures. For speakers of English, time is handled as if it were a material. English expressions include "saving time," "spending time," and "wasting time." Time is considered to be a commodity, and those who misuse this commodity earn disapproval.

With an awareness of mainstream U.S. conceptions of time, teachers become more understanding of students and their families whose time values differ from their own, and are willing to make allowances for such differences. In oral discourse, some students may need more time to express themselves, not because of language shortcomings per se, but because the timing of oral discourse is slower in their culture.

Example of Concept: Time and Culture

Parents who were raised in cultures with radically different concepts of time may not be punctual to the minute for parent conferences. One group of teachers allowed for this by not scheduling specific individual conference times. Instead, they designated blocks of three hours when they would be available for conferences, and parents arrived when they could.

Language allows speakers a means for rich and dynamic expression. By knowing about language and its various properties and components, teachers are in a position to promote English-language development while welcoming students' primary languages as an alternative vehicle for self-expression. Languages have universal features; so, regardless of the language of the student, teachers are assured that by having successfully acquired one language, students will also be successful in a second (or third or fourth). Understanding the basics of language helps to make language learning a meaningful, purposeful, and shared endeavor. ∎

LEARNING MORE

Thinking It Over

What do people need to know to talk to one another? List as many rules as you can that you think must be followed by people who are interacting in face-to-face conversations. How do children learn these rules? (Adapted from Farrell, 2006)

Web Search

To learn more about the subsystems of language, Dr. R. Beard provides short, amusing, enlightening essays.

- How to Pronounce "Ghoti" . . . and Why (www.facstaff.bucknell.edu/rbeard/phono.html)
- There Are No Such Things as Words (www.facstaff.bucknell.edu/rbeard/words.html)
- You Have to Pay Your Syntax (www.facstaff.bucknell.edu/rbeard/syntax.html)
- Can Colorless Green Ideas Sleep Furiously? (www.facstaff.bucknell.edu/rbeard/semantic.html)

Exploration

Go through the checkout line at a grocery store. Pay attention to the verbal and non-verbal elements of the checkout procedure. Record as much as possible of the procedure. Repeat this procedure, observe others going through the same procedure, or engage in the exploration with several colleagues. Look for patterns. What signals the beginning? What words are exchanged? What topics of conversation are permissible? How does the interaction terminate? Once you've discovered the script for the checkout, begin to pay attention to the scripts in your classroom.

Try It in the Classroom

Engage students in an activity to determine personal comfort in distance. Have students stand in two opposing lines. At a signal, have one line move one step toward the other. Repeat, alternating the line that moves until a student says, "Stop." Mark that distance. Continue until all students have said "Stop." Discuss the implications of the various distances. The activity can also be done sitting.

The Power of Classroom Practice
www.myeducationlab.com

An ESL Vocabulary Lesson

In this video, the teacher demonstrates a vocabulary lesson in which she first pronounces each word, has the children pronounce each word, and then asks students to make vocabulary cards of the words for study. Next, she gives a definition of each word, sometimes has children act out a word, and describes each word in ways that will help the children know them. Finally, they write their own sentences with the words and play games with the words to build fluency.

> To access the video, go to MyEducationLab (www.myeducationlab.com), choose the Díaz-Rico and Weed text, and log in to MyEducationLab for English Language Learners. Select the topic Vocabulary, and watch the video entitled "An ESL Vocabulary Lesson."

Answer the following questions:
1. How could these words be taught differently?
2. Would this lesson be very different for older students who are beginners in English-language development? Intermediate in English-language development? How?
3. What difference does it make in long-term retention if vocabulary words are presented with or without an accompanying context?

3 | Learning about Second-Language Acquisition

Students develop communicative competence as they use language to interact with one another.

Without communication the world would be so dark. Life would be boring. It is through language that we find a way into people's hearts, their lives, and their culture. Through language we explore into the secrets of other cultures.

I was born in Afghanistan. I came to the United States when I was sixteen years old. This was my new home and yet, because I could not speak any English, I was a stranger to my new home. How I wished to express my gratitude to people who helped my family and me, but all I could do was to give them an empty look and a confused smile. I was living among the people and yet I was not one of them. I thought everybody was cold and unfriendly. Sometimes I got angry and wanted to scream at the whole world.

Slowly the ice broke. I started learning English. New windows started opening. The once cold and unfriendly became warm and caring. My family and I found a way into hearts of the people.

Ahmad Shukoor, grade 12, in Shukoor (1991, p. 34)

Almost five million students in the United States face the daily challenge of attending school in a new language—English. By knowing about language acquisition and use, teachers (particularly those who are monolingual) can come to recognize and use communication strategies that help break down barriers.

As an introduction to the study of language teaching and learning, this chapter presents an overview of historical and contemporary theories that will help the teacher place issues of English-language development within an orienting framework.

Historical Theories of Language Teaching and Learning

Humans have been describing and analyzing language for over 2,300 years. Many methods of second-language teaching have been used throughout recorded history, each based on an underlying rationale or set of beliefs about how language is best learned. As early as the fourth century BC, Greek philosophers were debating the nature of language. In about the second century BC, Dionysius Thrax identified eight different word classes. His book *The Art of Grammar* became a model for both Greek and Latin grammars. Latin was the model for grammar throughout the Middle Ages. When grammarians finally began writing grammars for vernacular languages, they generally copied the Latin grammars, using the same terminology and the same word classes. Unfortunately, Latin was not an appropriate model for all languages, but the model persisted nonetheless.

Grammar-Translation Methodology

Throughout the Middle Ages and even until the earliest years of the twentieth century, the educated classes in Europe used the method by which Latin grammar was taught as a model for learning language: drilling on vocabulary, verb tenses, and parts of speech. Teachers were expected to have a thorough knowledge of grammar rules.

This grammar-translation method of instruction is still widely used throughout the world in settings in which the main goal of instruction is reading and grammar knowledge of the second language. Students learn only what is required and are rewarded for precisely defined goals such as memorizing word lists or correct translation. Grammar-translation pedagogy can be seen as a traditionalist form of behaviorism.

The strengths of this methodology are twofold. First, desirable results are clearly defined, and success can be precisely correlated to the amount of effort expended. Second, the curriculum can be carefully structured and controlled, with students' access to the second language limited to that which the teacher or other authorities determine to be valuable.

Drawbacks are that students have little choice in what they learn, little contact with actual speakers of the language they are acquiring, almost no actual use of the language in a social context, and little stimulation of curiosity, playfulness, and exploration—aspects of learning that are intrinsic to the nature of the mind. In contrast, current second-language teaching, especially in the elementary school, features extensive social interaction and active language use among learners (see Takahashi, Austin, & Morimoto, 2000).

Structural Linguistics

In the eighteenth and nineteenth centuries, scholars began to notice similarities among languages. Studying written documents of earlier forms of languages, they traced the origins of words and sounds, attempted to show that languages had undergone changes over time, and traced historical relationships among various languages. Linguists developed a method for identifying the sound units of languages, for analyzing the ways that morphemes form words and words form sentences.

This *descriptive* linguistics led to the comparison of languages for the purpose of teaching. Knowledge of the grammar and sound structure of one language was believed to transfer to a second language so that the second language could be explained in terms of the first.

However, this contrastive analysis—with its premise that the more similar two languages, the easier a speaker of the first would learn the second—proved to be an unworkable predictor of learning ease or difficulty in a second language. (See Gass & Selinker [2001] for a discussion of contrastive analysis.) For example, Chinese and English are comparatively different in many aspects (writing system, tonal system, word structure, verb tense system, etc.), but these differences do not exactly predict what difficulties a particular learner might experience. Therefore, descriptive linguistics and contrastive analysis are largely ineffectual in second-language teaching.

Behaviorism

Although behaviorism is not strictly a linguistic theory, its vast influence on learning theory has affected second-language teaching. Behaviorists claim that the mind is a "blank slate"; a learner must be filled with content during the course of teaching (see Skinner, 1957). Strict principles of timing, repetition, and reward led to classroom methodology that incorporated extensive drill and practice of language components, from sounds to complex sentences. Three aspects of behaviorism are still used in contemporary language teaching: audiolingualism, direct teaching/mastery learning, and total physical response (TPR). The latter is explained in Chapter 4.

Audiolingualism. The audiolingual method of language learning is based on behavioral principles. Oral practice is believed to be the primary means to language learning. Teachers provide oral pattern drills that are based on specific grammatical forms; for example, a complete lesson can be centered on a tag question ("It's cold today, *isn't it?*"). The goal for the learner is to learn new habits of speech, including correct pronunciation, in the second language. Students develop correct language behavior by repetitious training, often using technology such as tape recordings in language laboratories. The role of the teacher is to direct and control students' behavior, provide a model, and reinforce correct responses (Doggett, 1986).

Direct Teaching and Mastery Learning. Direct teaching and mastery learning are both forms of behaviorist instruction, and their widespread use in classrooms of English learners with reading programs such as Open Court and Direct Instruction demonstrates that behaviorism is still widely practiced. Direct teaching incorporates explicit instructional objectives for students and promotes the learning of facts, sequenced steps, or rules. The instructor maximizes learning time by using carefully scripted lessons. Students are regularly tested over the material that is covered and receive immediate remediation if performance lags.

Mastery learning resembles direct teaching. In both methods, the course of study is divided into small units with specific objectives. In mastery learning, rather than learning in strict unison, students progress at their own rates and demonstrate mastery of each unit before proceeding to the next. As in other systems of behavioral management, mastery learning provides immediate feedback and reinforcement of performance. In the best use of mastery learning, students are gradually taught how to self-monitor, regulate, and reward their own actions.

Advantages and Disadvantages of Behavioral Methods for Second-Language Teaching.
The strength of the audiolingual method is its focus on correct pronunciation. An advantage of direct teaching and mastery learning is the focus on the subskills of language, including word recognition and low-level comprehension skills, and the focus on immediate remediation when these skills are weak.

A weakness of audiolingual pedagogy is that it limits exposure to the target culture and fails to emphasize self-motivated language acquisition; it also places pressure on learners to perform accurately under classroom or laboratory conditions instead of equipping learners with a language repertoire that would enable them to communicate spontaneously with native speakers.

Example of Concept: Communicating with Language Learned by Audiolingual Instruction

In 2000 I spent a week in Beijing. Unfortunately, due to a busy schedule, before departing to the People's Republic of China I had no opportunity to review the Chinese-language materials I still have from my graduate years at the University of Pittsburgh, a training that had consisted in part of long hours in a language laboratory repeating phrases in Mandarin. During the second taxi trip across Beijing, I gathered up my courage to speak Mandarin. I strung together every word I could remember and—not sounding too bad, at least to myself!—I asked the driver if he thought it would rain.

That one sentence was my downfall! In return for my one sentence, I was treated to a twenty-minute treatise on local weather conditions—I guess—I could understand so little of it! When I asked the question, my adequate pronunciation—a result of audiolingual instruction—must have sounded like I knew what I was saying, but my comprehension certainly did not keep pace with my accent!

The weakest part of direct teaching is that students are seldom asked to set their own goals in learning or pursue their own interests (as they might do in a literature-based program that encouraged free choice in reading), and they have little time to explore language creatively. Balancing the strengths and weaknesses of behavioral-based pedagogy, one might conclude that these teaching approaches have a distinct, yet limited, role in instruction.

Current Theories of Language Development

Starting in the mid-twentieth century, several important new theories have shaped current understanding of language acquisition and development. In 1959, Noam Chomsky claimed that language is not learned solely through a process of memorizing and repeating, but that the mind contains an active language processor, the language acquisition device (LAD), that generates rules through the unconscious acquisition of grammar.

In 1961, Hymes directed attention toward the idea of communicative competence: that the *use* of language in the social setting is important in language performance. Halliday (1975) elaborated on the role of social relations in language by stating that the social structure is an essential element in linguistic interaction. Current theories of language have thus moved away from the merely linguistic components of a language to the more inclusive realm of language in use—which includes its social, political, and psychological domains.

Current language teaching is being shaped by several important ideas. First, the shift toward a cognitive paradigm means that *learning* has taken precedence over *teaching*. What the student learns is the important outcome of the teaching–learning process, not what the teacher teaches. Second, learning is maximized when it matches the processes that take place naturally within the brain. Third, thematic integration across content areas unifies the language processes of reading, writing, speaking, listening, thinking, and acting. Thus, current perspectives on second-language learning align with brain-compatible instruction that emphasizes higher-order thinking skills.

Transformational Grammar

Following Chomsky's lead, transformational grammarians envision language as a set of rules that human beings unconsciously know and use. They believe that human beings, once exposed to the language(s) of their environment, use their innate ability to understand and produce sentences they have never before heard, because the mind has the capacity to internalize and construct language rules. The goal of transformational grammar is to understand and describe these internalized rules. In the early 1970s, some grammar texts included the use of transformational grammar to explain language structures, but this never became a popular approach to teaching grammar.

Krashen's Monitor Model

Krashen (1981, 1982) theorized that people acquire second-language structures in a predictable order only if they obtain comprehensible input, and if their anxiety is low enough to allow input into their minds. A *monitor,* or internal editing device, gradually acquires and applies a sense of correct language usage. Krashen's theory included five hypotheses: the *acquisition-learning hypothesis,* the *natural order hypothesis,* the *monitor hypothesis,* the *input hypothesis,* and the *affective filter hypothesis.*

The Acquisition-Learning Hypothesis. Krashen defined *acquisition* and *learning* as two separate processes in the mastering of a second language. Learning is formal knowledge about the rules of a language. Acquisition, on the other hand, is an unconscious process that occurs when language is used for real communication. Acquirers gain a "feel" for the correctness of their own utterances as their internal monitor is gradually adjusted.

For the classroom teacher, Krashen's distinction between acquisition and learning is important in that teachers acknowledge the fact that students will produce some language unself-consciously and will need rules and help for others. Thus, when children chat with one another as they work in cooperative groups, they are learning not only content (science, social studies) but also the English language.

The Natural Order Hypothesis. Krashen formulated the hypothesis that there appears to be a natural order of acquisition of English morphemes. The order is slightly different for second-language learners from the first-language order, but there are similarities.

Here is an example of the developmental sequence for the structure of negation (Krashen, 1982):

1. Negative marker outside the sentence
   No Mom sharpen it. (child L1 acquisition)
   Not like it now. (child L2 acquisition)

2. Negative marker between the subject and the verb
   I no like this one. (L2 acquisition)
   This no have calendar. (L2 acquisition)

3. Negative marker in correct position
   I don't like this one.

This example demonstrates that children acquire correct usage of grammatical structures in their second language (L2) gradually, as do children acquiring a first language (L1).

The Monitor Hypothesis. The monitor is an error-detecting mechanism; it scans an utterance for accuracy and edits—that is, confirms or repairs—the utterance either before or after attempted communication. However, the monitor cannot always be used. In a situation involving rapid verbal exchange, an individual may have little time to be concerned with correctness.

The monitor hypothesis is not without flaws. Krashen's claim that children are more successful language learners because they are not burdened by the monitor is disputed by McLaughlin (1987), who argues that adolescents are more successful learners than are children.

However, through his monitor construct, Krashen has changed the orientation that previously drove language instruction. The notion that language is best learned through conscious study of grammatical rules has been replaced by the realization that a "natural" language-rich environment facilitates acquisition.

The Input Hypothesis. The input hypothesis claims that language is acquired in an "amazingly simple way—when we understand messages" (Krashen, 1985, p. vii). Language must contain what Krashen calls "comprehensible" input.

Comprehensible input has generally been assumed to contain predictable elements: shorter sentences; more intelligible, well-formed utterances; less subordination; and more restricted vocabulary and range of topics with a focus on communication. Simpler structures roughly tuned to the learner's ability are used, and speech is slower. To conceptualize the input hypothesis, Krashen introduced the expression $i + 1$, where i stands for the current level of the acquirer's competence and 1 is the next structure due to be acquired in the natural order. Input needs to contain structures at the $i + 1$ level for the acquirer to proceed.

For the classroom teacher, the relevance of this hypothesis lies in its emphasis on "comprehensible." When working with English learners, teachers need to use a variety of techniques and modalities, including visual and kinesthetic, to ensure that their speech is understandable.

The Affective Filter Hypothesis. This hypothesis addresses emotional variables, including anxiety, motivation, and self-confidence. These are crucial because they can block or facilitate input from reaching the language acquisition device (LAD). If the affective filter blocks some of the comprehensible input, less input enters the learner's LAD, and thus less language is acquired. A positive affective context increases the input. Most teachers understand that a nonthreatening and encouraging environment promotes learning, and that it is important to increase the enjoyment of learning, raise self-esteem, and blend self-awareness with an increase in proficiency as students learn English.

Cummins's Theories of Bilingualism and Cognition

Jim Cummins's work falls within the cognitive approach to language, with its emphasis on the strengths the learner brings to the task of learning a second language. Dispelling the notion that bilingualism impedes classroom learning, Cummins's research has furthered the belief that being bilingual is a cognitive advantage and that knowledge of the first language provides a firm foundation for second-language acquisition.

Separate or Common Underlying Proficiency. Some critics of bilingual education have charged that educating children in the primary language reduces their opportunity to acquire English. This argument assumes that proficiency in English is separate from proficiency in a primary language and that content and skills learned through the primary language do not transfer to English—a notion that Cummins (1981b) has termed *separate underlying proficiency (SUP)*. In contrast, Cummins asserted that cognition and language fundamentals, once learned in the primary language, form a basis for subsequent learning in any language. This position assumes a *common underlying* *proficiency (CUP)*, the belief that a second language and the primary language have a shared foundation, and that competence in the primary language provides the basis for competence in the second language.

For example, children learning to read and write in Korean develop concepts about print and the role of literacy that make learning to read and think in English easier, despite the fact that these languages do not share a similar writing system. The surface differences in the languages are less important than the deeper understandings about the function of reading and its relationship to thought and learning. Cummins (1981b) cited much evidence to support the idea of a common underlying proficiency. Students do not have to relearn in a second language the essentials of schooling: how to communicate, how to think critically, and how to read and write.

Basic Interpersonal Communication Skills and Cognitive Academic Language Proficiency.
Cummins (1979, 1980) posited two different yet related language skills: basic interpersonal communication skills (BICS) and cognitive academic language proficiency (CALP). BICS involve those language skills and functions that allow students to communicate in everyday social contexts that are similar to those of the home, as they perform classroom chores, chat with peers, or consume instructional media as they do television shows at home. Cummins called BICS *context embedded* because participants can provide feedback to one another, and the situation itself provides cues that further understanding.

In contrast, CALP is the language needed to perform school tasks successfully. Such tasks generally are more abstract and decontextualized. Students must rely primarily on language to attain meaning. Cummins (1984) called CALP *context-reduced* communication because there are few concrete cues to aid in comprehension. Successful educators are aware that students need skills in both language domains.

During the elementary school years, and then even more so throughout middle and high school, students who may appear to be fluent enough in English to survive in an all-English classroom may in fact have significant gaps in the development of academic aspects of English. Conversational skills have been found to approach nativelike levels within two years of exposure to English, but five or more years may be required for minority students to match native speakers in CALP (Collier, 1987; Cummins, 1981a; Hakuta, Butler, & Witt, 2000).

Both BICS and CALP are clearly more than words. BICS involves the totality of communication that takes place between two or more people in their everyday activities. Some exchanges with people involve no words at all; for instance, a nod of the head while passing in the hallway at work may serve the same communicative purpose as a greeting. CALP, on the other hand, is more difficult to define. Beyond words, it also involves systematic thought processes. It provides the human brain with necessary tools to systematically categorize, compare, analyze, and accommodate new experiences, a cognitive toolbox—the in-depth knowledge that characterizes the well-educated individual in a complex modern society.

Cognitive academic language proficiency requires a complex growth in many linguistic areas simultaneously. This growth is highly dependent on the assistance of teachers because, for the most part, CALP is learned exclusively in school. The complexity of CALP can be captured by examination of the five Cs: communication, conceptualization, critical thinking, context, and culture (see Table 3.1). Many of the skills that are a part of CALP are refinements of BICS, whereas others are more exclusively school centered.

Table 3.1

Components of Cognitive Academic Language Proficiency (CALP)

Component	Explanation
Communication	Reading: Increases speed; uses context cues to guess vocabulary meaning; masters a variety of genres in fiction (poetry, short story) and nonfiction (encyclopedias, magazines, Internet sources) to "read the world" (interprets comics, print advertising, road signs). Listening: Follows verbal instructions; interprets nuances of intonation (e.g., in cases of teacher disciplinary warnings); solicits, and profits from, help of peers. Speaking: Gives oral presentations, answers correctly in class, and reads aloud smoothly. Writing: Uses conventions such as spelling, punctuation, and report formats.
Conceptualization	Concepts become abstract and are expressed in longer words with more general meaning (*rain* becomes *precipitation*). Concepts fit into larger theories (*precipitation* cycle). Concepts fit into hierarchies (rain → precipitation cycle → weather systems → climate). Concepts are finely differentiated from similar concepts (*sleet* from *hail, typhoons* from *hurricanes*). Conceptual relations become important (opposites, subsets, causality, correlation).
Critical thinking	Uses graphic organizers to represent the structure of thought (comparison charts, Venn diagrams, timelines, "spider" charts). Uses textual structures (outlines, paragraphing, titles, main idea). Uses symbolic representation (math operators [$<, >, +, =$]; proofreading marks, grade indications [10/20 points, etc.]). Reads between the lines (inference). Employs many other kinds of critical thinking. Plans activities, monitors progress, evaluates results, employs self-knowledge (metacognition). Increases variety and efficiency in use of learning strategies.
Context	Nonverbal: Uses appropriate gestures (and is able to refrain from inappropriate ones); interprets nonverbal signs accurately. Formality: Behaves formally when required to do so. Participation structures: Fits in smoothly to classroom and schoolwide groups and procedures.
Culture	Draws on experience in mainstream culture (background knowledge). Uses social class markers, such as "manners." Moves smoothly between home and school. Marshals and controls parental support for school achievement. Deploys primary-language resources when required. Maintains uninterrupted primary-culture profile ("fits in" to neighborhood social structures). Develops and sustains supportive peer interactions.

Example of Concept: Teaching Students to Use CALP

A look at an elementary classroom shows the integrated work that takes place across these CALP areas.

Mrs. Gómez found in her second-grade transitional bilingual class that although the students were fairly fluent English conversationalists they were performing poorly in academic tasks. Students seemed to understand English when pictures and other visual clues were present. However, when she gave instructions or briefly reviewed concepts, the students appeared lost. She realized that students needed lessons that eased them along the continuum from their interpersonal language usage to the more abstract academic requirements.

When Linda and several of her classmates were jumping rope during recess, Mrs. Gómez wrote down many of the patterned chants the girls were reciting. She transferred these to wall charts and read and recited them with the children. Next she introduced poems with more extensive vocabulary on wall charts, supplementing the charts with tapes that children could listen to in learning centers. The instructions for these centers featured patterned language similar to that already encountered in the rhymes. Gradually Mrs. Gómez was able to record more complex and abstract instructions in the learning centers. This progression and integration of activities helped the children to move along the continuum from BICS to CALP.

Communicative Competence

Language is a form of communication that occurs in social interaction. It is used for a purpose, such as persuading, commanding, and establishing social relationships. Knowing a language is no longer seen as merely knowing grammatical forms. Instead, the competent speaker is recognized as one who knows when, where, and how to use language appropriately.

Communicative competence is the aspect of language users' competence, or knowledge of the language, that enables them to "convey and interpret messages and to negotiate meanings interpersonally within specific contexts" (Brown, 1987, p. 199). Canale (1983) identified four components of communicative competence: grammatical competence, sociolinguistic competence, discourse competence, and strategic competence. Each of these is discussed in the following paragraphs.

Grammatical Competence. Some level of grammar is required when learning vocabulary, word formation and meaning, sentence formation, pronunciation, and spelling. This type of competence focuses on the skills and knowledge necessary to speak and write accurately, and becomes increasingly important to the English learner in more advanced stages of proficiency.

Sociolinguistic Competence. To communicate well, one must know how to produce and understand language in different sociolinguistic contexts, taking into consideration such factors as the status of participants, the purposes of the interaction, and the norms or conventions of interaction. One of the tasks of teachers is to help learners use both appropriate forms and appropriate meanings when interacting in the classroom.

Discourse Competence. In both speaking and writing, the learner needs to combine and connect utterances (spoken) and sentences (written) into a meaningful whole. A speaker may be both grammatically correct and appropriate socially but lack coherence or relevance to the topic at hand. Such a disconnected utterance shows a lack of discourse competence.

Example of Concept: Discourse Competence in Kindergarten Students

An example of discourse competence can be seen in the following conversation between two kindergarten boys, one a native-English speaker and the other an English learner:

Andrew: Can I play?
Rolando: No.
Andrew: There're only three people here.
Rolando: Kevin went to the bathroom.
Andrew: Can I take his place 'til he comes back?
Rolando: You're not playing.

Rolando was able to respond appropriately (though not kindly) to Andrew's request and to add information about his decision at the proper moment. This conversation shows that Rolando has discourse competence.

Strategic Competence. A speaker may use strategic competence in order to compensate for breakdowns in communication (as when a speaker forgets or does not know a term and is forced to paraphrase or gesture to get the idea across) and to enhance the effectiveness of communication (as when a speaker raises or lowers the voice for effect).

Language-Use Strategies Involving Communicative Competence. Chesterfield and Chesterfield (1985) found a natural order of strategies in students' development of second-language proficiency. These are strategies the mind uses in an untutored way to try to retain and process information when faced with the task of communicating in a second language. Teachers who are aware of these language-use strategies can incorporate them into instruction to build on students' developing competence. These strategies, in their order of development, include the following:

- *Repetition in short-term memory:* Imitating a word or structure used by another
- *Formulaic expressions:* Using words or phrases that function as units, such as greetings ("Hi! How are you?")
- *Verbal attention getters:* Using language to initiate interaction ("Hey!" "I think . . .")
- *Monitoring:* Correcting one's own errors in vocabulary, style, and grammar
- *Appealing for assistance:* Asking another for help
- *Requesting clarification:* Asking the speaker to explain or repeat

Teachers can specifically plan to increase students' skills in discourse and sociolinguistic and strategic competence by building experiences into the curriculum that involve students in solving problems, exploring areas of interest, and designing projects. Students carry over knowledge of how to communicate from experiences in their first language. This knowledge can be tapped as they develop specific forms and usage in English.

Example of Concept: Developing Communicative Competence

In a high-school economics class, Mr. Godfried often demonstrated consumer economics to the students by having them role-play. In the fifth-period class, several students were recent immigrants who had been placed in this class as a graduation requirement despite their limited English. Mr. Godfried's job became more complicated than in the past; now he had to teach not only economics but also basic communication skills in English. The process of opening a checking account was not difficult for Takeo, a Japanese student, who had had a checking account as a student in Japan. But Vasalli, an immigrant from Byelorussia, found the task mystifying. He had had limited experience with consumerism in general and no experience with the concept of a checking account. What he did have, however, was a general knowledge of how to interact with an official. Through the role-plays, Mr. Godfried was able to help the students use their background knowledge to conduct appropriate verbal interactions in the banking situation and use their communication experience to expand their content knowledge.

The Social Context for Language Learning

Learning a language is not strictly a communicative endeavor; it includes social and cultural interaction. The Russian psychologist Lev Vygotsky emphasized the role played by social interaction in the development of language and thought. According to Vygotsky (1978), teaching must be matched in some manner with the student's developmental level, taking into consideration the student's "zone of proximal development." Vygotsky defines this zone as "the distance between the actual developmental level as determined by independent problem solving and the level of potential development . . . under adult guidance or in collaboration with more capable peers" (p. 86).

Vygotsky's theory of cognitive development was sociocultural: He believed that teachers must understand the historical and cultural contexts of each child's background in order to understand how that person's mind has developed. He also emphasized the important role that language plays in human development—we internalize the language we learn in our social context, and this language is the basis of our mental "tool kit." Children hear others talking, and as they take in this language they use it to create their own understanding.

Using peer conversation as a means of enriching a student's exposure to language maximizes the opportunity for a student to hear and enjoy English. Mixing more-skilled with less-skilled speakers supplies more advanced language models to English learners. Thus, the context of instruction plays as critical a role in language development as does the actual language exchanged.

The teacher who is aware of the social uses of language provides a classroom environment in which students engage in communicative pair or group tasks. These can include practicing a readers' theater with other students in order to perform for their class or school, developing interview questions in order to survey local opinion on a timely topic, and planning an exhibition of art or written work to which to invite parents or other students.

Just as important as providing ample opportunity for students to interact within an information-rich environment is the assurance that such interaction takes place between language equals. Placing equal value on the primary language and its speakers creates a classroom in which there is no unfair privilege for native-English speakers.

Discourse Theory

Discourse theorists have analyzed conversation to understand how meaning is negotiated. According to them, face-to-face interaction is a key to second-language acquisition. By holding conversations (discourse), non-native speakers attend to the various features in the input they obtain. Through their own speech output, they affect both the quantity and the quality of the language they receive. The more learners talk, the more other people will talk to them. The more they converse, the more opportunity they have to initiate and expand topics, signal comprehension breakdowns, and try out new formulas and expressions.

In constructing discourse, second-language learners use four kinds of knowledge: knowledge about the second language, competence in their native language, ability to use the functions of language, and their general world knowledge. The language they produce is an *interlanguage*, an intermediate system that they create as they attempt to achieve nativelike competence (Selinker, 1972, 1991). Through a variety of discourse opportunities, learners sort out the ways language is used and gradually achieve proficiency.

Based on this understanding of the active role of the language learner, teachers need to provide many opportunities for English learners to engage in discourse with native speakers of English, in a variety of situations. ELD programs that restrict English learners to certain tracks or special classrooms, without incorporating specific opportunities for native–non-native-speaker interaction, do a disservice to English learners.

Adapted Instruction: Encouraging Native-Speaker/Non-Native-Speaker Interaction

- Students can interview others briefly on topics such as "My favorite sport" or "My favorite tool." The responses from the interviews can be tallied and form the basis for subsequent class discussion.
- English learners can also interact with native-English speakers during school hours through cross-age or peer interactions.

Understanding how discourse is used during instruction and modifying classroom discourse to encourage participation by English learners is a large part of specially designed academic instruction in English (SDAIE; see Chapter 5) and also culturally compatible teaching (see Chapter 10).

Meaning-Centered versus "Bottom-Up" Approaches to Language Acquisition

Meaning-Centered Approaches. Researchers (Goodman, 1986; Smith, 1983) looking at children learning to read in naturalistic settings noticed that they actively seek meaning. They work to make sense of text. They combine text clues with their own prior knowledge to construct meanings. The theory called *whole language* arose from the idea that meaning plays a central role in learning, and that language modes (speaking, listening, reading, writing) interact and are interdependent. Whole language, a philosophy of reading instruction, complemented many of the findings of studies in first- and second-language acquisition.

Meaning-centered systems of language acquisition (also called *top-down* systems—see Weaver, 1988) support the view that learners are generating hypotheses from and actively constructing interpretations about the input they receive, be it oral or written. Language is social in that it occurs within a community of users who attach agreed-upon meaning to their experiences. This view of language and literacy underlies a "constructivist" perspective. Constructivist-oriented classrooms tend to be those in which students' lives and experiences are valued, and in which they explore the multiple functions of literacy, reading, and writing to satisfy their own needs and goals.

Bottom-Up Approaches. Advocates of *bottom-up* approaches are concerned that learners connect the individual sounds of language with its written form as soon as possible, leading to the ability to decode whole words. Once words are identified, meaning will take care of itself. Instruction in decoding the sound–symbol relationship includes a set of rules for sounding out words.

To present the learner with easily decodable text, basal reading materials with controlled vocabulary are used to present simplified language, and teachers are encouraged to "preteach" vocabulary words that appear in reading passages. The emphasis is on skills for identifying words and sentence patterns, rather than on strategies for creating meaning from text.

Research and observation of children learning to read indicates that in fact readers use both top-down strategies and bottom-up skills as they read. Current reading instruction now favors a balanced approach (see Tompkins, 2005, particularly Chapter 1, for further discussion; also see Fitzgerald, 1999).

Semiotics

Not all second-language acquisition depends on verbal language. Semiotics is a discipline that studies the ways in which humans use signs to make meaning. According to semiotic theory, there are three kinds of signs: symbols, icons, and indexes. *Symbols* are signs for which there is an arbitrary relationship between the object and its sign; the word *table,* for example, is arbitrarily linked to the object "table." *Icons* are signs that resemble what they stand for, such as a drawing of a table. *Indexes* are signs that indicate a fact or condition; for instance, thunderclouds indicate rain.

Signs are organized into systems of objects and behaviors. Thus, the way chairs are arranged in a classroom and the manner in which students are expected to respond to the teacher are both signs that signal meaning. Signs—and the meanings they carry—

vary across cultures and languages, adding richness to the study of second language that words alone seldom express fully.

Semiotics provides a perspective for examining human development through the interplay of multiple meaning systems. As students learn English, wise teachers provide and accept various ways through which students demonstrate their knowledge.

Adapted Instruction: Using Semiotics to Acquire a Second Language

- Students can view themselves, other students, teachers, the community, and culturally authentic materials (phone books, voicemail messages, advertising brochures, music videos, etc.) to examine ways that meaning is communicated using both verbal and nonverbal messages.
- Students can engage in a variety of cross-media activities— produce music, create collages, and write poems, journal entries, or advertising slogans—to display their identities, values, or ideas.
- Students can "people-watch" using semiotics to read nonverbal messages sent by dress styles, posture, demeanor, and so forth as a way to increase their interactions with one another at all levels of language proficiency.

Source: Díaz-Rico and Dullien (2004).

Semiotics has become increasingly important within the last decade as visual information, rather than primarily text, has become increasingly available and salient in the lives of students. Sophisticated computer art, animation, and graphics programs available through the Internet have opened up a language of two-dimensional shape and color that supplements, if not replaces, text as a source of information and experience for many young people. To learn more about this field, see Chandler (2005), Kress and Van Leeuwen (1995), Martin and Ringham (2006), Scollon and Scollon (2003), Ryder (2005).

Contributions of Research about the Brain

A basic question concerning second-language acquisition is, "What is the role of the brain in learning language?" Neurolinguists attempt to explain the connection between language function and neuroanatomy and to identify, if possible, the areas of the brain responsible for language functioning. Recent studies have looked at the role of emotions and visual and gestural processing in second-language acquisition, tracing the brain processing not only of verbal language but also of nonverbal input such as gestures, facial expressions, and intonation (Paradis, 2005; Schumann, 1994).

Several contemporary educators have specialized in developing learning methods that take into consideration brain processing. According to research (Caine & Caine, 1994; Hart, 1975, 1983), learning is the brain's primary function. Many parts of the brain process reality simultaneously, using thoughts, emotions, imagination, and the senses to interact with the environment. This rich reaction can be tapped to facilitate language acquisition (see Table 3.2). For further information about brain-based learning, see *Brain/Mind Learning Principles in Action: The Fieldbook for Making Connections, Teaching, and the Human Brain* by Caine, Caine, McClintic, and Klimek (2004); Jensen's *Teaching with the Brain in Mind* (1998); Lyons and Clay's *Teaching Struggling Readers: How to Use Brain-Based Research to Maximize Learning* (2003); and Smilkstein's *We're Born to Learn* (2002).

Adapted Instruction: Using Principles of Brain-Based Learning in Oral Presentations

Before a Presentation
■ Have students lower anxiety by taking a few deep breaths, visualizing success, and repeating positive self-talk phrases (brain-based principle 2: Learning engages the entire physiology).
■ Remind students to review the structure of the information, especially how the parts of the presentation fit together (brain-based principle 6: The brain processes parts and wholes simultaneously).

During the Presentation
■ The speaker concentrates on the task while staying tuned to the needs of the audience (brain-based principle 7: Learning involves both focused attention and peripheral perception).
■ Tenseness that is redefined as "eustress" ("good stress") supplies energy for learning rather than inhibits performance (brain-based principle 11: Learning is enhanced by challenge and inhibited by threat).

After the Presentation
■ Students evaluate their accomplishment, ask for feedback and tune in to the reactions of others, identify problem areas, and make a plan for improvement (brain-based principle 10: Learning occurs best when facts and skills are embedded in natural, spatial memory—including the memory of positive performance).

Theories of second-language acquisition provide the rationale and framework for the daily activities of instruction. Teachers who are aware of the basic principles of contemporary language acquisition and learning are better equipped to plan instruction and explain their practices to peers, parents, students, and administrators.

Although the teacher's role is valuable as students learn a second language, the actual language learned is the responsibility of the learner. Research on cognitive processes shows that learners construct and internalize language-using rules during problem solving or authentic communication. The shift from *what the teacher does* to *what the learner does* is a characteristic of contemporary thinking about learning in general and language acquisition specifically and has wide implications for teaching English learners. ■

LEARNING MORE

Further Reading

Excellent general background reading on discourse and context is Mercer's *Words and Minds* (2000), which traces the codevelopment of language and thinking. Mercer gives

Table 3.2

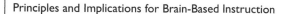

Principles and Implications for Brain-Based Instruction

Principle	Implications for Instruction
1. The brain can perform multiple processes simultaneously.	Learning experiences can be multimodal. As students perform experiments, develop a play from the text of a story, or take on complex projects, many facets of the brain are involved.
2. Learning engages the entire physiology.	Stress management, nutrition, exercise, relaxation, and natural rhythms and timing should be taken into consideration during teaching and learning.
3. The search for meaning is innate.	Language-learning activities should involve a focus on meaning; language used in the context of interesting activities provides a situated, meaningful experience.
4. The brain is designed to perceive and generate patterns.	Information is presented in a way that allows brains to extract patterns and create meaning rather than react passively.
5. Emotions are crucial to memory.	Instruction should support the students' backgrounds and languages. Interaction should be marked by mutual respect and acceptance.
6. The brain processes parts and wholes simultaneously.	Language skills, such as vocabulary and grammar, are best learned in authentic language environments (solving a problem, debating an issue, exploring) in which *parts* (specific language skills) are learned together with *wholes* (problems to be solved).
7. Learning involves both focused attention and peripheral perception.	Music, art, and other rich environmental stimuli can enhance and influence the natural acquisition of language. Subtle signals from the teacher (processed peripherally by students) communicate enthusiasm and interest.
8. Learning always involves conscious and unconscious processes.	Students need opportunities to review what they learn consciously so they can reflect, take charge, and develop personal meaning. This encourages and gives shape to unconscious learning.
9. There are at least two types of memory: spatial memory and rote learning systems.	Teaching techniques that focus on the memorization of language bits—words and grammar points—use the rote learning system. Teaching that actively involves the learner in novel experiences taps into the spatial system.
10. Learning occurs best when facts and skills are embedded in natural, spatial memory.	Discrete language skills can be learned when they are embedded in real-life activities (demonstrations, field trips, performances, stories, drama, visual imagery).
11. Learning is enhanced by challenge and inhibited by threat.	Teachers need to create an atmosphere of acceptance. Learners are taken from the point where they are at present to the next level of competence through a balance of support and challenge.
12. Each brain is unique.	Teaching should be multifaceted. English learners can express developing understanding through visual, tactile, emotional, and auditory means.

many examples of how people use discourse to shape events, such as arguing, persuading, laying the ground rules for conversation, and even giving and receiving a bribe. The discussion of the role of the teacher in fostering communicative talk in the classroom is broadly applicable across many levels of schooling.

Web Search

The *Open Court Reading* Website (online at www.sraonline.com/oc_home.html) gives the rationale for teaching reading through a structured program based on systematic and explicit scaffolding of skills. In contrast, the Heinemann Website (online at www.heinemann.com) offers reading materials such as Pransky's *Beneath the Surface: The Hidden Realities of Teaching Culturally and Linguistically Diverse Young Learners, K–6* (2008) that present a child-centered view of the reading process. Use these two Websites to contrast top-down and bottom-up reading practices and their related underlying theories of learning.

Exploration

Visit several local ESL teachers to investigate the second-language learning theories underlying their classroom practice. Ask what they know about Krashen's monitor theory, or such terms as *comprehensible input* and *affective filter*. Ask if they recognize the terms *basic interpersonal communication skills* (BICS) and *cognitive academic learning proficiency* (CALP). If not, ask what techniques they use to make instruction understandable to their English learners, and if they believe that lowering anxiety (the affective filter) increases learning.

Experiment

Ask a friend to learn ten names in a foreign language (you supply). If the friend agrees, see how long it takes him or her to memorize the names to your satisfaction. Next, ask the same friend if he or she would have learned the names faster for a reward. If so, what reward would have been sufficient? Does your friend think the reward would have increased the speed of learning? Why or why not?

The Power of Classroom Practice
www.myeducationlab.com

Peers Provide Scaffolding for Language Learning

In this video, two English-language learners in a multilingual classroom participate in a peer/buddy reading activity guided by their teacher. With their teacher's help, the older student reads to the younger student. Both of the students are Hmong, but the older student is much more proficient in English than the younger student, who only speaks in Hmong on the video. As you watch the video, observe the children's interaction with the book and with each other. Try to identify portions of the video that illustrate how this interaction has a positive effect on each student's ability to respond to the text. Also think about what theory of cognitive development is being applied.

To access the video, go to MyEducationLab (www.myeducationlab.com), choose the Díaz-Rico and Weed text, and log in to MyEducationLab for English Language Learners. Select the topic Comprehensible Input, and watch the video entitled "Peers Provide Scaffolding for Language Learning."

Answer the following questions:
1. How might the peer interaction in this video provide examples of the following teaching and learning principles in action?
   • Active engagement
   • Cultural relevance
   • Collaboration
   • Comprehensible input
   • Prior knowledge
2. Not all children are "born teachers." How can the classroom teacher assist peer tutors to assist others?
3. How does the classroom teacher monitor the situation to assess the effectiveness of peer tutoring?

part two

Instruction

Oracy and Literacy for English-Language Development, Content-Area Instruction, and Bilingual Education

Part Two examines methods for enhancing listening, speaking, reading, and writing skills in English for English learners (Chapter 4); models of schooling for academic development in the content areas of social studies, literature, mathematics, science, visual/performing arts, and physical instruction (Chapter 5); and various models of bilingual education that serve students with varying degrees of support for heritage-language proficiency (Chapter 6). The figure below highlights Part Two of the theoretical model presented in the introduction.

Theoretical Model for CLAD Instruction: Oracy and Literacy for English-Language Development, Content-Area Instruction, and Bilingual Education.

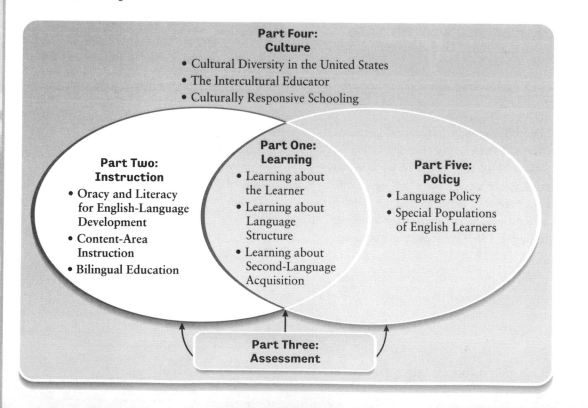

Part Four: Culture
- Cultural Diversity in the United States
- The Intercultural Educator
- Culturally Responsive Schooling

Part Two: Instruction
- Oracy and Literacy for English-Language Development
- Content-Area Instruction
- Bilingual Education

Part One: Learning
- Learning about the Learner
- Learning about Language Structure
- Learning about Second-Language Acquisition

Part Five: Policy
- Language Policy
- Special Populations of English Learners

Part Three: Assessment

4

Oracy and Literacy for English-Language Development

Listening centers help students to hear authentic spoken language as well as literary language in the form of books, poems, or songs.

As part of our immigration unit, the children and I read *How Many Days to America?* (Bunting, 1990). Because so many of the children had immigrated to our southern California community, they had a lot to share about their own experiences. Prior to reading our next book, *If You Sailed on the Mayflower in 1620* (McGovern, 1969), we looked at a detailed poster of a drawing of the *Mayflower*. This familiarized the children with the different parts of the ship and the story we would be drawing, talking, writing, and reading about.

K. Weed and M. Ford (1999, p. 70)

Developing proficiency in English is a multifaceted task. Not only must students *read* and *write* at a level that supports advanced academic success, but they must also use their skills of *listening* and *speaking* to gain information and demonstrate their knowledge. A fifth necessary skill is the ability to *think* both critically and creatively. The teacher's role is to integrate these separate, but interrelated, skills in a unified curriculum that moves students from beginning to advanced proficiency in classroom English.

In this chapter, we first discuss English-language development standards that help teachers organize and develop their programs. Next, we explore the four language modalities and provide suggestions for specific lessons and activities that foster English-language oracy and literacy development. Because of the pervasiveness of technology in today's world, a separate section on oracy, literacy, and technology provides information and activities to integrate technology with literacy instruction.

English-Language Development Standards

To provide educators with directions and strategies to assist English learners, the international professional organization Teachers of English to Speakers of Other Languages, Inc. (TESOL, Inc.) developed an ESL standards document (TESOL, 1997) to draw attention to English learners' needs. This document served as a complement to other standards documents and specified the language competencies that English learners need in order to become fully fluent in English. In 2006, TESOL published its revised standards that expanded the scope and breadth of the 1997 standards (see Figure 4.1). The former ESL standards were consolidated (Standard 1) and four new standards address the language of the core curriculum areas (Standards 2–5). Information on this document is available at the TESOL Website, www.tesol.org.

Figure 4.1 PreK–12 English Language Proficiency Standards

The English language proficiency standards are broad statements encompassing the range of language competencies required of all English-language learners for success in the classroom.

Standard 1: English-language learners communicate for social, intercultural, and instructional purposes within the school setting.

Standard 2: English-language learners communicate information, ideas, and concepts necessary for academic success in the area of language arts

Standard 3: English-language learners communicate information, ideas, and concepts necessary for academic success in the area of mathematics

Standard 4: English-language learners communicate information, ideas, and concepts necessary for academic success in the area of science

Standard 5: English-language learners communicate information, ideas, and concepts necessary for academic success in the area of social studies

Source: Teachers of English to Speakers of Other Languages (TESOL; 2006), p. 2.

Numerous states have also produced documents to assist teachers working with English learners. California, for example, has prepared *English-Language Development Standards* (California Department of Education [CDE], 2002) to ensure that English learners develop proficiency in both the English language and the concepts and skills contained in the English-Language Arts (ELA) Content Standards (CDE, 1998a). This document provides teachers with guidelines to move students toward fluency within the language-arts curriculum. Because California's English-Language Development standards were designed with the same categories as the English-Language Arts standards for mainstream students, teachers are able to identify "big ideas" in both sets of standards (such as "Follows directions") so that in a tightly focused lesson, English learners and English-only students are learning the same core skill. To make this easier, WestEd publishes a Map of Standards for English Learners (Carr & Lagunoff, 2006).

The importance of these standards documents is that teachers now have specific behaviors and goals to help them work with English learners. They can work with students through a developmental framework, recognizing that students cannot be forced to produce beyond their proficiency level, but knowing that students are expected to attain certain levels of competency commensurate with their proficiency.

Integrating Language Skills

Instead of teaching reading apart from writing, listening, and speaking, educators now recommend that these skills be combined smoothly into instruction that develops language skills in a unified way. For example, students tell stories as the teacher writes them down for later reading aloud (Language Experience Approach); students listen to stories and then retell them or write a new ending; and students write poems and then read them aloud. This reinforces one skill using another, allowing vocabulary words to be seen, heard, and spoken, and language to convert from receptive (listening and reading) to productive (speaking and writing) and vice versa.

Example of Concept: Integrated Language Skills

Mrs. Ford's story, which begins this chapter, provides a concrete example of how one teacher integrated the language modalities in her multigrade (2, 3, 4), multilingual (Spanish, English, Samoan, Tongan, Armenian, Indonesian) classroom. The story continues:

I then started the story (*If You Sailed on the Mayflower in 1620*). After reading a segment, I stopped and asked the children to draw what they thought was most important about what they had heard. They quickly sketched their main ideas, knowing they could go back later to add details (similar to writing a rough draft). We continued for several days until we finished the book.

At the end of each daily reading and sketching session, the children got together in groups and shared a drawing that the group discussed. If a child did not fully understand a concept, the group discussed it. . . . During this small-group time, I rotated among the different groups and prompted where necessary, "What more can you tell me about your picture?" "Why did you decide to include this detail?" . . . "What could you do differently to make your ideas clearer?"

Although the text and my questions were in English, the students' discussion ranged across languages. Often, a long exchange occurred in Indonesian or Spanish or Tongan as the students sorted out ideas, clarified their interpretations, and then drafted their written work. . . . The students were gaining rich conceptual knowledge through their talk. Notions understood through the English medium were being massaged and expanded in the primary language.

After their discussions, the artists wrote a sentence or two about the drawing, pulling from their own and their group members' ideas. By the end of the week, the children had a series of drawings in a folder. . . . They got into groups again and collectively sequenced their pictures. They were creating their own book based on the story of the *Mayflower*.

More discussion went on during this group work. Although the published work would be in English, pairs and trios of students continued to discuss in their primary languages, and the braver, sometimes the more proficient, would present ideas in English to the whole small group. I often saw three- and four-way conversations—discussion in first language, tentative idea presenting in English, some exploring among members in English, with questions and discussion going back and forth in various respective primary languages. From their initial "story map," students elaborated on their writing, adding details and clarifying thoughts. The editing evolved as a part of group discussion as students prepared their story for publication. They also refined their artwork, adding details, . . . and going back to the book for ideas.

Throughout this sequence of activities, the children generated ideas through different systems. Writing would prompt new ideas for pictures, and pictures generated new ideas for writing. Discussion clarified, suggested, and supported. Sometimes students would even completely change a picture or their writing based on a new understanding. . . . [O]ften a student who was reticent in speaking was nonetheless an important idea generator for a group.

During the editing sessions, I introduced small strategy lessons depending on the group's needs. These lessons focused on issues, questions, and dilemmas that had come up in the natural course of discussion and writing. In this manner, specific skills could be addressed in the context of the students' writing.

When the final products were ready, a representative from each group read the group's book aloud and showed the illustrations. These students were not always the most proficient in English, but rather those whom the group decided would best represent it. The books were then placed in the classroom library for all to read. These student-produced books were so popular that they often wore out.

Source: Weed and Ford (1999). Reprinted with permission.

English learners, like native speakers of English, do not necessarily demonstrate a balance in language acquisition and ability. Some prolific speakers lag behind in reading, whereas some capable readers are shy about speaking, and so forth. The integrated skills approach supports those language skills that may be underdeveloped, while allowing students with strong skills in other areas to shine.

Listening

Part of the knowledge needed to comprehend oral discourse is the ability to separate meaningful units from the stream of speech. Although listening has been classified along with reading as a "receptive" skill, it is by no means a passive act. Listeners draw on their store of background knowledge and their expectation of the message to be conveyed as they actively work at understanding conversational elements.

The role of the teacher is to set up situations in which students feel a sense of purpose and can engage in real communication. In this way, students can develop a personal agenda—their own purposes and goals—for listening, and the English they acquire is most useful in their daily lives. Although the current emphasis is on communicating for authentic purposes, activities are discussed under the categories of listening to repeat, listening to understand, and listening for communication.

Listening to Repeat

A common listening strategy is *minimal pair* pattern practice, in which students are asked to listen to and repeat simple phrases that differ by only one phoneme—for example: "It is a ship/It is a sheep"; "He is barking/He is parking." Little attention, however, is paid to meaning. Current methods encourage students to listen to minimal pairs within meaningful contexts. Not only do these activities help students to hear the language, but the work with sounds also provides opportunities for preliterate students to develop phonemic awareness, "the insight that every spoken word is made up of a sequence of phonemes" (CDE, 1999, p. 278) and considered by many to be a prerequisite for learning to read.

Adapted Instruction: Listening for Sounds

- Use poems, nursery rhymes, and songs to introduce words that differ by only one phoneme.
- Ask students to orally fill in the blanks at the end of lines, demonstrating their knowledge of the sound and the word within the context.
- Read aloud wordplay books, alliterative books, and books with tongue twisters.

Students also need to listen attentively to longer sections of discourse to hear sentence intonation patterns. Jazz chants provide rhythmic presentations of natural language in a meaningful context: "The rhythm, stress, and intonation pattern of the chant should be an *exact* replica of what the student would hear from a native speaker in natural conversation" (Graham, 1992, p. 3).

Example of Concept: Sentence Intonation

Mr. Pang used "Late Again" (Graham, 1978) not only to help students with intonation in short phrases but also as a means to get them ready to leave for the day. After learning the chant, students brainstormed words like *backpack, homework,* and *pencil case* to substitute for *keys, socks,* and *shoes* in the original chant. Mr. Pang would start the chant, "Are you ready?" and students would respond as they gathered their things and lined up at the door.

Listening to Understand

Students perform tasks such as writing the correct response or selecting the correct answer to demonstrate comprehension (Morley, 2001). To be successful, they must listen carefully. Typical classroom tasks are listening to an audiotape and completing true/false exercises based on the content, listening to a prerecorded speech and circling vocabulary items on a list as they appear in the text, and listening to a lecture and completing an outline of the notes.

Listening objectives in language tasks can vary from simply identifying words or facts, to comprehending details, or getting the main idea. Listeners can respond by choosing from two alternatives, taking notes, transferring what has been heard to a chart, answering questions, making a summary, or discussing or acting out what was heard (Lund, 1990).

Total Physical Response. Total physical response (TPR) is based on the association between language and body movement and can be an engaging, lively addition to classroom techniques. In studying and observing children learning their first language, Asher (1982) noted three elements that he made the basis for his approach:

1. Listening, and hence understanding, precedes speaking.
2. Understanding is developed through moving the body.
3. Speaking is never forced.

In TPR, students respond to an oral command that is simultaneously being modeled. For example, the teacher says, "Stand" while standing up, and "Sit" while sitting down, and students follow along. The instructor repeats the commands followed by the appropriate action until students perform without hesitation. The instructor then begins to delay his or her own action to allow students the opportunity to respond and thus demonstrate understanding. Eventually, the students, first as a whole group and then as individuals, act on the instructor's voice command alone. Novel commands are given that combine previously learned commands in a new way. For example, if the students were familiar with "Run" and "Walk to the chair," they might be given "Run to the chair." Students continue to respond in a nonverbal manner until they feel comfortable issuing their own commands.

Reading and writing are also introduced through commands. The instructor may write "Stand" on the board and gesture to the students to perform the action. After practice with the written form in class, students can be given lists of familiar commands that they can then manipulate in their own fashion. The concrete, hands-on methodology recommended by Asher is associated with early stages of second-language learning and is recommended by Krashen and Terrell (1983) for promoting comprehension in a low-anxiety environment. (For TPR used in storytelling, see Ray and Seely [1998].)

Ong and Murugesan (2007, p. 26) list some options that can accompany or follow listening for understanding:

- Mime what is heard
- Follow the leader
- Identify/point
- Follow cues to perform actions
- Put pictures in order
- Draw/color according to verbal directions

Example of Concept: Orienting Students to Classroom Procedures

Ms. Knight reviews her classroom procedures and selects five that she wants students to learn the first week; for example, "Take out your reading book"; "Look at the directions on the board." She says and models the behavior. The students mimic her first as a whole group and then in table groups. By having all students participate, Ms. Knight allows her English learners to become confident members of the class without singling them out.

Listening for Communication

Current language-teaching methods emphasize the interactional aspects of language and recognize the importance of the listener's construction of meaning. During the initial "silent period," learners actively listen, segmenting the sound stream, absorbing intonation patterns, and becoming comfortable in the second-language environment. They demonstrate comprehension through nonverbal means. With this methodology, academic subjects can be included even in the early stages of language acquisition.

Adapted Instruction: Preparing for a Speaker

Before the Talk
- Discuss the topic of an upcoming talk (by a guest speaker, cross-age, or grade-level peer).
- Brainstorm questions and comments the students might like to make.

During the Talk
- Ask students to listen for answers to their questions.
- Record the talk.

After the Talk
- With the recording at a listening center, have students listen again, making note of ideas they want to share in the class follow-up activities. The recording also serves as a mediator when students have varying recollections of a particular point. The students can listen carefully to the tape in order to reconcile their points of view.

Table 4.1

Activities for Listening Comprehension

Repetition	Understanding	Communication

To hear sound patterns:
  Rhyming poems
  Songs
  Couplets
  Tongue twisters
  Jingles
  Alliterative poems and books
To listen to sentences:
  Jazz chants
  Dialogues
  Skits
	Listening to answer factual
	questions orally or in writing:
	  Dialogues
	  Talks
	  Lectures
	  Arguments
	Listening to make notes:
	  Support an argument
	  Persuade
		Playing games:
		  Twenty Questions
		  Pictionary
		  Password
		  Simon Says
		  Mother May I?
		Interviews
		Conversation starters
		Cooperative problem-solving
		activities:
		  Riddles
		  Logic puzzles
		  Brainteasers

Listening, far from merely being a receptive skill, can be successfully combined with other language modes as part of an integrated approach to English acquisition. Table 4.1 provides listening comprehension activities within each of the three categories discussed.

A favorite activity to develop speaking and listening skills is Information Gap. In this activity, two students have copies of the same materials, but they sit with a manila folder between them. One describes a picture, and the other identifies which one is the subject of the description. In the same manner, one student can be seated to watch a movie segment in order to describe it to another student whose back is turned. The one listening must summarize the action after the description, and then both can watch the segment again together. This activity is easily adapted for various levels of language proficiency.

Speaking

Speaking involves a number of complex skills and strategies. Spoken discourse involves not only stringing words together in proper grammatical sequence but also organizing those strings into coherent wholes. This produces an oral text, one that has an inherent form, meaning, purpose, and function.

Spoken discourse can be informal, such as conversations between friends, or formal, such as lectures or presentations. Informal conversations are interactive; speaker and listener share common knowledge and support one another with nonverbal cues. In a formal presentation, the speaker assumes the listener can supply a complex background or context. The listener is less able to interact with the speaker to negotiate meaning. In addition to these different dimensions of formality, conversations and presentations take place in a variety of social contexts, with differing amounts of contextual cues that help the speaker to communicate.

Part of the role of the teacher is to help students understand and produce discourse not only for the purpose of basic interpersonal communication (informal) but also for the comprehension and production of cognitive/academic language (formal). In addition, the teacher provides opportunities for students to express themselves in the wide range of language functions (see Chapter 2).

Situations for Spoken Discourse

Students need opportunities to talk in natural interactional contexts and for a variety of purposes: to establish and maintain social relationships; to express reactions; to give and seek information; to solve problems, discuss ideas, or teach and learn a skill; to entertain or play with language; or to display achievement. In addition, students learn needed discourse skills by interacting with different conversational partners: other students, the teacher, other adults at school, cross-age peers, classroom visitors, and so on. Beginning language learners may need basic survival language:

- Can they give their name, address, and telephone number?
- Can they say their parents' names?
- Can they ask for help politely, using "please" and "thank you"?
- Can they understand simple classroom procedures, such as how to ask to use the bathroom?
- Can they name several classmates?

For students to have the opportunity to develop discourse proficiency, teachers create environments that challenge students to use language to meet the social, emotional, and cognitive demands of their lives in and out of school. The following three principles (Dudley-Marling & Searle, 1991) help teachers set up such environments:

1. *Consider the emotional setting.* Teachers set up a climate of trust and respect by encouraging students to respect the language of their peers, by listening respectfully when students speak, and by working with students to establish classroom rules of respect and support.

2. *Create a physical setting for talk.* Classrooms need to be arranged so that students have flexibility in working and interacting. Some desks can be replaced with round or rectangular tables; other desks can be arranged in clusters.

3. *Group students for instruction.* Students need frequent opportunities to talk. Flexible grouping allows students to work with a variety of classmates; cross-age tutors provide one-on-one time with an older student; and aides, parent volunteers, and volunteer "grandparents" can lead small-group discussions.

Improving Oral Proficiency

English learners must have a comprehensible control of the English sound system. Pronunciation involves the correct *articulation* of the individual sounds (phonemes) of English as well as the proper *stress* and *pitch* within syllables, words, and phrases. Longer stretches of speech require correct *intonation* patterns (see Chapter 2).

Example of Concept: Chant and Dance Syllable Work

Artist, guitarist, and literacy coach Eduardo García has a novel way of introducing fifth-grade English learners to syllables using the African-based rhythms of Latin America. Students each wear flash cards around their necks with one syllable of a long word. They sit in a circle. The coach-as-drummer sits in the center, and calls out a syllable: "o." Everyone chants "o." The student wearing the *o* dances to the center, soon to be joined by the "per," "a," and "tion." Soon everyone chants "operation" and they all sit down. Next come the syllables of the word *recommendation*, then *cooperation* until a roomful of words has been danced into memory. (García, 2004, p. 49)

The goal of teaching English pronunciation is not necessarily to make second-language speakers sound like native speakers of English. Some English learners do not wish to have a nativelike pronunciation but prefer instead to retain an accent that indicates their first-language roots and allows them to be identified with their ethnic community (Morley, 2001). Still others may wish to integrate actively into the mainstream culture and thus are motivated to try to sound like a native speaker of English. The teacher's role is to create a nonthreatening environment that stimulates and interests students enough that they participate actively in producing speech. Finders and Hynds (2007) point out that a strong focus on correctness may stifle students' enthusiasm and creativity—the emphasis should be on "progress, not perfection" (p. 97).

In other cases, however, teachers may want to intervene actively. Clarification checks may be interjected politely when communication is impaired. Correction or completion by the teacher may be given after the teacher has allowed ample "wait time." Older students may be given the task of comparing speech sounds in their native language with a sound in English in order to better understand a contrastive difference. Students' attempts to produce English may be enhanced if they are taught strategies that help them to overcome anxiety and are given opportunities to speak in the context of reading and other content activities.

Adapted Instruction: Acquiring the Oracy Strategy—"Self-Talk for Speaking"

As a warm-up, ask students if they talk to themselves as they prepare to do something new. Elicit positive and negative examples. Tell students they will practice positive *self-talk* as they prepare for and carry out speaking tasks in English. Next, model self-talk when making a telephone call.

Then, hand out a worksheet with several blank lines, with the heading, "When I prepare for a presentation, I can tell myself _____" (students will fill in the blanks with several self-selected phrases).

For homework, students should prepare and rehearse a one-minute presentation using self-talk. They give the presentation the next day, and then report which phrases they found most helpful before and during delivery.

Source: Adapted from Chamot, Barnhardt, El-Dinary, and Robbins (1999, pp. 231–232).

Example of Concept: Cued Story Retelling

Beginning language learners can use pictures from the stories they read to cue story retellings. To prepare them for retelling, each student is given a set of pictures. As the story is read aloud, each student holds up a relevant picture. After the story is read, students mix up their pictures and then arrange them in order of events, telling the story as they go (Malinka, 2006).

Table 4.2 organizes representative oral activities into the three categories suggested by Allen and Vallette (1977). These categories range from tightly structured (on the left) to freely constructed (on the right).

Vocabulary Development

According to educational researchers, English-language learners will never catch up with native speakers unless they develop a rich vocabulary. Native-English speakers typically know at least 5,000 to 7,000 English words before kindergarten—a huge vocabulary, as anyone who has struggled to learn a second language knows. English-language learners must close that initial gap, but also keep pace with the native speakers as they steadily expand their vocabulary mastery.

The vocabulary of academic language goes well beyond that used in most social conversations. It is only through structured talk about academically relevant content that students learn the words needed to engage in class discussions and to comprehend what they read in various subjects. Memorizing word lists rarely helps. Words must be learned and used in context (American Educational Research Association, 2004, p. 2).

Table 4.2

Formats for Oral Practice in the ELD Classroom

Guided Practice	Communicative Practice	Free Conversation
Formulaic exchanges:	Simulations	Discussion groups
Greetings	Guessing games	Debates
Congratulations	Group puzzles	Panel discussions
Apologies	Rank-order problems	Group picture story
Leave-taking	Values continuum	Socializing
Dialogues	Categories of preference:	Storytelling/retelling
Mini-conversations	Opinion polls	Discussions of:
Role-plays	Survey taking	Films
Skits	Interviews	Shared experiences
Oral descriptions	Brainstorming	Literature
Strip stories	News reports	
Oral games	Research reports	
	Storytelling	

Example of Concept: Discussion about Vocabulary

Group discussions can also take place about new words. Tinker Sachs and Ho (2007) described Ms. Wu's vocabulary-building lesson, in which small groups grappled with the definitions, synonyms, and antonyms for new words they acquired during an exercise in which they classified books into genres such as classics, humor, drama, and autobiography. After small-group discussion, Ms. Wu invited one member of each group to teach the whole class about a new word that the group acquired.

Vocabulary instruction is multifaceted. Students need a variety of strategies to gain meaning from context, including ways to guess what part of speech a word is, to look for embedded definitions in which the following text explains the meaning, and to find theme-related clues in the surrounding text. Students can learn to distinguish connotative from denotative meanings of words, so they can acquire the emotions and nuances that accompany new words as they are learned. They can identify words with multiple meanings to avoid confusion (Newman, 2006).

New vocabulary words can be presented in a variety of ways:

- Say the word clearly and show its spelling.
- Provide a definition or examples.
- Show or draw a picture.
- Act it out; use gestures.
- Give examples of the word in use.
- Translate the word into L1.
- Present the word through chants and songs. (Ong & Murugesan, 2007, p. 44)

Example of Concept: Vocabulary through Visualization

Especially when faced with a new language, many learners rely on visuals for understanding, such as textbook illustrations, gestures, photos, drawings, and charts. Zemach (2007) encourages students to illustrate new vocabulary words with sketches, and then to quiz one another with their homemade flash cards. Instead of making an outline to brainstorm for an essay, she encourages students to use mind maps. These visuals reduce the stress of all-verbal learning.

Reading

Literacy instruction is a crucial aspect of K–12 schooling in the United States. For decades, educators have debated the best way to help children learn to read and read to learn. Recent research has revealed a dismal literacy level for students who are classified as "formerly English learners"—only 20 percent scored at the proficient or advanced levels of the reading portion of the 2005 NCES testing (Calderón, 2007). However, a complicating factor that is sometimes not considered by monolingual reading researchers is the varying background experiences that English learners bring to the reading task. California TESOL (CATESOL, 1998) provided the following five classifications for English learners that help teachers to understand the varying backgrounds of English learners.

1. Young learners [K–3] whose beginning literacy instruction is in their primary language
2. Young learners [K–3] acquiring initial literacy in English because they do not have access to primary-language reading instruction
3. Older learners with grade-level primary-language literacy, who are beginning to develop literacy in English
4. Older learners with limited formal schooling in their home country
5. Older learners with inconsistent school history, with limited development of either the primary language or English (p. 1)

Even when teachers use this classification to understand that English learners' literacy backgrounds differ widely, standards documents such as the one for California (CDE, 1999) are written with the expectation that teachers can raise English learners quickly to the literacy levels of monolingual English speakers. The document specifically states that the ELD standards "are designed to move all students, regardless of their instructional program, into the mainstream English-language arts curriculum" (p. 2).

What, then, characterizes literacy instruction for English learners? Evidence from research in second-language acquisition indicates that the natural developmental processes that children undergo in learning their first language (oral and written) also occur in second-language acquisition (oral and written). For reading, these processes include using knowledge of *sound–symbol relationships* (graphophonics), *word order and grammar* (syntax), and *meaning* (semantics) to predict and confirm meaning, and using background knowledge about the text's topic and structure along with linguistic knowledge and reading strategies to make an interpretation (Peregoy & Boyle, 2008).

Adapted Instruction: Characteristics of Classrooms That Support English Learners' Literacy Development

- Activities are meaningful to students and are often jointly negotiated with the teacher.
- Instruction is cognitively demanding yet is scaffolded—that is, temporarily supported—to ensure student success.
- Learning is organized into topics and themes so that students can build on previous learning.
- Students work collaboratively and grouping is flexible.
- Students are immersed in a print-rich environment so that they have constant opportunities to interact with the written word.

Source: Adapted from Hamayan (1994) and Peregoy and Boyle (2008).

Several important issues for teachers working with reading and English learners are discussed here. These include transferring literacy from first to second languages, students without literacy in their first or second language, and phonics for English learners. These discussions are followed by explanations of specific strategies that support English learners' literacy development.

Transferring Literacy from First to Second Languages

Many English learners already have basic understandings of the reading/writing process that they can transfer to a second language. One of the most important of these is the concept that print carries meaning. Others involve directionality, sequencing, and visual discrimination—concepts about print that kindergarten and first-grade teachers work with in teaching students to read.

In classrooms where English learners are already literate in their first language, they transfer that knowledge to reading and writing in English. (See Snow, Burns, and Griffin [1998] for a review of research findings supporting transfer.) Table 4.3 lists concepts that transfer from the first language to the second.

However, even though learners may be literate in their first language, they are still English learners and as such need support to develop their English proficiency and to have the background information necessary to read and produce English texts. Teachers' tasks are more difficult if students are not literate in their first language.

Students without Literacy in First or Second Languages

Preschoolers without a knowledge of print, older students without previous schooling, and the partially literate who may have acquired some decoding skills in their primary language but whose overall level of literacy does not provide them useful access to print—these groups need special treatment. Appropriate programs for these learners adhere to three important principles of literacy instruction:

1. Literacy is introduced in a meaningful way.
2. The link between oral language and print is made as naturally as possible.
3. Students have the opportunity to enjoy reading and writing.

Table 4.3

Literacy Skills That Transfer from the First Language to the Second

Concepts and Skills Shown to Transfer from First-Language Literacy to Second-Language Literacy

- Print has meaning
- Reading and writing are used for various purposes
- Concepts about print
    - Book-orientation concepts (how to hold a book, how to turn pages)
    - Directionality (in English, left to right, and top to bottom)
    - Letters (letter names, lowercase, uppercase)
    - Words (composed of letters, spaces mark boundaries)
- Knowledge of text structure
- Use of semantic and syntactic knowledge
- Use of cues to predict meaning
- Reading strategies (hypothesizing, constructing meaning, etc.)
- Confidence in self as reader

Example of Concept: A Reading Program for Nonliterates

In a five-year study of English learners in New York City schools, the Center for Applied Linguistics identified a group they called "students with interrupted formal education" (SIFE)—immigrant students who may have had only a few years of schooling in their country of origin. Educators devised an intervention program entitled Reading Instructional Goals for Older Readers (RIGOR), taught by ESL dual-language educators, tutors, or reading specialists. Levels 1 and 2 feature decoding and comprehension tools using high-interest narratives with phonetically regular vocabulary words (Calderon, 2007).

In situations in which literacy development in the first language is not possible (no materials or resources in L1; few L1 speakers; limited school resources), teachers need to teach students to read directly in English. Seven instructional procedures have proved successful in leading students to literacy in their second language (Hamayan, 1994). (Although these strategies are especially important for preliterate second-language learners, they are also helpful for English learners in general, even those who are literate in their first language.)

Environmental Print. The classroom is saturated with meaningful environmental print. Students see labels, announcements, names, and signs with as many contextual clues as possible. Labels can be bilingual or trilingual, thus incorporating students' native languages into their beginning literacy experiences.

Meaning-Based. Literacy activities move from the "known" to the "unknown." They revolve around content of interest to the learners. One way of starting with the known is to base literacy activities on the learners' oral language (see LEA later in this chapter).

A Silent Period in Reading. Literacy is allowed to emerge naturally. Students go through a silent period in reading, often mouthing words while the teacher reads aloud. Dialogue journals are a means of allowing language to emerge in a natural, developmental way.

Low-Anxiety Environment. Effective literacy environments are free of anxiety. Learners' attempts at reading and writing are greeted with enthusiasm. When they see their efforts are rewarded, students feel encouraged to continue.

Motivating Activities. Activities stimulate thinking and have value beyond that of a classroom exercise. Learners sense the intrinsic worth of reading when it leads to a dramatic presentation or sharing with a buddy.

Integration of Structure and Function. Students' attention is focused on specific structures and forms of written language within the context of meaningful activities. Their own oral-language stories, dialogue journals, and so on provide the basis for specific instruction.

Integration of Content and Literacy. Content-area instruction is integrated with literacy. Vocabulary, grammatical structures, and language functions needed in academic areas are incorporated into literacy activities.

Table 4.4 provides examples of materials and reading and writing activities that have been found to support English learners.

Balanced Literacy Instruction for English Learners

In 1995, the California Reading Task Force recommended that, "every school and district must organize and implement a comprehensive and balanced reading program that is research-based and combines skill development with literature and language-rich activities" (n. p.).

To receive part of the billion dollars that was allocated for the teaching of reading in the 1996 California Reading Initiative, school districts had to certify that 90 percent of their teachers in K–3 classes received training in specifically targeted elements of instruction that were shown by research to lead to reading success: phonemic awareness; systematic, explicit phonics instruction; sound–symbol relationships; decoding; word attack skills; spelling instruction; comprehension instruction; and independent reading of high-quality books.

The task force concluded that a *balanced reading program* should include the following:

- A strong literature, language, and comprehensive program that includes a balance of oral and written language
- An organized, explicit skills program that includes phonemic awareness, phonics, and decoding skills to address the needs of the emergent reader

Table 4.4

Materials and Activities to Support English Learners' Literacy Development

Materials	Activities with a Reading Focus	Activities with a Writing Focus
Literature, literature, and more literature	Read-aloud	Dialogue journals
Big books, pattern books	Readers' theater	Buddy journals
Wordless picture books	Storytelling	Writing workshop
Ads, posters, pamphlets, brochures	Shared reading	Response groups
Songbooks	Oral reading activities:	Peer editing groups
Poetry, rhymes, riddles, tongue twisters	Choral reading	Author's chair
Journals, diaries	Buddy reading	Classroom/school newspaper
Magazines	Repeated reading	Literature response journals
Comic books	Independent reading	Content-area journals
How-to books	Directed Reading–Thinking Activity (DR–TA)	Developing scripts for readers' theater
Dictionaries, encyclopedias	Language Experience Approach (LEA)	Language Experience Approach (LEA)
		Pattern poems

- An ongoing diagnosis that informs teaching and assessment that ensures accountability
- A powerful early intervention program that provides individual tutoring for children at risk for reading failure (CDE, 1995, n.p.)

Teachers who use a "balanced literacy" approach employ a variety of components to help students become better readers and writers:

- Shared reading: The teacher reads an enlarged text aloud as students read along; students use various strategies when they encounter difficulty.
- Read aloud: The teacher reads a text while students listen; the teacher models thinking aloud about how to interpret the information.
- Reading workshop: Students work independently, with partners, or in a small group; the teacher gives mini-lessons to teach reading strategies.
- Shared writing: The teacher composes texts with students, modeling the thought process by thinking aloud.
- Interactive writing: Students and teacher write a text together; the teacher helps students build up structure and meaning.
- Writing workshop: Students work independently, with partners, or in a small group; the teacher gives mini-lessons to teach writing strategies.
- Word study, which might include phonemic awareness, phonics, and/or spelling. (Mermelstein, 2006)

Phonics. The alphabetic principle is the idea that the sounds of spoken words correspond to written words in systematic ways. Phonics instruction teaches readers sound–letter correspondences in order to recognize words. Quick recognition of words is the basis for fluent reading, which in turn is the basis for comprehension—the real goal of reading.

Bottom-up, or part-to-whole phonics approaches, work in this fashion:

[T]eachers isolate letter–sound correspondences, teach students how to synthesize the sounds represented by letters, provide blending and spelling practice with words that contain the targeted letter–sound correspondence, and supervise application of this knowledge as students read connected text that is composed primarily of . . . decodable (i.e., contrived) texts. (Villaume & Brabham, 2003, p. 479)

In contrast, in the top-down (embedded) phonics approach:

[T]eachers assist students in developing explicit understandings of the alphabetic principle through guided discovery and analysis. They draw students' attention to a targeted letter–sound correspondence found in a familiar text or a writing experience. Teachers engage students in reading and spelling words with the targeted sound–letter correspondence as they make words and break them apart using a variety of materials such as dry-erase boards, magnetic letters, or letter tiles. They also coach students in word recognition during authentic reading and writing events. (Villaume & Brabham, 2003, p. 479)

The goal is to provide what Villaume and Brabham (2003, p. 478) called "varied, flexible, and responsive" phonics instruction.

Phonics for English Learners. Cummins (2003) reviewed and synthesized research on teaching reading both to native- and non-native-English speakers. He found that almost all studies agree that the following four areas led to success in decoding skills and reading comprehension and were "by far the major determinant of reading comprehension development as students progress through the grades":

1. Immersion in a literate environment
2. The development of phonemic awareness, letter knowledge, and concepts about print
3. Explicit instruction in phonemic awareness, letter knowledge, and concepts about print, *together with a significant instructional focus on actual reading*
4. Access to print and actual reading (p. 28; italics in original)

Phonological Awareness. According to Ehri (1995), students develop phonemic awareness in two general stages: After a preliminary stage in which they do not use sound cues, they first use phonetic cue reading (perhaps using the first or last letter of a word) to decode a word, before developing full alphabetic awareness, in which children use all letters and sounds. This corresponds to the way learners use *temporary,* or *invented,* spelling to approximate the sounds of words. Many tasks have been used to teach phonemic awareness. These are presented in Table 4.5.

Explicit Phonics Instruction. Educational regulators have insisted that "explicit" phonics instruction is the key to higher reading scores; by this they seem to mean clearly

Table 4.5

Tasks for Teaching Phonemic Awareness

Task	Sample Activity
Rhyming	Recognize or produce rhymes.
Word-to-word matching	Which of three words does not begin or end the same as the others?
Sound-to-word matching	Is this sound found in this word? (Is there an /m/ in *man*?)
Initial (or final) sounds	The child gives the first (or last) sound in the spoken word (Give the last sound in *dish*).
Segmentation	The child identifies each sound heard in a word by putting the correct letter in a separate box (number of boxes available for letters matches number of phonemes in the word).
Blending	Given a sequence of phonemes, the child blends them to form a word.
Reading words in isolation	The learner is given a set of words to read, perhaps having the same phonics principle.
Reading words in stories	The learner applies phonics knowledge to achieve comprehension of words in context.
Writing words: dictation	The learner practices writing words that are given in spoken form.
Writing words: using invented spelling	The learner writes without achieving perfect spelling in a transitional focus on fluency over accuracy.

Source: Adapted from Stahl, Duffy-Hester, & Stahl (1998).

◼Did You Know?◼

The principal concern that teachers may have in developing word recognition skills in English is the students' tendency to be *too* good at transferring their word-unlocking strategies from Spanish to English. "Because the techniques have served them well in Spanish, the students may become very successful at *calling words*. This apparent prosperity must be monitored thoughtfully to ensure that students are obtaining meaning from the English words they have recognized" (Thonis, 2005, p. 108).

expressed instructions that teachers should follow to ensure that students understand and use the alphabetic principle when they read. Many districts require teachers to follow scripted reading lessons, as if adhering to the letter of a teaching routine is in itself sufficient to create effective readers. But as Villaume and Brabham (2003) pointed out, "Scripts cannot capture the interactive and dynamic conversations expert teachers have with their students about the ways that words work" (p. 479).

Frustrations with Phonics. Since the National Reading Panel stated in 2000 that phonics produces significant benefits as a part of reading instruction, the federal government has been influencing school districts to adopt programs with a strong phonics component. The rules of English phonics are complex, and not easy for children to learn. Research has shown that children who rely on phonics read slowly, paying more attention to the form of the word than its meaning. As a consequence, they are easily bored with reading. Uribe (2008) summarizes educators' frustrations with phonics-based instruction:

> [T]he most frustrating in all this is that many educators now think of phonics as a substitute for reading and devote more class time to sound and spelling correspondences than to literary experiences. And that is unfair. Phonics is a tool that students can use to help understand a text in some situations, but what really makes the difference is reading itself, the social event that takes place between reader and book. This, not phonics, nurtures students' positive attitudes to books and reading. To say that phonics is an essential element in the reading process is outrageous. And the consequences for our students and for our society in the long run will be incalculable. (p. 37)

One elementary teacher, using the phonics-based program Success for All, identified the following problems in using the program with his English learners: Reading (decoding) is separated from comprehension; emphasis is on sound and sound-blend identification to the detriment of coherent, logical reading material; specially written stories focus on targeted sounds and do not include commonly occurring English words and natural language use; and unnatural, awkward syntax contradicts English learners' growing knowledge of spoken English and/or reinforces use of problematic language (Lee, 2000).

Approaches to Teaching Reading

Reading is an essential skill. Children who do not learn to read in elementary school enter secondary education as severe underachievers and are at risk for dropping out.

Did You Know?

Reading First

Reading First is a $1 billion-a-year reading program, an integral part of the No Child Left Behind Act, by which the federal government funnels money through state educational agencies to eligible school districts to promote reading skills in grades K–3. The state departments of education are mandated to fund those programs that show the most promise for raising student achievement and for successful implementation of reading instruction. Only programs that are founded on "scientifically based" reading research—a term that has been hotly debated—are eligible for funding through Reading First. Funds are allocated to states according to the proportion of children age five to seventeen who reside within the state and who are from families with incomes below the poverty line. The funds that are provided to school districts also support professional development for teachers, as well as the use of screening and diagnostic tools and classroom-based instructional reading assessments to monitor students' progress (U.S. Department of Education, 2008).

Supporters of Reading First have long believed that its emphasis on phonics, phonemic awareness, scripted instruction by teachers and regular, and detailed analyses of children's skills, will raise reading achievement, especially among the low-income kids it

targets. However, critics such as Jim Cummins have questioned the use of phonics for English learners: "Phonics instruction soon reaches the point of diminishing returns" (Cummins, 2008). In 2008, the U.S. Education Department's National Center for Education Evaluation and Regional Assistance carried out a large-scale study that looked at students in first through third grade from 2004 through 2006. The results show that the reading skills of children in schools receiving Reading First funding are virtually no better than those of children in schools that didn't get the funding. These disappointing findings, coupled with a U.S. congressional investigation in 2007 that looked into funding improprieties in the implementation of Reading First, indicate that phonics-based approaches may not continue to be the only reading method funded in the near future under the No Child Left Behind Act.

Others have been kinder to Reading First: "Whatever the problems with Reading First, at least it infuses funds in professional development, provides direct support to teachers, promotes local assessments and supports teacher collaboration. All of that has a greater chance of making a difference in the long run than diverting funds to private tutors" (Cox, 2008, p. A20).

How can teachers encourage English learners to acquire skills that will result in academic achievement and an enjoyment of reading?

Standards-Based Reading Instruction. New reading materials in the marketplace reflect the current insistence on standards-based instruction, with explicit references to standards on each page. *High Points* from Hampton-Brown (Schifini, Short, & Tinajero, 2002) is a typical ELD series, complete with teaching tips designed to facilitate comprehensible input, decodable small books, learning strategies for enhancing cognitive academic language, ways to increase reading fluency, writing support for students with non-Roman alphabets, and cultural tips. The texts themselves do not contain ESL standards, however, leaving the integration of standards and instruction up to the classroom teacher.

Emergent Literacy. When children—or adolescents or adults, for that matter—are first learning to read, they are in the stage of *emergent literacy;* their reading and writing behaviors precede and develop into conventional literacy. Emergent literacy involves a combination of components. Emergent readers must learn to:

- Draw upon their prior knowledge of the world to connect the printed word with its meaning; for example, most preschool children connect a red octagonal sign at a street corner with the meaning "stop."
- Use phonemic awareness to understand that sounds correspond to symbols.
- Recognize a set of sight words that are frequently used in English but may not be phonetically predictable ("the" is not "ta-ha-ay").
- Acquire reading behaviors, such as handling books, using a library, and reading for enjoyment.
- Participate in a culture of reading, sharing their pleasure in reading with others and working in the company of others to acquire meaning from books.

Most learners read and write because they see others doing it—reading directions, newspapers, or road signs for information; or notes they have written to themselves to jog their memory; or novels, just to pass the time. However, many English learners do not see their families reading or writing, even in their home language. It is important, then, that the classroom as a community be a place in which reading is an everyday, enjoyable feature. This socializes students into a culture of literacy. By creating shared contexts, modeling language and literacy behaviors such as reading and writing, encouraging peer interactions, relating to students' cultural backgrounds, and according high status to students' first languages, teachers can successfully develop language and literacy skills in multilingual classrooms.

The Basics of Learning to Read. Within the social context of shared enjoyment among a group of readers, there are four important facets of learning to read: skill with print, decoding text, utilizing prior knowledge, and comprehension.

Skill with print involves understanding that a printed text contains words which carry meaning, and that printed words correspond to spoken language. Words, not pictures, are read. Learners note that language is divided into words which can be written down, with spaces in between; letters make words and words make sentences; sentences begin with capital letters and end with punctuation; a book is read from front to back, and reading goes left to right and top to bottom; a book has a title, an author, and sometimes an illustrator. In a *print-rich environment,* children see print wherever they turn—on bulletin boards, calendars, book displays, labels on objects in several languages, shopping lists at play centers, and so forth.

In *decoding text,* as in a sentence with an unknown word, various readers use distinct strategies. One type of reader uses *semantic knowledge.* If a sentence reads, "Joey pushed open the door of the haunted . . ." a reader might guess that the next word is not *hose,* because its meaning would not make sense. Another type of reader might use *syntactic knowledge* on the sentence "Joey drives a small . . ." to reject the word *care* as the wrong choice for that part of the sentence. Still a third type of reader might use *orthographic shape* in the sentence "Joey drove a load of trees to the paper mill," knowing that the words *pap* and *paperwork* look wrong. A single reader might use these three types of meaning making equally often, or one might detect a preference for one type of decoding. Interventions would be designed accordingly (Newman, 1985).

The Three-Stage Reading Process. Activities prior to reading prepare students to get "into" the reading. Other strategies help students read "through" the material, and, finally, follow-up activities help students organize and retain their understanding "beyond" the act of reading. Actually, in a classroom in which literacy is socially constructed, reading is more complex—students are moving into, through, and beyond their own reading on an individual basis as they dip into some books, pick up and discard others, or "surf" the Internet. Therefore "into–through–beyond" activities represent reading for an entire topic.

"Into" activities generate interest. Background knowledge may be activated or developed through classroom activities that include all of the language processes. Two such activities are brainstorming and KWL (What do I *know*? What do I *want* to learn? What have I *learned*?). Asking "What do I know?" allows students to place new knowledge in the context of their own episodic memories and existing concepts. KWL not only taps into what students already know but also elicits from them what they would like to learn. The students list everything they know about a topic. They then tell the teacher what they would like to learn. A chart is maintained for the duration of the unit and students refer to it from time to time to talk about what they have learned. Starting each topic or unit with KWL actively engages students in reviewing their own experiences relevant to the topic. This activates prior knowledge.

Example of Concept: Activating Prior Knowledge

Two distinct scenarios illustrate the importance of teachers' making connections when introducing a work of literature.

Scenario One

OK guys, today we're going to be getting a new book called *The House on Mango Street* by a Latina author. I thought it was really important that we read an author from a different culture since many students here are Latinos.

Scenario Two

(*After reading a brief section from Cisneros's book*) So, we've been talking about this whole idea of growing up, about creating an identity for oneself, what it means, how and when it happens. *Huck Finn* allowed us to talk about some important aspects of that whole experience. And Nathan McCall's book told us what it was like for him to grow up as a young black man in the sixties. I thought it would be interesting to see what this other book has to say about the experience since unlike Huck she didn't take off but stayed on Mango Street. I love this book a lot. It took her five years to write this 120-page book. It's like a poem almost, the language and images are so intense.

The second scenario is clearly preferable in that the teacher aroused students' interest by reading an excerpt and then linked the book to the theme that the class had been developing in their prior reading. In the second scenario, the teacher emphasized the book's literary quality and added a sense of personal enthusiasm, instead of giving students the feeling that the book was chosen simply for its ethnic focus (Burke, 1999, p. 252).

"Through" activities help students as they work with the text. Teachers find reading aloud a useful strategy that gives the students an opportunity to hear a proficient

Table 4.6

In-Class Reading Methods for English Learners

Method	Description
Page and paragraph	Teacher or fluent reader reads a page, then an English learner reads a paragraph, then group discusses what has been read.
Equal portions	Students work in pairs, and each reads aloud the same amount of text.
Silent with support	Students read silently in pairs, and can ask each other for help with a difficult word or phrase.
Choral reading	A passage is divided into sections, and different members of the audience read various sections.
Radio reading	One student reads while others close their books and listen. After reading, the reader can question each student about what was read.
Repeated reading	Students read silently a book that has been read aloud, or independently re-read books of their choice.
Interactive read-aloud	Students can join in on repetitious parts or take parts of a dialogue.
Echo reading	For rhythmic text, students echo or repeat lines.
Nonprint media support	Students can follow along with a taped version of the book.

Source: Adapted from Hadaway, Vardell, and Young (2002).

reader, to get a sense of the format and story line, and to listen to the teacher "think aloud" about the reading. To help students develop a sense of inflection, pronunciation, rhythm, and stress, a commercial tape recording of a work of literature can be obtained for listening and review, or native-English-speaking students or adult volunteers may be willing to make a recording. Various activities can be used for students to perform the actual reading. Table 4.6 offers a variety of reading methods for in-class use.

"Beyond" activities are designed to extend students' appreciation of literature, usually in another medium, such as poems, book reviews, letters to authors or to pen pals, cued retelling, or mock television shows. This encourages students to read for a purpose. *Story mapping* is a way for students to use a graphic organizer to summarize the plot. Younger students can work with four boxes (*Who? Wants? But? So?*) to fill in their knowledge of what happens in the story. Older students can use the terms *Characters, Intent, Opposition,* and *Resolution.* Using this device, students can follow the story grammar, or progression of events in the plot.

Example of Concept: Daily Reading Interventions

Based on observations during the previous school year of those children who had made unexpected progress in reading skills, Mrs. Hedberg, the ELD teacher, and Mrs. Greaver-Pohzehl, the second-grade homeroom teacher, devised a new program. The program included additional opportunities for practice and fluency through the use of volunteers and a take-home reading program.

In the classroom, the students received daily directed, guided reading instruction with one of the teachers during which they were introduced to new texts, participated in oral discussion, and

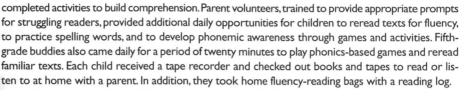

completed activities to build comprehension. Parent volunteers, trained to provide appropriate prompts for struggling readers, provided additional daily opportunities for children to reread texts for fluency, to practice spelling words, and to develop phonemic awareness through games and activities. Fifth-grade buddies also came daily for a period of twenty minutes to play phonics-based games and reread familiar texts. Each child received a tape recorder and checked out books and tapes to read or listen to at home with a parent. In addition, they took home fluency-reading bags with a reading log.

Although the program did not always run smoothly (bags and tapes left at home, for example), by the end of the year, every child in the program made progress—all of them advanced at least two reading divisions on the district's literacy scale; developed a greater range of reading and writing skills; developed a stronger, more fluent voice while reading; and showed positive attitudes toward reading and writing (Greaver & Hedberg, 2001).

Strategies for English Learners' Literacy Instruction

An explanation of all the strategies appropriate for English learners is beyond the scope of this book. However, certain strategies that encompass the main principles for suitable instruction with English learners are explained here. These include the Language Experience Approach (LEA), a strategy particularly helpful for nonliterate students; Directed Reading–Thinking Activity (DR–TA), a strategy that develops students' abilities to predict text; self-monitoring; enhancing reading comprehension; literature-based reading; and a postreading strategy that invites active student participation.

Language Experience Approach. A language-development activity that encourages students to respond to events in their own words is the Language Experience Approach (LEA). As a student tells a story or relates an event, the teacher writes it down and reads it back so that students can eventually read the text for themselves. Because the students are providing their own phrases and sentences, they find the text relevant and interesting and generally have little trouble reading it. The importance of LEA in developing the language of English learners cannot be overemphasized. Its advantages include the following:

- LEA connects students to their own experiences and activities by having them express themselves orally.
- It reinforces the notion that sounds can be transcribed into specific symbols and that those symbols can then be used to re-create the ideas expressed.
- It provides texts for specific lessons on vocabulary, grammar, writing conventions, structure, and more.

Example of Concept: Using LEA after Reading

Sixth-grade teacher Laura Bowen used LEA after her students read about the Qin dynasty to help reinforce key concepts.

After finishing the lesson on the Qin dynasty, I had my class brainstorm key ideas. I wrote their points on the board and then asked them to tell a story about a fictional family of three living during that era. The only restriction I put on them was that they had to keep in mind the key points. Their story follows:

> Chang, Li, and their son, Wei, lived during the Qin dynasty. Li was excited because Chang was able to *buy* the family some *land.* A few days later, Chang was taken by the emperor to go *build* the *Great Wall.* Li and Wei were sad. They did not like the emperor, because he had strict *laws* and *punishments.* Li wrote Chang a letter telling him how the emperor tried to bring the people in China together by *standardizing writing, money,* and *measurement.* Chang never received the letter because he died on the long walk to the Great Wall. Li and Wei grew crops so they could survive. They hoped a new and better emperor would come and *overthrow* the mean one.

After the students decided they were finished with their story, they read it out loud many times. They then chose the twelve key words (underlined above) they wanted to focus on. I erased the key words from the story, leaving blanks where they were supposed to go. The class read the story again. The next day I had individual copies for the students. We worked with the story again by reading, matching key words to the appropriate blanks, and so on.

Directed Reading–Thinking Activity. Students need to understand that proficient readers actively work with text by making predictions as they read. Directed Reading–Thinking Activity (DR–TA) is a teacher-guided activity that leads students through the prediction process until they are able to do it on their own. The teacher asks students to make predictions and then read to confirm their ideas. Although initially students believe there are absolute "right" and "wrong" predictions, through teacher guidance they begin to see how the text helps them predict and understand that general ideas serve equally as well as specific details.

The key to successful DR–TA lessons is for teachers to accept all student responses. The teacher's goal is to help students see that correctness is not as important as plausibility, and that they need to check the text continually as new information is revealed.

Self-Monitoring. Sentence-by-Sentence Self-Monitoring (SSSM; Buettner, 2002) helps students to chunk texts into small units. The teacher selects a section of text, and the student counts the sentences. The student reads the text silently, and when ready, reads aloud. The teacher notes miscues, and sometimes reads back the sentence exactly as the student read it, asking, "Does that make sense?" or "Is that what we see in the picture?" The reading process becomes like coaching, a conversation about the meaning of the text and the strategy that the reader is using. A score sheet may be used to help students track their own progress and strategies.

Reading Comprehension. The key to meaning is reading *comprehension.* Readers generally form some initial hypothesis about the content or main idea of a book or a reading passage, based on their expectations, title, first sentence, previous knowledge of genre, or other clues. Reading further, the reader modifies the initial prediction. Getting the gist of a passage is the most important concept a reader can develop, because getting the main idea makes further reading more purposeful, facilitates recall, and helps to make sense of the supporting details.

Even though visual images bombard students through the Internet, films, and television, students may not have the capacity to form their own visual images as they read. Many struggling readers focus solely on decoding words; without forming images of the plot or content, and do not achieve comprehension. Research on visual imagery indicates that students may need to be prompted repeatedly as they read to produce mental images ("television in the mind"). To facilitate this process, students may learn to sketch illustrations as they read, draw upon pictures in the text to assist comprehension, or even go back and forth between a movie and the associated work of literature to learn to work interactively with images (Hibbing & Rankin-Erickson, 2003).

Adapted Instruction: Sticky Notes for Reading Comprehension

One sixth-grade teacher models aloud to students the process of thinking aloud about the type of connections made during reading—such guidance as details linked to main ideas (MI), connections made to world knowledge (W) or personal experience (ME), and connections made to causal knowledge (C) drawn from other parts of the text.

After the teacher models this process, students use sticky notes to code texts as they read with these codes (Dewitz & Dewitz, 2003).

To paraphrase Stahl, Duffy-Hester, and Stahl (1998), an effective reading program in the early grades might entail direct instruction in decoding using easily decodable texts, including some contrived texts that sound interesting and authentic (*not* "Dan takes Fran to the prom in the fog"). Authentic literature may be chosen for repetition of a taught pattern. Children's comprehension growth can be aided by the teacher's reading aloud. Children practice their knowledge of sound–symbol correspondence as they use temporary spelling when writing, using these experiments to hypothesize about the sounds they hear and refine their developing phonemic awareness. These efforts are augmented by an extensive program of choice reading.

Literature-Based Reading. More and more teachers are using literature as the core of their reading program. For an overview of the use of literature in a children's reading program, see Tunnell and Jacobs (2000). A literature-based approach to reading uses *controlled readers* (literature-based basal reader is tailored for the target reading level), *text sets* (thematically related books, such as books on sports and hobbies, or sets of multicultural readers on the Cinderella theme), *core books* (those specifically featured in a statewide adoption list for all classrooms to use), and *thematic units* (literature as integrated content with science, social studies, and art/music/performing arts) to provide reading experiences that are rich in meaning and interest for students.

Multicultural literature helps students to see life from a variety of points of view, to compare cultures on different aspects of life, and to see their own culture represented in the curriculum. *Multicultural Voices in Contemporary Literature* (Day, 1994) presents thirty-nine authors and illustrators from twenty different cultures. A follow-up book, *Latina and Latino Voices in Literature for Children and Teenagers* (Day, 1997) has biographies of thirty-eight authors with synopses of their work, as well as an extensive list of resources for books in English on Latino themes. Day (2003) is a follow-up extending the Latina and Latino theme.

As students become better readers, they begin to read their own *self-selected books*. As they read independently, they are encouraged to use familiar techniques for comprehension: making mental images, surveying a book and making predictions, and monitoring their reading to make sure they understand. Students keep a simple reading log of the books they finish. Several sources are available that suggest *age-level appropriate reading material*. Public libraries have detailed reference books that list thousands of children's books, including the Caldecott and Newbery Medal books. *Book conferences* with the teacher, if there is time, allow students to benefit from the teacher's direct guidance.

Picturebooks are becoming increasingly popular, with growing recognition that text and visual elements can separately contribute to increased literary enjoyment and comprehension. The postmodern picturebook (Wolfenbarger & Sipe, 2007) moves the reader into a nonlinear pattern, often including elements that are satirical, self-referential, or anticonventional. *The Stinky Cheese Man* (Scieszka & Smith, 1992) is the epitome of such a genre, a tale in which the clever protagonist avoids being eaten because he steps outside the text and uses its features to trick and trap his assailant. These texts delight readers because they simultaneously employ and undermine accepted conventions, provoking meta-literary insights into fiction and nonfiction.

Example of Concept: New Literacy Genres

Many young adults are fond of comic books and graphic novels, comparatively new forms of literature. Stephanie Craig, a young *manga* lover, relates what she enjoys about the Japanese genre: "I can buy either *shoujou* (girls') manga, featuring fantasy, action, and adventure, or *shouman* (boys') manga, in which romance will not play as large a role in the plot." She goes on to explain *manga* has many of the same archetypes (warriors, heroes, sages, magicians, creators, innocent fools, etc.) that are in young adult Western literature, but characters in *manga* are not as black and white (evil versus good) as in Western literature, but instead are interesting shades of gray. She also likes ways in which the serial form of the novels furthers the plots (Nilsen & Donelson, 2009, pp. 178–179).

Literacy Communities. When teachers encourage English learners to enjoy reading, the classroom becomes its own literacy community. Books are exchanged and so are the ideas they contain. Students write books, and everyone is an audience for each other's literacy. The enthusiasm is contagious.

Example of Concept: Literacy Communities

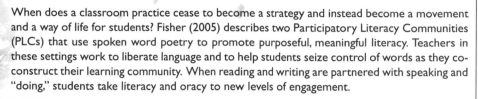

When does a classroom practice cease to become a strategy and instead become a movement and a way of life for students? Fisher (2005) describes two Participatory Literacy Communities (PLCs) that use spoken word poetry to promote purposeful, meaningful literacy. Teachers in these settings work to liberate language and to help students seize control of words as they co-construct their learning community. When reading and writing are partnered with speaking and "doing," students take literacy and oracy to new levels of engagement.

When students do not like to read, schooling becomes a cycle of failure—poor reading habits exacerbate poor academic work, leading in turn to the dislike to read. Minority students reported to Zanger (1994) that their literacy was adversely affected by their feelings of low status in high school, with classroom experiences and curriculum that alienated them from the teacher and from other students, and with their home language and cultures not included in a respectful and meaningful way. Literacy is fostered by inclusionary, multicultural learning environments in which English learners feel accepted, productive, and successful.

Writing

Writing is more than just an exercise for the teacher to assign and critique. It is an opportunity for students to link with the social and cultural heritage of the United States and to begin communicating effectively across cultures. At the heart of the classroom writing task is its relation to the real world. Through writing, students perform a purposeful social action, an action that takes them beyond a mere school assignment. Communicating with one another—with others outside the classroom, with home and family, with presidents and corporate officers, with city officials and nursing home residents—establishes real discourse and helps students to convey information that is real and necessary. This is the essence of writing as a communicative task.

After careful study of students learning to write in their second language, Fitzgerald and Amendum (2007) drew the following conclusions:

- For preschool and primary-grade English learners, features of ESL writing may develop in ways that are similar to certain features of early writing development in native-English speakers (such as phases of developmental spelling).
- For primary- and intermediate-grade students, knowledge and skills in writing (such as concepts about print) can transfer between their first and second language.
- For intermediate-grade and secondary-level students, some composing processes resemble those used by native-English speakers (such as prewriting and planning strategies).

Based on these findings, Fitzgerald and Amendum (2007) suggest that writing techniques used for native-English speakers be adapted for English learners, taking into consideration the length of time it takes to master the syntax, semantics, and sociocultural features of a second language. They promote an adaptation of the Language Experience Approach they call Daily News, in which students dictate their ideas about current events to a scribe who uses chart paper. They also suggest the use of dialogue journals and the writing of structured persuasive essays as ways for students to benefit by sharing authentic purposes for writing and employing a limited set of well-rehearsed genres.

Texts and Contexts

Children learning to write create *texts;* within the classroom these texts are part of the school *context.* Discourse experts are now able to use tools of analysis to deconstruct the more complex levels of children's writings in ways never before thought possible. Instead of seeing childish jumbles of words and pictures, analysts can note the development of concepts about signs and messages, embedded references to other texts and contexts (intertextuality and intercontextuality); mixtures of genres and voices, developing forms of visual and verbal syntax, and hybrid representations of information the children have received at home, from mass media, and from schooling (Kamberelis & de la Luna, 2004). According to Kamberelis and de la Luna (2004):

> Because children have only nascent control over the tools and strategies for graphically representing their messages, their writing may actually be shorthand for richer, longer, and more complex messages than meets the eye. . . . Therefore, [we] need to find ways to make visible the sometimes invisible richness, complexity, and variability that are often embodied in children's texts. (p. 242)
>
> Writing contexts are not simply containers in which actions, practices, and activities occur. Instead, they are dynamic streams of overlapping and integrated discourses, spaces, sociocultural practices, and power relations. . . . A more ecologically apt term might be something like text-context-activity relations. (p. 243)

The child brain as it manifests itself in writing is as much or more of a creative and meaning-seeking organ as is the adult brain, even though its surface manifestation may seem to lack sophistication. Drawing forth this depth and complexity from students requires teaching that is subtle, evocative, and capable of understanding the myriad symbol systems that may be combined within the seemingly primitive expressions of children.

Thus the texts and contexts of children's writing are far deeper than first imagined. The texts and contexts of English learners' writing mirror this complexity.

The Writing Process

Writing as a process has become increasingly accepted as an alternative to the "product" view of writing. The shift from a focus on *product* to a focus on *process* is "the most significant single transformation in the teaching of composition" (Kroll, 1991, p. 247). It changes the way students compose, provides situations in which language can be used in a meaningful way, and emphasizes the *act* of writing rather than the result. The process approach is particularly important for English learners who are developing their oral language skills at the same time as their written skills, because it involves more interaction, planning, and reworking. Students are not moving from topic to topic quickly, but instead have an opportunity to work with a topic (and therefore vocabulary and structures) over a sustained period.

The three general stages—*prewriting, writing,* and *editing*—allow students to organize, develop, and refine concepts and ideas in ways that the product approach to writing does not. For example, during prewriting, students are involved in oral-language experiences that develop their need and desire to write. These activities may include talking about and listening to shared experiences, reading literature, brainstorming, or creating role-plays or other fantasy activities (Enright & McCloskey, 1988).

Example of Concept: Brainstorming

The students gather at the front of the room and brainstorm the topic—butterflies. Mrs. Dowling writes their ideas on the board. A student says, "I have my first sentence" and tells the class how she will start her writing. Mrs. Dowling dismisses the student so she can begin writing. When only a few children remain, Mrs. Dowling rereads the list and helps each decide how he or she will start.

During the writing stage, students write quickly to capture ideas, doing the best they can in spelling, vocabulary, and syntax without a concern for accuracy. They then rewrite and redraft as necessary, again working with other students and/or the teacher to share, discuss, expand, and clarify their ideas.

Example of Concept: Drafts

Each Tuesday morning, cross-age tutors and parent volunteers (many of whom share the primary language of their group of students) work with Mrs. Dowling's students on their drafts. They listen and comment but know that the actual writing needs to be done by the child.

In the final stages, editing and publishing, students are helped to fix up their mechanics of usage and spelling, particularly when their writing is going to be shared in a formal way. If a perfected or final version is not necessary, students may file their rough drafts in a portfolio. By using the writing process, students have generated writing that is satisfying in its ability to capture and share ideas—the essence of writing for the purpose of communication. If, however, the writing is published or publicly shared, students also achieve the pride of authorship. Ways of publishing may vary: a play performed, a story bound into a book for circulation in the class library, a poem read aloud, an essay posted on a bulletin board, a video made of a student reading aloud, a class newspaper circulated to the community (Enright & McCloskey, 1988).

Example of Concept: Publishing

At the "bookmaking" center, Mrs. Dowling provides samples of book types (circle, small, folded, accordion, pop-up). Students choose which story they wish to "publish," decide which type of book will best show off the story, and copy their edited draft. Three times a year they write invitations to family members to come to their "publishing party." They read their books and then enjoy snacks and drinks with their proud families.

The Six Traits Approach

The "six traits" approach to writing has become popular due to the wealth of associated materials available from Great Source publishers. The six traits are as follows: *ideas,* the content for writing; *organization,* the way the content is structured; *voice,* the effectiveness of personal experience or authentic flavor of writing; *word choice,* using powerful vocabulary well adapted to the purpose of the writing; *sentence fluency,* employing direct, well-structured sentences that are varied in form, logical, and well connected; and *conventions,* appropriate punctuation, capitalization, citations, and other rules of usage (Spandel & Hicks, 2006). A good writer adapts each of these components to genre, audience, and purpose.

Writing Strategies

Graham and Harris (2005) have developed an approach called Self-Regulated Strategy Development (SRSD) in which students with special needs learn specific strategies for writing, including planning, self-evaluating, and revising. Teachers help students by explicitly presenting each strategy, then training students to take responsibility for strategy use.

De La Paz (2007) teaches her students to use the PLAN and WRITE strategies. PLAN is a strategy for writing as follows:

P = Pay attention to the prompt.
L = List the main ideas.
A = Add supporting ideas.
N = Number your ideas.

Did You Know?

Lori M. Carlson's *Cool Salsa: Bilingual Poems on Growing Up Latina in the United States* was a surprising best seller of the 1990s. In 2005, she followed up with *Red Hot Salsa: Bilingual Poems on Being Young and Latino in the United States.* The poems, in both Spanish and English, are by such well-known poets as Gary Soto, Martin Espada, and José Antonio Burciaga, as well as some written by teenagers in New York City's public schools (Nilsen & Donetson, 2009, p. 148).

WRITE continues the composition process:

W = Work from your plan to develop the thesis statement.
R = Remember your goals.
I = Include transition words for each paragraph.
T = Try to use different types of sentences.
E = Use exciting, interesting, million-dollar words.

Example of Concept: Writing Letters

Judith LeVine uses letter writing to make writing more meaningful. She writes to students to announce daily activities ("Dear Friends, Today we will bake bread. Love, Mrs. LeVine"). She also takes dictation from the class to compose group letters to thank classroom visitors. The children also write to Tommy Bear, the classroom teddy bear who takes turns spending the night at home with each child. Tommy is also gifted with word processing skills, as he writes back to each child! (LeVine, 2002)

Writing Poetry

Ingrid Wendt uses poetry writing as a motivator for learning English. In her class, students can write in their first language and then translate their work into English. She uses poems as models that speak of shared dreams, fears, hopes, and values from many ethnicities and cultures. "Whatever the student's age or ability level in English or Spanish, I find that writing poetry is an empowering experience," she says. "Students discover that poetry can come from real-life experience, and when they wrote poetry, words become tools for them to share their own experience. There is a reason for them to read and write these words" (Harris, 2006).

Adapted Instruction: Poetry Slam

What is required to hold a poetry slam? An uninhibited master of ceremonies; numbered "tickets" on which students write their name and the name of their poem, which make it easier for the master of ceremonies to introduce the next performer; simple refreshments to add to the "coffee house" atmosphere; two sets of judges' score cards, wielded by student volunteers seated on opposite sides of the room; and small prizes such as pencils and erasers for the "winning" poets (Nilsen & Donelson, 2009).

Error Correction and Grammar in Oracy and Literacy Instruction

Teachers do need to focus on form. English learners cannot be expected to merely absorb the language as they listen to teachers and interact with peers in learning groups.

After all, native-English speakers spend twelve years studying English—why shouldn't English learners have some of the same opportunities? However, for English learners, indiscriminate error correction and decontextualized grammatical practice do not appear to enhance language acquisition. Instead, teachers need to provide both formal and informal language-learning opportunities in meaningful contexts (Dutro & Moran, 2003).

Treatment of Errors

In any endeavor, errors are inevitable, and language learning is certainly no exception. People generally accept errors (or do not even notice them) when children are learning their first language, but teachers expend much energy noting, correcting, and designing lessons to address errors when students are learning a second language. Often, no allowance is made for the learner's age, level of fluency, educational background, or risk-taking behavior. These, however, are relevant factors in determining how a teacher should deal with language errors.

In the early stages of language learning, fluency is more important than accuracy. Thus, the teacher, instead of monitoring and correcting, should converse in and model appropriate language. When a student says, "My pencil broken," the teacher's response is, "Go ahead and sharpen it." In this interchange, language has furthered meaning despite the imperfection of syntax. Error correction is not necessary. The teacher focuses on the student's message and provides correction only when the meaning is not clear.

Younger children in particular appear to learn more when teachers focus on meaning rather than form. Older students and those with more English proficiency need and can benefit from feedback on recurring errors. The teacher can observe systematic errors in the class and discuss them with the class, or provide mini-lessons with small groups who display the same error. By observing systematic errors, the teacher will recognize that random errors do not need to be corrected.

Adapted Instruction: Error Correction

The following suggestions focus on error correction in writing:

- Assess students' needs based on several writing samples.
- Provide mini-lessons to the whole class, a small group, or individual students.
- Have students keep a journal that lists their errors and ways to correct them.

Treatment of Grammar

Historically, grammar has been seen as the organizational framework for language and as such has been used as the organizational framework for language teaching. In many classrooms, second-language instruction has been based on learning the correct use of such items as the verb *to be,* the present tense, definite articles, subject–verb agreement, and so forth. Ellis (1988) called this the "structure of the day" approach (p. 136). Linguists dispute the value of such a structured approach for the attainment of grammatical competence. The effective language teacher, therefore, organizes instruction around meaningful concepts—themes, topics, areas of student interest—and deals with grammar only as the need arises.

How can teachers help English learners to improve their grammar? McVey (2007) offers these suggestions:

- Give students the opportunity to self-correct, or peer-correct by having students read their writing aloud to a partner.
- Encourage students to use the grammar-check function when they use the computer for writing assignments.
- Teach grammar structures in the order in which they are acquired (do not attempt to have students master the definite and indefinite article at the beginning level of proficiency).
- Be selective in correcting students' grammatical errors, focusing only on those areas that interfere with meaning.

Oracy, Literacy, and Technology

The digital revolution is changing the way people spend their free time—playing video and computer games, chatting on the Internet, conducting business transactions, and much more. The social changes of the digital revolution, many cultural observers believe, will be as vast and far-reaching as those generated by Gutenberg's invention of moveable type (Hanson-Smith, 1997). Language classrooms can be similarly transformed with the capabilities now available through multimedia computing, the Internet, and the World Wide Web. Computer-assisted language learning (CALL) has the potential for extending learning beyond the four walls of the classroom to include the whole world.

Computer-Assisted Language Learning/ Computer-Mediated Communication

Computer-assisted instruction has long been available for classrooms. Computer-assisted language learning (CALL) applied to English learning has moved beyond skill drills into more innovative applications. *Computer-mediated communication* (CMC) is a term that describes the role of computers in facilitating virtual communication by people. Both CALL and CMC have proved useful in the education of English learners.

Learning has been transformed through multimedia computing and the Internet— the digital revolution. Lesson plans, quizzes, chat rooms, and bulletin boards are

Personalized Learning

What counts as literacy achievement? Brass (2008) describes one at-risk student's involvement in an after-school literacy program called the Technology and Literacy Project. A Latino teenager, Horatio received poor grades on school-based measures of literacy achievement, yet he created complex digital movie text on a digital movie-composing platform, using his local knowledge and out-of-school literacy practices in a sophisticated way. How is school literacy, with its negative labeling of his skills, serving Horatio?

available that allow learners to sample English idioms, prepare for standardized tests, or connect with English learners around the world. Desktop and laptop computers and the Internet have had a huge impact on the accessibility of learning. E-mail is used to deliver course content and facilitate online discussions; information of all kinds is readily accessible; and learners can post to bulletin boards and download materials at their leisure (Ryan, 2008).

The World Wide Web delivers authentic texts, images, streaming audio and video recordings, video and sound clips, virtual reality worlds, and dynamic, interactive presentations. Students can listen to live radio stations from around the world or hear prerecorded broadcasts of music, news, sports, and weather. Search engines help students find a wealth of material for classroom, group, or individual research topics.

Current classroom computer use will undergo even more rapid change in the near future as broadband power becomes available to mobile personal devices. Commonly known as "third generation" (3G), this means that vast amounts of multimedia content will be accessible through handheld devices, including television programs, movies, videoconferencing, and music. Next will come 4G, in which data rates are expected to be 100 times faster than 3G. As the delivery platform of broadband content and functionality shifts from computer to personal devices, learning will be unlike anything humans have yet experienced (March, 2007, p. 213).

CALL Impacts Literacy Instruction. Literacy practices are changing in the twenty-first century under the influence of Web-based technologies. Penrod (2008) calls this "Literacy 2.0" in contrast to Literacy 1.0, the traditional reading and writing based on the innovations introduced by Gutenberg's printing press. Literacy 2.0 is more than academic literacy—it is on-demand and flexible, with multiple modalities of input. This literacy extends beyond the school walls to involve its users in social networking sites, blogs, podcasts, wikis, and Moodles, and provokes teachers to design instruction that addresses a spectrum of literacies. According to Penrod (2008, p. 52), such literacy has created "a cultural and technological wave" in which learners demand "immersive educational experiences that are socially rich and informationally engaging." These multimodal literacies are extending the reach of the human mind and creativity.

One of the major innovations at the end of the twentieth century was the use of hypertext in digital media. By clicking on active links in a Webpage, a reader can jump between texts or text segments in a nonlinear way. Information is interactive—connections are set up through a database of sources and links. Because texts are intertextually linked, documents become "multidimensional and dynamic" (Yates, 1996, p. 122).

However, this means that current notions of reading comprehension may have to change to accommodate technology. A Webpage—typically nonlinear, interactive, often in multimedia format—may have multiple forms of hypertext links; for example, leading to word definitions, parallel topics, linked activities, or e-mail. In addition to new kinds of text comprehension, users of Web-based text need the ability to navigate cyberspace, avoid distracting commercial messages, and stay focused on a topic despite a myriad of textual distractions (Coiro, 2003). Reading on the Internet produces the need for guidance in the use of complex communication tools.

Reading software that leverages the most current advances in media design and culturally- and kid-sensitive iconography, combined with rigorous research-based content, has the capacity to create "flow," the feeling of energized and enjoyable focus in an activity. Using technology, literacy opportunities built around solid reading content can maintain "flow" while increasing the learner's fluency, comprehension, and language skills (Quinn, 2007, p. 26).

A host of programs are available that provide reading intervention for struggling English learners. Zeiler (2007) described several of these. One Web-based learning system, Let's Go Learn, combines online diagnostic assessment with differentiated instruction so educators can assess, provide individualized intervention, and then monitor and track the growth in a student's reading ability. This is typical of computer-assisted reading systems.

However, the world of the future may be "postliterate." Futurist William Crossman sees this as a positive development for human evolution. Using voice in/voice out (VIVO) technology, computers will "allow the world's millions of functionally illiterate people to access information via the Internet and the Web without having to learn to read and write. They will become as skillfully literate in the information technology of their generation as we are in ours" (Labbe, 2007).

CALL Supports Strategic Learning. Computers have become an integral part of classroom activities. For example, word processing supports the writing process by allowing students to electronically organize, draft, revise, edit, and publish their work. Students can develop oral skills by using authoring software to create professional-looking oral presentations, developing English skills as they learn content.

Researchers have found that students' attitudes toward writing improve when they use word processing programs (Bitter & Pierson, 2006); students are motivated to produce longer writing, and find revision easier. Students who use word processing enjoy reading their own writing aloud, and are more likely to return to their writing for revision. Teachers find students more willing to exchange feedback about their writing with peers when working on a computer screen.

Both software programs and online resources are used in classrooms to help students achieve their language-learning goals. Software programs include traditional drill-and-practice programs that focus on vocabulary or grammar; tutorials; games; simulations that present students with real-life situations in the language and culture they are learning; and productivity tools (word processing, databases, spreadsheets, graphics, desktop publishing, and presentation-authoring programs). Material from encyclopedias and even the *National Geographic* is available on CD-ROMs.

Example of Concept: WebQuests

WebQuests are a popular form of Internet-based instruction because teachers can use the *WebQuest.org* template to adapt to their own lessons. Ideally, WebQuests involve students using the Internet to carry out inquiry-based tasks in which students pose interesting, open-ended questions. Such questions spark true learning: They require students to think for themselves, and to analyze, synthesize, and evaluate the information they find on the Web (Cunningham & Billingsley, 2006).

CALL and CMC Increase Communicative Abilities. The Internet connects students with other parts of the world, with speakers of English, and with rich sources of information. E-mail, bulletin boards, online chat rooms, and social networking sites make such interaction available both spontaneously in real time (synchronously) and asynchronously (students can take their time to draft responses). A new kind of English (English as a lingua franca) is emerging as non-native speakers of English converse with one another, with syntactic differences from Standard English—not to mention the influences of cyberspeak on English (CYL on this).

CALL Supports Learner Autonomy. The computer is a powerful learning tool that requires the teacher's input to organize, plan, and monitor. Egbert and Hanson-Smith (2007) found that computer technology can provide students with the means to control their own learning, to construct meaning, and to evaluate and monitor their own performance.

However, the computer should not be viewed as something students use without benefit of teacher guidance. Hanson-Smith (1997) described three levels of CALL implementation in the classroom, noting the teacher's role in each. At a modest level, language-learning software can provide a passive listening experience as students click on a word or sentence to hear it repeatedly, look up a meaning, analyze grammar, view a related picture or video clip, and/or read a related text. The teacher monitors students' progress, encouraging, instructing, and modeling as appropriate. At a higher level, students can research current events, historical and cultural topics, business matters, art or literature, weather or geography—any topic of interest to them consonant with the learning goals of the class. Again, the teacher's role is crucial in maximizing the use of computer tools.

CALL Enhances Creativity. English learners in well-equipped schools are already experiencing ways in which computers afford creative learning, whether through digital storytelling, student-created PowerPoint projects, or student-made podcasts and Webcasts. Rennebohm Franz uses a classroom Website to publish students' writing (www.psd267.wednet.edu/~kfranz/index.htm).

Students in schools across the United States are using multimedia computer tools for video and film production, using Quicktime and other digital video production techniques to add sound effects, animation, and other presentation enhancements to

---

Personalized Learning

Paula uses the Internet in her sheltered high-school American History class to research current events for her weekly "news" assignment, as well as to find information for her PowerPoint talk on Robert E. Lee. She uses SDAIE-classroom-adapted American history software that enables her to click on a word or sentence to hear it repeatedly, look up the meaning, see a related picture or video clip, and/or read a related text. Her teacher and peers provide help as needed.

create unique works. Bitter and Legacy (2006) have included a host of classroom-friendly multimedia production tools, both software and hardware. English learners should have access to these tools on a par with other learners.

Example of Concept: Digital Storytelling

"A digital story is a 2- to 5-minute movie-like production that learners create using one of several readily available software programs" (Rance-Roney, 2008, p. 29). Each student writes and records a short script and adds digital images such as text, pictures, drawings, and photographs, as well as music. Creating a digital story engages the learners' skills in reading, writing, and speaking, as well as stimulates the flow of creative juices. Rance-Roney adds, "I have found the process of putting together the story is not linear; students continue to revise the script, edit images, change the music, and re-record their voice, giving them the opportunity to practice language more and more at each stage" (p. 29).

CALL Brings Together a Classroom Learning Community. Internet technologies have been developed that support a community of learning in the classroom. Holding e-mail discussions by means of a listserv or group e-mail list automates the process of broadcasting one posting to an entire group. Listervs can also distribute electronic journals, e-magazines, or newsletters. A teacher can "prime" the list by asking thoughtful questions, recommending useful resources, or by requiring students post a minimum number of messages or responses. Bulletin board discussions resemble e-lists, but the discussions can be structured to maintain the order and topics of discussion and make the entire "conversation" visible (Mills, 2006).

Teachers have found creative ways to use the Internet to develop collaborative projects between classrooms (Karchmer-Klein, 2007). Susan Silverman (www.kids-learn.org), Dale Hubert (www.flatstanleyproject.com), and Marci McGowan (www.mrsmcgowan.com) have used the Internet to open the classroom window and invite in the world.

Computers can also be the subject of debates and conversations in class as a means of improving students' oral proficiency. Teske and Marcy (2007) offer speaking topics that engage students in lively discussions about the world of cybernetics.

Unfortunately, computer use also has the potential to undermine a sense of community. Willard (2007) relates interesting insights into the minds of cyberbullies and the rationalizations they use to justify their actions. Understanding this reasoning may help teachers to combat such behaviors.

Technological Literacy

The education of English learners must involve more than CALL—students also need a broader technological literacy. Hansen (2000) defined technological literacy as "a personal ability to adopt, adapt, or invent proper technological tools in an information society to positively affect his or her life, community, and environment" (p. 31). As people recognize its importance, technological literacy will become a growing field. English learners will need in-depth computer skills for the workplace of the future.

One problem inherent in the use of technology in education is the "digital divide" in terms of race, culture, and economics. If access to digital information or the ability to use technology separates students across geographic, ethnic, language, financial, disability, gender, or political barriers, then technology becomes problematic. The U.S. Department of Education has found that 41 percent of African American and Latino students use a computer at home, compared with 77 percent of European American students; 31 percent of students from families with a total income less than $20,000 use computers, whereas 89 percent of students from families earning more than $75,000 per year are using computers (Ryan, 2008).

Moreover, schools with predominantly minority enrollments are more likely to use technology for drill, practice, and test taking. Thus, race, culture, and economics act as dividers in students' acquisition of computer skills at school (Cavanaugh, 2006). In contrast, computers can be used in more exciting ways, to model weather systems, to visualize molecular science, and to map complex ideas and concepts (Jonassen, 2006). English learners who use computers in boring ways are not well served by the digital revolution. Teachers in CLAD classrooms need to advocate for their own continual training in CALL and CMC in order to ensure that English learners are at the cutting edge of technology-enhanced learning.

The ELD classroom is a complex environment. The classroom teacher orchestrates a wide variety of language-acquisition activities, involving students whose English-language abilities vary greatly. Standards documents developed by TESOL that provide expectations for English learners, and those developed by individual states and localities, provide teachers with frameworks within which they can design their language-development program and maintain the momentum their learners need to progress through the grades. Often, oracy and literacy instruction is integrated so that students can benefit from repeated exposure to themes, concepts, language, and vocabulary.

Teachers of English learners have a wide array of strategies available to them as they help students develop oracy and literacy skills. With the current emphasis on "every child a reader," teachers are under pressure to help all students attain grade-level competencies. Teachers invariably face the complication of mixed levels of student ability—in any single class they may have students who are literate in their first language, students who may have decoding skills only in that language, and/or students who have no literacy in either their first or their second language. Fortunately, various strategies have proved helpful for diverse learners, including activities that integrate oracy, literacy, and technology. Although classrooms with English learners are complex, they are also joyful places where teachers see students making daily progress. ■

LEARNING MORE

Further Reading

Reading, Writing, and Learning in ESL (Peregoy & Boyle, 2008) is an indispensable resource for K–12 teachers of English learners. It orients the reader to English learners, explores second-language acquisition, discusses oracy and literacy for English learners, and provides practical strategies for developing these skills.

Web Search

For resources to help students with speaking, listening, and reading, see G. Carkin's (2004) article "Drama and Pronunciation" in Compleat Links (*Essential Teacher, 1*[5]) at the TESOL Website (www.tesol.org). In addition to discussing the advantages of drama for English learners, Carkin provides several additional Websites.

Exploration

Choose one of your English learners to observe. Note the student's use of English in different contexts (class, playground, arrival/departure from school, lunchtime). Write down specific examples of the student's language. Sit down with the student to find out about his or her prior literacy experience in both L1 and L2. What instruction has he or she had? In which language? What variety of materials? What computer experiences? What literacy experiences are available in the home?

Collaboration

Based on your findings about your student, design a lesson addressing one or more of his or her needs. If possible, engage a colleague in the same exploration and experiment so you can discuss your findings, lessons, and results together. What specifically did you learn by working with the student? How will what you learn change your teaching? What are the next steps?

PEARSON
myeducationlab
The Power of Classroom Practice
www.myeducationlab.com

Additional Sentences

This clip shows a teacher working with several students to sharpen their language skills. The teacher has her entire class work together to form sentences to create a story. She then asks each student to be responsible for writing part of the story on chart paper.

> To access the video, go to MyEducationLab (www.myeducationlab.com), choose the Díaz-Rico and Weed text, and log in to MyEducationLab for English Language Learners. Select the topic Speaking, and watch the video entitled "Additional Sentences."

Answer the following questions:
1. How does the teacher in the clip include all of her students in the writing process? Why is this essential to the development of language skills for this group of students? How do the students learn from each other in this situation?
2. In the clip, the teacher is able to teach language skills by
   a. having students read alone.
   b. having students read aloud, write the story together, and format their sentences together as a class.
   c. creating the story for her class to write.
   d. assigning the story to be written for homework.
3. How does the teacher include all students in the group? Is there individual accountability for each student's speaking level?

5 | Content-Area Instruction

Science activities incorporate English-language-learning opportunities.

In a sheltered seventh-grade science class, students improve their English-language skills while studying about the universe. The science teacher in this class has received special training in working with English learners. Because the students are all still acquiring English as a second language, she modifies her presentation style to help the students comprehend the material. The teacher's primary goal is for students to understand the content materials (in this case, about the origin of the universe). But she also spends some time helping students with language-related issues (e.g., academic vocabulary, reading skills) that pertain to the science unit they are studying. The exposure to higher-level language (through the content materials) and the explicit focus on language issues by the teacher set the stage for successful language acquisition.

Donna Brinton (2003, p. 203)

Educators in schools, school districts, and state and federal agencies are working to develop programs and lessons to educate the growing number of second-language students in the nation's schools. Fortunately, programs that include sheltered instruction address this specific need.

Sheltered instruction is an approach used in multilinguistic content classrooms to provide language support to students while they are learning academic subjects, rather than expecting them to "sink or swim" in a content class designed for native-English speakers. Sheltered instruction may take place either in mainstream classes made up of native-English speakers mixed with non-native-English speakers of intermediate proficiency, or in classes consisting solely of non-native speakers who operate at similar English proficiency levels (Echevarria, Vogt, & Short, 2004).

Sheltered instruction is, ideally, one component in a program for English learners that includes ELD classes for beginning students, primary-language instruction in content areas so students continue at grade level as they learn English, and content-based ESL classes.

Sheltered English, or as it is often called, Specially Designed Academic Instruction in English (SDAIE), combines second-language-acquisition principles with those elements of quality teaching that make a lesson understandable to students. Such instruction enables them to improve listening, speaking, reading, and writing through the study of an academic subject. A SDAIE (pronounced "sah-die") classroom has content objectives identical to those of a mainstream classroom in the same subject but, in addition, includes language and learning-strategy objectives. Instruction is modified for greater comprehensibility. Augmenting mainstream content instruction with SDAIE techniques is the subject of this chapter.

Principles of Specially Designed Academic Instruction in English (SDAIE)

English learners can succeed in content-area classes taught in English. If they can follow and understand a lesson, they can learn content matter, and the content-area instruction—if modified to include English-language development—becomes the means for acquiring English. Basically, SDAIE addresses the following needs of English learners: (1) to learn grade-appropriate content; (2) to master English vocabulary and grammar; (3) to learn "academic" English (i.e., the semantic and syntactic ways that English is used in content subjects); and (4) to develop strategies for learning how to learn.

To accomplish these goals, SDAIE teachers provide a context for instruction that is rich in opportunities for hands-on learning and student interaction. Teachers devote particular attention to communication strategies. By altering the means of presenting material to make it more accessible and understandable, the teacher maintains a challenging academic program without watering down or overly simplifying the curriculum

SDAIE teachers have knowledge of second-language acquisition and instructional techniques for second-language learners. In mainstream elementary and content classrooms, English is an invisible medium. In SDAIE classrooms, English is developed along with content knowledge.

It is sometimes helpful to understand a concept by defining what it is *not*. The following statements put SDAIE into perspective by stating what it is *not*:

- SDAIE is *not* submersion into English-medium classrooms—that is, placing students in mainstream classes in which the teacher makes *no* modifications to accommodate English learners.
- SDAIE is *not* a substitute for primary-language instruction. Even in a sheltered classroom, students still are entitled to, and need support in, their primary language for both content and literacy development.
- SDAIE is *not* a watered-down curriculum. The classroom teacher continues to be responsible for providing all students with appropriate grade-level content learning objectives.

A Model for SDAIE

The model for SDAIE provides a frame for discussing appropriate instruction in sheltered classes (see Figure 5.1). This model originally used the four critical components of the Los Angeles Unified School District (1993) SDAIE model—*content, connections, comprehensibility,* and *interaction*—as a guiding framework. Often, however, teachers could be technically proficient in many of the SDAIE elements yet not be successful with English learners. Discussion and observation revealed that the teacher's attitude played such a critical part in the success of the class that it needed to be explicitly incorporated into the model. Thus, *teacher attitude* was added as an overarching component.

In addition to the model, an observation form (Figure 5.2) provides more explicit elements and strategies within each component. It allows teachers to focus on, observe,

Figure 5.1   **A Model of the Components of Successful SDAIE Instruction**

Teacher Attitude	
The teacher is open and willing to learn from students	
Content	**Connections**
Lessons include subject, language, and learning-strategy objectives.	Curriculum is connected to students' background and experiences.
Material is selected, adapted, and organized with language learners in mind.	*Tap prior knowledge*
Comprehensibility	**Interaction**
Lessons include explicit strategies that aid understanding:	Students have frequent opportunities to:
Contextualization	Talk about lesson content
Modeling	Clarify concepts in their home language
Teacher speech adjustment	Re-present learning through a variety of ways
Frequent comprehension checks through strategies and appropriate questioning	*Modeling expectations*
Repetition and paraphrase	

Figure 5.2 Specially Designed Academic Instruction in English (SDAIE) Observation Form

Date: _____

Duration of observation: _____

Subject: _____

Number of students: _____

SDAIE Component	✓	Evidence (describe with specific evidence the components observed)

CONTENT
Content objective
Language objective
Learning-strategy objective
Materials and text
   Clear and meaningful
   Support objectives
		Positive Affective Domain

CONNECTIONS
Bridging1
   Concepts/skills linked to student experiences
Bridging2
   Examples used/elicited from students' lives
Schema building
   New learning linked to old through scaffolding strategies (webs, semantic maps, visual organizers, etc.)
		con text
		
		TEACH STUDY SKILLS

COMPREHENSIBILITY
Contextualization
   Use of pictures, maps, graphs, charts, models, diagrams, gestures, labels, and dramatizations to illustrate concept clearly
   Appeal to variety of learning styles
Modeling
   Demonstration of skill or concept to be learned
Speech adjustment
   Slower rate
   Clear enunciation
   Controlled use of idioms
Comprehension checks
Teacher and student strategies
   Appropriate questioning
   Recitation and paraphrase
		Visuals
		~~strict to~~
		Modify use of Text

INTERACTION
Opportunities for students to talk about lesson content
   Teacher to student
   Student to teacher
   Student to student
   Student to content
   Student to self
Clarification of concepts in L1
   Primary-language material
   Student interaction
Re-presentation of understanding
   Students transform knowledge through illustration, dramatization, song creation, dance, story rewriting, critical thinking
		Use self. assessments
		role play
		✓

and incorporate SDAIE elements into their lessons. Teachers find they do not use every aspect of the model in every lesson, but by working within the overall frame they are more assured of providing appropriate learning opportunities for their English learners. In the following sections, each of the five SDAIE components is explained and illustrated.

Teacher Attitude

Previous chapters have mentioned affective aspects of learning and classroom environments that foster meaningful language acquisition, but they have not specifically addressed the role of the teacher's attitude. Good teachers find delight and satisfaction in their students' learning. It is this sense of delight that is important in working with all learners, particularly English learners.

Three aspects characterize a successful attitude in working with second-language learners:

1. Teachers believe that all students can learn. They do not assume that because a student does not speak English he or she is incapable of learning.
2. Teachers recognize that all students have language. Students have successfully learned their home languages and have understandings and skills that transfer to their second language.
3. Teachers recognize that a person's self-concept is involved in his or her own language and that at times students need to use that language.

In SDAIE classrooms, it is not only the students who are learning. Successful teachers themselves are open, not only *willing* to learn but also *expecting* to learn. Teachers using SDAIE reflect on their teaching using videotapes of themselves, peer observation, reflective journals, informal discussions with colleagues, and summative notations on lesson plans. They also set aside a quiet time for contemplation about the effectiveness of their teaching.

Example of Concept: A Positive Environment

An ELD teacher observed and interviewed her colleagues at her school. She discovered that accomplished teachers set up effective learning environments for the English learners. They understood the needs of their culturally and linguistically diverse students and created an atmosphere in the classroom that helped newly arrived students integrate into the life of the school. For example, they encouraged friendships by asking a classmate to sit with the English learner at lunch. They provided appropriate instruction for their English learners and applauded their successes. This environment helped relieve much of the newcomers' anxiety (Haynes, 2004).

Content

Teaching SDAIE-modified academic content involves the careful planning of content, language, and learning-strategy objectives and the selecting, modifying, and organizing of materials and text that support those objectives. A lesson with a clear objective focuses the instruction and guides the teacher to select those learning activities that accomplish the goal. Once objectives are clearly stated, the teacher selects material that will help students achieve those objectives.

What are the benefits of lesson planning? Teachers can reuse a good plan without tedious replanning. For evaluation purposes, a good plan can be used as a checklist to see what has been accomplished. With a good plan in place, teachers can focus on students rather than worrying what should come next. Finally, a thorough plan helps teachers to evaluate material needs in advance as well as to estimate the duration of the activity.

Content Objectives. Planning begins by the teacher's first specifying learning goals and competencies students must develop. Standards documents that spell out what students should know and be able to do are available to provide an overview of the goals. Curricular programs follow the goals put forth in the documents. The teacher divides these overall goals for the year into units. These units are further divided into specific lessons. Each lesson contains the essential content-area objectives.

In developing their sequence of content objectives, teachers should keep two important questions in mind: (1) Have I reviewed the objectives for the year and organized them for thematic flow? and (2) Have I considered the sequence of objectives and rearranged them, if necessary, putting more concrete concepts before more abstract ones (i.e., those that can be taught with hands-on materials, visuals, and demonstrations before those that are difficult to demonstrate or that require more oral and/or written skills)?

Language Objectives. Each content area has specific language demands. Language objectives take these into account. The teacher considers the various tasks that language users must be able to perform in the different content areas (e.g., describing in a literature lesson, classifying in a science lesson, justifying in a mathematics lesson, etc.). A language objective takes into account not only vocabulary but also the language functions and discourse of the discipline.

In working with teachers, Short and Echevarria (1999) noted that incorporating language objectives has been problematic for both content teachers, who tend to see language only as vocabulary development. For many content teachers, language is still an invisible medium. *The CALLA Handbook* (Chamot & O'Malley, 1994) is a valuable resource for helping teachers understand the language demands of various disciplines.

In reviewing the language objectives, a teacher can keep the following questions in mind:

- What is the concept focus of the unit and what are the key concepts students must master?

- What are the structures and discourse of the discipline and how can these be included in the language objectives?
- Are all four language modes included—listening, speaking, reading, writing?

Learning-Strategy Objectives. Learning strategies help students learn *how* to learn. These include cognitive strategies (critical thinking, using graphic organizers); social-affective strategies (learning to work cooperatively, appreciating art); and metacognitive strategies (planning, self-monitoring, and self-evaluating). Chamot and O'Malley's CALLA is discussed later in this chapter.

Figure 5.3 shows how content, language, and learning strategies can be used in a high-school social studies lesson on liberty. The objectives align with national and state standards.

Materials and Texts. A critical aspect of any lesson is the proper selection and use of materials. Textbooks have become a central tool in many classrooms, but they often need to be supplemented by other materials. The SDAIE teacher must select and modify text materials to best accommodate the needs of English learners.

Because texts can be problematic for English learners, teachers need to include specific objectives (either language or learning strategy) that teach students how to read and study academic discourse. Students need to understand the structure of a text as well as the actual content. Teachers teach students how to preview or "walk through" a text by noting the structure of the assigned chapter(s), including the main headings, subheadings, specialized words in bold or italic, maps, graphs, and pictures that are included to assist comprehension.

Figure 5.3 Liberty: Content, Language, and Learning-Strategy Objectives

Social Studies. The students will . . .

Examine the causes and course of the American Revolution and the contributions of South Carolinians

Identify and explain historical, geographic, social, and economic factors that have helped shape American democracy

Describe the means by which Americans can monitor and influence government

Language. The students will . . .

Listen to, speak, read, and write about subject-matter information

Gather information both orally and in writing

Select, connect, and explain information

Learning Strategies. The students will . . .

Apply basic reading comprehension skills (skimming, scanning, previewing, reviewing text)

Take notes to record important information and aid their own learning

Determine and establish the conditions that help them become effective learners (when, where, how to study)

Source: Adapted from Majors (n.d.).

Teachers should also familiarize students with the difference in the style and structure of texts depending on the particular discipline. Content texts are more information-rich than stories, have specialized organizing principles that may be discipline specific, and use abstract and specialized vocabulary. The language may feature complex sentence structures and reference may be made to background knowledge that is restricted to that discipline (Addison, 1988).

Selecting materials involves an initial choice of whether the teacher wishes to have one primary content source or a package of content-related materials (chapters from various texts, video- and audiotapes, magazine and newspaper articles, encyclopedia entries, literary selections, Internet sources, software programs, etc.). Regardless of what is chosen, the teacher must consider two main criteria: Are the content objectives for the lesson adequately presented by the material? Is the material comprehensible to English learners? The following list enumerates additional items to consider when selecting materials:

- Is the information is accurate, up-to-date, and thorough?
- Are the tasks required of students appropriate to the discipline?
- Is the text clearly organized, with print and layout features that assist students' comprehension?
- Does the text appeal to a variety of learning styles?
- Is the language of the text straightforward, without complex syntactic patterns, idioms, or excessive jargon.
- Is new content vocabulary clearly defined within the text or in a glossary?
- Are diagrams, graphs, and charts clearly labeled and complement and clarify the text?
- Will most of the students have prior experience with the content, or will much time be necessary for schema building? (Allan & Miller, 2005)

Content area teachers must also consider the use of primary-language resources, such as dictionaries, books, software programs, and Internet sites, as well as people resources, such as cross-age tutors, parents, and community volunteers, in helping students to understand concepts.

Example of Concept: Primary Language Support

One teacher organized a schoolwide Translation and Bridging Committee of students in grades 2 through 6 that prepared notes for parents and programs for school assemblies in Tagalog and Spanish. This gave students a sense of pride in the contributions their native-language skills made to the school (Echevarria & Graves, 2007).

Modifying materials may be necessary to help English learners comprehend connected discourse. Some learners may need special textual material, such as excerpts taken from textbooks or chapters from the readings that have been modified. Rewriting text selections requires a sizable time investment, however, so one of the following alternative approaches may be preferable:

- Supply an advance organizer for the text that highlights the key topics and concepts in outline form, as focus questions, or in the form of concept maps.
- Change the modality from written to oral. By reading aloud, the teacher can also model the process of posing questions while reading to show prediction strategies used when working with text.
- Tape-record selected passages for students to listen to as they read along in the text.
- Develop a study guide for the text. For each reading section create ten sentences that reflect the main ideas, then turn each sentence into a question or selectively omit key words that students must supply.
- Ask students to work in groups so they can share their notes and help one another complete missing parts or correct misunderstood concepts.

Example of Concept: Using Multiple Sources

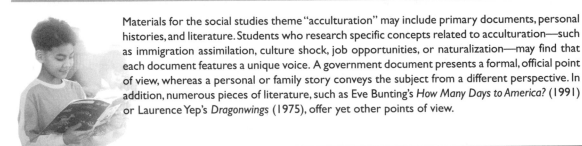

Materials for the social studies theme "acculturation" may include primary documents, personal histories, and literature. Students who research specific concepts related to acculturation—such as immigration assimilation, culture shock, job opportunities, or naturalization—may find that each document features a unique voice. A government document presents a formal, official point of view, whereas a personal or family story conveys the subject from a different perspective. In addition, numerous pieces of literature, such as Eve Bunting's *How Many Days to America?* (1991) or Laurence Yep's *Dragonwings* (1975), offer yet other points of view.

Connections

Students engage in learning when they recognize a connection between what they know and the learning experience. This can be accomplished in several ways: *bridging*— linking concepts and skills to student experiences (bridging1) or eliciting/using examples from students' lives (bridging2)—and *schema building*—using scaffolding strategies to link new learning to old.

Bridging1: Developing Experiences. Students bring a wealth of experiences to the learning task, and SDAIE teachers help students relate those experiences to the concepts to be learned. In addition, teachers provide new experiences that arouse interest in and attention to a topic. These experiences may include field trips, guest speakers, films and movies, experiments, classroom discovery centers, music and songs, poetry and other literature, computer simulations, and so on. To deepen these experiences, the teacher can guide the students to talk and write about them, associating what they already knew with these new experiences.

Example of Concept: Experiences That Focus Instruction

The firsthand experiences of a field trip piqued the interest of Dorothy Taylor's students in Virginia history and prepared them for the colonial unit she had planned (Taylor, 2000, pp. 53–55).

In the fall, all of the fourth-grade classes in the school went on a field trip to Jamestown, Virginia. The children returned from their trip eager to talk about what they had learned. The field trip and students' enthusiasm were a perfect introduction to the social studies unit on the hardships faced by the Jamestown colonists. The students shared with each other what they knew about Jamestown and colonial America and added to their knowledge and vocabulary by reading and watching a video.

Bridging2: Linking from Students' Lives.   Prior knowledge of a topic may be tapped to determine the extent of students' existing concepts and understandings. Many students may have relevant experiences to share. Tapping prior knowledge allows them to place new knowledge in the context of their own episodic memories rather than storing new information solely as unrelated concepts.

Adapted Instruction: Tapping into Previous Knowledge

The following strategies elicit information from students and help the teacher understand the extent of students' understanding:

- Brainstorming
- K-W-L (What do I *know*? What do I *want* to learn? What have I *learned*?)
- Venn diagrams
- Twenty Questions
- Interviews

Schema Building.   If they have little prior knowledge about the topic at hand, students will need more instructional support to construct a framework of concepts that shows the relationships of old and new learning.

Graphic organizers help students order their thoughts by presenting ideas visually. Semantic mapping and webs are ways of presenting concepts to show their relationships. After a brainstorming session, the teacher and students could organize

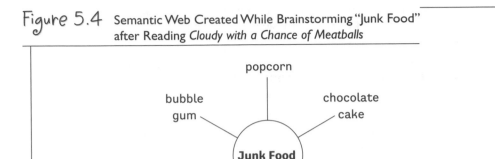

Figure 5.4 Semantic Web Created While Brainstorming "Junk Food" after Reading *Cloudy with a Chance of Meatballs*

their ideas into a semantic map, with the main idea in the center of the chalkboard and associated or connected ideas as branches from the main idea.

Alternatively, a teacher could be more directive in creating a map by writing the central topic and branching out from it with several major subtopics. Students could provide information that the teacher then writes into the appropriate category. Figure 5.4 shows the results of a brainstorming session after second-grade students had heard *Cloudy with a Chance of Meatballs* (Barrett, 1978). They brainstormed on the questions "What junk food can you think of?" and "What is in junk food that our bodies don't need?"

Comprehensibility

A key factor in learning is being able to understand. Through all phases of a lesson, the teacher ensures that students have plenty of clues to understanding. This is one of the aspects of SDAIE that makes it different from mainstream instruction. Teachers increase the comprehensibility of lessons in four ways: *contextualization, modeling, speech adjustment,* and *comprehension checks.*

Contextualization. The verbal presentation of a lesson is supplemented by the use of manipulatives, realia, media, and visual backup as teachers write key words and concepts on the chalkboard or butcher paper; the use of graphs, pictures, maps, and other physical props to communicate; or the use of the overhead projector or a computer hooked to a television monitor. By presenting concepts numerous times through various means and in a rich visual, auditory (for example, software programs and Websites that offer sounds and experiences), and kinesthetic (drama and skits, "gallery" walks) environment, lessons also appeal to students' different learning styles.

Example of Concept: Supplementing the Verbal Presentation

In a biology class, when teaching about flowers, the teacher refers students to the explanation in the text (paragraph form), a diagram of a flower in the text (graphic form), a wall chart with a different flower (pictorial form), a text glossary entry (dictionary form), and actual flowers that students can examine. Through these numerous media, the concepts "petal," "stamen," "pistil," and "sepal" are understood and provide a basis for future study about life-forms. The teacher's task here is to ensure that these multiple sources are organized to communicate clearly each concept.

Table 5.1 provides a list of both object and human resources that can help contextualize classroom content.

Example of Concept: Resources for English-Language Development

Jasper Elementary is one of four schools in the Waterloo (Iowa) Community School District that is designated to offer services to ELD students. Because the ELD students are integrated into mainstream classes, each teacher must find resources to help the students in his or her classroom. One fourth/fifth-grade teacher makes use of the Minnesota Migrant Resource Center, a repository of hands-on materials that can be borrowed. These include objects and pictures for bulletin boards and centers, song lyrics, worksheets, books, and other materials. The staff of the center is trained to help teachers match materials to student needs (Milambiling, 2002).

Table 5.1

Media, Realia, Manipulatives, and Human Resources to Contextualize Lessons

Object Resources		Human Resources
Picture files	Science equipment	Cooperative groups
Maps and globes	Manipulatives:	Pairs
Charts and posters	M&Ms	Cross-age tutors
Printed material:	Buttons	Heterogeneous groups
Illustrated books	Cuisinaire rods	Community resource people
Pamphlets	Tongue depressors	School resource people
News articles	Gummy bears	Parents
Catalogs	Costumes	Pen pals (adult and child)
Magazines	Computer software	Keypals
Puzzles	Internet	

In addition to contextualizing the content of a lesson, teachers of English learners must also make accessible the organization and management procedures in the classroom. During the lesson, verbal markers provide structure so that students can understand what is expected of them. Markers for key points, such as *now, note this, for instance,* or *in conclusion,* cue students to material that is especially important. Terms such as *first, second,* and *last* clearly mark the steps of a sequence. To help students with these verbal markers, teachers can provide students with a list and ask students to listen for them during a lesson. To help with directions, teachers can determine the ten most frequently used verbal markers and provide mini-TPR-type lessons to help students learn them.

Modeling. Demonstrating new concepts can involve hands-on, show-and-tell explanations in which students follow a careful sequence of steps to understand a process. The teacher ensures that the demonstration illustrates the concept clearly and that there is a one-to-one correspondence between the teacher's words and the demonstration.

Speech Adjustment. Teachers in SDAIE classrooms modify their speech to accommodate the various proficiency levels of their students. One way they do this is by monitoring their own language usage and reducing the amount of their talking in the classroom. This provides more opportunities for students to talk both with the teacher and among themselves.

By slowing their delivery and articulating clearly, teachers allow English learners greater opportunity to separate words and process the language. Teacher speech modification exists at all linguistic levels: phonological (using precise pronunciation); syntactic (less subordination; shorter sentences that follow subject-verb-object format); semantic (more concrete, basic vocabulary); pragmatic (more frequent and longer pauses, exaggerated stress and intonation); and discourse (self-repetition, slower rate).

As students become more proficient in English, teachers again adjust their speech, this time increasing speed and complexity. Ultimately, English learners will need to function in an all-English-medium classroom; therefore, over time, SDAIE teachers need to lessen the speech-modification scaffolds they use to accommodate their students' evolving proficiency.

Comprehension Checks. Teachers use strategies to continually monitor students' listening and reading comprehension. During formal presentations, they use devices such as asking students to put their thumbs up or down, to paraphrase to another student, or to dramatize, write, or graph their understanding. Depending on student response, teachers may need to rephrase questions and information if the students do not initially understand.

When asking questions, the teacher can consider a linguistic hierarchy of question types. For students in the "silent period" of language acquisition, a question requiring a nonverbal response—a head movement, pointing, manipulating materials—will elicit an appropriate and satisfactory answer. Once students are beginning to speak, either/or questions provide the necessary terms, and the students need merely to choose the correct word or phrase to demonstrate understanding: "Is the water evaporating or condensing?"; "Did explorers come to the Americas from Europe or Asia?" Once students are more comfortable in producing language, *wh-* questions are appropriate: "What is happening to the water?"; "Which countries sent explorers to the Americas?"; "What was the purpose of their exploration?"

In addition to using comprehension strategies, teachers may also need to teach students how to verbalize their understanding. Teachers may need to find ways in which English learners can voice their need for clarification, such as accepting questions that are written on index cards (Díaz-Rico, 2008).

An important part of providing a comprehensible learning environment for students is the teacher's use of the same type of direction throughout various lessons. For example, an elementary teacher might say, "Today we are going to continue our work on . . ."; "Who can show me their work from yesterday?" These sentences can be repeated throughout the day to introduce lessons so that students know what to expect and how to proceed.

Adapted Instruction: Strategies for Comprehensibility

- Use sentence structures that expand the students' output by supplying needed phrases and vocabulary.
- Use gestures to convey instructions.
- Concentrate on understanding and communicating rather than on error correction.
- Provide alternative grouping procedures so that students can share their understanding with one another and with the teacher.
- Maintain regular classroom procedures and routines.

Interaction

The organization of discourse is important for language acquisition in content classes. Teacher-fronted classrooms are dominated by teacher talk. The teacher takes the central role in controlling the flow of information, and students compete for the teacher's attention and for permission to speak. More recent research (Gass, 2000), however, points to the role of the learner in negotiating, managing, even manipulating conversations to receive more comprehensible input. Instead of English learners being dependent on their ability to understand the teacher's explanations and directions, classrooms that feature flexible grouping patterns permit students to have greater access to the flow of information.

The teacher orchestrates tasks so that students use language in academic ways. Students are placed in different groups for different activities. For example, when learning new and difficult concepts, English learners who speak the same language are placed together so that they can use their native language, whereas students of varying language backgrounds and abilities are grouped for tasks that require application of key concepts and skills. Teachers themselves work with small groups to achieve specific instructional objectives.

In planning for interaction in the SDAIE lesson, the teacher considers opportunities for students to talk about key concepts, expects that students may clarify the concepts in their primary language, and allows a variety of means through which students can demonstrate their understanding.

Student Opportunities to Talk. Classrooms in which teachers use SDAIE are noisy places as students engage in a variety of opportunities to explore, express, debate, chat, and laugh, with numerous conversational partners. Interaction patterns include teacher to student, student to teacher, student to student, student to content, and student to self.

Cooperative learning activities, both formally and informally structured, allow English learners to work with one another in a noncompetitive, equal opportunity environment. In the Complex Instruction model (Cohen, Lotan, & Catanzarite, 1990), students are assigned well-defined roles that rotate among all members. Equal opportunity at all roles eliminates notions of high and low status within the group. Students further practice cooperative rules while working with content materials.

Probably one of the most powerful strategies teachers can use to ensure both content and language development in an interactional setting is the Instructional Conversation (IC). The lessons in this discussion-based strategy focus on an idea or concept that has educational value as well as meaning and relevance for students. The teacher encourages expression of students' own ideas, builds on students' experiences and ideas, and guides them to increasingly sophisticated levels of understanding.

The following summarizes the use of the IC in the classroom.

Adapted Instruction: The Instructional Conversation

1. Arrange the classroom to accommodate conversation between the teacher and a small group of students on a regular and frequent schedule.
2. Have a clear academic goal that guides conversation with students.
3. Ensure that student talk occurs at higher rates than teacher talk.
4. Guide conversation to include students' views, judgments, and rationales, using text evidence and other substantive support.
5. Ensure that all students are included in the conversation according to their preferences.
6. Listen carefully to assess levels of students' understanding.
7. Assist students' learning throughout the conversation by questioning, restating, praising, encouraging, and so forth.
8. Guide the students to prepare a product that indicates the goal of the instructional conversation was achieved.

Source: Center for Research on Education, Diversity, and Excellence (2002).

Clarification of Concepts in the Primary Language. In SDAIE classrooms, students are afforded opportunities to learn and clarify concepts in their own language. When possible, the teacher provides primary-language resources (print, electronic, personnel) that can help students with key concepts. Research continues to show that when students are able to use their first language, they make more academic gains in both content and language than if they are prohibited from using it (Collier, 1995).

Re-Presentation of Understanding. After students have had the opportunity to learn new material in a meaningful way, they can transform that knowledge through other means, such as illustrating, dramatizing, creating songs, dancing, and rewriting stories. By re-presenting information in another form, students must review what they know and think about how to organize and explain their knowledge in the new format. By sharing their discoveries in a variety of ways—in learning centers; through dramatic, visual, or oral presentations; by staging readers' theater; by developing slide, video, or computer-based audiovisual shows; through maps and graphs—they also use their developing language skills in a more formal setting.

Re-presentation of knowledge is also an important means for teachers to assess student learning and to pinpoint areas for reteaching, expansion, and/or modification. In this manner, assessment becomes a part of the learning cycle instead of something divorced from classroom practices.

Example of Concept: Re-Presenting Knowledge

In one fifth-grade class, the students produced a news program with a U.S. Civil War setting. The program included the show's anchors; reporters in the field interviewing generals, soldiers, and citizens; a weather report; and reports on sports, economics, and political conditions. There were even commercial breaks. The students engaged in much research in order to be historically accurate, but enthusiasm was high as they shared their knowledge in a format they knew and understood. In addition, students were able to work in the area of their particular interest.

When a unit of instruction is completed, it is time to evaluate its success. The teacher should reflect on and record:

- What students learned (both content and language)
- The appropriateness of resources used
- Students' engagement
- The design and appropriateness of tasks
- The effectiveness of instruction, both by the main teacher and by aides and/or volunteers (Gibbons, 2006, p. 223)

SDAIE offers English learners an important intermediate step between content instruction in the primary language, an environment in which they may not advance in English skills, and a "sink-or-swim" immersion, in which they may not learn key content-related concepts. Although standards-based instruction emphasizes the acquisition of content, SDAIE requires additional lesson objectives that foster English-language acquisition. This supplementary focus on language development is the key that unlocks the core curriculum for English learners.

Content-Area Application

Each content area has standards that guide curriculum development. Applying the standards for English learners has been a thorny issue. The No Child Left Behind legislation (2002) states that English learners will develop high levels of academic proficiency in English and meet the same challenging state academic standards as do their native-English-speaking peers. How do they have access to the same challenging content as their peers? How do they meet the standards? While native-English-speaking students are learning content, English learners have the dual task of learning content *and* language, sometimes in sheltered classes, but more frequently in mainstream ones (McKeon, 1994).

The Cognitive Academic Language Learning Approach (CALLA) is an approach specifically developed to address these issues. By incorporating principles of CALLA, teachers can adapt their content-area lessons to help students meet content-area challenges. CALLA is explained below, followed by a discussion of the individual content areas. In each, reference is made to the respective content standards, and then strategies organized around the SDAIE model are presented as specific means to help teachers provide challenging and accessible content to their English learners.

Cognitive Academic Language Learning Approach (CALLA)

CALLA, designed for English learners at the advanced beginning and intermediate levels of English-language proficiency, includes the development of academic language skills and explicit instruction in learning strategies for both content and language acquisition (Chamot & O'Malley, 1994). To acquire academic language skills, students learn not just vocabulary and grammar but also language functions important for the specific curricular areas, such as analyzing, evaluating, justifying, and persuading.

A central component of CALLA is instruction in learning strategies. These strategies are divided into three major categories: *cognitive, social-affective,* and *metacognitive.*

Cognitive strategies include using reference materials resourcefully; taking effective notes; summarizing material adequately; applying rules of induction or inference; remembering information using visual images, auditory representation, or elaboration of associations to new knowledge; transferring prior skills to assist comprehension; and grouping new concepts, words, or terms understandably. Social-affective strategies teach how to elicit needed clarification, how to work cooperatively with peers in problem solving, and how to use mental techniques or self-talk to reduce anxiety and increase a sense of personal competency.

Metacognitive strategies help students to plan, monitor, and evaluate their learning processes. Teachers help students learn to preview the main concepts in material to be learned, plan the key ideas that must be expressed orally or in writing, decide in advance what specific information must be attended to, check comprehension during listening or reading, and judge how well learning has been accomplished when the lesson is completed.

When acquiring a new learning strategy, students first use guided practice so they can be exposed to clear examples. Grade-level appropriate practice follows, so that students can try a strategy with material that is within their range of understanding. Independent practice follows when students are familiar and comfortable with a learning strategy and have tried it with supervision in a variety of contexts (Echevarria & Graves, 2007).

Explanatory Models for Academic Disciplines

Educators have become wary of simply expecting student performance to increase by using visuals, manipulatives, and other types of modified instruction. Researchers have shown that students need to acquire explanatory models for each discipline. These are typical ways that practitioners use to make sense of the world, to use patterns of ideas to solve problems.

According to Duran, Dugan, and Weffer (1997), more successful students are those who are socialized into specific ways to think about the academic subjects they are studying. It is not enough to use the language of a scholar; one must also acquire a specific worldview and orientation toward particular kinds of knowledge. This way of thinking is an integral part of modified instruction.

Social Studies

According to the social studies standards document *Expectations for Excellence,* the primary purpose of social studies is to help young people develop the ability to make informed and reasoned decisions for the public good as citizens of a culturally diverse, democratic society in an interdependent world (National Council for the Social Studies [NCSS], 1994). This purpose represents a tall order for teachers working with English learners who may have limited background with the social studies program in U.S. schools. However, by implementing certain strategies on a regular basis, teachers have found that their English learners are able to achieve the goals outlined in the social studies standards documents.

Content: Flexible, Thematic Curricula. A recent trend in many public schools has been to organize instruction around broad themes. Students learn social studies by researching, reading, and experimenting to answer real-world questions that they have posed themselves. The question-driven or problem-posing format forces a reconceptualization of the curriculum away from a narrow focus on subject areas to broader concepts that connect to significant ideas and issues (Freeman & Freeman, 1998). For English learners, this reconceptualization allows for more interactive engagement with a number of other speakers, for continuous concept development, and for an expanding base of vocabulary and language structures that can be used in a variety of contexts.

Example of Concept: Using Multiple Resources for Depth of Content

Students studying a fifth-grade unit on Settlement of the West can examine the legal issues involved in the Treaty of Guadalupe-Hidalgo, compare the various cultures that came into contact in the Southwest, delve into the history of land grant titles, and pursue many more issues of interest. Through filmstrips, films, videos, computer simulations, literature, nonfiction texts, and oral discussions, students develop conceptual knowledge. Such a unit incorporates history, geography, sociology, economics, values, information-seeking skills, group participation, and perhaps dramatic skills as students act out the signing of treaties and other cultural events.

Connections: Linking to Prior Knowledge. By starting each class with an activity that actively engages students in reviewing their own experiences relevant to the topic, the teacher not only gains valuable insights that can help in teaching, but he or she also gives students an opportunity to see how their experiences fit into the realm of the social studies.

Using an oral history approach actively involves students in gathering information from their families and communities. Furthermore, not only do students learn that history is composed of their own and their family's stories, but also, by delving into their own backgrounds, they may learn about complex issues, such as religious persecution, tyranny of autocratic rulers, and the rights and responsibilities of self-governance. Through such oral history projects, students are engaging in many of the historical thinking skills outlined in the U.S. history standards (e.g., chronological thinking, reading historical narratives, describing the past through the perspectives of those who were there, and preparing a historical analysis and interpretation) (Anstrom, 1999b).

Example of Concept: History with a Hip-Hop Beat

"Gandhi, the freedom fighta!" is an unconventional phrase for a sixth-grade history class. Scott Sayre, a teacher at Jackson Elementary School in Los Angeles who is also an amateur musician, called on friends in the music-recording industry to help students record a rap song. Students plan to continue their research on civil rights to record a complete album featuring eight to ten songs. The class is selling its first single, "Taking a Risk for Justice," for $2.50 to cover the album's production costs. Twelve-year-old Cristela Gomez likes this novel approach. "I'm really shy," she says. "It helps me get rid of the shyness" (Green, 2007, p. B3).

Comprehensibility: Contextualizing Instruction. Specific strategies can increase the ability of English learners to understand content and to experience history "come alive." Graphic organizers provide students with visual means to represent their content knowledge. A timeline can be used to place important events in chronological sequence. A population graph can show the effect of events on people, and maps can place significant events in their geographical locale. Pictures from a variety of sources can bring past events to life. Pictures, charts, and diagrams help students identify main concepts. Classmates can help one another evaluate the information they read in order to write group reports.

Interaction: Cooperative Learning. Social studies topics in particular have been difficult for English learners because the topics are generally abstract, cognitively complex, and highly language dependent. Cooperative learning can be used to structure the classroom so that English learners have increased opportunities to verify their comprehension by receiving explanations from their peers and sharing prior knowledge. Encouraging students to exchange information helps them to clarify and familiarize themselves with the lesson content. In this way, students are involved in their own learning and teachers can rely less on lectures and worksheets.

Adapted Instruction: Cooperative Learning Structures

- *Three-step interview.* One student interviews another and then the two reverse roles. They share with each other what they have learned.
- *Roundtable.* In a small group, the first student writes a contribution and then passes the paper to the next student. Each contributes in turn. The group discusses their findings. (This procedure can be done orally.)
- *Think-pair-share.* After the teacher asks a question, students think of a response. Students use the interview technique to share answers.
- *Solve-pair-share.* The teacher poses a problem and students work on solutions individually. Students explain their various solutions in interview or roundtable procedures.
- *Numbered heads.* Each team member has a number. The teacher asks a question. The teams put their heads together to find the answer and make sure everyone knows it. The teacher calls a number and the student with that number in each team raises his or her hand.
- *Jigsaw.* Each student is in a home team and an expert team. Expert teams work together on specific material different from other expert teams. Students return to their home team and share what they have learned.

Re-Presenting Knowledge: Linking Instruction to Assessment. Many of the tasks, projects, and role-plays that students are engaged in to learn content can be further used in assessment. Such authentic tasks provide a richer means of assessing students who are still struggling with the language than the traditional paper-and-pencil tests.

Example of Concept: Re-Presenting Knowledge

The culminating activity for the Holocaust unit in Kathy Reckendorf and Wilma Ortiz's class was the creation of a quilt based on the *Diary of Anne Frank*. The class was separated into teams and each team created one quilt square based on their depiction of a theme or message that they felt was the most relevant in the book. The teams referred to the text and wrote one or two lines or phrases that captured their attention. They sketched these ideas and selected the one that they agreed represented the theme and message they had identified. The students then displayed their quilt in the school cafeteria (Reckendorf & Ortiz, 2000).

Adapted Instruction: The Importance of Review

Schedule time for review at the end of each lesson; point out key concepts and vocabulary while making connections to lesson objectives and state standards. This is essential, because English learners may concentrate so intently on processing language during instruction that they forget the importance of the information (Friend & Bursuck, 2006, p. 320).

In summary, among the principles and practices recommended for SDAIE are the following (Chamot & O'Malley, 1994; Schifini, 1994):

1. Content and language are integrated.
   - Instruction is organized around grade-level content, with special techniques to increase access for English learners.
   - The level of students' English fluency determines the language objectives.
   - New words are defined in context or pretaught, and are repeated and recycled to increase exposure and retention.
2. Varied instruction increases comprehensibility.
   - Multiple modes include reading, drawing, discussing, and looking at realia and visuals (drawing, maps, charts, etc.).
   - Teachers build on students' prior knowledge, including cultural background.
3. Language is modified for comprehensible instruction.
   - Complex or sophisticated language expressions (e.g., idioms, jargon, slang) are simplified.
   - Gestures and actions reinforce verbal delivery.
4. Students are explicitly taught learning strategies.
   - Strategies build content knowledge, English proficiency, and thinking skills.
   - Group work is designed for maximum support and participation.
5. Assessment is varied to enable students to demonstrate growth in content knowledge and language proficiency.

Literature

Of the twelve standards in the *Standards for the English Language Arts* (National Council of Teachers of English [NCTE] & International Reading Association [IRA], 1996, online at www.ncte.org/about/over/standards/110846.htm), two provide support for English learners: Standard 9, "Students develop an understanding of and respect for diversity in language use, patterns, and dialects across cultures, ethnic groups, geographic regions, and social roles"; and Standard 10, "Students whose first language is not English make use of their first language to develop competency in the English language arts and to develop understanding of content across the curriculum." In addition, Standard 1 calls for wide reading, including texts about the cultures of the United States and the world.

Content: Material Selection. An appropriate selection of genre may be one way to help English learners develop their conceptual and linguistic schemata. The literature curriculum can be a planned sequence that begins with familiar structures of folktales and myths and uses these as a bridge to more complex works of literature. Myths and folktales from many cultures are now commonly available in high-quality editions with vibrant illustrations. Students can move from these folktales and myths to selected short stories by authors of many cultural backgrounds, then to portions of a longer work, and then to entire works.

Students who read books that interest them are more motivated to read. A study of sixth-grade students' reading preferences found that most preferred books with scary stories, comics, and content about popular culture, sports, cars and trucks, and animals (Worthy, Moorman, & Turner, 1999). The features of the text make a motivational difference. Frey and Fisher (2007) described common features of various text genres: Chapter books are largely text-only, whereas graphic novels are based on pictures, with text used largely for dialogue—these are often recommended to jump-start reading for the reluctant adolescent.

Example of Concept: A Variety of Materials

William Pruitt (2000, pp. 33–49) describes how his students benefit from studying different versions of a folktale:

One of the goals of the story unit is for students to examine how the same story may differ as it appears in different perspectives, media, and cultures, and compare and contrast these forms. Over the course of the 2-week unit, we read and compare and contrast an original (translated) version of "Beauty and the Beast," a poem entitled "Beauty and the Beast," and three video versions of the story. Once students have gained experience with this folktale and understand the pattern of activities, we move to other texts that have film adaptations, for example, *Tuck Everlasting* (Babbitt, 1976) or *To Kill a Mockingbird* (Lee, 1960).

Connections and Comprehensibility: *Into, Through,* and *Beyond.* "Into" activities activate students' prior knowledge. Once students are ready for the text, they can make predictions about the story. Some teachers put these predictions into short-term "time capsules" that can be opened and analyzed once the text has been read. Students can discuss what happened later in the book to confirm or disprove their original predictions.

Adapted Instruction: Ways "into" Literature

- *Anticipation/reaction guides:* A short list of statements provokes students to agree or disagree
- *Pictures, art, movies:* Visual means build a feeling for the setting
- *Physical objects:* Items relating to the reading selection allow students to identify and discuss
- *Experiences:* Field trips can interest students in the topic

"Through" activities help students as they work with the text. Teachers find reading aloud a useful strategy that gives the students an opportunity to hear a proficient reader, to get a sense of the format and story line, and to listen to the teacher "think aloud" about the reading. In the think-aloud, teachers can model how they monitor a sequence of events, identify foreshadowing and flashback, visualize a setting, analyze character and motive, comprehend mood and theme, and recognize irony and symbols (Anstrom, 1998a).

Adapted Instruction: Ways "through" Literature

- *Character review.* Specific students become a character and provide background for other students' questions throughout the reading.
- *Image/theme development.* Charts, graphs, pictures, and symbols can trace the development of images, ideas, and themes.
- *Read-along tapes.* Tapes encourage slower readers, allow absent students to catch up, and provide auditory input for students who learn through that modality.
- *Visual summaries.* Groups of students create chapter reviews, character analyses, or problem–solutions on overhead transparencies.

"Beyond" activities are designed to extend the students' appreciation of literature. These can be analytical, creative, or communicative and use language in an integrative manner to deepen comprehension and spur thoughtful reactions.

Interaction: Literature Response Groups. To help develop a community of readers and assist students in understanding the richness of the literacy experience, teachers engage them in literature response groups. After having read a piece of literature, the teacher and a small group meet to discuss the piece. Each student is given an opportunity to express ideas about the story before a general discussion begins. The teacher listens and, after each student has had a turn, opens the discussion with a thought-provoking question. As points are made, the teacher guides the students to deeper understandings by, for example, asking them to support their point with words from the text and asking what words or devices the author used to invoke a mood, establish a setting, describe a character, move the plot along, and so on.

Interaction: Maintaining the First Language. As the standards document makes clear, students are encouraged to use and develop their native language (NCTE/IRA, 1996). Teachers can use several strategies that support students' first language within the context of the classroom program. Aides and tutors can assist in explaining difficult passages and helping students summarize their understanding. Native-language books, magazines, films, and other materials relating to the topic or theme of the lesson can support and augment students' learning (Tikunoff, Ward, Romero, Lucas, Katz, Van Broekhuisen, & Castaneda, 1991). Students can also keep reading logs or journals in their native language.

Example of Concept: Primary-Language Poetry

Judith Casey (2004) encourages students to share their native language with their classmates during a poetry activity. When Ms. Casey invites students to bring in and read aloud a poem in their L1, someone always shouts out, "But we won't be able to understand them!" But she tells them that everyone can enjoy the sounds and rhythms of the various languages. On Poetry Day, the atmosphere of the class is charged. No one knows exactly what to expect but the students are excited. Amazingly, hearing each other read in their L1 lets the students see each other in a new light. The class is forever changed as students recognize the value, contributions, and abilities of their classmates.

Mathematics

The National Council of Teachers of Mathematics' (NCTM) standards document, *Principles and Standards for School Mathematics* (NCTM, 2000), provides six principles: equity, curriculum, teaching, learning, assessment, and technology. Those specifically relevant for English learners (although they are never directly addressed) include equity (high expectations and strong support for all students), teaching (challenging and supporting students to learn mathematics well), and learning (actively building new knowledge from experience and prior knowledge to learn mathematics with understanding). For non-native speakers of English, specially designed activities and teaching strategies must be incorporated into the mathematics program in order for them to have the opportunity to develop their mathematics potential.

Example of Concept: Teaching to a Standard

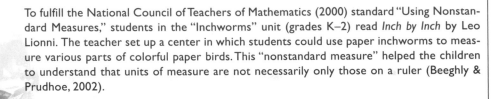

To fulfill the National Council of Teachers of Mathematics (2000) standard "Using Nonstandard Measures," students in the "Inchworms" unit (grades K–2) read *Inch by Inch* by Leo Lionni. The teacher set up a center in which students could use paper inchworms to measure various parts of colorful paper birds. This "nonstandard measure" helped the children to understand that units of measure are not necessarily only those on a ruler (Beeghly & Prudhoe, 2002).

The Language of Mathematics. Instead of being "language neutral," mathematics does in fact pose numerous problems for English learners. These difficulties lie in four major areas: vocabulary skills, syntax, semantics, and discourse features.

Vocabulary in mathematics includes words of a technical nature such as *denominator, quotient,* and *coefficient,* and words such as *rational, column,* and *table* have a meaning different from everyday usage. Often, two or more mathematical concepts combine to form a different concept: for example, *least common multiple* and *negative exponent.* The same mathematical operation can be signaled with a variety of mathematics terms: *add, and, plus, sum, combine,* and *increased by* all represent addition. Moreover, special symbols are used to stand for vocabulary terms (Dale & Cuevas, 1992).

Example of Concept: Specialized Vocabulary

Many words in mathematics are special uses of words with common meanings outside of math. *Base* is a word also used in baseball; a teacher can explain that just as it is a place to rest between plays, it can mean a surface upon which an object rests. A *yard* is a grassy area around a house, but can also be a unit for measuring this area. Developing a list of content words for each year's math instruction and explicitly teaching these words helps students to gain math literacy (Adams, 2003).

Syntax problems arise because of the complexity of the language of mathematics. Students may not recognize that a concept is made up of the relationship between two words (for example, *greater than, less than, as much as, the same as*). Complex structures such as "Twenty is five times a certain number. What is the number?" can confuse students. In addition, students often do not understand the use of the passive voice: "Nine is divided by 3," "Thirty is represented by one-half of 60" (Carrasquillo & Rodríguez, 2002).

Semantic problems occur when students are required to make inferences from natural language to the language of mathematics. For example, in the problem "Five times a number is two more than ten times the number," students must recognize that "a number" and "the number" refer to the same quantity.

Discourse features that are unlike natural language characterize the texts used in mathematics. The tendency to interrupt for the inclusion of formulae is confusing and perhaps frightening to the reader of mathematics textbooks. Such texts require a reading rate adjustment because they must be read more slowly and require multiple readings.

Adapted Instruction: Developing Mathematical Language

- Pairs or small groups of students discuss the mathematics in their everyday language and relate it to everyday uses before moving to mathematics terms and concepts.
- Use mathematical language together with appropriate actions and concrete objects.
- Relate new terms to what students already know.
- Recycle vocabulary to reinforce understanding and familiarity with the language in context.
- Verbalize the strategies used to solve problems.
- Provide both oral and written forms of new structures and vocabulary.

Source: Teaching Mathematics to ESL Students (n.d.).

Content: Learning Strategies. Metacognitive strategies are especially important during math instruction. Students who can monitor their own thinking while reading a math textbook are likely to discover for themselves when they need to reread, summarize, question, or clarify what they are reading (Unrau, 2008). Mathematics textbooks have a predictable lesson structure, consisting of the following sequence: preview concept set; present concept 1, give example of concept 1, demonstrate sample problem using concept 1; present concept 2, give example of concept 2, demonstrate sample problem using concept 2, and so on; then a problem set utilizing concepts in order of presentation, then a final problem set ranging in difficulty from those using simple algorithms to those requiring more advanced application of concepts, including bonus problems. At any point in this sequence, a student can reread, attempt problems, check for understanding, and review. Monitoring this process for comprehension is a skill that each math student can learn and use to increase success.

Connections: Using Students' Experiences. Teachers can find out from their students what activities they engage in after school and then capitalize on those for mathematics instruction. For example, those students who participate in sports can learn to calculate their batting average, points per game, race times, average speed, and so on. Older students with after-school jobs can use their pay stubs to figure the percentages of their various withholding categories (Anstrom, 1999a). Younger students may be able to assist their parents with shopping by helping to keep purchases within the budget and determine the best-priced item. They can also help calculate the tax that will be added to the total.

Comprehensibility: Modeling Technology and Other Tools. Many English learners are unfamiliar with the basic tools associated with mathematics (rulers, protractors, calculators, computers, etc.). After demonstrating each, teachers can provide students with real-life opportunities to use them. For example, students are told that the classroom needs to be recarpeted. They first have to estimate the area, then check their estimates with the actual tools (using both standard and metric measuring instruments, as they will not know which system the carpet company uses). Computer programs can also be used to provide estimates and calculations.

Comprehensibility: Differentiated Instruction. Teachers should vary the classroom instructional routine, design tasks that appeal to students' various intellectual gifts, and allow students some choice in the types of learning in which they engage. In *Mathematics Teaching Today,* NCTM makes this clear: "Students may use the Internet to research and collect data, use interactive geometry software to conduct investigations, or use graphing calculators to translate among different mathematical representations. . . . [T]eachers should use various arrangements and tools flexible to pursue their goals" (NCTM, 2007, p. 41).

Interaction: Working in Groups. Strategies for reading math texts and for supplementing students' math with language instruction involve more student interaction and small-group work. Students need to be encouraged to think aloud about mathematics and to talk with one another about the processes involved. In this way, they use language as a tool for tackling mathematics concepts. Working in groups, students can discuss with one another the activities they engage in at math centers or stations in various parts of the classroom. This gives them an opportunity to try out ideas and learn various mathematical strategies from their peers.

Re-Presenting Knowledge: Alternative Assessment. Alternative assessment requires students to perform tasks similar to those used to teach and learn the material. In mathematics, tasks such as asking students to develop a series of graphs based on student characteristics, to run a school store, or to pretend playing the stock market (Anstrom, 1999a) keep students actively engaged in mathematics while allowing the teacher to assess their understanding.

Adapted Instruction: Alternative Means of Demonstrating Math Knowledge

- Produce or find three different drawings for the number x.
- Write three story problems that have the number x as an answer.
- Find out the favorite ice cream flavor of ten people you know. Invent a way to show this information to the class.

Source: Adapted from Rowan and Bourne (1994).

In response to teachers' requests for materials that would help students of nonmainstream cultures acquire the knowledge, skills, and most importantly, dispositions to succeed in mathematics, NCTM published a series of books called *Changing the Face of Mathematics,* with separate volumes addressing adapted mathematics education for African Americans, Asian Americans and Pacific Islanders, Latinos, and multiculturalism and gender equity. For example, in the book targeted to help educators interest Native American students in mathematics (Hankes & Fast, 2002), an article describes a Rug Task designed for Navajo students that challenges them to connect the mathematic concepts of symmetry and area to the skill of weaving a rug.

Science

The *National Science Education Standards* (National Research Council, 1996) emphasize inquiry as the means for students to become scientifically literate. Inquiry is described as

> a multifaceted activity that involves making observations; posing questions; examining books and other sources of information to see what is already known; planning investigations;

Profile of an Educator:

Despite Poverty, Students Pass Advanced Math

Basil Lee teaches trigonometry at Benjamin Banneker High School in College Park, Georgia. Lee left a job as a factory manager in 1991 to work as a teacher for one-third of his previous salary. Banneker High School had not made adequate yearly progress (AYP) on No Child Left Behind measures. Students in Mr. Lee's class were poor; 63 percent of students in the school receive free or reduced-rate lunch. Sixteen-year-old Lucie Kamga took Lee's advanced algebra and trigonometry class last year. "He really cares about whether we learn or not," she says. Almost every day he would stand in front of the class and explain. He would break it down and make sure we understood it. If it wasn't for his class, I would be lost in AP calculus now" (Copeland, 2008, p. 9D).

reviewing what is already known in light of experimental evidence; using tools to gather, analyze, and interpret data; proposing answers, explanations, and predictions; and communicating the results. Inquiry requires identification of assumptions, use of critical and logical thinking, and consideration of alternative explanations. (p. 23)

Working in inquiry classrooms with English learners can be challenging but extremely rewarding for teachers who recognize the connections between inquiry and SDAIE and who organize learning activities to maximize their students' experiences. Teachers need to recognize that as English learners construct science knowledge, they have linguistic and cultural demands placed on them over and above those placed on native-English-speaking students (Kessler, Quinn, & Fathman, 1992).

Example of Concept: Scaffolded Science

Hammond (2006) defines scaffolding as "specific help that enable[s] students to engage in tasks and develop understandings that they could not do on their own" (p. 152). At the end of scaffolded instruction, students should be able to transfer their understanding and skills to new tasks with a sense of independence as learners. Instead of simplifying the curriculum, a key idea is to provide high levels of systematic support.

Hammond teaches science in a cycle, beginning with hands-on experiments and discussion, followed by students' reading and reflecting in a structured cooperative-learning format; they then make charts of key information and use these charts to write about what they have learned. This cycle distributes the responsibility for learning among peer groups in a carefully structured way.

In a paragraph about instruction for English learners, the addendum to the standards document, *Inquiry and the National Science Education Standards* (Olson & Loucks-Horsley, 2000), notes that "learner-centered environments in which teachers build new learning on the knowledge, skills, attitudes, and beliefs that students bring to the classroom, are critical to science learning of English language learners" (p. 122).

The following sections present the language of science and the problems it can pose for students. Specific strategies that need to be incorporated to facilitate English learners' science learning are then provided.

The Language of Science. The four major language areas (vocabulary, syntax, semantics, and discourse features) detailed in the section on mathematics are also relevant for science. Students not only have to learn scientific definitions of some common words they may already know (e.g., *energy, sense, work*) but they must also learn complex syntactic structures, which include passive voice, multiple embeddings, and long noun phrases (Chamot & O'Malley, 1994). Furthermore, English learners need to understand the structure of scientific text.

A number of types of text structures are common in science content materials. The *cause–effect* structure links reasons with results or actions with their consequences.

The *compare–contrast* structure examines the similarities and differences between concepts. The *time–order* structure shows a sequential relationship over the passage of time (Pérez & Torres-Guzmán, 2002). To assist in their comprehension, students can receive special training in following written instructions for procedures or experiments and can be shown ways to organize their recognition of science vocabulary.

Example of Concept: What's the Structure?

Often science texts have structures such as problem–solution, cause–effect, sequence of events, comparison, or detail–description. Students who recognize the structure of a text have an advantage in comprehension and recall. Richards and Gipe (1995) invented a game called What's the Structure? to assist students' content reading. The game is played by forming groups of six to eight students. Each group receives a game board with nine spaces (the center space has the words, "What's the Structure?"). Members of each group receive an identical card with a content passage structured in one of five ways (see above). They work together to answer the following eight questions.

1. What are the connective words and phrases in the passage? How is the information organized?
2. How do the connective words and phrases provide clues to the writing pattern or combination of patterns in the passage? What is the top-level structure?
3. Why do you think the author of this passage used this particular text structure?
4. What other text structures at lower levels, if any, are used?
5. Share some connections between the facts and concepts in the passage and your own experiences and background knowledge.
6. Create a map showing how the facts and concepts in the passage are connected to each other.
7. What are the most important ideas in the passage?
8. Write a short summary of the information in the passage.

The game is played on repeated days with each group receiving a differently structured passage.

Adapted Instruction: Developing Scientific Language

- Provide appropriate contexts for new vocabulary, syntactic structures, and discourse patterns. Isolated lists or exercises do not appear to facilitate language acquisition.
- Engage students in hands-on activities in which they discuss concepts in a genuine communicative context.
- Promote activities in which students actively debate with one another about the truth of a hypothesis or the meaning of data gathered.

Source: Adapted from Carrasquillo and Rodríguez (2002); Kessler et al. (1992).

Content: Common Themes. Organizing instruction around broad themes—such as the nature of matter, the pollution and purification of water, or the impact of drugs on the physiology and behavior of living organisms—puts science in a comprehensible context that can have relevance to students' lives. Such contextualizing increases the probability that students will continue to want to learn science on their own; extends the time a single topic is studied, thus allowing more time for understanding and reflection as well as repetition of key English words and phrases; and reduces the tendency toward superficial treatment of subjects.

In planning around themes, teachers often prepare a choice of projects for students to complete to strengthen their comprehension of difficult science material. Caution needs to be taken in developing the list of projects, however. Each project needs to be tied to a central objective. For example, if students are to understand the basic properties of a cell, the list of projects might include drawing and labeling a cell diagram, preparing an oral report on the structure and function of a cell, or summarizing the current research on cloning. Sometimes, "fun" activities do not provide equal access to central objectives and concepts. Teachers need to review project lists and be clear about the objectives.

Connections: Keeping a Science Notebook. Writing is one way students can connect with science. The science notebook is more than a place where students record data they collect, facts they learn, or procedures they conduct. "It is also a record of students' questions, predictions, claims linked to evidence, conclusions, and reflections—all structured by an investigation leading to an understanding of "big ideas" (not factoids) in science. A science notebook is a central place where language, data, and experience work together to form meaning for the student" (Klentschy, 2005, p. 24).

Example of Concept: Science Vocabulary through Music and Drama

Students in the second grade experienced the water cycle in guided imagery as they listened to Tchaikovsky's "Waltz of the Snowflakes" from the *Nutcracker Suite*. They began as a water drop, turned into vapor, condensed, and fell to ground as a snowflake. Later, students created a "sound sculpture," making different sounds for each stage of the cycle. These activities motivated a deeper interest in the science they learned as they tried to embody abstract concepts: accumulation, evaporation, and precipitation (Jacobs, Goldberg, & Bennett, 2004, pp. 93–94).

Comprehensibility: Modeling. If the teacher feels the need to lecture, a helpful strategy for English learners is to videotape the lesson. Students should be encouraged to listen to the lecture, concentrating on understanding and writing down only questions or parts of the lecture they do not understand. Later, the videotape is played and the teacher and several students take notes on the board. The teacher can model the type of outline that emphasizes the main ideas and clearly indicates supporting details. The students use whatever strategies are comfortable for them, including use of their native language. After a few minutes, the videotape is stopped and the notes compared. The discussion then highlights various note-taking strategies and provides new strategies for everyone involved. This activity can be used on a periodic basis to determine students' ability to comprehend lectures and take effective notes (Adamson, 1993).

Interaction: Talking about Lesson Content. Scientific investigation provides a natural setting for students to talk about science concepts. Discovery learning, problem posing and solving, experiments, and hypotheses testing all give students numerous opportunities to interact with various members of the class, with the teacher, and potentially with experts.

Example of Concept: Talking in Science

Debbie Zacarian described the way in which students interact with one another during a science unit about the solar system. During the first week of the solar system unit, the names of the planets were tossed into a hat. Each of nine pairs of native-English-speaking and English-learning students selected one planet and developed a poster session about their planet based on resources in the school library. After each pair presented their planet, the teacher combined pairs into small groups. Each group was to create a tenth planet based on what they had learned during the paired experience. Each group engaged in a lively discussion developing ideas about their tenth planet. After a short lesson on papier-mâché making, each group created a papier-mâché model of their planet and presented it to the class. This activity extended the amount of social and academic interactions and understandings about the content.

The Visual and Performing Arts

The visual and performing arts are often used as a medium for English learners to illustrate their understandings of concepts in other disciplines. Ideas that were originally presented in linguistic form can be translated into the artistic medium so that students can demonstrate their comprehension. However, arts lessons in themselves help students develop language skills. The *Visual and Performing Arts Standards* (CDE, 1998b) provide specific objectives and sample tasks for each of the five strands: artistic perception; creative expression; historical and cultural context; aesthetic valuing; and connections, relations, applications (p. x).

Teachers knowledgeable about SDAIE techniques can organize instruction so that it meets the content objective while addressing the needs of English learners. For example, English learners in any of the primary grades would be able to participate in the following, learning not only artistic principles but also vocabulary. For the theater objective "Replicate the sound and movement of objects, animals, and people," the following is a sample task: "After a walk around the school during which students have observed the movement of natural objects, they pantomime the actions of such objects as leaves, branches, clouds, and the animals they saw" (CDE, 1998b, p. 81). For creative expression (music), third graders need to sing or play, with increasing accuracy, a varied repertoire of music, alone and with others (CDE, 1998b, p. 58).

Obviously, songs from their own cultures can be included in this repertoire. English learners can find their culture valued as well by the objective in historical and cultural context (dance): "Learn and perform dances from their own and other cultures. After viewing a dance performed by a visiting dancer and being assisted in learning some movements to the dance, students perform the movements in unison" (p. 11). SDAIE techniques have been used successfully to introduce students to art concepts.

Physical Education

The *Physical Education Framework* (CDE, 1994) divided its seven standards into three areas: movement skills and movement knowledge, self-image and personal development, and social development. Students who participate in a high-quality physical education program can expect the following: to develop various motor skills and abilities related to lifetime leisure skills; to value the importance of maintaining a healthy lifestyle; to improve their understanding of movement and the human body; to know the rules and strategies of particular games and sports; and to gain self-confidence and a sense of self-worth in relation to physical education and recreation programs (p. vi).

Physical education is more than activity—it is "a discipline that encourages the thoughtful development of body and mind" (Unrau, 2008, p. 379). Experts in the field emphasize the connection between language and physical education, including the acquisition of a vocabulary that includes physiology (names of muscles), rules of sports, and so on. Acquiring cognitive and metacognitive strategies is as important in physical education as in other disciplines. Students can be encouraged to develop their own philosophies and plans for personal recreation, discuss healthy attitudes toward athletic participation, and debate the dangers of extreme risks. In this way, the PE class is focused on the development of the whole student and the acquisition of lifelong dispositions and habits (Griffin & Morgan, 1998).

California's Standard 7 pertains to the interrelationship between history and culture and games, sports, play, and dance. Teachers can elicit from students what they know about their own cultures' games, sports, and so on; invite guest speakers to demonstrate various activities; and build their curriculum from their students' own knowledge base.

Additionally, physical education activities can be carefully structured to motivate students' cooperation and sense of group cohesiveness. This is particularly important in a class in which English learners of various cultures are together.

Example of Concept: Modeling and Working Together

According to Debbie Zacarian, a physical education teacher helped an English learner by modeling and placing the student with carefully selected peers. When Tien attended his first PE class in the United States, he was not sure what to do. Fortunately, his teacher used many physical movements to model the desired activities, enabling Tien to follow along and imitate the movements. When the teacher separated the class into teams, he carefully placed Tien with two students who modeled the volleyball activity. Tien continued to participate because he was able to see what he needed to do to be successful in class.

Instructional Needs beyond the Classroom

To be successful in their academic courses, English learners often need assistance from organizations and volunteers outside of the classroom. This assistance can come from academic summer programs, additional instructional services such as after-school programs and peer tutoring, and Dial-a-Teacher for homework help in English and in the primary language. Support in the affective domain may include special home visits by released-time teachers, counselors, or outreach workers and informal counseling by teachers.

Example of Concept: Meeting Instructional Needs beyond the Classroom

Escalante and Dirmann (1990) profiled the Garfield High School calculus course in which Escalante achieved outstanding success in preparing Hispanic students to pass the Advanced Placement (AP) calculus examination. Escalante was the organizer of a broad effort to promote student success. In his classroom, he set the parameters: He made achievement a game for the students, the "opponent" being the Educational Testing Service's examination; he coached students to hold up under the pressure of the contest and work hard to win; and he held students accountable for attendance and productivity. But beyond this work in the classroom was community support.

Community individuals and organizations donated copiers, computers, transportation, and souvenirs such as special caps and team jackets. Parents helped Escalante emphasize proper conduct, respect, and value for education. Past graduates served as models of achievement, giving pep talks to students and hosting visits to high-tech labs. The support from these other individuals combined to give students more help and encouragement than could be provided by the classroom teacher alone. The results were dramatized in the feature film *Stand and Deliver.*

Escalante's successful AP calculus program at Garfield High School involved much more than excellent classroom instruction. It is not surprising that the five key features of SDAIE were incorporated in his teaching: *content* and *language* teaching, the latter through an extensive attention to specific mathematics vocabulary; *connections* between the math curriculum and the students' lives and development of appropriate schema when background was lacking; *comprehensibility* through use of realia and visual support for instruction and modification of teacher talk; *interaction* with one another through cooperative learning; and *teacher attitude,* a positive coaching approach that conveyed high expectations. This is the instructional enhancement that opens the door to success for English learners. ■

LEARNING MORE

Further Reading

Making Content Comprehensible for English Language Learners (Echevarria et al., 2004) presents the sheltered instruction observation protocol (SIOP) model, a tool for observing and quantifying a teacher's implementation of quality sheltered instruction.

Web Search

Visit the Website of the professional organization of your field or of the field that interests you the most. Search under "English learners" to find what standards, criteria, lessons, and advice are provided.

Exploration

Using the SDAIE model observation form, elicit from a number of teachers at your site specific activities, approaches, and methods they use. If possible, observe the teachers and together discuss the lessons and their results for English learners.

Discussion

You firmly believe in the use of cooperative learning and seat your students in tables of four in your classroom. Students with special education Individualized Educational Plans (IEPs) who are mainstreamed, some of whom are English learners, are mixed with other students, including other English learners. However, parents of some students have contacted you to express concerns that their students are more occupied teaching others than learning new things (Brahier, 2009). What arguments can you use to continue your practice of heterogeneous grouping?

PEARSON
The Power of Classroom Practice
www.myeducationlab.com

Literature for a Range of Learners Part 2

Roberta Sejnost discusses how to use both fiction and nonfiction in all three steps of the reading process. A teacher talks about how she chooses articles to use with her students. Her class discusses an article and practices finding the main idea.

> To access the video, go to MyEducationLab (www.myeducationlab.com), choose the Díaz-Rico and Weed text, and log in to MyEducationLab for English Language Learners. Select the topic Content Area Reading and Writing, and watch the video entitled "Literature for a Range of Learners Part 2."

Answer the following questions:
1. How does the teacher accommodate the needs of learners who might not be able to benefit from a grade-level reading text?
2. Where does the teacher look for resources to match the thematic content of a unit?
3. What steps does the teacher use to help students find the main idea?

chapter

6 Theories and Methods of Bilingual Education

Dual-language immersion bilingual education employs two languages for academic purposes.

When we hear the child speak, we see only what is above the surface of the water, the water lily itself. But the roots of the mother tongue lie deep beneath the surface, in the more or less unconsciously acquired connotative and non-verbal meanings. When the child learns a foreign language, that language easily becomes . . . a splendid water lily on the surface which superficially may look just as beautiful as the water lily of the mother tongue. . . . But it is often the case that for

a very long time the second language is a water lily more or less floating on the surface without roots.

If at this stage we allow ourselves to be deceived by the beautiful water lily of the foreign language into thinking that the child knows this language . . . well enough to be able to be educated through it . . . the development of the flower of the mother tongue may easily be interrupted. If education in a foreign language poses a threat to the development of the mother tongue, or leads to its neglect, then the roots of the mother tongue will not be sufficiently nourished or they may gradually be cut off altogether.... [A] situation may gradually develop in which the child will only have two surface flowers, two languages, neither of which she commands in the way a monolingual would command her mother tongue. ... And if the roots have been cut off, nothing permanent can grow any more.

Tove Skutnabb-Kangas (1981, pp. 52–53)

Bilingual education has existed in the United States since the colonial period, but over the more than two centuries of U.S. history it has been alternately embraced and rejected. The immigrant languages and cultures in North America have enriched the lives of the people in American communities, yet periodic waves of language restrictionism have virtually eradicated the capacity of most U.S. citizens to speak a foreign or second language, even those who are born into families with a heritage language other than English. For English learners, English-only schooling has often brought difficulties, cultural suppression, and discrimination even as English has been touted as the key to patriotism and success.

In many parts of the world, people are not considered well educated unless they are schooled in multiple languages. Many young people in the United States enter school fluent in a primary language other than English, a proficiency that can function as a resource. Programs that assist students to sustain fluency and develop academic competence in their heritage language offer bilingual education in its best sense. Exemplary bilingual education programs are explicitly bicultural as well so that students' natural cultures as well as their heritage languages can be fostered.

Despite the argument—and the evidence—that bilingual education helps students whose home language is not English to succeed in school, bilingual education continues to be an area of contention. Figure 6.1 presents ten common misconceptions about bilingual education.

The challenge to any English-language-development program is to cherish and preserve the rich cultural and linguistic heritage of the students as they acquire English. One means of preserving and supplementing the home languages of our nation's children is through bilingual instruction (see figure on page 67).

In this chapter, three important areas of bilingual education are discussed: (1) the foundations of bilingual education, bilingual education's legal evolution, issues related to educating students in two languages, and the role of teachers, students, parents, and the community; (2) various organizational models currently used in the United States; and (3) instructional strategies.

Foundations of Bilingual Education

Progress in bilingual education in the United States has taken place on three fronts: cultural, legislative, and judicial. Culturally, the people of the United States have seemed to accept bilingualism when it has been economically useful and to reject it

Figure 6.1   Ten Common Fallacies about Bilingual Education

Since its inception, bilingual education has been controversial. Although much research has documented its potential benefits, many people in the United States hold misconceptions about bilingual education that run counter to research findings. Ten such common fallacies are presented below.

Fallacy 1: English is losing ground to other languages in the United States.

In fact, there are more speakers of English in the United States than ever before. Between 1980 and 1990, the number of immigrants who spoke non-English languages at home increased by 59 percent, while the portion of this population that spoke English very well rose by 93 percent (Waggoner, 1995).

Fallacy 2: Newcomers to the United States are learning English more slowly now than in previous generations.

Although the number of minority-language speakers is projected to grow well into the twenty-first century, the number of bilinguals fluent in both English and another language is growing even faster. About three in four Hispanic immigrants, after fifteen years in this country, speak English on a daily basis, while 70 percent of their children become dominant or monolingual in English (Veltman, 1988).

Fallacy 3: The best way to learn a language is through "total immersion."

There is no credible evidence to support the claim that children who are exposed to all-English instruction learn more English. According to Krashen (1996), L2 input must be comprehensible to promote L2 acquisition. If students are left to sink or swim in mainstream classrooms, they learn neither English well nor the subject matter—they need native-language support and instruction to make lessons meaningful.

Fallacy 4: Children learning English are retained too long in bilingual classrooms, at the expense of English acquisition.

Well-designed bilingual programs present knowledge and skills about subject matter in the native language that transfer to English, as well as actually teaching English. Therefore, time spent in primary-language instruction does not detract from learning English.

Fallacy 5: School districts provide bilingual instruction in many different native languages.

Rarely are there sufficient numbers of each language group in a school district to make bilingual instruction practical for every language; nor are there qualified teachers to make this possible. For example, in 1994 immigrants from 136 different countries enrolled in the public schools in California, but bilingual teachers were certified in only seventeen languages, 96 percent of them in Spanish (CDE, 1995).

Fallacy 6: Bilingual education means instruction mainly in students' native languages, with little instruction in English.

In fact, the vast majority of U.S. bilingual education programs promote an early exit to mainstream English-language classrooms, whereas only a tiny fraction of programs are designed to maintain the native tongues of students.

Fallacy 7: Bilingual education is far more costly than English-language instruction.

All programs serving English learners—regardless of the language of instruction—require additional staff training, instructional materials, and administration. So they all cost a little more than regular programs for native-English speakers. In-class approaches to L1 maintenance and English-language development are the most cost-effective.

Fallacy 8: Disproportionate dropout rates for Hispanic students demonstrate the failure of bilingual education.

Bilingual programs touch only a small minority of Hispanic children. Other factors, such as recent arrival in the United States, family poverty, limited English proficiency, low academic achievement, and being retained in grade, place Hispanic students at much greater risk.

Fallacy 9: Research is inconclusive on the benefits of bilingual education.

Meta-analysis, an objective method that reviews a wide range of studies to weigh numerous variables, has yielded positive findings about bilingual education (Greene, 1998; Willig, 1985).

Fallacy 10: Language-minority parents do not support bilingual education, because they feel it is more important for their children to learn English than to maintain the native language.

Truly bilingual programs seek to cultivate proficiency in both tongues, and research has shown that students' native language can be maintained and developed at no cost to English. When polled on the principles underlying bilingual education, a majority of parents are strongly in favor of maintenance bilingual programs (Krashen, 1996).

Source: Crawford (1998).

when immigrants were seen as a threat. In periods when the economic fortunes of the United States were booming, European immigrants were welcome and their languages were not forbidden. (Immigrants of color, however, faced linguistic and cultural barriers as they strove for assimilation.)

In times of recession, war, or national threat, immigrants, cultures, and languages were restricted or forbidden. Periodically throughout history, English has been proposed as the national language. Although the United States has no official language, twenty-three states have passed laws proclaiming English as official (Crawford, 2003).

Because the states reserve the right to dictate educational policy, bilingual education has depended on the vagaries of state law. When the U.S. Congress enacted legislation to begin Title VII of the Elementary and Secondary Education Act, federal funding became available for bilingual education programs. Almost simultaneously, the courts began to rule that students deprived of bilingual education must receive compensatory services. Together, the historical precedents, federal legislative initiatives, and judicial fiats combined to establish bilingual education in the United States. However, it has been left to the individual states to implement such programs, and this has at times caused conflict.

Historical Development of Bilingual Education

Early Bilingualism. At the time of the nation's founding, at least twenty languages could be heard in the American colonies, including Dutch, French, German, and numerous Native-American languages. In 1664 at least eighteen colonial languages were spoken on Manhattan Island. Bilingualism was common among both the working and educated classes, and schools were established to preserve the linguistic heritage of new arrivals. The Continental Congress published many official documents in German and French as well as in English. German schools were operating as early as 1694 in Philadelphia, and by 1900 more than 4 percent of the United States' elementary school population was receiving instruction either partially or exclusively in German. In 1847, Louisiana authorized instruction in French, English, or both on the request of parents. The Territory of New Mexico authorized Spanish–English bilingual education in 1850 (Crawford, 1999).

Language Restrictionism. Although there were several such pockets of acceptance for bilingual education, other areas of the country effectively restricted or even attempted to eradicate immigrant and minority languages. Under an 1828 treaty, the U.S. government recognized the language rights of the Cherokee tribe. Eventually, the Cherokees established a twenty-one-school educational system that used the Cherokee syllabary to achieve a 90 percent literacy rate in the native language. In 1879, however, the federal government forced the Native-American children to attend off-reservation, English-only schools where they were punished for using their native language. In the East, as large numbers of Jews, Italians, and Slavs immigrated, descendants of the English settlers began to harbor resentment against these newcomers. New waves of Mexican and Asian immigration in the West brought renewed fear of non-English influences. Public and private schools in the new U.S. territories of the Philippines and Puerto Rico were forced to use English as the language of instruction (Crawford, 1999).

World War I brought anti-German hysteria, and various states began to criminalize the use of German in all areas of public life (Cartagena, 1991). As World War I ended, Ohio passed legislation to remove all uses of German from the state's elementary schools, and mobs raided schools and burned German textbooks. Subsequently, fifteen states legislated English as the basic language of instruction. This repressive policy continued in World War II, when Japanese-language schools were closed. Until the late 1960s, "Spanish detention"—being kept after school for using Spanish—remained a formal punishment in the Rio Grande Valley of Texas, where using a language other than English as a medium of public instruction was a crime (Crawford, 1999).

Assimilationism. Although the U.S. Supreme Court, in the *Meyer v. Nebraska* case (1923), extended the protection of the Constitution to everyday speech and prohibited coercive language restriction on the part of the states, the "frenzy of Americanization" (Crawford, 1999) had fundamentally changed public attitudes toward learning in other languages. European immigrant groups felt strong pressures to assimilate, and bilingual instruction by the late 1930s was virtually eradicated throughout the United States. Discrimination and cultural repression became associated with linguistic repression.

After World War II, writers began to speak of language-minority children as being "culturally deprived" and "linguistically disabled." The cultural deprivation theory rejected genetic explanations for low school achievement for English learners and pointed to such environmental factors as inadequate English-language skills, lower-class values, and parental failure to stress educational attainment. On the basis of their performance on IQ tests administered in English, a disproportionate number of English learners ended up in special classes for the educationally handicapped.

The Rebirth of Bilingual Education. Bilingual education was reborn in the early 1960s in Dade County, Florida, as Cuban immigrants, fleeing the 1959 revolution, requested bilingual schooling for their children. The first program at the Coral Way Elementary School was open to both English and Spanish speakers. The objective was fluency and literacy in both languages. Subsequent evaluations of this bilingual program showed success both for English-speaking students in English and Spanish-speaking students in Spanish and English. Hakuta (1986) reported that by 1974 there were 3,683 students in bilingual programs in the elementary schools nationwide and approximately 2,000 in the secondary schools.

The focus of bilingual education on dual-language immersion and developmental bilingualism that had been featured in the Dade County bilingual programs was altered when the federal government passed the Bilingual Education Act of 1968 (Title VII, an amendment to the 1965 Elementary and Secondary Education Act). This act was explicitly compensatory. Children who were unable to speak English were considered to be educationally disadvantaged, and bilingual education was to provide the resources to compensate for the "handicap" of not speaking English.

Thus, from its outset, federal aid to bilingual education was seen as a "remedial" program rather than an innovative approach to language instruction (Wiese & García, 1998). The focus shifted again in 1989, when developmental bilingual programs were expanded. Maintaining and developing the native language of students became an important goal for bilingual education.

The English-as-Official-Language Movement. In the early 1980s, during a period of concern about new immigration, a movement arose to seek the establishment of English as the nation's official language. The goals of the English-only movement are the adoption of a constitutional amendment to make English the official language of the United States, repeal of laws mandating multilingual ballots and voting materials, restriction of bilingual funding to short-term transition programs, and universal enforcement of the English language and civics requirement for naturalization (Cartagena, 1991).

Emergence of a New Nativism. Many U.S. communities are feeling the pressure not only of increased immigration but also of immigration from underdeveloped nations. (See Chapter 1 for demographic trends.) Since the mid-1980s, language loyalties have become a subtle means of reframing racial politics, and bilingual education has become an integral part of the issue. Bilingual education is a subject that is bound up with individual and group identity, status, intellect, culture, and nationalism.

Maceri (2007) points out the difficulty some Americans have with the concept of dual-language use. Although 47 million residents of the United States speak a language other than English at home, according to figures of the U.S. Census, the presence of these languages is a problem for Americans who believe in the concept of one language, one country. The most serious concern is caused by the preponderance of Spanish, which some people see as challenging the supremacy of English. The presence of the Spanish language in banks, ATMs, hospitals, and even some government services may create the image that one does not have to learn English. Maceri notes:

> Although it is true that some services are available in Spanish, not speaking English means a very limited horizon and few opportunities. However, these days some third-generation Americans are beginning to [regret] having lost the language of their grandparents. . . . Now they try to correct it and study some of these languages in school as they try to recapture their roots. (p. 15)

Bilingualism in the Modern World. Many countries in today's world are officially bilingual, including Canada, Belgium, Finland, Cameroon, Peru, and Singapore. Official bilingualism, however, does not imply that all inhabitants of a country are bilingual; it simply means that more than one language may be used in government or education. But as the world becomes progressively smaller and more and more regions interact in economic, political, and cultural exchanges, bilingualism, and even multilingualism, has become a fact of daily life. In the global society, proficiency in more than one language is a highly desirable trait—what Cook (1999) called *multicompetent language use.*

Legal Evolution

The use of English and other languages in public life, particularly language use in the schools, has been affected by "cycles of liberalism and intolerance" (Trueba, 1989) in which conflicting beliefs and policies about language have influenced legislation and judicial actions. Together, Congress and the state and federal courts have supported bilingual education through a combination of federal mandates and legal protections for the rights of non-English-speaking students.

Federal Law and Judicial Decisions. Since the initial legislation in 1968, there have been six reauthorizations of the Bilingual Education Act (1974, 1978, 1984, 1988, 1994, and 2001). The 2001 reauthorization was contained within the No Child Left Behind Act (2002). Numerous court cases have upheld or clarified the rights of English language learners.

Title VI of the Civil Rights Act (1964) set a minimum standard for the education of any student by prohibiting discrimination on the basis of race, color, or national origin in the operation of a federally assisted program (National Clearinghouse for English Language Acquisition [NCELA], 2002). The Title VI regulatory requirements have been interpreted to prohibit denial of equal access to education because of an English learner's limited proficiency in English (U.S. Office for Civil Rights, 1999).

The Bilingual Education Act of 1968 was the first federal law relating to bilingual education. It authorized $7.5 million to finance seventy-six projects serving 27,000 children. The purpose of these funds was to support education programs, train teachers and aides, develop and disseminate instructional materials, and encourage parental involvement.

The May 25 Memorandum from the U.S. Office for Civil Rights (1970) informed school districts with more than 5 percent national-origin minority children that the district had to offer some kind of special language instruction for students with a limited command of English, prohibited the assignment of students to classes for the handicapped on the basis of their English-language skills, prohibited placing such students in vocational tracks instead of teaching them English, and mandated that administrators communicate with parents in a language they can understand.

Serna v. Portales Municipal Schools (1972) was the first case in which the federal courts began to enforce Title VI of the Civil Rights Act. A federal judge ordered instruction in native language and culture as part of a desegregation plan.

Lau v. Nichols (1974) was a landmark case in which the U.S. Supreme Court ruled:

> There is no equality of treatment merely by providing students with the same facilities, textbooks, teachers and curriculum, for students who do not understand English are effectively foreclosed from any meaningful education.

Lau v. Nichols made illegal those educational practices that excluded children from effective education on the basis of language. By finding school districts in violation of a student's civil rights based on discriminatory *effect*, rather than on proof of discriminatory *intent,* it extended the protection afforded under the *Brown v. Board of Education* decision to language-minority students under Title VI of the 1964 Civil Rights Act.

Moreover, *Lau v. Nichols* assumed that private individuals—the Chinese-speaking students in San Francisco for whose benefit the lawsuit was put forward—could sue for discriminatory effect to ensure that the mandates of Title VI were met. This last assumption was subsequently overturned in *Alexander v. Sandoval* (2001), when the U.S. Supreme Court ruled that private individuals could sue successfully under Title VI only if discriminatory intent could be proved (see Moran, 2004).

To further define the civil rights of students, the Equal Education Opportunities Act (EEOA) of 1974 states the following:

> No state shall deny equal educational opportunities to an individual on account of his or her race, color, sex, or national origin by the failure of an educational agency to take appropriate action to overcome language barriers that impede equal participation by its students in its instructional programs.

The 1974 reauthorization of Title VII specifically linked equal educational opportunity to bilingual education. Bilingual education was defined as "instruction given in, and study of, English, and, to the extent necessary to allow a child to progress effectively through the educational system, the native language" (Bilingual Education Act, 1974, p. 2).

Other changes in the legislation included eliminating poverty as a requirement; mentioning Native-American children as an eligible population; providing for English-speaking children to enroll in bilingual education programs; and funding for programs for teacher training, technical assistance for program development, and development and dissemination of instructional materials (Bilingual Education Act, 1974).

The 1975 *Lau Remedies* were guidelines from the U.S. Commissioner of Education that told districts how to identify and evaluate children with limited English skills, what instructional treatments to use, when to transfer children to all-English classrooms, and what professional standards teachers need to meet (U.S. Office for Civil Rights, 1976).

Ríos v. Read (1977) was a federal court decision that a New York school district had violated the rights of English learners by providing a bilingual program that was based mainly on ESL and that included no cultural component (Crawford, 1999). Although no specific remedy was mandated, the U.S. Office for Civil Rights began to visit school districts with large numbers of English learners to ensure that districts met their responsibilities.

Between 1974 and subsequent reauthorizations, public opinion moved toward an assimilationist position, that public funds should be used for English-language acquisition and assimilation toward the mainstream (Crawford, 1999). The 1978 Title VII reauthorization added to the definition of bilingual education: Instruction in English should allow children to achieve competence in English and English-speaking students in bilingual programs were to help children with limited English proficiency to improve their English-language skills. Additionally, parents were included in program planning, and personnel in bilingual programs were to be proficient in the language of instruction and English (Wiese & García, 1998).

Castañeda v. Pickard (1981) tested the EEOA statute. The Fifth Circuit Court outlined three criteria for programs serving English learners. District programs must be (1) based on "sound educational theory," (2) "implemented effectively" through adequately trained personnel and sufficient resources, and (3) evaluated as effective in overcoming language barriers. Qualified bilingual teachers must be employed, and children are not to be placed on the basis of English-language achievement tests. The outcome of the *Idaho Migrant Council v. Board of Education* (1981) case was a mandate that state agencies are empowered to supervise the implementation of federal EEOA requirements at the local level.

Plyler v. Doe (1982) was a Supreme Court decision stating that under the Fourteenth Amendment a state cannot deny school enrollment to children of illegal immigrants (NCELA, 1996). *Keyes v. School District #1* (1983) established due process for remedies of EEOA matters.

The 1984 reauthorization of Title VII provided for two types of bilingual programming: transitional and developmental. Thus, for the first time, the goal of bilingual education was competence in two languages. However, limited funding was provided for these programs (NCELA, 2002).

Gómez v. Illinois State Board of Education (1987) was a court decision that gave state school boards the power to enforce state and federal compliance with EEOA regulations. Children must not sit in classrooms where they cannot understand instruction, and districts must properly serve students who are limited in English. In none of the rulings did the courts mandate a specific program format, but in all they clearly upheld the notion that children must have equal access to the curriculum.

The Title VII reauthorization of 1988 increased funding to state education agencies, placed a three-year limit on participation in transitional bilingual programs, and created fellowship programs for professional training (NCELA, 2002).

The Improving America's Schools Act (IASA; 1994) amended and reauthorized the Elementary and Secondary Education Act of 1965 within the framework of the Goals 2000: Educate America Act (1994). The comprehensive educational reforms called for in Goals 2000 entailed reconfiguration of Title VII programs, with new provisions for reinforcing professional development programs, increasing attention to language maintenance and foreign-language instruction, improving research and evaluation at state and local levels, supplying additional funds for immigrant education, and allowing participation of some private school students. IASA also modified eligibility requirements for services under Title I so that English learners became eligible for services under that program on the same basis as other students (U.S. Office for Civil Rights, 1999).

Title III of the most recent reauthorization of ESEA, the No Child Left Behind (NCLB) Act of 2001, provides funding for language instruction programs for limited-English-proficient and immigrant students, provided these students "meet the same challenging State academic content and student academic achievement standards as all children are expected to meet" (NCLB, Title III, Part A, Sec. 3102. Purposes [1]). However, the program has been criticized for its rigid adherence to standards without providing additional financial assistance to schools with large populations of English learners.

According to James Crawford, executive director of the National Association for Bilingual Education, the No Child Left Behind Act

> does little to address the most formidable obstacles to the achievement [of English learners]: resource inequities, critical shortages of teachers trained to serve ELLs, inadequate instructional materials, substandard school facilities, and poorly designed instructional programs. Meanwhile, its emphasis on short-term test results—backed up by punitive sanctions for schools—is narrowing the curriculum, encouraging excessive amounts of test preparation, undercutting best practices based on scientific research, demoralizing dedicated educators, and pressuring schools to abandon programs that have proven successful for ELLs over the long term. (Crawford, 2004a, pp. 2–3)

Instead of supporting bilingual instruction, NCLB heavily emphasizes English-language proficiency not only for students but also for teachers, who must be certified in written and oral English. The elimination of federal support for bilingual education represents the culmination of several decades of heated debate, among lawmakers and educators, as well as the general public. Arguments against bilingual education have often centered on the effectiveness of bilingual instruction in teaching English, with no attention given to the potential benefits of bilingualism or primary language use and maintenance (Peregoy & Boyle, 2008, p. 21).

The online article *Federal Policy, Legislation, and Education Reform: The Promise and the Challenge for Language Minority Students* (Anstrom, 1996), provides a clear discussion of educational reform and the challenges faced by English learners, chiefly whether they will have access to the kind of curricula and instruction necessary for them to achieve the high standards stipulated by government mandates. In sum, the kinds of legislative support for bilingual education changed according to the social politics of each era. As Freeman (2004) reported,

> During the 1960s and 1970s, the dominant discourses emphasized tolerance, civil rights, and inclusion. Bilingual education was encouraged, but no particular model or program type was endorsed. During the 1980s, we saw increasing English-only activity across the country, and Title VII supported bilingual and/or English programs that emphasized a quick transition to English. In the 1990s, we saw competing discourses about linguistic and cultural diversity on the national level as well as increasing support for dual-language programs at school. (p. 25)

State Law. Although federal protections of the rights of English learners continue, many states are at present more concerned about achieving compliance with federal NCLB mandates than about safeguarding their requirements regarding bilingual education. Educational agencies operate under legislative provisions for limited-English-proficient-student instructional programs in each specific state; these provisions may specify ELD instructional programs, bilingual/dual-language instructional programs, or both.

In 1998, California, with a school enrollment of approximately 1.4 million limited-English-proficient children, passed Proposition 227, a measure rejecting bilingual education. The proposition stipulates that

> all children in California public schools shall be taught English by being taught in English. In particular, this shall require that all children be placed in English language classrooms. Children who are English learners shall be educated through sheltered English immersion during a temporary transition period not normally intended to exceed one year. . . . Once English learners have acquired a good working knowledge of English, they shall be transferred to English language mainstream classrooms. (California State Code of Regulations [CSCR], 1998, Article 2, 305)

Article 3, Provision 310, of the CSCR provided parents with waiver possibilities if their children met criteria spelled out in the law: "Under such parental waiver conditions, children may be transferred to classes where they are taught English and other subjects through bilingual education techniques or other generally recognized educational methodologies permitted by law."

Unfortunately, laws such as this one often result in a lack of support for the education of English learners. Dismantling bilingual education and expecting children to learn English (along with academic subjects) in a single year flies in the face of contemporary research on language acquisition (see, in particular, Collier, 1995). After thirty-five years of legislation supporting the rights of English learners, it can only be assumed that such laws will be found to infringe on students' rights.

Educational Issues Involving Bilingual Education

What obligation does a community have toward newcomers—in particular, non-native, non-English-speaking children? When education is the only means of achieving social mobility for the children of immigrants, these young people must be given the tools necessary to participate in the community at large. When school dropout rates exceed 50 percent among minority populations, it seems evident that the schools are not providing an adequate avenue of advancement. Clearly, some English learners do succeed: Asian-American students are overrepresented in college attendance, whereas Hispanics are underrepresented.

The success or failure of ethnic minority students has caused concern and has prompted various explanations for students' mixed performances. A *genetic inferiority* argument assumes that certain populations do not possess the appropriate genes for high intellectual performance. The *cultural deficit* explanation attributes lower academic achievement to deficiencies in the minority culture. The *cultural mismatch* perspective maintains that cultures vary and that some of the skills learned in one culture may transfer to a second but that other skills will be of little value or, worse, will interfere with assimilation to the new culture. The *contextual interaction* explanation posits that achievement is a function of the interaction between two cultures—that the values of each are not static, but adapt to each other when contact occurs.

In schools, three phenomena occur in which language-minority students are disproportionately represented: underachievement, dropping out, and overachievement. In response to the perception that some students underachieve or overachieve or drop out or are pushed out, schools have designed various mechanisms to help students succeed. Some of these have been successful, others problematic.

Underachievement. Several measures of achievement reveal discrepancies in the achievement of Whites in comparison with ethnic minorities. On the Scholastic Assessment Test in 2003, the average score for Whites on the verbal subtest was 529, whereas those of all ethnic minority groups (Hispanic, Black, Mexican American, Puerto Rican, Asian American, and American Indian) were between 48 and 97 points lower. With the exception of Asian Americans (average score 575), all ethnic groups were lower than Whites (534) on the mean score of the mathematics subtest (College Entrance Examination Board, 2003).

Ethnic minority groups, except for Asian Americans, attain lower levels of education. Hispanic Americans, for example, are particularly hard hit by the phenomenon of educational underachievement. In 2001, of the 62 percent of high-school graduates who attended college, 54.6 percent were White and only 5.6 percent were of Hispanic origin (National Center for Education Statistics [NCES], 2003a).

In addition, Hispanic Americans represent only a small number of faculty members and administrators in higher education; they hold 3.3 percent of such positions

(NCES, 2003b). Low educational levels have resulted in poor subsequent incomes and a lower likelihood of high-prestige occupations.

It is unclear that underachievement is the real problem. Even ethnic minorities who achieve in school may not be able to attain positions of responsibility in society. It is equally unclear to what extent English proficiency—or lack of it—is linked to underachievement and discrimination.

Dropouts. There is a disparity in graduation and dropout rates among various ethnic groups in the United States.* An important marketplace repercussion of graduation and dropout statistics is the differential rate of employment of these two groups: Sixty-one percent of high-school dropouts are in the labor force versus 80 percent of graduates who were not in college (Kaufman, Alt, & Chapman, 2004).

In fact, recent data show that the school districts serving the nation's largest cities have shockingly high dropout rates; only 52 percent—about one half—of students in the principal school systems in America's fifty largest cities complete high school with a diploma. Using a measure called the cumulative promotion index, researchers estimated the likelihood that a ninth-grader would complete high school on time with a regular diploma. Four districts—Baltimore, Cleveland, Detroit, and Indianapolis—had less than 32 percent. Clearly, to be young and urban in the United States is to be educationally at risk. Limited-English-proficient students drop out of school at a rate five times as high (51 percent) as their English-speaking peers, citing lack of English language knowledge as the primary reason for leaving school early (Rahilly & Weinmann, 2007).

Example of Concept: Segregation and Dropping Out

The predominantly Puerto Rican community in North Philadelphia is located in an economically depressed part of the city that is plagued by many of the problems of low-income urban neighborhoods across the United States. Latinos make up between 85 and 99 percent of the total student population in this community, and the Latino dropout rate is disproportionately high in the district. According to a Harvard University report that examined issues of racial justice in the United States, such segregation of Latinos in poorly performing schools in low-income neighborhoods is pervasive in cities in the Northeast (Harvard Civil Rights Project, online at www.civilrightsproject.harvard.edu/research/reseg03/resegregation03.php) (Freeman, 2004, p. 88).

Many English learners who are new immigrants to the United States are not prepared for the racism, anger, and suspicion they face. A persistent myth is that immigrants can achieve the "American dream" through hard work and determination. In reality, immigrants face barriers such as the need to work multiple low-paying jobs to provide for their families, lack of access to English classes, separation from their

---

*A Harvard University report released March 23, 2005, claimed nearly half of the Latino and African-American students who should have graduated from California high schools in 2002 failed to complete their education. The Harvard report said that current education policies—including those that require annual standardized testing of students—may exacerbate the dropout crisis by creating "unintended incentives for school officials to push out low-achieving students" (Helfand, 2005, p. A26).

home culture, and ethnocentrism. One study reported that Latino students who dropped out of school did so because of discrimination: They felt they were "not part of the school or the classroom . . . being treated as if they were less worthy than other students" (Valdes, 2007, p. 31).

Noting the alarmingly high percentage of Hispanic dropouts, U.S. Secretary of Education Richard W. Riley in 1995 initiated a special project to study issues related to the problem. In its final report, *No More Excuses,* the Hispanic Dropout Project (1998) highlighted the continuing stereotypes, myths, and excuses that surround Hispanic-American youth and their families:

> What we saw and what people told us confirmed what well-established research has also found: Popular stereotypes—which would place the blame for school dropout on Hispanic students, their families, and language background, and that would allow people to shrug their shoulders as if to say that that was an enormous, insoluble problem or one that would go away by itself—are just plain wrong. (p. 3)

The Hispanic Dropout Project found that teachers may make one of two choices that undermine minority students' school achievement: either to blame the students and their families for school failure or to excuse the students' poor performance, citing factors such as low socioeconomic status or lack of English proficiency (Lockwood, 2000). The three recommendations the report made for teachers are consistent with the principles, concepts, and strategies outlined in this text: (1) provide high-quality curriculum and instruction—methods and strategies provided in Part Two of this book; (2) become knowledgeable about students and their families, as discussed in Part Four of this book; and (3) receive high-quality professional development—an ongoing task for which this entire text can be an impetus. The online article *Transforming Education for Hispanic Youth: Exemplary Practices, Programs, and Schools* (Lockwood & Secada, 1999) provides more in-depth information about, and examples of, exemplary schools for Hispanic-American youth.

Overachievement. An equally pernicious view ascribes exceptional achievement to a specific group, such as is the case for Asian Americans. The term *model minority* has been evoked for Asian Americans, connoting a supergroup whose members have succeeded in U.S. society despite a long history of racial oppression.

Example of Concept: Seeing Beyond the Myth

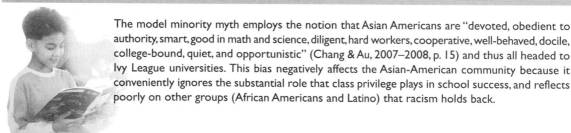

The model minority myth employs the notion that Asian Americans are "devoted, obedient to authority, smart, good in math and science, diligent, hard workers, cooperative, well-behaved, docile, college-bound, quiet, and opportunistic" (Chang & Au, 2007–2008, p. 15) and thus all headed to Ivy League universities. This bias negatively affects the Asian-American community because it conveniently ignores the substantial role that class privilege plays in school success, and reflects poorly on other groups (African Americans and Latino) that racism holds back.

This stereotype plays out in at least two ways with equally damaging results. First, ascribing a "whiz kid" image to students can mask their individual needs and problems and lead the teacher to assume a student needs little or no help. This may ultimately lead to neglect, isolation, delinquency, or inadequate preparation for the labor market among these students (Feng, 1994). Second, by lumping all Asian Americans together into this stereotype, it ignores the different cultural, language, economic, and immigration status of the various groups and severely limits those most in need of help.

Among Southeast-Asian students, the Khmer and the Lao have a grade point average (GPA) below that of White majority students, whereas Vietnamese, Chinese Vietnamese, Japanese, Korean, Chinese, and Hmong students are well above this GPA (Trueba, Cheng, & Ima, 1993).

Bias toward Asian Americans has also been found in college admissions. When voters in several states passed measures that ended affirmative action programs as a basis for college admissions, Asian-American enrollment increased significantly, indicating that race-conscious admission policies actually had unfairly held Asian Americans to higher standards of performance to gain entrance to universities (Schmidt, 2008).

Adapted Instruction: Countering the Model Minority Myth

To avoid reenacting the model minority myth in the classroom,

- Treat students as individuals.
- Do not ascribe high or low expectations based on national origin or ethnicity.
- Recognize that Asian-/Pacific-American students speak different languages and come from different cultural areas.

Source: Nash (1991).

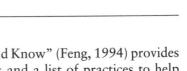

"Asian-American Children: What Teachers Should Know" (Feng, 1994) provides general information about Asian-American students and a list of practices to help teachers become more knowledgeable about Asian cultures.

Placement. Educators have responded to these educational issues by developing special programs and procedures and by placing students in special classes.

Special education referrals and placements for culturally and linguistically different students have been disproportionate (Cummins, 1984; Rodríguez, Prieto, & Rueda, 1984). Explanations for this overreferral include the following: low level of acculturation, inadequate assessment, language problems, poor school progress, academic/cognitive difficulties, and special learning problems (Malavé, 1991). Biased assessment has resulted in negative evaluation of English learners, largely because intelligence testing has been derived from models of genetic deficiency, cultural deprivation, and other deficit models (Payan, 1984; Rueda, 1987). Chapter 12 provides a more in-depth discussion of the issues and challenges facing special education for English learners and their teachers.

Retention/promotion policies are not carried out with equity. Unfortunately, some students begin falling behind their expected grade levels almost immediately on entering school.

In 2007 The National Center for Education Statistics (NCES) reported the following:

> In 2003, some 17 percent of Black students had been retained, a higher percentage than that of White, Hispanic, or Asian/Pacific Islander students. The percentage of Hispanic students (11 percent) who had been retained was higher than the percentage of White students (8 percent) retained, while the percentage of Asian/Pacific Islander students (5 percent) was lower than that of Whites. (NCES, 2007)

Students who repeat at least one grade are more likely to drop out of school. On the other side of the coin, students are also differentially distributed in Advanced Placement courses, a type of "in-house" promotion. Table 6.1 illustrates this distribution.

Tracking offers very different types of instruction depending on students' placement in academic or general education courses. Tracking has been found to be a major contributor to the continuing gaps in achievement between minorities and European Americans (Oakes, 1985, 1992).

Several reform efforts have attempted to dismantle some of the tracking programs previously practiced in schools. These have included accelerated schools, cooperative learning, restructured schools, and "untracking." A particularly noteworthy high-school program is Advancement Via Individual Determination (AVID). This "untracking" program places low-achieving students (who are primarily from low-income and ethnic or language-minority backgrounds) in the same college-preparatory academic program as high-achieving students, who are primarily from middle- or upper-middle-income and "Anglo" backgrounds (Mehan, Hubbard, Lintz, & Villanueva, 1994).

Segregation in schools has been steadily increasing, with particularly disastrous effects on minority students. Although during the 1970s and 1980s, districts were working at desegregating their schools, the 1990s witnessed an increasing number of

Table 6.1

Percentage of High-School Graduates Taking Advanced Placement Courses in High School, by Race/Ethnicity, 1998

	White	Black	Hispanic	Asian/Pacific Islander	Native American
AP calculus	7.5	3.4	3.7	13.4	0.6
AP/honors biology	16.7	15.4	12.6	22.2	6.0
AP/honors chemistry	4.8	3.5	4.0	10.9	0.9
AP/honors physics	3.0	2.1	2.1	7.6	0.9

Source: Digest of Educational Statistics (2003a).

court cases that released districts from these efforts (Weiler, 2000). Inequity follows segregation. In a study in the Boston metro area, "97 percent of the schools with less than a tenth white students faced concentrated poverty compared to 1 percent of the schools with less than a tenth minority students" (Orfield & Lee, 2005). In addition, segregation makes it difficult for English learners to be grouped with native speakers of English during the school day.

Compensatory education was the impetus behind the success of the Bilingual Education Act. However, compensatory programs are often reduced in scope, content, and pace, and students are not challenged enough, nor given enough of the curriculum to be able to move to mainstream classes that provide a richer academic preparation (Mehan, Hubbard, Lintz, & Villanueva, 1994).

ELD as compensatory education is all too common. Unfortunately, ELD has been identified with remediation of linguistic deficiencies. Too often ELD instruction has consisted of skill-and-drill worksheets and other decontextualized methods.

Submersion in English is too often an alternative to bilingual education: English learners are placed with native speakers in classrooms where teachers have no training in language-teaching pedagogy or sheltered content practices (McKeon, 1994). Research has shown that parents of students in submersion programs have been less involved in helping their children with homework than parents of students in bilingual programs (Ramírez, 1992). Expecting children to acquire English without help has long-term adverse consequences for school achievement.

Inclusion of English learners in mainstream classrooms is now the trend. In a study of "good educational practice for LEP [Limited English Proficient] students," researchers found numerous schools that have successfully been educating English learners to high standards (McLeod, 1996). In these schools, programs for English learners were an integral part of the whole school program, neither conceptually nor physically separate from the rest of the school.

> The exemplary schools have devised creative ways to both include LEP students centrally in the educational program and meet their needs for language instruction and modified curriculum. Programs for LEP students are so carefully crafted and intertwined with the school's other offerings that it is impossible in many cases to point to "the LEP program" and describe it apart from the general program. (p. 4)

Access for English Learners. School programs that recognize the rights and abilities of minority students and strive to reverse the discriminatory patterns of the society at large have proved more successful in helping these students through the schooling process (Cummins, 1984, 1989). *School Reform and Student Diversity: Exemplary Schooling for Language Minority Students* (McLeod, 1996) details features of exemplary schools, goals for ensuring access to high-quality teaching, ways to improve teaching and learning for EL students, and an appendix of the featured schools.

Parent and Community Participation

"Strong parent involvement is one factor that research has shown time and time again to have positive effects on academic achievement and school attitudes" (Ovando & Collier, 1998, p. 270). Fortunately, over the past decade successful programs have developed and various guidelines are available to help school personnel, parents, and communities work together to ensure parental rights, parental involvement, successful programs, and school–community partnerships that benefit students.

Recognizing Parental Rights. Parents have numerous rights that educators must respect and honor in spite of the challenges they may present to the school. These include (1) the right of their children to a free, appropriate public education; (2) the right to receive information concerning education decisions and actions in the language parents comprehend; (3) the right to make informed decisions and to authorize consent before changes in educational placement occur; (4) the right to be included in discussions and plans concerning disciplinary action toward their children; (5) the right to appeal actions when they do not agree; and (6) the right to participate in meetings organized for public and parent information (Young & Helvie, 1996).

Issues in Parental Involvement. Schools attempting to increase parental involvement have encountered issues in five areas of concern: language, survival and family structure, educational background and values, knowledge about education and beliefs about learning, and power and status. Ovando and Collier (1998) offered questions within each area that can provide a valuable guide as school personnel begin to address and overcome misconceptions regarding parents and that will open dialogue for fruitful collaborations and programs (see Table 6.2).

Table 6.2

Questions Regarding Parent–School Relationships

Area of Concern	Questions
Language	How does educators' language (jargon?) affect home–school communication?
	Do community members support using the home language in school?
Family structure	How do the struggles of day-to-day survival affect the home–school partnership?
	How will differences in family structure affect the relationship?
Educational background, attitudes toward schooling	Do school expectations match the parents' educational backgrounds?
	What do educators assume about the attitudes of parents toward schooling?
Knowledge and beliefs about education	How do parents learn about school culture, their role in U.S. schools, and the specific methods being used in their child's classroom? Would they be comfortable reinforcing these methods at home?
	How do parents and teachers differ in the perception of the home–school relationship?
Power and status	How does the inherent inequality of the educator–layperson relationship affect the partnership?
	Do programs for parents convey a message of cultural deficiency?
	To what degree are language-minority community members a part of the school in instructional and administrative positions?

Source: Adapted from Ovando and Collier (1998, pp. 301–309).

Programs in Action. As schools and parents have looked for ways in which they can partner in order to help children achieve success in school, several have developed family literacy projects. One of the first was the Párajo Valley Family Literacy project in Watsonville, California. Project founder and author Dr. Alma Flor Ada designed a parental involvement program that would help parents recover a lost sense of dignity and identity. She began with a "meet the author" program by telling her own stories and explaining her feelings about writing in Spanish. Each subsequent session included reading and discussing children's books and sharing experiences. Videotapes showing parents discussing and enjoying the books were circulated in the community. The major components of this project were the collaboration of the school and parents in a shared enterprise and the reciprocal interaction between parents and children that encourages both to enjoy literature (Ada, 1989).

A second such project was the Hmong Literacy Project initiated by Hmong parents in Fresno, California. As their children became more assimilated in the United States and less appreciative of their cultural roots, the parents felt the need to preserve their oral history and maintain their culture through written records. Therefore, they asked for literacy lessons in Hmong (a language that has been written for about only thirty years) and in English. Throughout the program, these parents developed not only the asked-for literacy skills but also skills in math and computers that allowed them to help their children academically. Through the *Hmong Parents Newsletter,* communication was increased between the school and the community, leading to greater parent participation in school activities (Kang, Kuehn, & Herrell, 1996).

A different type of program is the Parent Resource Center in Texas, affiliated with the University of Houston–Clear Lake. It provides a system of social and educational support for language-minority parents. Based on a needs assessment, the parent community identified four priorities: (1) ESL instruction, (2) strategies to help their children at home, (3) understanding the school system, and (4) understanding their rights and responsibilities (Bermúdez & Márquez, 1996). The words of one of the program participants illustrate the value of such a program not only in helping immigrant parents but also in dispelling negative stereotypes regarding parents:

> Learning English helps us overcome the obstacles we encounter in this country. It gives us the opportunity to go to a doctor without having to find an interpreter. . . . Look, my children are growing, I need to learn to help my children with their school work. Although I only completed nine years of school in my country [Guatemala], one day I want to go back to school so I can obtain a job. This is my dream. We are very appreciative of all that the program has done for us. We are in this country and we need to communicate with others in their language. (Bermúdez & Márquez, 1996, p. 4)

PreK–3 education environments for young Hispanic children should feature rich language stimuli, with many opportunities for students and teachers to talk with one another in both Spanish and English. This also includes families as part of the dialogue. As Garcia and Jensen (2007) note, "Spanish-speaking parents are more likely to involve themselves in schools and classrooms in which Spanish is regularly spoken" (p. 37).

School–Community Partnerships. In addition to developing partnerships with parents, schools are also reaching toward communities to help them in educating all children. Community-based organizations (CBOs)—groups committed to helping people obtain health, education, and other basic human services—are assisting students in ways that go beyond traditional schooling (Dryfoos, 1998). Adger (2000) found that school–CBO partnerships support students' academic achievement by working with parents and families, tutoring students in their first language, developing students' leadership skills and higher education goals, and providing information and support on issues such as health care, pregnancy, gang involvement, and so on (see Chapter 11).

Organizational Models: What Works for Whom?

Bilingual education is an umbrella term used to refer to various types of programs and models. It is a term used in two ways: first, for education that promotes academic and linguistic development in two languages; and second, to denote programs that include students who speak languages other than English. In the first instance, bilingualism is being fostered; in the second, English learners are present but bilingualism is not a goal of the curriculum (Baker, 2001). Obviously, the school experience for language-minority students varies depending on the aim of the program in which students participate. The program can support and extend the home language and culture, or it can consider the students' language and culture irrelevant to schooling.

The term *bilingual education* rarely includes a discussion of foreign-language instruction for native-English-speaking students. Traditionally, this instruction has consisted of three to four years of high-school classes. In recent years, a limited number of school districts in the United States have begun programs of foreign language in the elementary school (FLES) in which students in K–6 classrooms receive one or more hours a week of instruction from a foreign-language specialist. Because this language is used neither as the language of academic instruction nor as a language of peer conversation, however, it is difficult for native-English-speaking students to achieve a high level of dual-language proficiency through FLES.

The bilingual education program models discussed in the following sections vary in the degree of support provided for the home language in the context of multicompetent language use (Cook, 1999). The most supportive is dual-language instruction that actively promotes bilingualism, biliteracy, and biculturalism for native-English-speaking students and language-minority students alike. The models reflect different goals—for example, remediation or enrichment—as well as the influence of federal, state, and local policies. In this discussion of bilingual programs, an ideal goal of instruction will be proposed: multicompetent language use not only for those students with a primary language other than English but also for native-English speakers.

Submersion

The default mode for educating English learners in U.S. classrooms is submersion—no provisions are made for the language and academic needs of English learners. Students receive instruction in English, with English monolingualism as the goal. The associated social difficulties experienced by English learners in a language-majority classroom are not addressed. Moreover, submersion programs do not utilize the language skills of English learners to enrich the schooling experience of native-English speakers.

In addition to being academically disabling, submersion denies students their rights under law:

> Submersion is not a legal option for schools with non-native-English speakers; however, oversight and enforcement are lax, and many smaller schools with low populations of NNS [non-native-speaking] students are simply unaware that they are required to provide some sort of services to these students. Parents of these children, for cultural and other reasons, tend not to demand the services their children are entitled to; thus it is not uncommon to find submersion in U.S. public schools. (Roberts, 1995, pp. 80–81)

A meta-analysis of program effectiveness for English learners found that bilingual or English-Plus rather than English-only or English-immersion approaches to curriculum and instruction help students to succeed academically (Rolstad, Mahoney, & Glass, 2005).

The Teaching of English-Language Development (ELD)

Before describing the various models of bilingual education, it is useful to survey the programs that teach English-language development (ELD). English instruction is delivered in a variety of ways, and studies have shown varying degrees of student success depending on the program model (Thomas & Collier, 1997). However, if ELD is the only component, then the program is not a bilingual program.

In few of the ELD models is the primary language of the students explicitly acknowledged or used—ELD teachers are seldom required to be fluent in the primary languages of the students. Individual teachers may have second-language competencies with which to support students on an individual basis, but this is not part of the program design.

Pull-Out ELD. English learners leave their home classroom and receive instruction in vocabulary, grammar, oral language, and spelling for separate half-hour- to one-hour-per-day classes with a trained ELD teacher. Such instruction rarely is integrated with the regular classroom program; and, when they return to the home classroom, children usually are not instructed on curriculum they missed while they were gone. Of the various program models, ELD pull-out has been the most implemented (Thomas & Collier, 1997).

Profile of an Educator:

ELD Specialist

Cindy Wilcox is employed by Lincoln Intermediate Unit #12, a regional state-funded educational agency. She works at Mary B. Sharpe Elementary School in Chambersburg, Pennsylvania. Throughout the day, students are pulled from their classrooms to receive intensive ELD tutoring in small classes for forty-five to ninety minutes. Although most of her students speak Spanish as a first language, she also serves students from Pakistan, Haiti, and Indonesia. In the three-county service area, thirty-four languages are represented. Focusing largely on mastery-learning reading materials and vocabulary development, Cindy wishes she had more time to teach writing.

ELD Class Period. Students in the secondary school often have separate ELD classes that help them with their English skills. The effect of such segregation is that students may not receive rich academic instruction. Moreover, in some school districts, students who are placed in separate ELD classes at the high-school level do not receive college-entrance-applicable credits for these classes—to be placed in an ELD class is to preclude the chance for college admission. Students should be placed in SDAIE-enhanced high-school English classes that bear college-entry credit value.

Content-Based ELD. Although content-based ELD classes are still separate and contain only English learners, students learn English through academic content in a curriculum organized around grade-level academic objectives (see Chapter 4). The most effective of these models is when the ELD teacher collaborates with content-area teachers and some team teaching occurs (Ovando & Collier, 1998).

Sheltered Instruction (SDAIE). As discussed in Chapter 5, sheltered instruction is provided by teachers who have both content background and knowledge of best practices in second-language acquisition. Lessons have content, language, and learning-strategy objectives. English learners and native-English speakers are often together in sheltered classrooms.

Transitional or Early-Exit Bilingual Education

The overriding goal of transitional bilingual education (TBE) programs is to mainstream students into English-only classrooms. In these programs, students receive initial instruction in most, if not all, content areas in their home language while they are being taught English. Most of these programs last only two to three years, long enough for students to achieve basic interpersonal communication skills (BICS) but not long enough for children to build cognitive academic language proficiency (CALP) in either their native tongue or English. As a consequence, they may not be able to carry out cognitively demanding tasks in English and may be considered to be "subtractively bilingual."

There are numerous problems with a TBE program. It may be perceived as remedial compensatory education. The program rests on the common misconception that two or three years is sufficient time to learn a second language for schooling purposes (Ovando & Collier, 1998).

Adapted Instruction: Easing the Transition Phase

Transitioning from the bilingual to the mainstream classroom has always been problematic for students and teachers. One program developed to ease this transition includes the following components:

- *Challenge.* Students think, learn, and engage intellectually as they study novels and short stories in depth over an extended period (six to eight weeks). Content and theme

are emphasized along with the traditional linguistic/phonological approach to language arts.

■ *Continuity.* Curriculum and instruction are connected as students move from the primary, to the middle, to the upper grades and from L1 to L2 language arts. In all grades, instruction includes literature units, instructional conversation, literature logs, assigned independent reading, comprehension strategies, pleasure reading, writing projects, dictation, and grammar lessons.

■ *Connections.* Transition teachers build on students' existing knowledge, skills, and experiences and make explicit connections to the academic curriculum. They connect and build on the literature studies of the pretransition period: Themes studied in a Spanish-language story are revisited in an English-language story; strategies introduced during pretransition are continued to help students recognize commonalities of reading and writing in Spanish and in English.

■ *Comprehensiveness.* The grades 2–5 program addresses both meaning and skills. Teachers teach directed lessons, facilitate group work, confer with individuals, and demonstrate strategies. Students have both assigned and pleasure reading, develop written projects and do dictation, participate in literary discussions, and receive formal lessons. For further information about the program, see Saunders and Goldenberg (2001).

Maintenance or Developmental Bilingual Education

A maintenance bilingual education (MBE) program supports education and communication in the students' primary language as well as students' heritage and culture. The major assumption in such a program is that bilingualism is a valuable asset, not only for the individuals who are bilingual but also for society as a whole. Students in an MBE design are not quickly transitioned but are encouraged to be proficient in both English and their native tongue. Literacy in two languages is often an important goal (Roberts, 1995). These goals enhance self-concept and pride in the cultural background.

For the most part, maintenance/developmental programs have been implemented at the elementary level. They are rarely continued into the intermediate grades. Programs that offer continuing support for students' academic learning in their first language have also been called *late-exit* to distinguish them from the transitional *early-exit* programs (Ramírez, 1992).

A particularly compelling use of maintenance bilingual programs is in the education of Native Americans. The attempt to increase the number of speakers of Native-American languages is sometimes called "restorative" bilingual education. Further information about restorative maintenance bilingual Native-American education is available in Hinton and Hale (2001).

Example of Concept: A Typical Day in a Second-Grade Kaiapuni (the Hawaiian-Language Immersion Program) Classroom

The Kaiapuni students lined up at 8:00 outside their classroom and began to *oli*—chant in Hawaiian—asking their teachers to allow them to enter their classrooms. The teachers chanted back, granting permission and welcoming the children, and everyone sang *Hawai'i Pono'i*, the state song.

Once in the room, the children turned in their homework and sat on the floor for the daily morning routine. One child reviewed the month and day of the week, and charted the temperature and the phase of the moon. The children all counted the number of days left until the end of the year. Leialoha, the teacher, reviewed the agenda for the rest of the day. Students wrote a "morning letter" and collectively corrected the spelling and grammar.

During recess, students interacted with other Kaiapuni students and students from the English-language program. After recess, the class read for fifteen minutes (sustained silent reading) and then engaged in another language arts activity based on a book about how Native Alaskans made mittens. The students read the book in small groups and followed instructions written on the board about how to make their own mittens. After lunch was journal writing time, followed by an art activity. Then students went outside for a music class with a resource teacher in preparation for an upcoming assembly. The school day ended at 2:30.

This description probably appears similar to classrooms in which English and not Hawaiian is the language of instruction. However, Kaiapuni is not just a Hawaiian translation of the English program. Hawaiian values, knowledge, and teaching methods are incorporated into classroom activities. For example, beginning the day with the *oli* reflects Hawaiian beliefs about social relationships and learning. Having students read about Native Alaskans reflects a curriculum that emphasizes indigenous peoples and their perspectives on life (Yamauchi & Wilhelm, 2001, p. 86).

Immersion Bilingual Education

Immersion bilingual education provides academic and language instruction in two languages, ideally from grades K through 12. The goal of immersion programs is for students to be proficient in both languages—to achieve *additive bilingualism*. The term has come from program models in Canada where middle-class, English-speaking children are instructed in French. In the United States, English-only submersion programs for English learners are sometimes mischaracterized as immersion. This misconception has led to confusion. Canadian immersion is not, and never has been, a monolingual program, because both English and French are incorporated into the programs as subjects and as the medium of instruction (Lambert, 1984). In addition, the social context of French immersion is the upper-middle class in Quebec Province, where both English and French have a high language status for instructional purposes. In contrast, when English learners are submerged in mainstream English classes, instruction is not given in their home language, and they do not become biliterate and academically bilingual.

Example of Concept: Distinguishing Features of the Inter-American Magnet School in Chicago

Inter-American Magnet School (IAMS) is dedicated to teaching and learning in two languages. From PreK through eighth grade, English-dominant, Spanish-dominant, and fully bilingual students learn and teach in their classrooms. IAMS is one of twenty-eight elementary magnet schools in Chicago. Students are selected to attend through a lottery system based solely on racial–ethic categories and gender. There are approximately 600 students: 70 percent Latino, 14.6 percent European-American, 12.7 percent African-American, and 1.9 percent Asian/Pacific Islander or Native-American.

The school's innovative model is regularly featured in national and international publications. It is the oldest dual-immersion school in the Midwest and the second oldest in the country. At all grade levels, English-dominant and Spanish-dominant students study together in the same

classrooms. Teachers at the same grade level collaborate on designing thematic units, incorporating as much cooperative grouping as possible in activities to encourage peer assistance. However, despite its dedication to dual-language equality, for various reasons, English dominates in schoolwide competitions and few Spanish learners use Spanish for authentic communication. (Potowski, 2007)

Three features distinguish this immersion program: a model program, parent involvement, and studies of the Americas. IAMS is a model for other two-way bilingual immersion programs, and teachers model best practices for those just entering the teaching profession. Parents actively participate at various levels within the school as a whole and in individual classrooms. They take lead roles on school committees and they help develop schoolwide policies and effect positive change.

The Studies of the Americas program, which guides the school's entire social studies curriculum, represents and reflects the language and cultural diversity of the IAMS student body. By the end of sixth grade, students have studied the three predominant cultures of Latin America today: indigenous, Hispanic, and African. In addition, students take their new knowledge beyond the classroom. Many teachers are involved in social causes and encourage students to "connect classroom studies to the outside world and use Spanish and English to communicate for authentic purposes" (Urow & Sontag, 2001, p. 20).

U.S. Enrichment Immersion. In the United States, a comparable social context to Canadian-style immersion is the exclusive private schools of the upper class, in which foreign languages are highly supported. This program model can be considered "enrichment immersion." This model is distinguished from FLES in that academic instruction may be delivered directly in a foreign language; and tutoring, travel abroad, and frequent, structured peer-language use (such as "French-only" dinners) are often an integral part of the program.

Example of Concept: U.S. Enrichment Immersion

The International School of Indiana (ISI) offers French and Spanish enrichment immersion programs in the heart of Indianapolis, a city with a two universities that attract scholars from around the world. Students with no prior experience in the target languages must enroll before grade 2 in order to benefit from the immersion opportunity (classes are 100 percent in the target language in the pre-elementary grades, 80 percent in grades 1–3, and 50 percent in grades 4–7). The curriculum has an international content, with high standards—the French and Spanish curricula are imported from France and Spain respectively. Community support has been generous in the form of large grants from local foundations and corporations. Teachers are recruited for their language skills and well as their teaching abilities, are paid well, and work hard, using crosslinguistic cooperation to offer innovative activities (Weber, 2001).

Dual or Two-Way Immersion. A two-way immersion model enhances the status of the students' primary language by providing instruction in that language to English learners. This allows English learners to be in a position to help their English-speaking peers (see the Point/Counterpoints on pages 167 and 168).

In the two-way immersion design, a high level of academic competence is achieved in two languages by both English learners and native-English speakers. Both groups of

Point/Counterpoint:

Does Dual Immersion Enhance English Learning?

Dual-immersion programs are designed to provide an enriched program of academic and language study in which students and teachers use both languages as the medium of communication for specific areas of the curriculum. But do immersion programs help English learners to develop English-language skills?

POINT: Dual Immersion Promotes English Learning. Research has shown that students who enter school in the United States with limited or no proficiency in English make more progress in acquiring English and in developing academically if they receive schooling in their primary language as they are introduced to English as a second language (Cummins, 1981b; Ramírez, 1992; Thomas & Collier, 1997). Strong literacy skills in the primary language can be applied to the acquisition of English literacy. Dual-language immersion schools help English learners to develop their primary language fully while adding proficiency in English through enriched, challenging curricula. Students who act as language hosts—for example, Spanish-speaking children who serve as language models for native-English-speaking students in a dual-immersion program—gain self-esteem and increased cultural pride (Lindholm, 1992), leading to increased motivation to learn.

COUNTERPOINT: Dual Immersion Delays English Learning. Some critics charge that dual-language immersion programs fail to teach English to English learners. Because programs teach content in the primary language, they do not emphasize communication in English, as do transitional bilingual programs. Amselle (1999) argued that "dual immersion programs are really nothing more than Spanish immersion, with Hispanic children used as teaching tools for English-speaking children" (p. 8). Experts concede that the greatest challenge in two-way bilingual programs is to "reduce the gap" between the language abilities of the two groups (English learners and native-English speakers acquiring the second language). This gap appears as content classes in English are modified (slowed down) for English learners to catch up, or as content delivery in the primary language is slowed for Spanish learners (SSLs). As Molina (2000) advised, "Without a watchful approach to the quality of two-way programs, schools will find themselves tragically exploiting the English learners they had hoped to help for the benefit of the language-majority students" (p. 12).

Implications for Teaching

Careful attention to a high-quality bilingual program in the context of primary-language maintenance and second-language acquisition is key.

Source: Adapted from Veeder and Tramutt (2000).

students participate in content-area instruction in the minority language as well as in English, although the two languages are not mixed. Both groups receive language instruction in both their native and the second language. This encourages English learners to develop their primary language and native-English-speaking students (for example, Spanish-as-a-second-language [SSL] learners) to attain advanced levels of functional proficiency in the second language by performing academic tasks in that language.

Newcomer Centers

Newcomer programs offer recent immigrants an emotionally safe educational atmosphere that fosters rapid language learning, acculturation, and enhancement of self-esteem. Common goals for various newcomer program models include helping students acquire

Point/Counterpoint:

Are Two-Way Immersion Programs the Best Model of Bilingual Education?

POINT: Two-Way Immersion Promotes Academic Achievement and Broad-Based Support for Bilingual Education. Two-way programs appeal to English-speaking parents who value bilingualism, offering peer models who are native speakers. Bilingual educators were initially attracted to this model, believing it offered more political support (Crawford, 2004b). Many educators believe it is a way to bridge the persistent achievement gap between English-speaking and language-minority students.

COUNTERPOINT: Two-Way Immersion Works Best with Economically Advantaged Students Who Are from Bilingual Homes. Studies have shown that, despite these programs, English learners still lag behind English-only students in achievement. For English learners who face challenges of poverty and parental illiteracy, two-way programs have not been shown to be superior to one-way developmental bilingual education (Crawford, 2004b).

Implications for Teaching
Like other school programs, two-way immersion programs vary in quality. Parental involvement is key to maintaining high standards.

enough English to move into the regular language support program, developing students' academic skills, helping them gain an understanding of U.S. schools and educational expectations, and introducing students to their new communities. Programs may be organized as a school-within-a-school, as a separate program in its own location, or in district intake centers (Genesee, 1999; Short, 1998).

Programs vary in both length of day and length of time in program. Some are full-day, in which students have various content courses along with ELD, whereas others are half-day or after school. The majority of newcomers enroll for one year, although some may attend four years and others only one semester or one summer. Programs also distinguish themselves by whether they are primarily ELD or bilingual, and by the manner in which they exit students (Genesee, 1999; Short, 1998).

Newcomer centers should not be considered a substitute for bilingual education. Programs that offer only English, while disregarding instruction in content subjects, are not effective in the long run for three reasons. First, researchers have documented that learning a second language takes three to five years. A short-term program (three months, sixth months, or even a year) cannot create mastery. Second, students who do not receive content instruction suffer delayed or disrupted schooling. Finally, language—including content vocabulary—is best learned in the context of rich, meaningful academic instruction.

Example of Concept: Newcomer Centers in Denver

The Newcomer Centers at Merrill Middle and South High Schools welcome new students to Denver Public School. The centers serve English learners who have been identified as having

limited or interrupted education as well as minimal literacy skills in their native languages and English. At the centers, students receive instruction on listening, speaking, reading, and writing improvement. Classes feature low student–adult ratios and state-of-the-art computer systems. English instruction is supported by Spanish when appropriate. After spending one or two semesters at one of the centers, students transition into an ELD program (Denver Public Schools, 2002, p. 1).

Research Studies on Program Effectiveness

Bilingual education continues to be controversial, entangled as it is with societal conceptions and misconceptions, issues of power and status, and climates of acceptance and fear. Despite variables that might predict school failure (such as poverty, the school's location in an impoverished area, and low status of the language-minority group), Thomas and Collier (1997) found three key predictors of academic success. Those schools that incorporated all three predictors were "likely to graduate language-minority students who are very successful academically in high school and higher education" (p. 15).

The three predictors are as follows: (1) cognitively complex on-grade-level academic instruction through students' first language for as long as possible, combined with cognitively complex on-grade-level academic instruction through the second language (English) for part of the school day; (2) use of current approaches to teaching the academic curriculum through two languages, including discovery learning, cooperative learning, thematic units, activities that tap into the "multiple intelligences" (Gardner, 1983), and bridging techniques that draw on students' personal experiences; and (3) a transformed sociocultural context for English learners' schooling, with two-way bilingual classes frequently used to achieve this goal.

The task facing English learners is daunting. Consider that they need to acquire English and academic subjects while their native-English-speaking (NES) peers are learning academic subjects. Each school year the NES student sustains ten months of academic growth. If an English learner initially scores low on tests in English (say two or three years below grade level), he or she has to make fifteen months' progress (an academic year and a half) on the tests each year for five or six years to reach the average performance of an NES student. In studying the various program models for English learners, Thomas and Collier (1997) found that students who received on-grade-level academic work in their primary language were able to make these gains and, most important, sustain them.

Krashen (2006) summarizes the positive aspects of bilingual education:

Bilingual education helps English in two ways. First, teaching subject matter in the child's first language provides knowledge, which helps the child understand instruction when it is presented in English.

The second way bilingual education accelerates English is by providing literacy development in the first language. . . . It is much easier to learn to read in a language you already know, and once you can read, you can read. The ability to read transfers rapidly across languages, even when the writing systems are different.

> Good bilingual programs provide exposure to comprehensible English from the very first day and introduce subject matter teaching in English as soon as it can be made comprehensible.
>
> Children in bilingual programs typically do better than children in all-English programs on tests of English reading. [This] has been established using scientific, controlled studies, which compare the progress of two groups of children with very similar backgrounds. (n. p.)

Instructional Strategies

Good classroom teaching must be a part of a bilingual classroom in the same way that good teaching is required in any classroom. When students are viewed as active participants in the learning process rather than as empty receptacles to be filled with knowledge, teachers organize classroom experiences for "reciprocal interaction" (Cummins, 1986). Teachers also recognize the importance of incorporating students' culture(s) into classroom tasks (see Chapter 10 for suggestions). In characterizing effective bilingual instruction, the following sections focus on the use of two languages and exemplary means of classroom organization.

Language Management

If instruction is to be effective for children who potentially can function at a high level in two languages, the use of these languages must maximize cognitive and academic proficiency. Programs using two languages can separate them by time, personnel, subject, and manner of delivery. These strategies are particularly relevant to the two-way immersion context.

Time. Bilingual programs may devote a specific time to each language. In an "alternate use" model, languages are used on alternating days: Monday, primary language; Tuesday, English; Wednesday, primary language; and so on. In a "divided day" model, the morning may be devoted to the primary language and the afternoon to English. In both these models, academic instruction is occurring in both languages.

Example of Concept: Divided Day

The two-way immersion program at Hueco Elementary School in El Paso, Texas, uses the 50–50 model for academic instruction. Fifty percent of daily instruction in grades K–6 is given in English and 50 percent in Spanish. Both Spanish-dominant and English-dominant students are in the same classes and serve as language models for one another during instruction in their dominant language (Calderón & Slavin, 2001).

Requiring that students use one language or the other in a dual-language environment is often frustrating for the teachers:

> Ms. Torres was frustrated that students used English during their "Spanish" time. She tried posting signs demarking which language should be used, and when, but everyone

ignored the signs. She did not require students from the other fifth grade to use Spanish when they visited during Spanish time. In addition, the teacher often accepted public use of English without sanction during teacher-front lessons. Spanish-only was only successfully enforced by students who chastised each other during groupwork in classes where prizes were lost for not using Spanish. (Potowski, 2007, pp. 98–99)

Personnel. Languages can be separated by teacher. In a team-teaching situation, one teacher may speak in English, the other in the primary language. When working with an aide, the teacher will use English and the aide the primary language. A caution in using this latter design is the association of the minority language with school personnel who do not have fully credentialed teaching status.

Subject. Language can be organized by subject—primary language for mathematics, English for science. Again, with this model school personnel need to be cognizant of which subjects are taught in which language. Models in which the primary language is used only for language arts, music, and art, and English is used for science and mathematics, send a message about the status of the primary language.

Example of Concept: Language Distribution by Subject

In the two-way development bilingual program at the Valley Center Union School District in California, students study core subjects (language arts, math, science, and social studies) in their L1 as they gain fluency in their L2. In fourth grade, students transition to studying the core in their L2, and by fifth grade they are able to use either language for the district's grade-level curriculum (Richard-Amato, 2003).

Manner of Delivery. The novice bilingual teacher may say everything twice, first in English and then in the primary language. This *concurrent-translation* model is ineffective because students tune out when their subordinate language is spoken. Moreover, concurrent translation is pedagogically random, and may not furnish enough time spent in English or even in the primary language. However, when used in a mindful way, to reinforce concept understanding or help students to review material, a structured form of code switching may be used concurrently to reinforce content delivery.

A better approach is *preview–review*, in which the introduction and summary are given in one language and the presentation in the other. When content-area materials are not available in the minority language, preview–review has been found to be particularly useful (Lessow-Hurley, 2009).

Example of Concept: Preview–Review

In a science lesson on measurement of temperatures, students receive an explanation in Korean of the general content of the upcoming lesson as well as the meaning of such English words as *increase* and *decrease*. After the lesson, delivered in English, students are divided into groups according to their dominant language and discuss what they have learned. This discussion allows the teacher to expand on concepts and correct misunderstandings (Ovando & Collier, 1998).

Primary-Language Use

In bilingual programs, the primary language can be used as the language of instruction in teaching students academic material, just as English is used for native-English-speaking students in mainstream programs. In addition to being a medium of instruction, the primary language is offered as an academic subject in its own right. Moreover, it can be used to help students in their acquisition of English.

Academic Learning. Primary-language instruction is defined as "instruction focused on the development of the language itself (oral and literacy skills) through use of authentic written and oral literature and discourse as well as academic instruction through the primary language" (Sánchez, 1989, p. 2). Instruction by means of the primary language allows students to capitalize on their life experiences and transfer their knowledge into an understanding of the purposes of reading and writing. Once they have a well-developed conceptual base in their primary language, they can translate into English concepts and ideas that are firmly established rather than facing the far more difficult task of learning fundamental concepts in an unfamiliar language (Lessow-Hurley, 2009).

For example, hearing and reading familiar songs, poems, folktales, and stories in the native language exposes students to literary language and various genres. Once literacy is established in the native language, children can use these resources as they move into English, creating their own English texts and reading English material written by others.

Second-Language Acquisition. There are several educationally sound as well as logical and psychological reasons for the judicious use of the primary language in learning English (and vice versa). Certainly in bilingual settings, in which two language groups are working and learning together, a disciplined approach to the use of L1 can enhance and facilitate language learning. The Point/Counterpoint on page 173 outlines the reasons for and against the use of L1 in learning L2.

Code Switching

As students become more proficient in English, several factors help to determine which language they use. The primary factor is the students' free choice. They should be allowed to respond in whichever language is comfortable and appropriate for them. Teacher proficiency and material availability are other factors. In some cases, teachers may provide instruction in English while students, in their groups, talk and write in the home language. Bilingual teachers and students may habitually alternate between the two languages that are used in their community. Code switching is accepted in this model, although students are expected to make final presentations, both oral and written, in whichever is the language of instruction.

Classroom Organization

Recent studies on school reform and education for English learners support the finding that students learn better when actively engaged in a nurturing environment that

Point/Counterpoint:

What Should Be the Role of L1 in Learning L2?

Many of the teaching techniques used for English-language teaching in the twentieth century were developed for use in multilingual, often urban, classes in which learners do not share a sole primary language. In these classes, the use of L1 was not feasible or was strongly discouraged because of the belief that L1 would interfere with learning L2. However, in schools in the United States that feature a student population that shares an L1, this argument does not hold. Debate is now raging over the use of the learner's first language in the classroom: What should be the role of L1 in learning L2?

POINT: L1 Is a Useful Tool in Learning English

■ Many words—especially concrete nouns—are learned fastest when translated. Teaching a simple word such as *garlic* involves a great deal of description or use of a picture. (Does every teacher have a picture of garlic?)

■ L1 is useful to highlight false cognates (*embarazada* is not *embarrassed*).

■ L1 can be used to discuss grammar differences between languages (*English* does not use an article, as does *el ingles*) and abstract grammar ideas (how the rules of using the subjunctive differ in L1 and in English).

■ Use of L1 lowers stress in learning L2.

■ Most learners naturally use L1; rather than creating a new language store, they mentally map the L2 directly on to the existing L1, drawing connections, contrasting ideas, and viewing the L2 through their L1.

COUNTERPOINT: L1 Is Not Useful in Teaching L2

■ Overuse of L1 can cause dependency.

■ Learners may misunderstand an exact translation of a word's many meanings, especially because English has multiple synonyms for words.

■ Use of L1 can also lead to a loss of useful language practice.

■ Teachers who do not use English socially in class may communicate a low value for speaking and listening to English.

■ Use of L1 may replace opportunities for listening and speaking practice in L2.

Implications for Teaching

Use of the L1 with beginners reduces anxiety, increases student–teacher rapport, and increases the effectiveness of instructional management. As students reach higher levels of proficiency in L2, less L1 may be used. Code switching should not be discouraged, however, if it promotes group solidarity, increases comprehension of more difficult topics, and lowers anxiety.

Source: Adapted from Buckmaster (2000).

honors and respects their language and culture (McLeod, 1996; Nelson, 1996; Thomas & Collier, 1997). The active strategies and techniques outlined in Chapters 4 and 5 are equally valid for bilingual classrooms as for ELD and SDAIE classrooms, if not more so, as two groups of students are learning two different languages. Curriculum that is organized around themes, that strives for depth of a topic rather than breadth, that is cross-disciplinary, and that has meaning to students and is relevant to their lives provides students with the opportunity to achieve academic success.

Cooperative Grouping. Cooperative grouping, in which English learners work cooperatively with native speakers of English or with one another, increases students' opportunities to hear and produce English and to negotiate meaning with others. Cohen's

Complex Instruction (Cohen et al., 1990) encourages equal access for all students in a cooperative group by assigning well-defined roles to each group member and ensuring that these roles rotate frequently. In addition to encouraging academic learning and language proficiency, cooperative learning helps children learn classroom conventions and rituals and become an active part of the culture of the classroom. To be most effective, grouping needs to be flexible and heterogeneous in language, gender, ability, and interest.

Example of Concept: Cooperative Grouping

A school in south Texas with a large number of migrant children implemented a cooperative grouping program for writing (Hayes, 1998). During their fifth-grade year, students were empowered to teach themselves—they talked and wrote about their lives outside the classroom and about what they were learning and the effect this learning had on their lives. Students were given choices and opportunities to express themselves using daily journals and class-made books. Writing conferences helped them evaluate their own writing and that of their classmates. A rich supply of stories and nonfiction books encouraged them to read.

Collaborative Teaching. When teachers have the opportunity to collaborate, they can share interests and experiences and build on one another's strengths for the benefit of their students. Dual-immersion teaching fosters collaboration between L1 and L2 teachers. ELD teaching often utilizes teaching assistants and paraprofessional resource people who provide support for English learners as a second resource person in and out of the classroom, acting as tutors, language informants, and small-group facilitators (Porter & Taylor, 2003).

Working with a paraprofessional can be a satisfying experience in what Villa, Thousand, and Nevin (2004) call "co-teaching." If the teacher and the instructional assistant are *team teaching*, they have equal, collaborative roles. Instruction is co-planned and divided so students can receive benefit from each teacher's strengths. If the model is that of *complementary teaching*, the teacher and the aide each have equal, alternating duties, and each follows up or enhances the other's instruction. In a *parallel teaching* model, the paraprofessional and the teacher work with different groups of students in different sections of the classroom, each with separate duties. The most common model, however, is that of *supportive teaching*, with the teacher in the lead instructional role while the aide circulates among students to provide support in a subordinate role.

Working with Classroom Volunteers. Activities that a classroom volunteer can assist a teacher with include:

- Instructional review and practice for groups
  - Dictating spelling words
  - Listening to reading practice
  - Conducting drills on words, phrases, and flash cards

- Individual tutoring or assessment
  - Helping with written compositions
  - Helping children who were absent from class to make up work
  - Giving reinforcement to children new to the class
  - Supervising individual testing
  - Repeating a lesson for a child who needs extra help
  - Teaching a special enrichment skill
  - Recording primary-language stories

- Supervision of small-group activities
  - Helping students to publish a class newspaper
  - Supervising student research committees
  - Accompanying small groups to the library

- Other teacher assistance
  - Setting up learning centers
  - Working with projectors, recorders, listening posts
  - Serving as an interpreter for non-English-speaking children
  - Informing about local culture

Well-implemented bilingual education programs have been found to be successful in educating not only English learners but also native-English-speaking students. In a world that is constantly getting smaller, in which the majority of people are bilingual, it is incumbent on the United States to utilize the linguistic facilities of its citizens and to develop these resources to their maximum potential. This argument speaks to the international arena. Equally important is the education of these citizens for the nation itself. As Thomas and Collier (1997) so eloquently express:

> By reforming current school practices, all students will enjoy a better educated, more productive future, for the benefit of all American citizens who will live in the world of the next 15–25 years. It is in the self-interest of all citizens that the next adult generations be educated to meet the enormously increased educational demands of the fast-emerging society of the near future. (p. 13)■

LEARNING MORE

Further Reading

Dual Language Instruction (Cloud, Genesee, & Hamayan, 2000) details ways to develop and sustain high-quality instruction in the context of dual-immersion education, what the authors call "enriched education." The book features interviews called "Voices from the Field," in which bilingual teachers share their experiences in dual-language education. One such vignette by Eun Mi Cho recounts her successes in teaching Korean to native-English speakers. She invites students to join the Korean Club, in which they play Korean traditional games. Students learn to make Korean crafts, sing Korean songs, read Korean literature, and meet Korean authors. They visit local Korean markets and cook traditional dishes. In this interesting and comfortable learning environment, students then begin to learn oral and written Korean.

Web Search

The NCELA Website offers a variety of Web-based resources about two-way immersion programs. Because parents are crucial to the success of such programs, Craig's (1996) article "Parental Attitudes toward Bilingualism in a Local Two-Way Immersion Program" is particularly relevant. This study describes why both European-American and Latino parents in one public school district chose to enroll their children in a local Spanish–English two-way immersion program, and how ongoing program evaluation was used to sustain a high level of support and participation.

Exploration

Visit a grocery store in which products from other countries are sold. Find a packaged product for which the product information is given only in a foreign language that you do not speak or read—without translation into English. When these conditions are met, examine the product you have chosen. Is it an item that you might already know how to cook? Or is it totally unfamiliar? Is the product labeling or packaging in a familiar format, or is the information represented in a way that is totally unlike a similar label might look in English? What can you predict about the meaning of words based on your familiarity with the item or with the packaging? If you were teaching that language to native-English-speaking students, what part of the product or the label might be easiest to match with its English counterpart?

Looking at Classrooms

Visit a bilingual program at a local school. With permission, interview several language-minority students to ask if they would like to attend a program in which native-English-speaking students would learn their language while they learned English. See if they can explain what they believe might be the advantages and disadvantages of such a program.

PEARSON
myeducationlab

The Power of Classroom Practice
www.myeducationlab.com

Family Literacy Program

A family literacy program has many benefits for families who speak English as a second language. In this video, parents visit the school regularly to participate in activities of their children's choosing.

> To access the video, go to MyEducationLab (www.myeducationlab.com), choose the Díaz-Rico and Weed text, and log in to MyEducationLab for English Language Learners. Select the topic Programs for English Learners, and watch the video entitled "Family Literacy Program."

Answer the following questions:
1. Name three positive outcomes that occur when parents are involved in their child's education.
2. Why is it sometimes difficult to get parents who speak English as a second language, or not at all, to become involved in school activities? What can schools do to make these parents feel more welcome? And more specifically, what could you, as a teacher, do to involve parents more in your classroom?

Assessment

Assessment plays a key role in determining academic progress. Chapter 7 surveys the current emphasis on standards-based instruction and the various ways in which English learners are assessed and placed in appropriate instruction. The accompanying figure highlights Part Three of the theoretical model presented in the introduction. In the figure, one can see the key role assessment plays not only in instruction but also in learning about the learner, in the process of classroom instruction, and in the policy decisions that affect the organization and management of schooling.

Theoretical Model for CLAD Assessment

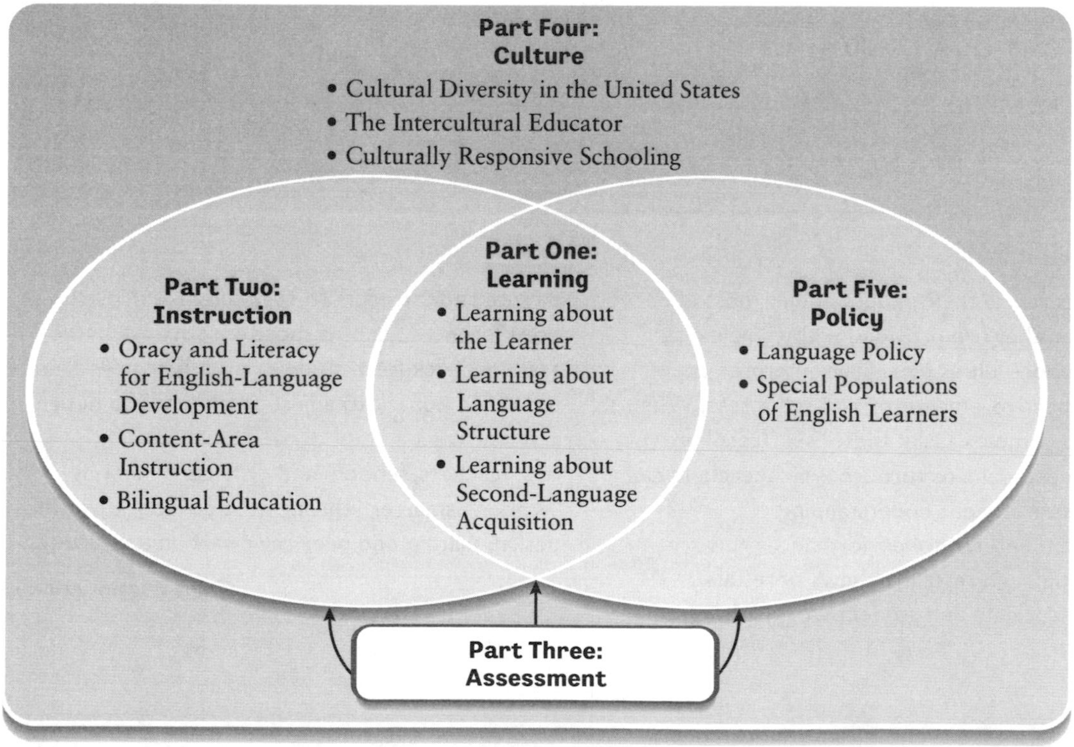

**Part Four:
Culture**
- Cultural Diversity in the United States
- The Intercultural Educator
- Culturally Responsive Schooling

**Part Two:
Instruction**
- Oracy and Literacy for English-Language Development
- Content-Area Instruction
- Bilingual Education

**Part One:
Learning**
- Learning about the Learner
- Learning about Language Structure
- Learning about Second-Language Acquisition

**Part Five:
Policy**
- Language Policy
- Special Populations of English Learners

**Part Three:
Assessment**

Language and Content-Area Assessment

Peers can use scoring rubrics to give one another feedback before a final grade is recorded.

Students reveal their understanding most effectively when they are provided with complex, authentic opportunities to explain, interpret, apply, shift perspective, empathize, and self-assess. When applied to complex tasks, these "six facets" provide a conceptual lens through which teachers can better assess student understanding.

Student and school performance gains are achieved through regular reviews of results (achievement data and student work) followed by targeted adjustments to curriculum and instruction. Teachers become most effective when they seek feedback from students and their peers and use that feedback to adjust approaches to design and teaching.

Teachers, schools, and districts benefit by "working smarter" through the collaborative design, sharing, and peer review of units of study.

Grant Wiggins (2005)

Assessment is a process for determining the current level of a learner's performance or knowledge. The results of the assessment are then used to modify or improve the learner's performance or knowledge. Assessment informs educators about the strengths and needs of language learners so that students are properly placed and appropriately instructed. Assessment is also used to inform school authorities, parents, or other concerned parties of student progress. A final use of assessment is to compare student achievement against national goals and standards, which poses a significant problem for English learners.

Various evaluation methods have been used with English learners. Some are required by government programs and legal mandates, and others are a part of standard classroom practice. In the domain of reading instruction, for example, teachers use a variety of assessment tools, including informal reading inventories, literacy skills checklists, running records, miscue analysis, guided observations, and portfolio assessment (Swartz, Shook, Klein, Moon, Bunnell, Belt, & Huntley, 2003).

Aside from the usual concerns that such assessment practices be valid, reliable, and practical, teachers of English learners must be careful to ensure that tests are fair (free from cultural and linguistic bias) and normed for English learners—that is, that they do not unfairly measure English learners against a standard designed for native speakers of English. Furthermore, tests must advance students' understanding and abilities if they are to constitute a valid part of education. Tests should not be merely instruments of diagnosis for labeling, placing, and designing remediation.

Ideally, assessment provides information about students' abilities and enables teachers to use this information humanistically—that is, for the benefit of the student's academic and personal development. However, the use of testing to further second-language development is problematic. If testing is aligned with curricular goals that emphasize "correct" English rather than authentic communication, the learners may passively submit to acquiring a minimum level of achievement without intrinsic motivation. Testing must therefore be an integral part of a learning environment that encourages students to seek meaning and use a second language to fulfill academic and personal goals. In the model presented in the figure on page 177, assessment has an impact on instruction, learning, and culture and is itself affected by culture.

Educational Standards and Standardized Assessment

The educational standards movement is an attempt on the part of educators and others to specify exactly what students are expected to learn in each content area and at each grade level (see Chapter 5). The emphasis on standards dovetails with outcome-based learning, a philosophy of education that relies on explicit connections between goals specified and outcomes produced. Assumptions that underlie this approach are straightforward. In order to achieve learning, teachers must first describe in detail what students are expected to accomplish, or perform; they then propose the kind of evidence that will substantiate this performance; they then design learning activities that will accumulate the desired evidence. Thus, curricula are planned according to state content standards. Achievement of these standards is measured on statewide achievement tests as mandated by the 2001 federal NCLB law. Table 7.1 offers terms that are currently associated with NCLB.

Advantages of Standards-Based Instruction for English Learners

An advantage of establishing content and performance standards for English learners is that by using these standards, teachers can focus on what students need to know. Teachers can pursue an articulated sequence of instruction, integrating the teaching of English into increasingly sophisticated levels of language and meaningful discourse, fluent communication skills, and cognitive academic language proficiency.

Table 7.1

Assessment Terms Associated with No Child Left Behind

Adequate yearly progress (AYP)	A federal requirement that schools make progress in approaching the goal specified in No Child Left Behind that 100 percent of students perform at a "proficient" level. AYP is calculated at a given percentage above the school's baseline measure. Ninety-five percent of students in all subgroups and 100 percent of the school must make AYP for the school as a whole to make AYP (Guillaume, 2008, p. 181).
National Assessment of Educational Progress (NAEP)	A measure of academic achievement that is designed to provide a picture of student progress over time. The assessment is conducted periodically in mathematics, reading, science, writing, the arts, civics, economics, geography, and U.S. history, with assessments in world history and in foreign language anticipated in 2012. Because NAEP assessments are administered uniformly and essentially the same year after year using the same sets of test booklets across the nation, the results can serve as a common metric for all states and selected urban districts.
High-stakes evaluation	When students—or teachers, for that matter—are assessed, the results have important consequences for the test subjects, such as the possibility of placement in special services or graduation for students, career ramifications for teachers, and either reduced or compensatory funding for schools.
Low-performing school	A school that has achievement scores below expectations on a continual basis leads it to qualify for extra resources coupled with a mandated school-improvement plan.
Multiple measures	Because NCLB requires at least one measure in addition to standardized testing be used to determine progress, school districts use more than one instrument to increase the evidence on which decisions are made.

Source: Adapted from Guillarme (2008).

The use of standards avoids what has been a too-frequent practice in the past: the use in ELD of materials and practices designed for younger students or for special education students (Walqui, 1999). Gándara (1997) reported vast discrepancies between the curricula offered to English speakers and to English learners. The use of standards can alter this practice. Moreover, surveys show that parents of all ethnic groups support standards and testing as a means to improve schools (Wadsworth & Remaley, 2007).

Why do standards matter? When learning is standardized, every student is expected to learn a specific, predetermined "amount" of knowledge, and that learning is measured by evidence of attainment of that knowledge. This protects students from being neglected, or from learning something that only one individual teacher believes is important. Such practices as giving students credit merely for occupying a seat in a class or giving a weak grade that is nevertheless sufficient for passing are no longer acceptable (Reeves, 2002).

Achievement Testing and No Child Left Behind

The federal No Child Left Behind Act of 2001 (NCLB, 2002) requires that all students be "proficient" in reading and mathematics by the 2013–14 school year. Beginning in 2005–06, all public school students in grades 3 through 8 must be tested annually, using state achievement tests. This group includes English learners, who must be assessed in a valid and reasonable manner that includes reasonable accommodations and, to the extent practicable, testing in the primary language. Those students who have completed thirty months of schooling must, however, be tested in English reading (special exemptions can be applied for on a case-by-case basis, and students living in Puerto Rico are automatically exempted). States must establish baseline proficiency goals to which yearly progress is compared (Gunning, 2005).

Although the noblest goal of assessment is to benefit the student, in the current climate of standards-driven instruction, the results of assessment are often used to assess the effectiveness of the teacher's instruction. This is called "high-stakes" assessment—and much is at stake: Often, funds are augmented for schools that show increased test scores or, conversely, withheld from schools in which test scores have not risen over a given period. Under NCLB, schools that fail to make acceptable yearly progress (AYP) for two years in a row are subject to corrective action.

A key drawback to NCLB is that although it mandates that all students reach "proficiency" by 2014, it allows each state to set its own definition of what constitutes proficiency. There is no real incentive for states to define proficiency rigorously.

Many states find that students are passing reading proficiency tests in lower grades, but on eighth-grade tests, results take a nosedive (Cronin, Dahlin, Adkins, & Kingsbury, 2007). Obviously middle school has more complex subject matter, but there may be other reasons why reading skills decline dramatically. It may be that students have not been taught to enjoy reading, and thus do not read very much—and whatever skills they have gained atrophy.

Example of Concept: The TAKS Measure of Proficiency

At the heart of NCLB is the call for all schoolchildren to become proficient in reading and mathematics by the year 2014—but each state is free to define and measure its own version of "proficiency." Texas uses the Texas Assessment of Knowledge and Skills (TAKS). Yet in a report published by the Fordham Institute (Cronin, Dahlin, Adkins, & Kingbury, 2007), researchers found TAKS to be of below-average difficulty—in other words, a misleading indicator of proficiency. Using this measure, fewer of Texas's schools would be labeled "low-performing"—thus leading parents to believe a student was "proficient," even though the child scored below two-thirds of students in other states. Obviously, "standards" are relative (Julian, 2007).

NCLB insists that the status of English learners not be hidden among the averages, but specifically disaggregated. The rationale for testing is to promote accountability: to determine the level of English proficiency of students so appropriate services can be rendered, to ensure that English learners access the core curriculum, to identify individuals who are falling behind, and to report to parents what children have and have not accomplished (Rahilly & Weinmann, 2007).

The aim of using standardized measures is to ensure that all students are held to the same level of performance. Yet the net result is often to penalize schools whose English learners do not score well on tests designed for native-English speakers. This poses a dilemma: On the one hand, high standards across schools do not permit school districts to lower academic standards for schools with high percentages of English learners. On the other hand, forcing students to undergo frustrating experiences of repeated testing in English when they are not ready can discourage students. Alternatively, testing students in their primary language is not effective if schools do not offer primary-language instruction.

Example of Concept: Standardized Testing and Bilingual Students

Sara Monempour was two years old when her family moved from Tehran to Los Angeles. Then she did what most new Americans do: learned English. Attending Los Angeles County public schools, Monempour excelled in class but scored "unbelievably low" on standardized reading tests, up to and including the SAT. Then she noticed that most of her bilingual classmates did poorly, too.

"We were raised here . . . and yet this pattern was always a factor," says Monempour, who speaks Farsi at home. "People who speak a different language at home or with their friends and family would have issues with testing" (Toppo, 2004).

Disadvantages of Standards-Based Instruction for English Learners

Although the overall goal is noble—devising a set of very broad standards for all students and measuring success according to a common set of criteria—the ongoing needs of English learners mandate that school districts remain flexible about the specific means for addressing standards and determining student achievement (Nelson-Barber, 1999). The heavy emphasis on high-stakes testing—and the attendant punitive consequences for schools with low test scores—places English learners at risk of failure (August, Hakuta, & Pompa, 1994). In fact, schools across the United States report low test scores for students who are linguistically "nonmainstream," including those who speak dialects of English at home that do not correspond to the academic English used in schools. Math test scores on the California Achievement Test show a gradual decline for English learners compared to all students, from a 14 percent gap in grade 2 to a 26 percent gap in grade 10 (Bielenberg & Wong Fillmore, 2004/2005). Clearly, it is not the testing itself causing this decline; but the emphasis on testing leaves little time for teachers to focus on teaching the academic subjects and the language that English learners need to acquire to perform well on high-stakes tests.

The high-stakes testing that drives the school-accountability movement has been shown to have important consequences for racial and ethnic minority students of low socioeconomic status. Valencia and Villareal (2003) predicted that Texas's requirement that all third-grade students take the Texas Assessment of Knowledge and Skills (TAKS) to be promoted would result in a 23 percent retention rate for English learners. Previous studies have shown that once retained, such students typically fall behind in their academic achievement and have a higher probability of dropping out of school.

The chief critique of standards-based school reform is that it treats the symptoms of school failure (poor achievement) rather than the cause (inferior schools). School failure is assigned to the individual rather than the systemic denial of equal educational opportunity by unequal school funding resulting in poor schools and lack of resources (Valencia & Villareal, 2003).

Standards work best when expectations are held constant for all groups of students at the same time that equal curricula and instruction are offered to all groups. This is not the case in most schools; students are tracked into classes of perceived high-, medium-, and low-instructional rigor. As Ryan (2008) points out, there is no quality education without equality in education.

Haycock (2001) has documented that students at risk of failure are more likely to have insufficient resources, less experienced teachers who are not prepared for the subjects they teach, and a watered-down curriculum, combined with low expectations for student achievement. This calls into question whether state standards and assessments can achieve educational equity.

Under NCLB, schooling is viewed as a market commodity: Schools whose students do not meet standards are perceived as "failing," and parents can obtain vouchers to take their children elsewhere. The burden, then, is on the family to find an alternative placement. Oakes and Lipton (2007) counter this rationale with the argument that every school should be given the funds to provide students with high-quality opportunities to learn, and families should not bear the burden of locating an alternative school.

Example of Concept: Testing Replaces Teaching

Facing standardized tests has become a frequent school experience for immigrant children who are learning the English language. Under the NCLB law, schools must make sure all their students, including English-language learners (ELLs), pass standardized tests or face consequences such as state takeover or privatization. Such high-stakes testing programs are encouraging schools to drop untested subjects from the school day, cancel English as a second language (ESL) classes, eliminate native-language instruction, and focus on lower-level academic skills

I saw all this firsthand when I took a teaching position in 2004–2005 at an elementary school in the Maryland suburbs of Washington, DC, in the heart of a Salvadoran immigrant community. ELL students in the fifth-grade classroom where I was assigned took five different standardized tests during the school year, some of them more than once. During the course of the year, my students missed thirty-three days of ESL classes, or about 18 percent of their English instruction, due to standardized testing.

Source: Monroe (2008, n.p.)

The answer to this dilemma is for school districts to invest in high-level, late-exit primary-language instruction and allow students to be tested in their primary language. The catch is the NCLB provision that students must be tested in English reading after three years of schooling. This regulation pressures schools to begin English reading early. English learners, then, are assumed to attain grade-level expectations in English reading that are set for native-English speakers, resulting in pressure toward submersion—or, at best, early-exit transition bilingual education programs—as a preferred model.

Linking Assessment to Progress for English Learners

Aside from their performance on standardized tests, English learners' achievement in English is measured and directed by standards-based curricula. This is made possible by a linkage between standards, placement testing, instruction, and careful record keeping.

Placement tests that are directly linked to standards-based classroom instruction for English learners permit teachers to begin use of effective instructional practices as soon as students enter the classroom. Placement tests that align with standards, which in turn align with daily instruction, provide a seamless system that helps teachers to track students' continuous progress toward mainstream instruction. Each linkage—from standards to assessment to instruction and back to assessment—is explained in the following sections.

The English-Language Development (ELD) Framework

English-language development takes place in stages. Rather than using the four stages introduced in the Natural Approach (preproduction, early production, speech emergence, and intermediate fluency), the California English Language Development Standards (CDE, 2002) are divided into five stages: Beginning, Early Intermediate, Intermediate, Early Advanced, and Advanced. The ELD standards describe expected proficiency on the part of the English learner in each of six key domains of language (Listening and Speaking, Reading/Word Analysis, Reading Fluency and Systematic Vocabulary Development, Reading Comprehension, Reading Literary Response and Analysis, and Writing Strategies and Application). For example, in the domain of Listening and Speaking, expected language proficiency increases gradually from Beginning to Advanced levels. Table 7.2 depicts the expectations for each of the five levels.

The ELD standards are incorporated into academic lessons as language objectives. For example, an English learner at the Beginning level is capable of the following: "Answer[ing] simple questions with one- or two-word responses." In order to advance to Early Intermediate, this student must become capable of "Ask[ing]/ answer[ing] instructional questions using simple sentences." Therefore, the Early Intermediate standard becomes an appropriate language objective not only for reading and language arts instruction but also for mathematics, social studies, or science.

If the lesson offers ample opportunity to develop this skill, and the teacher collects enough evidence (anecdotal/observational in the case of listening/speaking objectives) that the student has mastered it, the teacher may use this evidence to advance the learner to the next level using an ELD checklist or other tracking device. For example, Alhambra School District in Alhambra, California, uses the English Language Development Progress Profile, a folder with the ELD standards printed in checklist format, with spaces for yearly test scores (see Sasser, Naccarato, Corren, & Tran, 2002).

Linking Placement Tests to Language Development

Several states have developed or use commercially available language-development tests (Loop & Barron, 2002). California, for example, uses the California English Language Development Test (CELDT) to identify new students who are English learners in kindergarten through grade 12, determine their level of English proficiency, and assess their progress annually toward becoming fluent-English proficient (FEP). A student's score on the CELDT (see www.cde.ca.gov/ta/tg/el) corresponds to a

Table 7.2

Listening and Speaking Expectations in the California English-Language-Development Standards for English Learners at Five Levels

ELD Level	Expectations
Beginning (K–2)	• Begins to speak with a few words or sentences, using some English phonemes and rudimentary English grammatical phrases • Answers simple questions with one- or two-word responses • Responds to simple directions and questions using physical actions and other means of nonverbal communication • Independently uses common social greetings and simple repetitive phrases
Early Intermediate	• Begins to be understood when speaking, but may have some inconsistent use of Standard English grammatical forms and sounds • Asks/answers questions using phrases or simple sentences • Retells familiar stories and short conversations by using appropriate gestures, expressions, and illustrative objects • Orally communicates basic needs • Recites familiar rhymes, songs, and simple stories
Intermediate	• Asks/answers instructional questions using simple sentences • Listens attentively to stories/information and identifies key details and concepts using both verbal and nonverbal responses • Can be understood when speaking, using consistent Standard English forms and sounds; however, some rules may not be in evidence • Actively participates in social conversations with peers and adults on familiar topics by asking and answering questions and soliciting information • Retells stories and talks about school-related activities using expanded vocabulary, descriptive words, and paraphrasing
Early Advanced	• Listens attentively to stories/information and orally identifies key details and concepts • Retells stories in greater detail including characters, setting, and plot • Is understood when speaking, using consistent Standard English forms, sounds, intonation, pitch, and modulation, but may have random errors • Actively participates and initiates more extended social conversations with peers and adults on unfamiliar topics by asking and answering questions, restating and soliciting information • Recognizes appropriate ways of speaking that vary based on purpose, audience, and subject matter • Asks and answers instructional questions with more extensive supporting elements
Advanced	• Listens attentively to stories/information on new topics and identifies both orally and in writing key details and concepts • Demonstrates understanding of idiomatic expressions by responding to and using them appropriately • Negotiates/initiates social conversations by questioning, restating, soliciting information, and paraphrasing • Consistently uses appropriate ways of speaking and writing that vary based on purpose, audience, and subject matter • Narrates and paraphrases events in greater detail, using more extended vocabulary

Source: Adapted from the California English-Language Arts Framework, online at www.cde.ca.gov/re/pn/fd/documents/englangdev-stnd.pdf.

student's skill level as defined in the California ELD standards. The CELDT was one of the first assessments to use a standards-based instrument to measure the proficiency of English learners. It has been used since 2003 to meet requirements of NCLB. The use of the CELDT was revised in 2006 to raise the cut scores, or the levels at which English learners were deemed "proficient," in order for students' proficiency to make more sense when aligned with the mainstream English-language arts proficiency.

The CELDT measures four language domains in grades 2–12: listening, speaking, reading, and writing (listening and speaking only in grades K–1). Students can score at five levels (Beginning, Early Intermediate, Intermediate, Early Advanced, or Advanced), and are reclassified based on this score (plus their score on the state English language-arts test, teacher evaluation, and parent consultation). They are tested once upon entry (initial CELDT) to determine their status, and then annually (annual CELDT) to determine their progress (Linquanti, 2008).

Each classroom lesson features one or two language-development goals. Record keeping consists of the teacher's checking off such goals as they are attained. This progress is tested annually during the CELDT readministration.

When students attain a redesignation level on the CELDT and are transitioned into mainstream English classes, teachers use the California English-Language Arts (ELA) standards (CDE, 1998a) to create standards-based language arts lessons. Because the ELD and ELA standards are closely related, the expectation is that English learners will make a smooth transition from one set of standards to the other.

WestEd publishes an ELD Student Report Card to accompany the Map of Standards for English Learners (Carr & Lagunoff, 2006), consisting of a template with essential ELD skill clusters with five columns for the five ELD levels (downloadable from www.wested/org/reportcard in English or Spanish). If teachers use the recording system to note the grading period and year in which a student has met an ELD standard, it is easy to track an English learner's progress as part of the required individual student progress monitoring system.

Linking Standards-Based Classroom Instruction to Assessment

In standards-based instruction, assessment is linked to instruction in two fundamental ways. First, instruction is designed with assessment in mind. The concern of the teacher is that instructional activities produce evidence that can be used to document student progress. Therefore, the assessment is embedded and authentic—the activities are designed in advance to be assessed. For formative assessment, the teacher helps students prepare this evidence by circulating during instruction to be available to them, by providing explicit feedback, and by encouraging students to self-monitor their progress toward completion of the lesson objective. Summative, or final, assessment shows that students have fulfilled the given standard.

Example of Concept: Linking Standards, Instruction, and Assessment

Mr. Phelan has two groups of third-grade English learners, twelve who are at the Early Advanced level and thirteen who are at the Advanced level. These levels share two similar ELD standards in the category Reading Comprehension: "Reads and uses basic text features such as title, table of contents, and chapter headings" (Early Advanced) and "Reads and uses basic text features such as title, table of contents, chapter headings, diagrams, and index" (Advanced). He prepares a treasure hunt assignment for the two groups. During their science class, the Early Advanced students answer questions from the science chapter that require them to list the source of the answer (title, table of contents, etc.) as well as the answer itself. The Advanced group has the same questions, as well as three bonus questions derived from the book's index and a chapter diagram. Mr. Phelan uses the results of the treasure hunt activity as evidence that both groups have met their corresponding ELD standards.

Second, assessment and instruction are linked through standardized testing. Because the classroom teacher does not know the test questions in advance, and because the tests sample the instructional content, there is no one-to-one match between instruction and assessment as there is in the first instance. Teachers can only hope that their efforts to meet the requirements of the standards-based curriculum produce high standardized test scores.

Purposes of Assessment

Assessment instruments can be used for a number of purposes: to make decisions about student placement, to make day-to-day instructional decisions such as when to provide a student with additional mediation, to make resource decisions such as allocation of instructional time or materials, and to measure student achievement against standards. Various types of tests are used for these purposes: *Proficiency tests, diagnostic* and *placement tests, achievement tests, student work samples, observations while students are working, performance-based tests,* and *competency tests.* Each will be discussed in turn.

Teachers who use assessment skillfully can choose which methods of assessment are most useful for classroom decision making; develop effective grading procedures; communicate assessment results to students, parents, and other educators; and recognize unethical, illegal, and otherwise inappropriate assessment methods and uses of assessment information (Ward & Murray-Ward, 1999).

Formative versus Summative Assessment

Before discussing types of tests, it is important to make one distinction. Not all assessment is end measurement (summative), used for final "sum-up" of student performance. Formative assessment is increasingly important as a way of providing an early measure of student performance so that corrective adjustment can be applied. Because many instructional activities are observable (such as guided, shared, and interactive reading), they can provide information about how well the student is doing. The teacher who monitors these activities and offers feedback can improve the quality of student work during the process of learning.

Formative assessment takes place through five means: teacher questioning, offering feedback through grading, peer assessment, self-assessment, and the formative use of summative tests (Black, Harrison, Lee, Marshall, & Wiliam, 2004). Table 7.3 summarizes key points for using these types of formative assessment.

Table 7.3

Key Points of Five Types of Formative Assessment

Type of Formative Assessment	Key Points
Teacher questioning	• Framing questions worth asking pinpoints essential understandings. • Increasing wait time after a question allows students time to create more thoughtful answers. • Brainstorming with a peer before answering increases a student's oral participation.
Feedback through grading	• Key written tasks focus on essential understandings. • Teacher feedback identifies what has been done well, what still needs improvement, and how to make that improvement. • Students need opportunities to respond to written feedback.
Peer assessment	• Teach students the habits and skills of collaborative assessment. • Students learn by teaching one another. • Peers are usually more willing to ask for help from one another than from the teacher. • Peer marking can isolate problems everyone is having. • Peer tutoring can help with specific individual problems.
Self-assessment	• Self-assessment helps students attain clarity about an assignment's goals and criteria. • Students benefit from concrete examples and scoring rubrics.
Formative use of summative assessment	• Students can generate sample test questions or take a sample examination.

Source: Adapted from Black et al. (2004).

Example of Concept: Using Formative Assessment

In order for formative assessment to be done by way of peer assessment, students need to practice giving feedback, as demonstrated by this account:

> I begin by having the class participate in several mock peer review sessions, in which students look at early drafts of student writing from previous semesters to discuss how they could be improved. . . . They pose questions to help clarify their understanding of the reading as they jot their commentary on the paper. Then the class critiques this commentary, or feedback, by discussing how it could help writers improve their texts.
>
> Initially, most students struggle to produce comments that are specific—and thus useful to the writer. . . . Eventually, students are able to tell the writer specifically what kind of information is needed, where it is necessary, and why it is important to the text as a whole. When students begin to pose these key questions to the writer, they are truly interacting with the text and will ultimately help shape it. (Anderson, 2004, p. 55)

Table 7.4 compares attributes of formative and summative assessment.

Table 7.4

Formative Versus Summative Assessment

Attribute	Formative	Summative
Purpose(s)	Monitor the learning to provide feedback about the progress of the student in order to reteach if necessary	Apply a final grade to the progress of the student
Who assesses	Self, peer, or the teacher	Usually the teacher
When work is assessed	During the lesson	At the end of the lesson
Form of assessment	Teacher observation, self-check, peer assessment	Final test, or final grade of classwork/homework
How work is assessed	Monitoring includes checking on students while they are working, collecting work samples, or checking work against rubrics	Use of scoring criteria—points are assigned to each question
How grade is obtained	No grade given, or tentative grade is given to indicate progress	Points are assigned to each item, and grades are connected with different ranges of point totals
Timing	During learning	After learning
How work is improved	Students may be given individual feedback, or class as a whole may be retaught; students may be grouped to be retaught portions that they have not mastered	The teacher may use results to rank or group students for subsequent teaching; results may inform next year's teaching—but it is too late to change current grades for current students
Who is informed by results	Teacher and students, in order to reteach what has not yet been learned	Teacher, students, administrators, and parents
Example	The teacher circulates, randomly checking progress of worksheet completion	Fill-in-the-blanks Short-answer test Multiple-choice test

Proficiency, Diagnostic, and Placement Tests

Proficiency tests measure a test taker's overall ability in English, usually defined independently of any particular instructional program. Proficiency tests are sometimes divided into subskills or modes of language (speaking, listening, writing, reading, vocabulary, and grammar), but experts in the field of second-language acquisition recommend that tests be a measure of communicative competence more than solely of grammar or vocabulary.

The proliferation of standardized tests has often resulted in an emphasis on the testing of decontextualized skills such as sentence-level punctuation, grammar, and spelling. This undermines the mode in which cognition is most effective: the ability of the brain to seek out and assemble personal meaning. Proficiency tests are poor tests of achievement because, by design, their content has little or no relationship to the content of an instructional program. They may also poorly diagnose what specific knowledge a student has or is lacking.

Diagnostic and placement tests are administered to determine specific aspects of a student's proficiency in a second language. Placement tests determine the academic level or the grade level into which students need to be placed. In addition to identifying students who are English learners and determining the level of proficiency, placement tests can be used to monitor progress of English learners in acquiring English and to assist in redesignating English learners to mainstream classrooms (Slater, 2000).

In the best case, however, the proficiency test used as a diagnostic or placement test is directly linked to subsequent instruction, such as the close link between California's ELD framework and the CELDT. Using the proficiency level designated by the test, the teacher can begin immediately to design appropriate instructional experiences for the English learner.

Example of Concept: Aligning CELDT Levels and Instruction

Sara, an eight-year-old third grader, is from Honduras, and her family returns to Tegucigalpa periodically to visit the extended family. She has been in the United States for a year. She began Spanish-language schooling at the age of four in Honduras and has attained a basic level of reading in Spanish. Her mother was a teacher in Tegucigalpa and helps her to maintain her Spanish reading skills. Her CELDT scores were Listening and Speaking 165, Reading 190, and Writing 100.

Sara's total score, 455, places her at the Early Intermediate level for students in the third grade. Her teacher recognizes that at the level of Early Intermediate, Sara can already "read familiar vocabulary, phrases, and sentences chorally and independently," and therefore will design reading instruction to provide evidence that Sara can, among other objectives drawn from the Intermediate level of the ELD standards, "use complex sentences and appropriate vocabulary to express ideas and needs in social and academic settings."

Achievement Tests

An achievement test measures a student's success in learning specific instructional content, whether language (knowledge about English) or another subject (e.g., mathematics, science). A curriculum-based achievement test is given after instruction has taken place and contains only material that was actually taught. The staff of the instructional program usually prepares such a test.

Rather than testing samples of a student's storehouse of knowledge, testing might measure a student's ability to think knowledgeably. For example, a beginning English learner may be given clues to a treasure hunt to practice the vocabulary associated with the schoolroom (eraser, chalk, globe), and a teacher may observe the student's ability to collect all the relevant items in an informal assessment. During the exercise, the student's English development is combined with critical and creative thinking.

However, the contemporary trend toward implementing national standards for achievement has caused a proliferation of achievement tests that are not aligned with specific curricular content. The pressure for students to perform well on these tests, which are often used by administrators as an index of academic success, may detract from time spent on language-development activities. Teachers who understand the needs of English learners can adjust their instruction to balance lesson planning with the need to prepare students to perform well on standardized achievement tests.

Example of Concept: Preparing Students for Standardized Tests

Third-grade teacher Jim Hughes does two particular things to prepare his students for standardized tests:

One is to expand their vocabulary—the vocabulary specifically found in the tests they must take. For example, the vocabulary of math includes words such as *about, approximately, estimate, round off, total, twice, double*—words they may know, but not their mathematical meanings. But, of course, the students have to know the words in context, so we practice, practice, practice.

Second, I spend a lot of time encouraging the kids that they can do well on the standardized tests. I ask them to "try their best." I try to lower anxiety as much as possible by being nearby. Motivation, then, as well as reassurance are a big part of the "special" thing I try to give the children.

Competency Tests

Almost half the states use minimum-competency testing programs to identify students who may be promoted or graduated (NCES, 2001). In some states, such as Florida, English learners in certain grades who have been in an ELD program for two or fewer years may be exempt from the state minimum-competency testing program. Many school districts mandate remedial instruction between terms for students who fail to meet minimum-competency standards. It is important that such supplementary instruction take into consideration the needs of English learners.

Example of Concept: Competency Requirements

The state of North Carolina requires that students pass "rigorous" competency tests in reading and mathematics in order to receive a North Carolina high school diploma. English learners must pass the competency tests as well as meet all state and local graduation requirements to graduate and receive a high school diploma. These students are eligible for certain types of accommodations while taking the tests—testing in a separate room; scheduled extended time; multiple test sessions; test administrator reads test aloud in English; students mark in test book; use of English or native-language dictionary or electronic translator. The student's committee for limited English proficiency determines the need and the type of accommodation. The use of accommodations must be documented and should be used routinely with the student by the classroom teacher (Public Schools of North Carolina, 2004, p. 3).

Methods of Assessment

Test scores, classroom grades, and teacher observation and evaluation are common bases for determining student progress. The judgments resulting from this testing may affect students' present adjustment to school and their future academic and social success. The social and economic pressures from testing often overshadow the curriculum and the affective goals of schooling.

Performance-based testing is a growing alternative to standardized testing, although standardized testing persists because of the economic and political investment in this type of assessment. For classroom purposes, teacher observation and evaluation—supplemented by other sources of data—remain potent allies for students' academic progress. Students can play a role in the assessment process by evaluating their own language development, content knowledge, and strategies for learning. This helps students become self-regulated learners who can plan their own learning activities and use of time and resources (O'Malley & Pierce, 1996).

Linking Assessment to the Integrated Curriculum

The use of an integrated curriculum promotes language and academic development for English learners. Units of study in literature, math, science, and social studies may be combined into an interdisciplinary program in which students can use a variety of communication systems (e.g., language, art, music, drama) to pursue open-ended assignments. Assessment is a natural part of this curriculum. Student outcomes are documented in a variety of ways—time capsules, surveys, creative works, posters, and so forth. Good records allow teachers to track individual progress and also reflect and store many observations about students' skills and interests. The book *Scenarios for ESL Standards-Based Assessment* (TESOL, 2001) uses actual classroom settings to illustrate how teachers integrate ongoing assessment with instructional activities.

Authentic Assessment

O'Malley and Pierce (1996) defined authentic assessment as "the multiple forms of assessment that reflect student learning, achievement, motivation, and attitudes on instructionally relevant classroom activities" (p. 4). Examples of authentic assessment include the use of portfolios, projects, experiments, current event debates, and community-based inquiries. Assessments are considered "authentic" if they stem directly from classroom activities, allow students to share in the process of evaluating their progress, and are valid and reliable in that they truly assess a student's classroom performance in a stable manner. The advantage of authentic assessment is that it is directly related to classroom performance and permits teachers to design and offer the extra mediation students may need as determined by the assessment.

Example of Concept: Authentic Assessment

At International High School in Queens, New York, authentic assessment is deeply embedded into all activities. In the Global Studies and Art interdisciplinary cluster, students researched a world religion that was unfamiliar to them. Their assignment was to create or re-create a religious artifact typical of the religion.

To begin the project, students brainstormed possible research questions. Project activities included visiting a museum that exhibits religious artifacts, researching in dyads, and communicating their research in progress to peers.

On the day of the final performance, students sat at tables of six, shared their findings, asked questions, and clarified what they had learned. The culminating activity was an informal conversation in yet another grouping so that students could expand their perspectives. Although students had their written reports at hand, they could not rely on them for their initial presentations or during the discussion (Walqui, 1999, p. 74).

Performance-Based Assessment

Performance-based testing corresponds directly to what is taught in the classroom and can easily be incorporated into classroom routines and learning activities. Methods for assessing a performance can be divided into two main types: *standardized* (e.g., tests, checklists, observations, rating scales, questionnaires, and structured interviews, in which each student responds to the same instructions under the same conditions) and *less standardized* (e.g., student work samples, journals, games, debates, story retelling, anecdotal reports, and behavioral notes, in which the scoring is tailored to the product in a less standard fashion). Using a combination of standardized and less standardized assessments provides a cross-check of student capabilities (Peregoy & Boyle, 2008). Students may be assessed through standardized means such as teacher-designed examinations that are intended to be scored quickly. (These, of course, are not as elaborately "standardized" using national norms as are large-scale, commercially published tests.)

Adapted Instruction: Administering a Classroom Test

- Teach to the assessment; let students know throughout the unit how their achievement will be measured.
- Align instructional methods and assessment methods.
- Check comprehension frequently throughout instruction.
- Supplement tests with other measures (observation, participation, discussions with students and projects).
- Review tests "through the eyes of an English learner." Look for difficult language and cultural bias; provide support such as word banks.
- Read tests to beginning English learners.
- Allow more time for English learners or give the test in sections.

Source: Grognet, Jameson, Franco, and Derrick-Mescua (2000).

Questionnaires and surveys can help teachers learn about many students' skills and interests at once. An observation checklist allows teachers to circulate among students while they are working and monitor specific skills, such as emergent literacy skills, word-identification skills, and oral reading (Miller, 1995). The advantage of standardized assessment is its speed of scoring, using predetermined questions and answer keys.

Less standardized, or open-ended, assessments may feature longer problem-solving exercises, assignments that involve performances or exhibitions, and portfolios that contain student work gathered over a longer period of time. Despite the potential drawbacks of open-ended assessment, it can furnish valuable information about students' abilities.

Not all open-ended assessments are difficult to grade; teacher-made *scoring rubrics* can be determined in advance of an assignment and assist both teacher and student by communicating in advance the basis for scoring. Like objectives, scoring rubrics help to specify the outcome that is expected from a learning activity. McDaniel and Wilde (2008, p. 94) point out four ways that rubrics clarify expectations:

1. They state the level of knowledge that is expected.
2. They establish the dimensions of quality that are expected.
3. They describe the levels of achievement that can be performed (e.g., the minimal level that will be accepted, as well as clear descriptions of what higher levels of quality may look like).
4. They define explicit criteria for rating each achievement level.

Adapted Instruction: Developing a Rubric

- Identify desired results: What should students *know* and *be able to do* at the end of the lesson/unit?
- Determine acceptable evidence: What *performance* (task) will the students do? The performance should *integrate* and *apply* learning from the unit in a real-life task, such as present a position to an authentic audience, gather and report data, design and conduct an experiment, solve a real-life math problem.
- Check with students periodically to be sure their work is on target.
- Whenever possible, give students a chance to revise the "final draft" so it better meets the criteria (conference with students before they submit the draft; allow students to work in dyads or small groups to exchange and critique one anothers' work according to the rubric).
- Plan learning experiences and instruction to lead to the performance.

Source: Grognet et al. (2000).

Teachers play an important role in assessing the developing skills of English learners. To assess bilingual students fairly, teachers must consider three sources of information: the results of assessment, their own understanding of the thinking processes that students use, and an understanding of the background knowledge from which students draw (Brisk, 1998). Overall, the responsibility for documenting the success of English learners is shared between teachers and school administrators, who work together to monitor students' progress and showcase the success of effective programs (Torres-Guzmán, Abbate, Brisk, & Minaya-Rowe, 2002).

Classroom Tests. Tests may be highly convergent (one right answer required) or may be open-ended, with many possible answers. Authentic tests of ability require students to have a repertoire of responses that call for judgment and skill in using language, skills, and knowledge.

Portfolio Assessment. The purposes of portfolio assessment are to maintain a long-term record of students' progress, to provide a clear and understandable measure of student productivity instead of a single number, to offer opportunities for improved student self-image as a result of showing progress and accomplishment, to recognize different learning styles, and to provide an active role for students in self-assessment (Gottlieb, 1995).

Portfolios can include writing samples (compositions, letters, reports, drawings, dictation); student self-assessments; audio recordings (retellings, oral think-alouds); photographs and video recordings; semantic webs and concept maps; and teacher notes about students (Glaser & Brown, 1993). Portfolio records about students should be descriptive (what the child does when learning). Once every few weeks, the teacher reviews these records and makes interpretations, making notes on the file about a student's strengths and weaknesses, and making tentative conclusions that plan ways to help the student succeed. These reflections and insights are the basis for emerging understanding about that student (Barr, Blachowicz, Bates, Katz, & Kaufman, 2007).

Example of Concept: What's in a Student Portfolio?

Mr. Zepeda gets baseline data from his students in order to assess their levels and to group them for instruction. He takes a running record as he listens to students read individually. Students write a friendly letter so Mr. Zepeda can determine their spelling development and their ability to express themselves in writing. In addition, he schedules individual conferences to learn about students' interests. He sets up a schedule so that he is collecting material for the portfolios on a regular basis, and he encourages the students to select work for their portfolios as well.

By the time of parent conferences, the students' portfolios contain writing samples; anecdotal records; photos; periodic running records; periodic assessments; records of books the student has read; a complete writing project including prewriting, drafts, and final, published copy; a summary of the student's progress; and a list of goals set and accomplished. In preparation for the conference, Mr. Zepeda tells the students, "I want you to select the one piece of work that you feel best about. Write a one-page note to your parents explaining why you are proud of that piece of work and what you learned from doing it" (Herrell, 2000, p. 160).

Example of Concept: What's in a Teacher's Portfolio?

What do teachers file in an assessment portfolio? Faltis and Coulter (2008) describe Mrs. MacPherson's language arts assessment for a sample student in her tenth-grade English class. In a three-ring binder she maintains a section for each student. In the section "Alex as a reader," she files a copy of the miscue analysis she did at the beginning of the year, along with other, shorter such assessments, some with annotations of her observations. She also has a set of sticky notes from informal observations she has made while walking around the class with a clipboard. A similar page of notes is entitled "Alex as a writer." She keeps a page of skills and strategies that Alex has agreed to work on throughout year—Alex also has a set in his student portfolio that he refers to periodically. Again, she and he keep a similar page for writing. In this binder she also files results from district and state assessments and samples of Alex's work. In the front of the binder is a large spreadsheet with each student's name across the top and a set of English-language arts standards down the side—she checks off students' names when they have met the standards.

Portfolio Conference. When it is time for parent conferences, portfolios can provide the basis for dialogue. Juliana Ferry, a teacher at the Sequoyah School in Pasadena, California, asks students to make a presentation of their work to their parents. "The relationship shouldn't be adversarial," she says, "It's more of a collaboration" (Rivera, 2008, p. B6).

Standardized Tests

Although teacher-made tests can be standardized—that is, prepared with standard means of scoring across individuals—the term *standardized test* has come to mean large-scale, widely used tests standardized and published by large testing corporations. The benefits of standardized tests include speed in administration and convenience in scoring. Such tests are also considered to be unbiased, although questions arise as to their impartiality.

Between 2005 and 2007, twenty-three states across the United States added more than 11.3 million reading and math tests to their school curricula in order to keep up with NCLB requirements. New York alone has added more than 1.7 million tests. The school testing and testing services industry (which includes tutoring, test prep courses, and the tests themselves) is now estimated to be a $2.3 billion a year enterprise, with just five big companies controlling 90 percent of the statewide testing revenue (*Parade,* p. 10).

Norm-Referenced Tests. Large-scale standardized tests can be norm-referenced or criterion-referenced, or a combination of both. Norm-referenced tests compare student scores against a population of students with which the test has been standardized or "normed." Examples of norm-referenced tests are the Language Assessment Scales (LAS), a test designed to measure oral language skills in English and Spanish, and the Woodcock-Muñoz Language Assessment.

Criterion-Referenced Tests. A criterion is a level of performance against which students are measured. Criterion-referenced tests are used principally to find out how much of a clearly defined domain of language skills or materials students have learned. The focus is on how the students achieve in relation to the material, rather than to one another or to a national sample. On this type of test, all students may score 100 percent if they have learned the material well. In an ELD program with many levels, students may be required to pass criterion-referenced tests to progress from one level to the next.

Preparing Students for Standardized Tests. Many sources offer hints for successful test taking. Beck (2004) directed these to the student: Focus on one question at a time. Read the question carefully, making sure you understand the task involved. Read all the answer choices given, especially when the test asks for the *best* answer. If the question depends on reading comprehension, reread the selection as you consider each question. Make sure that each answer you mark corresponds to the question you are answering. If you do not understand a question, go on to the next one, answering the questions you know first—but make sure you mark an answer for each question. Go on to the next page if the test says "Continue" or "Go on." In a useful practice book for high-school students, Beck (2004) offered a series of sample examination questions covering multiple standards on the California English-Language Arts Content Standards.

Adapted Instruction: Thinking Skills for Standardized Tests

Standardized tests raise the persistent question, "Should teachers 'teach to the test'?" Should teachers rehearse students through sample test items in the hope that this will improve test performance? A more useful approach would be to teach the thinking skills that are required on most tests. These include the following:

- Analyzing questions
- Organizing a response
- Selecting and eliminating response possibilities
- Distinguishing between major and minor ideas
- Bringing prior knowledge to the fore

Source: Adapted from Conley (2008).

Williams (2007) questions the long-term effects of standardized testing on culturally and linguistically diverse students:

> What effect does the unrelenting emphasis on standardized literacy testing have on students' perception of the purposes and possibilities of literacy? By extension, what effect does testing have on their perception of the possibilities for themselves as readers and writers? Many concerns about identity and standardized testing have been framed in terms of race and social class. . . . [T]eachers and researchers have argued that standardized testing works not from a set of objective standards somehow as constant as the North Star but from a set of cultural conceptions about literacy that are neither objective nor static. Students whose race or social class is not a part of the dominant culture often face more complex challenges in meeting the standards of that dominant culture. (pp. 70–71)

Nieto and Bode (2008) urge teachers to be proactive about testing:

> With a group of interested colleagues and parents, you can approach the local school committee and ask that standardized tests be kept to a minimum, that the results be used in more appropriate ways, and that students not be placed at risk because of the results of such tests. . . . [Y]ou can start an after-school tutoring program for students at your school. Try to get funding from your school system or the PTA, or even from a local business. (p. 128)

Teacher Observation and Evaluation

Teachers can document student progress and diagnose student needs by observing and evaluating students on an ongoing basis. They then communicate students' progress to students, to parents, and to administrators.

Observation-Based Assessment. As students interact and communicate using language, an observant teacher can note individual differences. Observations may be formal (e.g., miscue analysis, running record, Student Oral Language Observation Matrix [SOLOM]) or informal, such as anecdotal reports to record a cooperative or collaborative group working together; students telling a story, giving a report, or explaining information; or children using oral language in other ways. Observations should extend across all areas of the curriculum and in all types of interactional situations. The may be based on highly structured content or on divergent and creative activities. Multiple observations show student variety and progress (Crawford, 1993).

Example of Concept: Anecdotal Observations

Mrs. Feingold keeps a pad of 3″ × 3″ Post-it™ notes in the pocket of her jacket. When she observes a student's particular use of language, use of a particular learning style, or other noteworthy behavior, she jots the information on a note, including the student's name, date, and time of day. She then transfers this note to a small notebook for safekeeping. Periodically, she files the notes by transferring them to a sheet of paper in each student's file. Just before parent conferences she duplicates this page—which contains as many as twelve notes side by side—as a permanent observational record of the student's language behaviors.

Adapted Instruction: Offering Feedback

There are various methods by which teachers can offer feedback: verbal praise, explaining a point of confusion, and informing if an answer is right or wrong; nonverbal feedback such as smiles, frowns, or nods; written feedback; individual, pair, group, or whole-class observations; promoting peer feedback; and immediate or delayed responses (Ong & Murugesan, 2007).

Student Self-Assessment.　Student self-assessment can take several forms. Students can discuss their progress with one another; write reflection logs; use checklists and inventories; and participate in reading and writing conferences to determine their progress and needs for growth. They can ask themselves the following questions: What did I learn? What did I do well? What am I still confused about? What do I need help with? What do I want to learn more about? What am I going to work on next? (Gottlieb, 2007, p. 67).

Grading.　A variety of approaches has been used to assign grades to English learners. Trying to fit nontraditional students into a traditional evaluation system can be frustrating for teachers. Some schools that assign a *traditional A–F grade scale* in accordance with grade-level expectations do not lower performance standards for English learners in sheltered classes, although assignments are adjusted to meet the students' language levels. A *modified A–F grade scale* uses A–F grades based on achievement, effort, and behavior, with report card grades modified by a qualifier signifying work performed above, at, or below grade level. A third type of grade system is the *pass/fail grade scale* used by schools whose English learners are integrated into the regular classroom. This scale avoids comparing the English learners with English-proficient classmates (From the Classroom, 1991).

　　Some schools have begun to assign a numerical grade (1–4, with 4 being the highest score) according to a student's knowledge of state standards. For example, in second grade, if a child is required to "read fluently and accurately and with appropriate

Point/Counterpoint:

Self-Assessment

Should students assess themselves? Farrell (2006) presents two sides of the argument:

POINT: Self-Assessment Works. "Self-assessment is easy to administer and it is quick. Also, students take more ownership in the assessment process, and may be more motivated to improve their language proficiency as a result" (p. 131).

COUNTERPOINT: Self-Assessment Is Not Helpful. "Both teachers and students may wonder if the students themselves are capable of assessing their own proficiency

levels. Also, some peer assessment may be perceived of as a waste of time and unfair by the students if the teacher is not involved in the assessment process" (p. 131).

Implications for Teaching
Peer assessment works best when balanced with the teacher's formative and summative assessment.

intonation and expression," the number grade reflects the mastery of this standard. Such ancillary factors as attendance and class participation do not influence this grade (Hernández, 2005). Administrators prefer standards-based grading because the scores align with state testing programs, which in turn align with the accountability system required under the federal NCLB legislation.

Grading and assessment issues concern teachers of all students, but teachers of English learners face additional challenges. English learners' limited English affects their ability to communicate their content knowledge. If teachers recognize English learners' efforts and progress, will they be setting two standards of achievement, one for English learners and one for native-English speakers? Teachers and English learners may have different expectations and interpretations of the grade (Grognet et al., 2000). Answers to these issues are not easy. By working collaboratively with other teachers in the school, an overall schoolwide plan can be developed.

Adapted Instruction: A Grading and Assessment Plan

- ■ Grade a combination of *process* and *product* for all students.
- ■ Early in the class, explain to students what and how you grade. Show examples of good, intermediate, and poor work.
- ■ Use rubrics.
- ■ Involve students in developing criteria for evaluating assignments.
- ■ Use a variety of products to assess (some less dependent on fluent language skills, such as art projects, dramatizations, portfolios, and graphic organizers).
- ■ Adapt tests and test administration (allow more time for English learners; read the test aloud).

- Teach test-taking skills and strategies.
- Use criterion-referenced tests because grading on a curve is often unfair to English learners.
- Teach students to evaluate their own work.
- Talk to students after grading if you find their expectations were different from the grade they received.
- Grade beginning ESOL students as satisfactory/unsatisfactory or at/above/below expectations until the end of the year. Then assign a letter grade for the year.
- Put a note on the report card or transcript to identify the student as an English learner. Write comments to clarify how the student was graded.

Source: Grognet et al. (2000).

Cautions about Testing

Tests are a significant part of the U.S. schooling system and are used in every classroom. When choosing standardized tests, teachers can consider the following guidelines (Worthen & Spandel, 1991) to help them determine the benefits and limitations of the test:

- Does the test correspond to the task that it measures?
- Does the score approximate the students' ability?
- How can the score be supplemented with other information?
- Does the test drive the curriculum?
- Is the test a fair sample of the students' skills and behaviors?
- Is the test being used unfairly to compare students and schools with one another?
- Are tests that involve minimum standards being used to make critical decisions regarding classification of students?

Cole (2007) explains what happens when testing dominates the conversation—and instruction—in the classroom:

> Teachers begin to explain the relevance or purpose of materials and activities not in terms of learning but in terms of state or national testing. When students ask "why" they have to do something, they are told it's for the test. . . . [W]e are not encouraging our students to learn for learning's sake. We are not showing them that the identities that they have available to them in this situation are valued because of their literacy, their numeracy, or their position in civic engagement. We are sending them the message that they are blips on a chart." (p. 7)

Best Practices in Testing

The most effective assessment of what has been learned is that which most closely matches what is taught. Test content should reflect the curriculum, build on the experiences of students and be relevant to their lives, and be matched to their developmental level. If possible the conditions for instruction and assessment should be identical; the same type of material should be tested as was presented during instruction, with the same language and student interaction (Gottlieb, n.d.). The use of similar conditions helps students to access and remember what they have learned.

Identification, Assessment, and Placement of English Learners in the Schools

Over half the states have specific laws and provide procedural guidelines regarding identification procedures for English learners. Many states also have procedures for redesignating students and for placing them in mainstream classes. Some states do not have state laws but do provide guidelines for the assessment of English learners. Generally speaking, students are first evaluated; then, if identified as needing ELD services, they are placed in suitable programs, if available. Ideally, the placement test results correspond directly to an instructional plan that can be implemented immediately by a classroom teacher. Once in a program, students are then periodically reevaluated for purposes of reclassification.

Identification Procedures for English Learners

A variety of methods are used to identify English learners needing services. The *home language survey,* a short form administered by school districts to determine the language spoken at home, is among the most frequently used methods of identifying students whose primary language is not English. *Registration* and *enrollment* information collected from incoming students can be used to identify students with a home language other than English. A teacher or tutor who has informally observed a student using a language other than English often does identification through observation. *Interviews* may provide opportunities to identify students. School districts are required by state and federal mandates to administer a placement test before assigning a new student to an instructional program if a home language survey indicates that the student's primary language is not English.

Assessment for Placement

Once students are identified, their level of English proficiency needs to be determined. Ideally, the assessment is done by staff with the language skills to communicate in the family's native language. Parents and students should be provided with orientation about the assessment and placement process and the expectation and services of the school system. Most important, the school staff needs to be trained, aware, and sensitive to the backgrounds and experiences of the student population.

Various states in the United States use a mixture of measures to evaluate students for ELD services. These include the following: oral proficiency tests, teacher judgment, parent request, literacy tests in English, prior instructional services, writing samples in English, achievement tests in English, teacher ratings of English proficiency, oral proficiency tests in the native language, and achievement tests in the native language (Hopstock & Stephenson, 2003).

Specific tests have been designed to help districts place English learners. For example, the Language Assessment Scales (LAS), a standardized test with mean scores and standard deviations based on various age groups, is designed to measure oral-language skills in English and Spanish. Another frequently used proficiency test is the Bilingual Syntax Measure (BSM), which measures oral proficiency in English and/or

Spanish grammatical structures and language dominance. The IDEA Proficiency Test (IPT) also measures oral-language proficiency in English. As students point to and name objects, complete sentences, and respond verbally, these responses are scored for accurate comprehension and production.

Educators who draw from a variety of information sources can view students' needs in a broader context and thus design a language program to meet these needs. Teacher-devised checklists and observational data gathered as students participate in integrated learning activities can be used to confirm or adjust student placement (Lucas & Wagner, 1999).

As a caution, teachers and school personnel need to be aware that even after administering these placement tests and gathering placement information, appropriate academic placement may be difficult. First, placement tests measure only language proficiency. They say nothing about a student's academic background. Students may be highly prepared in certain subject areas and very weak in others. They may be very strong academically but have poor English skills, or, conversely, have excellent English skills and few academic skills. Placement by age can be a problem. Students may need much more time in the system to learn English, but placement in a lower grade may lead to social adjustment problems.

While acknowledging that NCLB has not provided enough help for urban school districts that are impacted by large numbers of English learners, some educational leaders recognize that the data provided by frequent testing can assist teachers in identifying students who need additional help (Domenech, 2008). Using ongoing assessment, teachers can help struggling students catch up before the end-of-year summative assessment documents school failure.

One example of assessment tracking is the English Language Proficiency Collaboration and Research Consortium (ELPCRC), a group of six states that use CTB/McGraw-Hill's LAS Links, a student tracking system that ties together assessment and instruction. Students are tested online, and the computer software evaluates performance and provides needed remediation. This system provides assessment–instruction integration that changes the role of teachers into managers rather than direct providers of instruction.

In summary, the procedures to identify and place English learners are as follows: When a student enrolls in a school district, administer the Home Language Survey. If the student has a primary language other than English, administer an English-language proficiency test. If the student is an English learner, administer achievement and placement tests in English and in the primary language. If the student is eligible for support services, notify parents of options and proceed with placement (Gottlieb, 2006).

Redesignation/Exit Procedures

School districts need to establish reclassification criteria to determine when English learners have attained the English-language skills necessary to succeed in an English-only classroom. The reclassification process may utilize multiple criteria (Rico, 2000) including, but not limited to, the following:

- Be based on objective standards
- Measure speaking, comprehension, reading, and writing
- Ensure that all academic deficits are remediated
- Include district evidence that students can participate meaningfully in the general program

Some districts organize bilingual education advisory committees to ensure ethnic parent representation and participation in implementing redesignation criteria that are reliable, valid, and useful. Norm-referenced tests using national norms or district, regional, or state nonminority norms can be employed for purposes of reclassification, as can standardized criterion-referenced tests. States set various cutoff scores on language and achievement tests that are used as criteria for proficiency in the process of redesignation.

Example of Concept: Criteria for Redesignating English Learners

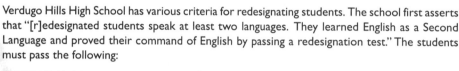

Verdugo Hills High School has various criteria for redesignating students. The school first asserts that "[r]edesignated students speak at least two languages. They learned English as a Second Language and proved their command of English by passing a redesignation test." The students must pass the following:

- CELDT (California English Language Development Test)
- ELA (English Language Arts) section of the CST (California Standards Test) with a score of Basic or higher
- Math and English or ESL 3/4 classes with a C or higher (Verdugo Hills High School, 2004)

Limitations of Assessment

Tests play a significant role in placing and reclassifying English learners. Often, pressure is applied for programs to redesignate students as fluent English-speaking in a short period of time and tests may be used to place English learners into mainstream programs before they are ready. Continuing support—such as tutoring, follow-up assessment, and primary-language help—is often not available after reclassification.

Standardized tests, though designed to be fair, are not necessarily well suited as measures of language ability or achievement for English learners. In fact, some have argued that the very use of tests is unfair because tests are used to deprive people of color of their place in society. As Sattler (1974) comments, "No test can be culture fair if the culture is not fair" (p. 34). The goal of tests notwithstanding, both the testing situation and the test content may be rife with difficulties for English learners.

Anxiety. All students experience test anxiety, but this anxiety can be compounded if the test is alien to the students' cultural background and experiences. Certain test formats such as think-aloud tasks may provoke higher levels of anxiety because students may fear that these assessments inaccurately reflect their true proficiency in English (Oh, 1992). Allowing students to take practice exams may familiarize them with the test formats and reduce test anxiety.

Time Limitations. Students may need more time to answer individual questions due to the time needed for mental translation and response formulation. Some students may need a time extension or should be given untimed tests.

Rapport. When testers and students do not share the same language or dialect, the success of the testing may be reduced. Students may not freely verbalize if they are shy or wary of the testing situation. Students who ostensibly share the primary language with the test administrator may not have in common certain dialectic features, resulting in reduced understanding. Rapport may also suffer if students are defensive about teachers' negative stereotypes or if students resent the testing situation itself.

Cultural Differences. Students from some cultural groups may not feel comfortable making eye contact with a test administrator. Students from cultures that discourage individuals from displaying knowledge may not be quick to answer questions and may be reluctant to guess unless they are certain they are accurate. They may be embarrassed to volunteer a response or receive positive feedback about their performance (Cloud et al., 2000).

Problematic Test Content

For the most part, language placement tests are well suited for assessing language. Other tests, however, particularly achievement tests, may contain translation problems or bias that affect the performance of English learners.

Equivalent First- and Second-Language Versions. Translating an English-language achievement test into another language or vice versa to create equivalent vocabulary items may cause some lack of correspondence in the frequency of the items. For example, *belfry* in English is a much less frequently understood term than its Spanish counterpart, *campanario*. The translation of a test is a hybrid belonging to neither culture.

Linguistic Bias. There are several forms of linguistic bias. *Geographic bias* happens when test items feature terms used in particular geographic regions but that are not universally shared. *Dialectical bias* occurs when a student is tested using expressions relevant to certain dialect speakers that are not known to others. *Language-specific bias* is created when a test developed for use with one language is used with another language.

Cultural Bias. Tests may be inappropriate not only because the language provides a dubious cue for students but also because the content may represent overt or subtle bias. The values of the dominant culture appearing in test items may be understood differently or not at all by English learners.

Cultural content appearing in tests may provide difficulty for students without that cultural background. Many students never experience common European-American food items such as bacon; common sports in the United States may be unfamiliar; musical instruments may be mysterious to students; even nursery rhymes and children's stories may refer only to one culture; and so on. In addition, students may be naïve about the process of testing and not recognize that these tests perform a gatekeeping function.

Example of Concept: Cultural Bias in Standardized Tests

Tae Sung, from Korea, looked at question number one.

1. Her tooth came out so she put it
On top of the refrigerator
Under the tree
Under her pillow
None of the above

In Korea, a child throws the lost tooth up on the roof so that the next one will grow in straight, but none of the answers said that. Tae Sung knew that "on top" meant *up* so he marked the first answer. Borden, from the Marshall Islands, also looked a long time at the question. In his country, you throw your tooth in the ocean for good luck. So Borden marked "none of the above" (Laturnau, n.d.).

Class Bias. Test content may represent a class bias; for example, the term *shallots* appeared on a nationally administered standardized achievement test, but only students whose families consume gourmet foods may be familiar with the term. Other such terms are *scallion* (another troublemaker from the onion family) and *vacuum cleaner*.

Content Bias. Even mathematics, a domain that many believe to be language-free, has been shown to cause difficulties, because language proficiency plays a relatively more important role than previously suspected.

Example of Concept: Language in Mathematics Testing

As one teacher found out, using open-ended questions that ask the students to explain or describe can change the difficulty level of a math test:

I ran into a problem when I administered the first test. The Asian English learners were highly skilled at the algebraic manipulation needed to solve problems, but they all had difficulty with the open-ended questions. I do not know if the obstacle was the nature of the question or the inability to communicate their ideas mathematically. I originally thought my test would be a diagnostic assessment tool for the students' understanding of mathematics. What the test turned out to be was a signal that raised questions of equity in regard to assessment. (Perkins, 1995)

Interpretation of Test Results

One last caution in the assessment of English learners is to understand the emphasis of the test: Is it on language proficiency or on content knowledge? When testing content, educators should select or devise tasks on which English learners can achieve, regardless of their language proficiency. When scoring the test, teachers must evaluate students' responses to distinguish those that are conceptually correct but may contain language problems from those that are conceptually incorrect.

The accompanying box offers attributes for the appropriate assessment of English learners.

Attributes of an Appropriate Assessment Plan for English Learners

- Both content knowledge and language proficiency are tested.
- Students' content knowledge and abilities in the native language as well as in English are assessed.
- Various techniques are used to measure content knowledge and skills (e.g., portfolios, observations, anecdotal records, interviews, checklists, exhibits, students' self-appraisals, writing samples, dramatic renditions, and criterion-referenced tests).
- The teacher is aware of the purpose of the assessment (e.g., whether the test is intended to measure verbal or writing skills, language proficiency, or content knowledge).
- Students' backgrounds, including their educational experiences and parents' literacy, are taken into account.
- Context is added to assessment tasks in the following ways:
    1. Incorporates familiar classroom material as a stimulus, such as brief quotations, charts, graphics, cartoons, and works of art

2. Includes questions for small-group discussion and individual writing
3. Mirrors learning processes with which students are familiar, such as the writing process and reading conferencing activities

- Administration procedures match classroom instructional practices (e.g., cooperative small groups, individual conferences, and assessment in the language of instruction).
- Extra time is given to complete or respond to assessment tasks.
- Other accommodations are made, such as simplifying directions in English and/or paraphrasing in the student's native language, as well as permitting students to use dictionaries or word lists.

Source: Adapted from August and Pease-Alvarez (1996) and Navarrete and Gustke (1996).

Technical Concepts

A good test has three qualities: validity, reliability, and practicality. A test must test what it purports to test (valid), be dependable and consistent (reliable), and be applicable to the situation (practical).

Validity

A test is *valid* if it measures what it claims to be measuring. If a test claims to measure the ability to read English, then it should test that ability. A test has *content validity* if it samples the content that it claims to test in some representative way. For example, if a reading curriculum includes training in reading for inference, then a test of that curriculum would include a test of inference. *Empirical validity* is a measure of how effectively a test relates to some other known measure. One kind of empirical validity is *predictive*: how well the test correlates with subsequent success or performance. A second type of empirical validity is *concurrent*: how well the test correlates with another measure used at the same time. Teachers often apply this concept of concurrent validity when they grade examinations. Intuitively, they expect the better students to receive better scores. This is a check for concurrent validity between the examination and the students' daily performance.

Reliability

A test is *reliable* if it yields predictably similar scores when it is taken again. Although many variables can affect a student's test score—such as error introduced by fatigue, hunger, or poor lighting—these variables usually do not introduce large deviations in students' scores. A student who scores 90 percent on a teacher-made test probably has scored 45 on one-half of the test and 45 on the other half, regardless of whether the halves are divided by odd/even items or first/last sequence.

Practicality

A test may be valid and reliable but cost too much to administer either in time or in money. A highly usable test should be relatively easy to administer and score. When a portfolio is kept to document student progress, issues of practicality still emerge. The portfolio should be easy to maintain, accessible to students, and scored with a rubric agreed on by teachers and students.

Many of the assessment practices and issues touched on in this chapter are further discussed in the online report "An Examination of Assessment of Limited English Proficient Students" (Zehler, Hopstock, Fleischman, & Greniuk, 1994).

One last criterion: Tests must be fair. This is not only true for individual tests, but for a testing system: "A legally defensible assessment system must stand on three pillars: validity, reliability, and fairness" (McDaniel & Wilde, p. 107).

Brewer, García, and Aguilar (2007), all key figures in Los Angeles Unified School District, call for an alternative accountability strategy for English learners:

> Congress should require and fund states to develop content-based standardized tests for EL students in their native languages. . . . [T]est scores shouldn't be factored into decisions about a school's proficiency until solid native-language tests are developed or EL students have time to learn the English they need to perform well. (p. A29)

Critics of NCLB are firm in contrasting its shortcomings with alternative visions. Alfie Kohn, author of *The Schools Our Children Deserve: Moving Beyond Traditional Classrooms and "Tougher Standards,"* has been a persistent critic of the standardized testing movement in general and of the emphasis on testing that underlies NCLB in particular. He points out that one does not need a federal law that tests children in order to identify schools that are underperforming; such schools are found in poor neighborhoods. A long-term plan to provide increased resources and better teachers is the necessary solution. He writes, "This law . . . must be replaced with a policy that honors local autonomy, employs better assessments, addresses the root cause of inequity and supports a rich curriculum" (Kohn, 2007, p. 7A).

Regardless of how valid, reliable, and practical a test may be, if it serves only the teachers' and the institution's goals, the students' language progress may not be promoted. Testing must instead be an integral part of a learning environment that encourages students to acquire a second language as a means to fulfill personal and academic goals. ■

LEARNING MORE

Further Reading

Scenarios for ESL Standards-Based Assessment (TESOL, 2001) is a useful resource offering principles for effective assessment of English learners, along with ideas for collecting and recording information, analyzing and interpreting assessment information, and using this information for reporting and decision making. An extensive set of examples drawn from K–12 instruction is included to assist the practitioner in using a wide range of assessment strategies including the use of journals and feedback forms, student conferences, performance tasks, commercially developed, norm-referenced tests, student observational and anecdotal records, rubrics, and assessment data-management systems.

Web Search

Using the Website www.ncela.gwu.edu/pubs/classics/focus/03mainstream.htm, compare the methods that various states use to assess and redesignate (exit) English learners. What are the procedures in your state? Compare the identification methods used in Idaho and Illinois, for example. What are the advantages of using multiple criteria to assess students' L1 and L2 proficiencies?

Exploration

Visit the language evaluation center in a local school district. Describe how English learners are identified. Ask for a copy of the home language survey (or equivalent), if available. Is there a coherent written plan available to parents about the process of identification, classification, and placement? Describe the testing procedure that follows the home language survey in which students are classified according to English-language level. Describe how this results in classroom placement. Once placed in classrooms, what kind of curriculum and instruction does each student receive?

Experiment

Go to the Web practice site for the Test of English as a Foreign Language (TOEFL; online at http://toeflpractice.ets.org) and take a practice test. Compare your score with acceptable score ranges for international students. Would you be admitted to study in the United States if you were not already a native-English speaker?

The Power of Classroom Practice
www.myeducationlab.com

Authentic Assessment for ELLs

Authentic assessment may take many forms. In this video, classroom examples demonstrate that how students communicate their understanding is as important as how they solve the problem.

> To access the video, go to MyEducationLab (www.myeducationlab.com), choose the Díaz-Rico and Weed text, and log in to MyEducationLab for English Language Learners. Select the topic Assessment, and watch the video entitled "Authentic Assessment for ELLs."

Answer the following questions:
1. Why does this student task qualify as an example of performance-based assessment? What benefits are there to this type of assessment for ELLs?
2. What scaffolds does the teacher provide for the assessment task? Can you suggest others that would be appropriate for ELLs at lower levels of language proficiency?

Culture

Cultural Diversity in the United States, the Intercultural Educator, and Culturally Responsive Schooling

Part Four contains a broad look at culture, offering a historical background on cultural diversity and its treatment in the United States (Chapter 8), and exploring how culture influences every aspect of life, including schooling, and how the intercultural educator becomes more aware of culture (Chapter 9). Specific insights for classroom teachers on the use and understanding of culture are available in Chapter 10. The accompanying figure highlights Part Four of the theoretical model presented in the introduction. It is evident in the model that culture is a pervasive influence on schooling, permeating every other aspect.

Theoretical Model for CLAD Culture: Cultural Diversity in the United States, the Intercultural Educator, and Culturally Responsive Schooling

**Part Four:
Culture**
- Cultural Diversity in the United States
- The Intercultural Educator
- Culturally Responsive Schooling

**Part Two:
Instruction**
- Oracy and Literacy for English-Language Development
- Content-Area Instruction
- Bilingual Education

**Part One:
Learning**
- Learning about the Learner
- Learning about Language Structure
- Learning about Second-Language Acquisition

**Part Five:
Policy**
- Language Policy
- Special Populations of English Learners

**Part Three:
Assessment**

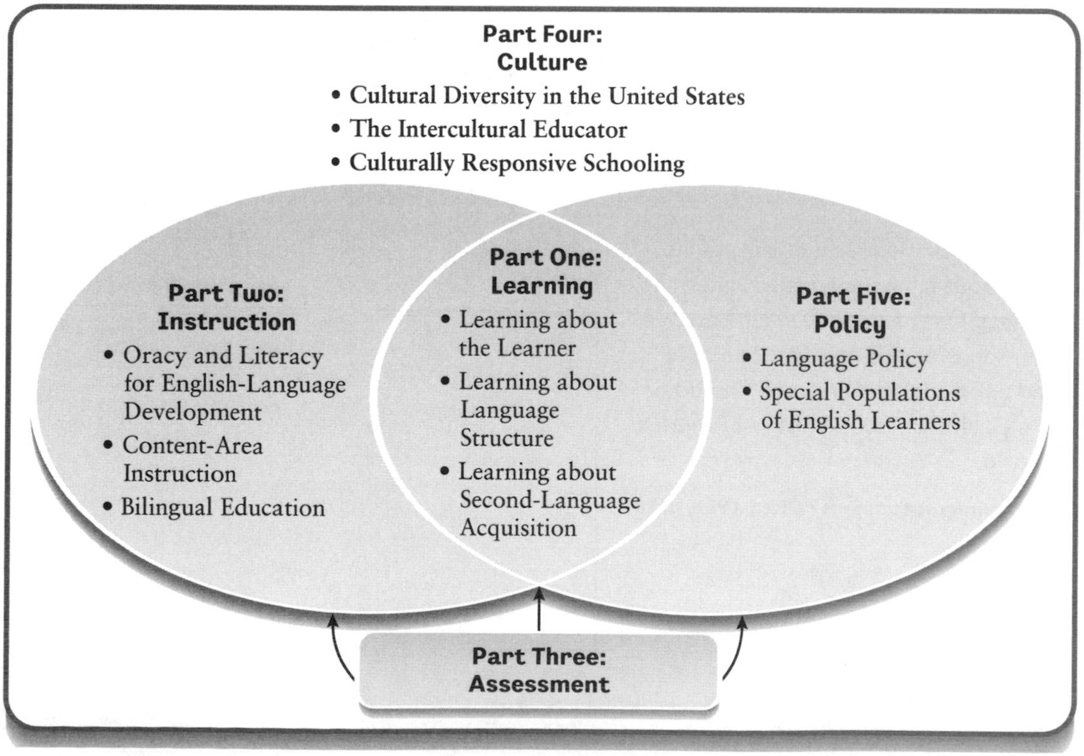

8 Cultural Diversity

Immigration has brought the world into U.S. schools.

Before I came to America I had dreams of life here. I thought about tall Anglos, big buildings, and houses with lawns. I was surprised when I arrived to see so many kinds of people—Black people, Asians. I found people from Korea and Cambodia and Mexico. In California I found not just America, I found the world.

Mexican immigrant student (Olsen, 1988, p. 10)

They still come—a medical student from India who remains in Knoxville to set up a practice; a Danish au pair worker who meets a U.S. college student and extends her work visa; a Vietnamese grandmother who follows her daughter, who followed her teenage sons; a Mexican lawyer who sets up an import–export practice in Tijuana and San Diego; Romanian orphans brought to the United States through an adoption service; a Hong Kong capitalist who settles his family in San José while he commutes by jet to maintain his businesses. The immigration that has enriched the United States shows little sign of abating.

Each successive wave of immigration has had unique characteristics and a distinct impact on U.S. education (see the figure on page 211). Whether attracted to the United States or forced here from their native country, immigrants have brought with them cultural, political, religious, and economic values, along with multiple tongues and various skills. Whether legally or illegally residing in the United States, immigrants contribute material aspects of their culture (crafts, foods, technology) as well as nonmaterial aspects (family values, spiritual beliefs, medical practices). During the process of settlement, these immigrants require social and educational services to help them adapt to their new environment.

The extent of immigration and the policies that shape it have been controversial issues since the founding of this country. This great experiment—the United States of America—has required the innovation, fabrication, and synthesis of whole new patterns of existence. Those who have participated in this great cultural amalgamation have been themselves transformed. This transformation has not ended and will not end in the foreseeable future. Not only do we need to live with it, but we also have the unique opportunity to enjoy and value it.

Historical Perspectives

The North American continent has received people from all over the world. Diverse ethnic groups have arrived on both coasts and have caused continuous intermingling and confrontation with indigenous populations and among themselves. In what was to become the United States, these contacts began when the Europeans arrived in the original thirteen colonies and met the many cultures of the Native Americans. Later, the colonists imported African slaves, who brought with them the various cultures of West Africa. Then, as settlers moved toward the interior, they encountered different native groups in the plains and pueblos. In the mid-nineteenth century, English-speaking Americans expanded into the Southwest, home to Native Americans as well as the Spanish-speaking heirs of land grants dating back to the sixteenth century. Finally, in the nineteenth and twentieth centuries, immigrant groups from all over the world poured into the United States, coming into contact with the descendants of all earlier groups.

From this contact came the expectation that these many cultures would merge into a homogeneous, shared national culture. The idea that the United States was a "melting pot" generated pressure on newcomers to conform in thought and behavior—and if this were not possible, pressure for the children of these newcomers to assimilate. For some, assimilation was easier than for others, and language, clothing, and other forms of distinction were easy to erase. For others, however, discarding traditions was not so easy. The Hassidic Jews, the Amish, the Hopi, the Navajo—those clinging to religious rites, lifestyles, or property without choosing to compromise—resisted assimilation pressures (Rubel & Kupferer, 1973). These groups and others have created a more modern metaphor, that of the salad bowl: a mix in which the individual ingredients are not melted but, rather, retain their flavor and texture.

Another powerful metaphor is that of the kaleidoscope, in which the shifting patterns of culture, language, and race combine and recombine ceaselessly, yet are bound together by an idea: that in the United States, diverse peoples are held together through common ideals. The contributions of different ethnic cultures to the United States cannot be underestimated, yet the picture is not uniformly sunny. Dark and sordid episodes of conflict between, and discrimination against, various groups cloud the history of this nation. Minorities have systematically been denied opportunities and rights accorded the more privileged. Those groups that are least similar to the original European-American immigrants have suffered exploitation and, in some cases, linguistic, racial, or cultural genocide. Despite the hardships many have endured, ethnic groups in this country have become inseparable threads in the cultural tapestry of the United States.

Contributions

The North American continent had a myriad of indigenous cultures characterized by high levels of civilization before the European invasion began. These civilizations were either obliterated or they accommodated the arrival of new cultures through the creation of a hybrid New World. The result has been a broad mix of lifestyles and contributions of both artifacts and patterns that reflect life in contemporary North America. For the most part, European invaders attempted to replicate the life they had lived in the Old World, and those who were not a part of this mainstream of culture had the choice of assimilating or leading a separate existence. Assimilation was never intended for everyone. Those who could not assimilate were largely left alone to carry on their linguistic and cultural traditions, albeit often treated as outsiders.

Many contributions of nonmainstream peoples remained just beneath the surface of the American dream—in some cases, *too* far beneath to influence the main paths of culture. For example, the spiritual heritage of the Native Americans—the deep and abiding respect for nature—has not had the impact on the dominant culture that may be necessary for the survival of the flora and fauna of the continent.

Did You Know?

According to author Kay Porterfield (2002), "Ancient American Indians were building pyramids before the Egyptians. They domesticated corn from a wild grass. They performed complicated surgeries. They also knew how to work with platinum and how to vulcanize rubber, two things Europeans could not do until the 1800s" (p. 1).

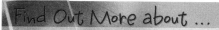
Find Out More about ...

Native-American Contributions

Porterfield, K., & Keoke, E. (2003). *American Indian Contributions to the World: 15,000 Years of Invention and Innovation.* New York: Checkmark Books.

This reference contains approximately 450 entries that detail and document the intentiveness of North, Meso-, and South American Indians.

Porterfield, K., & Keoke, E. (2005). *American Indian Contributions to the World: 15,000 Years of Invention and Innovation, Grades 4–9.*

A five-volume collection that introduces young readers to the advances that American Indians have made throughout history. Volumes include Food, Farming, and Hunting; Buildings, Clothing, and Art; Trade, Transportation, and Warfare; Medicine and Health; Science and Technology. (To order, visit www. factsonfile.com/ newfacts/FactsHome. asp).

Native Americans. In many ways, the indigenous civilizations of precolonial North America were more highly developed than European cultures. The cities and roads of the Aztec culture astounded the European conquerors. The agricultural systems featured advanced forms of irrigation, with the cultivation of foods that were unknown to the Old World. Some of these foods (potato, corn, peanuts, and other grains) were later to provide 60 percent of Europe's diet and were responsible for the greatest explosion of population since the Neolithic Age (Feagin & Feagin, 1993). Substances from the New World (cocoa, tobacco, coca) were to provide Europeans with exhilarating addictions in the centuries to come.

Medicinal products from the Americas revolutionized the treatment of disease in Europe and still fascinate pharmacologists with as yet untapped treasures. The political systems of native peoples ranged from the religious theocracies in Mexico, sources of advanced astronomical and mathematical achievement unparalleled in the world of that day, to the democratic councils of the Algonquin, Iroquois, and other nations that were much admired by Benjamin Franklin and Thomas Jefferson (Hardt, 1992).

African Americans. The culture of African Americans has evolved from an African base that survived despite harshly limiting circumstances: Slaves could bring little or none of the material aspects of African culture with them. The aspects that survived did so in the hearts and minds of those who were forcibly moved to the New World. The present-day legacies of the African past are evident not only in the dance, music, literature, and religion of contemporary African Americans, but also in the sheer power of the patterns of everyday life and language that were strong enough to survive despite centuries of oppression. Ironically, the genre of music most associated with the United States—jazz—is permeated with African-American influence. One could argue that the music of the United States would not exist in its current form without this influence. Even today the endlessly mutating forms of African-American culture

Did You Know?

Although African Americans comprise 12 percent of the U.S. population, they account for more than 42 percent of all students enrolled in public schools (Russell, 2008). The fact that only 2.4 percent of teachers are African-American men and 5.6 percent are African-American women leaves a racial and cultural gap in the preparation of African American teachers. In the top twenty urban school districts in America (with a total enrollment of 5 million students), over 80 percent of the students are African-American, yet over 70 percent of teachers in urban schools are European American.

constitute an ongoing avant-garde (Criston, 1993), aspects of which are alternately embraced and denigrated by the wider society (some say, appropriated and abused by European-American performers and producers—see Dyson, 1996).

Despite substantial discrimination, a long line of African-American writers, such as James Weldon Johnson, Claude McKay, Richard Wright, Ralph Ellison, James Baldwin, Imamu Baraka (LeRoi Jones), Maya Angelou, Toni Morrison, and Langston Hughes, have enriched U.S. literature and inspired new generations of poets, writers, and rappers. The religion of Black America has been a source of sustenance to African Americans since the arrival of the first slaves and has played a major role in fomenting protest for social justice. The nonviolent civil disobedience movement from the mid-1950s to the 1970s had religious underpinnings, with prominent minister-leaders such as the Reverend Martin Luther King Jr.

Find Out More about ...

African-American Contributions in the Arts

African-American Contributions to Theatrical Dance

www.theatredance.com

This Website lists the characteristics of African dance that have contributed to various dance movements. Different types of dances are described.

The Nathaniel C. Standifer Video Archive of Oral History: Black American Musicians

www.umich.edu/~/afroammu/standifer.html

This collection was begun in 1968 and contains approximately 150 videotaped interviews, primarily with black musicians who have made highly significant contributions to musical genres of African-American origin or influence.

Did You Know?

Over his lifetime, Elijah McCoy was granted fifty-two patents, most of which were for improvements in steam engines, although he did patent a folding ironing board and self-propelled lawn sprinkler. In 1916 he patented what he described as his greatest invention, the "graphite lubricator," which used powdered graphite suspended in oil to lubricate cylinders of "superheater" train engines. Others tried to copy his oil-dripping cup but none was as successful, prompting McCoy's customers to ask for "the real McCoy"—hence the expression (http://teacher.scholastic.com/activities/bhistory/inventors/mccoy.htm).

Find Out More about ...

African-American Inventors

The Top 10 African-American Inventors
http://teacher. scholastic.com/activities/bhistory/inventors/index.htm

    This teacher- and student-friendly Website provides short introductions to ten African-American inventors and links to other sites with further information.

American Chemical Society (ACS). (1994). *Inventing the Future: African-American Contributions to Scientific Discovery and Invention*. Washington, DC: Author.

This series of videotapes features highlights from the careers of many African-American scientists and inventors who have contributed to science and technology in the United States. Provided with the videotape is a teacher's guide that contains facts about each of the scientists and that includes hands-on activities for grades 3 through 6 that relate to the scientific fields practiced by the featured scientists and inventors.

    African Americans have made substantial contributions to science. In the years preceding 1900, more than 1,000 patents were awarded to African-American inventors, despite the fact that slaves were barred from applying for patents. For example, Jo Anderson, a slave in the Cyrus McCormick household, was the coinventor of the McCormick reaper. A slave of Jefferson Davis, president of the Confederate States of America, invented a boat propeller but was unable to patent the device. In the twentieth century, major scientists were active in such fields as aviation; electrical, mechanical, and construction engineering; rocketry; and many others. African Americans who have contributed in social science and philosophy include W. E. B. DuBois, Marcus Garvey, Elijah Muhammad, Frederick Douglass, E. Franklin Frazier, Oliver C. Cox, and Malcolm X (Appiah & Gates, 2003).

    The story of Ernest E. Just illustrates the difficulties faced by African-American scientists in their ascent to prominence. Just, a marine biologist, rose to become vice president of the American Society of Zoologists but was once refused admittance to Rockefeller Institute. Although Just authored over sixty scholarly papers and was a leading authority on egg fertilization, artificial parthenogenesis, and cell division, he was never appointed to a European-American university. By contrast, George Washington Carver never aspired to take his place alongside European-American scientists in their well-equipped, well-financed research facilities but revolutionized the agronomy of the peanut working in his small laboratory in Tuskegee.

Example of Concept: An African-American History Curriculum

A partnership between the Baltimore City School System, the Reginald F. Lewis Museum, and local businesses has resulted in a new curriculum of forty-three lessons for elementary- and middle-school students grades 4–8 that features African-American history. Field trips, primary-source reading materials, audio and video clips, and activities that provide for a variety of learning styles make history come alive for Baltimore's students. As of 2008, more than 1,400 students have visited local sites of importance to African-American history (Weber, 2008).

Hispanics/Latinos. Hispanic contributions, which predate the landing of the Pilgrims at Plymouth Rock, have also been significant. Hispanic settlers in the Southwest helped lay the foundations for the agricultural, mining, and cattle industries on which early city and state economies were built (Hispanic Concerns Study Committee, 1987). This influence continues today. With the influx of Cubans during the 1960s, Miami was transformed, becoming a vibrant international and bicultural metropolis. New York and its environs contain more Puerto Ricans than the island of Puerto Rico. Los Angeles is now the second-largest Latin-American city in the world.

Although Hispanics living in the United States can trace their roots to several different countries, a common denominator of Hispanic culture in the United States includes language, religious beliefs and practices, holidays, and life patterns. Values shared among Hispanics include the importance of interdependence and cooperation of the immediate and extended family and the importance of emotional relationships. As the mainstream culture comes into more contact with the Hispanic culture, it is beginning to recognize the importance of these family values.

In politics, Hispanic Americans have influenced urban life and education. The political impetus behind bilingual education stems from the culmination of Cuban immigrant pressure in Florida and the "Chicano Power" movement of the 1960s. A lasting contribution of this bilingual legislation may be current attempts to preserve the "small incidence" languages of Native Americans and Micronesia, linguistic resources that are endangered. Thus, Hispanic leadership has helped to preserve cultural resources in unforeseen ways.

In literature and the other arts, Hispanic Americans have made significant contributions. An impressive folk tradition of Spanish songs and ballads has maintained a musical current containing the history, joys, and sorrows of the Mexican-American, Puerto Rican, and Cuban experiences. Spanish radio and television stations and newspapers have played a major role in sustaining the language and reinforcing the values of Spanish America.

Spanish words have enriched the minds and tongues of North Americans. Fiction and poetry, in both languages, affirm Hispanic heritage and identity. Puerto Rican and Mexican-American theater has dramatized the struggles for a voice. The public

---

■Did You Know?■

The Spanish governor of the Louisiana Territory, Bernardo de Galvez, provided the armies of General George Washington and General George Rogers Clarke with gunpowder, rifles, bullets, blankets, medicine, and supplies. Once Spain entered the Revolutionary War on the side of the Americans, Galvez raised an army of Spanish and Cuban soldiers, Choctaw Indians, and black former slaves that beat off the British attack in 1780 and gained control of the Mississippi River, thus frustrating a British plan to encircle the American colonies. After the war, because of the generous assistance that Galvez gave some European Americans who wanted to settle Texas, they named their city after him, Galveston (Padilla, 1998).

Find Out More about . . .

Hispanic-American Contributions

Contributions of Americans of Hispanic Heritage

www.neta. com/f~lstbooks/dod2.htm

An excellent site that provides a historical account of Hispanic contributions as well as an annotated list of important Hispanics in fields such as politics, entertainment, sports, business, and the military.

Impacto, Influencia, Cambio

www.smithsonianeducation.org/scitech/impacto/graphic/index.html

This site highlights the lives and accomplishments of inventors, aviators, astronauts, and the everyday people of Latin America and the southwestern United States who have affected science and technology.

art of Mexico is a centuries-old tradition, with the colorful *steles* of the Aztecs and Mayans resonating through time and reappearing in the murals of the barrios and the public art of cities throughout the Southwest. Art, to the Hispanic, is a breath of culture, and artists, like intellectuals, are esteemed as cultural leaders. The culinary contributions of Hispanics are legion and include enchiladas from Mexico, black beans from Cuba, *mangú* from the Dominican Republic, and *pasteles* from Puerto Rico.

Asian Americans. Contributions of the Pacific Rim peoples to the United States will be of increasing importance in the twenty-first century. The economic power of Asian capital stems not only from Japanese post–World War II efforts but also from the Chinese diaspora that has provided capital for economic investment in much of Southeast Asia, Indonesia, Australia, and California. Although Chinese and Japanese immigration to western America was severely curtailed throughout the history of the United States, through sheer force of numbers and the volume of international trade, Asian economic and cultural influences on the United States have been consistent.

The cultures of Asia, characterized by unparalleled continuity from ancient times to the present, have contributed to Western culture in innumerable ways. The U.S. fascination with Asian cultures has included the martial arts, Eastern spiritual philosophies, fireworks, acupuncture, and Asian food, décor, and gardening.

Did You Know?

A Chinese-American horticulturist helped to develop Florida's frost-resistant citrus fruit and paved the way for the state to compete in the citrus industry against California. Another Chinese American patented the process to make evaporated milk. There are Chinese-American astronauts who go into space, and a Chinese-American scientist helped to develop the fabric to make the space suits.

Source: Lin (2002, pp. 2–3).

Table 8.1

Websites with Resources for Teaching Asian Americans	
www.asianamericanbooks.com	K–12 books and materials for Asian-American cultural awareness
www.teachingforchange.org	Books, DVDs, CDs, and videos on the Asian-American experience
www.chabotcollege.edu/Library/subjectindex/AsianAmericanStudies.htm	Asian-Americans/Pacific Islanders Studies Website index and list of reference books
www.csun.edu/asianamericanstudies	Resources for community activism, speakers' bureau
www.cetel.org/res.html	Gateway to online exploration of Asian-American history, culture, media, and curricular resources
http://sun3.lib.uci.edu/~dfsang/aas2.htm	A comprehensive guide to information about Asian Americans and Pacific Islanders
http://falcon.jmu.edu/~/ramseyil/asiabio.htm	Links to noteworthy Asian Americans in ten different fields as well as related sites about Asian Americans
http://inventors.about.com/od/astartinventor/a/AsiaInventors.htm	A brief description of the inventions of Asian Americans with links to more detailed sites

The chief stumbling block to greater acceptance of Asian influences in the United States is the perceived linguistic barrier. The fact that more Asians speak English than the reverse closes the doors to a deeper knowledge of Asian cultures for many Americans. Perhaps the current generation of high-school students will begin to bridge this gap; Japanese is now taught in 563 U.S. schools, approximately 125 of which are in Hawaii, and Chinese in 85, of which almost half are in Washington state (Center for Advanced Research on Language Acquisition, 2001). Table 8.1 offers a variety of Web-based resources for promoting the Educational success of Asian Americans.

Arab Americans. Other groups as well have been ignored or remain invisible in the mainstream literature and education. However, events can propel a particular group to the forefront. Such is the case of Arab Americans, who are suddenly the object of much media attention. Because words such as *terrorism* and *anti-Americanism* arise, the ELD teacher may need to help students fight stereotypes and misinformation about this group.

Did You Know?

In the summer of 1895, Kahlil Gibran arrived in New York from a small village in Lebanon. He became a well-known painter and writer. His most famous book, *The Prophet,* remains a bestseller sixty-two years after his death.

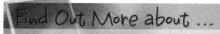

Find Out More about ...

Arab-American Contributions

Arab Americans: Making a Difference

www.aaiusa.org

Divided into areas such as military, politics, sports, activism, business, law, entertainment, education, art and literature, fashion, and science and medicine, this Website lists and briefly describes leading Arab Americans in the above fields.

Several waves of immigrants from Arabic-speaking countries have been settling in the United States since the 1880s. Unlike the previously mentioned groups, most Arab Americans have been able to assimilate into American life, and 80 percent of them are American citizens. They work in all sectors of society; are leaders in many professions and organizations; have a strong commitment to family, economic, and educational achievements; and are making contributions to all aspects of American life (Arab American Institute Foundation, n.d.).

Among other impressive contributions include those of surgeon Michael DeBakey, who invented the heart pump; comedian and actor Danny Thomas, the founder of St. Jude's Children's Research Hospital; and lawyer Edward Masry, who, along with Erin Brockovich, filed a class action lawsuit against Pacific Gas and Electric for polluting the drinking water of Hinkley, California. Through their efforts, PG&E paid out the largest toxic tort injury settlement in U.S. history, $333 million in damages (Suleiman, 1999).

Exploitation

The contributions of minorities to the cultural mainstream have not consistently been valued. On the contrary, many peoples in the cultural mix have been exploited. Their labor, their art, and their votes have been used and abused without adequate compensation.

From the beginning, European settlers exploited others. Many indentured servants worked at low wages for years to repay their passage to the New World. Native Americans brought food to the starving colonists and, in return, saw their fertile coastal lands taken away. Westward expansion features many a sordid tale of killing and robbery on the part of European settlers (Eckert, 1992). On the West Coast, Spanish missionaries also colonized native peoples, with somewhat more pious motives but a similar result. The Hispanic settlers in the West were in turn exploited by European Americans. Although superior firearms still carried the day, legal manipulations carried out in the English language systematically disenfranchised Hispanic settlers and caused a vast number of them to lose their property and water rights. Chinese settlers who were permitted into the West during the nineteenth century found that their labor was valued only in the meanest way, and the jobs available constituted "woman's work" such as laundry and cooking. And the story of exploitation of Africans brought to the New World is a tale of tears mixed with genocide and forced miscegenation.

Table 8.2

Poverty Rates, Educational Attainment, Average Earnings, and Health Insurance by Race and Origin

Race and Origin	Poverty Rates (3-year average 2001–2003)	Educational Attainment (high-school graduate or more)	Average Earnings in 2002 for All Workers, 18 Years and Older			Health Insurance: People without Coverage (3-year average 2001–2003)
			Total	Not High-School Graduate	High-School Graduate	
White	10.2%	85.1%	$37,376	$19,264	$28,145	14.2%
Non-Hispanic White	8.2%	89.45%	$39,220	$19,423	$28,756	10.6%
Black	23.7%	80.0%	$28,179	$16,516	$22,823	19.6%
American Indian/Alaska Native	23.2%	—	—	—	—	27.5%
Asian	10.7%	87.6%	$40,793	$16,746	$24,900	18.5%
Asian and/or Native Hawaiian and other Pacific Islanders	10.8%	—	—	—	—	18.6%
Hispanic origin (of any race)	21.9%	57.0%	$25,827	$18,981	$24,163	32.8%

Source: Adapted from U.S. Census Bureau (2004a, 2004b, 2004c).

In many cases, this exploitation continues to this day as the underclass of the United States, whether white, brown, or black, is inadequately paid and undereducated, forced to live without health benefits or adequate housing (see Table 8.2). Temporary jobs without benefits are the hallmark of the crueler, harsher world of the twenty-first century as economic and political forces polarize society.

The most difficult piece of the puzzle is the challenge of population growth. Creating jobs for a burgeoning population that will provide the financial means for the purchase of health care, education, housing, and an adequate diet is the issue. The population in 2050 is projected to consist largely of developing nations' peoples. The challenge is evident. Wrongs from the past cannot be righted, but present and future citizens can avoid those wrongs by understanding exploitative measures and working for change.

The Impact of a Changing Population

By the year 2010, one of every three Americans will be either African American, Hispanic American, or Asian American. (See Chapter 1 for demographic trends.) This represents a dramatic change from the image of the United States throughout its history. In the past, when Americans have looked in the mirror, they have seen a largely European-American reflection. Immigration, together with differing birthrates among various populations, is responsible for this demographic shift. Along with the change in racial and ethnic composition has come a dramatic change in the languages spoken in the United States and the languages spoken in U.S. schools.

In the midst of the changing demographics in the United States, two minority groups—immigrants and economically disadvantaged minorities within the country—face similar challenges. Both immigrants and indigenous minorities must adjust to the demands of modern technological societies and must redefine their cultural self-identity. Economic and educational achievement is not equally accessible to these minorities.

Poverty among Minority Groups

A key difficulty for many minorities is that of poverty. Almost one-quarter (24 percent) of African Americans and over one-fifth (22 percent) of Hispanic Americans live in poverty (U.S. Census Bureau, 2004c). Worse, Blacks and Hispanics are even more likely not to be simply poor, but to be *extremely* poor—with incomes under half the poverty level of Whites. In fact, at 16.1 percent, the share of the Black population that is extremely poor is over four times that of non-Hispanic Whites (3.7 percent), and well above that of Hispanics (10.5 percent) (Henwood, 1997).

Poverty is associated with a host of difficulties, such as underemployment, home-lessness, educational deprivation, single-parent homes, and other types of instability. However, not all poverty can be linked to these difficulties; some minorities continue in poverty because of social and political factors in the country at large, such as racism and discrimination. Poverty hits minority children particularly hard.

The number of children living in poverty in the United States has grown by 11.3 percent to approach 13 million (Reid, 2006). Although the vast majority of the poor are non-Latino Whites (4.3 million), since 2000, more than 600,000 Latino children have fallen into poverty; and in 2005, one in every three Black children living in America was poor.

Since 2002, for every five children who fell into poverty, four fell into extreme poverty (living with an annual income below $7,412 for a family of three, $18,660 for a family of four). Unfortunately the number of children in extreme poverty grew 11.5 percent, almost twice as fast as the 6.0 percent rate of increase for child poverty overall (Children's Defense Fund, 2004c).

Contrary to popular perceptions about poor families, 70 percent of children in poverty lived in a family in which someone worked full- or part-time for at least part of the year. Almost one in three poor children (31.4 percent) lived with a full-time year-round worker. One of the results of poverty, according to the Department of Agriculture, is that poor households are "food insecure" (without enough food to fully meet basic needs at all times due to lack of financial resources). This was the case for one out of every six households with children in 2002 (Children's Defense Fund, 2004a).

Poverty does not mean merely inadequate income; rather, it engenders a host of issues, including insufficient income and jobs with limited opportunity, lack of health insurance, inadequate education, and poor nutrition. Poor children are more likely to die in infancy, have a low birth weight, and lack health care, housing, and adequate food (Children's Defense Fund, 2004b). Poor children are at least twice as likely as nonpoor children to suffer stunted growth or lead poisoning or to be kept back in school. They score significantly lower on reading, math, and vocabulary tests when compared with similar nonpoor children (Children's Defense Fund, 2004c). Table 8.3 lists outcomes of health and education and the risk incurred by low-income children.

Among people living below the poverty line, 56 percent speak a language other than English, compared with 41 percent for those above the poverty line (Gorman & Pierson, 2007). English learners often face severe educational shortfalls, as one researcher noted: "Compared with affluent schools, ELs attend schools which are likely to experience higher teacher turnover, allocate fewer resources to classrooms, and face more challenging conditions overall" (Merino, 2007, p. 1).

Poverty plays a large role in the education of America's youth. It affects the ability of the family to devote resources to educational effort. This situation, coupled with social and political factors that affect minority children in schools, stacks the deck against minority-student success. Demographic trends ensure that this will be a continuing problem in the United States.

Table 8.3

Why Poverty Matters

Outcomes	Low-Income Children's Higher Risk
Health	
Death in infancy	1.6 times as likely
Premature birth (under 37 weeks)	1.8 times as likely
Low birth weight	1.9 times as likely
No regular source of health care	2.7 times as likely
Inadequate prenatal care	2.8 times as likely
Family had too little food sometime in the last 4 months	8 times as likely
Education	
Math scores at ages 7 to 8	5 test points lower
Reading scores at ages 7 to 8	4 test points lower
Repeated a grade	2 times as likely
Expelled from school	3.4 times as likely
Being a dropout at ages 16 to 24	3.5 times as likely
Finishing a four-year college	Half as likely

Source: Children's Defense Fund (2004a). Reprinted with permission.

Did You Know?

Each day in the United States . . .

	Among All Children	Among White Children	Among Black Children	Among Latino Children	Among Asian Children	Among Native American Children
Babies die before their first birthdays	76	36	22	13	3	1
Babies are born to mothers who received late or no prenatal care	390	139	98	128	18	9
Babies are born at low birth weight	860	434	216	157	45	8
Babies are born without health insurance	1,707	526	378	820	—	—
Babies are born into poverty	2,171	762	659	711	36	40
High-school students drop out	2,539	1,072	489	689	94	—

Source: Adapted from Children's Defense Fund (2004b).

Almost three-quarters (74 percent) of the Hispanic population are under thirty-five years of age, compared with a little more than half (51.7 percent) of the non-Hispanic White population. Hispanics were more than two and a half times more likely to live in families of five or more people than were non-Hispanic Whites (26.5 percent versus 10.8). Only 25.9 percent of Hispanic families consist of two people, whereas 48.7 percent of White families do (U.S. Census Bureau, 2003a). The average Hispanic female is well within childbearing age, and Hispanic children constitute the largest growing school population. Therefore, the educational achievement of Hispanic children is of particular concern.

The Education of Minorities

The economy of the United States in the future will rest more on Asian-American and Hispanic-American workers than at present. As a consequence, the education of these populations will become increasingly important. Consider that in 2000, 38.8 percent of students enrolled in public elementary and secondary schools were minorities—an increase of 30 percent from 1986, largely due to the growth in the Hispanic population (NCES, 2002). Of these minorities, 87.6 percent of Asian Americans have a high-school diploma and 49.8 percent have bachelor degrees. In contrast, only 57 percent of Hispanics have high-school diplomas and 11.4 percent have college degrees. Eighty-five percent of non-Hispanic Whites, on the other hand, have high-school diplomas and over a quarter (27.6 percent) have bachelor degrees (U.S. Census Bureau, 2004a). The extent of the problem becomes clearer.

Minority students typically live in racially isolated neighborhoods and are more likely to attend segregated schools. Over one-third (38 percent) of Hispanic students and Black students (37 percent) attended schools with minority enrollments of 90 to

100 percent. Seventy-seven percent of Hispanics and 71 percent of Blacks were enrolled in schools where minorities constitute 50 percent or more of the population.

In addition, minority children are overrepresented in compensatory programs in schools. In the 1999–2000 school year, 15 percent of Black and 14 percent of Native-American students were enrolled in special education, a significantly higher proportion than White and Hispanic (11 percent) and Asian/Pacific Islander students (6 percent) (NCES, 2003a, 2003b; University of Texas at Austin, 1991).

Thus, nearly a half-century after *Brown v. Board of Education,* a student who is Black, Latino, or Native American remains much less likely to succeed in school. A major factor is a disparity of resources—inner-city schools with large minority populations have been found to have higher percentages of first-year teachers, higher enrollments, fewer library resources, and less in-school parental involvement, characteristics that have been shown to relate to school success (U.S. Government Accounting Office, 2002).

The conclusion is inescapable: The educational system of the United States has been fundamentally weak in serving the fastest growing school-age populations. Today's minority students are entering school with significantly different social and economic backgrounds from those of previous student populations and therefore require educators to modify their teaching approaches to ensure that these students have access to the American dream.

Second-Language-Speaking Minority Populations

Many minority students come to school with home languages other than English. According to the 2000 census, one American in five, 47 million, speaks a language other than English at home. Almost 3 million school-age children spoke Spanish as a native language—more than three-quarters (76.9 percent) of English learners in schools. No other native language exceeded 3 percent. The five most common languages after Spanish were Vietnamese (2.4 percent), Hmong (1.8 percent), Korean (1.2 percent), Arabic (1.2 percent), and Haitian Creole (1.1 percent) (Hopstock & Stephenson, 2003).

How is the impact of these large numbers of students with English-learning needs felt in schools? Districts find themselves scrambling for teachers and staff with second-language competencies and for those knowledgeable about language, culture, and academic development for English learners; for primary-language as well as appropriate English-language materials; and for ways of working with and involving parents.

Immigration and Migration

The United States has historically been a nation of immigrants, but the nature and causes of immigration have changed over time. The earliest settlers to the east coast of North America came from England and Holland, whereas those to the South and West came mainly from Spain. In the early eighteenth century, these settlers were joined by

▪Did You Know?

The number of foreign-born people in the United States is now, in absolute numbers, at its highest point in history—representing about 10 percent of the population. According to U.S. Census Bureau 2000 data, approximately 51 percent are from Latin America, 25.7 percent from Asia, 15.2 percent from Europe, and 8.1 percent from other regions such as Africa and Oceania (Migration Policy Institute, 2004).

involuntary immigrants from Africa. Subsequent waves of immigrants came from Scotland, Ireland, and Germany, and later from central and eastern Europe. Immigration from the Pacific Rim countries was constrained by severe immigration restrictions until the last decades of the twentieth century.

However, imperialistic policies of the United States, primarily the conquest of the Philippines, Puerto Rico, Hawaii, and the Pacific Islands, caused large influxes of these populations throughout the twentieth century. The wars in southeast Asia and Central America throughout the 1970s and 1980s led to increased emigration from these areas. In the 1990s, immigrants arrived from all over the world. In 2000, 40 percent of all legal immigrants came from just five countries—Mexico, China, the Philippines, India, and Vietnam (Migration Policy Institute, 2004).

Immigrants have come to the United States for a variety of reasons. The earliest immigration was prompted by the desire for adventure and economic gain in a new world combined with the desire to flee religious and political persecution. These factors provided both attractive forces (pull) and expulsive forces (push). Later, U.S. foreign policy created connections with populations abroad that pulled certain groups to the United States. For example, the conquest of the Philippines at the turn of the century eventually resulted in significant Philippine immigration to the United States.

Once in the United States, both immigrants and natives have historically been restless populations. Much of the history of the United States consists of the migration of groups from one part of the country to another.

Causes of Immigration

Migration is an international phenomenon. Throughout the world, populations are dislocated by wars, famine, civil strife, economic changes, persecution, and other factors. The United States has been a magnet for immigrants seeking greater opportunity and economic stability. The social upheavals and overpopulation that characterized nineteenth-century Europe and Asia brought more than 14 million immigrants to the United States in the forty-year period between 1860 and 1900. A century later this phenomenon can be witnessed along the border between the United States and Mexico. Politics and religion as well as economics provide reasons for emigration. U.S. domestic and foreign policies affect the way in which groups of foreigners are accepted. Changes in immigration policy, such as amnesty, affect the number of immigrants who enter the country each year.

Find Out More about . . .

Economic Factors

U.S. Immigration Facts

www.rapidimmigration.com/usa/
1_eng_immigration_facts.html

This site provides general facts about recent U.S. immigration and then discusses immigrant entrepreneurs and economic characteristics of immigrants.

Economic Factors in Immigration. The great disparity in the standard of living attainable in the United States compared to that of many developing countries makes immigration attractive. Self-advancement is uppermost in the minds of many immigrants and acts as a strong incentive despite the economic exploitation often extended to immigrants (e.g., lower wages, exclusion from desirable jobs).

Immigration policy has corresponded with the cycles of boom and bust in the U.S. economy; the Chinese Exclusion Act of 1882 stopped immigration from China to the United States because of the concern that Chinese labor would flood the market. The labor shortage in the western United States resulting from excluding the Chinese had the effect of welcoming Japanese immigrants who were good farm laborers. Later, during the Great Depression of the 1930s, with a vast labor surplus in the United States, the U.S. Congress severely restricted Philippine immigration, and policies were initiated to "repatriate" Mexicans back across the border.

When World War II transformed the labor surplus of the 1930s into a severe worker shortage, the United States and Mexico established the Bracero Program, a bilateral agreement allowing Mexicans to cross the border to work on U.S. farms and railroads. The border was virtually left open during the war years (Wollenberg, 1989). However, despite the economic attractiveness of the United States, now, as then, most newcomers to this society experience a period of economic hardship.

Political Factors in Immigration. Repression, civil war, and change in government create a "push" for emigration from foreign countries, whereas political factors within the United States create a climate of acceptance for some political refugees and not for others. After the Vietnam War, many refugees were displaced in southeast Asia. Some sense of responsibility for their plight caused the U.S. government to accept many of these people into the United States. For example, Cambodians who cooperated with the U.S. military immigrated to the United States in waves: first, a group including 6,300 Khmer in 1975; second, 10,000 Cambodians in 1979; third, 60,000 Cambodians between 1980 and 1982 (Gillett, 1989a).

The decade of the 1980s was likewise one of political instability and civil war in many Central American countries, resulting in massive civilian casualties. In El Salvador, for example, such instabilities caused the displacement of 600,000 Salvadorans who lived as refugees outside their country (Gillett, 1989b). Through the Deferred Enforced Departure program of the U.S. government, nearly 200,000 Salvadoran immigrants were given the right to live and work legally in the United States.

Other populations, such as Haitians claiming political persecution, have been turned away from U.S. borders. U.S. policy did not consider them to be victims of political repression, but rather of economic hardship—a fine distinction, in many cases, and here one might suspect that racial issues in the United States make it more difficult for them to immigrate. It would seem, then, that the grounds for political asylum—race, religion, nationality, membership in a particular social group, political opinion—can be clouded by confounding factors.

In sum, people are pushed to the United States because of political instability or political policies unfavorable to them in their home countries. Political conditions within the United States affect whether immigrants are accepted or denied.

Religious Factors in Immigration. Many of the early English settlers in North America came to the New World to found colonies in which they would be free to establish or practice their form of religious belief. Later, Irish Catholics left Ireland in droves because their lands were taken by Protestants. Many eastern European Jews, forced to emigrate because of anti-Semitic pogroms in the nineteenth century, came to the United States in great numbers. Current immigration policies permit refugees to be accepted on the basis of religion if the applicant can prove that persecution comes from the government or is motivated by the government (Siskind Susser, n.d.).

Family Unification. The risks associated with travel to the New World have made immigration a male-dominated activity since the early settlement of North America. In some cases, such as that of the Chinese in the nineteenth century, immigration laws permitted only young men to enter. Initial Japanese immigration, which was not restricted as severely as Chinese, involved predominantly young men between the ages of twenty and forty. Similarly, today's Mexican immigrant population consists largely of young men who have come to the United States to work and send money home. Once settled, these immigrants seek to bring family members to the United States. Family unification is a primary motivation for many applications to the Bureau of Citizenship and Immigration Services (BCIS) in the Department of Homeland Security.

Unfortunately, too often the mainstream media in the United States focus on anti-immigration stories, particularly against Mexicans. Rarely featured in the media, however, are analyses of the reasons behind persistent Mexican emigration attempts: Today, the majority of Mexicans are poorer and more economically insecure that they were just a few years ago (Bigelow, 2007). Under the North American Free Trade Agreement (NAFTA), manufacturing wages in Mexico declined 9 percent between 1994 and 2004, poverty in rural areas increased from 54 percent to 81 percent, and almost 1.5 million Mexican farmers lost their land because of cheap corn imports from the United States. These facts argue for a more compassionate stance toward Mexican English learners who are recent immigrants.

Migration

Americans have always been restless. Historically, crowding and the promise of greater economic freedom were reasons for moving west. The gold rush attracted, for the most part, English-speaking European Americans from the eastern United States, but other minority groups and immigrants were also drawn to the search for instant wealth. Miners from Mexico, Peru, and Chile increased California's Latino population; Greeks, Portuguese, Russians, Poles, Armenians, and Italians flocked to the San Francisco Bay area. During the Depression, many of these populations migrated once again to California's central valley to find work as farm laborers (Wollenberg, 1989). With the rise of cities, rural populations sought economic advancement in urban environments. Many African Americans migrated to northern cities after World War I to escape prejudice and discrimination.

Today, many immigrants are sponsored by special-interest groups such as churches and civic organizations that invite them to reside in the local community. Once here, however, some groups find conditions too foreign to their former lives and eventually migrate to another part of the United States. For example, a group of Hmong families sponsored by Lutheran charities spent two years in the severe winter climate of the Minneapolis area before resettling in California. Hispanics, on the other hand, are migrating from cities in the Southwest, New York, and Miami toward destinations in the Midwest and middle South (Wilson, 1984).

Based on the 2000 census, Americans continue to move. The most mobile population between 1995 and 2000 was Hispanics (56 percent), followed by Asians (54 percent), Native Americans and Alaska Natives (50 percent), and Blacks (49 percent). The least mobile population was non-Hispanic Whites (43 percent). Of the regions in the United States, the South had the highest level of net domestic immigration of non-Hispanic Whites, Blacks, Asians, and Hispanics. Of the states, Nevada had the largest gain in numbers of Asians, Florida in numbers of Hispanics, and Georgia in numbers of Blacks (Schachter, 2003).

For newly arriving immigrants, historical patterns are also changing. California, which had attracted 33 percent of these immigrants, recently has only received 22 percent. Newer immigrants are settling in states such as Oregon, Arizona, Iowa, Arkansas, Georgia, North Carolina, Kentucky, Tennessee, and Virginia (Migration Policy Institute, 2004).

Immigration Laws and Policies

Economic cycles in the United States have affected immigration policies, liberalizing them when workers were needed and restricting immigration when jobs were scarce. These restrictive immigration policies were often justified with overtly racist arguments.

Did You Know?

Although Hispanics are the most urbanized ethnic/racial group in the United States (90 percent living in metropolitan areas in 2000), the nonmetro Hispanic population is now the most rapidly growing demographic group in rural and small-town America. By 2000, half of all nonmetro Hispanics lived outside traditional southwest cities. Many of these Hispanics are newly arrived undocumented young men from rural, depressed areas of Mexico. In spite of their relatively low education levels and weak English skills, employment rates exceeded those of all other nonmetro Hispanics and non-Hispanic Whites.

Source: Adapted from Kandel and Cromartie (2004).

Asian immigration was targeted for specific quotas. The first Asian population that was specifically excluded was the Chinese (the Chinese Exclusion Act of 1882), but the growth of Japanese immigration as a result of this quota prompted Congress to extend the concept of Chinese exclusion to Japan (1908) and the rest of Asia. The immigration laws of the 1920s (the National Origins Acts of 1924 and 1929) banned most Asian immigration and established quotas that favored northwestern European immigrants. The quota system, however, did not apply to Mexico and the rest of the Western Hemisphere. In 1943, Congress symbolically ended the Asian exclusion policy by granting ethnic Chinese a token quota of 100 immigrants a year. The Philippines and Japan received similar tiny quotas after the war.

U.S. Foreign Policy. As the United States grew as a capitalist nation, economic forces had a great influence on U.S. foreign policy. In the early growth of commercial capitalism from 1600 to 1865, new settlers were a source of labor; Africans were enslaved to provide plantation labor, and poor Europeans such as Irish Catholics were recruited abroad for low-wage jobs in transportation and construction. In the phase of industrial capitalism (1865–1920), U.S. treaties with Europe and intervention in European affairs (World War I) maintained the labor supply until the 1924 Immigration Act, which provided overall limits on immigration (favoring immigrants from Europe over other regions of the world). U.S. imperialist policies in Asia (conquest of the Philippines and Hawaii) ensured a supply of raw materials and a home for U.S. military bases in the Pacific, but immigration policy denied access to the United States for the majority of Asians.

The Immigration and Nationality Act Amendments of 1965 brought about vast changes in immigration policy by abolishing the national origins quota system and replacing it with a seven-category preference system for allocating immigrant visas—a system that emphasizes family ties and occupation. Although there is a per-country limit for these preference immigrants, certain countries—People's Republic of China, India, Mexico, and the Philippines—are "oversubscribed," and hopeful immigrants are on long waiting lists, some extending for as many as twelve years (U.S. Department of State, 2004).

An additional provision in the 1965 act is the diversity immigrant category, in which 55,000 immigrant visas can be awarded each fiscal year to permit immigration opportunities for persons from countries other than the principal sources of current immigration to the United States. No one country can receive more than 7 percent of the available diversity visas in any one year (U.S. Department of State, 2004).

The Refugee Act of 1980 expanded the number of persons considered refugees, again allowing more immigrants to enter the United States under this category. As a result of these policy changes, immigrants from Latin America and Asia began to enter the United States in unprecedented numbers, eclipsing the previous dominance of Europeans.

Legal Status. Many immigrants are *documented*—legal residents who have entered the United States officially and live under the protection of legal immigration status. Some of these are officially designated *refugees,* with transitional support services and assistance provided by the U.S. government. Most immigrants from Cambodia, Laos, Vietnam, and Thailand have been granted refugee status. *Undocumented* immigrants

Find Out More about ...

U.S. Immigration Policy

U.S. Department of State, Bureau of Consular Affairs, Visa Bulletin

http://travel.state.gov/visa/frvi/bulletin/bulletin_1360.html

The Visa Bulletin, updated monthly, provides information about immigrant numbers and eligibility criteria for various categories.

United States Immigration Policy

www.cbo.gov/doc.crfm?index-7051

This paper, written in 2007, provides an overview of U.S. immigration policy, a summary of current U.S. immigration law, statistics, enforcement efforts, and requirements for naturalization.

are residents without any documentation who live in fear of being identified and deported.

Being in the United States illegally brings increased instability, fear, and insecurity to school-age children because they and their families are living without the protection, social services, and assistance available to most immigrants. With the passage of the Immigration Reform and Control Act in 1986, however, undocumented children are legally entitled to public education. Often they and their families are unclear about this right, and school staff and authorities sometimes worsen the situation by illegally asking for immigration papers when children are being registered (Olsen, 1988).

Resources Available to Immigrants. The Emergency Immigrant Education Program (EIEP; No Child Left Behind, Title III, subpart 4) provides assistance to school districts whose enrollment is affected by immigrants. The purpose of the program is to provide high-quality instruction to immigrant children and youth, to help them with their transition into U.S. society, and to help them meet the same challenging academic content and student academic achievement standards as all children are expected to meet (NCLB, Sec. 3241). School districts and county offices of education qualify for EIEP funding if they have an enrollment of at least 500 eligible immigrant pupils and/or if the enrollment of eligible immigrant pupils represents at least 3 percent of the total enrollment.

How far have we come? The Puritans brought to New England a religion based on a monochromatic worldview. They outlawed Christmas and disapproved of celebration. The United States of America has struggled with this severe cultural reductionism since its founding. As the splendor and the celebratory spirit of the Native-American and immigrant cultures have been recognized, the people of the United States have opened up to accept the beauty and brilliant hues that Native-Americans and immigrants have contributed. As more and more diverse groups settle and resettle throughout the continent, customs and traditions mingle to create an ever-new mix. The salad bowl, the kaleidoscope—these are metaphors for diversity in taste, in pattern, and in lifestyle. The American portrait is still being painted, in ever-brighter hues. ∎

LEARNING MORE

Further Reading

Lies My Teacher Told Me by J. Loewen (1995) is a fascinating book that questions many of the "facts" presented in U.S. history textbooks. According to the author, "African American, Native American, and Latino students view history with a special dislike" (p. 12). Perhaps the Eurocentric every-problem-is-solved approach in the texts deadens students to the true nature of the controversies and to the richness of the stories of history.

Web Search

Using a search engine (Google, for example), enter "contributions of _____ " (the group of students who are most represented in your school). Based on what you find, share your findings with the school staff and then prepare a lesson (with the help of the students and their parents) that highlights the contributions of the group.

Exploration

Visit a local school district office (or use the Internet) to find out which ethnic groups are represented in your state and school district. Prepare a presentation for the staff at your school and brainstorm how you can be more proactive in including these groups in the curriculum.

Collaboration

Determine what school-site activities involve minority groups. Are the activities confined to flags, food, and fiestas? Are the activities confined to specific months (e.g., African Americans discussed only during Black History Month)? Work with other teachers to develop an overall year plan that incorporates contributions of various groups to the richness of the United States.

PEARSON
The Power of Classroom Practice
www.myeducationlab.com

Multicultural Education

Administrators from Hans Christian Andersen School discuss their conceptions of multicultural education. They also deal with issues of evaluating students' and their own performances. They share their thoughts about political correctness.

> To access the video, go to MyEducationLab (www.myeducationlab.com), choose the Díaz-Rico and Weed text, and log in to MyEducationLab for English Language Learners. Select the topic Cultural-Based Instruction, and watch the video entitled "Multicultural Education."

Answer the following questions:
1. What advantages of a multicultural curriculum are discussed? What do these administrators mean when they say that schools are desegregated but not integrated?
2. What is meant in this video by "politically correct"?
3. Several administrators describe students' pride in their cultural heritage. How does this relate to students' pride in being a successful student? Discuss the differences in the definition of a "successful student." How does one define success?

The Intercultural Educator

Teachers who take the time to chat with students can learn about their cultures, homes, and family lives.

Unlike my grandmother, the teacher did not have pretty brown skin and a colorful dress. She wasn't plump and friendly. Her clothes were of one color and drab. Her pale and skinny form made me worry that she was very ill. . . . The teacher's odor took some getting used to also. Later I learned from the girls this smell was something she wore called perfume. The classroom . . . was terribly huge and smelled of medicine like the village clinic I feared so much. Those fluorescent light tubes made an eerie drone. Our confinement to rows of desks was another unnatural demand made on our active little bodies. . . . We all went home for lunch since we lived a short walk from the school. It took coaxing, and sometimes bribing, to get me to return and complete the remainder of the school day.

Joe Suina (1985, writing his impressions on entering school at age 6)

The narrative of this Pueblo youth illustrates two cultural systems in contact. Neither is right or wrong, good or bad, superior or inferior. Suina was experiencing a natural human reaction that occurs when a person moves into a new cultural situation—culture shock. He had grown up in an environment that had subtly, through every part of his life, taught him appropriate ways of behavior—for example, how people looked (their color, their size, their dress, their ways of interacting) and how space was structured (the sizes of rooms, the types of lighting, the arrangement of furniture). His culture had taught him what was important and valuable. The culture Suina grew up in totally enveloped him and gave him a way to understand life. It provided him with a frame of reference through which he made sense of the world.

Culture is so pervasive that often people perceive other cultures as strange and foreign without realizing that their own culture may be equally mystifying to others. Culture, though largely invisible, influences instruction, policy, and learning in schools (see the figure on page 211). Members of the educational community accept the organization, teaching and learning styles, and curricula of the schools as natural and right, without realizing that these patterns are cultural. And the schools *are* natural and right for members of the culture that created them. As children of nondominant cultures enter the schools, however, they may find the organization, teaching and learning styles, and curricula to be alien, incomprehensible, and exclusionary.

Unfortunately, teachers—who, with parents, are the prime acculturators of society—often have little training regarding the key role of culture in teaching and learning. Too often, culture is incorporated into classroom activities in superficial ways—as a group of artifacts (baskets, masks, distinctive clothing), as celebrations of holidays (Cinco de Mayo, Martin Luther King Jr. Day), or as a laundry list of stereotypes and facts (Asians are quiet; Hispanics are family-oriented; Arabs are Muslims). Teachers who have a more insightful view of culture and cultural processes are able to use their understanding to move beyond the superficial and to recognize that people live in characteristic ways. They understand that the observable manifestations of culture are but one aspect of the cultural web—the intricate pattern that weaves and binds a people together. Knowing that culture provides the lens through which people view the world, teachers can look at the "what" of a culture—the artifacts, celebrations, traits, and facts—and ask "why."

Teachers in the twenty-first century face a diverse student population that demands a complicated set of skills to promote achievement for all students. As intercultural educators, teachers understand cultural diversity and can adapt instruction accordingly. Table 9.1 outlines the skills and responsibilities of the intercultural educator. This chapter addresses cultural diversity and the struggle to achieve equity in schooling. Chapter 10 focuses on using culturally responsive pedagogy to promote student achievement.

Understanding Cultural Diversity

As an initial step in learning about the complexity of culture and how the culture embodied within the school affects diverse students, the following sections examine the nature of culture. Knowledge of the deeper elements of culture—beyond superficial

Table 9.1

The Skills and Responsibilities of the Intercultural Educator

Understand Culture and Cultural Diversity

Explore key concepts about culture.
Investigate ourselves as cultural beings.
Learn about students' cultures.
Recognize how cultural adaptation affects learning.

Strive for Equity in Schooling

Detect unfair privilege.
Combat prejudice in ourselves and others.
Fight for fairness and equal opportunity.

Promote Achievement

Respect students' diversity.
Work with culturally supported facilitating or limiting attitudes and abilities.
Sustain high expectations for all students.
Marshal parental and community support for schooling.

Source: Díaz-Rico (2000).

aspects such as food, clothing, holidays, and celebrations—can give teachers a cross-cultural perspective that allows them to educate students to the greatest extent possible. These deeper elements include values, belief systems, family structures and child-rearing practices, language and nonverbal communication, expectations, gender roles, and biases—all the fundamentals of life that affect learning.

The Nature of Culture

Does a fish understand water? Do people understand their own culture? Teachers are responsible for helping to pass on cultural knowledge through the schooling process. Can teachers step outside their own culture long enough to see how it operates and to understand its effects on culturally diverse students? A way to begin is to define culture.

The term *culture* is used in many ways. It can refer to activities such as art, drama, and ballet or to items such as pop music, mass media entertainment, and comic books. The term *culture* can be used for distinctive groups in society, such as adolescents and their culture. It can be used as a general term for a society, such as the "French culture." Such uses do not, however, define what a culture is. As a field of study, culture is conceptualized in various ways (see Table 9.2).

The definitions in Table 9.2 have common factors but vary in emphasis. The following definition of culture combines the ideas in Table 9.2:

Culture is the explicit and implicit patterns for living, the dynamic system of commonly agreed-upon symbols and meanings, knowledge, belief, art, morals, law, customs,

Table 9.2

Definitions of Culture

Definition	Source
The sum total of a way of life of a people; patterns experienced by individuals as normal ways of acting, feeling, and being	Hall (1959)
That complex whole that includes knowledge, belief, art, morals, law, and custom, and any other capabilities acquired by humans as members of society	Tylor (in Pearson, 1974)
A dynamic system of symbols and meanings that involves an ongoing, dialectic process in which past experience influences meaning, which in turn affects future experience, which in turn affects subsequent meaning, and so on	Robinson (1985)
Mental constructs in three basic categories: *shared knowledge* (information known in common by members of the group), *shared views* (beliefs and values shared by members of a group), and *shared patterns* (habits and norms in the ways members of a group organize their behavior, interaction, and communication)	Snow (1996)
Partial solutions to previous problems that humans create in joint mediated activity; the social inheritance embodied in artifacts and material constituents of culture as well as in practices and ideal symbolic forms; semi-organized hodgepodge of human inheritance. Culture is exteriorized mind and mind is interiorized culture	Cole (1998)
Frames (nationality, gender, ethnicity, religion) carried by each individual that are internalized, individuated, and emerge in interactions	Smith, Paige, and Steglitz (1998)

behaviors, traditions, and/or habits that are shared and make up the total way of life of a people, as negotiated by individuals in the process of constructing a personal identity.

The important idea is that culture involves both observable behaviors and intangibles such as beliefs and values, rhythms, rules, and roles. The concept of culture has evolved over the last fifty years away from the idea of culture as an invisible, patterning force to that of culture as an active tension between the social "shortcuts" that make consensual society possible and the contributions and construction that each individual creates while living in society. Culture is not only the filter through which people see the world but also the raw dough from which each person fashions a life that is individual and satisfying.

Because culture is all-inclusive (see the figure on page 211), it includes all aspects of life. Snow (1996) listed a host of components (see Table 9.3).

Cultures are more than the mere sum of their traits. There is a wholeness about cultures, an integration of the various responses to human needs. Cultures cannot be taught merely by examining external features such as art and artifacts. For example, a teacher who travels to Japan may return laden with kimonos and chopsticks, hoping these objects will document Japanese culture. But to understand the culture, that teacher must examine the living patterns and values of the culture that those artifacts represent.

Table 9.3

Components of Culture

Daily Life			
Animals	Hobbies	Medical care	Sports
Clothing	Housing	Plants	Time
Daily schedule	Hygiene	Recreation	Traffic and transport
Food	Identification	Shopping	Travel
Games	Jobs	Space	Weather

The Cycle of Life		
Birth	Divorce	Rites of passage
Children	Friends	Men and women
Dating/mating	Old age	
Marriage	Funerals	

Interacting		
Chatting	Functions in communication	Parties
Eating	Gifts	Politeness
Drinking	Language learning	Problem solving

Society			
Business	Education	Government and politics	Science
Cities	Farming	Languages and dialects	Social problems
Economy	Industry	Law and order	

The Nation		
Holidays	Cultural borrowing	National issues
Geography	Famous people	Stereotypes
History		

Creative Arts		
Arts	Genres	Music
Entertainment	Literature	Television

Philosophy, Religion, and Values

Source: Adapted from Snow (1996).

Key Concepts about Culture

Despite the evolving definitions of culture, theorists agree on a few central ideas. These concepts are first summarized here and then treated with more depth.

Culture Is Universal. Everyone in the world belongs to one or more cultures. Each culture provides templates for the rituals of daily interaction: the way food is served, the way children are spoken to, the way needs are met. These templates are an internalized way to organize and interpret experience. All cultures share some universal characteristics. The manner in which these needs are met differs.

Culture Simplifies Living. Social behaviors and customs offer structure to daily life that minimizes interpersonal stress. Cultural patterns are routines that free humans from endless negotiation about each detail of living. Cultural influences help unify a society by providing a common base of communication and common social customs.

Culture Is Learned in a Process of Deep Conditioning. Cultural patterns are absorbed unconsciously from birth, as well as explicitly taught by other members. Culture dictates how and what people see, hear, smell, taste, and feel, and how people and events are evaluated. Cultural patterns are so familiar that members of a culture find it difficult to accept that other ways can be right. As cultural patterns are learned or acquired through observation and language, seldom are alternatives given. The fact that cultural patterns are deep makes it difficult for the members of a given culture to see their own culture as learned behavior.

Culture Is Demonstrated in Values. Every culture deems some beliefs and behaviors more desirable than others, whether these be about nature, human character, material possessions, or other aspects of the human condition. Members of the culture reward individuals who exemplify these values with prestige or approval.

Culture Is Expressed Both Verbally and Nonverbally. Although language and culture are closely identified, the nonverbal components of culture are equally powerful means of communication about cultural beliefs, behaviors, and values. Witness the strong communicative potential of the obscene gesture! In the classroom, teachers may misunderstand a student's intent if nonverbal communication is misinterpreted.

Example of Concept: Nonverbal Miscommunication

Ming was taught at home to sit quietly when she was finished with a task and wait for her mother to praise her. As a newcomer in the third grade, she waited quietly when finished with her reading assignment. Mrs. Wakefield impatiently reminded Ming to take out a book and read or start another assignment when she completed her work. She made a mental note: "Ming lacks initiative."

Societies Represent a Mix of Cultures. The patterns that dominate a society form the *macroculture* of that society. In the United States, European-American traditions and cultural patterns have largely determined the social behaviors and norms of formal institutions. Within the macroculture, a variety of *microcultures* coexist, distinguished

The first generation of Japanese immigrants, who often referred to themselves as *issei,* or first generation, came to the United States starting about 1900 and consisted, for the most part, of young men who became agricultural laborers or skilled craftsmen. Often seen as a threat by European Americans, these immigrants were often the target of discrimination, which peaked after the attack on Pearl Harbor. The *issei* were divested of their property and removed to relocation camps. Their children, the *nisei* generation, are often considered to have a very low ethnic profile, perhaps as a response to the treatment given to their parents (Leathers, 1967).

by characteristics such as gender, socioeconomic status, ethnicity, geographical location, social identification, and language use.

Generational experiences can cause the formation of microcultures. For example, the children of Vietnamese who immigrated to the United States after the Vietnam War often became native speakers of English, separating the two generations by language. Similarly, Mexicans who migrate to the United States may find that their children born in the United States consider themselves "Chicanos."

Individuals who grow up within a macroculture and never leave it may act on the assumption that their values are the norm. When encountering microcultures, they may be unable or unwilling to recognize that alternative beliefs and behaviors are legitimate within the larger society.

Culture Is Both Dynamic and Persistent. Human cultures are a paradox—some features are flexible and responsive to change, and other features last thousands of years without changing. Values and customs relating to birth, marriage, medicine, education, and death seem to be the most persistent, for humans seem to be deeply reluctant to alter those cultural elements that influence labor and delivery, marital happiness, health, life success, and eternal rest.

Culture Is a Mix of Rational and Nonrational Elements. Much as individuals living in western European post-Enlightenment societies may believe that reason should govern

The Persistence of Cultural Values

The Sarmatians, like their neighbors the Scythians, were nomadic people who lived just north of the Black Sea in ancient times. They had one outstanding trait in particular—a unique love of their horses, such that graves were almost always found with horse bones, bridles, and other accoutrements buried next to the human remains. Thousands of years later, in the twentieth century, their descendants, the Ossetians, waged a fierce cultural skirmish with government officials of the Union of Soviet Socialist Republics (USSR). The issue? The Ossetians insisted on killing a man's horse when he died and burying it with the corpse. The Soviets mandated that it was a crime to waste the People's resources. For many years, subterfuge persisted—a deceased man's horse mysteriously would become sick or disabled and had to be shot, and graves would be reopened in the dead of night to accommodate one more body. (More information at www.ossetians.com/eng.)

human behavior, many cultural patterns are passed on through habit rather than reason. People who bring a real tree into their houses in December—despite the mess it creates—do so because of centuries-old Yule customs. Similarly, carving a face on a hollow pumpkin is not a rational idea. Those who create elaborate altars in their homes or take food to the grave of a loved one for the Mexican celebration of Day of the Dead do so because of spiritual beliefs.

Cultures Represent Different Values.   The fact that each culture possesses its own particular traditions, values, and ideals means that the culture of a society provides judgments that may differ from those of other cultures about what actions are deemed right or wrong for its members. Actions can be judged only in relation to the cultural setting in which they occur. This point of view has been called *cultural relativism*. In general, the primary values of human nature are universal—for example, few societies condone murder. However, sanctions relating to actions may differ. The Native-American cultures of California before contact with Europeans were pacifists to the extent that someone who took the life of another would be ostracized from the tribe. In contrast, the U.S. macroculture accepts as heroes soldiers who have killed in the context of war (for example, Andrew Jackson and Ulysses S. Grant).

Attempting to impose "international" standards on diverse peoples with different cultural traditions causes problems. This means that some cardinal values held by teachers in the United States are not cultural universals but instead are values that may not be shared by students and their families. For example, not all families value children's spending time reading fiction; some may see this as a waste of time. Some families may not see value in algebra or higher mathematics; others might consider art in the classroom to be unimportant.

Diverse Societies Have a Mainstream Culture.   The term *mainstream culture* refers to those individuals or groups who share values of the dominant macroculture. In the United States, this dominant or core culture is primarily shared by members of the middle class. Mainstream American culture is characterized by the following values (Gollnick & Chinn, 2006):

- Individualism and privacy
- Independence and self-reliance
- Equality
- Ambition and industriousness
- Competitiveness
- Appreciation of the good life
- Perception that humans are separate from and superior to nature

Culture Affects People's Attitudes toward Schooling.   For many individuals, educational aspiration affects the attitude they have toward schooling: what future job or profession they desire, the importance parents ascribe to education, and the investment in education that is valued in their culture. The son of blue-collar workers, for example, may not value a college education because his parents, who have not attained such an education, have nevertheless prospered, whereas the daughter of a recent, low-wage immigrant may work industriously in school to pursue higher education and a well-paid job.

Cultural values also affect the extent to which families are involved in their children's schooling and the forms this involvement takes. Family involvement is discussed in Chapter 10.

Adapted Instruction: Working with Attitudes toward Schooling

In working with diverse students, teachers will want to know:

- What educational level the student, family, and community desire for the student
- What degree of assimilation to the dominant culture (and to English) is expected and desired

Culture Governs the Way People Learn.   Any learning that takes place is built on previous learning. Students have learned the basic patterns of living in the context of their families. They have learned the verbal and nonverbal behaviors appropriate for their gender and age and have observed their family members in various occupations and activities. The family has taught them about love and about relations between friends, kin, and community members. They have observed community members cooperating to learn in a variety of methods and modes. Their families have given them a feeling for music and art and have shown them what is beautiful and what is not. Finally, they have learned to use language in the context of their homes and communities. They have learned when questions can be asked and when silence is required. They have used language to learn to share feelings and knowledge and beliefs. Indeed, they are native speakers of the home language by the age of five, and can express their needs and delights.

The culture that students bring from the home is the foundation for their learning. Although certain communities exist in relative poverty—that is, they are not equipped with middle-class resources—poverty should not be equated with cultural deprivation. Every community's culture incorporates vast knowledge about successful living. Teachers can utilize this cultural knowledge to organize students' learning in schools.

Culture appears to influence learning styles, the way individuals select strategies and approach learning (Shade & New, 1993). For example, students who live in a farming community may have sensitive and subtle knowledge about weather patterns, knowledge that is essential to the economic survival of their family. This type of knowledge may predispose students to value learning in the classroom that helps them better understand natural processes like climate. These students may prefer kinesthetic learning activities that build on the same kind of learning that has made it possible for them to sense subtleties of weather. In a similar manner, Mexican-American children from traditional families who are encouraged to view themselves as an integral part of the family may prefer social learning activities. For more discussion on learning strategies and cognitive styles, see Chapter 1.

Example of Concept: Culturally Specific Learning Styles

Students can acquire knowledge by means of various learning modalities, which are often expressed in culturally specific ways. The Navajo child is often taught by first observing and listening, and then taking over parts of the task in cooperation with and under the supervision of an adult. In this way, the child gradually learns all the requisite skills. Finally, the child tests himself or herself privately—failure is not seen by others, whereas success is brought back and shared. The use of speech in this learning process is minimal (Phillips, 1978).

In contrast, acting and performing are the focus of learning for many African-American children. Children observe other individuals to determine appropriate behavior and to appreciate the performance of others. In this case, observing and listening culminates in an individual's performance before others (Heath, 1983b). Reading and writing may be primary learning modes for other cultures such as traditionally educated Asian students.

Adapted Instruction: Learning Modalities

- Observe students learning from one another in a natural, unstructured setting to determine their culturally preferred modalities of learning. For example, have students make a small beaded leather shield to celebrate Native American Day (the last Friday in September). By making beads and leather available—without tightly structuring the activity— you can see how students organize materials, teach, cooperate, or compete with one another.
- At a family conference, ask family members what kind of work is done at home and how the child participates.

Investigating Ourselves as Cultural Beings

The Personal Dimension. For intercultural educators, self-reflection is vital. By examining their own attitudes, beliefs, and culturally derived beliefs and behaviors, teachers begin to discover what has influenced their value systems. Villegas and Lucas (2002) summarized this self-reflection in eight components (see Table 9.4). Some of these components are further addressed in Chapter 10.

Table 9.4

Components of the Personal Dimension of Intercultural Education

Component	Description
Engage in reflective thinking and writing.	Awareness of one's actions, interactions, beliefs, and motivations—or racism—can catalyze behavioral change.
Explore personal and family histories by interviewing family members.	Exploring early cultural experiences can help teachers better relate to individuals with different backgrounds.
Acknowledge group membership.	Teachers who acknowledge their affiliation with various groups in society can assess how this influences views of, and relationships with, other groups.
Learn about the experiences of diverse groups by reading or personal interaction.	Learning about the histories of diverse groups—from their perspectives—highlights value differences.
Visit students' families and communities.	Students' home environments offer views of students' connections to complex cultural networks.
Visit or read about successful teachers.	Successful teachers of children from diverse backgrounds provide exemplary role models.
Appreciate diversity.	Seeing difference as the norm in society reduces ethnocentrism.
Participate in reforming schools.	Teachers can help reform monocultural institutions.

Source: Adapted from Villegas and Lucas (2002).

Cultural Self-Study:

Self-Exploration Questions

• Describe yourself as a preschool child. Were you compliant, curious, adventuresome, goody-goody, physically active, nature loving? Have you observed your parents with other children? Do they encourage open-ended exploration, or would they prefer children to play quietly with approved toys? Do they encourage initiative?

• What was the knowledge environment like in your home? What type of reading did your father and mother do? Was there a time when the members of the family had discussions about current events or ideas and issues? How much dissent was tolerated from parental viewpoints? Were children encouraged to question the status quo? What was it like to learn to talk and think in your family?

• What kind of a grade-school pupil were you? What is your best memory from elementary school? What was your favorite teacher like? Were you an avid reader? How would you characterize your cognitive style and learning

style preferences? Was the school you attended ethnically diverse? What about your secondary school experience? Did you have a diverse group of friends in high school?

• What is your ethnic group? What symbols or traditions did you participate in that derived from this group? What do you like about your ethnic identity? Is there a time now when your group celebrates its traditions together? What was the neighborhood or community like in which you grew up?

• What was your experience with ethnic diversity? What were your first images of race or color? Was there a time in your life when you sought out diverse contacts to expand your experience?

• What contact do you have now with people of dissimilar racial or ethnic backgrounds? How would you characterize your desire to learn more? Given your learning style preferences, how would you go about this?

Self-Study. Self-study is a powerful tool for understanding culture. A way to begin a culture inquiry is by investigating one's personal name. For example, ask, "Where did I get my name? Who am I named for? In which culture did the name originate? What does the name mean?" Continue the self-examination by reviewing favorite cultural customs—such as holiday traditions, home décor, and favorite recipes. More difficult self-examination questions address the mainstream U.S. values of individual freedom, self-reliance, competition, individualism, and the value of hard work. Ask, "If someone in authority tells me to do something, do I move quickly or slowly? If someone says, 'Do you need any help?' do I usually say, 'No, thanks. I can do it myself'? Am I comfortable promoting myself (for example, talking about my achievements in a performance review)? Do I prefer to work by myself or on a team? Do I prefer to associate with high achievers and avoid spending much time with people who do not work hard?" These and other introspective questions help to pinpoint cultural attitudes. Without a firm knowledge of one's own beliefs and behaviors, it is difficult to contrast the cultural behaviors of others. However, the self-examination process is challenging and ongoing. It is difficult to observe one's own culture.

Learning about Students' Cultures

Teachers can use printed, electronic, and video materials, books, and magazines to help students learn about other cultures. However, the richest source of information is local—the life of the community. Students, parents, and community members can provide insights about values, attitudes, and habits. One method of learning about students and their families, ethnographic study, has proved useful in learning about the ways that students' experiences in the home and community compare with the culture of the schools.

Ethnographic Techniques

Ethnography is an inquiry process that seeks to provide cultural explanations for behavior and attitudes. Culture is described from the insider's point of view, as the classroom teacher becomes not only an observer of the students' cultures but also an active participant (Erickson, 1977; Robinson, 1985). Parents and community members, as well as students, become sources for the gradual growth of understanding on the part of the teacher.

For the classroom teacher, ethnography involves gathering data in order to understand two distinct cultures: the culture of the students' communities and the culture of the classroom. To understand the home and community environment, teachers may observe and participate in community life, interview community members, and visit students' homes. To understand the school culture, teachers may observe in a variety of classrooms, have visitors observe in their own classrooms, audio- and video-tape classroom interaction, and interview other teachers and administrators.

Observations. Initial observations of other cultures must be carried out, ideally, with the perspective that one is seeing the culture from the point of view of a complete outsider. Observers need to be descriptive and objective and make explicit their own attitudes and values in order to overcome hidden sources of bias. This requires practice and, ideally, some training. However, the classroom teacher can begin to observe and participate in the students' cultures, writing up field notes after participating and perhaps summing up the insights gained in an ongoing diary that can be shared with colleagues. Such observation can document children's use of language within the community; etiquettes of speaking, listening, writing, greeting, and getting or giving information; values and aspirations; and norms of communication.

When analyzing the culture of the classroom, teachers might look at classroom management and routines; affective factors (students' attitudes toward activities, teachers' attitudes toward students); classroom talk in general; and nonverbal behaviors and communication. In addition to the raw data of behavior, the thoughts and intentions of the participants can also be documented.

Interviews. Interviews can be divided into two types: structured and unstructured. Structured interviews use a set of predetermined questions to gain specific kinds of information. Unstructured interviews are more like conversations in that they can range over a wide variety of topics, many of which the interviewer would not necessarily have anticipated. As an outsider learning about a new culture, the classroom teacher would be better served initially using an unstructured interview, beginning with general questions and being guided in follow-up questions by the interviewee's responses. The result of the initial interview may in turn provide a structure for learning more about the culture during a second interview or conversation. A very readable book about ethnography and interviewing is *The Professional Stranger: An Informal Introduction to Ethnography* (Agar, 1980).

Home Visits. Home visits are one of the best ways in which teachers can learn what is familiar and important to their students. The home visit can be a social call or a brief report on the student's progress that enhances rapport with students and parents. Scheduling an appointment ahead of time is a courtesy that some cultures may require and provides a means for the teacher to ascertain if home visits are welcome. Dress should be professional. The visit should be short (twenty to thirty minutes) and the conversation positive, especially about the student's schoolwork. Viewing the child in the context of the home provides a look at the parent–child interaction, the resources of the home, and the child's role in the family. One teacher announces to the class at the beginning of the year that she is available on Friday nights to be invited to dinner. Knowing in advance that their invitation is welcomed, parents and children are proud to act as hosts.

Example of Concept: A Home Visit

Home visits can be an effective way for a teacher not only to demonstrate accessibility and interest to students and their families, but also to learn about the family and the context in which the student lives, as seen in this story from Hughes:

Years ago a child named Nai persuaded her parents to let me visit them. Many people lived in the small apartment. One of the men spoke a little English as I tried a few Mien phrases that drew chuckles and good will. I ate with them. Recently a community college student dropped in at our school. "Nai!" I cried, delighted. . . . "How's your family?" "They OK." "I enjoyed my visit with them," I said. She smiled. "My parents . . . they talk still about 'that teacher,' they call you." (Hughes, 2004, p. 10)

Students as Sources of Information. Students generally provide teachers with their initial contact with other cultures. Through observations, one-on-one interaction, and group participatory processes, teachers gain understanding about various individuals and their cultural repertoire. Teachers who are good listeners offer students time for shared conversations by lingering after school or opening the classroom during lunchtime. Teachers may find it useful to ask students to map their own neighborhood. This is a source of knowledge from the students' perspectives about the boundaries of the neighborhood and surrounding areas.

Parents as Sources of Information. Parents can be sources of information in much the same way as their children. Rather than scheduling one or two formal conferences, PTA open house events, and gala performances, the school may encourage parent participation by opening the library once a week after school. This offers a predictable time during which parents and teachers can casually meet and chat. Parents can also be the source for information that can form the basis for classroom writing. Using the Language Experience Approach, teachers can ask students to interview their parents about common topics such as work, interests, and family history. In this way, students and parents together can supply knowledge about community life.

Community Members as Sources of Information. Community members are an equally rich source of cultural knowledge. Much can be learned about a community by walking or driving through it, or stopping to make a purchase in local stores and markets. One teacher arranged to walk through the neighborhood with a doctor whose office was located there. Other teachers may ask older students to act as tour guides. During these visits, the people of the neighborhood can be sources of knowledge about housing, places where children and teenagers play, places where adults gather, and sources of food, furniture, and services.

Through community representatives, teachers can begin to know about important living patterns of a community. A respected elder can provide information about the family and which members constitute a family. A community leader may be able to contrast the community political system with the city or state system. A religious leader can explain the importance of religion in community life. Teachers can also attend local ceremonies and activities to learn more about community dynamics.

The Internet. Websites proliferate that introduce the curious to other cultures. Webcrawler programs assist the user to explore cultural content using keyword prompts.

Participating in Growth Relationships. Self-study is only one means of attaining self-knowledge. Teachers who form relationships with individuals whose backgrounds differ from their own, whether teacher colleagues or community members, can benefit from honest feedback and discussions that help to expand self-awareness. Intercultural educators are not free from making mistakes when dealing with students, family and community members, and colleagues whose culture differs from their own. The only lasting error is not learning from these missteps or misunderstandings.

Sociocultural Consciousness. Villegas and Lucas (2007) invite teachers who were raised in middle-class, monolingual communities to develop a "sociocultural consciousness" (p. 31) that impels them to examine the role of schools in both perpetuating and challenging social inequities. Understanding the role that differential distribution of wealth and power plays in school success helps teachers to commit to the ethical obligation of helping all students learn.

How Cultural Adaptation Affects Learning

As immigrants enter American life, they make conscious or unconscious choices about which aspects of their culture to preserve and which to modify. These decisions affect learning. We cannot know all things about all cultures, but it is possible to understand what happens when the home culture comes into contact with the school culture and how this contact affects schooling. When cultures meet, they affect each other. Cultures can be swallowed up (*assimilation*), one culture may adapt to a second (*acculturation*), both may adapt to each other (*accommodation*), or they may coexist (*pluralism* or *biculturalism*). When an individual comes in contact with another culture, there are characteristic responses, usually stages, an individual goes through in adapting to the new situation. Contact between cultures is often not a benign process. It may be fraught with issues of prejudice, discrimination, and misunderstanding. Means of mediation or resolution must be found to alleviate cultural conflict, particularly in classrooms.

Since the 1980s, an unprecedented flow of immigrants and refugees has entered the United States. One of the impacts of this immigration is that many school districts not only have three or more languages spoken in a single classroom, but they also have students who speak the same non-English language but who come from different cultures. These demographic issues pose a number of questions about cultures in contact. Are there characteristic differences in the patterns of adaptation to schooling among individuals from various cultures? Can we understand how to increase the school success of all students by studying the process of cultural contact?

Fears about Cultural Adaptation. Pryor (2002) captured the nature of immigrant parents' concerns about their children's adjustment to life in the United States:

> In the United States, some immigrant parents live in fear that their children will be corrupted by what they believe to be the materialistic and individualistic dominant culture, become alienated from their families, and fall prey to drugs and promiscuity. Their fears are not unfounded, as research shows that the longer that immigrants live in the United States, the worse their physical and mental health becomes. . . . One Jordanian mother stated, "I tell my son (who is 8 years old) not to use the restroom in school. I tell him he might catch germs there that he could bring home, and make the whole family ill. I really am afraid he may get drugs from other kids in the restroom." (p. 187)

Many immigrant parents are overwhelmed with personal, financial, and work-related problems; they may miss their homelands and family members abroad and have few resources to which to turn for help. In the process of coming to terms with life in a foreign country, they may be at odds with the assimilation or acculturation processes their children are experiencing, causing family conflict.

Assimilation. When members of an ethnic group are absorbed into the dominant culture and their culture gradually disappears in the process, they are said to assimilate. For assimilation to be complete, there must be both cultural and structural assimilation (Gordon, 1964). *Cultural assimilation* is the process by which individuals adopt the behaviors, values, beliefs, and lifestyle of the dominant culture. *Structural assimilation* is participation in the social, political, and economic institutions and organizations of mainstream society. It is structural assimilation that has been problematic for many immigrants. Gordon found that only limited structural assimilation occurred for groups other than White Protestant immigrants from northern and western Europe.

Individuals may make a choice concerning their degree of cultural assimilation. However, the dominant society determines the extent of structural assimilation. These two related but different concepts have important consequences in classrooms.

Teachers may strive to have students assimilate but be blind to the fact that some of their students will not succeed because of attitudes and structures of the dominant society.

Acculturation. When individuals adapt effectively to the mainstream culture, they are said to *acculturate*. This concept should be distinguished from *enculturation*, the process through which individuals learn the patterns of their own culture. To acculturate is to adapt to a second culture without necessarily giving up one's first culture. It is an additive process in which individuals' right to participate in their own heritage is preserved (Finnan, 1987). Some researchers have emphasized the importance of acculturation for success in school. For example, Schumann (1978a) claims that the greater the level of acculturation in a particular individual, the greater the second-language learning will be for that individual.

Schools are the primary places in which children of various cultures learn about the mainstream culture. Sometimes culture is taught explicitly as a part of the ELD curriculum (Seelye, 1984). According to Cortés (1993):

> Acculturation . . . should be a primary goal of education. Schools have an obligation to help students acculturate because additive acculturation contributes to individual empowerment and expanded life choices. But schools should not seek subtractive assimilation, which can lead to personal and cultural disempowerment by eroding students' multicultural abilities to function effectively both within the mainstream and within their own ethnic milieus. . . . In our increasingly multicultural society, even traditional additive acculturation is not the only acculturation goal. Education for the twenty-first century should embrace what I call "multiculturation," the blending of *multiple* and *acculturation*. (p. 4)

Accommodation. A two-way process, accommodation happens when members of the mainstream culture change in adapting to a minority culture, the members of which in turn accept some cultural change as they adapt to the mainstream. Thus, accommodation is a mutual process. To make accommodation a viable alternative in schools, teachers need to demonstrate that they are receptive to learning from the diverse cultures in their midst, and they also need to teach majority students the value of "interethnic reciprocal learning" (Gibson, 1991).

Example of Concept: Accommodating Students' Culture

[I]n non-Indian classes students are given opportunities to ask the teacher questions in front of the class, and do so. Indian students are given fewer opportunities for this because when they do have the opportunity, they don't use it. Rather, the teacher of Indians allows more periods in which she is available for individual students to approach her alone and ask their questions where no one else can hear them. (Philips, 1972, p. 383)

Pluralism. Assimilation, not acculturation, was the aim of many immigrants who sought to become part of the melting pot. More recently, minority groups and their advocates have begun to assert that minority and ethnic groups have a right, if not a responsibility, to maintain valued elements of their ethnic cultures (Kopan, 1974). This *pluralist* position is that coexistence of multicultural traditions within a single society provides a variety of alternatives that enrich life in the United States. Pluralism is the condition in which members of diverse cultural groups have equal opportunities for success, in which cultural similarities and differences are valued, and in which students are provided cultural alternatives.

But does pluralism endanger society, as cultural purists have charged, by heightening ethnic group identity, leading to separatism and intergroup antagonism? In a healthy society, these groups may sometimes clash in the process of coexistence, but the strength of the society is founded on a basic willingness to work together to resolve conflicts. According to Bennett (2003), schools can evince *integrated pluralism* (actively trying to foster interaction between different groups) or *pluralistic coexistence* (different racial or ethnic groups informally resegregate). Integration creates the conditions for cultural pluralism. Merely mixing formerly isolated ethnic groups does not go far enough, because groups rapidly unmix and resegregate.

Biculturalism. Being able to function successfully in two cultures constitutes biculturalism. Darder (1991) defined *biculturalism* as

> a process wherein individuals learn to function in two distinct sociocultural environments: their primary culture, and that of the dominant mainstream culture of the society in which they live. It represents the process by which bicultural human beings mediate between the dominant discourse of educational institutions and the realities they must face as members of subordinate cultures. (pp. 48–49)

Everyone is to some extent bicultural. Every pluralistic society (take, for example, life in New York City) contains individuals who become a part of more than one culture. At a minimum level, everyone who works outside the home functions daily in two cultures—personal (home) and professional (work). For some individuals, the distance between the cultures of work and home are almost indistinguishable, whereas for others the distance is great. For example, Native-American children who were sent to Bureau of Indian Affairs boarding schools often experienced great difficulties in adjusting to the disparate cultures of home and school.

What is it like to be bicultural in the United States? Bicultural people are sometimes viewed with distrust. An example is the suspicion toward Japanese Americans during World War II and the resulting internment. Parents may also feel threatened by their bicultural children. Appalachian families who moved to large cities to obtain work often pressured their children to maintain an agrarian, preindustrial lifestyle, a culture that is in many ways inconsistent with urban environments (Pasternak, 1994). Similarly, families from rural Mexico may seek to maintain traditional values after immigrating to the United States even as their children adopt behaviors from the U.S. macroculture. The process of becoming bicultural is not without stress, especially for students who are expected to internalize dissimilar, perhaps conflicting, values.

Cultural Congruence. In U.S. schools, the contact of cultures occurs daily. In this contact, the congruence or lack thereof between mainstream and minority cultures has lasting effects on students. Students from families whose cultural values are similar to those of the European-American mainstream culture may be relatively advantaged in schools, such as children from those Asian cultures who are taught that students sit quietly and attentively. In contrast, African-American students who learn at home to project their personalities and call attention to their individual attributes (Gay, 1975) may be punished for efforts to call attention to themselves during class.

Teachers, who have the responsibility to educate students from diverse cultures, find it relatively easy to help students whose values, beliefs, and behaviors are congruent with U.S. schooling but often find it difficult to work with others. The teacher who can find a common ground with diverse students will promote their further education. Relationships between individuals or groups of different cultures are built through commitment, a tolerance for diversity, and a willingness to communicate. The teacher acting as intercultural educator accepts and promotes cultural content in the classroom as a valid and vital component of the instructional process and helps students to achieve within the cultural context of the school.

Stages of Individual Cultural Contact. Experiencing a second culture causes emotional ups and downs. Reactions to a new culture vary, but there are distinct stages in the process of experiencing a different culture (Brown, 2000). The stages are characterized by typical emotions and behaviors beginning with elation or excitement, moving to anxiety or disorientation, and culminating in some degree of adjustment (Levine & Adelman, 1982). These same emotional stages can occur for students. The intensity will vary depending on the degree of similarity between home and school culture, the individual child, and the teacher.

The first state, *euphoria,* may result from the excitement of experiencing new customs, foods, and sights. This may be a "honeymoon" period in which the newcomer is fascinated and stimulated by experiencing a new culture.

The next stage, *culture shock,* may follow euphoria as cultural differences begin to intrude. The newcomer is increasingly aware of being different and may be disoriented by cultural cues that result in frustration. Deprivation of the familiar may cause a loss of self-esteem. Depression, anger, or withdrawal may result. The severity of this shock will vary as a function of the personality of the individual, the emotional support available, and the perceived or actual differences between the two cultures.

The final stage, *adaptation to the new culture,* may take several months to several years. Some initial adjustment takes place when everyday activities such as housing and shopping are no longer a problem. Long-term adjustment can take several forms. Ideally, the newcomer accepts some degree of routine in the new culture with habits, customs, and characteristics borrowed from the host culture. This results in a feeling of comfort with friends and associates, and the newcomer feels capable of negotiating most new and different situations. On the other hand, individuals who do not adjust as well may feel lonely and frustrated. A loss of self-confidence may result. Certain aspects of the new culture may be actively rejected. Eventually, successful adaptation results in newcomers finding value and significance in the differences and similarities between cultures and in being able to actively express themselves and to create a full range of meaning in the situation.

Example of Concept: Language and Culture Shock

Zacharian (2004b) related the story of one student experiencing language and culture shock and the effect it had on his personality: "One student, whom I'll call Jin, shared some powerful feelings with his classmates. Through his tutor, he stated that he had been very popular in China, made friends easily, and loved to be with his friends. However, after a few weeks of attempting to ask short questions in English and not being able to understand the responses he received he had found it increasingly painful and frustrating to try to speak English. 'From being popular and having a lot of friends,' Jin stated through his translator, 'to being silenced by my lack of English is terrible for me'" (pp. 12–13).

Adapted Instruction: Students in Culture Shock

In the classroom, some students may show culture shock as withdrawal, depression, or anger. Mental fatigue may result from continually straining to comprehend the new culture. Individuals may need time to process personal and emotional as well as academic experiences. Teachers must take great care not to belittle or reject students who are experiencing culture shock.

Achieving Equity in Schooling

Teachers who were themselves primarily socialized in mainstream American culture may not be aware of the challenges faced by individuals from nondominant cultures as they strive to succeed in U.S. schools. Bonilla-Silva (2003) contended that European Americans have developed powerful rationalizations and justifications for contemporary racial inequality that exculpate them from responsibility for the status of people of color. This constitutes a new racial ideology he called "color-blind racism" (p. 2), which is a way of committing or participating in racist practices while not believing that oneself is racist (also called "racism without racists" [p. 1] and "new racism" [p. 3]).

To create school environments that are fair for all students, teachers need to achieve clarity of vision (Balderrama & Díaz-Rico, 2005) about the social forces that advantage some members of society and disadvantage others. This work entails recognizing that society is becoming increasingly polarized, moving toward a vast separation between the rich and the poor. Class and racial privilege, prejudice, and unequal opportunity are barriers to success. Awareness of unfair practices is the first step toward remedy.

Detecting Unfair Privilege

For European-American middle-class teachers to accept the work of achieving equity in education, they must at some point examine their own complicity in the privileges of being white and middle class in a society predicated on inequity. *Privilege* is defined as the state of benefiting from special advantages, favors, or rights accorded to

Figure 9.1 The Privileges of the Dominant Race/Class/Gender

I can rent or purchase housing in an affordable, desirable area, with neighbors who will be neutral or pleasant to me.

My children will see their race represented in curricular materials.

When I purchase, my skin color does not suggest financial instability.

I can criticize our government without being seen as a cultural outsider.

"The person in charge" is usually a person of my race.

Traffic cops do not single me out because of my race.

My behavior is not taken as a reflection on my race.

If my day is going badly, I need not suspect racial overtones in each negative situation.

I can imagine many options—social, political, or professional—without wondering if a person of my race would be allowed to do what I want to do.

Source: Adapted from McIntosh (1996).

some, to the exclusion of others. Although no one likes to think that one person's advantage is another person's disadvantage, in effect, the middle class is a socially privileged position, one that directly or indirectly benefits from the discomfort of others who are lower on the economic scale.

McIntosh's (1996) article "White Privilege and Male Privilege" is a useful tool for exploring the advantage experienced by those who are white, male, or middle-class in order to become aware of the many social advantages they have reaped at the expense of those who are nonwhite, non-middle-class, or female. According to McIntosh, the privileges of being male, white, and middle-class function as an invisible backpack, full of advantages that those in these categories can build on—but that are not available to those outside these categories, giving them an unfair handicap. Figure 9.1 presents some of the privileges that the dominant race/class/gender enjoys.

Fighting for Fairness and Equal Opportunity

Schools in the United States have not been level playing fields for those of nonmainstream cultures. Teachers can remedy this in both academic and extracurricular areas. According to Manning (2002), teachers should

> consider that all learners deserve, ethically and legally, equal access to curricular activities (i.e., higher-level mathematics and science subjects) and opportunities to participate in all athletic activities (i.e., rather than assuming all students of one race will play on the basketball team and all students of another race will play on the tennis or golfing teams). (p. 207)

Cultural fairness can extend to the social and interpersonal lives of students, those daily details and microinteractions that also fall within the domain of culture. Manning (2002) emphasized that listening to students' voices and requesting input on their concerns leads to fairness. For instance, is there only one kind of music played at school dances? Do teachers or administrators appear to show bias toward certain groups over others? Teachers who invest time to get to know their students, as individuals as well as cultural beings, address issues of fairness through a personal commitment to equality of treatment and opportunity.

Combating Prejudice in Ourselves and Others

If diversity is recognized as a strength, educators will "avoid basing decisions about learners on inaccurate or stereotypical generalizations" (Manning, 2002, p. 207). Misperceptions about diversity often stem from prejudice.

The Dynamics of Prejudice.   One factor that inhibits cultural adaptation is prejudice. Although prejudice can include favorable feelings, it is generally used in a negative sense.

Prejudice takes various forms: excessive pride in one's own ethnic heritage, country, or culture so that others are viewed negatively; *ethnocentrism*, in which the world revolves around oneself and one's own culture; a prejudice against members of a certain racial group; and stereotypes that label all or most members of a group. All humans are prejudiced to some degree, but it is when people act on those prejudices that discriminatory practices and inequalities result. A simple explanation for prejudice is that it is based on fear—fear of the unknown, fear of engulfment by foreigners, or fear of contamination from dissimilar beliefs or values.

A closer look at various forms of prejudice, such as racism and stereotyping, as well as resulting discriminatory practices can lead to an understanding of these issues. Teachers can then be in a position to adopt educational methods that are most likely to reduce prejudice.

Example of Concept: Xenophobia in U.S. History

Sutherland (1989) described the Centennial of 1876, which was held in Philadelphia:

> [T]he Centennial impressed everyone. Its 167 buildings and 30,000 exhibits covered 236 acres in Fairmount Park. The Main Exhibition Building, housing the principal exhibits of manufactured products and scientific achievements, measured 1,800 feet long and 464 feet wide, the largest building in the world. . . . [A] total of thirty-five foreign nations provided exhibits or entertainment in one form or another. . . . [W]herever they went on the fairgrounds, visitors saw and heard xenophobic expressions of prejudice. Foreign-looking people of all races and nationalities, were they Orientals, Turks, Slavs, Egyptians, or Spaniards, were "followed by large crowds of idle boys, and men, who hooted and shouted at them as if they had been animals of a strange species." (pp. 263, 264, 268)

Racism.   Racism is the view that a person's race determines psychological and cultural traits—and, moreover, that one race is superior to another. Racism can also be cultural when one believes that the traditions, beliefs, languages, artifacts, music, and art of other cultures are inferior. On the basis of such beliefs, racists justify discriminating against or scapegoating other groups. As important as is the facet of symbolic violence that racism represents, of equal importance is the fact that goods and services are distributed in accordance with such judgments of unequal worth.

Racism is often expressed in hate crimes, which are public expressions of hostility directed at specific groups or individuals. These may take the form of harassment (scrawling graffiti on people's homes; pelting houses with eggs; burning crosses on lawns; children playing in yards being subjected to verbal taunts; hate-filled e-mails sent to individuals or groups; swastikas carved into public textbooks, school desks, or other property; etc.) or, at the extreme, assaults and murder directed toward minorities. At present, data show that 60 percent of hate crimes are directed toward African Americans.

Youth at the Edge, a report from the Southern Poverty Law Center (1999), described a new underclass of disenchanted youth in the United States who are susceptible to hate groups. Perhaps due to feelings of frustration at social and economic forces they cannot control, those who are marginally employed and poorly educated often seek out scapegoats to harass. Too often, the targets are immigrants, particularly those of color. The availability of information on the Internet has unfortunately encouraged a resurgence of hate groups worldwide. Over 250 Internet sites foment white supremacy and other forms of racial hatred. Schools are often prime sites in which hate crimes are committed. This fact underscores the urgency of educators' efforts to understand and combat racism.

Stereotypes.   Often resulting from racist beliefs, stereotypes are preconceived and oversimplified generalizations about a particular ethnic or religious group, race, or gender. The danger of stereotyping is that people are not considered as individuals but are categorized with all other members of a group. A stereotype can be favorable or unfavorable, but, whether it is positive or negative, the results are negative: The perspective on an entire group of people is distorted.

Example of Concept: Comparisons within a Cultural Group

Mrs. Abboushi, a third-grade teacher, discovers that her students hold many misconceptions about the Arab people. Her goal becomes to present them with an accurate and more rounded view of the Arab world. She builds background information by using a world map on which the students identify the countries featured in the three books they will read: *Ibrahim* (Sales, 1989), *The Day of Ahmed's Secret* (Heide & Gilliland, 1990), and *Nadia, the Willful* (Alexander, 1983).

After reading and interactively discussing the books, students are divided into groups of four, each receiving a copy of one of the books. Students prepare a Cultural Feature Analysis chart that includes the cultural features, setting, character and traits, family relationships, and message. Groups share their information and Mrs. Abboushi records the information on a large chart. During the follow-up discussion, students discover that not all Arabs live the same way, dress the same way, or look the same way. They recognize the merging of traditional and modern worlds, the variability in living conditions, customs and values, architecture, clothing, and modes of transportation (Diamond & Moore, 1995, pp. 229–230).

Teaching against Racism.   Students and teachers alike must raise awareness of racism in the attempt to achieve racial equality and justice. Actively listening to students in open discussion about racism, prejudice, and stereotyping can increase teachers' understanding of how students perceive and are affected by these concepts. School curricula can be used to help students be aware of the existence and impact of racism.

Science and health teachers can debunk myths surrounding the concept of race. Content-area teachers can help students develop skills in detecting bias.

Adapted Instruction: Antiracist Activities and Discussion Topics

■ Recognize racist history and its impact on oppressors and victims.
■ Understand the origins of racism and why people hold racial prejudices and stereotypes.
■ Be able to identify racist images in the language and illustrations of books, films, television, news media, and advertising.
■ Identify specific ways of developing positive interracial contact experiences.
■ Extend the fight against racism into a broader fight for universal human rights and respect for human dignity.

Source: Bennett (2003, pp. 370–373).

Programs to Combat Prejudice and Racism. The Southern Poverty Law Center distributes *Teaching Tolerance* magazine, a free resource sent to over 600,000 educators twice a year that provides antibias strategies for K–12 teachers. Carnuccio (2004) describes the Tolerance.org Website, a Web project of the Southern Poverty Law Center (available at www.splcenter.org), as an "extremely informative resource":

> The project has done an excellent job of collecting and disseminating information on the advantages of diversity. . . . The site features pages designed specifically for children, teens, teachers, and parents. *Planet Tolerance* has stories for children to read and listen to and games for them to play. Teens can find ideas on how to bring diverse groups together in their schools. Teachers' pages feature articles, films and books to order, lesson ideas, and a forum in which to share ideas with other teachers. The pamphlet *101 Tools for Tolerance* suggests a variety of ideas for community, workplace, school, and home settings. *Parenting for Tolerance* offers ways for parents to guide their children to develop into tolerant adults. (p. 59)

Institutional Racism. "[T]hose laws, customs, and practices that systematically reflect and produce racial inequalities in American society" (Jones, 1981) constitute institutional racism. Classroom teaching that aims at detecting and reducing racism may be a futile exercise when the institution itself—the school—promotes racism through its policies and practices, such as underreferral of minority students to programs for gifted students or failing to hire minority teachers in classrooms where children are predominantly of minority background.

Classism. In the United States, racism is compounded with classism, the distaste of the middle and upper classes for the lifestyles and perceived values of the lower classes.

Although this classism is often directed against linguistic and cultural minorities—a typical poor person in the American imagination is urban, black, and young, either a single teen mother or her offspring—portraying poverty that way makes it easier to stigmatize the poor (Henwood, 1997).

Classism has engendered its own stereotype against poor European Americans—for example, the stereotyped European-American indigent who is called, among other things, "White trash" (Wray & Newitz, 1997). The distaste for "White trash" on the part of the U.S. middle class is compounded in part by ignorance and frustration. According to Wray and Newitz, "Americans love to hate the poor. . . . [I]n a country as steeped in the myth of classlessness, we are often at a loss to explain or understand poverty. The White trash stereotype serves as a useful way of blaming the poor for being poor" (p. 1). Often, middle-class teachers view the poor as unwilling or unable to devote resources to schooling. Ogbu (1978) postulated that indigenous minorities may be unable to accept the belief in the power of education to elevate individuals to middle-class status. Poor whites, who outnumber poor minorities (see Chapter 8), may bear the brunt of a "castelike" status in the United States as much as linguistic and cultural minorities do.

Discrimination. Discrimination refers to actions that limit the social, political, or economic opportunities of particular groups. Discriminatory practices tend to legitimize the unequal distribution of power and resources between groups defined by such factors as race, language, culture, gender, and/or social class. Blatant discrimination, in which differential education for minorities is legally sanctioned, may be a thing of the past, but discrimination persists. De facto segregation continues; most students of color are still found in substandard schools. Schools with a high percentage of minority enrollment tend to employ faculty who have less experience and academic preparation. Teachers who do not share the ethnic background of their students may not communicate well with their students or may tend to avoid interaction, including eye and physical contact. Teachers may communicate low expectations to minority students. The "hidden curriculum" of tracking and differential treatment results in schools that perpetuate the structural inequities of society. Thus, school becomes a continuation of the discrimination experienced by minorities in other institutions in society (Grant & Sleeter, 1986).

In the past, those in power often used physical force to discriminate. Those who did not go along were physically punished for speaking their language or adhering to their own cultural or ethnic customs. With the spread of literacy, the trend moved away from the use of physical force toward the use of shame and guilt. The school plays a part in this process. The values, norms, and ideology of those in power are taught in the school. Skutnabb-Kangas (1981, 1993) called this *symbolic-structural violence*. Direct punishment is replaced by self-punishment, and the group discriminated against internalizes shame associated with cultural differences. The emotional and intellectual bonds of internalized injustice make the situation of minorities more difficult.

Skutnabb-Kangas (1981) cited a variety of examples of discrimination that has taken place against minority students in Swedish and Norwegian schools. These examples demonstrate the internalization of shame.

The headmaster said, "You have a name which is difficult for us Swedes to pronounce. Can't we change it? . . . And besides, perhaps some nasty person will make fun of your name." "Well, I suppose I'd better change it," I thought. (p. 316)

I love my parents and I respect them but what they are and everything they know count for nothing. . . . Like lots of Turkish children here, [my parents] know lots about farming and farm animals, . . . but when is a Turkish child given the task at school of describing the cultivation of vines? (p. 317)

Reducing Interethnic Conflict

Students experiencing cultural conflict may meet racism and anti-immigration sentiment from others in their environment. Subtle incidents occur every day across campuses in the United States. Verbal abuse, threats, and physical violence, motivated by negative feelings and opinions, are all too common. The scope of these incidents, together with the increasing involvement of young adults, is a disturbing trend on today's campuses. Schools are crucial to the resolution of hate crime because the young are perpetrators and the schools are staging grounds. Policies, curricula, and antiracism programs are needed to prevent and control hate crimes.

Example of Concept: Cultural Conflicts

A Latina elementary teacher had this to say about cultural conflicts in the schools:

I am sensitive to cultural barriers that exist among educators. These barriers are created by lack of communication between people coming from different backgrounds and cultures. Unfortunately, we don't discuss cultural conflicts openly. We have learned that conflicts are negative and produce racial disharmony when, in fact, the opposite is true. (Institute for Education in Transformation, 1992, p. 12)

The Culturally Receptive School. In general, research suggests that substantive changes in attitudes, behaviors, and achievement occur only when the entire school environment changes to demonstrate a multicultural atmosphere. Parents are welcomed in the school; counselors, teachers, and other staff implement culturally compatible practices; and programs are instituted that permit interactions between students of different backgrounds. In such schools, all students learn to understand cultures different from their own. Minority students do not internalize negativity about their culture and customs. Cooperative learning groups and programs that allow interaction between students of diverse backgrounds usually result in fewer incidents of name-calling and ethnic slurs as well as in improved academic achievement (Nieto & Bode, 2008).

It is not easy for culturally and linguistically diverse (CLD) students to maintain pride in their cultures if these cultures suffer low status in the majority culture. Students feel conflict in this pride if their culture is devalued. When the languages and cultures of students are highly evident in their schools and teachers refer to them explicitly, they gain status. Schools that convey the message that all cultures are of value—by displaying explicit welcome signs in many languages, by attempts to involve parents, by a deliberate curriculum of inclusion, and by using affirmative action to promote hiring of a diverse faculty—help to maintain an atmosphere that reduces interethnic conflict.

Strategies for Conflict Resolution. If interethnic conflict occurs, taking immediate, proactive steps to resolve the conflict is necessary. Table 9.5 presents a scenario in which conflict resolution is needed and describes a twelve-skill approach to mediation.

Johnson and Johnson (1979, 1994, 1995) emphasized the usefulness of cooperative, heterogeneous grouping in the classroom in the resolution of classroom conflict. Explicit training for elementary students in negotiation and mediation procedures has proved effective in managing conflict, especially when such programs focus on safely expressing feelings, taking the perspective of the other, and providing the rationale for diverse points of view (Johnson, Johnson, Dudley, & Acikgoz, 1994).

Especially critical is the role of a mediator in establishing and maintaining a balance of power between two parties in a dispute, protecting the weaker party from intimidation, and ensuring that both parties have a stake in the process and the outcome of mediation. In contrast, those programs that teach about "group differences," involve exhortation or mere verbal learning, or are designed directly for "prejudice reduction" are usually not effective.

Example of Concept: Conflict Resolution in New Jersey

Real estate development in the West Windsor–Plainsboro School District in the 1980s and 1990s brought into one rural area a population that was diverse in income, culture, race, and ethnicity. Increasing incidents of racial unrest in the schools and in the community at large caused school administrators to set into motion a program of conflict resolution in K–12 classrooms. Among its components were the following:

- A peacemaking program at the elementary level to teach children how to solve problems without resorting to aggression
- Training for middle school students in facilitating positive human relations
- A ninth-grade elective course in conflict resolution
- An elective course for grade 11 and 12 students to prepare student mediators for a peer-mediation center
- An annual "human relations" retreat for student leaders and teachers that encouraged frank and open conversations about interpersonal and race relations
- A planned welcome program for newcomers at the school to overcome feelings of isolation
- A minority recruitment program for teachers
- Elimination of watered-down, nonrigorous academic courses in lieu of challenging courses, accompanied by a tutoring program for academically underprepared high-school students

Within three years, the number of incidences of vandalism, violence, and substance abuse in the school district was reduced considerably. The people of West Windsor and Plainsboro "accomplished much in their quest to rise out of the degradation of bigotry" (Bandlow, 2002, pp. 91–92; Prothrow-Smith, 1994).

Table 9.5

Applying a Twelve-Skill Approach to Interethnic Conflict

Scenario: A group of four European-American girls in tenth grade had been making fun of Irena and three of her friends, all of whom were U.S.-born Mexican Americans. One afternoon Irena missed her bus home from high school, and the four girls surrounded her when she was putting books in her locker. One girl shoved a book out of the stack in her hands. Irena shoved her back. Just then, a teacher came around the corner and took Irena to the office for discipline. The assistant principal, Ms. Nava, interviewed Irena to gain some background about the situation. Rather than dealing with Irena in isolation, Ms. Nava waited until the next day, called all eight of the girls into her office, and applied the twelve-skill approach to conflict resolution.

Skill	Application of Skills to Scenario
1. The win–win approach: Identify attitude shifts to respect all parties' needs.	Ms. Nava asked each girl to write down what the ideal outcome of the situation would be. Comparing notes, three of the girls had written "respect." Ms. Nava decided to use this as a win–win theme.
2. Creative response: Transform problems into creative opportunities.	Each girl was asked to write the name of an adult who respected her and how she knew it was genuine respect.
3. Empathy: Develop communication tools to build rapport. Use listening to clarify understanding.	In turn, each girl described what she had written above. The other girls had to listen, using eye contact to show attentiveness.
4. Appropriate assertiveness: Apply strategies to attack the problem not the person.	Ms. Nava offered an opportunity for members of the group to join the schools' Conflict Resolution Task Force. She also warned the group that another incident between them would result in suspension.
5. Cooperative power: Eliminate "power over" to build "power with" others.	Each girl was paired with a girl from the "other side" (cross-group pair) to brainstorm ways in which teens show respect for one another.
6. Managing emotions: Express fear, anger, hurt, and frustration wisely to effect change.	Ms. Nava then asked Irena and the girl who pushed her book to tell their side of the incident without name-calling.
7. Willingness to resolve: Name personal issues that cloud the picture.	Each girl was asked to name one underlying issue between the groups that this incident represented.
8. Mapping the conflict: Define the issues needed to chart common needs and concerns.	Ms. Nava mapped the issues by writing them on a wall chart as they were brought forth.
9. Development of options: Design creative solutions together.	Still in the cross-group pairs from step 5 above, each pair was asked to design a solution for one of the issues mapped.
10. Introduction to negotiation: Plan and apply effective strategies to reach agreement.	Ms. Nava called the girls into her office for a second day. They reviewed the solutions that were designed and made a group plan for improved behavior.
11. Introduction to mediation: Help conflicting parties to move toward solutions.	Each cross-group pair generated two ideas for repair if the above plan failed.
12. Broadening perspectives: Evaluate the problem in its broader context.	The eight girls were asked if racial conflict occurred outside their group. Ms. Nava asked for discussion: Were the same issues they generated responsible for this conflict?

Source: Adapted from www.crnhq.org.

Educators should not assume that cultural contact entails cultural conflict. Perhaps the best way to prevent conflict is to include a variety of cultural content and make sure the school recognizes and values cultural diversity. If conflict does occur, however, there are means to prevent its escalation. Teachers should be aware of conflict resolution techniques before they are actually needed.

Adapted Instruction: Resolving Conflicts in the Classroom

- Resolve to be calm in the face of verbalized anger and hostility.
- To defuse a problem, talk to students privately, encouraging the sharing of perceptions on volatile issues. Communicate expectations that students will be able to resolve their differences.
- If confrontation occurs, set aside a brief period for verbal expression. Allow students to vent feelings as a group.
- Do not tolerate violence or personal attacks.

This chapter has emphasized the profound influence of culture on people's perceptions, feelings, and actions, and the variety of ways in which individuals experience contact with other cultures. Let us revisit briefly Joe Suina, the Pueblo youth whose contact with school created cultural conflict for him. How could the school have been more accommodating? Ideally, Suina's teacher would be a Pueblo Indian and would share his culture. Classrooms in a Pueblo school would resemble the home, with intimate spaces and furniture designed for student comfort. If these conditions are not feasible, a non-Pueblo teacher would accommodate to the ways of the students in the same way that students are expected to accommodate to the school. Actually, students of any culture would appreciate schools that were more comfortable and less institutional, wouldn't they? ■

LEARNING MORE

Further Reading

Victor Villaseñor's *Rain of Gold* (1992) is a fascinating history of his family's experience as Mexican immigrants to southern California. Read the book and identify passages that illustrate the following Mexican values: the importance of religion, the woman as center of home and family, respect for the mother, protection of women's virtue, the ideal woman as pure, how to be a man, the role of the man as protector of the family, the importance of tradition, respect for life, death as a part of life, respect for work, respect for learning, importance of honor, and acceptance of passion as a part of life.

Web Search

Explore the Southern Poverty Law Center's Website at www.splcenter.org. The most current issue of *Teaching Tolerance,* the organization's magazine for teachers, is available to read online, and by clicking other buttons you can discover ideas and resources for teachers, parents, teens, and children. Also investigate www.tolerance.org. This site also provides invaluable information for teachers, parents, teens, and children. Share your findings with your colleagues and plan how to incorporate some of the lessons and ideas from this site into your overall school plan.

Exploration

Ask your parent or grandparent about a favorite family holiday. How was it celebrated differently in "the old days"? What aspects have changed? How might your family's favorite holiday be celebrated (if at all) by other groups? What holidays are favorites among the other teachers, and among your students? How are the celebrations different and the same?

Collaboration

With a colleague, enroll in a training program to acquire conflict-resolution skills. Compare what you learn with the needs of a nearby school. Discuss with your colleague how the program or skills you acquired could be useful.

PEARSON
myeducationlab
The Power of Classroom Practice
www.myeducationlab.com

Incorporating the Home Experience of Culturally Diverse Students into the Classroom, Part 2

In this video segment, we recognize that all students have experiences, yet not all of these experiences are acknowledged in schools. Oftentimes these behaviors conflict with the ideologies and norms of the schools and of teachers. As you are viewing this clip, try to recognize how biases of teachers can often be problematic for culturally diverse students. Try to identify how different cultural behaviors of students are unaccepted by teachers.

> To access the video, go to MyEducationLab (www.myeducationlab.com), choose the Díaz-Rico and Weed text, and log in to MyEducationLab for English Language Learners. Select the topic Cultural-Based Instruction, and watch the video entitled "Incorporating the Home Experience of Culturally Diverse Students into the Classroom, Part 2."

Answer the following questions:

1. Explain at least two different types of cultural behaviors students may exhibit in the classroom that may not be tolerated by the teacher as stated in the video clip. How can a teacher be better prepared to handle these types of cultural differences?
2. What is the role of an ethnographer?
3. Students of culturally diverse backgrounds have
   a. varied experiences.
   b. experiences that may not be acknowledged in schools.
   c. demonstrated behaviors that may conflict with the norms of the school.
   d. all of the above.

10 | Culturally Responsive Schooling

Multicultural festivals encourage students to share their cultures with others.

"Teacher," Maria said to me as the students went out for recess. "Yes, Maria?" I smiled at this lively Venezuelan student, and we launched into conversation. The contents of this talk are now lost on me, but not the actions. For as we talked, we slowly moved, she forward, me backward, until I was jammed up against the chalkboard. And there I remained for the rest of the conversation, feeling more and more agitated. She was simply too close. . . .

I did not ascribe any negative or aggressive tendencies to her. But knowing the difference in personal space requirements between my culture and hers did not lessen my anxiety. What it afforded me was the knowledge that we were behaving differently and that such differences were normal for our respective groups.

Kathryn Z. Weed

*C*ulture influences every aspect of school life (see the figure on page 211). Becoming an active member of a classroom learning community requires specific cultural knowledge. Students from a nonmainstream culture are acquiring a mainstream classroom culture that may differ markedly from their home culture.

Intercultural educators who understand students' cultures can design instruction to meet children's learning needs. They invite students to learn by welcoming them, making them feel that they belong, and presenting learning as a task at which students can succeed. Teachers and students do not necessarily share the same perceptions of what is acceptable behavior and what is relevant learning. Teaching styles, interaction patterns, classroom organization, curricula, and involvement with parents and the community are factors within the teacher's power to adapt.

The skills and responsibilities of the intercultural educator include understanding cultural diversity and striving to achieve equity in schooling (see Chapter 9). In addition, the intercultural educator uses culturally responsive schooling practices to promote the school success of culturally and linguistically diverse (CLD) students. As Richards, Brown, and Forde (2004) stated, "In a culturally responsive classroom, effective teaching and learning occur in a culturally supported, learner-centered context, whereby the strengths students bring to school are identified, nurtured, and utilized to promote student achievement" (n.p.).

The four major components of culturally responsive schooling that promote achievement (see Table 9.1 on page 236) are as follows.

- Respect students' diversity.
- Work with culturally supported facilitating or limiting attitudes and abilities.
- Sustain high expectations for all students.
- Marshal parental and community support for schooling.

This chapter examines each of these components in turn.

Respecting Students' Diversity

Traditionally, educators have used the word *diversity* to denote racial differences. However, today's school population is diverse in a number of ways: academic ability, multiple intelligences, learning styles, thinking styles, gender, attitudes, culture and ethnicity, socioeconomic status, home language, and developmental readiness (Kagan, 2007). Differentiated instruction has come to mean the responsibility that teachers must assume in diversifying classroom practices to ensure that individual students will succeed.

Differentiated instruction involves first assessing students to get to know them in a variety of ways. Then, instructional components must be diversified (see Table 10.1). Differentiated instruction is an approach in which teachers assess students to determine how they differ on an array of characteristics and then modify instruction to honor that diversity. Ongoing assessment helps teachers maintain a flexible understanding of students' needs, whether it be for solitary versus group learning experiences, preference for visual versus auditory channels, wholistic versus linear-sequential learning, or other personal qualities.

Table 10.1

Components of Differentiated Instruction

Component to Be Varied	Examples
Instructional strategies	Direct instruction, learning centers, Internet discovery, individual task cards
Instructional resources	Almanacs, computer software, magazines, manipulatives, research, films
Student support	Aides, specialists, tutors, classroom volunteers
Time and workload	More/fewer problems, more time to think, alternative tasks
Difficulty	Tiers and levels for projects, vary the required level of thinking skill, more/less modeling
Products and presentations	Individual oral presentations, team presentations, written reports, exhibits, demonstrations
Types of assessment	Portfolios, work samples, discussions, behavioral observation

Source: Kagan (2007).

Teachers who are members of the mainstream culture and who have an accommodating vision of cultural diversity recognize that they need to adapt culturally to culturally and linguistically diverse (CLD) students, just as these individuals, in turn, accept some cultural change as they adapt to the mainstream. In this mutual process, teachers who model receptiveness to learning from the diverse cultures in their midst help students to see this diversity as a resource. The first step toward communicating this vision is for teachers to build awareness and celebration of diversity into daily practice.

Acknowledging Students' Differences

Imagine a classroom of thirty students, each with just one unique fact, value, or belief on the more than fifty categories presented in Table 9.3 ("Components of Culture," p. 238). Yet this dizzying array of uniqueness is only the tip of the iceberg, because within each of these categories individuals can differ. Take, for example, the category "Food" under "Daily Life" in Table 9.3. Each student in a classroom of thirty knows a lot about food. What they know, however, depends largely on what they eat every day.

Example of Concept: Students Have Diverse Facts

When I first arrived in Puerto Rico to live, I thought I knew a lot about fruits. But Leo and Alejandro, the children who lived next door, knew so much that I didn't know! The fat, green fruit with the clawlike barbs on the skin and the milky white flesh with big brown seeds was a *guanábana.* The small bananalike fruits were finger bananas, *deditos.* The *quenepa,* a small fruit that appears in the summer, looks like bunches of large, green grapes. The *acerola* is tart and stains the fingers red. The *pepino* is a large, oval melon. . . . There was so much new to learn. And all from our back patios! (Díaz-Rico, n.d.)

Culture includes diversity in values, social customs, rituals, work and leisure activities, health and educational practices, and many other aspects of life. Each of these can affect schooling and are discussed in the following sections, including ways that teachers can respond to these differences in adapting instruction.

Values, Beliefs, and Practices. Values are "beliefs about how one ought or ought not to behave or about some end state of existence worth or not worth attaining" (Bennett, 2003, p. 64). Values are particularly important to people when they educate their young, because education is a primary means of transmitting cultural knowledge.

All the influences that contribute to the cultural profile of the family and community affect the students' reactions to classroom practices. Different cultures organize individual and community behavior in radically different ways—ways that, on the surface, may not seem compatible with school practices and beliefs. To understand these differences is to be able to mediate for the students by helping them bridge relevant differences between the home and the school cultures.

Example of Concept: Values Affect Schooling

Some student populations have very different cultures despite a shared ethnic background. Such is the case at Montebello High School in the Los Angeles area:

> Students at Montebello . . . may look to outsiders as a mostly homogenous population—93 percent Latino, 70 percent low income—but the 2,974 Latino students are split between those who are connected to their recent immigrant roots and those who are more Americanized. In the "TJ" (for Tijuana) side of the campus, students speak Spanish, take ESL classes, and participate in soccer, *folklorico* dancing, and the Spanish club. On the other side of campus, students speak mostly English, play football and basketball, and participate in student government. The two groups are not [mutually] hostile . . . but, as senior Lucia Rios says, "it's like two countries." The difference in values between the two groups stems from their families' values—the recent immigrants are focused on economic survival and do not have the cash to pay for extracurricular activities. . . . Another difference is musical taste (soccer players listen to Spanish music in the locker room, whereas football players listen to heavy metal and rap). (Hayasaki, 2004, pp. A1, A36–A37)

Social Customs. Cultures cause people to lead very different daily lives. These customs are paced and structured by deep habits of using time and space. For example, time is organized in culturally specific ways.

Example of Concept: Cultural Conceptions about Time

Adela, a Mexican-American first-grade girl, arrived at school about twenty minutes late every day. Her teacher was at first irritated and gradually exasperated. In a parent conference, Adela's mother explained that braiding her daughter's hair each morning was an important time for the two of them to be together, even if it meant being slightly late to school. This family time presented a value conflict with the school's time norm.

Other conflicts may arise when teachers demand abrupt endings to activities in which children are deeply engaged or when events are scheduled in a strict sequence. In fact, schools in the United States are often paced very strictly by clock time, whereas family life in various cultures is not regulated in the same manner. Moreover, teachers often equate speed of performance with intelligence, and standardized tests are often a test of rapidity. Many teachers find themselves in the role of "time mediator"— helping the class to adhere to the school's time schedule while working with individual students to help them meet their learning needs within the time allotted.

Adapted Instruction: Accommodating Different Concepts of Time and Work Rhythms

- Provide students with choices about their work time and observe how time spent on various subjects accords with students' aptitudes and interests.
- If a student is a slow worker, analyze the work rhythms. Slow yet methodically accurate work deserves respect; slow and disorganized work may require a peer helper.
- If students are chronically late to school, ask the school counselor to meet with the responsible family member to discuss a change in morning routines.

Space is another aspect about which social customs differ according to cultural experience. Personal space varies: In some cultures, individuals touch one another frequently and maintain high degrees of physical contact; in other cultures, touch and proximity cause feelings of tension and embarrassment. The organization of the space in the classroom sends messages to students: how free they are to move about the classroom, how much of the classroom they "own," how the desks are arranged. Both the expectations of the students and the needs of the teacher can be negotiated to provide a classroom setting in which space is shared.

Adapted Instruction: Accommodating Different Concepts of Personal Space

- If students from the same culture and gender (one with a close personal space) have a high degree of physical contact and neither seems bothered by this, the teacher does not have to intervene.
- The wise teacher accords the same personal space to students no matter what their culture (e.g., does not touch minority students more or less than mainstream students).

Some *symbolic systems* are external, such as dress and personal appearance. For example, a third-grade girl wearing makeup is communicating a message that some teachers may consider an inappropriate indicator of premature sexuality, although makeup on a young girl may be acceptable in some cultures. Other symbolic systems are internal, such as beliefs about natural phenomena, luck and fate, vocational expectations, and so forth.

Example of Concept: Beliefs about Natural Occurrences

One teacher noticed during a strong earthquake that the Mexican-American students seemed much less perturbed than their European-American peers. In succeeding days, several of the European-American children were referred to the school counselor because of anxiety, but the Mexican-American children showed no signs of anxiety. The principal attributed this difference to the Mexican-Americans' cultural belief that nature is powerful and that humans must accept this power. In contrast, most European-American cultures include the view that nature is something to be conquered. When natural forces are greater than human control, anxiety results. Thus, the students' different behavior during earthquakes is a result of different symbolic systems—beliefs—about nature.

Adapted Instruction: Culturally Influenced School Dress Codes

- Boys and men in some cultures (rural Mexico, for example) wear hats; classrooms need to have a place for these hats during class time and provision for wearing the hats during recess.
- Schools that forbid "gang attire" yet permit privileged students to wear student council insignia (sweaters with embroidered names, for instance) should forbid clique-related attire for all.
- A family–school council with representatives from various cultures should be responsible for reviewing the school dress code on a yearly basis to see if it meets the needs of various cultures.

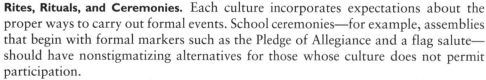

Rites, Rituals, and Ceremonies. Each culture incorporates expectations about the proper ways to carry out formal events. School ceremonies—for example, assemblies that begin with formal markers such as the Pledge of Allegiance and a flag salute—should have nonstigmatizing alternatives for those whose culture does not permit participation.

Rituals in some elementary classrooms in the United States are relatively informal. For example, students can enter freely before school and take their seats or go to a reading corner or activity center. Students from other cultures may find this confusing if they are accustomed to lining up in the courtyard, being formally greeted by the principal or head teacher, and then accompanied in their lines as they enter their respective classrooms.

Rituals are also involved in parent conferences. Greeting and welcome behaviors, for example, vary across cultures. The sensitive teacher understands how parents expect to be greeted and incorporates some of these behaviors in the exchange.

Adapted Instruction: Accommodating School Rituals

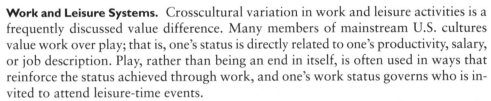

- Teachers might welcome newcomers with a brief explanation of the degree of formality expected of students.
- School seasonal celebrations are increasingly devoid of political and religious content. The school may, however, permit school clubs to honor events with extracurricular rituals.
- Teachers might observe colleagues from different cultures to view the rituals of family–teacher conferences and adapt their behavior accordingly to address families' cultural expectations.

Work and Leisure Systems. Crosscultural variation in work and leisure activities is a frequently discussed value difference. Many members of mainstream U.S. cultures value work over play; that is, one's status is directly related to one's productivity, salary, or job description. Play, rather than being an end in itself, is often used in ways that reinforce the status achieved through work, and one's work status governs who is invited to attend leisure-time events.

Young people, particularly those in the middle class, are trained to use specific tools of play, and their time is structured to attain skills (e.g., organized sports, music lessons). In contrast, other cultures do not afford children any structured time to play but instead expect children to engage in adult-type labor at work or in the home. In still other cultures, such as that of the Hopi Nation in Arizona, children's playtime is relatively unstructured, and parents do not interfere with play. Cultures also vary in the typical work and play activities expected of girls and of boys. All these values have obvious influence on the ways children work and play at school (Schultz & Theophano, 1987).

Did You Know?

In Japan, individuals compete fiercely for admission to prestigious universities, but accompanying this individual effort is a sense that one must establish oneself within a group. Competition in the Japanese classroom is not realized in the same way as in U.S. schools; being singled out for attention or praise by teachers may result in embarrassment (Furey, 1986).

Adapted Instruction: Accommodating Diverse Ideas about Work and Play

- Many high-school students arrange class schedules in order to work part time. If a student appears chronically tired, a family–teacher conference may be needed to review priorities.
- Many students are overcommitted to extracurricular activities. If grades suffer, students may be well advised to reduce activities to regain an academic focus.
- Plagiarism in student work may be due to unclear conceptions about the permissability of shared work.
- Out-of-school play activities such as birthday parties should not be organized at the school site, such as passing out invitations that exclude some students.

Medicine, Health, and Hygiene. Health and medicine practices involve deep-seated beliefs, because the stakes are high: life and death. When students come to school with health issues, teachers need to react in culturally compatible ways. Miscommunication and noncooperation can result when teachers and the family view health and disease differently. For example, community health practices, such as the Cambodian tradition of coining (in which a coin is dipped in oil and then rubbed on a sick person's back, chest, and neck), can be misinterpreted by school officials who, seeing marks on the child, call Child Protective Services.

Adapted Instruction: Health and Hygiene Practices

- Families who send sick children to school or, conversely, keep children home at the slightest ache may benefit from a conference with the school nurse.
- All students can profit from explicit instruction in home and school hygiene.

Institutional Influences: Economic, Legal, Political, and Religious. The institutions that support and govern family and community life have an influence on behavior and beliefs and, in turn, are constituted in accordance with these behaviors and beliefs. These institutions influence daily life in the United States by means of a complex web of law, custom, and regulation that provides the economic and legal infrastructure of the dominant culture.

Interwoven into this rich cultural–economic–political–legal texture are religious beliefs and practices. In the United States, religious practices are heavily embedded but formally bounded: witness the controversy over Christmas trees in schools but the almost universal cultural and economic necessity for increased consumer spending at the close of the calendar year.

Teacher Judy Haynes (2007) discusses the "December dilemma":

> The biggest issue of the December [holiday] wars is the traditional school concert that is at the heart of the celebration of Christmas. The dilemma arises when deciding what music to sing. The question is whether a school concert can include religious Christmas music without promoting a particular belief. The courts have decreed that some religious music may be included if the purpose is to teach about a particular religion and the program is balanced (Anti-Defamation League, 2004).
>
> I think the onus should be taken off December. Let's solve the December dilemma by learning about Diwali and Ramadan in September, Rosh Hashanah in October, and Christmas in December. We should not overemphasize one particular holiday. (pp. 6–7)

Religious beliefs underlie other cultures even more fundamentally. Immigrants with Confucian religious and philosophical beliefs, for example, subscribe to values that mandate a highly ordered society and family through the maintenance of proper social relationships. In Islamic traditions, the Koran prescribes proper social relationships and roles for members of society. When immigrants with these religious beliefs encounter the largely secular U.S. institutions, the result may be that customs and cultural patterns are challenged, fade away, or cause conflict within the family.

Adapted Instruction: Economic, Legal, Political, and Religious Practices

- On a rotating basis, teachers could be paid to supervise after-school homework sessions for students whose parents are working multiple jobs.
- Schools can legally resist any attempts to identify families whose immigration status is undocumented.
- Permission for religious garb or appearance (e.g., Islamic head scarves, Sikh ritual knives, Hassidic dress) should be a part of the school dress code.

Educational Expectations. In the past, educational systems were designed to pass on cultural knowledge and traditions, much the same learning that parents taught their children. However, in the increasingly complex society of the United States, schools have shifted their emphasis to teaching unforeseen kinds of content, including science and technology and multicultural education.

This shift affects all students but is particularly troublesome for children whose parents teach them differently than the school does. Students come to school already steeped in the learning practices of their own family and community. They come with expectations about learning and generally expect that they will continue to learn in

■Did You Know?■

Polynesian students coming from the South Pacific may have experienced classroom learning as a relatively passive activity. They expect teachers to give explicit instruction about what to learn and how to learn it and to carefully scrutinize homework daily.

When these students arrive in the United States and encounter teachers who value creativity and student-centered learning, they may appear passive as they wait to be told what to do (Funaki & Burnett, 1993).

school. Many of the organizational and teaching practices of the school may not support the type of learning to which students are accustomed. For immigrant children with previous schooling, experience in U.S. classrooms may create severe conflicts. Teachers who can accommodate students' proclivities can gradually introduce student-centered practices while supporting an initial dependence on the teacher's direction.

Teachers who seek to understand the value of education within the community can interview parents or community members (see Chapter 8).

Adapted Instruction: Accommodating Culturally Based Educational Expectations

- Classroom guests from the community can share methods for teaching and learning that are used in the home (e.g., modeling and imitation, didactic stories and proverbs, direct verbal instruction).
- Children from cultures that expect passive interaction with teachers (observing only) can be paired with more participatory peers to learn to ask questions and volunteer.

Roles and Status. Cultures differ in the roles people play in society and the status accorded to these roles. For example, in the Vietnamese culture, profoundly influenced by Confucianism, authority figures are ranked in the following manner: The father ranks below the teacher, who ranks only below the king. Such a high status is not accorded to teachers in U.S. society, where, instead, medical doctors enjoy this type of prestige. Such factors as gender, social class, age, occupation, and education level influence the manner in which status is accorded to various roles. Students' perceptions about the roles possible for them in their culture affect their school performance.

Gender. Immigrants to the United States often come from cultures in which men and women have rigid and highly differentiated gender roles. The gender equality that is an ostensible goal in classrooms in the United States may be difficult for students of these cultures. For example, parents may spend much time correcting their sons' homework while ascribing little importance to their daughters' schoolwork.

Sexual identification is also a part of gender issues. Gay, lesbian, or bisexual adolescents who face a hostile school climate or undergo harassment, and/or verbal or physical abuse may become truant, drop out, or resort to suicide or substance abuse (Nichols, 1999).

Adapted Instruction: Gender-Role Expectations

- Monitor tasks performed by boys and girls to ensure they are the same.
- Make sure that boys and girls perform equal leadership roles in cooperative groups.
- If families in a given community provide little support for the scholastic achievement of girls, a systematic effort on the part of school counselors and administrators may be needed to help families accommodate their beliefs to a more proactive support for women.

Social Class. Stratification by social class differs across cultures. Cultures that are rigidly stratified, such as India's caste system, differ from cultures that are not as rigid or that, in some cases, border on the anarchic, such as continuously war-torn countries. The belief that education can enhance economic status is widespread in the dominant culture of the United States, but individuals in other cultures may not have similar beliefs.

In general, individuals and families at the upper-socioeconomic-status levels are able to exert power by sitting on college, university, and local school boards and thus determining who receives benefits and rewards through schooling. However, middle-class values are those that are generally incorporated in the culture of schooling. The social class values that children learn in their homes largely influence not only their belief in schooling but also their routines and habits in the classroom.

Adapted Instruction: The Influence of Social Class on Schooling

- Students who are extremely poor or homeless may need help from the teacher to store possessions at school.
- A teacher who receives an expensive gift should consult the school district's ethics policies.
- A high grade on a school assignment or project should not depend on extensive family financial resources.

Age-Appropriate Activities. Age interacts with culture, socioeconomic status, gender, and other factors to influence an individual's behavior and attitudes. In various cultures, expectations about appropriate activities for children and the purpose of those activities differ. Middle-class European Americans expect children to spend much of their time playing and attending school rather than performing tasks similar to those of adults. Cree Indian children, on the other hand, are expected from an early age to learn adult roles, including contributing food to the family. Parents may criticize schools for involving children in tasks that are not related to their future participation in Cree society (Sindell, 1988).

Cultures also differ in their criteria for moving through the various (culturally defined) life cycle changes. An important stage in any culture is the move into adulthood, but the age at which this occurs and the criteria necessary for attaining adulthood vary according to what *adulthood* means in a particular culture.

Adapted Instruction: Accommodating Beliefs about Age-Appropriate Activities

- Child labor laws in the United States forbid students from working for pay before a given age. However, few laws govern children working in family businesses. If a child appears chronically tired, the school counselor may need to discuss the child's involvement in the family business with a responsible family member.
- Cultural groups in which girls are expected to marry and have children at the age of fifteen or sixteen (e.g., Hmong) may need access to alternative schools.

Occupation. In the United States, occupation very often determines income, which in turn is a chief determinant of prestige in the culture. Prestige is one factor in occupational choices. Other factors can include cultural acceptance of the occupation, educational requirements, gender, and attainability. Students thus may not see all occupations as desirable for them or even available to them and may have mixed views about the role education plays in their future occupation.

Some cultural groups in the United States are engaged in a voluntary way of life that does not require prolonged schooling (e.g., the Amish). Other groups may be involuntarily incorporated into U.S. society and relegated to menial occupations and ways of life that do not reward and require school success (e.g., Hispanics in the Southwest). As a result, they may not apply academic effort (Ogbu & Matute-Bianchi, 1986).

Example of Concept: Collaborative Relationships

Conchas (2006) studied the Medical Academy at Baldwin High School (California), a school-within-a-school that prepares students for careers in health-related occupations. A positive learning environment connected students and teachers across race, gender, and class differences. Both immigrant and U.S.-born Latinos formed a strong sense of belonging and identification with other students in the program; strong collaborative relationships led to academic success.

Adapted Instruction: Occupational Aspirations

- At all grade levels, school subjects should be connected with future vocations.
- Teachers should make available at every grade an extensive set of books on occupations and their requirements, and discuss these with students.
- Role models from minority communities can visit the classroom to recount stories of their success. Successful professionals and businesspeople can visit and explain how cultural diversity is supported in their place of work.

Child-Rearing Practices. The way in which families raise their children has wide implications for schools. Factors such as who takes care of children, how much supervision they receive, how much freedom they have, who speaks to them and how often, and what they are expected to do affect their behavior on entering schools. Many of the misunderstandings that occur between teachers and students arise because of different expectations about behavior, and these different expectations stem from early, ingrained child-rearing practices.

Because the largest group of English learners in California is of Mexican ancestry, teachers who take the time to learn about child-rearing practices among Mexican immigrants can help students adjust to schooling practices in the United States. An excellent source for this cultural study is *Crossing Cultural Borders* (Delgado-Gaitan & Trueba, 1991).

Food Preferences. As the numbers of school-provided breakfasts and lunches increase, food preferences are an important consideration. Furthermore, teachers who are knowledgeable about students' dietary practices can incorporate their students' background knowledge into health and nutrition instruction.

Students from Korean-American backgrounds may be accustomed to an authoritarian discipline style in the home. These parents often seek to influence their children's behavior by expecting reciprocity for the sacrifices made for them. Decision-making strategies reward conformity and obedience, and teachers are expected to reinforce this. An egalitarian classroom atmosphere may create conflicts for Korean-American students between the pressures they experience in their families and the school environment (CDE, 1992).

Besides customs of what and when to eat, eating habits vary widely across cultures, and "good" manners at the table in some cultures are inappropriate or rude in others. For example, Indochinese consider burping, lip smacking, and soup slurping to be common behaviors during meals, even complimentary to hosts. Cultural relativity is not, however, an excuse for poor or unhygienic eating, and teachers do need to teach students the behaviors that are considered good food manners in the U.S. mainstream context.

Adapted Instruction: Dealing with Food Preferences

- In addition to knowing in general what foods are eaten at home, teachers will want to find out about students' favorite foods, taboo foods, and typical foods.
- Eating lunch with students—even on a by-invitation basis—can provide the opportunity to learn about students' habits.
- If a student's eating habits alienate peers, the teacher may need to discuss appropriate behaviors.

Humanities and the Arts. In many cultures, crafts performed at home—such as food preparation; sewing and weaving; carpentry; home building and decoration; religious and ritual artistry for holy days, holidays, and entertaining—are an important part of the culture that is transmitted within the home. Parents also provide an important means of access to the humanities and the visual and performing arts of their cultures. Often, if immigrant students are to gain an appreciation of the great works of art, architecture, music, and dance that have been achieved by their native culture, it is the classroom teacher who must provide this experience and awareness by drawing on the resources of the community and then sharing these with all the members of the classroom.

Educating Students about Diversity

Both mainstream students and CLD students benefit from education about diversity, not only cultural diversity but also diversity in ability, gender preference, and human

Did You Know?

James Banks (1994) explained the difference between studying the cultures of other countries and the cultures within the United States. According to Banks, teachers may implement a unit on the country of Japan but avoid teaching about Japanese internment in the United States during World War II (Brandt, 1994).

nature in general. This engenders pride in cultural identity, expands the students' perspectives, and adds cultural insight, information, and experiences to the curriculum.

Global and Multicultural Education. ELD teachers—and mainstream teachers who teach English learners—can bring a global and multicultural perspective to their classes.

> Language teachers, like teachers in all other areas of the curriculum, have a responsibility to plan lessons with sensitivity to the racial and ethnic diversity present in their classrooms and in the world in which their students live. . . . [Students] can learn to value the points of view of many others whose life experiences are different from their own. (Curtain & Dahlberg, 2004, p. 244)

Table 10.2 lists some cultural activities that Curtain and Dahlberg recommended for adding cultural content to the curriculum.

The goal of multicultural education is to help students "develop cross-cultural competence within the American national culture, with their own subculture and within and across different subsocieties and cultures" (Banks, 1994, p. 9). Banks introduced a model of multicultural education that has proved to be a useful way of assessing the approach taken in pedagogy and curricula. The model has four levels, represented in Table 10.3 with a critique of strengths and shortcomings taken from Jenks, Lee, and Kanpol (2002).

Table 10.2

Sample Cultural Activities for Multicultural Education

Activity	Suggested Implementation
Visitors and guest speakers	Guests can share their experiences on a variety of topics, using visuals, slides, and hands-on materials.
Folk dances, singing games, and other kinds of games	Many cultures can be represented; cultural informants can help.
Field trips	Students can visit neighborhoods, restaurants, museums, or stores that feature cultural materials.
Show-and-tell	Students can bring items from home to share with the class.
Read books about other cultures	Age-appropriate fiction or nonfiction books can be obtained with the help of the school or public librarian.
Crosscultural e-mail contacts	Students can exchange cultural information and get to know peers from other lands.

Source: Curtain and Dahlberg (2004).

Table 10.3

Banks's Levels of Multicultural Education, with Critique

Level	Description	Strengths	Shortcomings
Contributions	Emphasizes what minority groups have contributed to society (e.g., International Food Day, bulletin board display for Black History Month).	Attempts to sensitize the majority white culture to some understanding of minority groups' history.	May amount to "cosmetic" multiculturalism in which no discussion takes place about issues of power and disenfranchisement.
Additive	Adding material to the curriculum to address what has been omitted (reading *The Color Purple* in English class).	Adds to a fuller coverage of the American experience, when sufficient curricular time is allotted.	May be an insincere effort if dealt with superficially.
Transformative	An expanded perspective is taken that deals with issues of historic, ethnic, cultural, and linguistic injustice and equality as a part of the American experience.	Students learn to be reflective and develop a critical perspective.	Incorporates the liberal fallacy that discussion alone changes society.
Social action	Extension of the transformative approach to add students' research/action projects to initiate change in society.	Students learn to question the status quo and the commitment of the dominant culture to equality and social justice.	Middle-class communities may not accept the teacher's role, considering it as provoking students to "radical" positions.

Sources: Model based on Banks (1994); strengths and shortcomings based on Jenks, Lee, and Kanpol (2002).

There is a clear distinction between multiculturalism and globalism, although both are important features of the school curriculum: "Globalism emphasizes the cultures and peoples of other lands, and multiculturalism deals with ethnic diversity within the United States" (Ukpokodu, 2002, pp. 7–8).

Nieto and Bode (2008) make the point that multicultural education does more than merely celebrate diversity:

[M]ulticultural education does not simply involve the affirmation of language and culture. Multicultural education confronts not only issues of difference but also issues of power and privilege in society. This means challenging racism and other biases as well as the inequitable structures, policies, and practices of schools and, ultimately, of society itself. Affirming language and culture can help students become successful and well-adjusted learners, but unless language and cultural issues are viewed critically through the lens of equity and social justices, they are unlikely to have a lasting impact in promoting real change. (pp. 4–5)

Similar to Banks's superficial-to-transformative continuum is that of Morey and Kilano (1997). Their three-level framework for incorporating diversity identifies as "exclusive" the stereotypical focus on external aspects of diversity (what they called the four *f*'s: food, folklore, fun, and fashion); "inclusive," the addition of diversity into a curriculum that, although enriched, is fundamentally the same structure; and "transformed," the curriculum that is built on diverse perspectives, equity in participation, and critical problem solving. Howard (2007) has suggested that a transformative approach to diversity has five basic phases: building trust, engaging personal culture, confronting issues of social dominance and social justice, transforming educational practices, and engaging the entire school community. Thus, it is clear that pouring new wine—diversity—into old bottles—teacher-centered, one-size-fits-all instruction—is not transformative.

Example of Concept: Action Research for Curricular Change

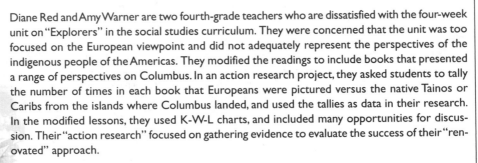

Diane Red and Amy Warner are two fourth-grade teachers who are dissatisfied with the four-week unit on "Explorers" in the social studies curriculum. They were concerned that the unit was too focused on the European viewpoint and did not adequately represent the perspectives of the indigenous people of the Americas. They modified the readings to include books that presented a range of perspectives on Columbus. In an action research project, they asked students to tally the number of times in each book that Europeans were pictured versus the native Tainos or Caribs from the islands where Columbus landed, and used the tallies as data in their research. In the modified lessons, they used K-W-L charts, and included many opportunities for discussion. Their "action research" focused on gathering evidence to evaluate the success of their "renovated" approach.

Source: Nolan and Hoover (2008).

Validating Students' Cultural Identity. "An affirming attitude toward students from culturally diverse backgrounds significantly impacts their learning, belief in self, and overall academic performance" (Villegas & Lucas, 2002, p. 23). Cultural identity—that is, having a positive self-concept or evaluation of oneself and one's culture—promotes self-esteem. Students who feel proud of their successes and abilities, self-knowledge, and self-expression, and who have enhanced images of self, family, and culture, are better learners.

Oakes and Lipton (2007) believe that students should view their cultural identities as integral to their school success, not as something they must "overcome":

> Perhaps schools' greatest challenge is to create a school culture that supports college attendance for students whose lives do not conform to [the profile of a person with high scores on standardized tests, whose parents went to college, whose main language is mainstream, unaccented English, and who have middle-class perspectives and financial support]. The school culture must position college success as expected and inevitable not just for students who change [identities] or for students who are exceptions to stereotypes, but for students who have no need or no intention to slight their family's background and culture as they acquire skills and knowledge that are genuinely useful for college success. (p. 354)

Of course, the most powerful sense of self-esteem is the result not solely of one's beliefs about oneself but also of successful learning experiences. Practices of schooling that damage self-esteem, such as tracking and competitive grading, undermine authentic cooperation and sense of accomplishment on the part of English learners.

Classroom Practices That Validate Identity. Díaz-Rico (2008) suggested that through observations, shared conversations during lunchtime or before or after school, and group participation, teachers can gain understanding about various individuals and their cultures. Teachers can also ask students to interview their parents about common topics such as work, interests, and family history and then add a reflective element about their relationship and identification with these aspects of their parents' lives.

Adolescents acquire identities through sociocultural groups, such as language and cultural groups, as well as through activities in which they engage (athletics, band, computers, gangsta, goth). They are also labeled by schools (students in honors or special education, English learners, "at-risk," "leaders"). These identities may influence school behavior, as some groups pressure members not to invest in school success, but rather to adopt resistance or apathetic attitudes.

Example of Concept: A Cultural Heritage Project

Promoting research projects is a way for students to participate in school in ways related to their personal identities. One teacher based a unit plan on this standard from the Michigan Curriculum Standard from Social Studies: *Students will gain knowledge about the past to construct meaningful understandings of our diverse cultural heritage.* In this unit, students were to compare two aspects of cultural heritage from information obtained from the Internet, culminating in an individual report on a favorite artist or inventor as well as a group PowerPoint presentation and simulated interview with the historical figure.

The Puerto Rican group compared Ladislao Martinez and Alvin Medina, one traditional and one contemporary *cuatro* (folk guitar) player. They contrasted the two players, drawing on sound clips that included current musical favorites. A rich context of time and place gave each participant a personal connection to the topic (Conley, 2008).

Instructional Materials That Validate Identity. Classroom texts are available that offer literature and anecdotal readings aimed at the enhancement of identity and self-esteem. *Identities: Readings from Contemporary Culture* (Raimes, 1996) includes readings grouped into chapters titled "Name," "Appearance, Age, and Abilities," "Ethnic Affiliation and Class," Family Ties," and so forth. The readings contain authentic text and may be best used in middle- or high-school classes.

The use of multicultural literature may enhance cultural and ethnic identity, but this is not always the case. In 1976 a committee of Asian-American book reviewers evaluated books to identify those that could be used effectively in educational programs. When they had evaluated a total of sixty-four books related to Asian-American issues or characters, they concluded that most of the existing literature was "racist, sexist, and elitist and that the image of Asian Americans [the books] present is grossly misleading" (Aoki, 1992, p. 133). The challenge, then, is to represent ethnic characters in a more realistic way.

A book that is useful for a comparison of Asian cultural values with those of mainstream American culture is Kim's (2001) *The Yin and Yang of American Culture.* This book presents a view of American culture—its virtues and vices—from an Eastern perspective and may stimulate discussion on the part of students. *Exploring Culturally Diverse Literature for Children and Adolescents* (Henderson & May, 2005) helps readers understand how stories are tied to specific cultural and sociopolitical histories, opening readers' minds to literature written from the "insider's" versus the "outsider's" point of view.

Promoting Mutual Respect among Students

The ways in which we organize classroom life should make children feel significant and cared about—by the teacher and by one another. Classroom life should, to the greatest extent possible, prefigure the kind of democratic and just society we envision and thus contribute to building that society. Together, students and teachers can create a "community of conscience," as educators Asa Hillard and George Pine call it (Christensen, 2000, p. 18).

Mutual respect is promoted when the curriculum includes multiple points of view and when students are given the chance to genuinely talk to one another about topics that concern them. The instructional conversation is a discourse format that encourages in-depth conversation (see Chapter 5).

Adapting to Students' Culturally Supported Facilitating or Limiting Attitudes and Abilities

A skilled intercultural educator recognizes that each culture supports distinct attitudes, values, and abilities. These may facilitate or limit the learning situation in U.S. public schools. For example, the cultures of Japan, China, and Korea, which promote high academic achievement, may foster facilitating behaviors, such as the ability to listen and follow directions; attitudes favoring education and respect for teachers and authorities; attitudes toward discipline as guidance; and high-achievement motivation. However, other culturally supported traits may hinder adjustment to the U.S. school, such as lack of experience participating in discussions; little experience with independent thinking; strong preference for conformity, which inhibits divergent thinking; and distinct sex-role differentiation, with males more dominant.

Example of Concept: Overcoming Reluctance to Participate Orally

Asian students are more likely to speak up in class when the participation is structured, such as in a debate that has definite rules for whose turn it is to talk. Unstructured class discussions in which one must aggressively promote one's turn may make many Asian students feel anxious and uncomfortable, because this does not mirror the home environment, where often students speak only when requested to do so by a parental authority (Tateishi, 2007–2008). Small-group discussion with leaders whose task is to involve all members can be a means of conducting classroom talk.

Similarly, African-American family and cultural values that encourage independent action, self-sufficiency, and imagination and humor may facilitate adjustment to the classroom, but dialect speakers with limited experiences with various types of Standard English patterns may be hindered. The Mexican-American cultural values that encourage cooperation; affectionate and demonstrative parental relationships; children assuming mature social responsibilities such as child care and translating family matters from English to Spanish; and eagerness to try out new ideas may facilitate classroom success. On the other hand, such attitudes as depreciating education after high school, especially for women; explicit sex-role stereotyping favoring limited vocational roles for women; and dislike of competition may go against classroom practices and hinder classroom success (Clark, 1983).

Cooperation versus Competition

Triandis (1995) stated that the most important difference between cultures that can be identified in schools is the contrast between individualist and collectivist value systems. Traditional U.S. classrooms mirror middle-class European-American values of competition: Students are expected to do their own work; are rewarded publicly through star charts, posted grades, and academic honors; and are admonished to do their individual best. In the Cree Indian culture, however, children are raised in a cooperative atmosphere, with siblings, parents, and other kin sharing food as well as labor (Sindell, 1988). In the Mexican-American culture, interdependence is a strength; individuals have a commitment to others, and all decisions are made together. Those who are successful have a responsibility to others to help them succeed.

Because about 70 percent of the world's population lives in a collectivist culture (including Native Americans, Native Hawaiians, Latin American, African Americans, Asians, and Arab groups), according to Tileston and Darling (2008), it is probably wiser for teachers to emphasize interdependence among students rather than aggressive and competitive competition. Some balance must be achieved in the classroom between the individual competitive culture of the dominant U.S. culture and the collaborative preferences of students from group-oriented, cooperative cultures.

Developing cooperative skills requires a focus in the classroom on communication and teamwork. Kluge (1999) emphasized the following elements:

- *Positive interdependence:* Members of a group depend on one another, and no one is exploited or left out.
- *Face-to-face interaction:* Students work in proximity to one another.
- *Individual accountability:* Each group member bears full responsibility for the work performed by the group.
- *Social skills training:* The teacher explicitly explains and models the kind of communication and cooperation that is desired.
- *Group processing:* The teacher makes time for reflection on how the group is working together and helps the group set goals for improvement.

The Use of Language

In learning a second language, students (and teachers) often focus on the form. Frequently ignored are the ways in which that second language is used (see the section on pragmatics in Chapter 2). The culture that underlies each language prescribes distinct patterns and conventions about when, where, and how to use the language (see Labov, 1972). Heath's (1983b) *Ways with Words* noted that children in "Trackton," an isolated African-American community in the South, were encouraged to use spontaneous verbal play, rich with metaphor, simile, and allusion. In contrast, the children of "Roadville," a lower-middle-class European-American community in the South, used language in more restricted ways, perhaps because of habits encouraged by a fundamentalist religious culture. Heath contrasted language usage in these two cultures: verbal and nonverbal communication (the "said" and the "unsaid"), the use of silence, discourse styles, the nature of questions, and the use of oral versus written genres.

Social Functions of Language. Using language to satisfy material needs, control the behavior of others, get along with others, express one's personality, find out about the world, create an imaginative world, or communicate information seems to be universal among language users. How these social functions are accomplished, however, varies greatly among cultures. For example, when accidentally bumping someone, Americans, Japanese, Koreans, and Filipinos would say "excuse me" or "pardon me." The Chinese, however, would give an apologetic look.

Verbal and Nonverbal Expression. Both verbal and nonverbal means are used to communicate a language function. Educators are oriented toward verbal means of expression and are less likely to accord importance to the "silent language." However, more than 65 percent of the social meaning of a typical two-person exchange is carried by nonverbal cues (Birdwhistell, 1974). *Kinesic* behavior, including facial expressions, body movements, postures, and gestures, can enhance a message or constitute a message in itself. *Physical appearance* is an important dimension of the nonverbal code during initial encounters. *Paralanguage*—the nonverbal elements of the voice—is an important aspect of speech that can affirm or belie a verbal message. *Proxemics,* the communication of interpersonal distance, varies widely across cultures. Last but not least, *olfactics*—the study of interpersonal communication by means of smell—constitutes a factor that is powerful yet often overlooked.

The Role of Silence. People throughout the world employ silence in communicating. Silence can in fact speak loudly and eloquently. As with other language uses, however, silence differs dramatically across cultures. In the United States, silence is interpreted as expressing embarrassment, regret, obligation, criticism, or sorrow (Wayne in Ishii & Bruneau, 1991). In Asian cultures, silence is a token of respect. Particularly in the presence of the elderly, being quiet honors their wisdom and expertise. Silence can also be a marker of personal power. In many Native-American cultures, silence is used to create and communicate rapport in ways that language cannot.

The Nature of Questions. Intercultural differences exist in asking and answering questions. In middle-class European-American culture, children are exposed early on to their parents' questioning. While taking a walk, for example, a mother will ask, "See the squirrel?" and, later, "Is that a squirrel? Where did that squirrel go?" It is obvious to both parent and child that the adult knows the answer to these questions. The questions are asked to stimulate conversation and to train children to focus attention and display knowledge. In the Inuit culture, on the other hand, adults do not question children or call their attention to objects and events in order to name them (Crago, 1993).

Did You Know?

Heath (1983b) described differences in questions that adults ask children between the Roadville (lower-middle-class European-American community) and the Trackton African-American community. Roadville parents used questions to ask their children to display knowledge ("What is three plus three?"). In contrast, Trackton adults challenged the child to display creative thinking: "What's that like?"

Responses to questioning differ across cultures. Students from non-Western cultures may be reluctant to attempt an answer to a question if they do not feel they can answer absolutely correctly. Students do not share the European-American value of answering questions to the best of their ability regardless of whether that "best" answer is absolutely correct or not.

Discourse Styles. Cultures may differ in ways that influence conversations: the way conversations open and close, the way people take turns, the way messages are repaired to make them understandable, and the way in which parts of the text are set aside. These differences in discourse are stressful for second-language learners. Multiply this stress by the long hours children spend in school, and it is no wonder that English learners may feel subjected to prolonged pressure.

Example of Concept: Classroom Discourse Patterns

Discourse in the classroom can be organized in ways that involve children positively, in ways that are culturally compatible. A group of Hawaiian children, with the help of an encouraging and participating adult, produced group discourse that was co-narrated, complex, lively, imaginative, and well connected. Group work featured twenty-minute discussions of text in which the teacher and students mutually participated in overlapping, volunteered speech and in joint narration (Au & Jordan, 1981). In contrast, Navajo children in a discussion group patterned their discourse after the adults of their culture. Each Navajo student spoke for an extended period with a fully expressed statement, and other students waited courteously until a clear end was communicated. Then another took a similar turn. In both communities, children tended to connect discourse with peers rather than with the teacher functioning as a central "switchboard." If the teacher acted as a central director, students often responded with silence (Tharp, 1989a).

Adapted Instruction: How Students Tell You They Don't Understand

Arabic (men): *Mish fahem*
Arabic (women): *Mish fahmeh*
Armenian: *Yes chem huskenur*
Chinese (Cantonese): *Ngoh m-ming*
Chinese (Mandarin): *Wo bu dung*
Persian: *Man ne'me fah'mam*
Japanese: *Wakarimasen*

Korean: *Juh-neun eehae-haji mot haget-ssum-nida*
Russian: *Ya nye ponimayu*
Spanish: *No comprendo*
Vietnamese: *Toi khong hieu*
Yiddish: *Ikh veys nikht*

In addition to ways to say "I don't understand" in 230 languages, J. Runner's Webpage has translations in many languages for the following phrases: "Hello, how are you?" "Welcome," "Good-bye," "Please," "Thank you," "What is your name?" "My name is . . . ," "Do you speak English?" "Yes," and "No." There is also a link to Internet Language Resources; see www.elite .net/~runner/jennifers/understa.htm.

Source: Runner (2000).

Oral versus Written Language. Orality is the foundation of languages. Written expression is a later development. In fact, of the thousands of reported languages in use, only seventy-eight have a written literature (Edmonson, 1971). Research has suggested that acquiring literacy involves more than learning to read and write. Thinking patterns, perception, cultural values, communication style, and social organization can be affected by literacy (Ong, 1982; Scribner & Cole, 1978).

In studying oral societies, researchers have noted that the structure and content of messages tend to be narrative, situational, and oriented toward activity or deeds, although abstract ideas such as moral values are often implicit. In contrast, the style of literacy is conceptual rather than situational. Words are separate from the social context of deeds and events, and abstract ideas can be extracted from written texts. In an oral society, learning takes place in groups because narration must have an audience. This contrasts with a literate society, in which reading and writing can be solitary experiences. In an oral society, much reliance is placed on memory, as this is the principal means of preserving practices and traditions (Ong, 1982).

Example of Concept: Characteristics of One Oral Culture

Hmong immigrants in the United States demonstrate the comparative disadvantage faced by individuals from an oral culture when expected to perform in a literate environment. Hmong individuals may become frustrated in the abstract world of school. The very concept of independent study is alien to this culture because learning always occurs in community groups. Learning among strangers and doing homework, a solitary endeavor, run counter to traditional group practices and may distance children from their families. As Hmong children become literate and engage in independent study, parents may become disturbed over the loss of centrality and power in their children's lives, which may produce family tension (Shuter, 1991).

Participation Styles

The way teachers are taught to teach is a reflection of the expectations of U.S. culture. Teachers raised in a mainstream culture have elements of that culture embedded in their personal teaching approach. The selection of a particular teaching method reflects cultural values more than it argues for the superiority of the method. Some of these elements may need to be modified to meet the needs of students from other cultures. The accompanying Example of Concept illustrates the way the culturally preferred participation style of one group of students differed from their teachers'.

Example of Concept: Culturally Preferred Participation Styles

In classrooms on the Warm Springs (Oregon) Reservation, teacher-controlled activity dominated. All the social and spatial arrangements were created by the teacher: where and when movement took place; where desks were placed and even what furniture was present in the room; and who talked, when, and with whom. For the Warm Springs students, this socialization was difficult. They preferred to wander to various parts of the room, away from the lesson; to talk to other students while the teacher was talking; and to "bid" for one another's attention rather than that of the teacher.

For the Native-American children, the small-reading-group structure in which participation is mandatory, individual, and oral was particularly ill fitting. They frequently refused to read aloud, did not utter a word when called on, or spoke too softly to be audible. On the other hand, when students controlled and directed interaction in small-group projects, they were much more fully involved. They concentrated completely on their work until it was completed and talked a great deal to one another in the group. Very little time was spent disagreeing or arguing about how to go about a task. There was, however, explicit competition with other groups.

A look at the daily life of the Warm Springs children revealed several factors that would account for their willingness to work together and their resistance to teacher-directed activity. First, they spend much time in the company of peers with little disciplinary control from older relatives. They also spend time in silence, observing their elders and listening without verbal participation. Speech seems to be an optional response rather than a typical or mandatory feature of interaction. One last characteristic of community life is the accessibility and openness of community-wide celebrations. No single individual directs and controls all activity, and there is no sharp distinction between audience and performer. Individuals are permitted to choose for themselves the degree of participation in an activity. Schooling became more successful for these students when they were able to take a more active part.

Source: Adapted from Philips (1972, pp. 370–394).

Even in monocultural classrooms, the teacher's style is more in accordance with some students than with others. Flexibility becomes a key in reaching more students. In a multicultural classroom, this flexibility is even more crucial. With knowledge of various teaching styles, teachers can examine their own style, observe students' reactions to that style, ask questions about a teacher's expected role and style in the community, and modify their style as necessary.

Teacher–Student Interactions

The teacher–student relationship is culturally mandated in general ways, although individual relationships vary. Teacher–student interaction may derive from parent–child relationships or from values transmitted by the parent toward teachers and schooling. Students who have immigrated may bring with them varying notions of teacher–student interactions. For example, in some cultures, learning takes place in an absolutely quiet classroom where the teacher is in complete control and authority is never questioned. In other cultures, students talk among themselves and are able to engage with teachers in cooperative planning. Attitudes toward authority, teacher–student relationships, and teacher expectations of student achievement vary widely. Yet the heart of the educational process is in the interaction between teacher and student. This determines the quality of education the student receives.

Adapted Instruction: Encouraging Positive Relationships

Although it may appear daunting to be able to accommodate the various teacher–student relations represented by different cultural groups in a classroom, there are several ways teachers can learn about their students to provide a learning environment.

- Express care and respect equally to all students.
- Openly communicate acceptance of students and be accessible to them.
- In classroom discussions and in private, encourage students to talk about their expectations for learning.
- Be sensitive to home conditions and try to make students' class experiences positive.
- Welcome and respect parents in classrooms.
- Understand that you are not only helping students academically but that you may also be helping families adjust.

Source: Adapted from Lemberger (1999).

Power and Authority. Most students expect power and authority to be vested in the teacher, and teachers expect respect from students. Respect is communicated verbally and nonverbally and is vulnerable to cultural misunderstanding. In the United States, respect is shown to teachers by looking at them, but in some cultures looking directly at the teacher is a sign of disrespect. Moreover, students are expected to raise their hands in North-American classrooms if they wish to ask or answer a question. In general, one must not conclude that a particular behavior is disrespectful; it may be that the child has learned different customs for communicating with those in authority.

Adapted Instruction: Understanding Behaviors Related to Power and Authority

- Seek alternative explanations to unexpected behavior rather than interpreting the behavior according to your own cultural framework.
- Ask "Why is this behavior occurring?" rather than "What is the matter with this child?"

Source: Adapted from Cushner (1999, p. 75).

Teacher–Student Relationships. The relationships that are possible between teachers and students also show cultural influences. The role of teachers in multicultural classrooms is to make explicit their understandings of the teacher–student relationship and to build a mutually satisfying classroom community. Sometimes this means going that extra mile to sustain a relationship that is at risk.

Example of Concept: "Retooling" to Improve Teacher–Student Relationships

Even teachers of color find they need to "retool" their practice when assigned to a classroom of culturally and linguistically diverse students. An African-American teacher who taught for many years in a predominantly white suburban school said, "When I first found myself teaching classes of mostly black kids, I went home frustrated every night because I knew I wasn't getting through to them, and they were giving me a hard time. It only started getting better when I finally figured out that I had to re-examine everything I was doing" (Howard, 2007, p. 17).

Kottler (1997) proposed that teachers take a cultural view when learning about students, asking these reflective questions:

- How are my cultural values and biases getting in the way of honoring those among my students who are different from what I am used to?
- What is it that I do not know or understand about this child's background that might help me to make sense of what is happening?
- What is it about where this student comes from that leads him or her to respond to others the way he or she does?
- How might I investigate further the customs of this child's family? (p. 98)

Classroom Organization

The typical organization of U.S. classrooms is that of a teacher-leader who gives assignments or demonstrates to the students, who act as audience. Teacher presentations are usually followed by some form of individual study. Learning is then assessed through recitation, quizzes, or some other performance. Small-group work, individual projects, or paired learning require distinct participation structures, ways of behaving and speaking. Learning how to behave in these settings may require explicit cultural adaptation. Many students new to U.S. classrooms have never before taken part in group problem solving, story retelling, or class discussion. Such activities entail social as well as linguistic challenges. Teachers can help students by providing clear instructions and ample models, by calling on more self-confident students first, and by assigning self-conscious students minor roles at first in order not to embarrass them.

The ability to ask for help when needed involves cultural norms and discourse competence. The common practice in teacher-directed classrooms is for students to bid to answer a teacher's question or for the teacher to call on a specific individual. Both procedures can be problematic for English learners, who may be reluctant to bring attention to themselves, either because they see such an action as incompatible with group cohesiveness and cultural norms or because they may be reluctant to display knowledge in front of others. Teachers who are sensitive to varying cultural styles organize other means for students to demonstrate language and content knowledge, and they act as observers and guides rather than directors or controllers of student activity.

Example of Concept: Class Discussions

A Vietnamese student who moved to the United States describes his reaction to a class discussion:

> As a student in Vietnam, I learned not to ask questions, not to raise my hand, or to have much contact with the teacher. I listened, took notes, and memorized the material. The teacher was always right. Imagine my surprise when I entered a U.S. classroom and listened as my classmates talked, argued, and discussed! The teacher encouraged discussion and even listened to what the students had to say. This felt very different to me.

Source: Dresser (1993, p. 120).

The explicit cultural knowledge needed to function well in a classroom is evident when students first encounter school, in preschool or kindergarten. For the children in two communities studied by Heath (1983b), those from Roadville were able to comply with teachers' rules for various activity centers (block building, reading, playing with puzzles). They had learned in their homes to play only certain kinds of games in certain areas and to put away their toys when finished. Children from Trackton did not confine toys to specific areas but instead were creative and improvised new and flexible functions for the toys, often mixing items from different parts of the room. A puzzle piece that looked like a shovel, for example, was taken outside to the sandbox. As Heath points out:

[These] children . . . were accustomed to playing with toys outdoors almost all of the time and they insisted on taking the school's "indoor toys" outside; at home, almost all their toys stayed outside, under the porch, or wherever they were left when play ended. Moreover, at home, they were accustomed to using toys for purposes they created, not necessarily those which the toy manufacturer had envisioned. (p. 275)

Thus, the differences in the home culture created differences in the way the students played at school. This, in turn, was noted by teachers as they formed judgments about which students were more academically capable than others.

Curriculum

Many aspects of the school curriculum are highly abstract and contain themes and activities for which many CLD students have little referent. Some teachers, rather than finding ways in which students can become familiar with academically challenging content, are quick to devise alternative activities of lower academic worth. Research on Alaska Native education suggests a number of abuses perpetrated in the name of "being sensitive to children's cultural backgrounds." Teachers often exempt Alaska Native students from standards applicable to other students. For example, they assign an essay on "Coming to the City from the Village" as a substitute for a research paper. They justify the lack of challenging courses with comments such as, "Well, they are going home to live in their village. What do they need algebra for anyway?" Too many lessons are created featuring stereotypic content (kayaks and caribou) that demonstrates a shallow cultural relevance (Kleinfeld, 1988).

Teachers who lack a solid foundation of cultural knowledge are often guilty of trivializing the cultural content of the curriculum. The sole cultural reference may be to holidays or food, or they may have "ethnic" bulletin boards only during certain times of the year (e.g., Black History Month). People from cultures outside the United States are shown only in "traditional" dress and rural settings or, if they are people of color, are always shown as poor. Native Americans may be represented as peoples from the past. Moreover, students' cultures are misrepresented if pictures and books about Mexico, for example, are used to teach about Mexican Americans or books about Africa are used to teach about African Americans (Derman-Sparks and Anti-Bias Curriculum Task Force, 1988).

Avoiding bias means more than using "politically correct" terminology that does not incorporate prejudice. It also means protecting the authenticity of sources. Reese (2007) comments on the distortions often displayed when children are presented with literature about Native Americans: Indians are portrayed either as savages, or on the other extreme, as poetic, romantic figures with a message about living in harmony with the earth. Reese, a Pueblo Indian, calls for literature that reflects the heterogeneity of the Native-American experience in ways that counter culturally and historically inaccurate mythmaking. She offers valuable guidelines for evaluating and selecting Native-American literature for classroom use, especially featuring markers of cultural authenticity.

Example of Concept: The Eurocentric Curriculum

What is a Eurocentric perspective, and why is that limiting for today's students? Because the United States began as a set of British colonies, many perspectives published even in contemporary textbooks reflect a European point of view. For example, in geography, Europe and the United States are centered side-by-side, with the rest of the world at the margins. Parts of the world are named according to their position relative to Europe, for example, the "Middle East" (Hernandez, 2001). World capitals are named in English rather than using their indigenous names ("Moscow" rather than "Moscova"). Students may become depressed when their native countries and regions play so small a role in the curricula and texts, and the world of information does not include their issues and perspectives.

In her article "Educating Teachers for Cultural and Linguistic Diversity: A Model for All Teachers," Parla (1994) discussed issues related to the multicultural classroom and includes information on cultural sensitivity, linguistic diversity, and teaching strategies that can help teachers grow in their understanding of cultural issues and translate that understanding into classroom practice. The article can be found at www.ncela.gwu.edu/pubs/nysabe/vol9/model.htm.

Adapted Instruction: Assessing Ethnic, Linguistic, and Gender Biases in the Curriculum

The following checklist can help teachers assess the extent to which ethnic, linguistic, and gender biases exist in the curriculum:

- What groups are represented in texts, discussion, and bulletin board displays? Are certain groups invisible?
- Are the roles of minorities and women presented in a separate manner from other content, isolated or treated as a distinct topic?
- Are minorities (and women) treated in a positive, diversified manner, or stereotyped into traditional or rigid roles?
- Are the problems faced by minorities presented in a realistic fashion, with a problem-solving orientation?
- Is the language used in the materials inclusive, or are biased terms used, such as masculine forms (*mankind, mailman*)?
- Does the curriculum foster appreciation of cultural diversity?
- Are experiences and activities other than those common to middle-class European-American culture included?

Sustaining High Expectations for All Students

Jussim (1986) offered a general framework for the relationship between teacher expectations and student achievement. Teachers develop initial expectations based on a student's reputation, on previous classroom performance, or on stereotypes about racial, cultural, and linguistic groups. These expectations, which often resist change despite evidence to the contrary, form the basis for differential treatment of students and for the rationalization for such treatment. Students, in turn, react to this differential treatment in ways that confirm the teacher's expectations. Thus, teachers have a high degree of effect on student achievement: Student effort and persistence are shaped, in part, by students' perception of the teacher's expectations.

Teachers' expectations for student performance are culturally based, as are their criteria for evaluation. Pedagogical training can enable teachers to organize instruction that more accurately allows diverse students access to the curriculum.

Expecting high achievement from English learners and communicating these expectations require specific educational programs that draw attention to the hidden curriculum of the school, quality of interaction between teachers and students, diverse learning styles, the use of the community as a resource, and a commitment to democratic ideals in the classroom (Gollnick & Chinn, 2006). Overall, the effect of teacher expectations amounts to a continuous, de facto, day-to-day assessment of students' worth and capabilities.

Assessing Students' Ability and Achievement Validly

A major responsibility of the intercultural educator is to ensure that students' abilities are truly developed by instructional experiences. Many students' abilities are underestimated because their second-language skills do not adequately convey their talents. Sometimes unfamiliarity with the students' culture compounds the language barrier. Validity and bias in testing are addressed in Chapter 7.

Challenging Students to Strive for Excellence as Defined by Their Potential

Teachers tread a fine line between expecting too much of their students, causing frustration on students' part through stress and overwork, and expecting too little by watering down the curriculum, leading to boredom and low academic achievement. Ongoing formative assessment, combined with a sensitive awareness of students' needs and a willingness to be flexible, helps the teacher to monitor and adjust the instructional level to students' abilities.

Teachers' behavior varies with the level of expectation held about the students. Students of whom much is expected are given more frequent cues and prompts to respond to, are asked more and harder questions, are given a longer time to respond, are encouraged to provide more elaborate answers, and are interrupted less often (Good & Brophy, 1984). Teachers tend to be encouraging toward students for whom they have high expectations. They smile at these students more often and show greater warmth through nonverbal responses such as leaning toward the students and nodding their heads as students speak (Woolfolk & Brooks, 1985). The online report *Expectations and Student Outcomes* (Cotton, 1989) is a useful resource in learning about how expectations are communicated to students.

Students' responses to teacher expectations seem to be highly influenced by cultural background and home discourse patterns. Some cultures encourage students to set internal standards of worth, and peer pressure devalues dependence on teachers for approval.

Motivating Students to Become Active Participants in Their Learning

Learner autonomy is a key element of constructivist learning—teachers help students to construct new knowledge, providing scaffolds between what students already know and what they need to learn. Learner autonomy occurs when learners feel that studying is taking place due to their own volition. This autonomy is the basis for self-managed, self-motivated instruction. Such autonomy must be supported in a systematic way by the teacher and curriculum in order for the learner to benefit.

Educators acknowledge that it is impossible to teach learners everything they need to know while they are in class. Therefore, a major aim of classroom instruction should be to equip learners with learning skills they can employ on their own. These include the following:

- Efficient learning strategies
- Identification of their preferred ways of learning
- Skills needed to negotiate the curriculum
- Encouragement to set their own learning objectives
- Support for learners to set realistic goals and time frames
- Skills in self-evaluation (Nunan, 1989, p. 3)

Student autonomy is at risk in the climate of coercive adherence to standardized test scores as the sole criterion of effective instruction. Certainly there is a place for choice in topics and freedom to voice divergent views as the core of democratic schooling (see Giroux & McLaren, 1996).

Encouraging Students to Think Critically

An important aspect of schooling in a democracy is the ability to think for oneself, analyze ideas, separate fact from opinion, support opinions from reading, make inferences, and solve problems. The ability to think critically can enhance self-understanding and help students approach significant issues in life with analytical skills. This includes critical thinking, preparing students to be problem solvers who can analyze, evaluate, synthesize, and design when offered real-life situations—students who can make connections between divergent ideas and face the world with compassion and empathy (Mintz & Yun, 1999). An organized introduction to this complex field, presenting lesson plans that have been remodeled to include critical thinking strategies, is available from www.criticalthinking.org/resources/articles under "Sample Teaching Strategies for K–12 Teachers."

Critical thinking includes the ability to look for underlying assumptions in statements, to detect bias, to identify illogical connections between ideas, and to recognize attempts to influence opinion by means of propaganda. These skills are fundamental to the clear thinking required of autonomous citizens in a democracy.

Helping Students Become Socially and Politically Conscious

"Sociocultural consciousness means understanding that one's way of thinking, behaving, and being is influenced by race, ethnicity, social class, and language" (Kea, Campbell-Whatley, & Richards, 2004, p. 4). Students as well as teachers need to have clarity of vision about their sociocultural identities and their role in the institutions that maintain social and economic distinctions based on social class and skin color.

Political and social consciousness is hard-won. It requires teachers to offer students a forum in which to discuss social and political events without partisan rancor; to investigate issues in the national and local press that have possible multiple perspectives; and to find a way to support students' voices about their lives and feelings. Bulletin boards on which student writing can be posted, weekly current event discussions, and class newsletters are projects that can encourage autonomous student thinking, writing, and discussion.

Marshaling Family and Community Support for Schooling

Family and community involvement supports and encourages students and provides opportunities for families and educators to work together in educating students. Families need to become involved in different settings and at different levels of the educational process. Family members can help teachers to establish a genuine respect for their children and the strengths they bring to the classroom. They can work with their own children at home or serve on school committees. Collaborative involvement in school restructuring includes family and community members who help to set goals and allocate resources.

Parental involvement in the school is influenced by cultural beliefs. The U.S. system was developed from small, relatively homogeneous local schools with considerable community and parental control. The pattern of community and parental involvement continues today with school boards, PTAs, and parent volunteers in the schools. This pattern is not universal outside the United States. In cultures in which teachers are accorded high status, parents may consider it improper to discuss educational matters or bring up issues that concern their children. Many Asian-American parents, for example, have high expectations for their children's academic success, but are reluctant to become involved in the classroom, believing education is the responsibility of the school (Fuller & Olson, 1998).

Other factors that make family involvement difficult are school procedures such as restrictive scheduling for family–teacher conferences and notification to parents that students' siblings are not welcome at school for conferences and other events. These procedures tend to divide families and exclude parents. School staffs can involve the community by talking with parents and community liaisons to work out procedures that are compatible with cultural practices.

Example of Concept: A Parent Fosters Cultural Pride

One Chinese-American parent successfully intervened in a school situation to the benefit of her daughter and her classmates:

After my daughter was teased by her peers because of her Chinese name, I gave a presentation to her class on the origin of Chinese names, the naming of children in China, and Chinese calligraphy. My daughter has had no more problems about her name. What is more, she no longer complains about her unusual name, and she is proud of her cultural heritage. (Yao, 1988, p. 224)

It is important that parents not be used in a compensatory manner or given the message that they need to work to bring their children "up" to the level of an idealized norm. This approach often makes parents feel that they are the cause of their children's failure in school. Attributing students' lack of success to parental failure does not recognize that the school itself may be the culprit by failing to meet students' needs.

Whether parents are willing to come to school is largely dependent on their attitude toward school, a result in part of the parents' own school experiences. This attitude is also a result of the extent to which they are made welcome by the schools. Invitational barriers can exclude parents as well as students. On the other hand, teachers who are willing to reach out to parents and actively solicit information from them about their children and their hopes for their children's schooling are rewarded with a richer understanding of students' potential.

Example of Concept: Cultural Differences in Parent Involvement

A major difference between Russian parents and those from other cultural groups is the assertive way in which Russian parents often approach classroom teachers to inquire about their children's academic progress. Russian parents also approach teachers even though they do not speak English very fluently. The children translate for them as they inquire about homework or progress in class (Gaitan, 2006, p. 60).

Adapted Instruction: Involving Parents as Cultural Mediators

Parents can act as cultural mediators in several ways:

- Establish an explicit open-door policy so parents will know they are welcome.
- Send written information home about classroom assignments and goals, and encourage parents to reply.
- Call parents periodically when things are going well and let them know when they can call you.
- Suggest specific ways parents can help in assignments.
- Get to know the community by visiting the community, and letting parents know when you are available to visit homes or talk at some other location.
- Arrange several parent conferences a year and let parents talk about their child's achievement.
- Solicit parents' views on education through a simple questionnaire, telephone interviews, or student or parent interviews.

Source: Adapted from Banks (2004).

Example of Concept: Parent Training Sessions

Parents of kindergarten English learners at Lillian Elementary School in Los Angeles were invited to two Saturday workshops in October and two more in December, where they were taught by teachers how to help their children learn to recognize alphabet letters and learn sight words such as *here* and *the*.

In a math lesson, teacher Gloria Sigala urged parents to teach their children the concept of a pair, or circles, triangles, and rectangles. Even though many parents are immigrants who work long hours to support their families, educators are seeing that time parents spend helping their children pays off. Teachers say that the kindergarteners are more confident and attentive in class (Quinones, 2008).

Parents and older siblings can be encouraged to work with preschool and school-age children in a variety of activities. Rather than recommending that parents speak English more at home, teachers can encourage parents to verbalize in their home language with children in ways that build underlying cognitive skills. Parents can sit with the child to look at a book, pointing to pictures and asking questions; they can read a few lines and let the child fill in the rest or let the child retell a familiar story. Children can listen to adults discuss something or observe reading and writing in the primary language. Schools can assist communities with implementing literacy or cultural classes or producing a community primary-language newspaper. The school can also educate students and parents on the benefits of learning the home language of the parents and can find ways to make dual-language proficiency a means of gaining prestige at school.

Example of Concept: Home and School Connection

Here one teacher describes the success of a nonfiction publishing party hosted by the students:

Parents and many extended family members came, as did neighbors and youth organization leaders with whom the students were involved. At various places around the room, reports were visible with yellow comment sheets. Visitors could sit at a desk or table, read, and comment on what they had read.

Language was not a barrier: Many parents encouraged their children to read to them in English and translate the stories into the native language. They were proud of the English that their child had learned and proud that the child remembered the native language well enough to translate. Many students encouraged their parents to try saying the name of the objects in the pictures that accompanied many of the reports in English. Everywhere I looked, I saw proud children beaming as they showed their work off to the people they cared about and who cared about them. (Cho Bassoff, 2004, para. 9 and 10)

This chapter has emphasized the important role that teachers can play in learning about their students' communities and cultures and in reducing the culture shock between home and school by working actively toward the creation of culturally responsive instruction. The best way for a teacher to understand culture is first to understand himself or herself and the extent to which mainstream U.S. cultural values are explicitly or implicitly enforced during instruction. A teacher who understands his or her own teaching and learning styles can then ask to what extent each student is similar or dissimilar. This goes a long way toward understanding individual differences.

An understanding of cultural diversity leads to engagement in the struggle for equity and then to a commitment to promoting educational achievement for all students. A variety of activities—ones that appeal to different students in turn—may be the most effective approach. The observation cycle continues as teachers watch students to see *which* approaches meet *whose* needs. The key for the intercultural educator is to be sensitive, flexible, and open. ■

LEARNING MORE

Further Reading

Order a catalog online from the multicultural literature source www.Shens.com. How many crosscultural versions of the Cinderella story do they sell?

Web Search

Using a Webcrawler or a search engine, enter the terms *parent involvement* or *family–school connections.* Make a list of helpful suggestions from the most professional Websites on this topic.

Exploration

Ask several educators how they celebrate the birthday of Dr. Martin Luther King Jr. on the legal holiday of his birth. Find a commemoration in your area and attend. How does this stimulate you to follow the ideals of Dr. King?

Collaboration

View the movie *Stand and Deliver,* which is about the success of Jaime Escalante, the outstanding mathematics teacher at Garfield High School in Los Angeles. Watch the scene two or three times in which a grandmother comes to Escalante's house. Role-play with a friend the elaborate greeting ritual with which Mr. Escalante warmly welcomes the elderly woman. Discuss with a friend or classmate a form of greeting that might be appropriate for an elderly family member who visits a classroom.

PEARSON
myeducationlab
The Power of Classroom Practice
www.myeducationlab.com

The Importance of Culture

In this video, teachers and other English-learner education experts discuss the role of culture in the process of second language acquisition, especially as it plays out in classroom interactions among students and teachers. Various aspects of culture are highlighted, including what people do, think, and believe about what constitutes appropriate ways to interact in the classroom; cultural norms concerning the meaning of eye contact, gestures, and facial expressions; and how much distance to maintain from others during conversations. The importance of learning about and validating students' home cultures is emphasized.

> To access the video, go to MyEducationLab (www.myeducationlab.com), choose the Díaz-Rico and Weed text, and log in to MyEducationLab for English Language Learners. Select the topic Diversity, and watch the video entitled "The Importance of Culture."

Answer the following questions:

1. How would you define "culture"? Provide three examples of how it applies to classroom interactions and student learning.
2. The video emphasizes learning about and validating students' home cultures. Describe several ways you can modify instruction to better involve students' families and their resources.
3. In the video, mention is made of the friction and emotional stress that may occur when cultural norms are violated. Identify one specific cultural aspect that might be a source of friction or stress due to differences between home and school norms. How might you resolve the issue while at the same time respecting the home culture?
4. How can teachers promote tolerance by integrating home and school learning experiences? How can teachers solicit the help of parents as cultural mediators (see the section "Marshaling Family and Community Support for Schooling")?

part five

Policy

Language Policy and Special Populations of English Learners

Language policies and specific program models constitute Part Five. Rather than summarizing the policy "big picture"—at the national or state levels—Chapter 11 begins with the role of the classroom teacher in daily policymaking and proceeds from that level to a more comprehensive overview. Chapter 12 contains a description of the issues surrounding identification and referral of culturally and linguistically diverse (CLD) learners to special school services. (See accompanying figure.)

Model for CLAD Policy: Language Policy and Special Populations of English Learners

Part Four: Culture
- Cultural Diversity in the United States
- The Intercultural Educator
- Culturally Responsive Schooling

Part Two: Instruction
- Oracy and Literacy for English-Language Development
- Content-Area Instruction
- Bilingual Education

Part One: Learning
- Learning about the Learner
- Learning about Language Structure
- Learning about Second-Language Acquisition

Part Five: Policy
- Language Policy
- Special Populations of English Learners

Part Three: Assessment

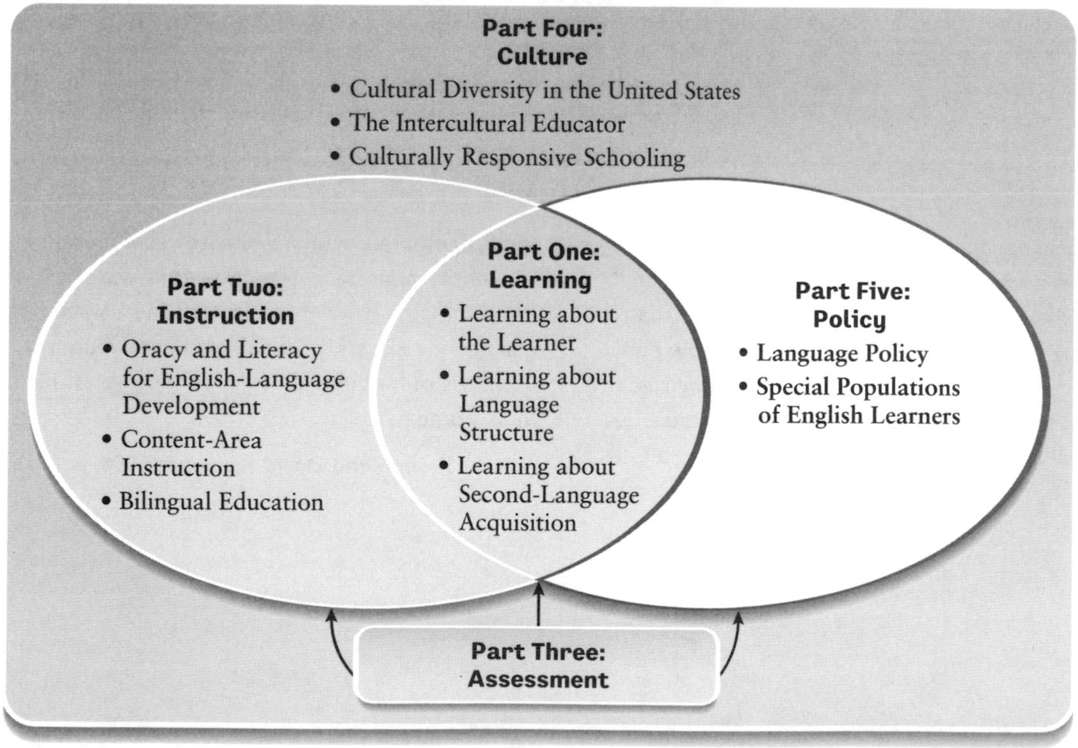

The Role of Educators
in Language Policy

Interacting with the community brings recognition to the student as well as the school.

The teacher had a new student who came from Ethiopia and spoke no English. She could not speak the student's language . . . but rather than allowing him to languish, she chose to allow him to teach the class enough of his native language so that they could all communicate a little bit. . . . The children got excited about discovering a new language. This led to the teacher doing a unit on Africa complete with a wall-size relief mural of the entire continent. The end result was that the Ethiopian student was treated as a valued part of the class. He was able to contribute the richness of his culture while learning about his new home.

Yvonne and David Freeman (1998, p. 124)

Teachers have a significant influence over the daily lives of students in their classroom. They can actively create a climate of warmth and acceptance for culturally and linguistically diverse (CLD) learners, supporting the home language while fostering the growth of a second language. Conversely, they can allow policies of the school to benefit only the students whose language and culture are in the majority by, for example, condoning the exclusive use of the dominant language. This permits majority-language students to gain advantage at the expense of those students who speak minority languages. Teachers make policy day by day, by the actions they take in the classroom, by the professional commitments they honor, and by the stance they take on the importance of their students' primary languages.

Policies about language—and, to a lesser extent, about culture (lesser only because the cultural patterns of schooling are less obvious)—determine the organization and management of schooling (see the figure on page 301). Such factors as class size, allocation of classrooms, availability of primary-language instruction, availability of support services for CLD learners, and funds for curricular materials are determined by policies that are made by decisions at the federal, state, local, or school level. The questions of *who makes policy* and *who influences policy* are important. Can teachers influence policy on a scale larger than their single classroom—on a schoolwide level, on a districtwide level, on the level of a community as a whole, on a statewide or national basis? Or are policy decisions too remote from the daily life of classrooms for teachers to be influential?

Policies can be formal and official, or they can be informal, such as efforts to create and manipulate attitudes toward languages and language variations (Corson, 1990). Both formal and informal policies have an impact on second-language teaching. Like it or not, teachers work under conditions that are highly affected by social and political conditions. Ideally, teachers' decisions further the academic success of English learners. If this is not the case, the academic future of these students is undermined or undone.

This chapter focuses on policy in language matters rather than on the more pervasive topic of cultural matters for two reasons. First, language policy is a current zone of contention for educators, and thus awareness in this area is urgent. Second, cultural patterns of schooling are more difficult to examine and, although equally important to the day-to-day lives of students and teachers alike, are not the subject of current controversy to the extent of such topics as bilingual education. However, the role of teachers in creating and executing policy in this area is also crucial.

A Critical Approach to Language Policy

Several sociologists and social philosophers who study language and society have urged a wider perspective on the social tensions that underlie arguments about the language(s) used in schooling. A critical perspective, one that looks at broad social issues of dual-language proficiency and language policy, has developed from the work of five theorists in particular: James Tollefson, Michel Foucault, Norman Fairclough, Pierre Bourdieu, and Jim Cummins.

Tollefson: Power and Inequality in Language Education

Tollefson (1995) has examined issues of language equity—the social policies and practices that lead to inequity for non-native language speakers—in various international contexts and laid the foundation for a worldwide vision of language equity issues. He contrasted two ways to study language behavior: *descriptive* and *evaluative* (Tollefson, 1991). A descriptive approach seeks to understand the relationship of language behavior and social participation. It examines such linguistic phenomena as *diglossia* (why low-status versus high-status language is used in various contexts); *code shifting* (why bilingual speakers choose one language over another in social contexts); *relations of dominance* (how language is used to establish and maintain social position); and *register shifts* (how the formality/informality of language shapes rules and norms of interaction).

An evaluative approach, on the other hand, looks at such language policy issues as efforts to *standardize* or *purify language,* attempts to *preserve* or *revive endangered languages,* and movements to *establish national languages* or *legislate language usage.* In these separate domains of inquiry, those who study language descriptively focus on language as it is actually used, and those who take an evaluative perspective describe shaping or changing language behavior.

Language diversity can be seen as a problem, as a right, or as a resource (Galindo, 1997; Ruíz, 1984). The view that dual-language proficiency is a *problem* that must be remedied is, at best, socially and economically shortsighted—and, at worst, the foundation for linguistic genocide (defined by Skutnabb-Kangas, 1993, as "systematic extermination of a minority language"; see also Skutnabb-Knagas, 2000). The position that language diversity is a *right* has been the basis for the court cases and congressional mandates that have created bilingual education; however, these movements have probably been successful because of the emphasis on transitional efforts, with bilingual education seen as a right that expires when a student makes the shift into English.

The idea that language diversity is a *resource,* that dual-language proficiency is a valuable asset, is gaining some adherents in the United States, particularly among those who do business with second-language populations in the United States and abroad. Unfortunately, current policy allows a young child's primary language to wither and die and then attempts to create foreign-language proficiency within a three-year high-school program. Many citizens maintain conversational proficiency in a primary language but do not attain a high level of cognitive academic proficiency either in the primary language or in English. The work of Tollefson and his colleagues (see Pennycook, 1994; Skutnabb-Kangas, 2000) has documented that fights for language equity have profound ramifications for social as well as economic policy on a worldwide basis.

Tollefson's work in providing a larger context for viewing the struggles of minority-language speakers is useful in policy settings in which an economic argument is made for English-only schooling (that English-only schooling furthers economic success for English learners). Ironically, English-only schooling will not be as valuable as dual-language proficiency—attaining advanced skills in more than one language—as the source of employment advancement for most job seekers in the coming global economy.

Foucault: The Power of Discursive Practices

Foucault, a twentieth-century social historian, traced the spread of power relations in the modern world, relations that are sustained by means of networks shaped largely by language practices. In several important treatises, Foucault outlined the links between power and language. He documented ways in which authorities have used language to repress, dominate, and disempower social groups in favor of social norms that are favorable to those in power; yet conversely, certain social groups have appropriated or acquired language practices that mimic those in power and thus have shaped power to their own ends. Foucault (1979, 1980) emphasized that the struggle for power is "a struggle for the control of discourses" (Corson, 1999, p. 15). In this same vein, Gramsci (1971) conceptualized social power as hegemonic; that is, people are influenced to follow invisible norms and forms of cultural power, even when it is not to their advantage to do so. Thus, the forms of power that benefit the dominant class influence and shape the behavior of subordinated classes, sometimes to their detriment.

Foucault's contribution to the study of language policy, although indirect, is profound. He has shown that language is not neutral; discursive practices are inseparable from the workings of power, and in fact are the direct vehicle for the circulation of power. Power, however, is neutral; it can be a creative force for those who use discourse masterfully, as well as a destructive force that excludes those without effective language practices.

Fairclough: Critical Language Analysis

Although Foucault laid the foundation for the study of the role of language in the workings of power, Fairclough (1989, 1997) has offered a structured means to analyze linguistic features of discourse in order to discover the power messages that are conveyed. Fairclough conceives of discourse as a nested set of boxes: first, the text itself that constitutes the message; second, the institutional influence on the message; and third, the social/cultural influence on the message. Any text, whether spoken or written, has features at these three levels. These levels constitute the power that the message carries. Fairclough's critical language analysis (CLA) offers tools to tease out the hidden messages of power in a discourse (Table 11.1).

CLA can be used to scrutinize a parent newsletter sent home from an elementary school to Spanish-speaking parents. The intent of the newsletter is to explain to parents how to help their child with homework:

- At the level of text, the newsletter appears to be a word-for-word translation of the reverse side, a letter to English-speaking parents. The text has been written on a word processor, in dual columns like a newspaper. There are no illustrations—merely a page full of text. The content has ten paragraphs, each explaining a different feature of "homework tips."
- At the institutional level, the sheet is part of a "School Open House" packet distributed with about six other papers, some of which are in Spanish and some of which are not. The text was written by an assistant principal and translated by an aide.

Table 11.1

Fairclough's Critical Language Analysis

Box Level	Description	Questions to Ask
First (innermost)	Describes features of the text	In order to read the message "between the lines," ask the following: What is the style of writing, level of vocabulary, complexity of syntax, and tone of the message? What is assumed that the reader knows? What features of gendered language are noticeable? Who is responsible for the actions, opinions, or stance taken in the text? Where did the text originate? What interaction generated it? What is said? What is unsaid but implied? What is the tone of the message?
Second (middle layer)	Probes the institutional influence on the text	To interpret this influence, ask: What social group or agency (a school, television, schooling, friendship, etc.) supplied the context for the message? What was the institutional origin of the message? Who supplied the platform, the paper, the computer, or the microphone? Who stands to benefit from the message? How was the text influenced by an institution?
Third (outermost layer)	Examines the sociocultural context	What sociocultural factors came into play? How did society's attitudes/treatment of age, gender, culture influence the text? How might the text have been different had its origin been a person of different culture, gender, or age? What hidden messages can be understood about this message knowing its social origin?

Source: Adapted from Fairclough (1989).

- At the sociocultural level, the text assumes that the parents welcome the advice of the school authorities and that the parents' role is to help the students complete the assignments sent home by the teachers. There is no mention of a role for parents as collaborating with the teacher to determine the worth or value of the assignments.

In contrast, another teacher works with students to write a "Homework Help" manual, a six-page "little book" composed by students themselves in cooperative groups. Each group decides on a title for their book and brainstorms the book's content. Will it include recommendations of a special place to study at home? Will it mention adequate lighting? Will it discuss how to deal with the distractions of television or of siblings? Will it advise students how to solicit help from parents? Will it advise parents how to communicate to teachers the comparative worth of different types of assignments? Will the book be in more than one language? Each group adds the ideas that the members choose. When the books are ready, the teacher asks each student to take the book home, discuss it with the family, and then come back to class with feedback about whether the suggestions are apt.

Examined with the analytical tools of CLA, these little books are a very different product from the parent newsletter previously described.

- At the level of text, this effort is an individual product, with personalized artwork, student-generated ideas, and student-generated language that is understandable to family members.
- At the institutional level, both the existing habits of the family and the needs of the school are respected, and communication between home and school is built into the project.
- At the sociocultural level, the student is positioned as a consultant on the family's habits and values, and family is positioned as a valued partner in teaching and learning.

Thus, CLA, a structured means of creating awareness of hidden levels of language, can be used to examine assumptions that lie beneath schooling practices. This awareness operates unconsciously but smoothly in skilled power players but is useful as a conscious tool for those who could benefit from an increased understanding of power, particularly as it operates at the institutional and sociocultural levels. As an analytic tool, it is simple yet easy enough to teach to children as they become aware of what is said—and not said—in discourse.

Bourdieu: Language as Social Capital

The French anthropologist Bourdieu considered language to be *cultural capital*—that is, a part of the social "goods" that people accumulate and use to assert power and social class advantage. In a capitalist society, those who are native speakers of a high-status language have cultural capital, whereas those who speak a lower-status language must work hard to overcome the lack of such capital. *Social capital* is a major form of cultural capital. Social capital for children in most middle-class families includes being provided transportation to public libraries, buying additional school-related materials, visiting museums, being given music or art lessons, traveling, having homework supervised, benefitting from tutors, attending school functions, and even moving into the best school districts (Chang, 2005).

Bourdieu (1977) emphasized that schools act as agents of an economic system to reproduce the existing distribution of capital. Schools permit the "haves" (those already possessing cultural capital) to succeed at the expense of the "have-nots," those who are comparatively lacking in the linguistic skills, prior knowledge, or other social

resources to succeed. Education plays a key role in the determination of social success, and permits further understanding of the challenges faced by those whose language skills are not deemed of social importance.

The unique contribution of Bourdieu was his recognition that language, along
with other intangible social factors, is an asset, as are physical resources. In a classroom, a teacher's predilection is to be attracted toward social capital—to those children who already appear to be successful—and to shun those who appear to lack this
attraction. One might also deduce that a teacher's attention, admiration, and reinforcement are therefore aspects of a teacher's social capital that he or she can deploy
at will. Bourdieu placed schooling, with its behaviors and practices, squarely in the
center of the surrounding economic reality, with policies that act as currency—currency
that functions every bit as powerfully as does hard cash.

Cummins: Language Policies as Emancipatory

Cummins (2001) clearly delineated educational practices that function as collaborative relations of power and set these against counterpractices that are coercive in nature. Cummins cautioned that children who enter schools in which diversity is *not*
affirmed soon grasp that their "difference" is not honored but, rather, is suspect. If
students are not encouraged to think critically, to reflect, and to solve problems, they
are being submitted to a "transmission model" of pedagogy. The resulting sense of
reduced worth undermines achievement. Pressuring students to conform, or to participate in schooling practices that are unfair or discriminatory, causes them to lose
their identity as human beings: They are subjected to what Cummins (1989) called
"identity eradication." To counteract this devaluation of students, teachers' and students' roles must be redefined.

Cummins thus took a critical pedagogy stance, in line with Paulo Freire's (1985)
call for a liberating education of "transforming action," in which teachers are dedicated to social change. Unfortunately, many teachers are unaware of the power practices that either help students to develop or hinder them from developing a sense of
control over their own lives. They are equally unaware of the ways in which spoken
and unspoken language can circulate messages of dominance or subordination—
features of institutional racism and disempowerment. Cummins's work, together with
the work of other critical pedagogists, highlights the need for structural changes within
schools that support positive attitudes, strong personal and social identities on the
part of English learners, and academic success.

To summarize the contributions of the critical language theorists, power relations
hidden within language issues are a characteristic of societies around the world. The
tools of the social language critic work to clarify and reveal the covert power relations that language enables. Language is a chief vehicle for deploying power, whether
constructively or destructively. The power potential of any message, verbal or nonverbal, can be systematically analyzed. Language is a kind of social asset, and schools
are agencies through which language is used to benefit or to detract from the accrual
of social wealth. Schooling practices can empower or disempower, depending on the
language and cultural policies within the school.

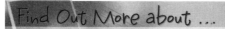

Find Out More about ...

Language Policy in the United States and the World

Language Policy

http://ourworld.compuserve.com/homepages/
JWCRAWFORD/langpol.htm

This article begins with a dictionary definition of *language policy* and then reviews language policy in the United States historically. The author, J.W. Crawford, ends the article with his opinion ("Today, in my view, the central question of U.S. language policy is how we should respond to demographic changes in ways that serve the national interest and uphold our democratic traditions") followed by three questions. The rest of the site provides links to issues in U.S. language policy and to articles and other sites that treat language policy.

Language Policies in Education: Critical Issues

www-writing.berkeley.edu/TESl-EJ/ej20/r11.html

This is an online review of the 2002 book edited by J. W. Tollefson. The initial chapters are described and the four articles that treat language education issues in Asia are examined. Because the book ranges the world, U.S. educators can view language policies in their schools from a broader perspective.

Language Policy: The Classroom

Teachers *can* influence language policy, and those who are experts on the education of English learners *should* be influential. If teachers do not influence policy, decisions will be made by others: by the force of popular opinion, by politicians, by bureaucrats, by demagogues. The influence of teachers will not be felt, however, by wishing or hoping. Teachers need to examine closely the possibilities that exist for influence on policy and then work hard to make this influence a reality. This influence can be wielded by teachers in different ways in various social and political arenas: by monitoring procedures and curricula within the classroom itself, at the school level, and at the level of the local school district; by encouraging support within the community; by working within state commissions and professional organizations; and by lobbying for federal policies that benefit English learners. As Villegas and Lucas (2007) note: "Teaching is an ethical activity, and teachers have an ethical obligation to help all students learn. To meet this obligation, teachers need to serve as advocates for their students, especially those who have been traditionally marginalized in schools" (p. 32).

Educational Equity in Everyday Practices

Equitable educational practices require discipline and vigilant self-observation on the part of classroom teachers (Tollefson, 1991). Practicing gender, socioeconomic, racial, and cultural equity means that males and females from minority and majority races and cultures, whether rich or poor, receive equal opportunity to participate, such as being given equally difficult questions to answer during class discussion, along with adequate verbal and nonverbal support.

Cultural equity calls for teachers to accept students' personalization of instruction; to use multicultural examples to illustrate points of instruction; to listen carefully to the stories and voices of the students from various cultures; and to tie together home and school for the benefit of the students. Issues of socioeconomic equity arise, for example, when assignments for at-home projects are evaluated more highly when they incorporate a wealth of resources that some families can provide and others cannot.

In a democratic classroom, even the teacher must not play an autocratic role, usurping the rights of others to be treated fairly and with respect. As Faltis and Coulter (2008) explain, students must be taught the interpersonal skills they need to solve problems that interfere with learning. In this way, the classroom functions smoothly and the focus is on learning.

Teachers must endeavor to extend the rich, close relationship of mentor and protégé to all students. Referrals to special education on the one hand, and to gifted or enriched instruction on the other, should not unfairly favor or target students of one gender, race, or culture. (If school site or district criteria result in de facto lack of equity in these areas, teachers may need to ask for a review of the criteria.) Practicing "everyday equity" ensures the possibility of equal opportunity for all. The following classroom policies promote inclusion for students:

- Teachers value the experiences of culturally different children.
- The primary language is seen as a worthy subject for instruction and as a means by which students can acquire knowledge.
- Classroom strategies guarantee boys and girls equal access to the teacher's attention.

Marshall and Oliva (2006) sum up the role of socially conscious educators:

School leaders sometimes do equity work when they implement equity-related policies. . . . Some go further, demanding better than the letter of the law, for example, by joining in political coalitions or in legal actions for school finance equity, for the preservation of bilingual programs, and the like. However, the activist, interventionist stance of social justice leadership goes even further, inspired not just by an intellectual ideal, but also by moral outrage at the unmet needs of students and a desire for a caring community where relationships matter. . . . Social justice leadership reconnects with emotional and idealistic stances. It supports leaders' . . . efforts to conceptualize and articulate models of leadership that incorporate democratic community engagement, spirituality and emotion, and caring and compassion. (pp. 7–8)

The Social Environment of the Classroom

Students come to school for social as well as academic reasons. School practices in noncurricular areas, such as discipline, and in extracurricular activities, such as school clubs, should be nondiscriminatory. These activities provide ways in which the school climate can foster or retard students' multicultural competence (Bennett, 2003). If the school climate is accepting of the linguistic and cultural identities of students, these identities will develop in ways that are consonant with an academic environment. If not, a resistance culture may develop that rejects schooling, with outcomes such as high dropout rates and high incidences of school vandalism. The formal and the hidden curriculum of a school need to be consistent with each other so that they support diversity and achievement. The social climate of the school can be one of acceptance for all students in the following ways:

- Culturally and linguistically diverse students are grouped heterogeneously.
- Children and staff learn about the cultural practices of the families represented in the school.
- Students can win prestige positions in extracurricular activities regardless of their ethnic or cultural background.
- Dress codes do not discriminate against some subcultures while allowing others to dress as they wish.
- School staff members (e.g., office personnel) are equally courteous to all students and visitors.

The Policies Embodied in Teachers' Plans

Teachers can be explicit about issues of equity and multicultural inclusion in planning yearly units and daily lessons. Teachers are responsible for obtaining materials that are nonbiased and promote positive role models from a variety of ethnic groups and for designing and planning instruction that makes success possible for all students (see Díaz-Rico, 1993). This responsibility cannot be transferred to other decision-making bodies. Materials are readily available that describe multicultural education (see Bennett, 2003; Harris, 1997; Nieto & Bode, 2008). Teachers can plan for culturally and linguistically fair instruction in the following ways:

- Students' interests and backgrounds are taken into consideration when planning instruction.
- Materials depict individuals of both genders and of various races and cultures in ways that suggest success.
- Materials for bilingual and multicultural instruction receive equitable share of budgeted resources.
- Daily plans include adequate time for development of primary-language skills.

Policy at the School Level

An exemplary teacher's greatest contribution at the school site may be the positive outcomes evident throughout the school as that teacher's students provide leadership, goodwill, and academic models for other students. However, a school site can be the setting for scores of such students when school personnel take explicit roles in school-site decision making.

Collaboration with Colleagues

Schools can benefit greatly when teachers work together. Sharing resources, working together to plan instruction, and teaching with one another add insight and vitality to a job that is often isolating. It is vital that personal relations be established and maintained with all colleagues at a school site to ensure that the staff are not polarized along lines of cultural, linguistic, or philosophical differences. Decisions that are often made collaboratively are the following:

- Extra-duty assignments are adjusted for teachers who must translate letters sent home to parents or develop primary-language materials.
- Primary-language materials and other materials are freely shared among professional staff.
- Primary-language instructors are socially integrated with the mainstream staff.

School-Site Leadership

School authorities, particularly principals, can support ELD and bilingual instruction in many ways. Often, principals are the leading advocates for funding increases at the district level. Principals can work with teachers to configure classes and class sizes to the benefit of English learners. Appointing a lead or mentor teacher can help new teachers adjust to and meet the needs of English learners. Lead teachers may be able to develop professional presentations that showcase student abilities or program features. Districtwide principals' meetings or school board meetings may be venues where these presentations can be seen and heard. By communicating to others about students' abilities as well as innovative program structures for English learners, principals begin to develop a climate of acceptance for linguistic and cultural diversity. This can be accomplished in the following ways:

- Marking policies are monitored to ensure that all students have equal opportunity to receive high grades.
- Staff members who have expertise in English-language development or expertise in primary-language instruction are given time to be of assistance to other teachers.

Find Out More about ...

School-Site Leadership

Professional Development for Teachers in Culturally Diverse Schools

www.cal.org/resources/digest/profdvpt.html

A digest that describes a set of necessary conditions concerning school and district policies in order for teachers to effectively teach second-language learners. In addition, it documents several schools that have successfully restructured their academic programs to include *all* students.

Leading for Diversity: How School Leaders Can Improve Interethnic Relations

www.cal.org/crede/pubs/edpractice/EPR7.htm

A report based on case studies of twenty-one schools across the United States in which the leadership had taken proactive steps to improve relations between the varying student groups. It provides two sample dilemmas and discusses how to assess the school context, set priorities, and develop a plan.

- Teachers with English-language development or primary-language assignments are given an equal share of mentoring and supervisory assistance.
- Leaders in the school set an example of respect and encouragement for diverse language abilities and cultures within the school.

The Academic Ambiance of the School

Schools that are noted for academic excellence attract community attention because of the success of their students and alumni. Academic competitions outside of schools are one way in which certain schools garner academic laurels and gain the reputation for an academic ambiance. The better examples of this type of competition tend to promote problem solving rather than simple recall skills. Competitions that require inventive thinking are also available, and the fact that these are less language dependent may be more attractive to English learners. Schools can foster an academic ambiance in a variety of ways:

- Teachers who sponsor academically oriented extracurricular activities are given extra pay, just as athletic coaches are.
- Funds are available for students to travel to intellectual competitions.
- Individuals from diverse cultural and linguistic backgrounds are actively solicited for teams that compete for academic awards.
- Some intellectual activities such as contests are held in the primary language.

Involving Parents/Families

Encouraging parents and families to participate in school activities is vital. The extra step of sending families letters, reports, and notices in their home language helps to build rapport and extend a welcome to the school. These language policies constitute the daily message that home languages are important and valued. Families can receive the message that they are valued in many ways:

- Representative family committees can advise and consent on practices that involve CLD students.
- Parents/guardians can use the school library to check out books with their children.
- School facilities can be made available for meetings of community groups.

Example of Concept: Involving Families and Communities

A simple invitation invited families, school district employees, local businesses, and community members to Community Literacy Day at the new elementary school in town. Each individual was asked to bring a favorite book to share. A table of book choices was available with volunteers to help match volunteer, book, and grade level. The program was a huge success. Each classroom had several readers, and some visitors went to more than one class (Guth, 2002).

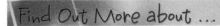

Find Out More about ...

Parental Involvement

Parental Involvement: Title I, Part A
www.ed.gov/programs/titleiparta/parentinvguid.doc

This guidance document from the U.S. Department of Education explains the parental involvement responsibilities of the state and local education agencies and the school under the No Child Left Behind legislation. .

Policy in Local School Districts

The policies of local school districts are shaped by the values of the community. This may create frustration for teachers who feel that educational decisions are not in the hands of educators. On the other hand, teachers who take responsibility for helping to shape the community's beliefs and values may find that their leadership as teachers is very welcome.

Professional Growth and Service

Serving on district curriculum adoption committees is one way in which teachers can share and contribute their expertise. Teacher-led presentations to other teachers, staff, or community members are also important contributions. These activities deliver the message that teachers are knowledgeable and interested in the community at large. Consider the following ideas for teacher involvement:

- Teachers' opinions are consulted for materials purchased by school district and community libraries.
- Teachers participate in leadership training for English-language-development programs.

The School Board

Teachers are very much aware that school policies are determined by the beliefs of school board members as well as by legal precedents set by state and federal laws and

Find Out More about ...

Professional Development

Professional Development for Language Teachers
www.cal.org/resources/digest/0303diaz.html

This digest discusses professional development and lists six strategies for teachers to help them with their development. .

court decisions. Part of the advocacy position suggested by Cazden (1986) is the need for teachers to espouse and support appropriate program for English learners before local boards. In cooperation with parent groups, teachers can be effective in marshaling support for programs designed for language-minority groups. School board policies can be influenced in positive ways:

- Policy committees can place recommendations before the school board in a timely manner, with clear, concise, well-researched presentations.
- Frequent attendance at school board meetings sends the message that the meetings are monitored by those who support language-minority students' achievement.

Community Support for English Learners

A supportive community offers a home for linguistic and cultural diversity. This support takes many forms: affirming variety in neighbors' lifestyles, patronizing minority businesses, fund-raising for college scholarships for English learners, and providing community services that are user-friendly for all.

The Public Forum

Communities accept other languages being spoken in the community if there is little fear of economic or political encroachment by immigrants. By supporting English learners and their rights, teachers can see that situations such as that which occurred in Monterey Park, California, do not recur. A Monterey Park city council member led a fight to halt the use of public funds for the purchase of Chinese-language books for the city's library. The criticism was that these books solely benefit the Chinese community. Those who supported the initiative did not recognize that the Chinese population has as much right to be supported by the government as any other group and that English-speaking Americans studying Chinese might benefit from these books (Dicker, 1992). In this case, local policy was being affected by the linguistic chauvinism of one community leader.

Policies of community agencies such as the library can be influenced by the following teacher-led activities:

- Librarians can file teachers' lesson plans in the library and make specific materials accessible to students.
- Teachers can justify to librarians the need for primary-language materials.
- Teachers can conduct classes open to parents in community arenas, including the library.
- Schools can work together with parents to encourage the use of community resources such as libraries.

Community Organizations

Service organizations are often run by community leaders who set the tone for the community and who are a source of employment for workers. Business leaders sometimes have strong ideas about education. They usually enjoy dialogue with professional educators and seek to be updated on current beliefs and practices. It is in this dialogue that professional educators need to present the foundation for current pedagogy. The leaders of community organizations want to help schools improve so that their children and their workers will be productive. Obtaining this help is easier when requests are concrete and the justification is strong. Ways in which community organizations can interact with schools include the following:

- Sending representatives to school career days to talk about the importance of more than one language in the workplace.
- Establishing partnerships with schools to support activities such as student internships, tutoring, and mentoring.
- Establishing partnerships with school districts to help finance language programs.

State Commissions and Professional Organizations

Outside the immediate community, a larger community awaits. Statewide commissions or state boards of education are opportunities for teachers to be involved in writing statewide curricula, adopting textbooks, and serving on advisory boards. National professional organizations often have state counterparts. Joining Teachers of English to Speakers of Other Languages (TESOL) or the National Association for Bilingual Education (NABE) puts educators in contact with language development specialists nationally and internationally. These organizations' publications carry news from state affiliates, and newsletters from the state organizations carry news of local associations. If there is no local organization, why not start one?

The Voice of the Expert

Attending district or regional professional conferences is a beginning step toward developing one's own expertise on linguistic and cultural issues and teaching practices. Successful teachers may be able to join with colleagues to develop school-level or district-level presentations about a particular area of instruction. Reading articles in professional magazines and journals helps to develop particular expertise, as does advanced university course work. Some journals, such as TESOL's *Essential Teacher* (see www.tesol.org for submission guidelines), and publishers solicit publications from teachers. This is one way to share successful classroom practices.

Professional Leadership Roles

A career is developed over a lifetime. Expertise in particular areas continues to grow along with teaching experience. One can envision a more just and equitable society thirty years from now as today's new teachers reap the harvest of the support for linguistic and cultural diversity that they have promoted. Those who are willing to take responsibility within professional organizations by serving on committees, drafting proposals, attending meetings, calling members, stuffing envelopes, and other activities are those who can be called on to serve in leadership positions. Leadership roles can come in various forms:

- Mentors and other experienced teachers can invite beginning teachers to professional meetings so the organizations can benefit from fresh energy.
- Teachers can start a local affiliation of a national organization.

Legislation and Public Opinion

State and national legislators are responsive to popular opinion as expressed by letters of support and phone calls on controversial issues. Bilingual education and language issues often arouse strong emotions, perhaps because language itself is so closely connected to the soul of a person or because language policies affect the criteria for employment vital to economic survival and success in the United States (Heath, 1983a). Legislators need to hear from professionals in the field to balance the effect of those who perceive language and cultural diversity as a threat. The debate that takes place within a legislature brings to public attention the issues involved in any complex area of public life and allows a public forum for criticizing government policies (Jewell, 1976). The strong backing of professional organizations supports legislators who have the courage to promote dual-language education. Public policy can be supported in the following ways:

- Organizations can send subscriptions to professional magazines to legislative libraries.
- Teachers and parents can organize letter-writing campaigns and visit legislators personally to convey interest in language-minority issues.

Influencing Federal Policies

In countries where more than one language is spoken, rarely do these languages share an equal social status. Speakers of the dominant language are those who make social policy, including language policy. These policies can range from support for the subordinate language, to benign neglect, to overt language suppression. Decisions are primarily made on political and economic grounds and reflect the values of those in political power (Bratt Paulston, 1992). Citizens have a duty to affect these policies.

Federal Funds for Innovation

The U.S. Department of Education provides billions of dollars in grants to states and school districts to improve elementary and secondary schools. With the help of these monies, numerous schools have restructured using dual-language and other enrichment models that actively engage CLD and mainstream students.

Notices about competitions for funds and special programs are usually available from state and county offices of education. By working with district grant specialists, teachers can write successful grant proposals. Individuals who have competed successfully for funding may be willing to offer workshops for others to increase the general expertise in such areas.

Federal Legislation

Programs such as Title III of the No Child Left Behind Act originate in Congress. Part of the Elementary and Secondary Education Act, this legislation must be reauthorized periodically. At such intervals, public opinion plays a large role in determining the continuation of programs that benefit English learners. When bills are introduced that commit federal funds on a large scale to minorities, conservative forces within Congress often target these programs for extinction. At these times, lobbying efforts are needed to communicate the need for these programs.

- Teachers can request that professional organizations send cards and letters to congressional representatives.
- E-mail campaigns can bring critical aspects of pending legislation to the attention of congressional leaders.

The National Spirit

A national spirit is created in part by individuals who voice their opinions freely. A national magazine, for example, offers a platform to writers whose opinions can be influential. Teachers need to exercise their writing skills frequently and at length in order to participate in national arguments that are rehearsed in the media.

Controversial actions and media figures also shape the national spirit. When demagogues arise who voice reactionary or incendiary viewpoints, the population at large must take steps to defuse their voices. Letters to national networks voicing opposition to and distaste for antiminority or racist viewpoints, for example, are necessary in order that these media do not glorify controversial figures and give them undue

---

Find Out More about ...

Grant Proposals and Exemplary Programs

U.S. Department of Education
www.ed.gov/fund/landing.jhtml

Provides links to sites that answer questions about the grant process, enables a search of the Department of Education's programs by topic (for example, English Language Acquisition), and makes available application packages along with information about deadlines and contacts.

School Reform and Student Diversity: Case Studies of Exemplary Practices for LEP Students
www.ncela.gwu.edu/pubs/schoolreform

This article describes programs in eight schools that "have created exemplary learning environments for language-minority students who have limited English proficiency" (Introduction, para. 4). All of them combine LEP program features with more general restructuring.

voice. The United States operates on a system of checks and balances. Those who oppose racism or bigotry must speak up and must speak as loudly as the voices of separation and intolerance. Often, teachers of English learners must become advocates for their concerns until the voices of the minority community become skilled enough to speak for themselves and powerful enough to be heard. Teachers who share the culture and language of the minority community have a natural function as community leaders.

- Teachers can make policymakers aware of the need for workers proficient in more than one language.
- With school administrators, teachers can generate community support to advocate for programs for CLD students.

In a nation consisting of more than 300 million people, the majority of whom share English as the language of daily interchange, the language skills and rights of minorities are a fragile resource. Social and political forces on a national scale may seem overwhelming. Indeed, as much as individualism is a part of the national mythology of the United States, by working together with colleagues and district personnel, by joining and becoming leaders in professional organizations, teachers can exert national influence for constructive change in the education of CLD learners. This constructive change is possible at every level from the national to the local by the use of appropriate professional activities.

At the classroom level where teachers are most comfortable, language policy means creating an educational and social climate that makes school a place where all students are comfortable, where all students meet success in learning. The days are past when the failure of large numbers of CLD learners can be blamed on students' personal shortcomings or supposed deficiencies in family background. When students fail to learn, schools and teachers have failed.

If teachers are willing to step outside the confines of the classroom to help students be successful, then it is time to learn how to influence policy on a larger scale. The belief that teachers have no role in language planning and language politics is a denial of professional responsibility, an abdication of authority. A teacher who believes in the potential for success of CLD learners is in a strong position to fight for the recognition of their rights and the allocation of resources that make educational success possible. ∎

LEARNING MORE

Further Reading

Rebecca Freeman's (2004) *Building on Community Bilingualism* demonstrates how schools that serve bilingual communities can promote English-language development, academic achievement, *and* expertise in other languages. Through an ethnographic account of bilingualism and education in the Puerto Rican community in Philadelphia, she shows how individual teachers and teams of educators have organized their policies, programs, and practices to promote bilingualism through schooling on the local school and school district levels. The book concludes by outlining how educators working in other contexts can develop language policies, programs, and practices that address the needs of the students and communities they serve.

Web Search

The Center for Applied Linguistics' Website (www.cal.org) provides several links to other organizations that deal with public policy and language issues (go to www.cal.org/links/policy.html). In addition, several language policy and planning digests provide insights into what teachers can do (www.cal.org/resources/digest/subject.html).

Exploration

The case studies of the eight exemplary schools in the School Reform and Student Diversity document (www.ncela.gwu.edu/pubs/schoolreform) are divided into the following sections: school and community context; learning environment; curriculum and instructional strategies; program for LEP students; school structure; and district support. Choose one of these areas and examine your school and district according to the model from the article.

Collaboration

Based on your exploration, work with colleagues and your administration to implement some of your findings. Conversely, collaborate with your district grant specialist to work on funding for a program at your site.

PEARSON
myeducationlab
The Power of Classroom Practice
www.myeducationlab.com

Community Support for Culturally Diverse Students and Families

In this video, Christine Slater expresses the need for pre-service teachers to bridge the gap between the school and the community. She discusses the importance of understanding the implications of a network of adults who are associated with each child.

> To access the video, go to MyEducationLab (www.myeducationlab.com), choose the Díaz-Rico and Weed text, and log in to MyEducationLab for English Language Learners. Select the topic Diversity, and watch the video entitled "Community Support for Culturally Diverse Students and Families."

Answer the following questions:

1. It is often a preconceived notion for teachers that mothers and fathers are the only adults in contact with their students. Explain how a community can provide a network of adults that provide support for children.
2. In what ways does the support community impact academic achievement for children learning English as a second language?
3. How can a teacher help to align community and schooling in a more coherent way?

Chapter

12

Culturally and Linguistically Diverse Learners and Special Education

English learners who are blind can achieve communicative competence by interacting with mainstream peers.

Srinivasa Ramanujan was born in 1887 in Erode, a town in southern India. . . . At the age of fifteen, he obtained a copy of Carr's *Synopsis of Elementary Results in Pure and Applied Mathematics,* a collection of 6,000 mathematical theorems. By himself, he verified the results of the 6,000 theorems and began to develop his own. . . . Through private correspondence with a leading mathematician of the time, he obtained a position as a visiting scholar at Cambridge. . . . He published brilliant papers in English and European journals and became the first Indian elected to the Royal Society of London. He died at the age of thirty-three from tuberculosis he contracted in London. . . . [H]e is recognized by mathematicians as one of the most phenomenal geniuses of all time. . . .

If [Ramanujan] had been in a U.S. school as an English learner, would his teacher have referred him to education designated for the gifted and talented?

James R. Newman (1956)

*C*ulturally and linguistically diverse (CLD) learners, as any other cross-section of today's learners, may need special education services. Often, mainstream classroom teachers find themselves responsible for teaching students with special education needs who also need to acquire English. A consultation model introduces constructive ways for teachers of CLD learners and other certified personnel to collaborate in order to meet the needs of such special learners.

> Given the rapid demographic changes that have occurred in schools, communities, and workplaces, a major concern in the field of special education and rehabilitation today is the provision of effective services to multilingual/multicultural diverse populations. . . . [C]hildren and youth of these diverse groups will form a major part of the future workforce in this country. Therefore, the services provided in schools as well as in rehabilitation play an important role in strengthening this workforce for our society. (Chang, 2005)

This chapter includes such topics as identifying CLD learners with special instructional needs, teaming with resource or special education teachers, and teaching strategies for inclusion. The emphasis will be on students who need additional instructional mediation, because those students' needs tend to surface in an obvious way. However, similar principles—if not strategies—can be applied to CLD learners who are gifted and talented.

Researchers who have looked at the special education services available to English learners (e.g., Baca & Cervantes, 1984; Figueroa, 1993; González, 1994) have found a host of issues, including cultural differences as well as language issues.

Both special education and special education–CLD learner interface have come under attack from those who criticize the current models of service delivery. Sleeter (1986) believed that the process that labels certain students as "handicapped" without a critical look at the social and cultural conditions of regular schooling needed to be examined. Stainback and Stainback (1984) advocated that special education and regular education be merged and that all students receive individualized education. Others (Artiles & Trent, 1994; Bernstein, 1989; Figueroa, Fradd, & Correa, 1989) have addressed the over- or underrepresentation of CLD students in special education. Few believe, however, that the current special education system, including the treatment of CLD learners within that system, will undergo vast systemic reform in the near future.

Jesness (2004) outlines the complexity of the situation when special education and ELD are mixed: "Placing learning disabled children in classes designed for English learners is as unethical and harmful as placing English learners in classes meant to serve the learning disabled and mentally challenged" (p. 82). Certainly those who have been educated in English for only a short time deserve an adequate period of adjustment. However, the Individuals with Disabilities Education Act (IDEA) specifically allows referral and placement for English learners and young children with developmental delays, which may include language acquisition.

In their call for a restructuring of bilingual special education, Baca and de Valenzuela (1994) offered three primary goals: (1) Classrooms should conform to the needs of students rather than students conforming to the classroom; (2) efforts should be made to increase the academic performance of CLD special education students; and

(3) teachers should be actively involved throughout the assessment process, with assessment-based curricular adaptations becoming a major part of the intervention process before a student is referred for special education services, and a diagnostic teaching model put in place instead of a remedial approach. These goals provide a direction for the efforts to augment and improve the overall delivery of education to CLD learners. But first, who are these learners? What educational and policy issues does their education raise?

Scenarios and Issues

The issues surrounding culture, learning, and second-language acquisition are complex. The needs of many students can be addressed only with the aid of careful diagnostic work and documentation of student progress. However, many cases involve similar situations and evoke consistent fundamental questions.

Who Are CLD Learners with Special Needs?

Because of the complexity of the issues that underlie special educational services for CLD learners, both personal and academic, it is helpful to personalize these issues with cases drawn from the field. Each scenario does not represent any student in particular but rather a composite of several students created from similar circumstances.

Elisa's Memory. Elisa's third-grade teacher, Stephanie Robinson, is wondering if Elisa has a memory problem. She did not attend kindergarten, and in first grade the instruction was primarily in Spanish. In second grade, the only class taught in English was social studies. Now that she is being asked to learn to read in English, Elisa doesn't seem to remember words that she has read before. When she reads aloud, she can decode most new words adequately but acts as though each word is new each time— there is little sense of recognition or increase in comprehension when she reencounters a word. Mrs. Robinson is just about to make a referral to special education. Does she have adequate grounds for referral?

Losing ELD Services after Referral. Alsumana comes from a family that recently emigrated from Papua New Guinea. His mainstream classroom teacher has successfully made a case for referral to testing, but Ron Patton, his pull-out ELD teacher, is not supportive of this referral because in the past, when a student was placed into a special education environment, that student lost access to ELD services. Because, in Ron's opinion, success in school ultimately depends on the child's acquisition of English, he would like to ensure that CLD learners are not deprived of any other services that would help them. How can he remain involved if Alsumana is placed in special education?

Conflict over Referral. Mrs. Espinoza, the fourth-grade classroom teacher, is struggling with Luke. Luke's parents emigrated from Romania and settled in a rural area in the school district. Luke attends school only reluctantly and says that he would rather be working with his father outdoors. Mrs. Espinoza insists his poor performance in school is due to his attitude toward schooling and not to a learning disability. The school social worker, however, has advocated all year for Luke to be referred for a special education evaluation. During this time, he has made little academic progress. Should he be referred to special education?

Social and Emotional Adjustment. New arrivals are "fresh meat" for the gangs in the area around Bud Kaylor's elementary school. Bud has taught ELD and fifth grade for six years, and although he finds rewards in the challenges of an urban school, he sees the fear and threats that students experience outside the school environment as detrimental to their learning. One student, José Luis, seems overcome by fear in the school setting and never speaks a word. Bud feels that psychological counseling could be a way to deal with the social and emotional problems José Luis seems to be experiencing. Should he refer José Luis for help?

Sonia Doesn't Read. Fifth-grader Sonia is a native-Spanish speaker from the Dominican Republic. She did not attend school until the second grade. She was taught to read in Spanish, but now that she does not have access to Spanish reading instruction, she is falling behind. She attends a resource program, but the resource teacher sees that the problems that show up in English (poor oral language, limited vocabulary development, difficulties with writing, and poor comprehension) limit Sonia's progress. Should Sonia be referred to special education?

Tran the Troubled. Tran is a new student in the fourth grade. His family lives a fairly isolated life in a community of immigrants from Vietnam, but his parents want Tran to grow up speaking English, so they speak to his sister and him in English. However, because the parents both work, they leave Tran for long periods with his grandmother, who speaks only Vietnamese. Tran acts like a dual personality. In class, his performance is uneven; he does not volunteer and does not complete work, yet he seeks constant attention and approval from his teacher. On the playground, his teacher sees in Tran a quick intelligence that comes out when he interacts with the other boys. The teacher is unsure how to handle Tran; he may have a learning disability, but his school problems may be due to extreme cultural differences between home and school. Does she have adequate grounds for referral for psychological testing?

Issues Underlying the Scenarios

Each of these scenarios reflects a particular aspect of the relationship between three distinct domains—learning, second-language acquisition, and special education services in the schools—and these domains are set in a background of cultural issues. Table 12.1 outlines the relationships between the scenarios and underlying issues.

These scenarios and the issues surrounding the education of CLD learners are centered on two basic questions: How can these students' language acquisition, cultural adjustment, and emotional/motivational difficulties be distinguished from learning problems? And how can these issues best be addressed? Special education–CLD learner issues are complex, yet a central dilemma focuses the essential debate: How

Table 12.1

Scenarios and Issues in Special Educational Services for English Learners

Scenario	Issues
Elisa's Memory. Does Elisa, a third-grade student who demonstrates low English reading skills, have a memory problem connected with a learning disability?	At what point is a learning problem considered a language-acquisition delay and not a learning disability?
Losing ELD Services after Referral. Will Alsumana, a recent immigrant, be deprived of ELD services if he is placed in special education?	Should ELD services be available to special education students?
Conflict over Referral. Does Luke's poor performance in school indicate a learning disability, or is it due to his low academic motivation?	What role do family attitudes and values play in the issue of special education referral?
Social and Emotional Adjustment. Should his teacher refer José Luis to psychological counseling to deal with his social and emotional problems in an urban school?	What is the role of psychological counseling in second-language acquisition?
Sonia Doesn't Read. Should Sonia, a fifth-grader with limited prior schooling experience and low English skills, be referred to special education?	What is the role of special education for immigrant students with little prior literacy experience?
Tran the Troubled. Tran's quick intelligence shines on the playground but not in the classroom. Is he learning disabled?	What role does cultural difference play in a case in which a student has classroom learning problems?

can a school district avoid inappropriate referrals and placements yet ensure access for CLD learners who are learning disabled? The ELD–special education interface brings with it a set of collaboration issues. What is the role of the ESL specialist (or the CLAD teacher) in referral, assessment, and subsequent services to students who may be placed in special education?

Principles for the Education of CLD–Special Education Students

Several basic principles characterize fair and effective processes for determining the educational services appropriate for the CLD learner who may be experiencing learning difficulties. These principles may be used to guide initial identification and early intervention, diagnostic evaluation and testing, and, if necessary, placement in a special education learning environment. The principles address five domains: the responsibility of students for learning, students' need for self-knowledge, goals for instruction, relationship of educational services to mainstream instruction, and the need for informed decision making. Table 12.2 presents each of these five domains and its accompanying principle.

Table 12.2

Principles for the Education of English-Learning Special Education Students

Domain	Principle
Responsibility of students for learning	English learners need to become self-responsible, active students who know how to learn. They need linguistic and nonlinguistic strategies, including metalinguistic and metacognitive, that may be generalizable across learning contexts.
Students' need for self-knowledge	Students need to understand their own learning styles and preferences, as well as discover their intrapersonal strengths and weaknesses in a variety of areas, including both linguistic and nonlinguistic (logical-mathematical, musical, and spatial) domains.
Goals for instruction	Students need meaningful and relevant language and academic goals that promote effective communication and learning, in social as well as academic domains.
Relationship of educational services to mainstream instruction	Any education setting must provide educational content and approaches that facilitate students' abilities to make smooth transitions to mainstream instruction.
Need for informed decision making	Educational decisions concerning CLD learners should involve ELD specialists, parents, and other professionals making collaborative, informed judgments that are based on a thorough, fair assessment of the child's language acquisition stage, culture, and individual needs and talents.

Source: Adapted from Wallach and Miller (1988).

The Disproportionate Representation of Culturally and Linguistically Diverse Children in Special Education

The Individual with Disabilities Education Act (IDEA) entitles all individuals with disabilities to a free, appropriate public education (FAPE) and mandates nondiscriminatory assessment, identification, and placement of children with disabilities. The law stipulates that children not be labeled "disabled" if their poor school achievement is due to ethnic, linguistic, or racial difference. Currently, the assessment and placement of CLD students have become major issues in special education (Burnette, 2000), including overidentification (i.e., students are classified into a disability category when they do not have genuine disabilities); underidentification (i.e., students' disabilities are overlooked and not addressed in their educational programs); and misidentification (i.e., students' disabilities are assigned to inappropriate disability categories) (Brusca-Vega, 2002).

Overrepresentation in Disability Programs

In the United States, some ethnic groups continue to be overrepresented in programs for those who are mildly mentally retarded (MMR) or seriously emotionally disturbed (SED). Overrepresentation of CLD learners in MMR programs was the basis for litigation in a number of court cases in the 1970s. The cases addressed the lack of due-process procedural safeguards, improper intelligence testing in the student's second language, and inadequate training of evaluators and special educators, resulting in mandated remedies in these areas (Coutinho & Oswald, 2004).

If the proportion of special education students of a given ethnic background exceeds the proportion of this group in the general population, then overrepresentation is a problem because the educational treatment that students receive is not equivalent to that received by the general student population (Macmillan & Reschly, 1998); because disproportionate placement in special education settings can segregate students by race; and because being labeled as a special education student has potentially negative effects on students' self-esteem and on teachers' perception of students (Valles, 1998).

Although the court cases of the 1970s helped to reduce the number of CLD students being sent into special education classes, recent expansion of disability categories to include mild learning disabilities and developmental delays has resulted in an increase in the number of bilingual students being served in remedial education classes (Connor & Boskin, 2001). Some researchers have cautioned that aptitude (or lack of it) is a cultural construction—cultural groups differ in what is considered a disability. For example, when students do not use expected classroom discourse rules, the teacher may judge them to be disabled.

Example of Concept: Misunderstanding Is Construed as Disability

Mrs. Patterson asked a "known-answer" question to the class to see who had read the science pages assigned as homework. "Who can tell me, in what system is 100 degrees the boiling point of water?" Mario looked down, but Mrs. Patterson was eager to have him participate. "Mario?" she asked. Mario looked up and squinted. "Metr?" he answered softly. Mrs. Patterson shook her head and asked, "Who can help Mario? Is it Fahrenheit or centigrade?" (She thought sadly, *Mario never knows the answer. Maybe he has a learning disability.* But Mario thought, puzzled, *What was wrong with "metric"?*)

Underrepresentation in Gifted Programs

Conversely, CLD students are underrepresented in gifted education with the exception of Asian-American students, who are overrepresented in proportion to the general population in the United States. According to Ryan (2008), African-American, Latino, and Native-American students have been historically underrepresented in gifted programs. These students may be underrepresented by as much as 30 to 70 percent (p. 53). Ford (1998) suggested that the issue of underrepresentation of Hispanic and African-American students is compounded by several problems: the widely differing definitions of *gifted* across the school districts of the United States, the inadequacy of relying solely on standardized tests for admission to such programs, the lack of training on the part of teachers to recognize diverse talents as they nominate students, the confusing nature of the nomination process for minority parents, the lack of self-nomination on the part of minority students, lack of diversity on the part of selection panels, and inadequate training of assessment personnel who act as gate-keepers for gifted programs. The following list provides recommended remediation for underrepresentation (Ford, 1998):

- Use valid identification instruments (for example, Raven's Matrices instead of the Wechsler Scale for Children–Revised).
- Collect multiple types of information from various sources (including both descriptive and quantitative data).
- Provide support services prior to identification (such as help with study skills and time management).
- Train teachers and school personnel on culturally derived learning styles.
- Increase family involvement in identification and support.
- Increase awareness of research on giftedness in minorities.

Identification, Referral, and Early Intervention

Classroom teachers, along with parents and other school-site personnel, are responsible for identifying CLD learners with special instructional needs. When a classroom teacher initially identifies a student who may need additional mediation, a phase of intensive focus begins that may, or may not, result in a placement in special education.

Typically, the most common reasons for referral to special education for English learners are the "high-incidence" diagnoses: learning disability (LD), mild cognitive delays, speech and language delays and disorders, attention-deficit/hyperactivity disorder (ADHD), and/or emotional or behavior disorders (EBD; De la Paz, 2007). However, lack of understanding of cultural and language issues has led some educators to be overly cautious about referring English learners for special education services (Echevarria & Graves, 2007).

The Referral Process: The Roles of the Classroom Teacher and the ELD Specialist

The School Screen Team or otherwise-named entity is a school-site committee that bears responsibility for receiving and acting on an initial referral by the classroom teacher for a student who is in need of additional mediation in learning. The team not only reviews the classroom teacher's specific concerns about the student but also makes suggestions for modifying the learning environment for the student within the regular classroom and provides guidance, training, and assistance in implementing *initial interventions* that may prove helpful in educating the student in question.

How can the classroom teacher decide if a student might have a disability requiring referral to special education? Friend and Bursuck (2006) offered these questions to assist in the decision-making process:

- What are specific examples of a student's needs that are as yet unmet in the regular classroom?
- Is there a chronic pattern that negatively affects learning? Or, conversely, does the difficulty follow no clear pattern?

- Is the student's unmet need becoming more serious as time passes?
- Is the student's functioning significantly different from that of classmates?
- Do you discover that you cannot find a pattern?

One last consideration is the discrepancy between the student's performance in the first and second languages. If the problem does not occur when the child receives instruction in the primary language, it is likely that the situation has resulted from second-language acquisition rather than from a learning disability.

After receiving a referral from the classroom teacher, the school ELD or bilingual specialist, as a member of the team, may be asked to fill out a data sheet containing test data, school history, language preferences, and other information about the student. Thus, this person plays an important role in investigating the following aspects of the CLD learner's case.

Background Experience and Previous School Settings. Does the student have a previous history of difficulty? In this case, contacting a previous teacher and checking records from previously attended schools can provide important background information. A file containing the history of special education services, if it exists, is not routinely transferred with a student unless specifically requested by the receiving school personnel.

Response to the Classroom Environment. Does the student seem uncomfortable or unaccustomed to a classroom environment? A history of previous schooling may uncover evidence of little or no prior schooling.

Cultural and Linguistic Background. The home language survey given on entering a school should properly identify the home language. If the home culture of the CLD learner is new to the classroom teacher, it may be useful to perform an ethnographic study of that culture (see Chapter 9).

Level of Acculturation. Contacting parents to determine the degree of acculturative stress that the family of the student is experiencing can provide important insights. Observing the student interacting with other students, staff, and parents in the home, school, and community can help the specialist identify possible acculturation problems.

Learning Styles. Observation of the student across a variety of academic tasks and content areas may show the need for curricular interventions that provide instructional variety.

Physical Health. The school nurse may provide or obtain a student's health record and developmental history, as well as a record of vision and hearing examinations and determination of overall physical health and diet.

Academic and Learning Problems That CLD Learners May Experience

CLD learners and students with learning disabilities may experience similar difficulties. This creates a challenge to determine whether a learning impairment is due to the students' second-language-acquisition process or to an underlying learning disability that warrants a special education placement. Gopaul-McNicol and Thomas-Presswood (1998) noted the following possible characteristics of CLD learners that may overlap with those of students with learning disabilities.

- *Discrepancies between verbal and nonverbal learning.* Exposure to enriching and meaningful linguistic experiences and activities may have been limited in a student's culture. Nonetheless, the student may have skills in nonlinguistic domains.
- *Perceptual disorders.* If a CLD student's home language is nonalphabetic, he or she may have difficulty with alphabetic letters. If a student was not literate in L1, he or she may have difficulty with sound–symbol relationships.
- *Language disorders.* A student may experience difficulty processing language, following directions, and understanding complex language.
- *Metacognitive deficits.* CLD learners without CALP may process information slowly. If from a nonliterate background, the student may lack preliteracy behaviors and strategies, such as regulatory mechanisms (planning, evaluating, monitoring, and remediating difficulties), or not know when to ask for help.
- *Memory difficulties.* Lack of transfer between the first and second language or limited information retention in the second language may be present.
- *Motor disorders.* Cultural differences and lack of previous education can influence motor performance such as graphomotor (pencil) skills.
- *Social–emotional functioning.* CLD learners may experience academic frustration and low self-esteem. This may lead to self-defeating behaviors such as learned helplessness. Limited second-language skills may influence social skills, friendships, and teacher–student relationships.
- *Difficulty attending and focusing.* CLD learners may exhibit behavior such as distractibility, short attention span, impulsivity, or high motor level (e.g., finger tapping, excessive talking, fidgeting, inability to remain seated). These may stem from cognitive overload when immersed in a second language for a long period of time.
- *Culture/language shock.* Students experiencing culture or language shock may show uneven performance, not volunteer, not complete work, or seek constant attention and approval from the teacher. The emotional reactions to long-term acculturation stress may lead to withdrawal, anger, or a pervasive sense of sadness.
- *Reading dysfunctions.* CLD learners may exhibit a variety of reading problems. These problems may include slow rate of oral or silent reading (using excessive lip movement or vocalization in silent reading); short perceptual span (reading word by word rather than in phrases); mispronunciation, omission, insertion, substitutions, reversals, or repetition of words or groups of words in oral reading; lack of comprehension; and inability to remember what has been read.
- *Written expression skill deficits.* Writing may present an additional area of difficulty for CLD learners, at the level of grammar and usage or at the level of content. Teachers often judge writing as "poor" if it lacks the following characteristics: variety in sentence patterns; variety in vocabulary (choosing correct words and using synonyms); coherent structure in paragraphs and themes; control over usage, such as punctuation, capitalization, and spelling; and evidence that the writer can detect and correct his or her own errors.

One cannot expect a newcomer to English to demonstrate proficiency in these skills immediately. Some writing skills may not be a part of the student's native culture, and thus acquiring these requires acculturation as well as second-language acquisition.

Similarities between Ethnic Language Variations and Learning Disability Symptoms

A systematic analysis of three sets of language users (native-English speakers, CLD learners, and students with learning disabilities) reveals similarities in abilities and dysfunctions between CLD learners and students who are learning disabled. This overlap in language characteristics highlights the difficulty in identifying an English learner as possibly learning disabled. Table 12.3 illustrates the three sets of language abilities

Table 12.3

Similarity in Language Abilities and Disabilities among Standard American English Speakers, English Learners, and Students with Learning Disabilities

Component of Oral Language	Definition	Expectations for Native Speakers of English	English Learners Often . . .	Learning Disabled Students May . . .
Pragmatics	The ability to use and manipulate language (including nonverbal language) in a given context	Know how to use language in a social context and to behave nonverbally with language	Use nonverbal language in a way that they learn from their native culture (e.g., eye contact)	Have difficulties with social rules in communicative exchanges (e.g., turn taking, reading social cues)
Prosody	An understanding of the correct use of rhythm, intonation, and stress patterns of a language	Understand and use different intonation to convey information	Use the intonation curves of sentences in LI when attempting L2	Have prosodic difficulties such as ambiguous intonation
Phonology	The speech sounds that constitute spoken language and the pronunciation rules	Produce and comprehend phonemes normally	Have difficulty with certain L2 phonemes that are not present in their LI	Have difficulty articulating or differentiating language sounds
Syntax	How words are organized to produce meaningful phrases and sentences	Use appropriate sentence structure	Have difficulty with articles, word order in sentences, noun–verb agreement, negation, and verb tenses	Have difficulty in sentence-level comprehension or understanding verb aspects such as mood
Semantics	The meaning of words and sentences	Use words that mean what they want to say	Have difficulties with connotation and denotation of words, as well as understanding *be* verbs	Have difficulty understanding multiple meanings of words or figurative language

Source: Adapted from Gopaul-McNicol and Thomas-Presswood (1998).

and disabilities according to five language components: pragmatics, prosody, phonology, syntax, and semantics.

Early Intervention

The classroom teacher's primary concern is to determine if a student's academic or behavioral difficulties reflect factors other than disabilities, including inappropriate or inadequate instruction. If a student is not responsive to alternative instructional or behavioral interventions over a period of several weeks or months, there is more of a chance that a placement in special education will be necessary (García & Ortiz, 2004; Ortiz, 2002).

The School Screen Team works with the classroom teacher to design intervention strategies that address the CLD learner's second-language-acquisition, language development, and acculturation needs, and decides if formal referral to testing is warranted.

A key to the diagnosis of language-related disorders is the presence of similar patterns in both the primary and the secondary languages. The classroom teacher adopts an experimental attitude, implementing strategies over a period of time and documenting the effect these innovations have on the student in question.

Adapted Instruction: Instructional Modifications for CLD Students

Although many of the strategies recommended below are appropriate for all students, they are particularly critical for CLD students suspected of a learning disability:

- Use reality-based or experiential models that feature visual, auditory, and tactile modeling.
- Teach skills and strategies explicitly (a direct instruction model in conjunction with an experiential approach).
- Focus on content over form.
- Provide understandable input and check frequently for understanding.
- Monitor the student for fatigue.
- Provide "wait time" and "think time."
- Respond positively to communication attempts.
- Use questions appropriate to students' second-language-acquisition stage.
- Explain behavioral expectations.

Source: Adapted from Nemmer-Fanta (2002).

The Web resource ldonline (www.ldonline.org/indepth/bilingual) provides suggestions for teaching English learners with learning disabilities. In addition, other checklists (Aladjem, 2000, www.ncela.gwu.edu/pubs/voices) assist in the initial intervention process. They include, among others, ways to ensure that the prereferral process fits the needs of bilingual learners, that initial assessment has taken place in the students' primary language, that family members have been adequately involved, and that any tests or alternative assessments that have been used are fair and free from linguistic or cultural bias.

Roles of Classroom Teachers and ELD Teachers during the Process of Determining Eligibility for Additional Services

Both classroom teachers and the ELD teacher may play a variety of roles during the process of determining a student's eligibility for additional services:

- *Organizer.* The classroom teacher, with the help of the ELD teacher, organizes student records, records of interventions attempted and the relative success thereof, records of parent contact, and records of contact with other community agencies.
- *Instructor.* The ELD teacher may be able to advise the classroom teacher about adapting learning environments to greater diversity in students' learning styles, devising initial intervention strategies, and using curriculum-based assessment to document student achievement.
- *Investigator.* The ELD teacher or a bilingual paraprofessional may accomplish preliminary testing in the student's L1, study students' culture and language, and interview parents.
- *Mentor to students.* The classroom and ELD teacher may get to know the student and family, suggest a testing environment compatible with the student's culture, and prepare the student for the evaluation process.
- *Colleague.* The ELD teacher and the classroom teacher act as helpful colleagues, sharing expertise about L2 acquisition effects, potential crosscultural misunderstandings, and possible effects of racism or discrimination on CLD learners and families. They collaborate to resolve conflicts, work with translators, and draw on community members for information, additional resources, and parental support. This collaboration is discussed later in this chapter.

Testing for Special Education

The School Screen Team, after reviewing the evidence provided by the classroom teacher and analysis of the early intervention accommodations, approves or denies the request for special education testing. If approved, such testing will take place only after parental approval has been secured in writing. A school psychologist or licensed professional evaluator performs the testing. Figueroa (1989) and the American Psychological Association's Office of Ethnic and Minority Affairs (1991) provided guidelines for the testing of ethnic, linguistic, and culturally diverse populations. Figure 12.1 offers some fundamentals that must be in place to ensure the validity of such testing.

Bilingual students must be tested in both languages to qualify for special education services. The most difficult students to refer to testing are those who may have language delay or mild learning disabilities, aggravated by the need to acquire English

Figure 12.1 Assumptions in Psychological Testing

1. The person administering testing is licensed and certified, and has adequate training concerning the following:
   - Administration, scoring, and interpretation of the test
   - Pitfalls and limitations of a particular test
   - Capability to establish rapport and understand the nonverbal language and cultural beliefs/practices of the person being tested
   - Oral ability in the language of the person or provision made for a trained interpreter
2. Instruments chosen for assessment have norms that represent the population group of the individual being tested.
3. The person being tested understands the words used and can operate from a worldview that understands what is expected from the testing situation.
4. Behavior sampled is an adequate measure of the individual's abilities.

Some caveats about the above assumptions:

1. Translated tests may not be equivalent to their English forms in areas such as content validity and the amount of verbalization that can be expected from different cultures. Even having discrete norms for different languages may not provide norms for different cultures.
2. Many individuals do not have testing experience or experience with test materials, such as blocks or puzzles. Conversely, what they do have expertise in may not be measured in the test. The individual's learning style or problem-solving strategies can be culturally bound.
3. Individuals who have the following characteristics will do well on tests. These are consistent with the dominant U.S. American mainstream culture and may not be present, or may be present to a limited degree, in an individual from another culture:
   - Monochronic orientation: focus on one task at a time
   - Close proximity: can tolerate small interpersonal space
   - Frequent and sustained eye contact
   - Flexibility in response to male or female examiner
   - Individual orientation: motivated to perform well in testing situation
   - Understanding of verbal and nonverbal aspects of majority culture
   - Internal locus of control: taking responsibility for one's own success
   - Field-independent cognitive style: can perceive details apart from the whole
   - Reflective, methodological, analytical cognitive style

Source: Adapted from Gopaul-McNicol and Thomas-Presswood (1998, pp. 46–50).

(Jesness, 2004). Some students may have had their prior schooling interrupted, making assessment of their ability a confusing process. The most important figure in this quandary is the bilingual psychologist, who can administer dual-language evaluation and make a reasoned determination for the student as to what kind of educational program is most appropriate.

The Descriptive Assessment Process

Evaluating CLD learners for possible placement in a special education classroom involves attention to linguistic and cultural factors that may impede the school success of the student. A *descriptive assessment* (Jitendra & Rohena-Díaz, 1996) process in three phases takes these factors into account.

The first phase is descriptive analysis, in which an oral monologue, an oral dialogue, and observation of the student in class are used together to ascertain if the student has a communicative proficiency problem. If this is the case, the assessment may end, and the student may be referred to a speech/language therapist for additional mediation in language development. Alternatively, the student may be referred for additional mediation in language development *and* the evaluation process may continue, indicating that the student has a communicative proficiency problem as well as other problems.

If there is evidence of some other learning problem, the second phase begins—explanatory analysis. The assessor examines extrinsic factors, such as cultural or ethnic background or level of acculturation, that determine if normal second-language-acquisition or crosscultural phenomena can account for the student's learning difficulties. If these factors do not account for the described difficulties, the examination continues to the third phase: assessment for the presence of intrinsic factors, such as a learning disability. This three-phase evaluation process helps to ensure that linguistic and cultural differences receive thoughtful consideration in the overall picture of the student's academic progress.

Family Support for Evaluation

During the evaluation process, the classroom teacher who keeps the family informed about the process reaps the benefit of knowing that family members understand the need for professional assessment and support the student's need for additional mediation of learning. Teacher–family conferences play an important part in sustaining support.

Example of Concept: Helping the Family Understand Their Child's Level of Achievement

Mrs. Said keeps three demonstration portfolio folders for use during family conferences. One folder displays average work for the grade level (all names have been removed from such work samples), one folder displays superior work, and a third folder contains work samples that are below grade level. During conferences, family members compare their child's work with these samples to gain a context for achievement at that grade level. If their child's performance is not at grade level, they often are more willing to support the provision of additional help for their child.

Collaboration among ESL–ELD Resource Teachers and Special Educators

Organizing a collaborative program requires cooperation between professionals who are concerned for the welfare of the student. Teachers can play a variety of collaborative and consultative roles within school contexts, using a variety of problem-solving strategies to design successful ways to create student success.

Definition and Principles of Collaboration

Collaboration is "a style for direct interaction between at least two coequal parties voluntarily engaged in shared decision making as they work toward a common goal" (Friend & Cook, 1996, p. 6). This definition pinpoints several necessary principles: Professionals must treat one another as equals; collaboration is voluntary; a goal is shared (that of finding the most effective classroom setting for the student under consideration); and responsibility is shared for participation, decision making, and resources, as well as accountability for outcomes. These are predicated on a collegial working environment of mutual respect and trust.

Collaboration among Professionals

In a well-designed program for educating English learners, much collaborative planning takes place among staff members. If there is an ELD specialist in the school, that professional often engages in planning with content teachers to integrate content instruction with language-development objectives; with classroom/mainstream teachers in grade-level team meetings; with bilingual teachers to choose complementary materials in the first and second languages; with resource teachers to share diagnostic tools and other forms of assessment; with program, school, and district administrators to design and implement services, offer in-service workshops, and set policies for grading, record keeping, and redesignation; and with curriculum coordinators to create model units of instruction that incorporate content and English-language-development standards (TESOL, 2006).

English-language-development services, whether delivered by the classroom teacher or by an ELD resource teacher, should continue during the period of referral and testing, and then continue if a student receives special education services.

Working with an Interpreter

Teachers who do not share a primary language with the student under consideration may benefit from collaborative relations with an interpreter. However, instructional aides who are hired as teaching assistants should not be automatically pressed into service as translators or interpreters. Interpretation is a professional service that should be provided by trained and certified personnel. Figure 12.2 gives guidelines for successful cooperative relations with interpreters.

Relationship of Continued ELD with Other Services

English-language-development services are a continuing resource for students throughout the initial intervention, testing, and recommendation phases of special education referral. An ELD teacher may work with the student directly, continuing to implement early intervention strategies, or help the student indirectly by working with other teachers, parents, and peers.

Direct Services. Working directly with the student, the ELD teacher may tutor or test the child in the curricular material used in the classroom, or chart daily measures of the child's performance to see if skills are being mastered. The ELD teacher may work

Figure 12.2   How to Work with an Interpreter

1. Meet regularly with the interpreter to facilitate communication, particularly before meeting with a student or parent.

2. Encourage the interpreter to chat with the client before the interview to help determine the appropriate depth and type of communication.

3. Speak simply, avoiding technical terms, abbreviations, professional jargon, idioms, and slang.

4. Encourage the interpreter to translate the client's own words as much as possible to give a sense of the client's concepts, emotional state, and other important information. Encourage the interpreter to refrain from inserting his or her own ideas or interpretations, or from omitting information.

5. During the interaction, look at and speak directly to the client. Listen to clients and watch their nonverbal, affective response by observing facial expressions, voice intonations, and body movements.

6. Be patient. An interpreted interview takes longer.

Source: Adapted from Lopez (2002).

specifically on those areas in which the student requires additional mediation or continue to teach the student as a part of an ELD group in the regular classroom.

Indirect Services. Supplementing the classroom teacher's role, the ELD teacher may consult with other teachers on instructional interventions; devise tests based on the classroom curricula and give instruction on how to develop and use them; show how to take daily measures of a child's academic and social behavior; establish parent groups for discussion of and help with issues of concern; train older peers, parent volunteers, and teacher aides to work with younger children as tutors; and offer in-service workshops for teachers that focus on special interest areas such as curriculum-based assessments, cultural understanding, and second-language-acquisition issues (West & Idol, 1990).

If the evaluation process results in the recommendation of special education services, the ELD teacher helps write the student's individual educational plan (IEP). Collaboration between ELD, special educators, the classroom teacher, parents, and the student is vital to the drafting and approval of an IEP that will result in academic success. The plan for continued ELD services are a part of the document.

Teaching Strategies for the CLD Special Learner

Modified instruction can accommodate different instructional needs within the classroom and foster learning across academic content areas. *Inclusion* is a term often used to describe the provision of instruction within the conventional/mainstream classroom for students with special needs or talents. Although primarily associated with the education of exceptional students, this term has also been used for the varying degrees of inclusion of CLD learners in the mainstream classroom (Florida Department of Education, 2003). The use of this term should not, however, be interpreted as encouraging an indiscriminate overlap of the instruction recommended for CLD learners and that of special education students.

The mainstream classroom of an included student is a rich, nonrestrictive setting for content instruction and language development activities. The three components of an exemplary program for CLD learners—comprehensible instruction in the content areas using primary language and SDAIE, language arts instruction in English, and heritage (primary) language maintenance or development—are present.

The teacher makes every effort for the student to be "as dynamically a part of the class as any student that is perceived as routinely belonging to that class" (Florida Department of Education, 2003, n.p.). Overall, teaching for inclusion features teaching practices that showcase learners' strong points and support the areas in which they may struggle. By using a variety of interactive strategies, teachers have ample opportunity to discover which methods and activities correspond to student success.

The task for the teacher becomes more complex as the increasingly varied needs of students—those who are mainstream (non-CLD/non-special-education), mainstream special education, CLD learner, CLD learner–special education—are mixed in the same classroom. Such complexity would argue that an inclusive classroom be equipped with additional educational resources, such as teaching assistants, lower student to teacher ratio, and augmented budget for instructional materials. The chief resource in any classroom, however, is the breadth and variety of instructional strategies on which the experienced teacher can draw. The following sections suggest multiple strategies in the areas of listening skills, reading, and writing.

Adapting Listening Tasks

Techniques to teach listening skills have been grouped in Table 12.4 into the three phases of the listening process (before listening, during listening, and after listening).

Table 12.4

Strategies for Additional Mediation for Included Students According to the Listening Process

Phase	Strategies
Before listening	• Directly instruct listening strategies.
	• Arrange information in short, logical, well-organized segments.
	• Preview ways to pay attention.
	• Preview the content with questions that require critical thinking.
	• Establish a listening goal for the lesson.
	• Provide prompts indicating that the information about to be presented is important enough to remember or write down.
During listening	• Actively involve students in rehearsing, summarizing, and taking notes.
	• Use purposeful, curriculum-related listening activities.
	• Model listening behavior and use peer models.
	• Teach students to attend to teacher cues and nonverbal signs that denote important information.
	• Use verbal, pictorial, or written prelistening organizers to cue students to important information.
	• Teach students to self-monitor their listening behavior using self-questioning techniques and visual imagery while listening.
After listening	• Discuss content. Use teacher questions and prompts to cue student response (e.g., "Tell me more").
	• Integrate other language arts and content activities with listening as a follow-up.

Source: Adapted from Mandlebaum and Wilson (1989).

Table 12.5

Strategies for Additional Mediation for Included Students According to the Reading Process

Phase	Strategies
Before/into reading	• Preview reading materials to assist students with establishing purpose, activating prior knowledge, budgeting time, and focusing attention. • Explain how new content to be learned relates to content previously learned. • Create vocabulary lists and teach these words before the lesson to ensure that students know these vocabulary words rather than just recognize them. • Ensure that readability levels of the textbooks and trade books used in class are commensurate with the student's language level. • Locate lower-reading-level supplements in the same topic so that tasks can be adapted to be multilevel and multimaterial. • Rewrite material (or solicit staff or volunteers to do so) to simplify the reading level, or provide chapter outlines or summaries. • Tape text reading or have it read orally to a student. Consider the use of peers, volunteers, and/or paraprofessionals in this process.
During/through reading	• Highlight key words, phrases, and concepts with outlines or study guides. • Reduce extraneous noise. • Use visual aids (e.g., charts and graphs) to supplement reading tasks.
After/beyond reading	• When discussing stories, paraphrase material to clarify content. • Encourage feedback from students to check for understanding. • Reteach vocabulary to ensure retention. • Provide the page numbers where specific answers can be found in a reading comprehension/content assignment. • Use brief individual conferences with students to verify comprehension.

Source: Adapted from Smith, Polloway, Patton, and Dowdy (2003).

Adapting Reading Tasks

Reading assignments for inclusion students, listed in Table 12.5, follow the three-part division of the reading process (before reading, during reading, and after reading, alternatively named "into," "through," and "beyond").

Adapting Writing Tasks

Writing is used in two main ways in classrooms: to capture and demonstrate content knowledge (taking notes, writing answers on assignments or tests) and to express creative purposes. If the acquisition of content knowledge is the goal, students can often use a variety of alternatives to writing that avoid large amounts of written work (both in class and homework). In general, teachers of students with special needs in inclusive settings change the response mode to oral when appropriate (Smith, Polloway, Patton, & Dowdy, 2003).

Adapted Instruction: Strategies for Content Writing

- Provide a written outline of key content from lecture notes to reduce the amount of board copying.
- Allow group written responses through projects or reports, with the understanding that each member takes an equal turn in writing.

A Focus on Self-Expression. When students write for self-expression, they should follow a well-defined writing process, with provision for generating ideas, drafting, and peer editing. Students can use a stamp that indicates "first draft" to distinguish drafts from polished, or recopied, versions; this helps to honor rough drafts as well as completed writing. (See Chapter 4 for a discussion of the writing process.)

Adapted Instruction: Strategies for Writing Conventions

- To help CLD learners with spelling, display a word bank on a classroom wall with commonly used words that native speakers would already know.
- Help students select the most comfortable method of writing (i.e., cursive or manuscript).
- For the purpose of improving handwriting, make available an optional calligraphy center where students can practice elegant forms of handwriting, with correct models available of cursive styles.

Adapting Homework Tasks

Special education students, like English learners, may need homework to be adapted to fit their needs:

- Adapted format—shorter assignments, alternative response formats (e.g., oral rather than written)
- Adapted expectations for performance—longer time until due date, grade based on effort rather than performance, provision for extra credit opportunities
- Scaffolded performance—arrangements made for teacher, aide, peer tutor, or study group assistance; auxiliary learning aids sent home with student (calculator, study guides)
- Monitored performance—student checks in frequently with teacher or parent (Hibbard & Moutes, 2006, p. 95)

Example of Concept: Adapting to a Student's Learning Style

Amber, a student in an inclusion classroom, describes what teachers have done to help her learn: "I am a relater and a visual learner. So I get along better if I work in groups, relate ideas, and make pictures of what I learn. After I read a chapter or listen to a lecture, I use something we call 'pegs'—to draw pictures. . . . [W]hen we studied the Bill of Rights, I used it to remember each of the Rights. For example, the first one is a picture of a Jewish man holding a pen. That kicks off peg 1 and reminds me of freedom of religion" (Sands, Kozleski, & French, 2000).

Assessing Student Performance in the Mainstream Classroom

A key feature of instruction for inclusion is continuous student assessment. Ongoing assessment accomplishes three purposes: It evaluates the curriculum using immediate, measurable results; diagnoses which instructional tasks and strategies are responsible for student success; and provides a basis for communicating this success to the student, parents, and collaborating team members. A variety of means are available to assess the success of the student in response to the curriculum, instructional strategies, and psychosocial aspects of the inclusion environment, and to judge if the inclusion placement of the student is appropriate.

Methods of Assessing the Success of Included Students

Direct observation and *analysis of student products* are two ways to assess the success of included students. Direct observation, by the teacher or by a collaborating team member, can determine if the student has opportunities to speak in class, has enough academic engaged time and time to complete assigned tasks, and is receiving teacher feedback that communicates high expectations and immediate contingencies for completion or noncompletion of work, correct responding, or misbehavior.

Analysis of student products can help team members determine which instructional activities have been successful and which may need to be modified. Throughout this process, formative assessment gives students feedback about their performance and ways they can improve.

Assessing Students' Work

For students who need a significantly modified curriculum, the issue of assigning grades should be addressed before the individualized education plan (IEP) is approved. The grading system used for included students should not differ significantly from that used for other students, although alternative grading systems are appropriate as long as the school district ensures that the grading practices and policies are not discriminatory. Teachers working together in the classroom collaborate to establish guidelines for achievement and assign grades. The grading process may include teachers' writing descriptive comments that offer examples of student performance or of certain instructional approaches or strategies that have proven successful, or observations about students' learning styles, skills, effort, and attitude.

The widespread emphasis on standards-based instruction means that grades should reflect student mastery of required material. A nationwide study (Bursuck, Polloway, Plante, Epstein, Jayanthi, & McConeghy, 1996) found that teachers were concerned about grading practices for special education students who are mainstreamed in regular classrooms. Most teachers found pass–fail and checklist-type grades more helpful for students with disabilities than letter and number grades; yet 80 percent of school districts mandate letter grades on report cards. This results in a high percentage of low grades given to included students. Bursuck et al. (1996) recommend that school districts allow multiple grades or multiple coding systems to be used with students who have learning disabilities (i.e., progress reports, grades for effort), perhaps modifying the modality depending on the recipient of the report (parents versus administrators, for example).

Using the Results of Assessment

Ongoing assessment monitors the extent to which the student's IEP is being fulfilled. Assessment activities should be detailed to the greatest extent possible when the IEP is approved so that all members of the collaborating team are aware of their roles and responsibilities. In this way, the results of assessment are immediately compared to the performance stipulated in the IEP and progress is ensured.

Keeping parents informed as full participating members of the collaborating team ensures that they know what they can do at home to assist their child. Persistence and positive feedback in this effort help parents stay motivated and engaged.

Universal Design for Special Populations of English Learners

English learners with special needs include those with learning disabilities and vision, hearing, health, and mobility impairments. These conditions add complexity to the second-language-acquisition challenges these learners face. Educators have begun to view the education of these learners from a unified perspective: Universal Instructional Design (UID), which is based on Universal Design (UD).

Principles of Universal Design, a model from the field of architecture and design, have been used to make products and environments "usable by all people, to the greatest extent possible, without the need for adaptation or specialized design" (Connell, Jones, Mace, Mueller, Mullick, Ostroff, Sanford, Steinfield, Story, & Vanderheiden, 1997, p. 1). The seven principles of Universal Design are as follows:

1. Equitable use (useful to people with diverse abilities)
2. Flexibility in use (accommodates individual preferences and abilities)
3. Simple and intuitive use (easy to understand, regardless of the user's experience, knowledge, language skills, or current concentration level)
4. Perceptible information (necessary information is communicated effectively to the user, regardless of ambient conditions or the user's sensory abilities)
5. Tolerance for error (adverse consequences of accidental or unintended actions are minimized)
6. Low physical effort (efficient, comfortable, and relatively effortless)
7. Size and space for approach and use (affords approach, reach, and manipulation regardless of user's body size, posture, or mobility)

Universal Instructional Design

With an augmented emphasis on learning styles and other learner differences, UD, now called *Universal Instructional Design,* has moved into education. Application of UID goes beyond merely physical access for all students (e.g., wheelchair ramps and sign language translators), ensuring access to information, resources, and tools for students with a wide range of abilities, disabilities, ethnic backgrounds, language skills, and learning styles. Burgstahler (2008) noted that

> Universal Instructional Design principles . . . give each student meaningful access to the curriculum by assuring access to the environment as well as multiple means of representation, expression, and engagement. (p. 1)

Table 12.6 offers an overview of the principles of UID and some suggested applications of these principles in the education of English learners with special needs. UID does not imply that one universal size fits all but rather that a diversity of opportunities will work for many different students.

Table 12.6

Principles of Universal Instructional Design Applied to English Learners with Special Needs

Principle	Definition	Application
Inclusiveness	A classroom climate that communicates respect for varying abilities	Use bilingual signage and Braille bilingual materials; welcome and respect aides and assistants; supply multiple reading levels of texts.
Physical access	Equipment and activities that minimize sustained physical effort, provide options for participation, and accommodate those with limited physical abilities	Use assistive technologies such as screen readers and online dictionaries; make online chatrooms available for deaf and hearing-impaired students.
Delivery methods	Content is delivered in multiple modes so it is accessible to students with a wide range of abilities, disabilities, interests, and previous experiences	Employ a full range of audiovisual enhancement, including wireless headsets and captioned video; build in redundant modes (e.g., audiotaped read-along books, typed lecture notes, and study guides).
Information access	Use of captioned videos and accessible electronic formats; in printed work, use of simple, intuitive, and consistent formats	Ensure that information is both understandable and complete; reduce unnecessary complexity; highlight essential text; give clear criteria for tests and assignments.
Interaction	Accessible to everyone, without accommodation; use of multiple ways for students to participate	Set up both heterogeneous groups (across second-language ability levels) and homogeneous groups (same language-ability level); instruct students on how to secure a conversational turn.
Feedback	Effective prompting during an activity and constructive comments after the assignment is complete	Employ formative assessment for ongoing feedback.
Demonstration of knowledge	Provision for multiple ways students demonstrate knowledge—group work, demonstrations, portfolios, and presentations	Offer different modes to all students so that special-needs students are not the only ones with alternatives.

Source: Adapted from Burgstahler (2002), Egbert (2004), and Strehorn (2001).

Table 12.7

Addressing the Needs of Blind Students

Aspects of Concern	Questions and Suggestions
Understanding degrees of blindness	Is the student partially or totally blind? Residual vision should be used to the maximum extent possible.
Understanding the background	How and when did the student become blind—at the age of eight or nine (certain visual memory will be retained) or blind at birth (ideas and images will be conceived differently)?
Setting up a readers service	Textbooks are usually translated into Braille one chapter at a time, but a pool of volunteers can read to blind students or tape-record books.
Technological help	Computer software can download material and transcribe it into Braille dots. Blind students can use the computer sound synthesis software such as text to speech and voice recognition—some software can be downloaded for free.
In the classroom	Because the blind student cannot see the classroom board, the teacher has to be more vocal and repeat every word put on the board. When plans or diagrams are used, they can be embossed by sticking string to cardboard.
Reactions of other students	Many sighted students come forward willingly to help their blind classmates both in the classroom and in the community.
Teaching tips	Use talking books and taped dialogues for reading comprehension lessons; use real objects in lessons; and use field trips to bring culture, exposure, and experiences to the blind students.

Teaching Blind English Learners

Because 80 percent of learning is visual (Seng, 2005), blind English learners are a special concern. Table 12.7 offers considerations to help teachers who are not trained to teach the blind so they can deliver effective instruction to these students.

Adapted Instruction: Assistive Technology for the Visually Impaired

Reese (2006) describes many ways that ELD programs can accommodate the visually impaired with assistive technology; audio books; and magnifiers, large print, print-enlarging devices, or Braille for written materials. For accessing materials at a distance such as a chalkboard, mildly impaired students can use monocular telescopes or bioptic lenses.

Teaching English Learners with Hearing Impairments

Over 40 percent of school-age deaf and hard-of-hearing students are from ethnically and racially diverse families (Schildroth & Hotto, 1994). Deaf students in the public school setting face the challenge of three different cultures: their own ethnic background, the

Deaf community, and that of mainstream hearing people (Qualls-Mitchell, 2008). Working with such cultural diversity, it is helpful to encourage students to appreciate and respect one another's differences, and to develop an awareness of the needs of others. Using signing, multimodal presentation of information, imagery, and highly motivating materials helps deaf students become active learners. Biographies that represent role models are motivating for all students. Qualls-Mitchell (2008) presents 15 different resources for teachers of hearing-impaired students, including Moore and Panara's (1996) *Great Deaf Americans,* a source book for biographies representing diverse populations.

Hearing loss can be *conductive* (damage or obstruction in the outer or middle ear), *sensorineural* (damage to the inner ear), *mixed* (both of previous), or *central* (involving the central nervous system and/or brain). Each type of hearing loss requires distinct intervention, conductive damage being the easiest to remediate using a hearing aid. Table 12.8 features teaching strategies for those with hearing impairments.

Table 12.8

Instructional Strategies for Students with Hearing Impairments

Services Available

- Speech/language training from a specialist
- Amplification systems
- Interpreter using sign language
- Captioned videotapes and television
- Note-taking assistance
- Instruction for teachers and peers in sign language
- Counseling
- Increased use of visual materials

Classroom Management

- Arrange desks in a semicircle to facilitate speech-reading.
- Reduce distracting ambient noise.
- Speak clearly, with good enunciation.
- Use gestures to facilitate understanding when speaking.

Student–Teacher Interaction

- Seat the student close to the teacher and face the student when talking.
- Speak face to face, using natural speech.

Academic Assistance

- List key points on the chalkboard.
- Use several forms of communication.
- Give short, concise instructions and have the student repeat key points privately to ensure comprehension.
- Appoint a peer buddy to help the student stay abreast of the class during oral reading.

Social Skills Development

- Create opportunities for group work.
- Model patience and respect during communication.
- Teach social cues and unspoken rules of conversation if the student seems to make inappropriate interactions.

Source: Adapted from Pierangelo and Giuliani (2001).

Teaching CLD learners in U.S. classrooms is a challenge on a scale without precedent in modern education. As the social and economic stakes are raised, students who fail to reach their potential represent a loss to society as a whole. Each student—including those with special needs, whether for additional mediation or acceleration of instruction—is a treasure box, with his or her individual and specific talents, cultural background, and life experiences locked inside. Opening this treasure chest and releasing these talents to the world is an educational adventure of the highest order. The teacher with crosscultural, language, and academic development training holds the key. ■

LEARNING MORE

Further Reading

Ask your school or local public librarian for a list of biographies, autobiographies, or other genres that will raise your awareness of a specific disability: autism, attention-deficit/ hyperactivity disorder, or a physical, emotional, or learning disability.

Web Search

Go online to see if the following organizations' Websites offer specific suggestions for the education of CLD students:

- Alexander Graham Bell Association for the Deaf
- American Association for the Deaf-Blind
- American Association on Mental Retardation
- American Council of the Blind
- American Society for Deaf Children
- Autism Society of America, Inc.
- Beach Center on Families and Disability
- Challenge (Attention Deficit Disorder Association)
- Children with Attention Deficit Disorders (ChADD)

Exploration

Visit a special education classroom in which instruction takes place in one or more primary languages. Discuss with the teacher the availability of special education materials in the language(s).

Experiment

Try "Second-Language Lead Me Blindfolded," a variation of the "Lead Me Blindfolded" game, in which a partner leads you around the block blindfolded and you must rely on that partner for cues. Choose a partner who will speak to you only in a foreign language with which you are not familiar as you are led around.

The Inclusive Classroom

With inclusion, students of all abilities are educated together in the general education classroom. Children with special needs are not isolated, but are involved in all aspects of the classroom, curriculum, and learning activities. The classroom diversity that results requires that the teacher function as part of a cooperative team that includes specialists that offer special services.

To access the video, go to MyEducationLab (www.myeducationlab.com), choose the Díaz-Rico and Weed text, and log in to MyEducationLab for English Language Learners. Select the topic Special Needs and Inclusion, and watch the video entitled "The Inclusive Classroom."

Answer the following questions:
1. What are the elements of an effective inclusive classroom for English learners?
2. What can the teacher of culturally and linguistically diverse (CLD) students do to create an effective inclusive classroom?
3. The inclusion of children with special needs adds to the diversity of the classroom. Evaluate the rewards and challenges of an inclusive classroom for culturally and linguistically diverse (CLD) students. Explain your answer.

References

Ada, A. (1989). Los libros mágicos. *California Tomorrow,* 42–44.

Adams, T. L. (2003). Reading mathematics: More than words can say. *The Reading Teacher, 56*(8), 786–795.

Adamson, H. (1993). *Academic competence.* New York: Longman.

Addison, A. (1988, November). Comprehensible textbooks in science for the nonnative English-speaker: Evidence from discourse analysis. *The CATESOL Journal, 1*(1), 49–66.

Adger, C. (2000). School/community partnerships to support language minority student success. *CREDE Research Brief #5.* Santa Cruz, CA: Center for Research on Education, Diversity and Excellence. Retrieved January 26, 2005, from www.crede.org/products/print/research_briefs/rb5.shtml.

Agar, M. (1980). *The professional stranger: An informal introduction to ethnography.* Orlando, FL: Academic Press.

Aladjem, P. (2000). *A suggested guide to the special education pre-referral process for bilingual learners.* Washington, DC: National Clearinghouse for Bilingual Education. Retrieved February 1, 2005, from www.ncela.gwu.edu/pubs/voices/aladjem.pdf.

Alexander v. Sandoval. (2001). 532 US 275, Docket No. 99-1908.

Alexander, S. (1983). *Nadia, the willful.* New York: Dial.

Allan, K. K., & Miller, M. S. (2005). *Literacy and learning in the content areas* (2nd ed.). Boston: Houghton Mifflin.

Allen, E., & Vallette, R. (1977). *Classroom techniques: Foreign languages and English as a second language.* San Diego: Harcourt Brace Jovanovich.

Alvarez, J. (2007). My English. In R. Spack (Ed.), *Guidelines: A cross-cultural reading/writing text* (pp. 30–35). New York: Cambridge University Press.

American Educational Research Association. (2004). English language learners: Boosting academic achievement. *Research Points, 2*(1).

American Psychological Association. (1991). *APA guidelines for providers of psychological services to ethnic, linguistic, and culturally diverse populations.* Retrieved February 10, 2005, from www.apa.org/pi/oema/guide.html.

Amselle, J. (1999). Dual immersion delays English. *American Language Review, 3*(5), 8.

Anderson, L. (2004). From mechanics to meaning through formative peer feedback. *Essential Teacher, 1*(5), 54–56.

Andrews, L. (2001). *Linguistics for L2 teachers.* Mahwah, NJ: Erlbaum.

Anstrom, K. (1996). Federal policy, legislation, and education reform: The promise and the challenge for language minority students. *NCBE Resource Collection Series No. 5.* Washington, DC: NCBE. Retrieved January 28, 2005, from www.ncela.gwu.edu/pubs/resource/fedpol.htm.

Anstrom, K. (1999a). Preparing secondary education teachers to work with English language learners: Mathematics. *NCBE Resource Collection Series No. 13.* Washington, DC: National Clearinghouse for Bilingual Education. Retrieved July 12, 2008, from www.ncela.gwu.edu/pubs/resource/ells/math.htm.

Anstrom, K. (1999b). Preparing secondary education teachers to work with English language learners: Social studies. *NCBE Resource Collection Series No. 12.* Washington, DC: National Clearinghouse for Bilingual Education. Retrieved July 12, 2008, from www.ncela.gwu.edu/pubs/resource/ells/social.htm.

Anti-Defamation League (2004). *The "December dilemma": December holiday guidelines for public schools.* Retrieved May 27, 2008, from www.adl.org/issue_education/december_dilemma_2004.

Aoki, E. (1992). Turning the page: Asian Pacific American children's literature. In V. J. Harris (Ed.), *Teaching multicultural literature in grades K–8* (pp. 109–135). Norwood, MA: Christopher-Gordon.

Appiah, K. A., & Gates, H. L. (2003). *Africana.* New York: Perseus.

Arab American Institute Foundation. (n.d.). *Quick facts about Arab Americans.* Washington, DC: Author. Retrieved January 13, 2005, from www.aaiusa.org/educational_packet.htm.

Arias, I. (1996). *Proxemics in the ESL classroom.* Retrieved September 2, 2004, from http://exchanges.state.gov/forum/vols/vol34/no1/p32.htm.

Artiles, A. J., & Trent, S. C. (1994). Overrepresentation of minority students in special education: A continuing debate. *Journal of Special Education, 27*(4), 410–437.

Asher, J. (1982). *Learning another language through actions: The complete teachers' guidebook*. Los Gatos, CA: Sky Oaks.

Au, K., & Jordan, C. (1981). Teaching reading to Hawaiian children: Finding a culturally appropriate solution. In H. Trueba, G. Guthrie, & K. Au (Eds.), *Culture and the bilingual classroom: Studies in classroom ethnography* (pp. 139–152). Rowley, MA: Newbury House.

August, D., Hakuta, K., & Pompa, D. (1994). *For all students: Limited English proficient students and Goals 2000*. Washington, DC: National Clearinghouse for Bilingual Education.

August, D., & Pease-Alvarez, L. (1996). *Attributes of effective programs and classrooms serving English language learners*. Santa Cruz, CA: Center for Research on Cultural Diversity and Second Language Learning.

Babbitt, N. (1976). *Tuck everlasting*. New York: Bantam Books.

Baca, L., & Cervantes, H. T. (1984). *The bilingual special education interface*. Columbus, OH: Merrill.

Baca, L., & de Valenzuela, J. S. (1994). *Reconstructing the bilingual special education interface*. Retrieved February 9, 2005, from www.ncela.gwu.edu/pubs/pigs/pig20.htm.

Baker, C. (2001). *Foundations of bilingual education and bilingualism* (3rd ed.). Clevedon, Eng.: Multilingual Matters.

Balderrama, M. V., & Díaz-Rico, L. T. (2006). *Teacher performance expectations for educating English learners*. Boston: Allyn & Bacon.

Bandlow, R. (2002). Suburban bigotry: A descent into racism and struggle for redemption. In F. Schultz (Ed.), *Annual editions: Multicultural education 2002–2003* (pp. 90–93). Guilford, CT: McGraw-Hill/Dushkin.

Banks, C. (2004). Families and teachers working together for school improvement. In J. Banks & C. Banks (Eds.), *Multicultural education: Issues and perspectives* (5th ed., pp. 421–442). Hoboken, NJ: Wiley.

Banks, J. (1994). *An introduction to multicultural education*. Boston: Allyn & Bacon.

Barna, L. M. (2007). Intercultural communication stumbling blocks. In R. Spack (Ed.), *Guidelines: A cross-cultural reading/writing text* (pp. 66–74). New York: Cambridge University Press.

Barr, R., Blachowicz, C. L. Z., Bates, A., Katz, C. & Kaufman, B. (2007). *Reading diagnosis for teachers: An instructional approach*. Boston: Pearson.

Barrett, J. (1978). *Cloudy with a chance of meatballs*. New York: Scholastic Books.

Beck, M. (2004). *California standards assessment workbook*. White Plains, NY: Longman.

Beeghly, D. G., & Prudhoe, C. M. (2002). *Litlinks: Activities for connected learning in elementary classrooms*. Boston: McGraw-Hill.

Bennett, C. (2003). *Comprehensive multicultural education: Theory and practice* (5th ed.). Boston: Allyn & Bacon.

Bermúdez, A., & Márquez, J. (1996). An examination of a four-way collaborative to increase parental involvement in the schools. *Journal of Educational Issues of Language Minority Students, 16*. Retrieved January 28, 2005, from www.ncela.gwu.edu/pubs/jeilms/vol16/jeilms1601.htm.

Bernstein, D. K. (1989). Assessing children with limited English proficiency: Current perspectives. *Topics in Language Disorders, 9*, 15–20.

Bielenberg, B., & Wong Fillmore, L. (2004/2005). The English they need for the test. *Educational Leadership, 62*(4), 45–49.

Bigelow, B. (2007). Rethinking the line between us. *Educational Leadership, 64*(6), 47–61.

Bilingual Education Act, Pub. L. No. (90-247), 81 Stat. 816 (1968).

Bilingual Education Act, Pub. L. No. (93-380), 88 Stat. 503 (1974).

Bilingual Education Act, Pub. L. No. (95-561), 92 Stat. 2268 (1978).

Bilingual Education Act, Pub. L. No. (98-511), 98 Stat. 2370 (1984).

Bilingual Education Act, Pub. L. No. (100-297), 102 Stat. 279 (1988).

Bilingual Education Act, Pub. L. No. (103-382) (1994).

Birdwhistell, R. (1974). The language of the body: The natural environment of words. In A. Silverstein (Ed.), *Human communication: Theoretical explorations* (pp. 203–220). Hillsdale, NJ: Erlbaum.

Bitter, G. G., & Legacy, M. E. (2006). *Using technology in the classroom*. Boston: Pearson.

Bitter, G. G., & Pierson, J. M. (2006). *Using technology in the classroom*. Boston: Pearson.

Black, P., Harrison, C., Lee, C., Marshall, B., Wiliam, D. (2004). Working inside the black box: Assessment for learning in the classroom. *Phi Delta Kappan, 86*(1), 9–21.

Bonilla-Silva, E. (2003). *Racism without racists: Colorblind racism and the persistence of racial inequality in the United States*. Lanham, MD: Rowman & Littlefield.

Bourdieu, P. (with Passeron, J.). (1977). *Reproduction in society, education, and culture*. Los Angeles: Sage.

Brahier, D. J. (2009). *Teaching secondary and middle school mathematics* (3rd ed.). Boston: Pearson.

Brandt, R. (1994). On educating for diversity: A conversation with James A. Banks. *Educational Leadership, 51*, 28–31.

Brass, J. J. (2008). Local knowledge and digital movie composing in an after-school literacy program. *Journal of Adolescent & Adult Literacy, 51*(5), 464–473.

Bratt Paulston, C. (1992). *Sociolinguistic perspectives on bilingual education*. Clevedon, Eng.: Multilingual Matters.

Brewer, D., García, M., & Aguilar, Y. F. (2007, September 7). Some children left behind. *Los Angeles Times*, A29.

Brinton, D. (2003). Content-based instruction. In D. Nunan (Ed.), *Practical English language teaching* (pp. 199–224). New York: McGraw Hill.

Brisk, M. E. (1998). *Bilingual education: From compensatory to quality schooling*. Mahwah, NJ: Erlbaum.

Brown, D. (1987). *Principles of language learning and teaching* (2nd ed.). Englewood Cliffs, NJ: Prentice Hall.

Brown, D. (2000). *Principles of language learning and teaching* (4th ed.). Englewood Cliffs, NJ: Prentice Hall.

Bruder, M. B., Anderson, R., Schultz, G., & Caldera, M. (1991). *Ninos especiales* program: A culturally sensitive early intervention model. *Journal of Early Intervention, 15*(3), 268–277.

Brusca-Vega, R. (2002). Disproportionate representation of English language learners in special education. In *Serving English language learners with disabilities: A resource manual for Illinois educators*. Retrieved February 9, 2005, from www.isbe.state.il.us/spec-ed/bilingualmanual2002.htm.

Buckmaster, R. (2000, June 22–28). First and second languages do battle for the classroom. *(Manchester) Guardian Weekly (Learning English* supplement), 3.

Buell, M. Z. (2004). Code-switching and second-language writing: How multiple codes are combined in a text. In C. Bazerman & P. Prior (Eds.), *What writing does and how it does it* (pp. 97–122). Mahwah, NJ: Erlbaum.

Buettner, E. G. (2002). Sentence-by-sentence self-monitoring. *The Reading Teacher, 56*(1), 34–44.

Bunting, E. (1990). *How many days to America? A Thanksgiving story*. New York: Clarion.

Burgstahler, S. (2008). *Creating video products that are accessible to people with sensory impairments*. Retrieved October 27, 2008, from www.washington.edu/doit/Brochures/Technology/vid_sensory.html.

Burgstahler, S. (2002). *Universal design of instruction*. Retrieved January 25, 2005, from www.washington.edu/doit/Brochures/Academics/instruction.html.

Burke, J. (1999). *The English teacher's companion: A complete guide to classrooms, curriculum, and the profession*. Portsmouth, NH: Boynton Cooke.

Burnette, J. (2000). *Assessment of culturally and linguistically diverse students for special education eligibility*. ERIC Clearinghouse on Disabilities and Gifted Education (ED #E604).

Bursuck, W. D., Polloway, E. A., Plante, L., Epstein, M. H., Jayanthi, M., & McConeghy, J. (1996). Report card grading and adaptations: A national survey of classroom practices. *Exceptional Children, 62*, 301–318.

Caine, R. N., Caine, G., McClintic, C., & Klimek, K. (2004). *Brain/mind learning principles in action: The fieldbook for making connections, teaching, and the human brain*. Thousand Oaks, CA: Sage.

Caine, R., & Caine, G. (1994). *Making connections: Teaching and the human brain*. Menlo Park, CA: Addison Wesley.

Calderón, M. (2007). Adolescent literacy and English language learners: An urgent issue. *ESL Magazine, 56*, 9–14.

Calderón, M., & Slavin, R. (2001). Success for all in a two-way immersion school. In D. Christian & F. Genesee (Eds.), *Bilingual Education*. Alexandria, VA: Teachers of English to Speakers of Other Languages.

California Department of Education (CDE). (1992). *Handbook for teaching Korean-American students*. Sacramento: Author.

California Department of Education (CDE). (1994). *Physical education framework*. Retrieved October 18, 2004, from www.cde.ca.gov/ci/cr/cf/allfwks.asp.

California Department of Education (CDE). (1995). Educational Demographics Unit. *Language census report for California public schools*. Sacramento: Author.

California Department of Education (CDE). (1998a). *English-language arts content standards*. Retrieved March 17, 2005, from www.cde.ca.gov/be/st/ss/engmain.asp.

California Department of Education (CDE). (1998b). *Visual and performing arts standards*. Retrieved

October 18, 2004, from www.cde.ca.gov/be/st/ss/vamain.asp.

California Department of Education (CDE). (1999). *Reading/language arts framework for California public schools.* Sacramento: Author. Retrieved September 10, 2004, from www.cde.ca.gov/cdepress/lang_arts.pdf.

California Department of Education (CDE). (2002). *English language development standards.* Sacramento: Author. Retrieved September 10, 2004, from www.cde.ca.gov.

California State Code of Regulations. (1998). *Title 5, Division 1, Chapter 11: English language learner education. Subchapter 4. English language learner education.* Retrieved May 16, 2001, from www.cde.ca.gov/prop227.html.

Canale, M. (1983). From communicative competence to communicative language pedagogy. In J. Richards & R. Schmidt (Eds.), *Language and communication* (pp. 2–27). New York: Longman.

Carkin, G. (2004). Drama and pronunciation. *Essential Teacher, Compleat Links, 1*(5). Retrieved January 27, 2005, from www.tesol.org/s_tesol/sec_document.asp?CID=724&DID=3021.

Carnuccio, L. M. (2004). Cybersites. *Essential Teacher, 1*(3), 59.

Carr, J., & Lagunoff, R. (2006). *The map of standards for English learners, Grades K–5 and Grades 6–12 versions* (5th ed.). San Francisco: WestEd. Retrieved May 30, 2008, from www.wested.org/cs/we/view/rs/796.

Carrasquillo, A., & Rodríguez, V. (2002). *Language minority students in the mainstream classroom.* Clevedon, Eng.: Multilingual Matters.

Cartagena, J. (1991). English only in the 1980s: A product of myths, phobias, and bias. In S. Benesch (Ed.), *ESL in America: Myths and possibilities* (pp. 11–26). Portsmouth, NH: Boynton/Cook.

Casey, J. (2004). A place for first language in the ESOL classroom. *Essential Teacher, 1*(4), 50–52.

Casteñada v. Pickard, 648 F.2d 989 (5th Cir. 1981).

CATESOL. (1998). *CATESOL position statement on literacy instruction for English language learners, grades K–12.* Retrieved September 14, 2004, from www.catesol.org/literacy.html.

Cavanaugh, C. (2006). *Clips from the classroom: Learning with technology.* Boston: Allyn & Bacon.

Cazden, C. (1986). ESL teachers as language advocates for children. In P. Rigg & D. S. Enright (Eds.), *Children and ESL: Integrating perspectives*

(pp. 9–21). Alexandria, VA: Teachers of English to Speakers of Other Languages.

Center for Advanced Research on Language Acquisition. (2001). *K–12 less commonly taught languages.* Retrieved January 12, 2005, from http://carla.acad.umn.edu:591/k12.html.

Center for Research on Education, Diversity, & Excellence. (2002). *Instructional conversation.* Retrieved October 24, 2008, from http://crede.berkeley.edu/Standards/5inst_con.shtml.

Center for Research on Education, Diversity, and Excellence (CREDE). (2004). *Observing the five standards of practice.* Retrieved April 8, 2005, from www.cal.org/crede/pubs/rb11.pdf.

Chamot, A. U., Barnhardt, S., El-Dinary, P. B., & Robbins, J. (1999). *The learning strategies handbook.* White Plains, NY: Longman.

Chamot, A., & O'Malley, J. M. (1994). *The CALLA handbook: Implementing the cognitive academic language learning approach.* Reading, MA: Addison-Wesley.

Chan, L. (2004). The inexorable demand for qualified ESL teachers. *Language Magazine, 3*(6), 30–31.

Chandler, D. (2005). *Semiotics for beginners.* Retrieved January 27, 2005, from www.aber.ac.uk/media/Documents/S4B/semiotic.html.

Chang, B., & Au, W. (2007–2008). Unmasking the myth of the model minority. *Rethinking Schools, 22*(2), 14–19.

Chang, J-M. (2005). *Asian American children in special education: Need for multidimensional collaboration.* Retrieved February 2, 2005, from www.dinf.ne.jp/doc/english/Us_Eu/ada_e/pres_com/pres-dd/chang.htm.

Chesterfield, R., & Chesterfield, K. (1985). Natural order in children's use of second language learning strategies. *Applied Linguistics, 6,* 45–59.

Children's Defense Fund. (2004a). *Defining poverty and why it matters for children.* Retrieved January 15, 2005, from www.childrensdefense.org/familyincome/childpoverty/default.asp.

Children's Defense Fund. (2004b). *Each day in America.* Retrieved January 15, 2005, from www.childrensdefense.org/data/eachday.asp.

Children's Defense Fund. (2004c). *2003 facts on child poverty in America.* Retrieved January 13, 2005, from www.childrensdefense.org/familyincome/childpoverty/basicfacts.asp.

Cho Bassoff, T. (2004). Compleat Links: Three steps toward a strong home–school connection. *Essential*

Teacher, 1(4). Retrieved February 8, 2005, from www.tesol.org/s_tesol/sec_document.asp?CID=658&DID=2586.

Chomsky, N. (1959). Review of B. F. Skinner "Verbal Behavior." *Language, 35,* 26–58.

Christensen, L. (2000). *Reading, writing, rising up: Teaching about social justice and the power of the written word.* Milwaukee, WI: Rethinking Schools.

Civil Rights Act, Pub. L. No. (88-352), 78 Stat. (1964).

Clark, B. (1983). *Growing up gifted: Developing the potential of children at home and at school* (2nd ed.). Columbus, OH: Merrill.

Cloud, N., Genesee, F., & Hamayan, E. (2000). *Dual language instruction.* Boston: Heinle and Heinle.

Cohen, E., Lotan, R., & Catanzarite, L. (1990). Treating status problems in the cooperative classroom. In S. Sharon (Ed.), *Cooperative learning: Theory and research* (pp. 203–229). New York: Praeger.

Coiro, J. (2003). Exploring literacy on the Internet. *The Reading Teacher, 56*(5), 458–460.

Cole, K. (2007). Pressures and promise in the mainstream classroom. In K. Cole, C. Collier, & S. Herrera (Eds.), *Making the right investments: Strengthening the education of English language and bilingual learners: Research conference proceedings* (pp. 3–11). Harrisburg, PA: Center for Schools and Communities.

Cole, M. (1998, April 16). *Cultural psychology: Can it help us think about diversity?* Presentation at the annual meeting of the American Educational Research Association, San Diego.

College Entrance Examination Board. (2003). *National report on college-bound seniors, by race/ethnicity: Selected years, 1986–87 to 2002–03.* Retrieved March 20, 2005, from http://nces.ed.gov/programs/digest/d03/tables/dt131.asp.

Collier, L. (2008). The importance of academic language for English language learners. *The Council Chronicle, 17*(3), 10–13.

Collier, V. (1987). Age and rate of acquisition of second language for academic purposes. *TESOL Quarterly, 21*(4), 617–641.

Collier, V. P. (1995). Acquiring a second language for school. *Directions in Language & Education.* Retrieved April 8, 2005, from www.ncela.gwu.edu/pubs/directions/04.htm.

Conchas, G. Q. (2006). *The color of success: Race and high-achieving urban youth.* New York: Teachers College Press.

Conley, M. W. (2008). *Content area literacy: Learners in context.* Boston: Allyn & Bacon.

Connell, B., Jones, M., Mace, R., Mueller, J., Mullick, A., Ostroff, E., Sanford, J., Steinfield, E., Story, M., & Vanderheiden, G. (1997). *The principles of universal design (Version 2.0).* Retrieved January 25, 2005, from www.design.ncsu.edu.8120/cud/univ_design/principles/udprinciples.htm.

Connor, M. H., & Boskin, J. (2001). Overrepresentation of bilingual and poor children in special education classes: A continuing problem. *Journal of Children and Poverty, 7*(1), 23–32.

Cook, V. (1999). Going beyond the native speaker in language teaching. *TESOL Quarterly, 33*(2), 185–209.

Copeland, L. (2008, March 3). Cold realities take back seat in this classroom. *USA Today,* 9D.

Corson, D. (1990). *Language policy across the curriculum.* Clevedon, Eng.: Multilingual Matters.

Corson, D. (1999). *Language policy in schools: A resource for teachers and administrators.* Mahwah, NJ: Erlbaum.

Cortés, C. (1993). Acculturation, assimilation, and "adducation." *BEOutreach, 4*(1), 3–5.

Cotton, K. (1989). *Expectations and student outcomes.* Retrieved April 6, 2005, from www.nwrel.org/scpd/sirs/4/cu7.html.

Coutinho, M. J., & Oswald, D. P. (2004). *Disproportionate representation of culturally and linguistically diverse students in special education: Measuring the problem.* National Center for Culturally Responsive Educational Systems. Retrieved July 12, 2008, from www.nccrest.org/publications.html.

Cox, K. B. (2008, May 14). Reading a little more closely. Letter to the editor, *Los Angeles Times,* A20.

Crago, M. (1993). Communicative interaction and second language acquisition: An Inuit example. *TESOL Quarterly, 26*(3), 487–506.

Craig, B. A. (1996). Parental attitudes toward bilingualism in a local two-way immersion program. *Bilingual Research Journal, 10*(3 & 4), 383–410.

Crawford, J. (1997). *Best evidence: Research foundations of the Bilingual Education Act.* Retrieved April 8, 2005, from www.ncela.gwu.edu/pubs/reports/bestevidence.

Crawford, J. (1998). *Ten common fallacies about bilingual education.* Retrieved April 8, 2005, from www.cal.org/resources/digest/crawford01.html.

Crawford, J. (1999). *Bilingual education: History, politics, theory, and practice* (4th ed.). Los Angeles: Bilingual Educational Services.

Crawford, J. (2003). *Language legislation in the U.S.A.* Retrieved March 19, 2005, from http://ourworld.compuserve.com/homepages/JWCRAWFORD/langleg.htm.

Crawford, J. (2004a). *Educating English learners: Language diversity in the classroom* (formerly *A bilingual education: History, politics, theory, and practice*). Los Angeles: Bilingual Educational Services.

Crawford, J. (2004b). Has two-way been oversold? *Bilingual Family Newsletter* (Multilingual Matters), *21*(1), 3.

Crawford, L. (1993). *Language and literacy learning in multicultural classrooms.* Boston: Allyn & Bacon.

Criston, L. (1993, May 23). Has he stepped out of the shadow? *Los Angeles Times Calendar,* pp. 6, 70, 72.

Cronin, J., Dahlin, M., Adkins, D., & Kingsbury, G. G. (2007). *The proficiency illusion.* Thomas B. Fordham Institute. Retrieved June 27, 2008, from www.edexcellence.net/detail/news.cfm?news_id=376.

Cummins, J. (1979). Cognitive/academic language proficiency, linguistic interdependence, the optimum age question and some other matters. *Working Papers on Bilingualism, 19,* 121–129.

Cummins, J. (1980). The cross-lingual dimensions of language proficiency: Implications for bilingual education and the optimal age issue. *TESOL Quarterly, 14*(2), 175–187.

Cummins, J. (1981a). Age on arrival and immigrant second language learning in Canada: A reassessment. *Applied Linguistics 2*(2), 132–149.

Cummins, J. (1981b). The role of primary language development in promoting educational success for language minority students. In *Schooling and language minority students: A theoretical framework* (pp. 3–49). Sacramento: California State Department of Education.

Cummins, J. (1984). *Bilingualism and special education: Issues in assessment and pedagogy.* San Diego: College-Hill.

Cummins, J. (1986). Empowering minority students: A framework for intervention. *Harvard Educational Review, 56*(1), 18–36.

Cummins, J. (1989). *Empowering minority students.* Sacramento: California Association for Bilingual Education.

Cummins, J. (2001). *Negotiating identities: Education for empowerment in a diverse society.* Los Angeles: California Association for Bilingual Education.

Cummins, J. (2003). Reading and the bilingual student: Fact and friction. In G. García (Ed.), *English learners reaching the highest level of English literacy* (pp. 2–33). Newark, DE: International Reading Association.

Cummins, J. (2008). *The role of culture in reading instruction.* Presentation at the annual conference of the Teachers of English to Speakers of Other Language.

Cunningham, C. A., & Billingsley, M. (2006). *Curriculum webs: Weaving the web into teaching and learning.* Boston: Pearson.

Curtain, H., & Dahlberg, C. A. (2004). *Language and children—Making the match: New languages for young learners, grades K–8.* Boston: Allyn & Bacon.

Cushner, K. (1999). *Human diversity in action.* Boston: McGraw-Hill.

Dale, T., & Cuevas, G. (1987). Integrating language and mathematics learning. In J. Crandall (Ed.), *ESL through content-area instruction: Mathematics, science, social studies.* Englewood Cliffs, NJ: Regents/Prentice Hall.

Dale, T., & Cuevas, G. (1992). Integrating mathematics and language learning. In P. Richard-Amato & M. Snow (Eds.), *The multicultural classroom* (pp. 330–348). White Plains, NY: Longman.

Dalle, T. S., & Young, L. J. (2003). *PACE yourself: A handbook for ESL tutors.* Alexandria, VA: Teachers of English to Speakers of Other Languages.

Darder, A. (1991). *Culture and power in the classroom.* New York: Bergin and Garvey.

Day, F. A. (1994). *Multicultural voices in contemporary literature: A resource for teachers.* Portsmouth, NH: Heinemann.

Day, F. A. (1997). *Latina and Latino voices in literature for children and teenagers.* Portsmouth, NH: Heinemann.

Day, F. A. (2003). *Latina and Latino voices in literature: Lives and works.* Westport, CT: Greenwood Publishers.

De la Paz, S. (2007). Best practices in teaching writing to students with special needs. In S. Graham, C. A. MacArthur, & J. Fitzgerald (Eds.), *Best practices in writing instruction* (pp. 308–328). New York: Guilford.

Delgado-Gaitan, C., & Trueba, H. (1991). *Crossing cultural borders: Education for immigrant families in America.* London: Falmer Press.

Denver Public Schools. (2002). *Newcomer centers.* Denver, CO: Author.

dePaola, T. (1981). *Now one foot, now the other.* New York: Putnam's.

Derman-Sparks, L., & Anti-Bias Curriculum Task Force. (1988). *Anti-bias curriculum: Tools for em-*

powering young children. Washington, DC: National Association for the Education of Young Children.

Dewitz, P., & Dewitz, P. K. (2003). They can read the words, but they can't understand: Refining comprehension assessment. *The Reading Teacher, 56*(3), 422–435.

Diamond, B., & Moore, M. (1995). *Multicultural literacy.* White Plains, NY: Longman.

Díaz-Rico, L. (1993). From monocultural to multicultural teaching in an inner-city middle school. In A. Woolfolk (Ed.), *Readings and cases in educational psychology* (pp. 272–279). Boston: Allyn & Bacon.

Díaz-Rico, L. T. (2000). Intercultural communication in teacher education: The knowledge base for CLAD teacher credential programs. *CATESOL Journal, 12*(1), 145–161.

Díaz-Rico, L. T. (2008). *Strategies for teaching English learners.* Boston: Allyn & Bacon.

Díaz-Rico, L. T. (2008). *Teaching English learners.* Boston: Allyn & Bacon.

Díaz-Rico, L. T., & Dullien, S. (2004). *Semiotics and people watching.* Presentation at the regional conference of the California Teachers of English to Speakers of Other Languages regional conference, Los Angeles.

Dicker, S. (1992). Societal views of bilingualism and language learning. *TESOL: Applied Linguistics Interest Section Newsletter, 14*(1), 1, 4.

Digest of Education Statistics. (2003a). *College enrollment and labor force status of 2001 and 2002 high school completers, by sex and race/ethnicity: October 2001 and October 2002* (Table 382). Retrieved January 28, 2005, from http://nces.ed.gov/programs/digest/d03/tables/dt382.asp.

Doggett, G. (1986). *Eight approaches to language teaching.* Washington, DC: Center for Applied Linguistics/ERIC Clearinghouse on Languages and Linguistics.

Domenech, D. (2008). Upholding standards. *Language Magazine, 7*(8), 24–26.

Dresser, N. (1993). *Our own stories.* White Plains, NY: Longman.

Dryfoos, J. (1998). *Safe passage: Making it through adolescence in a risky society.* New York: Oxford University Press.

Dudley-Marling, C., & Paugh, P. (2004). *A classroom teacher's guide to struggling readers.* Portsmouth, NH: Heinemann.

Dudley-Marling, C., & Searle, D. (1991). *When students have time to talk.* Portsmouth, NH: Heinemann.

Duran, B. J., Dugan, T., & Weffer, R. E. (1997). Increasing teacher effectiveness with language minority students. *High School Journal, 80*(4), 238–246.

Dutro, S., & Moran, C. (2003). Rethinking English language instruction: An architectural approach. In G. García (Ed.), *English learners reaching the highest level of English literacy* (pp. 227–258). Newark, DE: International Reading Association.

Dyson, M. E. (1996). *Between God and gangsta rap: Bearing witness to black culture.* New York: Oxford University Press.

Echevarria, J., & Graves, A. (2007). *Sheltered content instruction: Teaching English language learners with diverse abilities.* Boston: Allyn & Bacon.

Echevarria, J., Vogt, M. E., & Short, D. (2004). *Making content comprehensible for English language learners: The SIOP model* (2nd ed.). Boston: Allyn & Bacon.

Eckert, A. (1992). *Sorrow in our heart.* New York: Bantam.

Edmonson, M. (1971). *Lore: An introduction to the science of fiction.* New York: Holt, Rinehart and Winston.

EdSource (2008, March). *English learners in California: What the numbers say.* Mountain View, CA: Author.

Egbert, J. (2004). Access to knowledge: Implications of Universal Design for CALL environments. *CALL_EJ Online, 5*(2). Retrieved October 27, 2008, from www.tell.is.ritsumei.ac.jp/callejonline/journal/5–2/egbert.html.

Egbert, J., & Hanson-Smith, E. (2007). *CALL environments: Research, practice, and critical issues* (2nd ed.). Alexandria, VA: Teachers of English to Speakers of Other Languages.

Ehri, L. C. (1995). Phases of development in learning to read words by sight. *Journal of Research in Reading, 18*, 116–125.

Ellis, R. (1988). *Classroom second language development.* New York: Prentice Hall.

Enright, D., & McCloskey, M. (1988). *Integrating English: Developing English language and literacy in the multilingual classroom.* Reading, MA: Addison-Wesley.

Equal Educational Opportunities Act of 1974, Pub. L. No. (93-380), 88 Stat. 514 (1974).

Erickson, F. (1977). Some approaches to inquiry in school-community ethnography. *Anthropology and Education Quarterly, 8*(2), 58–69.

Escalante, J., & Dirmann, J. (1990). The Jaime Escalante math program. *Journal of Negro Education, 59*(3), 407–423.

Fairclough, N. (1989). *Language and power.* New York: Longman.

Fairclough, N. (1997). *Critical discourse analysis: The critical study of language.* Reading, MA: Addison-Wesley.

Faltis, C. J., & Coulter, C. A. (2008). *Teaching English learners and immigrant students in secondary schools.* Upper Saddle River, NJ: Pearson Merrill Prentice Hall.

Farrell, T. S. C. (2006). *Succeeding with English language learners: A guide for beginning teachers.* Thousand Oaks, CA: Corwin.

Feagin, J., & Feagin, C. (1993). *Racial and ethnic relations* (4th ed.). Englewood Cliffs, NJ: Prentice Hall.

Feng, J. (1994). Asian-American children: What teachers should know. *ERIC Digest,* ED 369577.

Figueroa, R. A. (1989). Psychological testing of linguistic minority students: Knowledge gaps and regulations. *Exceptional Children, 56*(2), 145–152.

Figueroa, R. A. (1993). The reconstruction of bilingual special education. *Focus on Diversity, 3*(3), 2–3.

Figueroa, R., Fradd, S. H., & Correa, V. I. (1989). Bilingual special education and this issue. *Exceptional Children, 56,* 174–178.

Finders, M. J., & Hynds, S. (2007). *Language arts and literacy in the middle grades: Planning, teaching, and assessing learning.* Upper Saddle River, NJ: Pearson.

Finnan, C. (1987). The influence of the ethnic community on the adjustment of Vietnamese refugees. In G. Spindler & L. Spindler (Eds.), *Interpretive ethnography of education: At home and abroad* (pp. 313–330). Hillsdale, NJ: Erlbaum.

Fisher, M. (2005). From the coffee house to the schoolhouse: The promise and potential of spoken word poetry in school contexts. *English Education, 37,* 115–131.

Fitzgerald, J. (1999). What is this thing called "balance"? *Reading Teacher, 53*(2), 100–107.

Fitzgerald, J., & Amendum, S. (2007). What is sound writing instruction for multilingual learners? In S. Graham, C. A. MacArthur, & J. Fitzgerald (Eds.), *Best practices in writing instruction* (pp. 289–307). New York: Guilford.

Florida Department of Education. (2003). *Inclusion as an instructional model for LEP students.* Retrieved February 10, 2005, from www.firn.edu/doe/omsle/tapinclu.htm.

Flynt, E. S., & Cooter, R. B. (1999). *The English–-Español reading inventory for the classroom.* Upper Saddle River, NJ: Merrill Prentice Hall.

Ford, D. Y. (1998). The underrepresentation of minority students in gifted education: Problems and promises in recruitment and retention. *Journal of Special Education, 32*(1), 4–14.

Foucault, M. (1979). *Discipline and punish: The birth of the prison.* New York: Vintage Books.

Foucault, M. (1980). *Power/knowledge: Selected interviews and other writings 1971–1977.* New York: Pantheon Books.

Frank, A. (1997). *The diary of Anne Frank* (O. Frank and M. Pressler, Eds.; S. Massotty, Trans.). New York: Bantam.

Freeman, D. E., & Freeman, Y. S. (2004). *Essential linguistics: What you need to know to teach.* Portsmouth, NH: Heinemann.

Freeman, R. (2004). *Building on community bilingualism.* Philadelphia: Caslon.

Freeman, Y., & Freeman, D. (1998). *ESL/EFL teaching: Principles for success.* Portsmouth, NH: Heinemann.

Freire, P. (1985). *The politics of education* (D. Macedo, Trans.). New York: Bergin and Garvey.

Frey, N., & Fisher, D. (2007). *Reading for information in the elementary school: Content literacy strategies to build comprehension.* Upper Saddle River, NJ: Pearson.

Friend, M., & Bursuck, W. D. (2006). *Including students with special needs: A practical guide for classroom teachers* (4th ed.). Boston: Allyn & Bacon.

Friend, M., & Cook, L. (1996). *Interactions: Collaboration skills for school professionals.* White Plains, NY: Longman.

From the Classroom. (1991). Teachers seek a fair and meaningful assessment process to measure LEP students' progress. *Teacher Designed Learning, 2*(1), 1, 3.

Fromkin, V., Rodman, R., & Hyams, N. (2003). *An introduction to language* (7th ed.). Boston: Heinle and Heinle.

Fuller, M., & Olson, G. (1998). *Home-school relations: Working successfully with parents and families.* Boston: Allyn & Bacon.

Funaki, I., & Burnett, K. (1993). *When educational systems collide: Teaching and learning with Polynesian students.* Presentation at the annual conference of the Association of Teacher Educators, Los Angeles.

Furey, P. (1986). A framework for cross-cultural analysis of teaching methods. In P. Byrd (Ed.), *Teaching across cultures in the university ESL program* (pp. 15–29). Washington, DC: National Association of Foreign Student Advisors.

Gaitan, C. D. (2006). *Building culturally responsive classrooms.* Thousand Oaks, CA: Corwin.

Galindo, R. (1997). Language wars: The ideological dimensions of the debates on bilingual education. *Bilingual Research Journal, 21*(2 & 3). Retrieved February 5, 2005, from http://brj.asu.edu/archives/23v21/articles/art5.html#issues.

Gándara, P. (1997). *Review of research on instruction of limited English proficient students.* Davis: University of California, Linguistic Minority Research Institute.

García, E. (2004). The many languages of art. In M. Goldberg (Ed.), *Teaching English language learners through the arts: A SUAVE experience* (pp. 43–54). Boston: Pearson.

García, E. E., & Jensen, B. (2007). Helping young Hispanic learners. *Educational Leadership, 64*(6), 34–39.

García, S. B., & Ortiz, A. A. (2004). *Preventing disproportionate representation: Culturally and linguistically responsive prereferral interventions.* National Center for Culturally Responsive Educational Systems. Retrieved January 25, 2005, from www.nccrest.org/publications.html.

Gardner, H. (1983). *Frames of mind: The theory of multiple intelligences.* New York: Basic Books.

Gardner, R., & Lambert, W. (1972). *Attitudes and motivation in second language learning.* Rowley, MA: Newbury House.

Gass, S. (2000, March 15). *Roundtable on interaction in classroom discourse.* Presentation at the annual meeting of the Teachers of English to Speakers of Other Languages, Vancouver, Canada.

Gass, S., & Selinker, L. (2001). *Second language acquisition.* Mahwah, NJ: Erlbaum.

Gay, G. (1975, October). Cultural differences important in education of black children. *Momentum,* 30–32.

Genesee, F. (Ed.). (1999). *Program alternatives for linguistically diverse students.* Santa Cruz, CA: Center for Research on Education, Diversity and Excellence. Retrieved April 8, 2005, from www.cal.org/crede/pubs/edpractice/Epr1.pdf.

Gibbons, P. (2006). Steps for planning an integrated program for ESL learners in mainstream classes. In P. McKay (Ed.), *Planning and teaching creatively within a required curriculum* (pp. 215–233). Alexandria, VA: Teachers of English to Speakers of Other Languages.

Gibson, M. (1991). Minorities and schooling: Some implications. In M. Gibson & J. Ogbu (Eds.), *Minority status and schooling. A comparative study of immigrant and involuntary minorities* (pp. 357–381). New York: Garland.

Gilbert, J. B. (2006). *Clear speech: Pronunciation and listening comprehension in North American English.* New York: Cambridge University Press.

Gillett, P. (1989a). *Cambodian refugees: An introduction to their history and culture.* Available from New Faces of Liberty/SFSC, P.O. Box 5646, San Francisco, CA 94101.

Gillett, P. (1989b). *El Salvador: A country in crisis.* Available from New Faces of Liberty/SFSC, P.O. Box 5646, San Francisco, CA 94101.

Giroux, H. (1983). Theories of reproduction and resistance in the new sociology of education: A critical appraisal. *Harvard Educational Review, 53,* 257–293.

Giroux, H., & McLaren, P. (1996). Teacher education and the politics of engagement: The case for democratic schooling. *Harvard Educational Review, 56*(3), 213–238.

Glaser, S., & Brown, C. (1993). *Portfolios and beyond: Collaborative assessment in reading and writing.* Norwood, MA: Christopher-Gordon.

Goals 2000: Educate America Act Pub. L. No. (103-227), (1994).

Gollnick, D. M., & Chinn, P. C. (2006). *Multicultural education in a pluralistic society* (7th ed.). Upper Saddle River, NJ: Merrill Prentice Hall.

Gómez v. Illinois State Board of Education, 811 F. 2d 1030 (7th Cir. 1987).

González, V. (1994). Bilingual special voices. *NABE News, 17*(6), 19–22.

Good, T., & Brophy, J. (1984). *Looking in classrooms* (3rd ed.). New York: Harper & Row.

Goodman, K. (1986). *What's whole in whole language?* Portsmouth, NH: Heinemann.

Gopaul-McNicol, S., & Thomas-Presswood, T. (1998). *Working with linguistically and culturally different children.* Boston: Allyn & Bacon.

Gordon, M. (1964). *Assimilation in American life.* New York: Oxford University Press.

Gorman, A., & Pierson, D. (2007, September 13). Not at home with English. *Los Angeles Times,* A1, A17.

Gottlieb, M. (1995). Nurturing student learning through portfolios. *TESOL Journal, 5*(1), 12–14.

Gottlieb, M. (2006). *Assessing English language learners.* Thousand Oaks, CA: Corwin.

Gottlieb, M. (2007). *Teacher's manual for Rigby ELL assessment kit.* Orlando, FL: Harcourt Achieve.

Gottlieb, M. (Prin. Writer). (n.d.). *The language proficiency handbook*. Illinois State Board of Education. Retrieved January 7, 2005, from www.isbe.net/assessment/PDF/lang_pro.pdf.

Graham, C. (1978). *Jazz chants*. New York: Oxford University Press.

Graham, C. (1992). *Singing, chanting, telling tales*. Englewood Cliffs, NJ: Regents/Prentice Hall.

Graham, S., & Harris, K. H. (2005). Improving the writing performance of young struggling writers: Theoretical and programmatic research from the Center on Accelerating Student Learning. *Journal of Special Education, 39*, 19–33.

Gramsci, A. (1971). *Selections from the prison notebooks of Antonio Gramsci* (Q. Hoare & G. N. Smith, Trans. and Eds.). New York: International Publishers.

Grant, C. A., & Sleeter, C. (1986). *After the school bell rings*. Philadelphia: Falmer Press.

Greaver, M., & Hedberg, K. (2001). Daily reading interventions to help targeted ESL and non-ESL students. Retrieved September 17, 2004, from www.fcps.k12.va.us/DeerParkES/TR/reading/reading.htm.

Green, A. (2007, March 12). This class is learning to its own beat. *Los Angeles Times*, B3.

Greene, J. P. (1998). *A meta-analysis of the effectiveness of bilingual education*. Claremont, CA: Tomas Rivera Policy Institute.

Griffin, J., & Morgan, L. (1998). Physical education—WRITE ON! *Strategies, 11*(4), 34–37.

Grognet, A., Jameson, J., Franco, L., Derrick-Mescua, M. (2000). *Enhancing English language learning in elementary classrooms study guide*. McHenry, IL: Center for Applied Linguistics and Delta Systems.

Guillarme, A. M. (2008). *K–12 classroom teaching: A primer for professionals* (3rd ed.). Upper Saddle River, NJ: Pearson Merrill Prentice Hall.

Gunning, T. G. (2005). *Creating literacy: Instruction for all students* (5th ed.). Boston: Allyn & Bacon.

Guth, N. (2002). Community Literacy Day: A new school develops community support. *The Reading Teacher, 56*(8), 234–235.

Hadaway, N. L., Vardell, S. M., & Young, T. A. (2002). *Literature-based instruction with English language learners, K–12*. Boston: Allyn & Bacon.

Hakuta, K. (1986). *Mirror of language*. New York: Basic Books.

Hakuta, K., Butler, Y. G., & Witt, D. (2000). *How long does it take English learners to attain proficiency?* Santa Barbara: University of California Linguistic Minority Research Institute Policy Report 2000–2001.

Hall, E. (1959). *The silent language*. New York: Anchor Books.

Halliday, M. (1975). *Learning how to mean: Explorations in the development of language*. London: Edward Arnold.

Halliday, M. (1978). *Language as a social semiotic*. Baltimore: University Park Press.

Hamayan, E. (1994). Language development of low-literacy students. In F. Genesee (Ed.), *Educating second language children* (pp. 278–300). Cambridge: Cambridge University Press.

Hammond, J. (2006). The potential of peer scaffolding for ESL students in the mainstream class. In P. McKay (Ed.), *Planning and teaching creatively within a required curriculum* (pp. 149–170). Alexandria, VA: Teachers of English to Speakers of Other Languages.

Han, Z. (2004). *Fossilization in adult second language acquisition*. Clevedon, Eng.: Multilingual Matters.

Hancock, C. (1994). Alternative assessment and second language study: What and why? *ERIC Digest*. ED376695.

Hankes, J. E., & Fast, G. R. (Eds.). (2002). *Changing the face of mathematics: Perspectives on indigenous people of North America*. Reston, VA: National Council of Teachers of Mathematics.

Hansen, J. W. (2000). Parables of technological literacy. *Journal of Engineering Technology, 17*(2), 29–31.

Hanson-Smith, E. (1997). *Technology in the classroom: Practice and promise in the 21st century*. Alexandria, VA: Teachers of English to Speakers of Other Languages.

Hardt, U. (1992, Spring). Teaching multicultural understanding. *Oregon English Journal, 13*(1), 3–5.

Harris, P. (2006). Teaching English language learners. *The Council Chronicle* (NCTE) 16(1), 1, 5–7.

Harris, V. (1997). *Teaching multicultural literature in grades K–8*. Norwood, MA: Christopher-Gordon.

Hart, L. (1975). *How the brain works: A new understanding of human learning, emotion, and thinking*. New York: Basic Books.

Hart, L. (1983). *Human brain, human learning*. New York: Longman.

Hayasaki, E. (2004, December 3). Cultural divide on campus. *Los Angeles Times*, A1, A36–A37.

Haycock, K. (2001). Closing the achievement gap. *Educational Leadership, 58*(6), 6–11.

Hayes, C. (1998). *Literacy con cariño: A story of migrant children's success.* Portsmouth, NH: Heinemann.

Haynes, J. (2004, Winter). What effective classroom teachers do. *Essential Teacher, 1*(5), 6–7.

Haynes, J. (2007). The December dilemma and English language learners. *Essential Teacher, 4*(4), 6–7.

Heath, S. (1983a). Language policies. *Society, 20*(4), 56–63.

Heath, S. (1983b). *Ways with words.* Cambridge, Eng.: Cambridge University Press.

Heide, F., & Gilliland, J. (1990). *The day of Ahmed's secret.* New York: Lothrop, Lee, & Shepard.

Heilman, A. W. (2002). *Phonics in proper perspective* (9th ed.). Upper Saddle River, NJ: Merrill Prentice Hall.

Helfand, D. (2005, March 24). Nearly half of Blacks, Latinos drop out, school study shows. *Los Angeles Times,* A1, A26.

Henderson, D., & May, J. (2005). *Exploring culturally diverse literature for children and adolescents.* Boston: Pearson.

Henwood, D. (1997). Trash-o-nomics. In M. Wray, M. Newitz, & A. Newitz, (Eds.), *White trash: Race and class in America* (pp. 177–191). New York: Routledge.

Hernández, B. (2005, January 12). Numerical grades help schools to measure progress. *Los Angeles Times,* B2.

Hernandez, H. (2001). *Multicultural education: A teacher's guide to linking context, process, and content* (2nd ed.). Upper Saddle River, NJ: Merrill Prentice Hall.

Herrell, A. (2000). *Fifty strategies for teaching English language learners.* Upper Saddle River, NJ: Merrill.

Hibbard, K. L., & Moutes, M. (2006). *Instructor's resource manual and test bank for Friend and Bursack's* Including students with special needs. Boston: Allyn & Bacon.

Hibbing, A. N., & Rankin-Erickson, J. L. (2003). A picture is worth a thousand words: Using visual images to improve comprehension for middle school struggling readers. *The Reading Teacher, 56*(8), 758–770.

Hinton, L., & Hale, K. (Eds.). (2001). *The green book of language revitalization in practice.* Burlington, MA: Elsevier.

Hispanic Concerns Study Committee. (1987). *Hispanic concerns study committee report.* Available from National Education Association, 1201 Sixteenth Street NW, Washington, DC 20036.

Hispanic Dropout Project. (1998). *No more excuses: The final report of the Hispanic Dropout Project.* Washington, DC: U.S. Department of Education, Office of the Under Secretary. Retrieved July 12, 2008, from www.ncela.gov/edu/pubs/hdp/.

Hopstock, P. J., & Stephenson, T. (2003). *Descriptive study of services to LEP students and LEP students with disabilities.* Washington, DC: U.S. Department of Education. Retrieved July 12, 2008, from www.ncela.gwu.edu/resabout/research/descriptivestudyfiles.

Howard, G. R. (2007). As diversity grows, so must we. *Educational Leadership, 64*(6), 16–22.

Hruska-Riechmann, S., & Grasha, A. F. (1982). The Grasha-Riechmann Student Learning Scales: Research findings and applications. In J. Keefe (Ed.), *Student learning styles and brain behavior* (pp. 81–86). Reston, VA: National Association of Secondary School Principals.

Hughes, J. (2004). On bridge making. *Essential Teacher, 1*(1), 8–10.

Hymes, D. (1961). The ethnography of speaking. In T. Gladwin & W. Sturtevant (Eds.), *Anthropology and human behavior* (pp. 13–53). Washington, DC: Anthropological Society of Washington.

Idaho Migrant Council v. Board of Education, 647 F. 2d 69 (9th Cir. 1981).

Improving America's Schools Act (IASA). 1994 (P.L. 103-382).

Institute for Education in Transformation. (1992). *Voices from the inside: A report on schooling from inside the classroom.* Available from the Institute for Education in Transformation, Claremont Graduate School, 121 East Tenth St., Claremont, CA 91711-6160.

Ishii, S., & Bruneau, T. (1991). Silence and silences in cross-cultural perspective: Japan and the United States. In L. Samovar & R. Porter (Eds.), *Intercultural communication: A reader* (6th ed., pp. 314–319). Belmont, CA: Wadsworth.

Jacobs, V., Goldberg, M., & Bennett, T. (2004). Experiencing science through the arts. In M. Goldberg (Ed.), *Teaching English language learners through the arts: A SUAVE experience* (pp. 87–98). Boston: Pearson.

Jenks, C., Lee, J. O., & Kanpol, B. (2002). Approaches to multicultural education in preservice teacher education: Philosophical frameworks and models for teaching. In F. Schultz (Ed.), *Annual editions: Multicultural education 2002–2003* (pp. 20–28). Guilford, CT: McGraw-Hill/Dushkin.

Jensen, E. (1998). *Teaching with the brain in mind.* Alexandria, VA: Association for Supervision and Curriculum Development.

Jesness, J. (2004). *Teaching English language learners K–12*. Thousand Oaks, CA: Corwin.

Jewell, M. (1976). Formal institutional studies and language. In W. O'Barr & J. O'Barr (Eds.), *Language and politics* (pp. 421–429). The Hague, Netherlands: Mouton.

Jitendra, A. K., & Rohena-Diaz, E. (1996). Language assessment of students who are linguistically diverse: Why a discrete approach is not the answer. *School Psychology Review, 25*(1), 40–56.

Johnson, D. W., & Johnson, R. T. (1979). Conflict in the classroom: Controversy and learning. *Review of Educational Research, 49*(1), 51–70.

Johnson, D. W., & Johnson, R. T. (1987). *Learning together and alone*. Englewood Cliffs, NJ: Prentice Hall.

Johnson, D. W., & Johnson, R. T. (1994). Constructive conflict in the schools. *Journal of Social Issues, 50*(1), 117–137.

Johnson, D. W., & Johnson, R. T. (1995). Why violence prevention programs don't work—and what does. *Educational Leadership, 52*(5), 63–68.

Johnson, D. W., Johnson, R. T., Dudley, B., & Acikgoz, K. (1994). Effects of conflict resolution training on elementary school students. *Journal of Social Psychology, 134*(6), 803–817.

Jonassen, D. H. (2006). *Modeling with technology: Mindtools for conceptual change* (3rd ed.). Upper Saddle River, NJ: Pearson/Merrill/Prentice Hall.

Jones, J. (1981). The concept of racism and its changing reality. In B. Bowser & R. Hunt (Eds.), *Impacts of racism on white Americans* (pp. 27–49). Beverly Hills, CA: Sage.

Julian, L. (2007, October 28). TAKS: Bar set so low, it hurts kids. *Houston Chronicle*, E1, E4.

Jussim, L. (1986). Self-fulfilling prophecies: A theoretical and integrative review. *Psychological Review, 93*(4), 429–445.

Kagan, S. (1986). Cooperative learning and sociocultural factors in schooling. *Beyond language: Social and cultural factors in schooling language minority students* (pp. 198–231). Los Angeles: Evaluation, Dissemination and Assessment Center, California State University, Los Angeles.

Kagan, S. (2007). *Differentiated instruction* (smart card). San Clemente, CA: Kagan Publishing.

Kamberelis, G., & de la Luna, L. (2004). Children's writing: How textual forms, contextual forces, and textual politics co-emerge. In C. Bazerman & P. Prior (Eds.), *What writing does and how it does it* (pp. 239–277). Mahwah, NJ: Erlbaum.

Kandel, W., & Cromartie, J. (2004). *New patterns of Hispanic settlement in rural America*. Retrieved January 16, 2005, from www.ers.usda.gov/publications/rdrr99.

Kang, H-W., Kuehn, P., & Herrell, A. (1996). The Hmong literacy project: Parents working to preserve the past and ensure the future. *The Journal of Educational Issues of Language Minority Students, 16*. Retrieved March 20, 2005, from www.ncela.gwu.edu/pubs/jeilms/vol16/jeilms1602.htm.

Karchmer-Klein, R. (2007). Best practices in using the Internet to support writing. In S. Graham, C. A. MacArthur, & J. Fitzgerald (Eds.), *Best practices in writing instruction* (pp. 222–241). New York: Guilford.

Kaufman, P., Alt, M. N., & Chapman, C. D. (2004). *Dropout rates in the United States: 2001*. Washington, DC: National Center for Education Statistics.

Kea, C., Campbell-Whatley, G. D., & Richards, H. V. (2004). *Becoming culturally responsive educators: Rethinking teacher education pedagogy*. National Center for Culturally Responsive Educational Systems. Retrieved January 29, 2005, from www.nccrest.org/publications.html.

Keefe, M. W. (1987). *Learning style theory and practice*. Reston, VA: National Association of Secondary School Principals.

Kessler, C., Quinn, M., & Fathman, A. (1992). Science and cooperative learning for LEP students. In C. Kessler (Ed.), *Cooperative language learning* (pp. 65–83). Englewood Cliffs, NJ: Regents/Prentice Hall.

Keyes v. School District Number One, Denver, Colorado, 576 F. Supp. 1503 (D. Colo. 1983).

Kim, E. Y. (2001). *The yin and yang of American culture*. Yarmouth, ME: Intercultural Press.

Kleinfeld, J. (1988, June). Letter to the editor. *Harvard Education Letter, 4*(3).

Klentschy, M. (2005). Science notebook essentials. *Science and Children, 43*(3). 24–27.

Kluge, D. (1999). A brief introduction to cooperative learning. (ERIC Document Reproduction Service No. ED 437 840). Retrieved April 6, 2005, from www.eric.ed.gov.

Kohn, A. (2007, June 1). Too destructive to salvage. *USA Today*, 7A.

Kopan, A. (1974). Melting pot: Myth or reality? In E. Epps (Ed.), *Cultural pluralism* (pp. 37–55). Berkeley, CA: McCutchan.

Kottler, J. A. (1997). *What's really said in the teacher's lounge: Provocative ideas about cultures and classrooms.* Thousand Oaks: Corwin Press.

Krashen, S. (1981). Bilingual education and second language acquisition theory. In C. F. Leyba (Ed.), *Schooling and language minority students: A theoretical framework* (pp. 51–79). Los Angeles: Evaluation, Dissemination and Assessment Center, California State University, Los Angeles.

Krashen, S. (1982). *Principles and practice in second language acquisition.* Oxford: Pergamon.

Krashen, S. (1985). *The input hypothesis: Issues and implications.* New York: Longman.

Krashen, S. (2006). *Bilingual education accelerates English language development.* Takoma Park, ND: Institute for Language and Education Policy. Retrieved May 16, 2008, from www.elladvocates.org/issuebriefs/Kranshen_bilingual.pdf.

Krashen, S., & Terrell, T. (1983). *The natural approach: Language acquisition in the classroom.* Oxford: Pergamon.

Krashen, S. D. (1996). *Under attack: The case against bilingual education.* Culver City, CA: Language Education Associates.

Kress, G. R., & Van Leeuwen, T. (1995). Reading images: The grammar of visual design. London: Routledge.

Kress, J. (1993). *The ESL teacher's book of lists.* West Nyack, NY: Center for Applied Research in Education.

Kroll, B. (1991). Teaching writing in the ESL context. In M. Celce-Murcia (Ed.), *Teaching English as a second or foreign language* (2nd ed., pp. 245–263). New York: Newbury House.

Labbe, J. R. (2007, September 1). Losing literacy. *The [Riverside, CA] Press-Enterprise,* B11.

Labov, W. (1972). *Sociolinguistic patterns.* Philadelphia: University of Pennsylvania Press.

Lambert, W. (1984). An overview of issues in immersion education. In California Department of Education, *Studies on immersion education* (pp. 8–30). Sacramento: California Department of Education.

Lapkoff, S., & Li, R. M. (2007). Five trends for schools. *Educational Leadership, 64*(6), 8–15.

Laturnau, J. (2001). Standards-based instruction for English language learners. Retrieved April 9, 2005, from www.prel.org/products/pc_standards-based.htm.

Lau v. Nichols. (1974). 414 U.S. 563.

Leathers, N. (1967). *The Japanese in America.* Minneapolis: Lerner Publications.

Lee, H. (1960). *To kill a mockingbird.* New York: Lippincott.

Lee, J. (2000). Success for all? *American Language Review, 4*(2), 22, 24.

Lemberger, N. (1999). Factors affecting language development from the perspectives of four bilingual teachers. In I. Heath & C. Serrano (Eds.), *Annual editions: Teaching English as a second language* (2nd ed., pp. 30–37). Guilford, CT: Dushkin/McGraw-Hill.

Lenneberg, E. (1967). *Biological foundations of language.* New York: Wiley.

Lessow-Hurley, J. (2009). *The foundations of dual language instruction* (5th ed.). Boston: Allyn & Bacon.

Levine, D., & Adelman, M. (1982). *Beyond language: Intercultural communication for English as a second language.* Englewood Cliffs, NJ: Prentice Hall.

LeVine, J. E. (2002). Writing letters to support literacy. *The Reading Teacher, 56*(8), 232–234.

Lin, S. (2002). *Remembering the contributions and sacrifices Chinese Americans have made to America: A time to give back.* Retrieved October 27, 2007, from www.scanews.com/spot/2002/august/s623/memory/ca.html.

Lindholm, K. (1992). Two-way bilingual/immersion education: Theory, conceptual issues and pedagogical implications. In R. Padilla & A. Benavides (Eds.), *Critical perspectives in bilingual education research* (pp. 195–220). Tucson, AZ: Bilingual Review/Press.

Linquanti, R. (2008). Assessing language proficiency of California's English learners and what it means for accountability. *University of California Linguistic Minority Research Institute (LMRI) Newsletter, 17*(2), 1–3.

Lockwood, A. T. (2000). *Transforming education for Hispanic youth: Broad recommendations for teachers and program staff.* Washington, DC: National Clearinghouse for Bilingual Education, 4. Retrieved January 28, 2005, from www.ncela.gwu.edu/pubs/issuebriefs/ib4.html.

Lockwood, A. T., & Secada, W. G. (1991). *Transforming education for Hispanic youth: Exemplary practices, programs, and schools.* Accessed July 12, 2008, from http://citeseer.ist.psu.edu/lockwood99transforming.html.

Loewen, J. (1995). *Lies my teacher told me.* New York: Touchstone.

Loop, C., & Barron, V. (2002). *Which states have statewide ELD standards and language proficiency assessments?* Retrieved March 22, 2005, from www.ncela.gwu.edu/expert/faq/eldstandardsdraft.htm.

Lopez, E. C. (2002). *Tips for the use of interpreters in the assessment of English language learners.* Retrieved February 14, 2005, from http://66.102.7.104/search?q=cache:8COtfXfYi-IJ:www.nasponline.org/culturalcompetence/recommend.pdf+working+with+an+interpreter&hl=en.

Los Angeles Times. (2008). Letters. January 6, p. M2.

Los Angeles Unified School District. (1993). *Sheltered instruction teacher handbook: Strategies for teaching LEP students in the elementary grades* (Publication No. EC-617). Los Angeles: Author.

Lucas, T., & Wagner, S. (1999). Facilitating secondary English language learners' transition into the mainstream. *TESOL Journal, 8*(4), 6–13.

Lund, R. J. (1990). A taxonomy for teaching second-language listening. *Foreign Language Annuals, 23,* 105–115.

Lyons, C. A., & Clay, M. M. (2003). *Teaching struggling readers: How to use brain-based research to maximize learning.* Portsmouth, NH: Heinemann.

Maceri, D. (2007). America's languages: Tower of Babel or asset? *Language Magazine, 6*(8), 15.

Maciejewski, T. (2003). *Pragmatics.* Retrieved August 31, 2004, from www.lisle.dupage.k12.il.us/maciejewski/social.htm.

Macmillan, D. L., & Reschly, D. J. (1998). Overrepresentation of minority students: The case for greater specificity or reconsideration of the variables examined. *Journal of Special Education, 32*(1), 15–24.

Majors, P. (n.d.). *Charleston County School District, Charleston, SC, sample standards-based lesson plan.* Retrieved September 29, 2004, from www.cal.org/eslstandards/Charleston.html.

Malavé, L. (1991). Conceptual framework to design a programme intervention for culturally and linguistically different handicapped students. In L. Malavé & G. Duquette (Eds.), *Language, culture and cognition* (pp. 176–189). Clevedon, Eng.: Multilingual Matters.

Malkina, N. (1996). Fun with storytelling. In V. Whiteson (Ed.), *New ways of using drama and literature in language teaching* (pp. 41–42). Alexandria, VA: Teachers of English to Speakers of Other Languages.

Mandlebaum, L. H., & Wilson, R. (1989). Teaching listening skills in the special education classroom. *Academic Therapy, 24,* 451–452.

Manning, M. L. (2002). Understanding diversity, accepting others: Realities and directions. In F. Schultz (Ed.), *Annual editions: Multicultural education 2002/2003* (pp. 206–208). Guilford, CT: McGraw-Hill/Dushkin.

March, T. (2007). The new WWW: Whatever, whenever, wherever. In F. Schultz (Ed.), *Annual editions 10/08: Education* (pp. 213–216). Dubuque, IA: McGraw-Hill Contemporary Learning Series.

Marinova-Todd, S., Marshall, D., & Snow, C. (2000). Three misconceptions about age and L2 learning. *TESOL Quarterly, 34*(1), 9–34.

Marshall, C., & Oliva, M. (2006). *Leadership for social justice: Making revolutions in education.* Boston: Pearson.

Martin, B., & Ringham, F. (2006). *Key terms in semiotics.* London: Continuum.

McDaniel, E., & Wilde, K. (2008). Candidate assessment. In C. E. Feistritzer (Ed.), *Building a quality teaching force* (pp. 88–109). Upper Saddle River, NJ: Pearson.

McGovern, A. (1969). *If you sailed on the Mayflower in 1620.* New York: Scholastic.

McIntosh, P. (1996). White privilege and male privilege: A personal account of coming to see correspondences through work in women's studies. In M. Anderson & P. Collins (Eds.), *Race, class, and gender: An anthology* (2nd ed., pp. 76–87). Belmont, CA: Wadsworth.

McKay, J. (2000). Building self-esteem in children. In M. McKay & P. Fanning, *Self-esteem* (3rd ed., pp. 279–313). New York: Barnes and Noble Books.

McKeon, D. (1994). When meeting common standards is uncommonly difficult. *Educational Leadership, 51*(8), 45–49.

McLaughlin, B. (1987). *Theories of second-language learning.* London: Arnold.

McLeod, B. (1996). *School reform and student diversity: Exemplary schooling for language minority students.* Retrieved March 20, 2005, from www.ncela.gwu.edu/pubs/resource/schref.htm.

McVey, D. C. (2007). Helping ESL students improve their grammar. *ESL Magazine, 56,* 16–18.

Mehan, H., Hubbard, L., Lintz, A., & Villanueva, I. (1994). *Tracking untracking: The consequences of placing low-track students in high-track classes.* Santa Cruz, CA: National Center for Research on Cultural Diversity & Second Language Learning. Retrieved April 8, 2005, from www.ncela.gwu.edu/pubs/ncrcdsll/rr10.

Mercer, N. (2000). *Words and minds: How we use language to think together and get things done.* London: Routledge.

Merino, B. (2007). Identifying critical competencies for teachers of English learners. *University of California Linguistic Minority Research Institute (LMRI) Newsletter, 16*(4), 1–7.

Mermelstein, L. (2006). *Reading/writing connections in the K–2 classroom.* Boston: Pearson.

Meyer v. Nebraska, 262 U.S. 390 (1923).

Meyer, E. F. (2008, May 9). Many immigrants are motivated to learn English. Letter to the Editor, *USA Today,* 20A.

Migration Policy Institute. (2004). *A new century: Immigration and the U.S.* Retrieved January 15, 2005, from www.migrationinformation.org/Profiles/display.cfm?ID=6.

Milambiling, J. (2002). Good neighbors: Mainstreaming ESL students in the rural Midwest. In E. P. Cochran, *Mainstreaming* (pp. 21–30). Alexandria, VA: Teachers of English to Speakers of Other Languages.

Miller, G. (1985). Nonverbal communication. In V. Clark, P. Eschholz, & A. Rosa (Eds.), *Language: Introductory readings* (4th ed., pp. 633–641). New York: St. Martin's Press.

Miller, W. H. (1995). *Alternative assessment techniques for reading and writing.* West Nyack, NY: Center for Applied Research in Education.

Mills, S. C. (2006). *Using the Internet for active teaching and learning.* Upper Saddle River, NJ: Pearson/Merrill/Prentice Hall.

Mintz, E., & Yun, J. T. (1999). *The complex world of teaching: Perspectives from theory and practice.* Cambridge, MA: Harvard Educational Review.

Molina, R. (2000). Building equitable two-way programs. In N. Cloud, F. Genesee, & E. Hamayan (Eds.), *Dual language instruction* (pp. 11–12). Boston: Heinle and Heinle.

Monroe, R. J. (2008). Standardized testing in the lives of the ESL students: A teacher's firsthand account. *Institute for Language and Education Policy.* Accessed July 28, 2008, from www.elladvocates.org/documents/nclb/Monroe_Standardized_Testing_for_ELLs.pdf.

Moore, M. S., & Panara, R. F. (1996). *Great deaf Americans* (2nd ed.). New York: DeafLife Press.

Moran, R. F. (2004). Undone by law: The uncertain legacy of *Lau v. Nichols. UC-LMRI Newsletter, 13*(4), 1, 3.

Morey, A., & Kilano, M. (1997). *Multicultural course transformation in higher education: A broader truth.* Boston: Allyn & Bacon.

Morley, J. (2001). Aural comprehension instruction: Principles & practices. In M. Celce-Murcia (Ed.), *Teaching English as a second or foreign language* (3rd ed.). Boston: Heinle and Heinle.

Nash, P. (1991). ESL and the myth of the model minority. In S. Benesch (Ed.), *ESL in America* (pp. 46–55). Portsmouth, NH: Boynton/Cook.

National Center for Education Evaluation and Regional Assistance (2008). *Reading First impact study: Interim report.* Washington, DC: Author.

National Center for Education Statistics. (2001). *States using minimum-competency testing, by grade levels assessed, and expected uses of standards: 1998–99.* Retrieved March 22, 2005, from http://nces.ed.gov/programs/digest/d01/dt155.asp.

National Center for Education Statistics (NCES). (2002). *Percentage distribution of enrollment in public elementary and secondary schools, by race/ethnicity and state: Fall 1986 and fall 2000.* Retrieved January 14, 2005, from nces.ed.gov/programs/digest/d02/dt042.asp.

National Center for Education Statistics (NCES). (2003a). *College enrollment and enrollment rates of recent high school completers, by race/ethnicity: 1960 to 2001.* Retrieved March 20, 2005, from http://nces.ed.gov/programs/digest/d03/tables/dt185.asp.

National Center for Education Statistics (NCES). (2003b). *Employees in degree-granting institutions, by race/ethnicity, primary occupation, sex, employment status, and control and type of institution: Fall 2001.* Retrieved March 20, 2005, from http://nces.ed.gov/programs/digest/d03/tables/dt228.asp.

National Center for Education Statistics (NCES). (2007). *Status and trends in the education of racial and ethnic minorities.* Retrieved October 24, 2008, from http://nces.ed.gov/pubs2007/minoritytrends/ind_4_16.asp.

National Clearinghouse for English Language Acquisition (NCELA). (1996). *Ask NCELA #7 What court rulings have impacted the education of language minority students in the U.S.?* Retrieved March 19, 2005, from www.ncela.gwu.edu/expert/askncela/07court.htm.

National Clearinghouse for English Language Acquisition (NCELA). (2002). *Ask NCELA #3 How has federal policy for language minority students evolved in the U.S.?* Retrieved March 19, 2005, from www.ncela.gwu.edu/expert/faq/03history.htm.

National Clearinghouse for English Language Acquisition and Language Instruction Educational Programs (2007). *2005–2008 Poster.* Retrieved July 3, 2008, from http://www.ncela.gwu/stats/2_nation .htm.

National Commission on Teaching and America's Future. (1996). *What matters most: Teaching and America's future.* New York: Author.

National Council for the Social Studies (NCSS). (1994). *Expectations for excellence: Curriculum standards for social studies.* Washington, DC: Author.

National Council of Teachers of English (NCTE) & International Reading Association (IRA). (1996). *Standards for the English language arts.* Urbana, IL & Newark, DE: Authors.

National Council of Teachers of Mathematics (NCTM). (2000). *Principles and standards for school mathematics.* Reston, VA: Author.

National Council of Teachers of Mathematics (NCTM). (2007). *Mathematics teaching today: Improving practice, improving student learning* (2nd ed., T. Martin, Ed.). Reston, VA: Author.

National Research Council. (1996). *The national science education standards.* Washington, DC: National Academy Press.

Navarrete, C., & Gustke, C. (1996). *A guide to performance assessment for linguistically diverse students.* Retrieved February 2, 2005, from www.ncela .gwu.edu/pubs/eacwest/performance.

Nelson, B. (1996). *Learning English: How school reform fosters language acquisition and development for limited English proficient elementary school students.* Santa Cruz, CA: National Center for Research on Cultural Diversity & Second Language Learning. Retrieved April 8, 2005, from www .ncela.gwu.edu/pubs/ncrcdsll/epr16.htm.

Nelson, C. (2004). Reclaiming teacher preparation for success in high-needs schools. *Education, 124*(3), 475–480.

Nelson-Barber, S. (1999). A better education for every child: The dilemma for teachers of culturally and linguistically diverse students. In Mid-continent Research for Education and Learning (McREL) (Ed.), *Including culturally and linguistically diverse students in standards-based reform: A report on McREL's Diversity Roundtable I* (pp. 3–22). Retrieved April 8, 2005, from www.mcrel.org/ PDFConversion/Diversity/rt1chapter2.htm.

Nemmer-Fanta, M. (2002). Accommodations and modifications for English language learners. In *Serving English language learners with disabilities: A resource manual for Illinois educators.* Retrieved February 9, 2005, from www.isbe.state.il.us/spec-ed/ bilingualmanual2002.htm.

Newman, C. M. (2006). *Strategies for test-taking success: Reading.* Boston: Thompson Heinle.

Newman, J. M. (1985). What about reading? In J. M. Newman (Ed.), *Whole language: Theory in use* (pp. 99–100). Portsmouth, NH: Heinemann.

Newman, J. R. (1956). Srinivasa Ramanujan. In J. R. Newman (Ed.), *The world of mathematics, Vol. 1* (pp. 368–376). New York: Simon and Schuster.

Nichols, S. L. (1999). Gay, lesbian, and bisexual youth: Understanding diversity and promoting tolerance in schools. *The Elementary School Journal, 99*(5), 505–519.

Nieto, S., & Bode, P. (2008). *Affirming diversity* (5th ed.). Boston: Allyn & Bacon.

Nilsen, A. P., & Donelson, K. E. (2009). *Literature for today's young adults* (8th ed.). Boston: Pearson.

No Child Left Behind Act of 2001. (2002). Retrieved October 14, 2004, from www.ed.gov/policy/elsec/ leg/esea02/index.html.

Nolan, J. F., & Hoover, L. A. (2008). *Teacher supervision & evaluation* (2nd ed.). Hoboken, NJ: Wiley.

Nunan, D. (1989). *Designing tasks for the communicative classroom.* Cambridge, Eng.: Cambridge University Press.

O'Malley, J. M., & Pierce, L. V. (1996). *Authentic assessment for English language learners.* Menlo Park, CA: Addison-Wesley.

O'Malley, J., Chamot, A., Stewner-Manzanares, G., Kupper, L., & Russo, R. (1985a). Learning strategies used by beginning and intermediate ESL students. *Language Learning, 35*(1), 21–40.

O'Malley, J., Chamot, A., Stewner-Manzanares, G., Kupper, L., & Russo, R. (1985b). Learning strategy applications with students of English as a second language. *TESOL Quarterly, 19*(3), 557–584.

Oakes, J. (1985). *Keeping track: How schools structure inequality.* New Haven, CT: Yale University Press.

Oakes, J. (1992). Can tracking research inform practice? Technical, normative, and political considerations. *Educational Researcher, 21*(4), 12–21.

Oakes, J., & Lipton, M. (2007). *Teaching to change the world* (3rd ed.). Boston: McGraw-Hill.

Ogbu, J. (1978). *Minority education and caste: The American system in crosscultural perspective.* New York: Academic Press.

Ogbu, J., & Matute-Bianchi, M. (1986). Understanding sociocultural factors: Knowledge, identity, and school adjustment. In *Beyond language: Social and cultural factors in schooling language minority students* (pp. 73–142). Los Angeles: Evaluation, Dissemination and Assessment Center, California State University, Los Angeles.

Oh, J. (1992). The effects of L2 reading assessment methods on anxiety level. *TESOL Quarterly, 26*(1), 172–176.

Olsen, L. (1988). *Crossing the schoolhouse border: Immigrant students and the California public schools.* San Francisco: California Tomorrow.

Olson, S., & Loucks-Horsley, S. (2000). *Inquiry and the national science education standards.* Washington, DC: National Academy Press.

Ong, M. F., & Murugesan, V. (2007). *Teaching English to young learners: Trainer's handbook.* Santa Fe Springs, CA: Compass.

Ong, W. (1982). *Orality and literacy.* London: Methuen.

Open Court Reading series. (2003). New York: McGraw-Hill/SRA.

Orfield, T., & Lee, C. (2005). *Why segregation matters: Poverty and educational inequality.* Retrieved March 20, 2005, from www.civilrightsproject.harvard.edu/research/deseg/deseg05.php.

Ortiz, A. A. (2002). Prevention of school failure and early intervention for English language learners. In A. J. Artiles & A. A. Ortiz (Eds.), *English language learners with special education needs: Identification, assessment, and instruction* (pp. 31–63). Washington, DC: Center for Applied Linguistics and Delta Systems Co.

Osgood, K. W. (2002). It takes a class to teach a child: The challenge program. In E. P. Cochran, *Mainstreaming* (pp. 43–51). Alexandria, VA: Teachers of English to Speakers of Other Languages.

Ovando, C., & Collier, V. (1998). *Bilingual and ESL classrooms: Teaching in multicultural contexts.* Boston: McGraw-Hill.

Oyama, S. (1976). A sensitive period for the acquisition of nonnative phonological system. *Journal of Psycholinguistic Research, 5,* 261–284.

Padilla, E. (1998). *Hispanic contributions to the United States.* Retrieved January 10, 2005, from http://members.aol.com/pjchacon/aims/contributions.html.

Pappamihiel, N. E. (2002). English as a second language students and English language anxiety: Issues in the mainstream classroom. *Research in the Teaching of English, 36,* 327–355.

Parade Magazine. (2007, October 28). Making a profit off kids, 10.

Paradis, M. (2005). *Neurolinguistics of bilingualism and the teaching of languages.* Retrieved January 23, 2005, from www.semioticon.com/virtuals/talks/paradis_txt.htm.

Parla, J. (1994). Educating teachers for cultural and linguistic diversity: A model for all teachers. *New York State Association for Bilingual Education Journal, 9,* 1–6. Retrieved February 7, 2005, from www.ncela.gwu.edu/pubs/nysabe/vol9/model.htm.

Pasternak, J. (1994, March 29). Bias blights life outside Appalachia. *Los Angeles Times,* A1, A16.

Payan, R. (1984). Language assessment for bilingual exceptional children. In L. Baca & H. Cervantes (Eds.), *The bilingual special education interface* (pp. 125–137). St. Louis, MO: Times Mirror/Mosby.

Pearson, R. (1974). *Introduction to anthropology.* New York: Holt, Rinehart and Winston.

Peñalosa, F. (1980). *Chicano sociolinguistics, a brief introduction.* Rowley, MA: Newbury House.

Pennycook, A. (1994). *The cultural politics of English as an international language.* New York: Longman.

Penrod, D. (2008). Web 2.0, meet Literacy 2.0. *Educational Technology, 48*(1), 50–52.

Peregoy, S., & Boyle, O. (2008). *Reading, writing, and learning in ESL* (5th ed.). Boston: Pearson.

Pérez, B., & Torres-Guzmán, M. (2002). *Learning in two worlds* (3rd ed.). New York: Longman.

Perkins, C. (1995). *Equity in mathematics assessment for English as a second language students.* Retrieved January 20, 2005, from http://jwilson.coe.uga.edu/EMT705/EMT705Perkins.html.

Philips, S. (1972). Participant structures and communicative competence: Warm Springs children in community and classroom. In C. Cazden, V. John, & D. Hymes (Eds.), *Functions of language in the classroom* (pp. 370–394). New York: Teachers College Press.

Phillips, J. (1978). College of, by, and for Navajo Indians. *Chronicle of Higher Education, 15,* 10–12.

Pierangelo, R., & Giuliani, G. A. (2001). *What every teacher should know about students with special needs.* Champaign, IL: Research Press.

Pinnell, G. S. (1985). Ways to look at the functions of children's language. In A. Jaggar & M. Smith-Burke (Eds.), *Observing the language learner* (pp. 57–72). Newark, DE: International Reading Association.

Plyler v. Doe, 457 U.S. 202, 102 S. Ct. 2382 (1982).

Pope, D. (2002). *Doing school: How we are creating a generation of stressed-out, materialistic, and miseducated students.* New Haven, CT: Yale University Press.

Porter, P., & Taylor, B. P. (2003). Experience is the best teacher: Linking the MA pedagogical grammar course with the ESL grammar classroom. In D. Liu & P. Master, *Grammar teaching in teacher education* (pp. 151–164). Alexandria, VA: Teachers of English to Speakers of Other Languages.

Porter, R. (1990). *Forked tongue: The politics of bilingual education.* New York: Basic Books.

Porterfield, K. (2002). *Indian encyclopedia wins Colorado book award.* Retrieved October 27, 2008, from www.kporterfield.com/aicttw/articles/award.html.

Potowski, K. (2007). *Language and identity in a dual immersion school.* Clevedon, Eng.: Multilingual Matters.

Pransky, K. (2008). *Beneath the surface: The hidden realities of teaching culturally and linguistically diverse young learners, K–6.* Portsmouth, NH: Heinemann.

Prothrow-Smith, D. (1994, April). Building violence prevention into the classroom. *The School Administrator, 8*(12), 8–12.

Pruitt, W. (2000). Using story to compare, conclude, and identify. In B. Agor (Ed.), *Integrating the ESL standards into classroom practice: Grades 9–12* (pp. 31–54). Alexandria, VA: Teachers of English to Speakers of Other Languages.

Pryor, C. B. (2002). New immigrants and refugees in American schools: Multiple voices. In F. Schultz (Ed.), *Annual editions: Multicultural education 2002/2003* (pp. 185–193). Guilford, CT: McGraw-Hill/Dushkin.

Public Schools of North Carolina. (2004). *The North Carolina competency tests: A handbook for students in the ninth grade for the first time in 2001–2002 and beyond.* Raleigh: Author. Retrieved February 2, 2005, from www.ncpublicschools.org/accountability/testing/competency.

Qualls-Mitchell, P. (2008). Reading enhancement for deaf and hard-of-hearing children through multicultural empowerment. *The Reading Teacher, 56*(1), 76–84.

Quinn, Q. (2007). Motivating reading. *Language Magazine, 6*(10), 24–26.

Quinones, S. (2008, February 25). A different kind of home schooling. *Los Angeles Times,* B4.

Rahilly, M. K., & Weinmann, A. (2007). *An overview of Title III programs.* Presentation at the annual conference of the Teachers of English to Speakers of Other Languages, Seattle.

Raimes, A. (Ed.). (1996). *Identities: Readings from contemporary culture.* Boston: Houghton Mifflin.

Ramírez, J. (1992, Winter/Spring). Executive summary, final report: Longitudinal study of structured English immersion strategy, early-exit and late-exit transitional bilingual education programs for language-minority children. *Bilingual Research Journal, 16*(1 & 2), 1–62.

Rance-Rooney, J. (2008). Digital storytelling for language and culture learning. *Essential Teacher, 5*(1), 29–31.

Ray, B., & Seely, C. (1998). *Fluency through TPR storytelling: Achieving real language acquisition in school* (2nd ed.). Berkeley; CA: Command Performance Language Institute.

Reckendorf, K., & Ortiz, F. W. (2000). *English and ESL inclusion model.* Unpublished article. Amherst, MA: Amherst Regional Middle School.

Reese, D. (2007). Proceed with caution: Using Native American folktales in the classroom. *Language Arts, 84*(3), 245–256.

Reese, S. (2006). When foreign languages are not seen or heard. *The Language Educator, 1*(2), 32–37.

Reeves, D. B. (2002). *Making standards work.* Denver, CO: Center for Performance Assessment.

Reid, J. (2006). New census data shows 1.3 million children have fallen into poverty since 2000. Children's Defense Fund. Retrieved May 16, 2008, from www.childrensdefense.org/site/News2?page=NewsArticle&id=7887.

Richard-Amato, P. (2003). *Making it happen* (3rd ed.). White Plains, NY: Longman.

Richards, H. V., Brown, A. E., & Forde, T. B. (2004). *Addressing diversity in schools: Culturally responsive pedagogy.* National Center for Culturally Responsive Educational Systems. Retrieved January 21, 2005, from www.nccrest.org/publications.html.

Richards, J., & Gipe, J. (1995). What's the structure? A game to help middle school students recognize common writing patterns. *Journal of Reading, 38*(8), 667–669.

Rico, H. (2000). *Programs for English learners: Overview of federal and state requirements.* Retrieved February 22, 2001, from www.cde.ca.gov/ccpdiv/eng_learn/ccr2000-el/index.htm.

Ríos v. Read. 75 Civ. 296 (U.S. District Ct. Ed. NY, 1977).

Rivera, C. (2008, March 10). Strife and solutions at school conferences. *Los Angeles Times,* B1, B 6.

Roberts, C. (1995, Summer/Fall). Bilingual education program models. *Bilingual Research Journal, 19* (3 & 4), 369–378.

Robinson, G. (1985). *Crosscultural understanding.* New York: Pergamon Institute of English.

Rodríguez, R., Prieto, A., & Rueda, R. (1984). Issues in bilingual/multicultural special education. *Journal of the National Association for Bilingual Education, 8*(3), 55–65.

Rolstad, K., Mahoney, K., & Glass, G. V. (2005). The big picture: A meta-analysis of program effectiveness research on English language learners. *Educational Policy, 19*(4), 572–594.

Rose, C. (1987). *Accelerated learning.* New York: Dell.

Rowan, T., & Bourne, B. (1994). *Thinking like mathematics.* Portsmouth, NH: Heinemann.

Rubel, A., & Kupferer, H. (1973). The myth of the melting pot. In T. Weaver (Ed.), *To see ourselves: Anthropology and modern social issues* (pp. 103–107). Glenview, IL: Scott Foresman.

Rueda, R. (1987). Social and communicative aspects of language proficiency in low-achieving language minority students. In H. Trueba (Ed.), *Success or failure? Learning and the language minority student* (pp. 185–197). Cambridge, MA: Newbury House.

Ruíz, R. (1984). Orientations in language planning. *NABE Journal, 8*(2), 15–34.

Runner, J. (2000). *"I don't understand" in over 230 languages.* Retrieved April 8, 2005, from www .elite.net/~runner/jennifers/understa.htm.

Russell, M. (2008). Solving the crisis of the male teacher shortage. *Teachers of Color, 3*(1), 12–14.

Ryan, M. (2008). *Ask the teacher: A practitioner's guide to teaching and learning in the diverse classroom.* Boston: Pearson.

Ryder, M. (2005). *Semiotics.* Retrieved January 23, 2005, from http://carbon.cudenver.edu/~mryder/ itc_data/semiotics.html.

Sales, F. (1989). *Ibrahim.* New York: Lippincott.

Sánchez, F. (1989). *What is primary language instruction?* Hayward, CA: Alameda County Office of Education.

Sands, D. J., Kozleski, E. B., & French, N. K. (2000). *Special education for the twenty-first century: Making schools inclusive communities.* Belmont, CA: Wadsworth.

Saslow, J., & Ascher, A. (2006). *Top Notch 2 Copy & go.* White Plains, NY: Pearson Longman.

Sasser, L., Naccarato, L., Corren, J., & Tran, Q. (2002). *English language development progress profile.* Alhambra, CA: Alhambra School District.

Sattler, J. (1974). *Assessment of children's intelligence.* Philadelphia: W. B. Saunders.

Saunders, W., & Goldenberg, C. (2001). Strengthening the transition in transitional bilingual education. In D. Christian & F. Genesee (Eds.), *Bilingual education* (pp. 41–56). Alexandria, VA: Teachers of English to Speakers of Other Languages.

Schachter, J. (2003). *Migration by race and Hispanic origin: 1995 to 2000.* Retrieved January 16, 2005, from www.census.gov/prod/2003pubs/censr-13.pdf.

Schifini, A. (1994). Language, literacy, and content instruction: Strategies for teachers. In K. Spangenberg Urbschat & R. Pritchard (Eds.), *Kids come in all language: Reading instruction for ESL students* (pp. 158–179). Newark, DE: International Reading Association.

Schifini, A., Short, D., & Tinajero, J. V. (2002). *High points: Teacher's edition.* Carmel, CA: Hampton Brown.

Schildroth, A., & Hotto, S. (1994). Inclusion or exclusion: Deaf students and the inclusion movement. *American Annals of the Deaf, 139,* 239–243.

Schmidt, P. (2008, February 20). Asians, not whites, hurt most by race-conscious admissions. *USA Today,* 13A.

Schultz, J., & Theophano, J. (1987). Saving place and marking time: Some aspects of the social lives of three-year-old children. In H. Trueba (Ed.), *Success or failure* (pp. 33–48). Cambridge, MA: Newbury House.

Schumann, J. (1978). The acculturation model for second-language acquisition. In R. Gringas (Ed.), *Second language acquisition and foreign language teaching* (pp. 27–50). Washington, DC: Center for Applied Linguistics.

Schumann, J. (1994). Emotion and cognition in second language acquisition. *Studies in Second Language Acquisition, 16,* 231–242.

Scieszka, J., & Smith, L. (1992). *The stinky cheese man and other fairly stupid tales.* New York: Viking Juvenile.

Scollon, R., & Scollon, S. W. (2003). *Discourses in place: Language in the material world.* London: Routledge.

Scribner, S., & Cole, M. (1978). Literacy without schooling: Testing for intellectual effects. *Harvard Educational Review, 48,* 448–461.

Seelye, H. (1984). *Teaching culture.* Lincolnwood, IL: National Textbook Company.

Selinker, L. (1972). Interlanguage. *International Review of Applied Linguistics, 10*(3), 209–231.

Selinker, L. (1991). Along the way: Interlanguage systems in second language acquisition. In L. Malavé & G. Duquette (Eds.), *Language, culture and cognition* (pp. 23–35). Clevedon, Eng.: Multilingual Matters.

Seng, C. (2005). *Teaching English to blind students.* Retrieved February 2, 2005, from www.teaching english.org.uk/think/methodology/blind.shtml.

Serna v. Portales Municipal Schools, 499 F. 2d 1147 (10th Cir. 1972).

Shade, B., & New, C. (1993). Cultural influences on learning: Teaching implications. In J. Banks & C. Banks (Eds.), *Multicultural education: Issues and perspectives.* Boston: Allyn & Bacon.

Short, D. (1998). Secondary newcomer programs: Helping recent immigrants prepare for school success. *ERIC Digest.* Retrieved January 28, 2005, from http://searcheric.org/scripts/seget2.asp?db= ericft&want=http://searcheric.org/ericdc/ED419385 .htm.

Short, D., & Echevarria, J. (1999). The sheltered instruction observation protocol: A tool for teacher-researcher collaboration and professional development. *ERIC Digest.* Retrieved January 28, 2005, from http://searcheric.org/scripts/seget2 .asp?db=ericft&want=http://searcheric.org/ericdc/ ED436981.htm.

Shukoor, A. (1991). What does being bilingual mean to my family and me? *NABE Conference Program.* Washington, DC: National Association for Bilingual Education.

Shuter, R. (1991). The Hmong of Laos: Orality, communication, and acculturation. In L. Samovar & R. Porter (Eds.), *Intercultural communication: A reader* (6th ed., pp. 270–276). Belmont, CA: Wadsworth.

Siccone, F. (1995). *Celebrating diversity: Building self-esteem in today's multicultural classrooms.* Boston: Allyn & Bacon.

Siegel, J. (1999). Stigmatized and standardized varieties in the classroom: Interference or separation? *TESOL Quarterly, 33*(4), 701–728.

SIL International. (2000). *Geographic distribution of living languages, 2000.* Retrieved August 24, 2004, from www.ethnologue.com/ethno_docs/distribution.asp.

Sindell, P. (1988). Some discontinuities in the enculturation of Mistassini Cree children. In J. Wurzel (Ed.), *Toward multiculturalism.* Yarmouth, ME: Intercultural Press.

Singleton, D., & Ryan, L. (2004). *Language acquisition: The age factor* (2nd ed.). Clevedon, Eng.: Multilingual Matters.

Siskind Susser. (n.d.). *The ABC's of immigration—grounds for asylum and refuge.* Retrieved January 16, 2005, from www.visalaw.com.

Skinner, B. (1957). *Verbal behavior.* New York: Appleton, Century, Crofts.

Skutnabb-Kangas, T. (1981). *Bilingualism or not: The education of minorities* (L. Malmberg & D. Crane, Trans.). Clevedon, Eng.: Multilingual Matters.

Skutnabb-Kangas, T. (1993, February 3). *Linguistic genocide and bilingual education.* Presentation at the annual conference of the California Association for Bilingual Education, Anaheim.

Skutnabb-Kangas, T. (2000). *Linguistic genocide in education—or worldwide diversity and human rights?* Mahwah, NJ: Erlbaum.

Slater, J. (2000, May 12). *ELD standards.* Presentation at the Linguistic Minority Research Institute Conference, Irvine, CA.

Sleeter, C. E. (1986). Learning disabilities: The social construction of a special education category. *Exceptional Children, 53*(1), 46–54.

Smilkstein, R. (2002). *We're born to learn: Using the brain's natural learning process to create today's curriculum.* Thousand Oaks, CA: Sage.

Smith, F. (1983). *Essays into literacy.* Portsmouth, NH: Heinemann.

Smith, S. L., Paige, R. M., & Steglitz, I. (1998). Theoretical foundations of intercultural training and applications to the teaching of culture. In D. L. Lange, C. A. Klee, R. M. Paige, & Y. A. Yershova (Eds.), *Culture as the core: Interdisciplinary perspectives on culture teaching and learning in the language curriculum* (pp. 53–91). Minneapolis: Center for Advanced Research on Language Acquisition, University of Minnesota.

Smith, T. E. C., Polloway, E. A., Patton, J. R., & Dowdy, C. A. (2003). *Teaching children with special needs in inclusive settings* (4th ed.). Boston: Allyn & Bacon.

Snow, C., & Hoefnagel-Hoehle, M. (1978). The critical period for language acquisition: Evidence from second language learning. *Child Development, 49,* 1114–1118.

Snow, C., Burns, S., & Griffin, P. (Eds.). (1998). *Preventing reading difficulties in young children.* Washington, DC: National Academy Press.

Snow, D. (1996). *More than a native speaker.* Alexandria, VA: Teachers of English to Speakers of Other Languages.

Sonbuchner, G. M. (1991). *How to take advantage of your learning styles.* Syracuse, NY: New Readers Press.

Southern Poverty Law Center. (1999). *Youth at the edge.* Retrieved April 8, 2005, from www.splcenter.org/intel/intelreport/article.jsp?pid=537.

Spandel, V., & Hicks, J. (2006). *WriteTraits advanced sampler.* Wilmington, MA: Houghton-Mifflin.

Spinelli, E. (1994). *English grammar for students of Spanish.* Ann Arbor, MI: Olivia and Hill Press.

Spring, J. (2001). The new Mandarin society? Testing on the fast track. *The Joel Spring Library.* Retrieved April 8, 2005, from www.mhhe.com/socscience/education/spring/commentary.mhtml.

Stahl, S. A., Duffy-Hester, A. M., & Stahl, K. (1998). Everything you wanted to know about phonics (but were afraid to ask). *Reading Research Quarterly, 33*(3), 338–355.

Stainback, W., & Stainback, S. (1984). A rationale for the merger of special and regular education. *Exceptional Children, 51*(2), 102–111.

Strehorn, K. (2001). The application of Universal Instructional Design to ESL teaching. *Internet TESL Journal.* Retrieved January 25, 2005, from http://iteslj.org/Techniques/Strehorn-UID.html.

Suina, J. (1985). . . . And then I went to school. *New Mexico Journal of Reading, 5*(2). (Reprinted in *Outlook, 59,* 20–26).

Suleiman, M. (Ed.). (1999). *Arabs in America: Building a new future.* Chicago, IL: Kazi.

Sutherland, D. E. (1989). *The expansion of everyday life 1860–1876.* New York: Harper & Row.

Swanson, C. B. (2008). *Cities in crisis.* America's Promise Alliance. Retrieved May 27, 2008, from www.americaspromise.org/APA.aspx.

Swartz, S. L., Shook, R. E., Klein, A. F., Moon, C., Bunnell, K., Belt, M., & Huntley, C. (2003). *Guided reading and literacy centers.* Carlsbad, CA: Dominie Press.

Takahashi, E., Austin, T., & Morimoto, Y. (2000). Social interaction and language development in a FLES classroom. In J. K. Hall & L. S. Verplaetse (Eds.), *Second and foreign language learning through classroom interaction* (pp. 139–162). Mahwah, NJ: Erlbaum.

Tannen, D. (n.d.). *Discourse analysis.* Linguistic Society of America, "Fields of Linguistics." Retrieved March 13, 2005, from www.lsadc.org.

Tateishi, C. A. (2007–2008). Taking a chance with words. *Rethinking Schools, 22*(2), 20–23.

Taylor, D. (2000). Facing hardships: Jamestown and colonial life. In K. Samway (Ed.), *Integrating the ESL standards into classroom practice* (pp. 53–81). Alexandria, VA: Teachers of English to Speakers of Other Languages.

Teachers of English to Speakers of Other Languages (TESOL). (2001). *Scenarios for ESL standards-based assessment.* Alexandria, VA: Author.

Teachers of English to Speakers of Other Languages (TESOL). (2006). *PreK–12 English language proficiency standards in the core content areas.* Alexandria, VA: Author.

Teaching Mathematics to ESL students. (n.d.). Retrieved September 29, 2004, from www.eduweb.vic.gov.au/curriculumatwork/esl/es_maprim.htm.

Teske, M., & Marcy, P. (2007). *Step up: Listening, speaking, and critical thinking.* Boston: Houghton Mifflin.

Tharp, R. (1989a). Culturally compatible education: A formula for designing effective classrooms. In H. Trueba, G. Spindler, & L. Spindler (Eds.), *What do anthropologists have to say about dropouts?* (pp. 51–66). New York: Falmer Press.

Tharp, R. (1989b, February). Psychocultural variables and constants: Effects on teaching and learning in schools. *American Psychologist, 44*(2), 349–359.

Thomas, W., & Collier, V. (1997). *School effectiveness for language minority students.* Retrieved April 8, 2005, from www.ncela.gwu/pubs/resource/effectiveness/index.htm.

Thonis, E. (2005). *The English-Spanish connection.* Miami: Santillana.

Tikunoff, W., Ward, B., Romero, M., Lucas, T., Katz, A., Van Broekhuisen, L., & Castaneda, L. (1991, April). *Addressing the instructional needs of the limited English proficient student: Results of the exemplary SAIP descriptive study.* Symposium at the annual meeting of the American Educational Research Association, Chicago.

Tileston, D. W., & Darling, S. K. (2008). Why culture matters. *Teachers of Color, 3*(1), 58, 60.

Tinker Sachs, G., & Ho, B. (2007). *ESL/EFL cases: Contexts for teacher professional discussions.* Hong Kong: City University of Hong Kong Press.

Tollefson, J. W. (1991). *Planning language, planning inequality.* London: Longman.

Tollefson, J. W. (Ed.). (1995). *Power and inequality in language education.* Cambridge, Eng.: Cambridge University Press.

Tollefson, J. W. (Ed.). (2002). *Language policies in education: Critical issues.* Mahwah, NJ: Erlbaum.

Tompkins, G. (2005). *Literacy for the 21st century: A balanced approach* (4th ed.). Upper Saddle River, NJ: Merrill.

Toppo, G. (2004). An answer to standardized tests. *USA Today.* Retrieved April 8, 2005, from www.usatoday.com/news/education/2004–10–12-tests-usat_x.htm.

Torres-Guzmán, M. E., Abbate, J., Brisk, M. E., & Minaya-Rowe, L. (2002). Defining and documenting success for bilingual learners: A collective case study. *Bilingual Research Journal, 26*(1). Retrieved April 9, 2005, from http://brj.asu.edu/v261/articles/art3.html#intro.

Triandis, H. C. (1995). *Individualism & collectivism.* Boulder, CO: Westview Press.

Trueba, H. (1989). *Raising silent voices.* Boston: Heinle and Heinle.

Trueba, H., Cheng, L., & Ima, K. (1993). *Myth or reality: Adaptive strategies of Asian Americans in California.* Washington, DC: Falmer Press.

Tunnell, M. O., & Jacobs, J. S. (2000). *Children's literature, briefly* (2nd ed.). Upper Saddle River, NJ: Merrill Prentice Hall.

Ukpokodu, N. (2002). Multiculturalism vs. globalism. In F. Schultz (Ed.), *Annual editions: Multicultural education 2002–2003* (pp. 7–10). Guilford, CT: McGraw-Hill/Dushkin.

U.S. Census Bureau. (2003). *USA Quickfacts.* Retrieved January 25, 2005, from http://quickfacts.census.gov/qfd/states/00000.html.

U.S. Census Bureau. (2004a). *Educational attainment in the U.S.: 2003.* Retrieved January 12, 2005, from www.census.gov/population/www/socdem/educ-attn.html.

U.S. Census Bureau. (2004b). *Health insurance data.* Retrieved January 12, 2005, from www.census.gov/hhes/www/hlthins/hlthin03/hlthtables03.html.

U.S. Census Bureau. (2004c). *Poverty tables 2003.* Retrieved January 12, 2005, from www.census.gov/hhes/poverty/poverty03/tables03.html.

U.S. Department of Education. (2008). *Reading First.* Retrieved June 24, 2008, from www.ed.gov/programs/readingfirst/index.html.

U.S. Department of State, Bureau of Consular Affairs. (2004). *Visa Bulletin, 8*(76). Washington, DC: Author. Retrieved January 18, 2005, from http://travel.state.gov/visa/frvi/bulletin/bulletin_1343.html.

U.S. Government Accounting Office. (2002). *Per-pupil spending differences between selected inner city and suburban schools varied by metropolitan area.* Retrieved January 14, 2005, from www.gao.gov/new.items/d03234.pdf.

U.S. Office for Civil Rights. (1970). *May 25 memorandum.* Retrieved March 19, 2005, from www.ed.gov/about/offices/list/ocr/docs/lau1970.html.

U.S. Office for Civil Rights. (1976). Office for Civil Rights guidelines: Task force findings specifying remedies available for eliminating past educational practices ruled unlawful under *Lau v. Nichols.* In J. Alatis & K. Twaddell (Eds.), *English as a second language in bilingual education* (pp. 325–332). Washington, DC: Teachers of English to Speakers of Other Languages.

U.S. Office for Civil Rights. (1999). *Programs for English language learners.* Retrieved from www.ed.gov/offices/OCR/ELL.

University of Texas at Austin. (1991, Spring). Individuals with Disabilities Education Act challenges educators to improve the education of minority students with disabilities. *Bilingual Special Education Perspective, 10,* 1–6.

Unrau, N. (2008). *Content area reading and writing: Fostering literacies in middle and high school cultures.* Upper Saddle River, NJ: Merrill Prentice Hall.

Uribe, D. (2008). Crazed on phonics. *Language Magazine, 7*(8), 37.

Urow, C., & Sontag, J. (2001). Creating commuity—*un mundo entero*: The Inter-American experience. In D. Christian & F. Genesee (Eds.), *Bilingual education.* Alexandria, VA: Teachers of English to Speakers of Other Languages.

Valdes, A. (2007). Top 10 immigration myths. *Colors^{NW} Magazine, 6*(12), 21–32, 43.

Valencia, R. R., & Villareal, B. J. (2003). Improving students' reading performance via standards-based school reform: A critique. *The Reading Teacher, 56*(7), 612–621.

Valles, E. C. (1998). The disproportionate representation of minority students in special education: Responding to the problem. *Journal of Special Education, 32*(1), 52–54.

Veeder, K., & Tramutt, J. (2000). Strengthening literacy in both languages. In N. Cloud, F. Genesee, & E. Hamayan (Eds.), *Dual language instruction* (p. 91). Boston: Heinle and Heinle.

Veltman, C. (1988). *The future of the Spanish language in the United States.* Washington, DC: Hispanic Policy Development Project.

Verdugo Hills High School. (2004). *Redesignated students*. Retrieved February 2, 2005, from www.lausd.k12.ca.us/Verdugo_HS/classes/esl/redes.htm.

Villa, R. A., Thousand, J. S., & Nevin, A. I. (2004). *A guide to co-teaching*. Thousand Oaks, CA: Corwin.

Villaseñor, V. (1992). *Rain of gold*. New York: Dell.

Villaume, S., & Brabham, E. (2003). Phonics instruction: Beyond the debate. *The Reading Teacher, 56*(5), 478–482.

Villegas, A. M., & Lucas, T. (2002). Preparing culturally responsive teachers: Rethinking the curriculum. *Journal of Teacher Education, 53*(1), 20–32.

Villegas, A. M., & Lucas, T. (2007). The culturally responsive teacher. *Educational Leadership, 64*(6), 28–33.

Vygotsky, L. (1978). *Mind in society*. Cambridge, MA: Harvard University Press.

Wadsworth, D., & Remaley, M. H. (2007). What families want. *Educational Leadership, 64*(6), 23–27.

Waggoner, D. (1995, November). Are current home speakers of non-English languages learning English? *Numbers and Needs, 5*.

Wallach, G. P., & Miller, L. (1988). *Language intervention and academic success*. Boston: Little, Brown.

Walqui, A. (1999). Assessment of culturally and linguistically diverse students: Considerations for the 21st century. In Mid-continent Research for Education and Learning (McREL) (Ed.), *Including culturally and linguistically diverse students in standards-based reform: A report on McREL's Diversity Roundtable I* (pp. 55–84). Retrieved March 17, 2005, from www.mcrel.org/topics/product Detail.asp?topicsID=3&productID=56.

Ward, A. W., & Murray-Ward, M. (1999). *Assessment in the classroom*. Belmont, CA: Wadsworth.

Weaver, C. (1988). *Reading process and practice*. Portsmouth, NH: Heinemann.

Weber, A. (2001). An international school in Indiana, USA. In D. Christian & F. Genesee (Eds.), *Bilingual education* (pp. 151–165). Alexandria, VA: Teachers of English to Speakers of Other Languages.

Weber, E. (2005). *MI strategies in the classroom and beyond*. Boston: Pearson.

Weber, G. (2008). A proud history: New African-American curriculum helps students realize cultural pride. *Teachers of Color, 3*(1), 44–45.

Weed, K., & Ford, M. (1999). Achieving literacy through multiple meaning systems. In E. Franklin (Ed.), *Reading and writing in more than one language* (pp. 65–80). Alexandria, VA: Teachers of English to Speakers of Other Languages.

Weiler, J. (2000). Recent changes in school desegregation. ERIC Clearinghouse on Urban Education. Retrieved April 8, 2005, from http://niusi.edreform.net/resource/5816.

Wells, M. C. (1996). *Literacies lost: When students move from a progressive middle school to a traditional high school*. New York: Teachers College Press.

West, J. F., & Idol, L. (1990). Collaborative consultation in the education of mildly handicapped and at-risk students. *Remedial and Special Education, 11*(1), 22–31.

Wiese, A. M., & García, E. (1998). The Bilingual Education Act: Language minority students and equal educational opportunity. *Bilingual Research Journal, 22*(1). Retrieved April 9, 2005, from http://brj.asu.edu/v221/articles/art1.html.

Wiggins, G. (2005). What is understanding by design? *Understanding by design*. Retrieved March 23, 2005, from www.grantwiggins.org/ubd.html.

Willard, N. E. (2007). *Cyberbullying and cyberthreats: Responding to the challenge of online social aggression, threats, and distress*. Champaign, IL: Research Press. 367C.

Williams, B. T. (2007). Standardized students: The problems with writing for tests instead of people. In Schultz, F. (Ed.), *Annual editions 10/08: Education* (pp. 71–75). Dubuque, IA: McGraw-Hill Contemporary Learning Series.

Willig, A. C. (1985). A meta-analysis of selected studies on the effectiveness of bilingual education. *Review of Educational Research, 55*, 269–317.

Wilner, L. K., & Feinstein-Whitaker, M. (2008). Accenting the positive. *Language Magazine, 7*(8), 34.

Wilson, W. (1984). The urban underclass. In L. Dunbar (Ed.), *Minority report*. New York: Pantheon Books.

Wilton, D. (2003). *How many words are there in the English language?* Retrieved August 30, 2004, from www.wordorigins.org/number.htm.

Wolfenbarger, C. D., & Sipe, L. R. (2007). A unique and literary art form: Recent research on picture books. *Language Arts, 84*(3), 273–280.

Wollenberg, C. (1989). *The new immigrants and California's multiethnic heritage*. Available from New Faces of Liberty/SFSC, P.O. Box 5646, San Francisco, CA 94101.

Woolfolk, A. (2007). *Educational psychology* (10th ed.). Boston: Allyn & Bacon.

Woolfolk, A., & Brooks, D. (1985). The influence of teachers' nonverbal behaviors on students' perceptions and performance. *Elementary School Journal, 85,* 514–528.

Worthen, B., & Spandel, V. (1991). Putting the standardized test debate in perspective. *Educational Leadership, 48*(5), 65–69.

Worthy, J., Moorman, M., & Turner, M. (1999). What Johnny likes to read is hard to find in school. *Reading Research Quarterly, 14,* 12–27.

Wray, M., & Newitz, A. (1997). *White trash: Race and class in America.* New York: Routledge.

Yamauchi, L., & Wilhelm, P. (2001). *e Ola Ka Hawai'i I Kona 'Olelo:* Hawaiians live in their language. In D. Christian & F. Genesee (Eds.), *Bilingual education* (pp. 83–94). Alexandria, VA: Teachers of English to Speakers of Other Languages.

Yao, E. (1988). Working effectively with Asian immigrant parents. *Phi Delta Kappan, 70*(3), 223–225.

Yates, S. (1996). English in cyberspace. In S. Goodman & D. Graddol (Eds.), *Redesigning English: New texts, new identities* (pp. 106–140). London: Routledge.

Yep, L. (1975). *Dragonwings.* New York: Harper & Row.

Young, M., & Helvie, S. (1996). Parent power: A positive link to school success. *Journal of Educational Issues of Language Minority Students, 16.* Retrieved April 8, 2005, from www.ncela.gwu.edu/pubs/jeilms/vol16/jeilms1611.htm.

Zacarian, D. (2004a). Keeping Tren in school. *Essential Teacher, 1*(2), 12–13.

Zacarian, D. (2004b). The road taken: "I was lost before the end of the first minute." *Essential Teacher, 1*(3), 11–13.

Zanger, V. V. (1994). "Not joined in": The social context of English literacy development for Hispanic youth. In B. M. Ferdman, R.-M. Weber, & A. G. Ramírez (Eds.), *Literacy across languages and cultures* (pp. 171–198). Albany: SUNY Press.

Zarate, M. E., Bhimji, F., & Reese, L. (2005). Ethnic identity and academic achievement among Latino/a adolescents. *Journal of Latinos in Education, 4*(2), 93–114.

Zehler, A., Hopstock, P., Fleischman, H., & Greniuk, C. (1994). *An examination of assessment of limited English proficient students.* Arlington, VA: Special Issues Analysis Center. Retrieved April 8, 2005, from www.ncela.gwu.edu/pubs/siac/lepasses.htm.

Zeiler, H. (2007). Successful interventions. *Language Magazine, 6*(9), 32–35.

Zemach, D. (2007). Picture this. *Essential Teacher, 4*(2), 12–13.

Author Index

Subject Index

PHOTO CREDITS

pp. 2, 212, Lindfors Photography; pp. 29, 49, 108, Bob Daemmrich Photography; p. 68, Elizabeth Crews; p. 143, Christina Kennedy/PhotoEdit; p. 178, Patrick White/Merrill Education; p. 234, Bill Aron/PhotoEdit; p. 264, Michael J. Doolittle/The Image Works; p. 302, David Young-Wolff/PhotoEdit; p. 321, Lawrence Migdale/Pix.

Ursula Meissner

AFGHANISTAN

Hope and Beauty in a War-torn Land

افغانستان

AFGHANISTAN

Hope and Beauty in a War-torn Land

1 *Widows beg in front of the ruins of Kabul in 2002.*
2 *From the window of this tearoom in Jalalabad, you get a good view of goings-on.* **3** *On the outskirts of Kabul, new shops are opening all the time.* **4** *Girls from Herat proudly carry their first schoolbooks and satchels.* **5** *Samina, a teacher, on her way to the village. It is one of the thousands that have no paved access.*

Next douple page *Sun-drenched riverbeds covered in vegetation are a sight for sore eyes in summer. War and crisis gets forgotten in the face of fields blooming with flowers and trees laden with fruits.*

Pages 6-7 *Gulbuddin Hekmatjar addresses the Mujahideen in the tribal area, on the border with Pakistan.*

MY AFGHANISTAN

When I crossed into Afghanistan from Pakistan in Spring 1986, I had no idea that this would be the first of 16 trips that I would make to this country. I was traveling with Mujahideen. I have been a photographer now for almost 20 years and I have worked in war zones and been caught up in crises all over the world. However, I have never been anywhere as often as I have to Afghanistan. Nor have I ever felt so singularly connected to any other country as I do to this one.

I have to thank someone in particular for that first trip over the Hindu Kush mountain range and through Jalalabad and the destroyed villages of Kabul province. It was Abdul Hack, a legendary figure, who rolled up the leg of my pants to check the size of my calf-muscles and decided that I was good enough to accompany him and his men. My legs, he thought, would hold out over the grueling terrain. None of the Mujahideen with us dared contradict Hack, but it was obvious that they were not entirely convinced about spending the fourteen days of their march in the company of a woman.

It was on this journey that I was astounded by the intensity and beauty of the country. Over time, my male companions developed a certain protectiveness towards me and I slowly learned something about the life of a "holy warrior". The majority of them were simple craftsmen and farmers, who could neither read nor write, let alone speak English. This made communicating with them rather difficult. Many of them had been forced to abandon their way of life in the wake of the Soviet invasion and had not seen their families for years. But these men were no religious fanatics. Rather they were combative, proud people who wanted the right to determine their own lives and who did not want to subject themselves to any foreign powers.

When we reached remote villages I was the only one from the group able to enter the houses and approach the families living

there. The heartiness of the welcome that I received and the hospitality that I encountered was overwhelming. Women made me tea and showed me their handicrafts. They proudly presented their children, complained about their domineering husbands and shared their meals with me. I learned how hard life in the mountains can be, cut off from civilization, and I was asked again and again whether this war would soon be over. This was a war they did not understand against an enemy they did not know.

Afghanistan is an incomparably beautiful country. There is nowhere else in the world that I have experienced such dramatic displays of nature as I have on the Hindu Kush. However, it is above all the people who make Afghanistan such a special place – their willingness to help, the dignity with which women in particular manage to overcome even the greatest deprivations and the enormous energy with which they constantly start all over again. They are living in the midst of a war which on paper ended long ago but which in reality has gone on for 30 years, a war that is constantly being stoked on the one side by fanatical Islamists and on the other by the most diverse political views and claims to power.

The extent to which Afghanistan has been subjected to the vagaries of power politics over the past few decades was most clearly expressed by Zbigniew Brezezinski, security advisor to U.S. President Jimmy Carter between 1977 and 1981. In an interview with the French magazine, "le Nouvelle Observateur", in 1988, he was asked if there was anything he regretted about U.S. policy on Afghanistan at the time. He replied: "Regret what? That secret operation was an excellent idea. It had the effect of drawing the Russians into the Afghan trap and you want me to regret it? The day that the Soviets officially crossed the border, I wrote to President Carter: 'We now have the opportunity of giving to the USSR its Vietnam war.' [...] What is most important to the history

of the world? The Taliban or the collapse of the Soviet empire? Some stirred-up Muslims or the liberation of Central Europe and the end of the cold war?" One might assume that had he been asked that question after September 11, 2001, his answer might have been a little different.

How Afghanistan will develop in the coming years and whether it will succeed in becoming a modern, peaceful society, is not a question that I feel able to answer. On behalf of this country, devastated as it is by war, I hope that it is the people who are central to the decisions being made by the international commu-

nity and that they are given the chance to rebuild their country. And then, perhaps, a generation can finally emerge who know what peace means.

Ursula Meissner, January 20, 2008

WOMEN – AN UNCERTAIN FUTURE

After 30 years of war, the people of Afghanistan are on the verge of making a fresh start, both politically and in terms of their society. But more than five years after the Taliban fell, the country's troubles are still far from over. And there is only a sketchy outline of how to tackle what is still to come.

THE BURQA – THE VIEW THROUGH THE BARS

A symbol of oppression?

It was not religious zeal but secular jealousy that led to the creation of the burqa. Legend has it that an Afghan ruler was surrounded by particularly charming wives. Their beauty was said to be so breathtaking that he begrudged his subjects' stares. He ordered the women to cover the curves of their bodies with a large piece of cloth as a simple veil would not suffice. Their entire body should be cloaked, aside from a small opening in front of the face. And since he was not only a jealous man but also a mistrustful one, the opening had to be covered with a mesh made from knitted wool, bound cloth or twisted horsehair. This is how the burqa was created.

To begin with, the burqa was little more than a fashionable piece of clothing. Women from well-to-do families coquettishly wore their full-body cover when they went out on walks or on shopping trips, promising much without giving away more than an indication of what lay beneath the wrapping. This changed radically in 1996 when the Taliban took control of Kabul and declared strict Islamic law. A radio broadcast in the capital city announced that women could no longer leave the house without a male member of their family to accompany them. Women could no longer go to work. Girls could no longer go to school. And wearing a burqa became obligatory. Shoes that might make a sound were forbidden because it was thought that they would disturb men. White shoes were forbidden, since white is the color of Islam. Woe betide those who trample it under foot! Woe betide the women who wear no socks! Woe betide those who paint their nails or wear colorful clothes under their burqa! Anyone who ignores these rules will be beaten in public!

Wherever one went, it was immediately apparent that the omnipresent clerical police were not joking. Women had strikingly

1 *Stopping by the roadside.* 2 *Fatima says she is just 50 years old.* 3 *This is how the farmers live in Nangahar, a village on the border with Pakistan.* 4 *Leamer and Leza – finally freed from the burqa.* 5 *Some women would be happy to lift the veil of their burqas so they can get a better look at what they are buying at the market.*

5

similar stories of their experiences. There were plenty of these stories around and the rumors would spread like wildfire. A neighbor saw something; a friend repeated the story; a mother warned her daughters. Men wearing black turbans patrolled the streets. The expressions on their faces were grim. They wielded menacing-looking wooden clubs and plastic-covered cords. They would grab any woman whose burqa did not properly cover their body and punish them publicly, with blows to the back and behind. Passers-by stood watching, dumbfounded. Fear was ever-present.

In December 1996, a Taliban-controlled radio station, Voice of Sharia, reported that 225 women in Kabul had been rounded up and publicly punished for disobeying the Taliban's rules on attire. A young girl was beaten because she had left the house without wearing socks. One woman with painted nails had her thumbs cut off.

The Taliban's strict regime was welcomed by a large part of Afghanistan's population, who hoped it would herald a new era in which their personal security would be guaranteed. While the United States and Europe criticised the fanatics, they overlooked the fact that it was not only Afghanistan but also it's neighbors who were failing to appreciate that gender equality was an inte-

SOMETHING NEW BENEATH THE BURQA

Bright red shoes worn beneath a burqa stand out on the streets of Kabul. So much so that even women rushing by stop to marvel at them. They are probably the only pair of shoes like it in the entire city.

With a note of pride in her young voice, the woman says her husband brought them back from England. Neither she nor her friends had ever seen anything like them before. The other women were envious. The woman said that there was a dress that matched the shoes but she only wore that at home for her husband.

I asked her if I could look at her face. The question shocked her and she scurried off. Freedom is a very gradual process. I took pictures of the shoes without anyone noticing.

gral part of free society. The Taliban countered domestic criticism in their own particular way with measures that were reminiscent of the Roman "bread and circuses" policy, used to pacify the local population. It was said that the Taliban in Kabul would publicly flog corrupt officials, having announced the event in advance. The same went for women convicted of crimes.

It was not the rocket-propelled grenades or the machine guns that became the symbol of the new Afghanistan, but rather the burqa. The streets of Afghanistan looked different. Women were no longer seen. They simply disappeared either from view or behind a burqa. This straightforward piece of clothing has become an enduring symbol of the physical and psychological oppression of women, of religious constraints and of the Taliban's totalitarian regime. Westerners felt anxious and uneasy at the sight of the full-body shroud. It was only after the Taliban fell in 2001 that the requirement to wear the burqa was dropped. At that moment, men and woman became equals in the eyes of the law. But the burqa remains to this day.

Top left *A girl's school in the provinces.* **Bottom left** *Samina, a school teacher, on her way home.* **Left** *Hawkers sell jewelry and nail polish at the bazaar.*

EQUAL IN THE EYES OF THE LAW

Self-determination for women is a life-and-death struggle

Here's an example of black humor from Afghanistan: in the old days, wives had to walk three paces behind their husbands. Now the men send their wives three paces in front. Is this a breakthrough for equality? No. The men are just scared of the land-mines that have been left lying around after the war.

According to the constitution, men and women in Afghanistan have the same rights. But even those who are aware of their rights would never dare to walk on the streets without their burqa. The fear of attack or the anxiety that the Taliban may someday return are simply too great. There is little faith in the new laws. And women scarcely have the opportunity to assert their newfound rights because no one is actually willing to support them in doing so. At present, the country is inundated with a flood of rules and laws. But while they exist on paper, the reality is quite different.

There have been very few actual changes in favor of women, and there has been a great deal of resistance. Abdullah Saleh, the chief magistrate of the tiny village of Asaf Khyl in the province of Karabagh, admits that mistakes were made in the past. But at the same time he is scandalized: the process has gone so far in the major cities that women working for the government or international organizations often get the same if not better jobs than the men. "That means the rights of men are now being trampled on," the old man says. But he comforts himself with the thought that everything is still quite different in the country. This stems from the fact that most women can neither read nor write out here. They are not even aware of what rights they have. And nobody bothers to explain the rights to them. The Afghanistan Independent Human Rights Commission confirms that the heads of families continue to use violence against women to get their way. Girls are still not allowed to go to school. Arranged marriages are still practiced as is the tradition of badal, a form of conflict resolution in which the victim's family is given a daughter by the family of the perpetrator. Up to 80 percent of marriages are arranged against the bride's will. More than half of those brides are under the age of 16 on their wedding day.

Women often choose horrible means of escaping violence in their marriages. They pour gasoline over their heads and then set themselves on fire. Self-immolation occurs almost daily in Afghanistan and there have been hundreds of cases.

There is just one female member of Afghanistan's first freely-elected government. She is the minister for family affairs. Around two dozen official advice centers for women were to have been created in the provinces. But because resistance was so high, they were never mentioned again.

The process of achieving equality in Afghanistan will be a lengthy battle and, for many women, a battle of life and death.

Above *A monument dating from the period of Soviet occupation in center of Kabul.* **Top right** *They say she burned herself while cooking. Very few people survive self-immolation.* **Bottom right** *A bedside visit – the husband has to remain outside.*

PLAYING WITH THE BURQA

One of my most pleasant encounters was with Fatma and her family in November 2001, shortly after the Taliban were driven out of Kabul by the Northern Alliance. It was a tough job to get Fatma, a widow, and her six daughters together in front of a camera for a group picture. One of them was always missing, which was hardly surprising. After the Taliban's regime of fear came to an end, women were allowed out of the house without male accompaniment. This meant they could go shopping again — which they did. With a passion. There are so many new things for them to discover, such as video clips and music, things that were never available on the market before. "The five years we spent under the Taliban were like being in prison," said Fatma. Her youngest, Freshta, adds: "It's not just that we were scared. You can't imagine how boring it was. For five years we couldn't do anything!" Finally, at the fourth attempt, all of them are sitting in the living room for the photo shoot, covered from head to toe in their burqas. The only face visible in the room is that of their late father, whose photo is hanging above the sofa. When I ask them to remove their burqas, they do so without hesitation. The oldest puts hers over a broom and carries it in through the living room door. Everyone laughs.

Left *Fatima goes to school for the first time.*
Top *An act of liberation — the burqa on a broomstick.*
Bottom *A group photo with veils.*
Next double-page *During the Taliban's rule, Mariam had to beg in front of the ruins. She was prevented from working as a teacher, but today she is back in the classroom.*

KABUL – THE KINGS HAVE ABDICATED

The King is dead. Long live the King? Not in Afghanistan. The era of absolute monarchy is long gone. But there is a ramshackle mausoleum on the hill that once served as the resting place for King Amanullah. It now houses the remains of Mohammed Sahir and his wife. It reminds Afghans of an era during which Kabul was a flourishing capital city. An era that the destroyed city of millions is now seeking to reclaim.

THE MIRACLE OF KABUL

The friendly official at the World Bank was absolutely right. "Just go take a look for yourself," he told me. "Only then are you going to be able to understand what Kabul's biggest problem really is. It's a problem that the European and Americans know very little about because it is apparently not yet spectacular enough to be reported about in the media."

He was not talking about the Taliban, but about the millions of people who have settled here in Kabul in a short space of time, as if hoping that the city's polluted rivers were full of gold.

Out of breath after clambering over the boulders, I am standing on one of the hills that encircle Afghanistan's capital city. I stare in disbelief at the women and children nearby who are hauling canisters of water from the bottom of the valley up to their families at the top, apparently with ease. All around me are simple stone huts and little buildings with walls made of clay bricks, dried in the sun. The roofs are invariably made from straw and clay, and look as if the next heavy rainstorm might wash them away. When viewed from the valley below, the little hilltop community looks almost picturesque. But the closer you get, the more apparent the reality becomes. There are clearly no toilets, nobody cares about the waste, everything is rotting and the stench is unbearable. But unlike in Africa, the people who live here under these appalling conditions are incredibly well-dressed. Old clothes are painstakingly repaired and I wonder to myself how they manage to keep everything so clean under these circumstances. Everyone is extremely friendly to me, as I've found just about everywhere in Afghanistan. But they don't want me to take pictures. They are too proud and therefore too ashamed of the conditions in which they are living.

Today, the picture one sees of Kabul is marked by these illegal communities, nestled on even the steepest of cliffs above the

1 Fresh bread from the baker. 2 Carpet dealers sometimes carry their goods for miles to reach their customers. 3 Something unusual for Afghanistan: this friendly looking old man was happy to have his picture taken. 4 Children are always hungry. 5 Kabul became a city of millions virtually overnight.

town. Attempts at urban planning date back 40 years when the population was expected to be rise to 700,000. A modern city was sketched out on the drawing board, complete with sewer systems, a power supply grid, paved roads and even a subway system. But before the ambitious plans could be turned into reality, Kabul was all but destroyed: first by the Soviet army, then in the civil war against the Taliban, and finally under American and British bombing raids.

During the decades of conflict, millions of Afghans fled to Pakistan and Iran. They came not only from the capital Kabul but also from surrounding villages that were destroyed in the war. After the Taliban fell, they were sent from the countries that had become their homes back to their homeland. The majority went to Kabul. Many of the people whom I have met there in the last few years – from street hawkers, taxi drivers, teachers to ordinary workers – have told me that their homes are, in fact, outside the city in the countryside. But there are precious few opportunities for them to work there. The only place that offers a livelihood is Kabul.

It is not just returning refugees who are drawn to the capital. More and more families from the surrounding villages are streaming into the city as well. There are no official figures but

experts estimate that in a relatively short period of time Kabul has increased in size from less than a million to more than three million inhabitants.

In an attempt to create a better life for themselves, many of these newcomers to Kabul try to buy tiny parcels of land but they often get ripped off by conmen who sell them plots whose ownership is uncertain or which are merely leased. As a result, the majority of Afghans have built property on land that belongs to the city. These "informal settlements", as they are politely de-

Under these conditions it is a minor miracle that Kabul has so far managed to avoid the sort of slums that are seen in Karachi or Calcutta. This is mainly because most of the new inhabitants all used to live in villages. In many ways, once they are in Kabul, they continue to lead their village lives. "When we were children in the villages, we learned how to build houses," residents of the "informal settlements" tell me. They are quite proud of what they have achieved and how they have achieved it. "If you don't have enough money, you go and ask a friend. We help each other out. It's usually just small amounts of money and the people here are all very hard-working." At least one person in the family usually manages to find a job in Kabul. And then the debts are paid straight back. It's a question of honor.

scribed in the World Bank's reports, have already spread across more than 80 square kilometers (30 square miles) around the city.

My translator, Zahir, says: "I don't know any more where my home town begins and where it ends." Up on the hilltops, there are neither water pipes nor any sort of sewage system. There are no refuse collectors, no schools, no hospitals, no power supplies. Basically, there is nothing that one might usually find in a residential urban area.

Left Page *In areas without power or telephone lines carrier pigeons are still an important means of communication (above). Blue mosques under a blue sky (below).* **Above** *Shopping at the market. The animals are slaughtered at home.* **Left** *A mountain of nuts at the bazaar.*

Next double-page *Those who can afford to take a pleasure trip with this carriage, which is drawn by an elaborately decorated horse. Usually it is the young girls who wear white burqas.*

A LIFE IN RUINS

50,000 widows and nobody cares

"The Russians are to blame for everything." In Kabul, I hear this comment more often than I hear other disparaging remarks about the Taliban, the Mujahideen or the Americans. The Russians probably had left behind the most spectacular ruins: the battle-scared Soviet cultural center in the west of Kabul. For years, the building housed the poorest members of Afghan society. In the meantime the Russians have rebuilt their cultural center. For the most part, they were widows and orphans seeking a home in slums. After 30 years of war, there are more than 50,000 women on the streets of Kabul, to a large extent illiterate and without any source of income.

International aid organizations like ADRA and others are often only capable of handling the major emergencies. There are scarcely any prospects for the future for these women.

Miriam is sitting opposite me in a windowless room with crumbling concrete walls. Tired and listless, she is poking at a little fire that is meant to be boiling water for the tea that she is about to serve. The Afghan people are always hospitable. Even under utterly adverse conditions, common courtesy says that guests must be offered something. Miriam tells me hesitantly that she sends her children out to beg instead of sending them to school.

"If the children don't bring home some money, then there is nothing to eat." I ask how many people, besides her, are living in these ruins. "At a least a couple of hundred," she says. "Perhaps even a thousand." She is not certain because every day more people arrive. "At least it is dry here and the aid organizations are able to locate us. Sometimes we get food and also some blankets and clothes. Otherwise, we would not be able to survive."

The ruins and the slums are slowly disappearing from Kabul. In the five years after the fall of the Taliban, much of the rubble has been removed, streets have been repaired and new buildings, in particular those of the Afghan authorities, have been erected. The many people without homes are being pushed out to the fringes of the city.

Left page *A ride on the big wheel costs one "Afghani" or less than one cent.* **Above** *Refugees in a former Soviet residence in Kabul.* **Left** *An aid organization distributes sunflower oil to refugees.*

Next double-page *Achmed is proud of this empty rice bag provided by the UN (above left). The tarpaulins that cover aid packages serve as protection against the wind and weather (below left). What will tomorrow bring? A mother and child in a tent in the refugee camp (right).*

Following double-page *Kabul is a fast-growing city. New houses built on rocky cliffs.*

Kabul's former Chief of Police Abdul Bassir Salangi was one of the first Afghan leaders to felt compelled to modernize the city. He ordered bulldozers to tear down an emergency accommodation in the Sherpur district, one of the poorest areas of Kabul, in order to make room for ostentatious villas built for the rich Afghans who were returning to the capital. The gold-covered columns on the facades of these houses glistened at me from afar. My translator pointed to a palace-like building. "That one belongs to the chief of police. And the one behind it too." Where did he get the money? I ask. My translator shrugs his shoulders. Apparently I am not the only one to be asking this question. Some western diplomats later protested to the Afghan president and Salangi was sent to work in another province. This settlement of villas will never be a choice destination for an excursion. Of more interest is the City Center, whose construction began in 2003, shortly after the end of the war. The building is made of steel and glass and its upper floors form part of a luxury hotel. Security there is tight, not just when state guests are staying in the hotel. The latest electronic gadgets, designer clothing and fine foods are on abundant display. These are things that people on the street or shopkeepers from the provinces have never even seen. It is an oasis of luxury, free of dust, in an otherwise chaotic city. Only officials, warlords and development workers can actually afford any of it. Normal Afghans are obliged to simply look in through the windows.

Afghanistan is a country on the cusp between the medieval and the modern. Centuries appear to separate village life in the far-off provinces and the modern image that Kabul shows off to its visitors. Sixteen banks have opened offices in the capital. Foreign automakers are tempting consumers with advertisements. There are numerous new restaurants where you can find Italian, Chinese, German or even Lebanese food. Modern Afghans use their cell phones to stay informed about what's new in the fast-changing city. What my translator does not show me during our trip through Kabul are the brothels. Since 2001 they have mushroomed all over the city and their doors are open not only to visitors from abroad.

Above *Art market in Kabul. The dealer is in high spirits so business must be good.*
Right page *The entrance to the shopping center is guarded. Luxury goods and images from the western world are a thorn in the Taliban's side. For that reason, the shops' owners are particularly wary of the threat of attacks (above). Afghan women go to Kabul beauty parlours to get their hair done in the style of Indian movie stars. The demure "Bollywood" romances are massively popular across Afghanistan (below).*

"WHAT'S A STREETCAR?"

Stoplights without power, drivers without licenses

There is blue sky up there somewhere. But from the ground you can't see it. I venture out into Afghanistan's capital city early one morning. There are already 400,000 cars, trucks, buses and motorbikes on the roads. Exhaust fumes mix with stirred-up dust to create thick, dark clouds. Nobody is concerned about environmental protection here. The air is so thick, that it is hard to make out the police officers gesticulating wildly at the intersections. "Why are there no streetcars in Kabul?" I ask the taxi driver. "What is a streetcar?" he asks in return. Traffic in Kabul is unbelievably chaotic. It progresses at walking pace, a blur of wheels, some of the vehicles just inches apart from each other. Farmers herd their goats and sheep across the road, threading them in

between the cars. They rub up against the old and new Japanese-built taxis with their yellow and white paint jobs, whose drivers always appear to decide at the very last minute which direction they wish to take. These are communal taxis that load up with as many passengers as they possibly can. It is cheaper for each individual passenger as result but they also stop constantly – and without warning – to let passengers on or off. Among the throng, you can also spot the modern SUVs belonging to foreigners and United Nations employees. They are driven around by Afghan drivers who earn 10 times as much as a police officer. In the midst of it all, rickety old bicycles squeak past pulling makeshift trailers laden with fruit and vegetables. The Afghan soldiers who guide their massive armored vehicles through the streets have to be particularly skillful in order to avoid accidents. The atmosphere is highly charged and it feels like it could go off at any minute. Ordinary traffic accidents have already been known to trigger bloody unrest.

A dozen stoplights have survived the vicissitudes of war. Since city's power supply is only on for a couple of hours at a time, I don't even know if they still function properly or if they just blink on and off. Abdul Shakoor Khairkhwah, head of the Kabul traffic

police force, has ordered new lights for 100 intersections. After they are installed, the look-out posts on the street corners, dating from the Soviet era, will disappear. But will the new lights actually work? The police chief is confident they will. A spokesman for the electricity authority warns, however, that the town has to pay $40,000 it owes in overdue power bills before that can be guaranteed. Also, because the cabling is so old, the traffic lights can only be connected close to generators themselves. Surely that will mean several more police officers will still be needed at every street corner? The people on the roads, for whom this matters most, are quite clear about it. "Of course. Drivers here are not going to pay attention to a stoplight. How are they supposed to know what the traffic laws are? Most of them simply bought their licenses anyway."

Left page *Some truck drivers indulge their fondness for the local children. A free trip through the streets of Kabul.*
Above *Chaotic traffic in Kabul. This police squad car was a gift from Germany.*
Left *Jeeps belonging to the security forces, yellow taxis and men on bicycles all fight for the right of way.*

"TITANIC" – THE RIVERBED MARKET

New designs on Afghan rugs

A dealer on Afghanistan's Chicken Street came up with the novel idea of weaving a carpet based on the September 11th attacks. And when it turned out that he could make money out of it everyone started copying him. Airplanes, skillfully woven from Afghan wool, can be seen flying into the burning World Trade Center. For a while the carpets were a top-seller among US soldiers, until they were stopped from going out in the evenings, like other uniformed foreigners, for fear of attacks.

Chicken Street is no ordinary bazaar. Apart from carpets, there are lots of items for sale that you might also find in a western supermarket. The normal bazaars in Kabul's old town, which have been rebuilt following their destruction during the war, look very much like those in Cairo, Damascus or Istanbul and will hopefully always retain their oriental charm, even if in future they will likely be overrun by tourists.

One of the peculiarities of the bazaars is that the traders do not sit patiently waiting behind their counters. They vie for your attention by gesturing wildly and calling out, even shouting, to get you to come over to where they can make deals with you. They lure buyers over to their stalls of dried fish, steaming pots of coffee, embroidered robes, herbs, radiant brass platters or tinny earrings said to be 1,000 years old. Whether it is little bottles of what is supposedly rosehip oil or bags of undefined spices, if you buy without bartering you will not be taken seriously.

The only exception is gold. This precious metal is weighed out precisely in front of the customer. The price for a gram of gold is determined by its value on the international market. The only point of negotiation is how much the goldsmith can charge for his handiwork. If a customer finds the price too high in one bazaar then no one comes running after him to try and change his mind, as is the case in many other aisles in the market.

If it is not raining, then Kabul has something rather special to offer its shoppers: a bazaar on the dried-out river bed of the Kabul river. Some wisecrack once dubbed the market "The Ti-

tanic Bazaar". The super-fast traders who lay out their tables on the river's sandy banks are relying on a prolonged drought. If the river were to suddenly flow again, then they might face the same watery fate that met the passengers of the ocean-liner.

Above *Hundreds of red carpets are rolled out on the dusty ground and offered for sale.*
Right page *If it does not rain then the bazaar takes place on the riverbed (above). This velvet cloth is mainly used to make pillow-cases (below).*

Next double-page *Afghan carpet dealers are not only good at driving a hard bargain. The attack on the World Trade Center inspired them to produce new designs. A lot of U.S. soldiers bought this carpet as a souvenir.*

HUSBANDS WHO TAKE THE LAW INTO THEIR OWN HANDS

Stories from imprisoned women

Nilop has just turned 17. Afraid, she sits on her bed in the prison cell, worrying that the visit might mean something sinister. I try to reassure her. The female prison-guard told me that the girl was supposed to marry a 60-year-old man. When she found out, she ran away from home. Her parents caught her and handed her over to the police. They put her in jail. The stinking prison cells house other women, some of whom have been handed over to the judicial authorities by their husbands for alleged adultery. One of the women threw boiling cooking fat into her cousin's face when he tried to rape her.

The imprisoned women live in unspeakable conditions. They are accommodated in the tiniest spaces, without access to sanitation, without sufficient food, sometimes without even drinking water, and constantly under threat of attack from the guards. The International Committee of the Red Cross and the international women's organization medica mondiale have been caring for these women since 2002. They receive food, clothes and blankets, and for the first time in their lives they sleep on proper bed-frames with mattresses. They ask me whether their cases will ever be brought to trial. I don't have any answers. Some of them have been waiting for three years for a hearing. Even after the fall of the Taliban, women who flee domestic violence are often treated like criminals by authorities and end up in jail. It could be years before a judicial reform announced by the government comes into effect. Women's equality exists officially but vast systemic changes are required before those changes become reality.

Right *An accusation from a husband is enough to get a wife and children sent to prison. Kafira, 19, does not know why she was locked up.*

Next double-page *The imprisoned women have to wait for months for a legal hearing. They are terrorized by the prison guards and are often raped. Private aid organizations take care of them. There are no lawyers to represent them, no medical assistance and hardly any contact with the outside world.*

ALONE WITH AFGHANS

An amusement park for the rich

The journey to a recreation park near Kabul was somehow not what I had imagined it would be. It was a Friday, the Islam equivalent to a Sunday in our calendar. The journey began through narrow streets. The sound was deafening. Clouds of dust tinged with diesel fuel wafted over us. There were cars stopped all along the way, some of them with flat tires in the soft sand. In this kind of traffic jam, even bikes and motorcycles can't get through. Any kind of delay is enough to bring out the beggars, who swarm around the day-trippers. They know that it is only those people with more money than average who can actually afford to make the trip into the hills.

The destination is a little spot of paradise on a small blue lake surrounded by green trees. There are swings for the children and even a carousel. Nestled along the sides of the lake are several small restaurants. Obviously they don't sell any beer but you can buy lurid colored soda and mineral water. There are also pavilions along the lakeshore with colorful awnings. But many of the guests have instead spread blankets out under the trees and can be seen sitting there eating food that they have brought with them. Some of them are dancing to Indian or Arabic music. Because power supplies in the capital of Kabul are irregular at best,

the calf and knee. But none of the women venture into the lake. Instead most of them are preparing the picnic for their families. They wander about up here without their burqas. If they are brave (most Afghans can't swim) and able to afford it, they rent out a colorful pedalo, designed to look like a swan. These are the only swans on the lake.

The amusement park was closed during the Taliban's reign. "Music was not even allowed in public," said Mohammed Sharif, a businessman from Kabul. Even now that the Taliban are gone foreigners clearly consider the trip to the idyllic lake too dangerous. The Afghans are pretty much on their own up here.

they are accustomed to hooking up their radios and tape decks to their car batteries in makeshift fashion. They can be seen expertly lifting out their cars' batteries and connecting them to their electronic equipment with an astonishing degree of confidence, almost as if this is what the car's user manual recommended.

The men leap into the warm, turquoise-colored water. For women, there is a particular kind of bathing suit, which covers

Left page *Stretched-out pieces of cloth are designed to protect the women from the gaze of other men (above). Grilled and spicy lamb with fresh flatbread is a much-loved delicacy in these parts and reserved mainly for the men (below).* **Above** *A deceptive idyll. Two landmines exploded in the park on this day. The visitors came nevertheless.* **Left** *Only the men take a dip.*

Next double-page *Young men enjoying each others' company. Music and dancing at a funfair in Kabul.*

SECURITY – A QUESTION OF WEAPONS?

In Afghanistan children play with destructed tanks. But this is not a game of soldiers. To the delight of their parents the children take them apart and salvage parts that can be sold for cash. Rusting wrecks that were once the pride of the Soviet army can be found all over the country. They were meant to have brought the Afghans the gift that they have been promised for years. A gift that they are still awaiting today. Peace and security.

SOLDIERS AS TOURISTS

A village becomes a munitions factory

If you're not careful in the bazaar, then your feet will get trodden on – without malice, of course. The guy that I am with knows this, too. He is a stocky non-commissioned officer in the German army. He is wearing his "war paint". That's what the soldiers call it when they are in uniform, with a loaded gun over their shoulders and on patrol without helmet, just a cap. We walk cross the market square and it is quite clear that he doesn't feel at home here in Kunduz among the noisy Afghans. He attempts to keep his distance from all the hustle and bustle. His job is to keep an eye on me, which in this babel of donkeys' hooves, flying tradesmen, begging children, burqa-clad women and bearded men is not exactly an easy task.

I am taking pictures among the tables, which are piled high with spices, or among the traders and the many sacks which they have been laid out in front of them.

My soldier companion finds it hard to move around with his cumbersome weapon. Instead, an unarmed, casually dressed officer from the Germany army camp remains at my side at all times. He is not at all bothered by the clothing and the sheets of cloth, which are draped from the shops' beams right up over the bazaar's pathways and which make me invisible to him at times. He is almost like a tourist. The only difference is that he is not buying anything. The Afghans pay more attention to me than they do to the German soldiers.

Since I knew my way around the country from my many previous visits, I was of the opinion that I didn't need protection and would have rather gone without my two chaperons. But as a guest of the German army, the rules said you have to have at least one person accompany you, even if on those days there had not been any trouble.

1 *Protection for aid workers: weapons are omnipresent.* 2 *A new bridge built not far from the Khyber Pass.* 3 *Men also dress up.* 4 *Construction materials are hard to obtain and only a few people can afford to rebuild their homes.* 5 *When the first German soldiers arrived in Afghanistan in 2002 they were welcomed with open arms.*

The Germany army had constructed a small camp on the outskirts of the town of Kunduz. The atmosphere was relaxed. It was harvest time. The farmers were out in the fields, the soldiers patrolled in their jeeps. Afghan farmers and German army soldiers would greet each other in a friendly way if they met far out of the town center. Once a week, the German army officers met the community elders. They discussed where the German soldiers could help with sanitation projects, where to sink a bore, and where a bridge needed to be constructed. It was clear to all involved that it was best if the German soldiers were not allowed out into the town given that the culture was completely alien to them. But if the dealers in the bazaar had their way they would welcome the soldiers with open arms. They asked me frequently where they all were. That was in 2003 – which in comparison to today meant that the security situation was pretty relaxed. No one imagined it would deteriorate as it has.

Today, trips to Afghanistan are either very tightly restricted or not at all possible. Soldiers stationed there no longer talk to the locals, because they rarely leave their quarters. It is inconceivable that a soldier would get out of their armored personnel carrier to visit a market. Even visiting members of German parliament are limited by and large to contact with the armed forces. If there are any meetings at all with the Afghan authorities then they invariably only take place in the German army's high-security compound.

A journey out to Derra makes clear how difficult it is dealing with Afghanistan. The border region between Pakistan and Afghanistan around the Khyber Pass is a kind of political no-man's land, for which there is no UN mandate. It has largely been spared the fighting seen in recent years.

As a result, the town of Derra is an oasis for all kinds of forms of trading. From high-tech electrical goods through drugs to weapons

SECURING PEACE

of all kinds, there is nothing that you can't get hold of in Derra. On the streets, there are only men. I am dressed like a man in my massoud hat and a salwar kameez that reaches down to my knees. My guards are nervous. They keep reminding me to keep my camera hidden. They are all armed to the teeth and the atmosphere is highly charged. The reason for this is quite apparent as soon as you look at the goods that are on offer. Dealers who would normally be selling sweet goods, embroidered burqas or

Left page *Placards like this one can be found wherever international troops are stationed. These symbols are meant to make clear that soldiers are friends and not occupiers.* **Top** *Hawkers share the street with German soldiers searching for mines. What was a normal occurrence in 2003 is impossible today.*
Above *An unscheduled stroll down Chicken Street would no longer be possible.*

Securing peace begins by creating confidence and winning the hearts of local children seems like a good place to start. When they arrived in Afghanistan, German soldiers gave the children kites adorned with white doves. The photographs of Taliban members, warlords and drug dealers that hang in the German army's quarters are designed to help the German soldiers get accustomed to the Afghans' facial features. Many of those who are wanted are hidden away in inaccessible mountain regions or in the Tribal Area on the border with Pakistan. Finding them is virtually impossible.

household items — that is to say everything that you would normally find in the bazaar — are conspicuous by their absence. Instead, younger and older men are touting infamous Russian Kalashnikov rifles and ammunition. You can find rocket launchers, homemade explosive devices in various sizes, weapons of all kinds, hand grenades and landmines. It's quite an impressive arsenal for such an ostensibly simple market.

The entire area is a weapons and munitions factory. Unfortunately I could not visit the workshops but it is there that original versions of various weapons are delivered, taken apart and faithfully copied. Kalashnikovs are particularly cheap. You can get a fully functioning weapon complete with ammunition for the equivalent of about $75. It is hard to say whether the imitation works as well as the original. It is also uncertain how many weapons Derra produces. "There would be a nationwide outcry if the government were to try to force the people of Derra into farming," one of my guards said.

According to Afghan tradition, every man should have at least one gun. And this is not just a result of the recent wars. Clan

rivalries meant that guns were necessary even in previous centuries for self-defence. The tradition of gun ownership stretches far back into Afghan history. There are so many rounds fired off at weddings and celebrations that you might think that there's a gunfight going on between two rival clans.

But in recent years the nature of the weapons that can be found in people's private arsenals has changed. Today, most of them would contain an anti-tank weapon. The weapons bazaar in Derra has until now outlasted all the wars in Afghanistan.

Left page *It is not just the bomb attacks that threaten the lives of people in Afghanistan. There are millions of mines spread around the country that pose a daily risk to the population (above). The German-Iranian writer Siba Shakib advises German troops (below).* **Above** *A short break with the farmers after searching for mines.* **Left** *Airmail for Kunduz.*

Next double-page *A business in the weapons hub of Derra.*

BILLIONS SPENT ON SECURITY

But who will pay?

Experts at the U.S. company Dyn.Corp. could not believe it at first. Young Afghans were to be given a crash course in becoming a police officer and were then sent out with new uniforms and new shoes to police stations across the country. There were no guns for them in the first year despite the fact that there was likely to be some firefights. Not even the training company had weapons or munitions. Shortly thereafter, the new police officers would return, happily, wearing the shabby clothes and the old beaten-up sandals that they had used before they had turned up for training in the first place. They had sold their new uniforms on the bazaar. When the Americans heard this, they put an end to the shoe and clothing program.

Afghanistan has never had a real police force. But now, in the shortest possible period of time, some 80,000 police officers are meant to be trained up and sent off to work. The reality of this is only slowly becoming apparent. And it is a far more complicated – and expensive – story than the episode with the uniforms. It appears that the Americans were completely unprepared for the level of illiteracy that they would encounter in the new recruits. Over 50 percent of the new police officers were incapable of reading or writing.

The American training company's approach to solving the problem was a supremely practical one, or so the story went in Kabul's cafes. Educated police officers took eight weeks to finish their training, while the illiterate recruits took only five weeks. This was because the training company dropped all the courses that illiterate recruits were unable to follow. Unfortunately, those were all the subjects that, from a European perspective at least, would be considered necessary for police work: ensuring law and order and giving the local communities the sense of security that they have been looking for.

Following a European model, some hundreds of Afghans have been put through three-year courses to become police officers

THE CLAN IS THE MOST IMPORTANT THING

For centuries, life in Afghanistan has been organized around the village community. Only men are allowed to sit on the council of elders which makes decisions on the future of the clan according to the rules of the Koran. Many Afghans, particularly those living in remote areas, do not feel bound to the rules imposed by the central government in Afghanistan. For as long as anyone can remember they have been looking out for themselves and are not about to start taking orders from a strange and distant government. This was the case during the war with the Soviet Union and it is exactly the same now with the Taliban – whether they are fighting with or against them. Decisions about which side of the conflict to support are often driven purely by economic necessity and the likelihood of the clan's survival. These deeply rooted structures mean that it is not easy today for those who are trying to help the Afghans stand on their own feet. Many of the former Mujahideen feel a greater sense of obligation towards their ex-leaders than they do towards the government in Kabul and therefore refuse to hand in their weapons. The Taliban are fully aware of this as well.

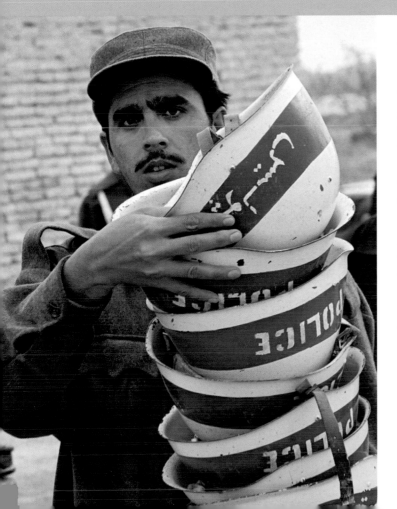

by German experts. A further 3,000 lower-ranking police officers have been given one-year training courses. The United States, however, has an entirely different concept of what the police force should actually be doing: their job is to make secure the regions that have been liberated from the Taliban, destroy poppy fields and win the war against the drug barons' armies – in effect, they should serve as gendarmes or military police officers. Training 70,000 police officers on this "conveyor belt" method has so far cost the US government more than $3 billion. Over the same timeframe, Germany has spent less than 100 million euros (a bit more than $150 million) on its police academy.

Afghan President Karzai has made an unusual contribution towards the process of police reform. In a surprise move, he founded an auxiliary police force: a 11,000-man group, formed by clan fighters, and based in the three southern provinces of the country. These former Mujahideen take their orders from their warlords. They don't need arming as they still have their

Left page *The army or police run drill exercises on the streets of Kabul.* **Left** *Aside from helmets soldiers are scarcely equipped with anything.*

weapons from the war. Karzai reassures critics by pointing out that they receive 10 days of training as police officers. These auxiliary forces are, however, a long way from the western concept of a police officer, serving the community as a friend and helper. The reality is that locals are actually scared of them.

Experts point to another major problem. Without a functioning justice system, police officers are operating in a vacuum which they have filled by collecting "fees" from criminals whom they arrest and then release again. This practice is prevalent even in the capital of Kabul. In the provinces there are hardly any police jails and no courts; there are no prosecutors nor judges. Moreover, so-called donor countries have failed to agree on who is going to pay the ongoing costs after the reform of the police service and the judiciary is complete. The system will require an estimated $2 billion every two years to keep running. Afghanistan cannot afford this alone.

Under a blanket of silence, the police force has been reduced in size. Instead of 319 police generals for 36,000 police officers, there are now only 120 generals for 80,000 officers. Instead of 2,447 colonels, there are now only 235. The number of police majors has declined from 1,067 to 474. Of 3,762 captains, there are now less than half that number, namely 1,140. The lower

ranks now earn three times more than what they made before. Soon there will be an electronic database at the Interior Ministry which will show how many of the freshly schooled police officers actually enter into service. In Kabul, the words of a U.S. general are oft repeated: "We trained tens of thousands of them. Where are they all?" It is safe to assume that of the new police officers around a third of them take better paying jobs from the drug barons, the warlords or the Taliban. The database should also help reduce the number of so-called "phantom" police officers. These are officers that the police station heads register as present, even though they do not exist. A comfortable means of pocketing extra cash when you are police chief. The computer will record peoples' personal details. In order to prevent unwanted people such as Taliban members from joining the police force, the recruits will be required to provide two guarantors. There has been little use for such character references in Afghan society until now.

"They came in the middle of the night," said the young woman sitting in the restaurant "Fontaine" in the Afghan capital. "There were several uniformed police officers. They claimed that we had given alcohol to Afghans. They were not interested in our papers. They took wine, beer and whisky off the shelves, took the money out of the cash register and put our cell phones in their pockets. They took my father with them. They released him the next day."

Omar, the father, had thought that the new Afghanistan would be quite different. The widower fled the Taliban with his daughter, went to the United States and earned a little money in a diner in California. After the end of the war, father and daughter returned to Kabul and intended to create a new life with a restaurant aimed at foreigners. Omar paid the state the equivalent of about $ 2200 for the license to sell alcohol. The rule was he could not serve Afghans. Shaking his head, Omar said: "Nothing has changed. First it was the Russians stealing from us, then the Taliban came, smashing everything up and beating us and now it is our very own police force who are ruining our livelihood."

Left page *Guard posts at the government palace in Kabul (above). Two generations – a former Mujahideen talks to a younger police officer (below).*
Above *The Soviets abandoned the wrecks of 147 tanks when they left Afghanistan. During the war they lost 333 helicopters and around 10,000 trucks. More than 14,000 Soviet soldiers were killed in Afghanistan.*

SMALL GIFTS, LARGE GIFTS

The government shies away from conflict with the warlords

The tanks are parked up in a courtyard in Kunduz, protected from inquisitive glimpses by a high, whitewashed wall of clay bricks. They appeared to have been well looked after, a bit like the warlord who was showing them to me. He was an Afghan who had made a name for himself fighting the Soviets and in the civil war. He was now leading a local militia. "The tanks are all ready for action," he boasted. He was wearing a smart black coat. It was 2003. Every time he came across German soldiers, who were at the time stationed in Kunduz, he exchanged pleasantries.

Two years after this conversation, the warlord from Kunduz became a General and was made Deputy Defence Minister. His tanks and militia army were incorporated into the Afghan army. The government is eager to avoid any kind of armed conflict with the warlords – as the odds would be stacked against them. The army and police are not equipped for these kinds of missions. A better strategy is to turn former opponents into allies. Opium dealers become ministers, and warlords become provincial governors or even members of parliament. The Americans and Europeans have grudgingly had to accept this road to peace. There is a less controversial method to secure peace, although its success is also questionable. "Farkhar is going to get power," the government of the province of Takhar in the north of the country announced. "Seven villages, 170 shops, the regional administration, the police force, a hospital and two schools will be supplied with electricity once the new small power station by the river is functioning." The one precondition for this is that the illegal groups operating in the district disband and hand in their weapons. The offer from the government is presented to the village elders and announced in the streets with megaphones. "Hand over your weapons and then we will build the power station which you so urgently need." The government hopes to create enough support and to motivate the local population to give up their guns. It does not work every time, however, because many of the illegal groups have such large arsenals of weapons that they just bring their less valuable weapons to the collection point and hide the better ones.

Above *This sight is not uncommon in Afghanistan – a heap of unexploded missiles at the entrance to a town.* **Right page** *The former warlord General Daud (right) is the government representative in charge of the war against drugs these days (above). Just because he has a rose does not mean this Mujahideen is bringing peace (below).*

Next double-page *Mujahideen clear a Soviet munitions dump in October 1987 (above left). At various times the Mujahideen have controlled broad swathes of Afghanistan (above right). Many of them are illiterate. However, it does not take them long to pick up the art of using modern weapons (below left). Red army prisoners with their Mujahideen guards in October 1987 in Kabul province (below right).*

DOUBLE-ENTRY ACCOUNTING

Where the billions in aid money goes

There's a significant number of modernizers in Kabul's new government. Of 31 ministers, 17 have been to a US university and returned to their native country with degrees. Others studied in Europe or in India. They did not simply come back to take part in the renaissance of their homeland. Their ambitions are greater than that: they believe Afghanistan should form closer ties to the western world. The reformers are fully aware that the West's greatest fear is that Afghanistan could again become the base for terrorists. The international community is therefore willing to support the democratization in Afghanistan with financial means. Afghanistan's young government is seeking transform the country into a modern state with the help of generous aid funding. But these reforms are long-term in nature and the population is seeing very little of them as yet. People are unhappy with the government because their standard of living is not getting noticeably better. Whether it's the drivers, the translators, the traders in the bazaar, every one asks me: "Where are the millions that you are supposed to be sending us?" They suspect the government is corrupt because the international aid program is far from transparent.

International financing has helped pay for prestige projects like the big road between Kabul and Kandahar or dams. But the farmers in the villages need wells, seeds and power.

On one of the new roads through the Panjshir Valley, we meet Abdul, a farmer, with his donkey. He is walking down the middle of a wide road that could be somewhere in Europe given the way it stretches out across the valley. I take a picture of him as he walks towards me and stops. He doesn't ask where I am from or who I am. He stands in front of me and gesticulates. He has not managed to harvest enough potatoes, he complains and takes a sack off his back and shows me the small, freshly-harvested crop. He has no idea how he will feed his wife and six children. His farmland is big enough but the trees that once yielded so many

apples and nuts were all burned down during the war. During the recent bitter conflicts, his farm was destroyed several times, he tells me. First by the Russians in the 1980s, then, again, when the Taliban moved in. Parts of the fields are still mined, meaning he can't grow anything there. He has been trying to get the local town council to agree to remove the mines since 2002. Again and again he is bought off with empty promises.

The road we are standing on was built by the government agency USAID. It leads directly to a monument to Massud, rises out of the almost romantic valley like a royal tomb. It could be a place of pilgrimage or a tourist attraction. Massud is a national hero for Abdul and most other Afghans, but no one is particularly proud of the road or of the new monument. Many families are starving, have no roofs over their heads and are awaiting support to help them in their daily struggle for survival.

Left page *A new dam in the province of Herat. During the summer the Murgh is dry.*
Above *Destroyed bridges and streets are a reminder of the war.*
Left *A village in the province of Kabul, destroyed and abandoned after the war. The former residents of this village moved into the nearby city.*

Coordinating international aid is difficult. The director of Siemens in Kabul put it this way: "The international community has still not managed to cooperate over reconstruction. Every donor country wants to lend a hand and give its support on its own terms. The Afghan authorities are overwhelmed by all the applications and suggestions by donor countries and there are mountains of paperwork building up in offices. In addition, economic reconstruction and the creation of sustainable agricultural projects are only now beginning to show limited success which means the fight against opium production is also rendered more difficult."

In order to keep corruption and embezzlement to a minimum, most monies are paid by the donor countries straight into individual projects. Much to its displeasure, the Afghan government only has an advisory role. It would rather manage the money itself and thus win more support from the population. At the moment, the government is only in charge of the so-called "core budget", from which teachers, border guards and other officials are paid.

Afghanistan is only able to muster around 10 percent of its state spending itself, the remainder comes from foreign sources. The country is broke, the population is poor, power and money lie with the drug barons, each of whom probably has more influence than the president. A large proportion of Afghanistan's farmers are still living off opium production: on the one hand, because they cannot defend themselves against the violence of the drug cartels and on the other hand, because they have no alternative way of feeding their families. It will take a long time to defeat the drug cartels, to disarm the country and create a stable peace.

President Karzai has said in the meantime, he was "naïve" when he entered office and that the reconstruction would take significantly longer than expected. According to current estimates, the United Nations reckon that it could take between 10 and 15 years. Only then will Afghanistan be able to stand on its own two feet again.

Above *This dam on the Khyber Pass has been back in operation for a relatively short period of time.* **Right page** *Scrap dealers in Kabul. Used screws, dismantled tanks, water pipes taken from ruins, iron rods – everything can be recycled.*

Next double-page *The wooden footbridge spans the Kabul river gorge.*

TORKHAM – OPEN BORDER AT KHYBER PASS

The famous Khyber Pass is open. Thousands of trucks cross back and forth between Pakistan and Afghanistan. Europe is financing a new customs post.

ROAD TOLL ON THE KHYBER PASS

Even "holy warriors" are willing to barter

Everyone has an experience that they will never forget. In my case, this is particularly true when the experience is linked to names like Torkham, the Khyber Pass and Jalabad. These places are hotspots of international politics and never cease to make headlines, mainly because they are under Taliban control. In September 2001, I was on my way to Jalabad. With hindsight, I know I could have met the same fate as that which befell a French colleague of mine just a couple of days beforehand. Some farmers found her corpse not far from the main road. She had been physically abused before she was killed.

Here's the setting: the Islamic Emirate of Afghanistan, which is what the Taliban called their state, was only recognized by Saudi Arabia, the United Arab Emirates and Pakistan. The Taliban had a consulate in the Pakistani border town of Peshawar. Wearing a white trouser suit and a white yashmak, I was sitting opposite two bearded Islamists. "Why do you want to go to Afghanistan?" one of them asked me. "I'm a photographer. I want to report on the problems that your farmers have because of the drought. I want to see what impact the latest earthquake had on your country."

The two turbaned men whispered to one another and then noted, apparently with admiration, that I was not wearing any lipstick and that my fingernails were not painted. I got a visa for $50. On that very same day, September 11, 2001, two planes crashed into the World Trade Center in Manhattan.

It was widely known that al-Qaeda was running training camps in Afghanistan and so an attack by the Americans was expected at any moment. As I got closer to the border in Torkham, I came across foreigners who had left Kabul and Jalabad. I listened to their warnings but I wanted to carry on. This was my 10th trip to Afghanistan and for the first time since the Soviets

1 *A truck on the Khyber Pass, decorated with brightly colored material.* **2** *Sometimes farmers' wives don't wear burqas.* **3** *The nomads' camels are still decorated according to local traditions.* **4** *A welcome for a patrolling soldier.* **5** *The border crossing at Torkham on September 11, 2001.*

were driven out, I had the opportunity to go to Kabul. I was not about to turn around having gotten this far. But nevertheless, Taliban soldiers sent me back after just a couple of hundred meters.

Two months later, I returned. The United States had already bombarded Kabul, Kandahar and Jalabad and the first ground troops had apparently just arrived in Northern Afghanistan. Pakistani border guards waved me over the border as if everything were completely normal. I was told that the Torkham border crossing was the easiest way for journalists to get into the country. No one knew, of course, how far the Northern Alliance troops had pushed and who was actually in charge of the command in Afghanistan at that time. Two local Afghans came with me as translators. Suddenly, four armed men blocked our path. I offered up my passport containing the unused visa. No one was interested in looking at it. My two unarmed companions were threatened with Kalashnikovs. They shoved me into a cabin, off to the side and under some trees. One of them locked the door. The group's leader carefully went through my luggage. It seemed to be taking hours. He took a sniff from a perfume bottle and stuck it in his pocket. Then he took it out of his jacket again and

held it towards me. Using his hands, he implied that there was something missing. I tried to tell him that the stopper was in Germany. Finally he started tugging at the arms of my jacket. Suddenly, it became clear that I had to get out of there. I hissed at him in English: "You are Muslim. You are not allowed to touch me."

To my surprise, he stopped immediately. He was probably not used to hearing a woman speak to him like that. He even allowed me to get up and to open the door. I said to him, loudly, that he should go and get someone to translate so that I can speak to him. The others got up and pointed their guns at me. The leader sent the men off and mumbled something menacingly in Pashto under his breath.

After a few minutes a young, tall Afghan appeared in the doorway. Accompanied by two armed men, he stammered again and again: "They want money."

Above *The proud kidnappers with their victim. They wanted to keep the picture as a souvenir.* **Right page** *Carrying everything that they own (above). January 1988: Afghan refugees make their way to Pakistan (below).*

My earlier experiences in Afghanistan convinced me that they were not about to kill me, at least not immediately. They were much more interested in the money. Now the trading began. The young Afghan was a skilled translator. They started at $1,000 and we agreed on $500. I told them I had no money with me but that in Jalabad, in the office where I was heading, I had dollars. If they'd take me there, then I could give them the money.

We got into a red Japanese truck. My two companions sat on the flatbed. The leader sniffed the perfume again and put it in his pocket. Then he locked the doors. It took us almost two hours to get to Jalabad, on a road that seemed to be made entirely of potholes. At times, I was sick to the stomach with fear that the gangsters might change their mind and kill me on the way.

Finally we arrived at the offices of the German aid organization ADRA where they knew who I was. As we walked into the room, I put my finger against my lips. But everyone knew anyway that it's best not to talk to men carrying weapons. I went behind the door and took out $500 that I actually had with me buried in my jacket. Fortunately, they had not checked there earlier. Then everything went very quickly. I gave them the money and said:

"Let's take a picture." My kidnappers actually stood beside me for a photograph. Their leader then took a faded passport picture out of his pocket, showed it to me and asked me to take a new one of him. I told him that if I did, I'd need to go to Kabul to get it developed. I was speechless after he answered: "Ok. When you return to Pakistan you will have to go via Torkham anyway. You are sure to find me there."

Left page *The Khyber Pass still looks medieval here. Soon afterwards the earthmovers descended.* **Above** *Nasim (left) and Ibrahim, my protection on the road to Afghanistan from Pakistan on September 11, 2001.*

Next double-page *Military controls on the Khyber Pass (above left). A view of the border crossing from the Pakistani side (below left). Everyone has to follow the new rules, including the trucks here on the Afghan side of the border crossing. In the background the newly opened duty free shops (above right). A recreational park just before the border with Pakistan. From the viewing platform you get a good glimpse of the colorful bustle flowing through the border crossing (below right).*

THE ROAD TO A NEW BEGINNING

Projects that don't make the headlines

Olav Bock is a German engineer. His tireless work will determine exactly when one of Afghanistan's most ambitious construction projects is completed. Bock, a man as big as a bear, smiles knowingly when asked for the umpteenth time when he will be finished. "We are almost there," he says, soothingly. Funded by EU money, the aim of the project is to create a modern, European-style border crossing for the famous Khyber Pass at Torkham. After putting the contract out to tender, the EU chose a Chinese company to carry out the construction. Olav Bock was put in charge of the project.

Counless thousands of trucks pass through here each month from Pakistan to Afghanistan. In the future, there will be not only customs duty to pay on all the goods that pass but also a toll fee. The faster the border crossing is finished, the sooner the Afghan government will start to receive the revenues. The first destination on this particular route is Jalabad. From there you can reach Kandahar and the south or Kabul and the north. Torkham will be linked to Afghanistan's road network.

The new, customs building, equipped with computers, is not likely to make international headlines when it opens. The same goes for the new roads that are being built in Afghanistan. Unless, of course, the government were able to announce not only the opening of the 400-km-long motorway (240 miles) between Kabul and Kandahar, but also guaranteed that you can drive on it without the threat of being attacked or kidnapped. But we are not that far yet. The American firm that has built

MULTICULTURAL PROJECT

The German engineer Olaf Bock was fed up with building commuter roads between German cities and decided on a whim to take on management of the border crossing at Torkham. The challenges were greater and more varied than he had expected. At first he was unsure whether he would be able to do it all: his workers are Chinese and Afghan, the border guards are Pakistani. He has to be able to deal with all of them and ensure that they can work together on a multicultural team. But the project was successful, thanks in no small part to the engineer's knowledge, acquired in Somalia and Sudan among other places, as well as his respect for everyone involved and above all else his boundless patience.

the motorway with the assistance of money from USAID (United States Agency for International Development) has had to employ hundreds of private security guards to protect its workers. And despite these measures there have still been numerous attacks.

The aim of the U.S. project is to build a new ring-road around the entire country, starting in Kabul, to Kandahar, down to the south and then west and to Herat. From there it will lead up to Mazar-i-Sharif in the north and then, via a mountain pass complete with a modern two-lane tunnel, back to Kabul. Feeder roads spreading out to the Panjshir Valley and other towns will link up the important markets.

Truck drivers used to need between two and three days to complete the journey between Kabul and Kandahar. Now, they can finish the journey in six hours. They drive so quickly that it is as if they are trying win a race. As a result, accidents are frequent. There is very little in the way of medical assistance along the road. The Afghans call it "George Bush Highway" be-

cause it was hurriedly finished in order that its opening could be used as an example of the success of the President's strategy. Yet just six months after it was opened there are sections of the road that already need repairs.

As in the past foreigners are only allowed to enter the dangerous tribal area on the Afghan-Pakistan border with a police escort. For the locals, however, a certain degree of normality has returned. For the first time in 28 years, busses are crossing the Khyber Pass again. They run five times a week between Peshawar in Pakistan and Jalabad in Afghanistan. Each bus carries 36 passengers. The operator is a private entrepreneur.

Left page *Huge market-halls and even bigger administrative buildings stand on the edges of new roads. This was meant to make things easier for customs guards.* **Top** *Donkeys and cars share the streets in the Panjir Valley.* **Above** *Accidents are not rare on the new highway.*

FORGOTTEN VILLAGES

Officials expect "sweeteners" from farmers

Mohammad Yousuf is the newly elected village chairman. He is an elderly and reserved man. Following the usual pleasantries, he asks me: "Do you know of an aid organization that could help us? We desperately need two new wells. Perhaps you could also help us get a fruit press and of course, we can't afford to build a new school all on our own. The children have to have open air classes." He is disappointed when I tell him I'm alone with my camera. "Why doesn't anybody help us?" he asks. "Everyone has forgotten us."

It's not that the international aid organizations don't want to help. But rather their resources are limited. The many billions of dollars destined for Afghanistan that the media are constantly talking about are predominantly used for the military budget. There are some aid programs for the rural population that the government in Kabul is running in cooperation with the World Bank. Some 13 million villagers already benefit from the program. A further 4,000 communities are still waiting for the project to be extended. This is scheduled to start "soon". Around here "soon" often means the same thing as "never".

Experts from the renowned U.S. RAND Corporation have drawn up estimates of how ineffective the aid program for Afghanistan ultimately was in the first years after the collapse of the Taliban regime. The international community invested 25 times as much money in Kosovo after the end of the war there and sent 50 times as many soldiers as there are currently in Afghanistan to act as a stabilization force. In Bosnia, the figures were even higher than that. The slow progress in terms of democratization and Afghanistan's meager annual economic growth has less to do with the population's motivation and more to do with the international community.

It's not only a question of development aid but also the fact that coordinating the various aid projects, whether they are state-backed or private-sector, is complicated. After the fall of the Taliban, there were lots of companies, including construction firms, security firms and international trading companies that registered as aid organizations in order to profit from various development and taxation benefits. The work of the real aid organizations, the so-called NGOs or non-governmental organizations, was hin-

Above *Five of 12 children belonging to one family in a nameless village. The village is one of thousands of forgotten communities in which there is no power, no running water, no school and no medical facilities.*
Right page *The babies are strapped into their cradles when the women carry them on their heads to neighboring villages or to the market (above). If possible, Afghan farmers build their homes on hillsides that offer shade and protection from storms (below).*

dered enormously. Alongside their actual work they often had to counter accusations that they were only interested in profits. A typical NGO has international experience in developing nations and, as far as is possible, they recruit locals for many of the positions of responsibility. Their projects are always long term and designed to be sustainable. They decided on an unusual step in Afghanistan: they created a "code of conduct", a rulebook for NGOs which made clear demands such as providing unlimited support for constitutional renewal in Afghanistan and requiring adherents to clearly reveal their finances. NGOs were obliged to work on a not-for-profit basis and to remain neutral in all political conflicts. More than 2,000 so-called aid orgnizations were stripped of their status after the publication of the "code of conduct". This has made the NGOs' work much easier.

Keeping out of the conflict means keeping away from NATO troops. They have created regional teams to rebuild Afghanistan. These consist of military bases whose soldiers are not just fighting the Taliban but also seeking to win the trust of the local population by getting involved in aid projects. The aid organizations welcome the military protection because that provides greater

security. However, they are eager to avoid blurring the boundaries between the military presence and civilian developmental aid. This is not always easy. The NATO vehicles that drive up and down Afghanistan's streets are painted white. The color is not just reserved for aid organizations. This means that the NGOs are now under attack, as I experienced first hand. We were trav-

its own employees. "I need a document confirming my election as village elder," he said. "When I went to the authorities, the official held out his hand, rubbed his thumb and index finger together as if he was counting money and then said 'shirni bee'. That means something like: 'Give me something sweet.' He meant a bribe. Such sweeteners are something that we have had to get used to in this country. Without sweeteners the officials are unwilling to do anything any more. How are they going to feed their families otherwise?"

eling around the Kunduz province when our white station wagon was shot at by militia. Some NGOs have changed the color of the vehicles again as white has become too dangerous. Back in the village forgotten by aid groups, the chairman tells me over tea what it means for Afghans on a day-to-day basis when the government does not have enough money to properly pay

Left page *Terraces are particularly difficult to build in Afghanistan where the ground is rocky. Sometime poppies are grown here (above). Even the road home from the fields is a tricky one (below).* **Above** *Maize and poppies do well here, the farmer says.* **Below** *For centuries, the mill stone has been driven by water.*

Next double-page *If you fall in the river, then you have to swim to Kabul, the Afghans say. I was very happy to reach the other side.*

POSTCARDS FROM AFGHANISTAN

A real census has never been taken

I owe my first impressions of Afghanistan's breathtaking beauty to Russian helicopters that circled from sunrise to sunset over this country's mountains and valleys, waiting for the moment to pounce on their unsuspecting prey. In fact, during my first visits to Afghanistan, between 1986 and 1988, I never once saw a road. I was with the Mujahideen, the "holy warriors", and that meant avoiding the paths well-trodden because they were too easy to see and were patrolled by the Russians.

It was not unusual to trek for eight days. We clambered over mountain crests and between rock falls, down into the valleys through ice-cold, crystal clear streams and then back up over the

emerald green slopes, past the grazing sheep and people who were so exhausted they could no longer even cry. My feet were bleeding after the all-day, all-night marches, during which we slept little and only rarely took breaks. Our diet consisted of flat bread with mutton fat and sometimes a few nuts. More than once I thought I had reached my limits and was about to simply sit down and wait for the Soviets to come.

Afghanistan's mountains, crowned by the 7,492-meter high (24,574 feet) ice-capped Noshaq peak in the Hindu Kush, are eerily beautiful and force man to adapt to their conditions. The winter temperatures sometimes fall to minus 50 degrees centigrade. The capital city, Kabul, is 1,500 meters (4,920 feet) above sea level. Forests that used to cover the peaks were bombed and razed years ago. The few trees that remained were felled in recent winters. Replanting is hard because there is not enough rain. Only in the region of Nuristan do the farmers still get an ample supply of firewood from the pine trees.

Even the Kunduz River has been touched by the war. The waterway gushes with melt water in spring and turns the area into a relatively fertile oasis in the midst of this dry landscape. Before the fighting, one might have seen a cluster of fishermen here with

boats and nets. Now there are hardly any fish left. Afghanistan is a country of extremes, where droughts come regularly. It also has the broadest span of temperatures anywhere in the world. In the desert and semi-arid deserts in the south of the country, where the sand tastes saltier than the sands of Syria or Egypt, temperatures of up to 53 degrees centigrade have been measured. Agriculture in most parts of Afghanistan is either heavily labor-intensive or completely impossible. The landscape is largely inhospitable and there are villages that can only be reached after a trek of several days on foot. As a result, there has not been a census taken since many years. The United Nations estimates that more than 30 million people live in Afghanistan. Around half of them are children aged under 15.

Left page *The sun shines in the valley but the mountains are covered in snow all year round.* **Above** *The Hindu Kush is one of the most imposing mountain ranges in the world.* **Left** *Even in this idyllic landscape the road leads through a minefield.*

Next double-page *The desert lives – even in Afghanistan, most of which is covered in arid sands.*

Above *Holy warriors under the prophet's banner. Their religion briefly united them.* **Right page** *A portrait of Massoud hangs above a shopping street in Charikar (above). A family prays in front of a memorial to Massoud (below).*

THE LION OF THE PANJSHIR VALLEY

"Holy warriors" as friends of the Taliban

I had assumed that after so many years of war and bitter experiences the Afghans would devote themselves wholeheartedly to the rebuilding of their country and to not have time to honor heroes of the past. That was a naive thought: the heroes of yesterday still wield their influence over the present. The country is blanketed with portraits of the man who would probably be one of the big players in Kabul today had al-Qaeda not murdered him. These are larger-than-life pictures of Ahmad Shah Massoud, the man they call "the lion of the Panjshir Valley." He was born in Panjshir and celebrated his victories as a warlord there. He became famous as a guerrilla fighter during the battle against the Soviet forces, largely through his bravery but also because of his brilliant military strategy. In the "holy warriors'" bloody struggle Massoud was considered to be one of the key figures. For a short period of time he was even Defence Minister of the Mujahideen government in the fight against the Taliban, a role that he would soon after have to hand over to Kabul. The Panjshir Valley was impregnable during Massoud's time.

On September 9th 2001, two days before the attacks in New York and Washington, Massoud was killed by suicide bombers who had disguised themselves as cameramen. They blew themselves up, killing him and demolishing his headquarters. One macabre detail spilled out later on. The FBI found out from a number printed on the camera that it had been stolen from a Frenchman at a Christmas market in Grenoble. A few months before the attacks, Massoud had warned the European Parliament of the likelihood of attacks by al-Qaeda. Today he is considered an official hero of Afghanistan.

I met Massoud once in March 1989. A well-groomed man, he was pleasant, open and without the affectations of some of the leaders of the Mujahideen, who are still active today as drug barons and warlords, guarded by their former "holy warriors". "Why are you Germans not helping us?" Massoud asked me. The Mujahideen and the Taliban had fought together between 1986 to 1989 against the Soviets. The Mujahideen were often farmers

or simple craftsmen who rallied around one of their clan elders. The Taliban, however, were largely students from the Koran schools. The Mujahideen and Taliban were supported generously at the time because the United States believed that it would help them in the Cold War against the Soviets. The Afghans got missiles, which became an effective means of bringing down Russian helicopters and which ultimately forced the Soviets to retreat. The rebels' base was in the neighboring state of Pakistan and in particular in the scarcely controlled and hard-to-access border area straddling Afghanistan and Pakistan on the Hindu Kush. During the guerrilla war against the Russians, I often accompanied the Mujahideen into the so-called "tribal area". This area had many caves and was therefore an ideal region for even a large group to hide itself.

The Mujahideen remained a united force during the war with the Soviets, but afterwards they split up. The presence of "holy warriors" in the government in Kabul and "holy warriors" in the opposition led to bloodshed. The Taliban used the chaos and the population's general fatigue over the war to create their own government. The defeated Mujahideen retreated to the north to await further developments and soon started to fight the Taliban once again. Energetic support came from the Americans who gave money and weapons to the Mujahideen as well as the warlords in the south. Therefore they were able finally to drive the Taliban out of Kabul in 2001. Without the Americans' intervention after the September 11th attacks, the Taliban government would have certainly held on for much longer.

Mujahideen from the north of the country now hold many of the most influential positions in the new government. Warlords in the south of the country and their militia, which they were able to recruit from the ranks of the former Mujahideen, are making life for the government in Kabul difficult. They have been able to finance their activities through protection money that they extract in the form of a "war" or "opium tax" from returning refugees and farmers in the provinces. Something that has evidently been conveniently forgotten both by the "holy warriors" as well as by the otherwise strict Taliban is that drugs are banned under their religious beliefs.

After their victory over the Soviets, the Mujahideen immediately ordered farmers to start planting poppies again: they were obliged to hand over a good proportion of their revenues. For a period of time during the Taliban government, the "opium tax" was actually enshrined in law. Since Afghanistan was at the time the main supplier of opium globally you can safely assume the Taliban and the Mujahideen got quite rich on payments from farmers.

Upon returning from exile in Pakistan, the Taliban were given a mixed reception by Afghanistan's population. Their strict religious regime had put off many Afghans during their time in government. Large parts of the population, however, still believed that they had brought a certain degree of security, and above all peace and stability, to the country. Parts of the population still support them as a result and several Mujahideen groups formed alliances with them.

Violence was still widespread. Continuing unrest in the country and the uncertainties about the future mean the heroes of the past have gained even more importance in the eyes of the population. Many believed that Ahmad Shah Massoud could have brought peace and prosperity. The film "Rambo III", in which Massoud is seen fighting the Russians alongside Sylvester Stallone, can still be found in every Afghan house in possession of a video recorder and it is still watched with undiminished enthusiasm.

Left page *1986: on the road with the Mujahideen. My first trip through Afghanistan. – Many older men dye their beards with henna (below).*
Above *There are more urgent problems to solve than to complete Ahmad Schah Massoud's mausoleum.*

A DIFFICULT HOMECOMING

No aid for those returning to Afghanistan

A burst of machine gun fire seems to be an odd way of welcoming Abdel Ali and his family as they return to Afghanistan after spending more than 20 years in a Pakistan refugee camp. American soldiers fire live rounds from a helicopter. The exercise is taking place at Bagram, a base established by the U.S. military not far from the Afghan capital of Kabul. When Abdel Ali fled with his wife and children to Pakistan from a village in the province of Nangarhar, the Soviet army's red flag was still flying above Bagram. The Soviets were the first to use Bagram as a military base. Between Bagram and the U.S. military's exercise facilities there are several square kilometers of rocky ground that belongs to the Afghan government.

The government sank wells on this piece of land. Those returning to Afghanistan are allowed to settle here if their home village has been destroyed or if another family has moved into their home and there is a dispute over who owns it. Some people simply do not know how they are expected to survive in their towns of birth and prefer to move to a place where they have opportunities. There is scarcely any work for those returning. Their home-towns are often less secure than they were when they left due

thanks to support from the international community. There were, of course, no paved roads, but there was fresh water, sanitary facilities, a school for the children, a medical center, police protection and even electricity for the radio which they managed to buy from funds raised selling their colorful woven carpets. They are going to find their homeland a little less welcoming because it can offer them none of the comforts that they have grown accustomed to.

After the fall of the Taliban, Pakistan's government made every effort to send the refugees back home again. They reduced the level of aid. Food distribution was stopped. Some of the camps

to the continuing fighting with the Taliban. The government offers those returning a small piece of rocky land. There is little else for them. Apart from an aid package from the UNHCR, the United Nations' refugee organization, there are no aid programs. The luckiest ones live in communities where international aid organizations like ADRA have built fountains and toilet facilities.

The Gul family, with their 10 children, enjoyed life in Pakistan. The refugee camp was transformed into a town over the years,

Left page *Rich and poor live alongside one another in Kabul. At the front of the picture are the refugees for whom the aid organizations are a lifeline. In the background stand the villas of those who have benefited from the opium trade (above). Expectations of the Ministry for Women are not high: it offers sewing courses (below).*
Above *If returning refugees are lucky they are granted a piece of land by the government. For the most part these plots are in parts of the countryside that no one else is willing to farm.*
Left *She wants to become a dressmaker because then she will only have to deal with women.*

were simply pulled down. Two million of the three million Afghan refugees living in Pakistan have already returned. Pakistan's ambassador to the United Nations, Muni Akram, tried to justify his country's behavior with an argument that quickly convinced the Europeans and Americans. He said the problems of warriors crossing over the Afghan-Pakistan border was closely linked to the situation with the Afghan refugees. The Taliban were among them, he said, and it was hard to find them. Therefore, he argued, we want to return these refugees as quickly as possible.

As a consequence, dozens of brightly colored trucks, laden to the limit, leave the Pakistan border area destined for Jalabad or Kabul. Tin decorations on the trucks jingle in accompaniment. Cows, sheep and goats stick their heads out of the boards on the sides of the vehicles. Five or six families pile into one truck with pans, pots, pails and sacks, embarking on a journey that will often take them several days. Some returning refugees do not any possesions aside from the clothes on their backs. When they arrive in Afghanistan, the United Nations is waiting for them again. The children are given inoculations; the fathers are given the equivalent of around $100 and then they are given warnings of the land mines that are still buried throughout the country.

After that, they are left to their own devices. The main subject of conversation in the reception centers in Afghanistan is how the returning refugees would rather have remained in Pakistan.

Iran is also attempting to get its Afghan refugees to return to their home country. Compared to the conditions that await them in their home countries, some Afghans have managed to elevate themselves to a position of significant wealth during their years in exile. They return bearing television sets and even refrigerators. The most popular items are large electric fans for the hot summer days. No one has apparently bothered to tell them about the power supply in Afghanistan. Or, perhaps they simply believe what everyone is telling them: "Things will get better soon."

Above *Women in Afghanistan wear their veils even when they are in exodus.* **Right page** *Refugee camp on the border with Pakistan (above). Hospital wards in Afghan cities: no heating, no water and not enough medicine. The situation is often better in the refugee camps that are supported by the international aid organizations (below).*

THE END OF ROMANTICISM

An uncertain fate for the nomads

Adam Khan Nasiri is a very talkative man. He is a "kuchi", or no-mad, who only rarely comes to Kabul and only then to enquire whether the government is finally willing to implement a long-promised aid program for his people. The father of six children is desperate: "In the past three years I have had to slaughter all 400 of my sheep because there has been no rain where they usually graze I don't have the money for hay or feed. I don't know what I am going to do."

Almost all the Nomads living in Afghanistan are in the same po-sition as Nasiri, with the exception of a small number of those who earn money as smugglers. The Kuchis have gotten used to allowing their sheep and goats to graze on huge expanses of land, a practice used for centuries. They would pitch their tents where the grass was at its most lush and where they could take cover from the heat and the cold. In the summer, they'd go north. In winter, they went south. This is also how the former kings of Afghanistan would lead their lives. They owned a resi-dence in Kabul and a second in the south, in Peschawar, in what is today Pakistan.

Before the most recent spate of fighting – a spate that lasted 30 years – there were an estimated two million nomads in Afghanistan. They supplied villages with fresh meat and fleeces in exchange for rice, flour and other items that they needed for daily life. The nomads were well known for their economical ways and would often give loans to farmers who had fallen into financial difficulty. The drought was just one of many strokes of fate that the Kuchi have had to deal with in recent years. While there were once two million nomads, the United Nations esti-mate that there are only about half as many now. Many of them did not survive the Soviets, the "holy warriors" and the Taliban. They were virtually defenceless in the face of attacks and kidnap-pings, and many more fell victim to the landmines that are

Right *The age when Afghanistan's nomads, like these in the province of Herat, could travel unimpeded through the valleys with their thousands of sheep and goats are almost gone. The water is too scarce and villagers are claiming the green land for themselves.*

littered around the country – especially because they had no access to either medicine or to medical aid.

My translator and I are looking for the Kuchi's brown tents in the hills of Logar. You can normally spot them by the groups of camels that are tied up alongside them. The nomads prefer camels over donkeys because donkeys are almost always thirsty. "There used to be dozens of tents here," my guide said. "As far as the eye could see. It's not just the grass that has shrivelled up but the streams have probably dried up too." We have to ask about the way to the nomads' tents. As soon as the nomads see the camera they ask for money. Foreigners are the only ones who can help them. Several years ago the charitable division of Germany's Protestant churches leant a hand when dozens of nomad tents were washed away after heavy rains.

I succeed in getting the chance to speak with one of the nomads' elders. "What was it like with the Taliban in power?" I ask. My guide translates for us.

The Taliban tried to recruit some of the young nomads as fighters, said the old man. After a lot of negotiating, we managed to swap the number of men they wanted with the same number of sheep, he continued. If they had not agreed to make the ex-

change, then they would probably have simply abducted the young men.

Kabul claims that it was the Kuchi who temporarily hid Osama bin Laden, the leader of al-Qaeda, as the Americas were trying to track him down. The claims are made on the grounds that the Kuchi always help those who are being pursued. Shinware, a young

nomad, explains why they would help a persecuted Arab like Osama bin Laden: "They come from the direction in which we pray. The come from Mecca and therefore we honor them. We are too poor ourselves to make a pilgrimage over there. Osama bin Laden is a prophet to us. We still honor him. We only heard about September 11th a long time after it had happened."

These days, the Kuchi live in terrible conditions in refugee camps in Pakistan or look for work as laborers in Afghan towns. Villagers in the provinces treat them with contempt and are not prepared to share their water supply and pasture land with them.

Left page *Female nomads generally don't wear a burqa. Instead they have traditional, brightly colored clothing that they wear even when tending the flock (above). A young nomad carries a goat back to the herd after it became separated (below).*
Above *Anyone who buys goats or sheep from the nomad checks first to make sure they are not too skinny.*
Left *Nomads prefer young goats to dogs.*

Next double-page *The nomads' tents are not made from animal pelts. They are in fact hand-woven blankets that offer protection from the sun. Even the camels get a place in the shade to rest.*

OPIUM MEANS MONEY AND DEATH

Afghanistan's farmers will only be able to wean them-selves off growing poppies when they are offered a viable alternative. In the province of Nangarhar, a private aid organization is attempting to find out whether it is possible to earn a living with roses.

OPIUM FOR THE MASSES

Drug barons in Afghanistan's parliament

They wave madly and welcome us with beaming faces as we arrive in our battered jeep. It is as if we had caught them by surprise picking berries in the garden rather than in the process of scraping opium in the poppy fields. Children, teenagers and adults flock around us and proudly show us what a huge harvest they have in 2007 thanks to last year's rainy winter.

Everyone wants their picture taken. The camera also captures how skilled they are at scraping the raw opium – a sticky, gelatinous, brown substance – from the inside of the poppy seeds. The seeds were slit open the day before. Over night, the white milk that spills from the seed has dried and turned brown.

I am traveling through the province of Nangarhar, a region that begins not too far east of the capital city of Kabul and spreads out to the Pakistani border. For many years it has been customary for workers from Pakistan to travel over the border into Afghanistan in order to work on the opium harvest, like workers coming into Germany from neighboring countries to help with our asparagus harvest. The Pakistanis are paid around $10 a day – a lot of money to these people.

"Either Afghanistan destroys the opium or the opium will destroy Afghanistan," said the country's president. His words have yet to make it as far as these villages. The farmers know the government has outlawed opium planting but they are not going to lose any sleep over the ban. They say that they can earn three times as much with the opium as they can with wheat or corn. As a result, they don't have to worry quite as much about how they will feed their families. Poppies yield much more than wheat. What they particularly like is the fact that the dealers always pay an upfront deposit for the goods.

1 *Even the men like the scent of roses.* 2 *The farmers' harvest is weighed and catalogued.* 3 *Rosehip oil or opium? Unfortunately the poppy crop is more lucrative.* 4 *Poppy blooms with frayed tips come from seeds that were originally imported from America.* 5 *The so-called opium bridge crosses the Murgh to Bala Margab and then continues to Turkmenistan. In the background sits a destroyed tank and a police station that appears to have been abandoned.*

5

The government in Kabul has passed a law under which it would be possible to ban the planting of poppies. The provincial governors have been called on to ensure that the poppy fields are bulldozed. The Afghans in the poppy fields smile knowingly when the bulldozers are mentioned. Of course, smaller poppy fields all over the country are being destroyed, but there has been little overall success. The official statistics showing how many fields have been destroyed need to be taken with a large grain of salt. In recent years, poppies have been planted continuously, apart from a very short period of time. That was in 2000, when the Taliban suddenly said that the Koran banned drug use. Before then they too had profited from the opium tax. Now they were calling for a ban on opium in the name of religion. Some experts believe that the Taliban's ban had been an attempt to inveigle themselves with the United States and the United Nations. Others claim that they were trying to send the price of opium skyrocketing because they had significant stockpiles of it at the time. Since the collapse of the Taliban regime and the presence of U.S. troops and NATO units in the region, more poppies then ever before are being planted and the production of opium has, according to a UN report, reached "worrying record levels". In 2006, Afghanistan produced 8,200 tons of opium – around

93 percent of the global market share according to the United Nations.

As a result of the boom in opiates farmers have been able fort he first time to buy themselves motorcycles. But they are not the only ones who benefit: it is also the drug dealers who ensure that the product reaches the international markets. They are reaping the most earnings. In total, opium trading makes up between 35 to 40 percent of Afghanistan's gross national product

of conflict in which all of the state's apparatus was destroyed, people were cast into poverty and the nation's sense of right and wrong was thrown into disarray.

The World Bank and the UN have publicly decried the fact that nothing is being done to stop the 25 to 30 biggest opium and heroin dealers in Afghanistan. The World Bank believes that it would be entirely feasible to block their bank accounts, to arrest them and send them to other countries for trial if the level of corruption in the Afghan system makes it impossible for them to be put on trial at home. The degree of entanglement is, however, so great that the Afghan government is only able to act slowly.

The government in Kabul is not in any situation at present to prevent the transportation of heroin into neighboring countries. Border police officers and customs officials, if there are any, are paid the equivalent of around $90 per month. Often they have

(GNP), according to a report written by the UN Development Programme (UNDP) in 2006.

Police officers and commanders in Afghanistan are bribed by the drugs runners. Provincial governors, army officers, customs officials, prosecutors, judges and even ministers all profit in some way. Bribes, known as baksheesh, have always been a way of life in this part of the world. But what is happening in Afghanistan to-day is the result of the 30 years of war that preceded it, a period

Left page *Planting wheat is not very lucrative for Afghanistan (above). Some 30 years ago Soviet tanks rolled across the bridge (below).* **Above** *Poppies grow well even in poor soil and do not need as much water as wheat. A farmer earns at least 10 times more from poppies.* **Left** *In the past they were famous as holy warriors. Not they are notorious opium dealers.*

to wait for several months before they get paid. The drugs mafia are far more punctual and offer a lot more money than the officials get paid. The border to Pakistan is also not very easy to monitor because there is a region between the two countries that is controlled by tribal leaders and which is the stomping ground of warlords and the Taliban. Heroin is also smuggled through Iran, even though there are great fears about the Iranian police.

In Herat I'm told that there is an "opium bridge" not far away, somewhere in the north on the road that leads to Turkmenistan and then on to Russia. Travelers have to use it to cross the river Murg in order to get to the little town of Bala Margab and the border.

The Soviet army destroyed the bridge as they attempted to ward off the Mujahideen or "holy warriors" during their Afghanistan occupation. That was at least 20 years ago and the bridge has only been provisionally put back in place. NATO troops don't care about it because it is not an important enough crossing. Those who drive their camels and their donkeys over the bridge or who thunder through the muddy river with their motorcycles appear to be happy enough with the corrugated iron construction that is being used for the moment.

The rusting remains of Russian tanks are strewn all over the area. They are an silent reminder of how important the little bridge was to the Soviet cause. There is also a wooden shed, probably also a remnant left by the Soviet army. A lonely Afghan solider wanders up and down. He doesn't even begin to try to make checks on anyone or anything that comes his way. He laughs and jokes with those who cross the bridge.

Among the travelers are many young men, on foot or with bicycles, who apparently have nothing to do. Unfortunately my companion and I failed to find out what they were doing there or whom they were waiting for. We went over to talk to them and I asked my translator to ask a particularly alert-looking young man about opium and the drug dealers. I also wanted to know if women smoked opium too in this region. The young guy appeared not to hear the questions. He was carrying a little pipe. He put it up to his lips and blew little soap bubbles that went floating off into the blue sky.

Left page *The town of Bala Margab appears to have slept through the past couple of centuries (above). This dealer is selling the little wooden knives that are needed to open the opium capsules (below).* **Above** *The Murgh, which becomes a torrent after heavy rains, is like a small mountain stream during the dry season.*

Next double-page *Girls during the poppy harvest (above left). When poppy fields were being burned in Kunduz some farmers built walls around their fields in order to protect their crops (below left). In order to extract the opium the capsule is first opened and scraped out on the following day (right).*

Above *The farmers have not yet adapted to growing roses. Rose petals are carefully weighed.* Right page *He looks a little skeptical. He has more experience in growing poppies (above). Norbert Burger, manager of the pilot project in Dare Noor, checks to see whether the rose petals are fresh (below).*

"WHERE WILL ALL THE ROSES BLOOM?"

Fragant oils as an escape from crisis

There are red roses everywhere. Cheerful children shower me with fragrant petals. Their mothers, emerging from the rose-filled fields with basket after basket stuffed with rose blooms, create piles of the flowers. Men, to whom it all seems rather strange, rub the buds between their fingers and sniff them, as if they can't quite believe that roses can smell this good.

I feel as if I'm standing at the edge of some huge European market garden, when in fact I clambered my way up through a rock field to this mountain village in Dare Noor, in the province of Nangarhar. In this province, as in many parts of Afghanistan, more and more poppies are being planted in order to harvest raw opium. The roads are so dangerous that American civilians have to give the U.S. military four days notice before they want to take any overland journey in the region in order that the appropriate arrangements for armed guards can be made. Otherwise the trip has to be cancelled.

So considering these circumstances the roses of Dare Noor appear all the more amazing. They are part of a pilot project that is attempting to rekindle farmers' affinity for the fragrant blooms. Depending on quality, a kilogram of rose oil can sell for the equivalent of around $ 6000 to $ 7500.

Around 120 former opium farmers have joined the experiment already. Many projects in Afghanistan these days are driven by optimism but they are also generally relatively modest in scope. This one, like many others, is not borne from an idea from a western government. The idea and the execution are both down to an initiative started by an private aid organization. Many non-governmental aid organizations could demonstrate over a number of decades and in many different countries that they are often able to help and give hope to more people in need than any official agency can.

The Afghans have been placed in good hands with Norbert Burger, Dare Noor's ambitious project manager, because he refuses to be limited by the official aims of the project, namely producing exclusively rose oil, as well as rose water and simple fragrant oil. He has also been experimenting in his apartment in the

provincial city of Jalabad. He is trying to find out what else can be made from roses. Several Afghans have been helping him as employees of the project.

The aid organization has granted the equivalent of around $2000 for the project. The lion's share of this is being funded with German government development aid. The roots of the rose bushes used in the 20 hectare (50 acre) rose gardens are being imported to Afghanistan from Bulgaria. Three small distilleries have been built in Dare Noor and its surrounding villages. The project has been a success so far. In the long term, the roses are expected to bring the farmers a better income than they would normally be able to earn from planting wheat. Another benefit is the fact that the rose bushes are easier to water than fields of corn: this is a significant advantage during the long periods of drought that Afghanistan endures on a regular basis.

Planting poppies is, however, still more attractive than growing roses because you can make more money with opium than with anything else. Burger, the project manager, believes however that the farmers are increasingly aware of how dangerous growing the drugs is, in particular for themselves. More and more men and women from families that produce opium are becoming dependent on drugs and therefore becoming a burden on their families.

Under the aegis of the west, Afghanistan became the number one producer of opium. Resorting to violence in order to try and wean farmers off the crop has had little effect so far: there is

still no functioning police force and no functioning justice system. Warlords and drug barons are earning so much money from opium that they can finance their own militias and use their power to have a greater say in Kabul. The average farmer, insufficiently protected from the drug barons and their militias, has few options left open to him: it is not exactly clear what he should grow instead of poppies and still be able to expect to feed his family.

After the fall of the Taliban, the English attempted to encourage farmers in Afghanistan to try other crops and grains. They paid them money, distributed expensive fertilisers, handed out seeds promised farmers they would have a rosy future. The aid program only lasted for a year, however. Then the farmers were left on their own. As a result they replanted poppies and realized that they could not put their faith in other people's promises. Another attempt to stop opium production by burning down the poppy fields also turned into an own goal. There were no plans at hand to replace the destroyed crop with anything else. The desperate farmers once again turned to the Taliban, who found willing volunteers among their ranks. The Americans also

believed that spraying the poppy fields with poisonous herbicides was the best approach. This was stopped at the very last moment by the Afghan president.

"Tell me when will roses bloom in Afghanistan instead of poppies?" I ask Norbert Burger. No one can predict, he says. I find one passage in documents from the United Nations that suggests it will be 20 years before opium production in Afghanistan falls to negligible levels. Habibullah Qaderi, head of the increasingly important ministry for drug prevention in Afghanistan, believes, however, that the problem will be solved within five years. "If we start talking about 20 years, then the farmers will be prepared for the fact that they can continue planting poppies for a long time yet."

Left page *Pressed rose petals are formed into briquettes, a by-product of rose harvesting. Unfortunately they do not smell like roses when they are burned (above). Rose water is not as valuable as rosehip oil. Rose water is sold on local markets but it is not exported (below).* **Above** *This set of scales looks like a museum piece but in fact it is used to weigh each rose bloom.*

HERAT – NOSTALGIA FOR ALEXANDER THE GREAT

Famous generals heaped honor and glory on Herat in the past. Now war only lives on in the memorials and the town is hoping for peace.

THE SECRET CAPITAL OF AFGHANISTAN

Herat has been the center of Islam since the 7th century

At first I thought the banners were calling on locals to take up arms once again. But then my Afghan acquaintances explained it to me. The expressions on the memorials in the center of Herat were urging locals to have their children vaccinated against polio. They were written in each of the dialects spoken around here, one of which is very similar to Persian. Persia, or what is now known as Iran, is just a stone's throw away and the Afghans are proud that Herat was once one of Persia's royal cities, more than a thousand years ago. Today Herat can look back on a long history, and traces of it can be seen everywhere. In the year 330 B.C., Alexander the Great created what was probably the first community here. The numerous stony historical relics, including a famous citadel dating back to those times, are enough to send archaeologists into raptures.

Since then Herat has been the scene of bloody violence. The people of Herat, with their violent spirit, made a significant contribution to the creation of modern Afghanistan. In March 1979 a bloody uprising was launched against the communist rulers who had been in power for less than a year. Many of the numerous advisers sent to Herat by the Soviets before their march on the country were killed. The resistance movement began in the barracks of the Afghan army under the leadership of Ismail Khan, one of the region's best-known Mujahideen. The government in Kabul decided that the situation in Herat was so dangerous that the communist party chief and premier Nur Taraki called the Soviet Prime Minister to plead for the assistance of Russian soldiers in Afghan uniforms. Moscow assumed that to be to risky. Therefore the Soviet tanks only came a half year later to Afghanistan. But the Communists in Kabul were not able to overcome the rebells of Herat which were supported by the civilian population. 25,000 deads were the result.

1 Women's fashions in Herat, imported from Iran. 2 Men at a tearoom in Herat. 3 A story teller applies decoration before his performance. 4 Witnesses of the past. 5 Herat in summer 2006. At first glance little has changed since Alexander the Great's time.

It wasn't until Soviet aircraft bombarded Herat that the central government managed to put down the rebellion. Many of the rebels, including Ismail Khan, fled into neighboring Iran or into the mountains. They formed the core of resistance in western Afghanistan, uniting the various factions of the Mujahideen against the advancing Soviet army. Khan took control of Herat in 1992 once the Russians were defeated following a fight that lasted several years, and the communist government was overthrown.

With help from the Iranians, a mini-state was created in the west of Afghanistan under the totalitarian control of Ismail Khan. Even before the Taliban took control in 1995 Khan pushed through a strict moral code. For the first time he introduced a law that made women wear burqas in Herat. But Khan had set himself up in opposition to the Taliban government. They arrested him in 1997. After two years imprisonment he managed to escape and returned to power after the fall of the

Taliban. He was celebrated as the "emir of Herat". He suppressed opposition and became a symbol of all warlords, of all former leaders of the Mujahideen who had turned their backs on the government in Kabul. He made it clear to journalists that he considered any form of criticism a fatal offense, particularly if it involved any details of his style of government making it into the foreign press. He once said that the money journalists earned working for Western radio stations should go towards buying their burial shrouds.

In 2004 Khan was finally overthrown as governor, an event that precipitated riots in Herat. The Americans soon succeeded in disarming his troops but his influence in Afghanistan remained considerable. True to his wishes for national reconciliation and the inclusion of each of the most powerful parties in his government, Afghanistan's President Karzai made the former "emir of Herat" his energy minister.

Herat is a city with a diverse past. A common thread running

A WEDDING BAND

A rock band such as one might find at a western wedding would be unthinkable in Afghanistan. The customs and music here are very traditional. Wedding guests sing, drum and dance. The high point of these musical performances are passionate love songs, performed by men and usually exclusively before a male audience. Even at weddings the men and women only meet at the ceremony. The celebrations which occur afterwards are strictly segregated. Only in Kabul are there public concerts like those we have in the West.

through its history, however, is the population's resistance to unwanted interference from outside. The people of Herat are incredibly proud of their town and its rich cultural history, a history that the people of Kabul have always been somewhat envious about. It has been called "The pearl of Persia" or "The town of poets, musicians and intellectuals with 3,000 years of history." This town was an important part of Persian and Muslim history for a long time and, quite rightly, its people hold their heads a little higher than the rest of Afghanistan.

Left page *The famous citadel of Herat.* **Top** *Alexander the Great once passed down this boulevard in the center of Herat.* **Center** *Herat is conservative even by Afghan standards. Women mainly stay in their homes.* **Left** *There are no such laboriously adorned palaces in Kabul.*

WHEN YOU'RE 44...

What a minimum-wage job is like in Afghanistan

An Afghan's average life expectancy is 44.5 years, according to the United Nations, if war-related deaths are excluded. Boys and girls born today in the western world can expect to reach an average age of 80. Students at the University of Herat refused to accept that this could be true until I explained how different the way of life is in the two countries. The numbers for Afghanistan are, like most figures about the country, only estimates. They are, however, a reflection of the reality.

Our life expectancy is continually increasing because medical care, nutrition and working conditions are steadily improving. There are about 300,000 doctors currently working in a state like Germany. In Afghanistan there are about 3,000 physicians. Measured against the population, that means there are 8,000

people for each. To make matters worse around 80 percent of Afghan doctors are to be found in the capital city, Kabul. In the villages, you would consider yourself lucky if you can even find a nurse. The only reason that there are no epidemics, such as cholera for example, is because of Afghanistan's climate. Students have heard how much better nutrition is in the western world. "Is it really true that so much people there are overweight?" one asks me. In Afghanistan, the majority of the population is malnourished. Without food aid from abroad, and from Europe in particular, many Afghans would be starving. These people can only dream of standards of living approaching those found in Europe or in the United States. It will take a long time before similarly high standards are introduced into Afghanistan. If you can find a job, you take it. No questions asked.

The majority of Afghanistan's unemployed can be found in the villages. They are largely invisible and manage to eke out an existence with the help of their extended families. In the cities unemployment is a much more visible problem. Increasing numbers of men looking for work go out onto the streets in the morning. Almost all of them seem to be wearing baggy long trousers, which have turned grey by years of washing, collarless shirts and an

embroidered jacket over the top. If a station wagon, a taxi or a truck stops in front of them, they will talk briefly to the driver and then one or more climb aboard. They typically get hired for a day job and they are willing to take on the dirtiest of assignments. A day's wage is usually about one dollar. Many are refugees who have returned and who prefer to remain in the city, or Afghans who have left their villages because their future prospects were dim. Their increasing numbers means the government in Kabul will, at some point in the future, have to consider some form of social security.

Left page *Most children accept that they have to work.*
Above *The heavy irons mean hard work for the children.*
Left *Sanad, age 12, is an apprentice in a mechanic's shop.*

Next double-page *Sand and stone to be used as building materials are collected with a great deal of effort from the bottom of the riverbed. There are no machines to do this kind of work in this country (left).* **Right** *Farming is very labor-intensive in Afghanistan (above). Families send their children to the river so that they can collect drinking water (below).*

THE TRAVEL AGENCY OPENS ITS DOORS

Personal security of $1,995

"The dignified sophistication of Herat gives this laid-back city a very different feeling than the rest of Afghanistan," reads the brochure for "Great Game Travel" in its description of Herat. If there is money to be earned then even the advertising wizards of Afghans are not shy about turning to flowery language. In a glossy magazine I pick up on an Ariana Afghan Airlines flight, I spotted the following sentence: "Famous for its poets and musicians, Heratis pride themselves in speaking eloquent and beautiful Persian. From the Arg castle sitting high above the city, to the Timurid mosques and minarets, visitors are enchanted by the medieval monuments scattered around Herat. Tree-lined boulevards and large parks complete the charm of this oasis at the edge of the desert." One thing that the tour guides fail to mention, however, is the particularly high number of women who commit suicide in the extremely conservative province of Herat, women driven to take desperate measures because their families treat them like slaves.

That the Afghans are eager to see a return of tourism in their country speaks volumes about their entrepreneurial spirit, espe-

If you are more accustomed to traveling around places such as the Caribbean or Egypt you may be in for some surprises in Afghanistan. "Our staff are sensitive to the cultural nuances of Afghanistan and can advise group members how to avoid drawing unwanted attention to themselves," the brochure reads.

In order to travel around Afghanistan safely it is important to always have the most up-to-date information about the location's situation so that you can react quickly. Tour guides are equipped with radio transmitters, mobile and satellite telephones and before the tours even start, they check the tour route for any last-minute changes in the situation on the ground in case they need to make alternative arrangements to ensure the safety of their clients. I have not yet heard any tales of adventure from tour participants.

cially when tourists still face a risk of encountering danger in many of the provinces.

The south and southeast of Afghanistan are not included in the brochures. All of the tours begin and end at Kabul airport, where military presence is high and security tight. A 10-day tour, which guarantees the highest possible levels of security, costs around $1,995.

Left page *Onion farmers in old Herat (above). Ice-cream vendors in a fancy restaurant in Kabul where many foreigners can be found (below).* **Above** *Rich Muslims, many of whom also come from abroad, are paying for the renovation of historic buildings in Herat.* **Left** *Gold is becoming increasingly expensive in Kabul since jewelry is held in high esteem.*

IN A BURQA AT THE GRAVESIDE

Spiritual encounters in no man's land

The taxi-driver was sullen and my translator was nervous as we made our way to the Pakistani-Afghan border region, the infamous tribal area where Mullah Omar, the former head of the Taliban and the man responsible for the destruction of the Buddha statues in Bamjam, continued to direct his militia army in their fight against the Americans and Europeans. Osama bin Laden is also alleged to be in the region after having gone into hiding in 2001.

On the side of the road I suddenly see a group of women wearing burqas, surrounded by a gaggle of children. They are placing carved stones on freshly dug graves and putting little flags with scraps of material on top of them. They are all conspicuously silent. It is not quite clear where the mourners came from as the area appears to be completely uninhabited.

I ask the taxi-driver to stop. My translator shakes his head: "We should carry on. I would not go up to the women if I were you." I convince him that it is okay, however, and I take my first pictures from inside the car. I walk slowly towards the women. I'm so nervous I can scarcely catch my breath. Foreigners are not supposed to attend burials in Afghanistan and taking photographs at a ceremony is completely unthinkable. The women act as if they have not seen me. Even the children remain at the graveside. Under normal circumstances they would have come running up to me and asked to look at the camera, or simply stared at me. My translator indicates that I should come back. The beauty of the situation casts some kind of spell on me, however, and I scarcely notice him. Finally he calls my name and I come around. I take a couple of quick shots and jump back into the car. With a note of seriousness in his voice, he tells me that I was lucky this time. If a man had been at the ceremony then he'd probably have shot me.

A couple of hundred meters further down the road a man on a bicycle approaches us. We stop and ask him if he knows who is being buried. He tells us that the Taliban are demanding a sort of "war tax" from those Afghans who have fled to the Pakistani refugee camps. It is a form of protection money to finance their war. The family being buried had refused to pay. Everyone in the family was killed. The jewels and stones on the gravestones are meant to reassure the dead that they will not be forgotten.

Above *Some of the women are pleased to have a visit from a stranger. A visit that would not be possible if men were present.*
Right page *Prayers at the graveside (above). Grave dressings. The stones are symbolically bound together with threads of cotton. Each stone represents the prayer of one of the deceased's relatives (below).*

Next double-page *Burial ceremony in the Tribal Area on the border with Pakistan. The young boy's glare shows quite clearly that the photographer's presence was unwelcome.*

EDUCATION – HOW DO YOU SPELL AFGHANISTAN?

The majority of Afghans can neither read nor write the name of their homeland. That will change. Millions of children are going to school and they are already dreaming of a future with computers.

CYBER CAFÉ IN KABUL

Logging on to the future

There is an Internet café in the center of Kabul that I sometimes visit. It seems to place a great emphasis on ensuring its customers' privacy. The computers are set up in such a way that you can surf the Web without anybody seeing you. And there may well be a good reason for that: the café's predominantly male clientele appear to use the place not just keep tabs on their business affairs or to read the news but also to surf erotic sites and look for partners. About a quarter of all Internet users in Kabul are, however, women. The majority of them are students. They use the Internet to do research for their lectures and to keep in contact with relatives and friends abroad. The cafés are full of men and women sitting next to one another at computers. The women mostly wear simple headscarves. A quick trip to one of Kabul's post offices is enough to convince you, however, that the World Wide Web has not yet been able to overcome all the barriers between men and women in Afghanistan. The postal service offers advice to customers who don't know how to use a computer yet, let alone write emails or surf the Internet: there is a female advisor for the women and a male advisor for the men.

That the World Wide Web made it so quickly to Afghanistan is due to an Afghan businessman who lives in New York. The Taliban had barely left the town center when he set up the Afghan Wireless Communications Company and offered the Ministry of Communications in Kabul a 20-percent stake in the promising firm. They were surprisingly quick to sign a 15-year contract. The American CEO of Afghan Wireless, Bennet Bayer, opened the first Internet café in the Intercontinental Hotel in Kabul in 2002. In the intervening period various different companies have set up Internet cafés in Kabul and other major cities. With an average daily wage of less than $3, it is still very much a luxury for Afghans to use the Internet. Nevertheless, there is still plenty of interest.

1 *There are only very few internet cafés in Afghanistan. Most people have yet to get to grips with computers.* **2** *Burqa-clad women sit with those in western dress: the internet café unites opposing worldviews.* **3** *Adult women learn to write their name.* **4** *Plastic bags serve as school satchels.* **5** *A word processing seminar at a University in Kabul. 25 Students share 5 computers.*

FAR TOO MANY ILLITERATE PEOPLE

Young Afghans dream of school

Hamid Karzai, Afghanistan's president, should consider himself lucky that he has access to a satellite telephone conference facility. He uses it whenever affairs of state oblige him to talk to his 34 provincial governors. He requires such a set-up because many of the governors from the provinces are unable to read or write. The majority of Afghan adults have never been to school and remain illiterate even to this day.

Sometimes a friend will write down the address of my next destination on a slip of paper. I often hand this over to the taxi-driver. The fact that he sometimes cannot read it can be quite irritating and usually costs me time and money. Sooner or later,

though, I always seem to get to where I want to go. When it comes to the reconstruction of Afghanistan, however, things tend to be a bit more complicated. The high illiteracy rate ranks third in terms of the problems this country faces, just behind the lack of any institutional structures and the ongoing fight against the Taliban. In urban areas between 70 and 80 percent of the population can neither read nor write. In the countryside this figure is closer to 90 percent.

The impact of this can be felt in all kinds of ways, both direct and indirect. Some of the consequences are things that one might never have considered before. Building new schools is all well and good, but who is going to actually teach in them? Even the justice ministry has a hard time finding men who can be trained up into prosecutors or judges to populate the modern judiciary it is trying to create. There is no new code of criminal procedure in Afghanistan because there are still not enough legal experts. The media are already asking the inevitable questions: what is the use of a new police force if there are no prosecutors and no functioning court system?

The new army is formed of recruits and former soldiers, many of

say that while there are enough officers in Afghanistan there are not enough qualified soldiers to fill the subordinate positions. The sub-officers, who are meant to lead the smaller units, are the backbone of the modern army. However, they first need to be able to read and write. That means training them costs more money and takes more time.

The new minister for education, Mohammad Haneef Atmar, recently presented an ambitious new program. It will cost around $2.5 billion. His white paper calls for all of Afghanistan's teachers to go back to school themselves in order to learn how to plan their curriculum properly. "Our teachers are very poorly educated," says the report. There are no indications what opportunities will exist for children once they have been through elementary

whom are illiterate. There is a plan to put the new military on its feet in a short period of time. But this appears to be overly optimistic and is unlikely to happen based on to the current timetable. According to German Foreign Minister Frank-Walter Steinmeier only 30,000 of the 70,000 soldiers due to be schooled by mid-2007 actually had their training. In Kabul people

Left page *Students in a good mood on their way home to the village of Qala-i-Naw, close to Herat.* **Above** *Most of the students in the Quran school have slates to write on. This boy proudly shows off his name.* **Left** *At this school in the province of Herat, teaching takes place in the open air. More than 200 students are forced to share this tiny school room.*

school. There are also no plans, no books and no teachers for further education. The minister admits there are still things that need changing and improving, even in his own ministry. "Modern technology has been unable to gain a foothold in the ministry," the minister wrote. That probably means there are no computers there – just old typewriters and handwritten card indices.

In order to make teaching more attractive the state will have to pay teachers more than it has done in the past. German aid workers say average monthly wages are around $ 45. Sometimes teachers have to wait for months to be paid. On top of all that students and teachers in the southern provinces face greater risks. The Taliban closed 226 schools within a year and killed more than 100 teachers and pupils, mainly females, in an attempt to stop girls from going to school.

But the efforts to raise the standard of education are all worth it, as I can testify after a visit to an elementary school in the province of Kunduz. It is almost as if I were in a different country altogether, a land unlike Afghanistan with its many problems. I have never seen as many enthusiastic children as I did at this school. They didn't seem to care whether they were sitting in the open air or at school desks, whether they had a canvas roof over their heads or whether they were being taught in a traditional classroom. Minister for Education Haneef Atmar tells me about the progress that is being made: "More than five million children are already attending school. Unfortunately, that is only half of the children in Afghanistan, but it is a big step. In order to go further we need a great deal more money. We have too few teachers, we have too few books and we need to equip thousands of distant villages. Many schools also do not have any sanitary facilities. The children even have to bring their own drinking water with them." Atmar pays a huge compliment to the international community, and in particular the NGOs: "Without them we could not have achieved what we have managed to achieve. We will do everything we can to ensure that more and more boys and girls can go to school."

Above *A lack of space means one has to be inventive. Lessons are taught in the stairwell.* **Right** *From his wheelchair, this teacher tells his students about the war.*

Above *Students on the campus of the University of Kabul. They only remove their burqas once they are in the lecture theatre.*
Right *It is mainly the men who are interested in natural sciences (above). Men and women sit together to listen to lectures about medicine. The female students, however, almost always sit at the back (below).*

BOOK-BURNING IN KABUL

The University of Kabul turns a new page

"Mrs. Bush was in Afghanistan for five hours. She brought $20 million with her. We didn't get a cent." Jamaludin, a 22-year-old history student at the University of Kabul, asks me: "Why is it that almost all of the money went to the new American University?" My Afghan companion manages to placate him a little by explaining that the old university will also benefit from various aid projects. Without international support, there probably wouldn't be any university lectures anywhere in Kabul. The "American University of Kabul" will enable specialists from various fields to obtain a top education. This will help not only in the reconstruction of Afghanistan but also accelerate the modernization of the country so desperately needed. Even Jamaludin thinks this is a positive step. There are many young Afghans currently learning in elementary school who say that they want to become university students later in life. The more opportunities there are for them later on the better it will be.

Afghanistan already boasted having a university back in the 1930s. One of the first in Asia, it was built with the help of the Americans and Germans. The members of the young elite who lined the benches of its lecture halls were soon seeking opportunities to transform their poor homeland into an advanced state, as they described it at the time. This is what they hoped the communists and the Soviet Union would bring them. But they were wrong. The visiting professors from Western countries disappeared from the University of Kabul and with them went the aid projects and development funds.

Soon after that the war between the Soviets and the Mujahideen began. The former students distinguished themselves early on as guerrilla leaders. Following the defeat of the Soviet forces, they wore one another down in a series of bloody conflicts which broke out between them. The university was well situated strategically for the battles that erupted around the capital city and the faculty became a focal point for the fighting between the "holy warriors". Instead of creating a united front in the interests of their homeland the various groups fought among themselves.

An elderly professor, who declined to give me his name, recalled the period: "The Mujahideen occupied various rooms in the

faculty buildings which they believed would provide protection thanks to their sturdy construction. Rival Mujahideen groups then literally forced them out of the buildings by firing rockets at them. The fighting lasted for several winters and bit by bit the entire inventory – chairs, cabinets, window-frames – was broken up and burned." Finally, the Mujahideen, with their long beards and armed with their Kalashnikovs, broke into the library, the professor explained. "The Mujahideen took as many books with them as they could carry. They were printed on good quality paper with excellent bindings and they burned for a long time in those fires."

When the Taliban came out on top in 1995 there was very little left of the university. There was no money available for reconstruction and teaching was severely restricted. The Taliban's minister for university education announced plans for a seminar on trauma aimed at former guerrilla fighters. The lectures never took place. The Taliban let it be known that everything a "holy warrior" required could be found in the pages of the Quran. The Taliban were eventually driven out of Kabul in 2001. However, as they retreated, they destroyed all of the university laboratories and took all the laboratory equipment with them with a view to selling it later on the bazaar.

Today several thousand young Afghans study at the University of Kabul. Among other things, they can attend lectures on economics, law and information technology. Young women, who were prevented from going to university during the Taliban's rule, now account for around one third of all students. Of the few women in Afghanistan who have so far been able to go to school many later attend one of the universities. There are numerous agreements with universities in Europe and the United States for exchange programs and guest lectureships.

BOOKS WERE HIDDEN ALL OVER THE HOUSE

It wasn't just television that the Taliban outlawed in Afghanistan. They were also suspicious of anyone who could read. In particular, the professors. Those teachers at the University of Kabul who were able to save some of their books during the war years and who did not see their home get destroyed had to develop some fairly cunning ways of hiding them from the Taliban. They also had to be wary of any visitor who might tell the Taliban that they had seen books in the house. I met a couple, the husband a professor, who had become particularly adept at hiding their books. They were generous enough to allow me to take pictures. They thought the Taliban would not come back. They had pulled curtains across the front of their bookshelves to make it look like there was a bed or a door or perhaps a window behind. The professor and his wife hid the books all over the house. They preferred to freeze in winter than to use the books to fuel the stove, as others in Kabul did.

Iran is a significant sponsor of the university in Kabul. It provided 25,000 books and also some computers. Germany was also quick to donate computers to the institution. But the university's directors failed to foresee the need for desks to put the computers on. The German lecturers who had brought the machines then had to go to a bazaar to buy the desks to put them on. An initiative organized by the German-Afghan University Society raised money to provide chairs for students and teachers. Afghanistan will find it difficult to build scientific links with univer-

sities in the West because it has been isolated for so many years. The first post-Taliban rector at the University of Kabul was a professor of botany. When choosing his successor, President Karzai named a man who was probably a better fit for his conception of a modern Afghanistan, a country resolutely oriented towards the West. Dr. Ashraf Ghani was graduated from Columbia University in New York. He taught as a professor in the United States, worked at the World Bank and was the country's Finance Minister for two years in the U.S.-backed interim government. Afghanistan's president will be relying on Ghani's international contact network and hoping that the new rector can become a successful fundraiser to further advance the University's modernization plans.

Left page *One of the few book dealers in the center of Kabul. At present, his selection of specialist texts is greater than that of the university's library (above). Medical students on their way to lectures (below).*
Left *In the two-hour break between his classes, this chemistry student is preparing a paper. The campus is still half in ruins. There are no cafés or common rooms.*

SCHOOL LESSONS AT A NEIGHBOR'S HOUSE

Women outsmart their husbands

The whispering and sniggering is never-ending. The young girls removed their burqas at the door and entered the room wearing just their headscarves. They are all happy to be here and excitedly tell stories about how they arrived. One was accompanied by her brother to the door. Another came with her father as far as the market stalls and then came the rest of the way on her own. A third girl even had to clamber over two fences and a roof because no one from her family had been able to accompany her. They each let out a sigh of relief: we managed to make it here again! Once they finish telling their stories, the girls look around the room and ask: "Where is our teacher?" She sits waiting in a room off to the side until she is sure that everyone who wants to come to class has managed to get here. Today's class is made entirely of young girls; sometimes there are also older women among them. Kalisa, the young teacher from Herat, introduces me to the girls and I am greeted with a mixture of approval and inquisitiveness. Strangers don't come here often. But I am very happy to be here, in part because the students have no objections to me taking pictures of them.

This is not always the case. We are in the small town of Bala Morghab in the Baghdis province close to the Turkmen border, a

are indebted to a private aid organization for the teaching they receive.

An internationally active aid organization has built wells in Afghanistan and taught local villagers how to irrigate tomato and apricot plantations. Creating schools for women and children is decidedly harder. Men are not allowed to teach girls and there are very few Afghan women who are able to work as teachers. The woman leading the project in Bala Morghab comes from Kenya. Catherine Oluoch has already had experience managing a school project in Eritrea. She thought it would be a fascinating challenge to teach Afghan women and help them discover their self-confidence and a greater sense of independence. Catherine is a caring and softly spoken woman. She told me how hard it was to convince others of the benefits of what she was doing. "I never imagined that it would be as hard as it was. Mainly because I thought I would be simply having to convince the male

region that has a reputation for being one of the more conservative parts of Afghanistan.

Women and girls are still required to wear the burqa here – even after the end of the Taliban regime. They are only allowed to walk on the streets or to cross the marketplace if they are accompanied by a male relative. The government plans to open schools for women and girls even in these distant regions. But at the moment the plans only exist on paper. These schoolgirls

Left page *Kalisa is happy that the Taliban are now gone. For the first time in years she can work again. She was 17 before she learned to write her name. (below).* **Above** *The transformation is clear. Happy girls in front of their school.*
Left *All ears for new learning – all ages are taught together.*

heads of the family how important it is that their wives and daughters all learn how to read and write. Then it turned out that the clan elders also had to agree to it. I spent hours talking to them. Most of them never went to school either and are illiterate. So it is quite hard to make them understand that letting women and girls go to school is important." She attempts to explain to the men what benefits it will bring them if they send their wives and daughters to school. A convincing argument often appears to be that besides learning how to read and write they will also acquire cooking and handicraft skills.

Setting up a school in an Afghan town or village requires consent not only from the relevant authorities and the clan elders, but also from the mullahs, the tradesmen who run the store next door, and the owner of the property. Catherine had to spend weeks convincing such men that all she planned to do was give the women some degree of education and not turn the women against them. Then, finally, she also had to find Afghan women teachers suitable for the job.

Catherine quickly realized that the circumstances under which these women and girls lived were worse than she had ever imagined they could be. Women were only allowed to meet at weddings. The Kenyan aid worker started to organize small

sowing classes in private homes in order to give the women an opportunity to meet one another. If women are alone, without accompaniment from a male member of their family, no other men are allowed to come near. This means they can talk freely with one another. Husbands leave the room when their wives meet other women. In many parts of Afghanistan this tradition is still strictly observed. "Sometimes women just have to try and out-smart their men," the Kenyan aid worker said. Men have their own rooms within the living quarters where they sit together to smoke or drink tea. Women are only allowed in to make the fire or, if they are fully covered by their burqa, to serve tea.

Catherine was so successful in the small town that she decided to set up a school for women in the next village. I was with her in the village of Moorichagh as she attempted to win the council of elders over to her project. She was optimistic because the bearded old men had welcomed us with mutton, rice, flatbread, tomatoes, grapes and melons. It was virtually unheard of for two women, one of them carrying a camera, to be visiting the village elders. The village elder first told us about the successful tomato harvest and how the aid organization had given the village 300 tomato plants. He thanked us for the support. Then they let

books and ballpoint pens to her pupils – things that they would never otherwise find here in the countryside. They are making good progress at school. I ask them what they want to be when they grow up. Many of them want to be teachers, others translators. All of them are looking forward to being able to read a book. Miriam, who at 44 is the oldest, says: "Men should also go to school in order that they can learn to understand women." Two days after I left, someone threw explosive devices into the private schoolhouse and into the teacher's home in the middle of the night. The buildings burned to the ground. Fortunately no one was hurt.

Catherine speak. They nodded meaningfully, listened carefully, sipped their tea and held their silence. Catherine told them about how important it was for the whole family that women learned how to read and write and how the entire village would benefit from that. The men, however, did not answer. "I will have to come again," she said. "Old traditions have to broken down slowly. It may take some time."
In the school in Bala Morghab, the teacher hands out school-

Left page *Catherine Oluoch from Kenya visits the families of female students in some of the more distant villages.* **Above** *Waheed (right), Catherine's translator, interprets for her while talking to the men.* **Left** *Radios are often the only means of communicating with the outside world from these distant valleys.*

Next double-page *Carpet weavers in the village of Qala-i-Naw. Even Shanaz, 7 years old, (center) helps out. A carpet of this size will take the women and children around two months to complete.*

GENERAL AMNESTY FOR "HOLY WARRIORS"

One woman leaves the men behind

According to the Afghan central bank, the average annual income for an Afghan worker is $335. Members of Afghanistan's houses of parliament earn $3,000 a month. They can thank President Karzai for the handsome paycheck, which is designed to make them more supportive of the government. It remains to be seen whether this policy has worked.

Modern Afghanistan is a presidential democracy. The president was elected in a vote with 70 percent voter turnout, astounding for a relatively new democratic system. Elections in countries where many voters are illiterate are always problematic because they require cumbersome ballot papers featuring the candidates' photographs. In Kabul alone the citizens had to choose between 390 candidates as provincial politicians were being elected at the same time. The documents for the vote were therefore sizeable. Bronwyn Curran, a spokeswoman for the international Joint Electoral Management Body, said: "Many people probably didn't even know what it was all about." Candidates were killed, ballot papers were falsified, polling stations were attacked by armed gangs and some people voted twice. However, the elections were deemed a success because they took place at all. Emma Bonino, head of a team of EU electoral observers, pointed out factors that had not been taken into account ahead of the vote: "Logistically, this election is a complete nightmare. People are now out there looking for horses and donkeys, for example, to fetch back the ballot boxes from some of the more distant villages."

Above *A tea break during a seminar at the Ministry for Women in Kabul.* **Right page** *There were separate polling stations for men and women at the first democratic elections held in Afghanistan on September 18, 2005 (above). One official stands in front of the women's polling station. She will explain the regulations to those women who come to vote (below).*

Members of parliament fulfilled one of the president's wishes by passing a law calling for "national reconciliation". It was one of the first laws they passed. All crimes committed during the war and the civil war were subject to a general amnesty. That means the deaths of thousands of innocent civilians will go unpunished, even if it is widely known who killed them. The majority of Afghans know that justice is hard to come by after all these years of violence. But in a country with such a long history of clan rivalries and bloody acts of vengeance it is not surprising that many worry that those involved could take the law into their own hands.

My acquaintances in Kabul are under no illusions about the trustworthiness of the new government. After all, parliament still represents all the groups who have held influence in Afghanistan over the past few years: from the warlords and the former Mujahideen, through the drug barons and communists to the Islamists, reformers and ex-Taliban leaders. Some senior positions are even held by war criminals. One of them was allegedly among those responsible for the infamous destruction of the

Buddha statues, carved out of rock in Bamyan. No one can prove it was him, however.

In order to strengthen the influence and rights of women as quickly as possible, parliament has a quota for women. A quarter of parliament seats are reserved for women. The most prominent election winner was the women's rights campaigner Fauzia Gailani, who has campaigned against arranged marriages and stood up for a woman's right to join any profession she chooses. She won more votes than the 100 men who ran against her. And this was in the conservative province of Herat, of all places. That might be down to the fact that voter turnout among women was higher than it was for the men.

Above *Entrance to the Ministry for Women in Kabul. The guards in the center keep an eye on the visitors.*
Right page *This calendar on sale in Kabul shows President Karzai together with other folk heroes from Afghanistan's past.*

A NEW BEGINNING —
WITH EMPTY HANDS

The majority of Afghans live in small villages where many of the basic essentials are lacking. That includes a means of providing for themselves beyond farming. Behind the scenes, the NGOs, the international non-governmental or private organizations, are doing their part, notching up successes even though they do not have millions of dollars to spend.

A SHINING EXAMPLE

Miriam provides for an entire village

In the village of Istalis, north of the capital of Kabul, it is not just the cold that has been a problem for locals in recent winters: they have also had nothing to eat for days on end. Before the Taliban withdrew from this region they burned down several villages, abducted young men and took with them anything that looked as if it could be of use. Many families fled because they were unable to live in the ruins of their homes and had no means with which to rebuild their houses. Despite the fact that it too was heavily affected by the war, the capital city itself took notice of the plight of the villages.

One of those who heard about the villages' fate decided he had to help straight away. Dr. Peter Jaggi and his wife Verena had just arrived in Afghanistan with the aid organization ADRA. They had worked for ADRA for three years already, helping people in the poor Nepalese mountain villages of the Himalayas and in the bamboo huts of Malawi in sub-tropical Africa. The couple had become adept at helping restore people's faith in the future no matter how hopeless their circumstances appeared to be.

ADRA and its employees assisted people in more than 120 countries and had already achieved a great deal in Afghanistan. By deploying a mobile sanitary team they had been able to prevent the spread of tuberculosis, an insidious and infectious respiratory disease, in the province of Bamyan. In the province of Jowzjan they

1 Sewing machines can only be found in places where international aid organizations are active. The majority of women still sew by hand. 2 A document proving that she is widow entitles this woman to a quilt. 3 Rahaila keeps herself and her family of eight from the money she makes sewing. 4 Children's clothes are made from the remains of the material. 5 ADRA distributes quilts among the ruins of Kabul's old town.

Next double-page *In the tiny village of Istali, Estory distributes the wool needed to stuff the quilts (above left). Medical supplies only reach the more distant villages sporadically. When a doctor comes to the village, a queue forms very quickly, as is here the case (below left). Fahrishta is one of the best seamstresses in the area. Before, like many other women, she used to sit by the side of the street and hope for handouts (right).*

5

helped farmers bore 80 new wells and installed new hand pumps for them. Verena Jaggi gave orphaned children teddy bears donated from the United States and Europe, providing many of them with the first toys they had ever had in their lives.

Through ADRA and other donors, the Jaggis' next achievement was to reach the desperate people in these destroyed villages with several trucks filled with tents, blankets and sacks of flour. The aid was at first welcomed with stares of disbelief and only a little later were there bursts of applause and celebration. Supporting the poorest of the poor is not just about providing temporary relief, however, but also about ensuring that they learn to help themselves, securing their way out of their predicament in the longer-term.

The idea of helping people to help themselves also lies behind ADRA's involvement in a program to create a healthcare system in the province of Bamyan.

In Istalis and the surrounding villages the recipe for success goes like this: ADRA provides the women with material for free. They use the material to produce blankets. The blankets are then given to other communities in need. The aid organization pays the women a modest daily wage, enough to support the families as they attempt to return to the way of life they used to have. Istalis and the neighboring villages used to be known for their pottery as far and wide as Kabul.

Miriam, a local baker, is playing a particularly important role in the rebirth of the village. She is a beaming young woman with a surprisingly attractive face.

When I saw her for the first time I could scarcely believe that she had already had six children and that she sat every day for eight hours in a tiny, smoke-filled mud-hut, kneading dough. Miriam let me taste her bread, and it was by far the best I had ever had the pleasure of eating in Afghanistan. Her bread feeds 500 people. She sells it very cheaply, but makes enough money to buy fresh flour and earn a little from it herself.

Above *A joyous reception for the truck.*
Right page *Before the quilts are delivered, the women are given the appropriate number of dockets for each member of their family (above). Many of the refugees returning home are living in tents in front of their destroyed homes (below).*

The winters can be bitterly cold, not just in the mountain villages on the Hindu Kush, but also in the valleys and on the plains. During the day, the women and girls keep warm thanks to their back-breaking work around the home or in the fields. Babies and little children are wrapped up in furs and cloth, sometimes so tightly that they start to resemble little parcels.

As night falls, they are keen to show me how they keep themselves and their homes warm. The women and girls gather in the living and sleeping quarters of their homes and sit around the relatively small, low wooden table. The men place hot stones, warmed in the embers of the fire, under the table. The stones retain their soothing heat for at least an hour. The women and girls keep their day clothes on overnight. Very rarely do they remove their headscarves. Before sleeping, they place their naked feet as close to the stones as possible and then hand around the hand-stitched, cotton quilts, stuffed with lambswool. The men sleep off in another room and use single, individual quilts in which they wrap themselves. Only the women and children get to enjoy the hot stones.

Right page *Miriam has been baking bread for the entire village for around five years now. With wet hands, she flattens the little balls of dough into flat shapes and then sticks them to the inside of the oven. The opening in the roof is the only source of light in the house and also provides a little fresh air.*

MEN DON'T LIKE IT

Photography – a tricky profession for a woman in Afghanistan

Somewhere on the outskirts of Kabul, a woman clad in rags collects cow-pies from the fields around her tattered tent to fuel her fire. Her five children help her. A young Afghan photographer – a woman – has just convinced her to let other people see how she lives. Suddenly a man storms out of the tent, gesticulating madly, and swearing at the photographer, shouting "Faischa" after her and finally throwing a stone in her direction. He shouts out that she is a whore and says she will bring shame on herself and her family in the eyes of God. She just manages to avoid the hurled stone. But this time she doesn't get her photos.

This story was relayed to me by 21-year-old Freshta Dunya as she described her latest attempt to record the daily lives of the beggars and refugees living in her home town. Day after day she wanders off with her camera. She wears just a headscarf, not the burqa that many women in Kabul still wear. "I wouldn't be able to see anything through the mesh opening," she says. "And I would be always tripping over the long hem."

Freshta became a photographer thanks to a seminar she attended, which was financed by the United Nations. She has seven sisters who helped her scrape together the money she needed to buy a second-hand camera in a bazaar.

She aims to capture the various facets of daily life and the various problems experienced by women living in her native country. From time-to-time she sells her pictures to foreign agencies. She has to be constantly tough because she is always being sworn at or spat at and she frequently has to avoid stones thrown in her direction.

Above *The young photographer Freshta Dunya has documented the suffering of her country.* **Right page** *Freshta is among the returning refugees who now live in a slum on the edges of Kabul. Other people moved into their homes while they were away (above). She often has to work hard to convince her subjects to let her take a photograph (below).*

"Men don't want to have their picture taken by a woman," she said. "And besides that they just don't like the fact that a woman can work as a photographer."

She has talent and could make a career for herself if her family situation did not pose such a problem. Freshta's father died fighting the Russians. When the Taliban was in power her mother promised her to the neighbor's son. She was 14 and he was three times her age. "He is called Abdul Wais," said my young colleague. "He used to be a tailor but now he is unemployed." She was supposed to marry him immediately after her mother had arranged the liaison but she has managed to keep putting off the wedding. Now her mother is putting her under pressure: the family will lose face if the wedding doesn't go ahead.

If Afghanistan had continued to develop in the way that the young photographer and the vast majority of the Afghan people had hoped following the fall of the Taliban then the young woman would likely have got her way and been able to avoid the arranged marriage by now.

For a time after the fall of the Taliban it seemed as if the situation for women would get easier. According to the constitution, women have the same rights as men and have to be 18 years old before they can marry, but the traditions run deep. They can't rely on the authorities to protect them either. Women are afraid to go onto the streets alone and have started wearing their burqas again. Rumors are circulating that the government intends to start paying more heed to Islamic values and traditions in order to take the wind from the sails of the Taliban, whose support is growing.

denly started punching and hitting me. My mother and my three sisters just stood and watched." Freshta's body was covered with bruises and a UN doctor found that she had broken a rib. Despite the hardships, she is determined to continue resisting the wedding.

Some young Afghan women simply give up when faced with such circumstances. Some women who see no way out pour oil over themselves and set themselves alight. Freshta has managed to win back some self-confidence through an exhibition of her photographs of women in dire straits. "Whenever I fight for the rights of women in Afghanistan then I am also fighting for my own rights." She knows her pictures can achieve far more than she would ever be able to achieve through words, simply because the overwhelming majority of men and women living in her home country are not able to read or write.

Left page *Later she was to give her soda bottle to the children (above). Freshta faces many forms of resistance but she is determined not to give up (below).* **Above** *Visiting the home of a poor Afghan woman.* **Left** *The photographer with her sister and two United Nations employees at her exhibition.*

Freshta can do very little in this situation to stop the daily visits from her future father-in-law. He brings sweets and pastries with him, inquires about the wedding preparations and asks to be told the date. On one occasion, I had arranged to meet Freshta but she told me she was ill and missed our meeting. Later, I found out why she didn't show up: "I told the neighbor that I would under no circumstances marry his son and he got angry and sud-

WAITING FOR CUSTOM

A trade in hand finds gold in every land

If you search for a factory chimneystack in Kabul you will be disappointed. It is not that the capital city's factories were destroyed during the war years but rather that there never were any in the first place. Neither Kabul nor any of the country's other major cities has ever had any industry to speak of. The new government is therefore eager to attract more foreign investors to help stimulate a modest process of industrialization in Afghanistan. But the security situation will have to improve radically to attract them to the country. Around 85 percent of the population live from agriculture and for the foreseeable future that is likely to remain the case. Without opium production and the proceeds from the drug trade they would be significantly worse off. Many Afghans are supported by relatives who live abroad, income that is rarely mentioned but which is vital. Afghans living in Pakistan, Iran and the Gulf States transfer around $500 million each year to their families in Afghanistan.

Abdul Baqi is a joiner who makes windows in Herat. Without the support of his brother in Tehran he would have had to shut his shop a long time ago. Everything he sells is handmade: he has never even seen machines like electric saws or other devices that are taken for granted elsewhere. Wherever he can he uses old pieces of glass for his windows, all of which look incredibly well-made. A young boy, whom he refers to as his assistant, helps him. Like his boss, the assistant didn't go to school and can neither read nor write.

The joiner complains that even though there are lots of houses in the town and in surrounding villages that were destroyed in the fighting, their owners would rather do the repairs themselves. He knows some people who would gladly buy windows from him but who have not got the money. "If no customers come then I'll go join the Taliban," he says. It is not entirely clearly whether he is joking.

Nasrullah lives in the province of Herat as well. He was trained as a welder by an aid organization. He sits waiting for custom. His

The non-governmental aid organization assists these men not only in learning a handicraft, but it also lends them small amounts of money so they can set up on their own.

The education program also offers courses in producing simple prosthetic devices that are in high demand in Afghanistan. During the war years, many people lost limbs due to landmines, which are still lying around in many places. Medical facilities are scarce and the prostheses that are available from the government are so old, uncomfortable and heavy that they are rarely of any use. There is an enormous need for this kind of hand-made products but there is simply not enough money around for people to buy them. It would only require a small improvement in the economy to increase demand for these products among the wider population. Such a boost would ensure that these tradesmen become sought-after individuals.

specialty is iron doors. His line of work is not as labor intensive because Nasrullah has got all the appropriate equipment and knows how to use it. All the same he too is waiting for customers to show up.

An international aid organization also tries to help former Mujahideen fighters who found themselves without jobs at the end of the war and who don't know any trade other than fighting.

Left page *Craftsmen are in demand in Afghanistan. Their jobs are often made harder by the fact that they do not have enough tools and lack modern aids.* **Above** *A businessman in Kabul produces prostheses for Afghans who can afford them.* **Left** *There are few customers for modern kitchens.*

Above *The centerpiece is this sowing machine.* **Right page** *Samina (right) shows the women how to trim the material (above). Progress on the aid project is documented (below).*

Next double-page *A pause during the sewing lessons. Samina (left) with one of her pupils (above left). The village of Safar Qualar in the province of Nangahar can only be reached by foot (above right). There is no school for the children of Safar Qualar (below right).*

VILLAGE BANKING

An aid organization's small-scale activities

There is a group of women dressed in brightly colored clothes waiting for us on the road leading into the village of Safar Quala in the province of Nangahar. One of them, standing right at the front of the group, has a sewing machine balanced on her head. The other women point at her and laugh heartily. They spin around on the spot and would very likely start dancing if it were not for the stones lying all over the ground. In the end they invite us into a nearby house. Samina, an Afghan woman who is accompanying me, says the women have been waiting for us all day. "All they knew is that we would come today. I couldn't tell them when."

Inside a shed with a low ceiling located in a farmyard there are 20 women clustered around eight sewing machines. These are not modern devices but the kind that you operate with your feet, like something my grandmother might have used many years ago. They are ideal for this village, however, because there is no power. They are used for sewing lessons and to produce clothing. The women have been practicing for six weeks already and proudly show me the first fruits of their labors. Samina learned how to be a seamstress when she was in Pakistan. Her parents went there during the war years. Now that she has returned to Afghanistan she comes to Safar Quala once a week and passes her knowledge on to the women in the village.

A private aid organization has organized sewing lessons and the production of children clothes, which are then passed on to other people in need of them. Samina is in charge of this unspectacular but important project. She has already built up 31 self-help groups, each of them based on the same principle. The women have to set up an organization with a president, a treasurer and a secretary first, and then they receive the equivalent of around $2,200. They sometimes find it hard to get even this far as there are very few women in Afghanistan who can read and write.

The women in the group can then decide for themselves how they use the loan. Some of them use it to make clothes; others make jams or press fruit. The system is known as "village banking". The aid organization also offers seminars that explain to women the importance of earning money for themselves and make them aware of the opportunities it could create for them.

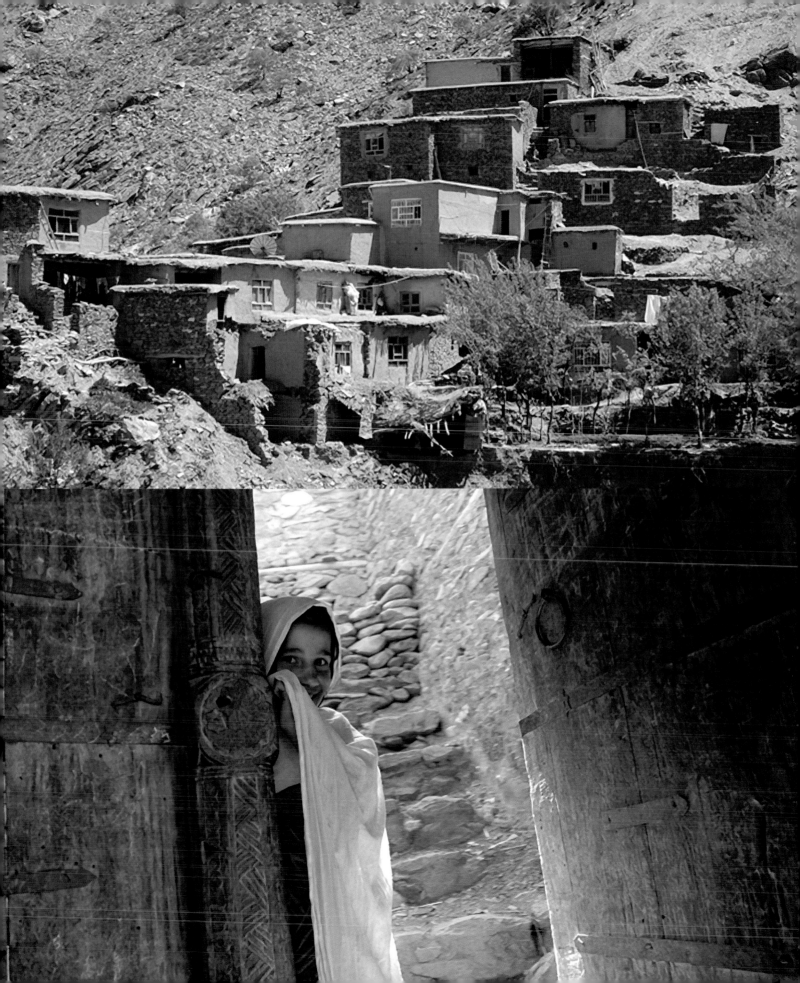

EVERYONE'S A HARD WORKER

The Afghans are too proud to beg

They may not be the most typical Afghan farming family but there are nevertheless many others like Bibbi and her husband Mohammed. He sells wheat and vegetables on the market with his first wife while Bibbi stays at home with the children and, when she has time, shells pistachios. "No pain, no gain" might be one appropriate way of describing the way of life in Afghanistan. The family consists of five children, all of them Bibbi's. They live in a house built from clay bricks and wood, surrounded by a crumbling clay wall. They also have a well.

Bibbi is 34 and her husband Mohammed is over 60 years old. His first wife, with whom he had no children, is around 50. Many Afghans don't know exactly how old they are. Bibbi was promised to Mohammed when she was a child. She was 14 years old

when she was forced into the arranged marriage. She protested strongly. She had five children over the next five years. Three girls and two boys. They are all still at school, something that has only been possible for the girls since the end of the Taliban's rule. Mohammed expects the children to earn their keep as well. He brings in the equivalent of around $ 60 a month from the market stall, just about enough to keep the family fed. Even after he married Bibbi, Mohammed's first wife stayed with him – as tradition dictates. She helps in the fields. Bibbi is also expected to contribute to the family's coffers. One thing she would never do, however, would be to go begging – and the same applies for the children.

It's hard for a woman in Afghanistan to earn even a few cents if she has no vocation and never went to school. Bibbi decided she would go with the children after school and sit on the side of the road in one of the nearby towns and sell pistachios. Pistachios are quite popular in Afghanistan where they are eaten either as a snack or used as the basis for various sweets and pastries. Bibbi and the children can shell up to 30 kilos of pistachios a day, breaking them open either with stones or with a small hammer. I met Bibbi at a school for women, located in a private house. At first the women were just there for a sewing class. After a while

can't do that. I think it's amazing that my daughters are now able to go to school as well. The girls' school was set up by you Germans."

At first Bibbi did not tell her husband about her visits to the school. He was just happy if he received a regular bit of income from her and didn't seem to care where she spent her time. She saved everything she could over and above what went to her husband and spent it on schoolbooks and equipment for her children. I asked her how she had managed all of this and whether spending time at school meant that she earned less money? "No, not all," she said. "I simply spent my evenings shelling pistachios by the light of the oil lamp when Mohammed was asleep."

they started to learn to read and write. Bibbi struck me because she asked the most questions and immediately wrote down the teacher's answers down in a book. I was allowed to accompany her back home to take some pictures of her house and the way she lived. This was quite a rare privilege.

Bibbi told me the story of her challenging life. She repeatedly burst into tears. "I am a completely different person since I have been able to read and write. Even Mohammed, my husband,

Left page *Bibi with two of her daughters in the courtyard of her house.* **Above** *Schooling in a private house. Even Bibi (to the left, against the wall) is learning how to read and write.*
Left *Pistachio shells are broken individually with a hammer.*

Next double-page *This community on the Salang Pass is on the up. New houses are being built, tiny shops in a village bazaar and perhaps, God willing, there will soon be a school.*

1747 The Persian ruler Nader Shah, whose empire encompasses what is now Afghanistan, is assassinated. He is replaced by the leader of his personal guard, Ahmed Durrani, who later succeeds in uniting the Pashtun, Tajik, Hazara, Uzbek, Kyrgyzs and Turkmen tribes. He becomes the first shah to carry the title of king or emir of a country still known as Khorasan. This is the beginning of modern Afghanistan. For the first century following its foundation, the country was characterized by war between India and Persia and by the rebellion of its tribesmen. Once again the country was divided. Later still, Russia's desire to gain access to the Indian Ocean, together with Great Britain's efforts to try and secure its colony India and to prevent the Russians from gaining influence in Afghanistan, had far-reaching consequences for this strategically important country.

1838–1842 The arrival in Kabul of a delegation sent by the Russian Tsar sparked the first Anglo-Afghan war. England's attempt to occupy Afghanistan and annex it for India failed. British envoys in the Afghan capital and a king supported by the British were killed.

1878–1880 Second Anglo-Afghan war. By this time the British are better prepared militarily. Afghanistan yields its foreign policy to the British and becomes a de-facto British protectorate. Southern Afghanistan becomes an Indian crown colony.

1893 Afghanistan is forced to accept a vaguely defined border to the south and the east. Even today, the border is still referred to as the Durand Line, named after the then foreign secretary of India, Sir Henry Mortimer Durand. It runs straight through the center of the Pashtuns' territory. Modern Pakistan adopted the Durand Line as its international border with Afghanistan. Afghanistan considers it to be invalid and claims the Pashtun territories in Pakistan. The border is not protected by either country and there are only very few crossings. One of them is the Khyber Pass.

1919 The third Anglo-Afghan war was started by the Afghans and lasted a month. Supported by the newly-created Soviet Union, Amir Amanullah is able to hold his own against the British. Territories were returned to Afghanistan and the country declared independence from Britain in August 1919. August 19th is therefore a national holiday.

1921–1928 Afghanistan wins international recognition under King Amanullah. In the following 50 years, Afghanistan signs numerous agreements with the Soviet Union in order to prevent further British influence in the country. Amanullah is open towards the rest of the world and visited Europe. In Berlin, he was particularly fascinated by the metro system. From the beginning of the 1920s, German engineers came to Kabul to construct various modern buildings. They also trained hundreds of locals in the art of construction when they undertook the creation of the Darul Aman Palace.

1929 Amanullah's attempts to institute European-style reforms fail. He is attacked by conservatives for having done away with the obligation to wear the veil and banned arranged marriages and polygamy. A civil-war like situation is brewing. For nine months, a bandit chief rules the country who was said to have been supplied with weapons and money by the British.

1933 Amanullah's rightful successor, Mohammed Nadir, was assassinated in 1933. His son, Mohammed Zahir Shah, bestowed an unusually long, peaceful period on the people of Afghanistan. He strove to find a balanced approach to domestic and foreign affairs.

1973 A military coup occurs, led by Mohammed Daoud, one of the King's relatives. Mohammed Zahir abdicates. Daoud declares Afghanistan a republic.

1978 The Communist Party win a civilian coup. The incumbent president is assassinated. The Communist writer Nur Muhammad Taraki becomes leader. His number two is the similarly ultra-left leaning teacher, Hafizullah Amin. Afghanistan becomes a People's Republic and an ally of the Soviet Union. American President Jimmy Carter signs a confidential directive to support the anti-Communists in Afghanistan. They are generously furnished with weapons and money.

1979 The Russians are incapable of preventing a power struggle developing in Kabul. Taraki is assassinated, most likely on the orders of Amin. Amin is then shot by Soviet troops storming the seat of government during the Soviet invasion of Afghanistan. This sparks a guerrilla war between the "holy warriors", the Mujahideen, and the Red Army with the soldiers of the Afghan communist government. The Mujahideen's base is in Pakistan. The Taliban, mainly Koranic students from Pakistan, also belong to the Mujahideen as do many Saudis, in particular Osama bin Laden who was unknown at the time. Every day, a "holy warrior" manages to shoot down a Russian helicopter, thanks to handy rocket launchers provided by the US and the British.

1988 The Red Army's losses continue to mount. Mikhail Gorbachev takes over the leadership at the Kremlin, a man who from the start was against the deployment of troops in Afghanistan. He pursues a policy of reforms, known as "Perestroika". A peace accord is signed in Geneva between the United States, the Soviet Union, Afghanistan and Pakistan.

1989 Soviet troops withdraw. A left-wing government remains in power in Kabul under pro-Soviet Mohammad Najibullah. The Mujahideen continues to wage war against the government while feuding among themselves.

1992 Some of the "holy warriors" form a government, but other Mujahideen members continue to undermine their power. The country is the throes of a civil war. Fighting around the capital Kabul is particularly intense. Thousands die and Kabul is deserted by its own people.

1996 The Taliban benefit from the chaos. With backing from Pakistan and Saudi Arabia, they very quickly gain control of Afghanistan right up to a small strip of land in the far northern area. The Taliban government is now recognized by Pakistan, Saudi Arabia and the Gulf Emirates. Their fanatical Muslim state attracts international condemnation because of practices such as the stoning of alleged adulteresses and a ban on anything that is considered tainted by the west. Their own people are lashed in cases of corruption and thieves are publicly punished by having one hand cut off. Afghanistan's population shows a certain degree of sympathy for such measures since they bring an element of security after years of chaos.

1997 The Taliban gives permission to Osama bin Laden and his al-Qaeda group to set-up a training camp in Afghanistan where fanatical Muslims from various countries were taught how to use modern weapons and explosives.

2001 On September 9th, al-Qaeda suicide attackers disguised as a camera crew attempt to assassinate the Taliban's arch enemy in the north of the country, the legendary Mujahideen leader Ahmad Shah Massoud. Massoud died of his injuries on September 12th.

2001 In the wake of the hijack attacks on the World Trade Center in New York on September 11th, the US and Great Britain invade Afghanistan with the support of the former Mujahideen. The Taliban is beaten decisively and many of its members flee to Pakistan. An interim government is put in place in Kabul by the US authorities.

2001 International Afghanistan Conference is held in Petersberg near Bonn, Germany. The legal conditions for stationing international troops in Afghanistan to support the government was agreed upon with the United Nations. Promises were made for an increase in international aid to support the reconstruction of the country, but no binding agreements were reached.

2001 The United Nations Security Council approves the deployment of the International Security Assistance Force in Afghanistan. German soldiers are also among the forces. The US maintains its own anti-terror group in the country, under the name "Operation Enduring Freedom".

2003 NATO takes over leadership of ISAF. By fall 2007, there are soldiers from 37 countries involved in "peace enforcement" in Afghanistan.

2004 Afghanistan's "loya jirga" or "grand assembly" approves a new constitution for Afghanistan. It guarantees equality for women, freedom of speech, condemns terrorism and drugs and calls for a presidential democratic system and a democratic vote for the president.

2004 Hamid Karzai, a Pashtun, is elected president with 55.4 percent of the vote.

2005 Parliamentary elections. Among the 249 members of parliament, there are 68 women.

2007 Six million children, still just half the number of children in Afghanistan, go to school. They are often taught in the open air because there are too few schoolrooms to accommodate them and too few qualified teachers. A teacher earns only the equivalent of around $45 a month.

2007 International criticism of a lack of civil support for reconstruction in Afghanistan. Governments are advised to devolve more tasks to aid organizations or Non-Governmental Organizations (NGOs). Western governments, however, increase their support for "provincial reconstruction teams" (PRT), whose activities they believe will increase Afghan sympathy for foreign troops.

Heinz Metlitzky

The author and photographer – Ursula Meissner worked in the Southeast Asia bureau of Germany's ZDF TV before trading in her keyboard for a camera. Her first photo essay documented the siege of Sarajevo in August 1992. She has worked as a freelance photographer in zones of war and crisis around the globe for 15 years. From Afghanistan to Sierra Leone, and Kosovo to Iraq, she puts faces on the many victims of war and humanitarian catastrophes. Her photographs have received numerous awards, and have been published internationally.

Thanks – I thank Heinz Metlitzky; without him this book would not exist.

Credits – Jacket, front flap: Photo of the author by Sandra Gätke, Hamburg, Germany. All others: Ursula Meissner.

Jacket pictures – Front: The Burqa, symbol of the new Afghanistan; rose harvest in Nangahar; poppy with raw opium; tank with flowers. Back: Ursula Meissner and young nomads.

This work has been carefully researched by the author and kept up to date as well as checked by the publisher for coherence. However, the publishing house can assume no liability for the accuracy of the data contained herein.

We are always grateful for suggestions and advice. Please send your comments to: C.J. Bucher Publishing, Product Management, Innsbrucker Ring 15, 81673 Munich, Germany
E-mail:
editorial@bucher-publishing.com
Website:
www.bucher-publishing.com

See our full listing of books at
www.bucher-publishing.com

Translation: Tom Armitage, Zurich, Switzerland
Proofreading: Erik Kirschbaum, Berlin, Germany
Product management for the English edition: Dr. Birgit Kneip
Product management for the German edition: Joachim Hellmuth
Map: Astrid Fischer-Leitl, Munich
Dust jacket and design: Frank Duffek, Munich
Production: Bettina Schippel
Technical reproduction: Repro Ludwig, Zell am See, Austria
Printed in Slovenia by MKT Print, Ljubljana
© 2008 C.J. Bucher Verlag GmbH, Munich, Germany

ISBN 978-3-7658-1688-8

www.bucher-publishing.com

Experience the colors of our world

Happiness
408 pages, 460 illustrations,
ISBN 978-3-7658-1658-1

Forest Planet
208 pages, 230 illustrations,
ISBN 978-3-7658-1689-5

Buddhist Views
144 pages, 200 illustrations,
ISBN 978-3-7658-1584-3

The Earth as Art
300 pages, 380 illustrations,
ISBN 978-3-7658-1628-4

China
200 pages, 320 illustrations,
ISBN 978-3-7658-1672-7

Colors of the Tropics
176 pages, 250 illustrations,
ISBN 978-3-7658-1691-8

www.bucher-publishing.com **BBUCHER**